Unilateralism and U.S. Foreign Policy

**CENTER ON
INTERNATIONAL
COOPERATION**

Studies in Multilateralism

UNILATERALISM AND U.S. FOREIGN POLICY

International Perspectives

edited by
David M. Malone
Yuen Foong Khong

LYNNE
RIENNER
PUBLISHERS

BOULDER
LONDON

Published in the United States of America in 2003 by
Lynne Rienner Publishers, Inc.
1800 30th Street, Boulder, Colorado 80301
www.rienner.com

and in the United Kingdom by
Lynne Rienner Publishers, Inc.
3 Henrietta Street, Covent Garden, London WC2E 8LU

Library of Congress Cataloging-in-Publication Data
Unilateralism and U.S. foreign policy : international perspectives /
    edited by David M. Malone and Yuen Foong Khong.
    Includes bibliographical references and index.
    ISBN 1-58826-143-3 (hc : alk. paper)
    ISBN 1-58826-119-0 (pb : alk. paper)
    1. United States—Foreign relations—2001– 2. Unilateral acts
(International law) I. Malone, David   II. Khong, Yuen Foong
JZ1480 .U544   2003
327.73—dc21   2002073986

British Cataloguing in Publication Data
A Cataloguing in Publication record for this book
is available from the British Library.

Printed and bound in the United States of America

        The paper used in this publication meets the requirements
⊗   of the American National Standard for Permanence of
        Paper for Printed Library Materials Z39.48-1984.

    5 4 3 2 1

Contents

Part 3 The International Political Economy

Part 4 U.S. Regional Policies

Part 5 Conclusion

Foreword

Apart from traditional diplomatic channels, the process of making U.S. foreign policy is remarkably insulated from international perspectives. Although the United States develops its policies partly in response to global events, the U.S. foreign policy community tends to give short shrift to the ideas and opinions of international observers. Foreign attitudes are often overlooked, ignored, or dismissed rather than being integrated into U.S. conversations about the country's global engagement. It is a rarity, for example, for a foreign leader to address Congress. Thanks to weak international coverage by the media—which tends to focus on criticism from European public intellectuals or dramatic denunciations from implacable U.S. foes—the U.S. public has only limited access to the views of non-Americans about the U.S. role in the world.

This book makes the case that U.S. foreign policy must be informed by a deeper appreciation of the way the United States is perceived abroad, arguing that unilateralism undercuts U.S. national interests. Given the scale of U.S. dominance in the early twenty-first century, other countries are increasingly sensitive to the manner in which the country uses its massive power. At the same time, the U.S. foreign policy agenda is being transformed by a wide range of challenges that cannot be addressed successfully by any single state, no matter how powerful. Given these trends, vigorous support for multilateral cooperation offers the firmest foundation for U.S. engagement.

This book is the second in a series on multilateralism and U.S. foreign policy sponsored by the Center on International Cooperation at New York University. The center was founded in 1996 to conduct policy research and international consultations on the political, financial, and organizational factors that impede or advance the effective use of multilateral means to resolve pressing global problems. The first in this series, *Multilateralism and U.S. Foreign Policy: Ambivalent Engagement,* edited by Stewart Patrick and Shepard Forman (Lynne Rienner Publishers, 2002), examined the costs and consequences of U.S. ambivalence toward multilateral arrangements. This volume pushes the analysis and findings farther by clarifying international reactions to U.S. decisions to "go it alone."

I am extremely grateful to David Malone and Yuen Foong Khong for agreeing to edit the volume and to the excellent group of authors they convinced to be part of this effort. Profuse thanks are due to my colleague, Stewart Patrick, who coordinated the project on multilateralism and U.S. foreign policy and provided much of its intellectual ballast. It is our hope that these two books and an accompanying policy paper, "The U.S. in a Global Age: The Case for Multilateral Engagement" (Center on International Cooperation, May 2002), will contribute to an important international dialogue on the place of the United States in world affairs.

The Center on International Cooperation is extremely grateful to the Rockefeller Brothers Fund for its support of the project on multilateralism and U.S. foreign policy and to the Ford Foundation and the John D. and Catherine T. MacArthur Foundation for their continuing support for the center's activities.

—Shepard Forman
Director, Center on International Cooperation

I

Unilateralism and U.S. Foreign Policy: International Perspectives

David M. Malone and Yuen Foong Khong

"THE UNITED STATES SERVED FORMAL NOTICE YESTERDAY THAT IT IS PULLING out of the Anti-Ballistic Missile (ABM) treaty . . . a move that clears the way for the development of its own missile defense system, but which will exacerbate fears of a new surge of American unilateralism." So goes the opening line of Rupert Cornwell's reporting of the U.S. withdrawal from the ABM Treaty in December 2001. Cornwell, the respected Washington, D.C., correspondent of *The Independent* (United Kingdom), goes on to cite several other recent instances of the George W. Bush administration "going it alone": opting out of the Kyoto Protocol on global warming, scuppering the tightening up of the 1972 Biological and Toxin Weapons Convention, and "refusing to ratify the statutes of the International Criminal Court of Justice."[1] The unstated premise of Cornwell's piece is that U.S. refusal to go along with the international consensus is detrimental to the general well-being of the international community.

Has there been a new surge of American unilateralism? Why is the world fearful of a United States that goes it alone? What are the consequences, for both the United States and the world, of a unilateral America? This book seeks to answer these questions. An earlier volume, also sponsored by the Center on International Cooperation of New York University, explored the same issue from a different angle: U.S. attitudes toward multilateralism.[2] The main finding of the earlier book was that the United States was profoundly ambivalent about multilateral engagement. The book also argued that at a time when the U.S. foreign policy agenda was being transformed by transnational challenges that no single country, even one possessing the unchallenged power of the United States, could resolve, this ambivalence carried serious costs for U.S. national interests and for the vitality of international institutions. The discussions and debates among the U.S. contributors that presaged these conclusions were sufficiently passionate as to suggest that a parallel investigation, this time by international scholars, about U.S. approaches to multilateralism and unilateralism would prove illuminating.

Americans are sometimes startled by the strong foreign reactions to and criticisms of its foreign policy. Although some of these criticisms are unjust, others cannot be readily dismissed. At any rate, analysis—preferably dispassionate analysis—must precede criticism. This book seeks to elucidate, for the U.S. policy community as well as for a broader global audience, the manner in which U.S. "unilateralism" is perceived abroad; some of the reactions that U.S. policies have stimulated in other countries; and the likely consequences of this dynamic for U.S. national interests and international institutions. To this end, we sought to identify several of the most significant post–Cold War international issues involving the United States and invited a set of distinguished international scholars and practitioners to explore these issues. The nationalities of our contributors are appropriately diverse, but authors were chosen for their substantive expertise on the issues they address.

In order to achieve a degree of policy relevance, we have given the book a contemporary focus. We concentrate particularly on the foreign policy record during Bill Clinton's presidency and the first year of George W. Bush's administration, although the success of the administration under his father, George H. W. Bush, in forging an impressive international coalition to address the 1990–1991 Gulf crisis has obvious relevance to our undertaking.

Definitions and Guidelines

What concerns us is the degree to which the United States, in addressing global or regional challenges, has committed itself to (or departed from) multilateral frameworks of cooperation, including working within and alongside international institutions as well as paying heed to international norms or law. In addition, we also seek to establish how other countries have perceived and responded to trends in U.S. behavior—and to probe the consequences of these dynamics for the realization of U.S. national interests and international cooperation on common global challenges.

For the purpose of this volume, "multilateralism" refers to the cooperation of three or more states in a given area of international relations. As John Ruggie has suggested, what is distinctive about this form of cooperation is the practice of coordinating relations among the parties on the basis of "generalized principles of conduct," that is, "principles which specify appropriate conduct for a class of actions, without regard to the particularistic interests of parties or the strategic exigencies that may exist in any specific occurrence."[3] Accordingly, multilateralism is "a highly demanding institutional form";[4] it is unsurprising that great powers would find such generalized principles of conduct constraining.

Multilateral frameworks of cooperation can vary along a number of dimensions. These include their level of institutionalization, which may range from ad hoc coalitions, to international regimes, to formal multilateral organizations; the nature of the commitments and obligations implied, whether they be voluntary, legal (in the case of treaties and conventions), ethical, or political; and their balance between egalitarianism and hierarchy—that is, whether they operate on the basis of equal treatment (like the United Nations [UN] General Assembly) or give certain privileges to their most powerful members (e.g., the UN Security Council, the World Bank, or the acknowledged leadership of the United States in the North Atlantic Treaty Organization [NATO]).

"Unilateralism," by contrast, refers to a tendency to *opt out* of a multilateral framework (whether existing or proposed) or to *act alone* in addressing a particular global or regional challenge rather than choosing to participate in collective action. States opt out of a multilateral framework or act alone because they do not wish to subject themselves to the generalized principles of conduct being negotiated or enforced, or they may find such principles inimical to their national interests. We recognize, however, that there is no clear dichotomy between unilateralism and multilateralism. There are many possible gradations between the two orientations, and there may be complex situations where elements of unilateralism and multilateralism coexist. One of the central conclusions of the previous book in this series (Patrick and Forman's *Multilateralism*) was that it is not only "unilateralism" that is distinctive in U.S. foreign policy but also the frequently "ambivalent," "inconsistent," and "selective" nature of U.S. multilateralism.

With these working definitions as a point of departure, our authors were invited to write in-depth chapters that explored the balance between unilateralism and multilateralism in post–Cold War U.S. foreign policy. We asked them to begin by analyzing the recent behavior of the United States in a particular issue area (e.g., trade) or region (e.g., Africa). If they detected a trend toward or away from unilateralism, to what causes and motivations could this be attributed? What were the consequences of perceived U.S. unilateralism?

We were particularly interested in the form and consequences of U.S. action for efforts to address global challenges (e.g., nonproliferation, protection of the environment); for relations with allies and adversaries; for the strength and credibility of international regimes and institutions; and for the interests of both the United States and its international partners. We hoped, in addition, that each author would offer an opinion about whether U.S. policy had served U.S. interests or had proven counterproductive. We hoped that the resulting chapters would capture a broad range of international views about recent U.S. conduct. We left open the possibility that recent U.S. policy had been more, rather than less, multilateral than in the past and that U.S. unilateralism might sometimes have beneficial effects for U.S. national interests and/or international institutions.

We also encouraged those authors who detected a trend away from multilateralism, and who argued that this had negative consequences, to offer an opinion as to what an "optimal" form of multilateralism might be, how the United States might have approached the issue differently, and what kind of results would have been possible in such cases. We were particularly interested in any policy implications of findings and ideas on changes in the content and style of U.S. global engagement to correct current weaknesses.

Argument

Virtually all the chapters address these questions head-on, although the emphasis varies. The answers add up to a common theme and constitute the argument of this book. In brief, it is possible to discern a trend on the part of the United States, since the late 1980s, toward unilateral action across a wide range of issues and with a variety of international implications, particularly for the partners and allies of the United States that we aim to discuss. What the earlier book characterized as "ambivalent engagement" on the multilateral front, this book interprets as growing unilateral disengagement. This difference in analysis and tone reflects the more recent focus of this book (including U.S. and international reaction to the terrorist attacks of September 11, 2001), the different issue areas investigated, and the non-U.S. lens through which the investigators examined the issues. As the synopses of the individual chapters below suggest, the causes of this trend include the unchallenged power of the United States, U.S. attachment to the preservation of its sovereignty, the influence of notions of U.S. exceptionalism, and the domestic political structure of the United States. Although the reactions of other countries to this trend vary, our findings point to the sensitivity of most governments to the conduct of U.S. diplomacy, notably the willingness (or otherwise) of U.S. administrations to engage them multilaterally. When Washington has adopted multilateral approaches, as during 1990–1991 in the Persian Gulf, allies and partners have tended to meet the United States if not all the way, then at least some of the way. In contrast, an aggressively unilateralist stance has often met with international defiance (which may or may not impinge on core U.S. national interests). However, we also argue that even though recent instances of U.S. unilateral action may provide short-term gains for the United States, they act to undermine its long-term interests. When the United States opts out of international agreements that it has played a leadership role in initiating, for example, it seriously weakens the relevant regimes and hinders the prospects for greater global cooperation. These missed opportunities detract from the vitality of an increasingly connected world and make the realization of future U.S. objectives more difficult.

U.S. Unilateralism and
Multilateralism Across Issue Areas

The chapters that follow analyze U.S. behavior since 1990 across a range of issue areas. The first chapter, by David Malone, provides a *tour d'horizon* of U.S. foreign policy, with special emphasis on the 1990s. It highlights the importance of U.S. sovereignty as a defining principle in U.S. dealings with others; it explores the tension between this principle and multilateralism, as well as the way these two principles worked themselves out in the Clinton and George W. Bush administrations. Malone's chapter sets the stage for the sixteen chapters that follow, each assessing the extent to which the United States adopted multilateral or unilateral approaches in the given issue area. The spectrum of issues dealt with by the sixteen chapters includes: (1) *rule of law issues*; (2) *peace and security;* (3) *economics and development;* and (4) *regional policy.* The findings and arguments are as follow:

Part I: The Rule of Law

The United States and the development of public international law. The United States, according to Nico Krisch, has historically been ambivalent about international law. The founding fathers, cognizant of the republic's relative weakness, saw international law as helpful to its security. They even viewed treaties as "the supreme Law of the Land," a view that was included in Article VI of the U.S. Constitution. But they were also extremely cautious about entering into new treaty obligations, as manifested by their writing into the constitution the requirement of a two-thirds majority in the Senate in order to ratify any treaty. Krisch argues that this ambivalence can be seen throughout the twentieth century. On the one hand, the United States took a leading role in the writing of treaties such as the Covenant of the League of Nations, the Kellogg-Briand Pact, the United Nations Charter, the Nuclear Non-Proliferation Treaty (NPT), and the Human Rights Covenants. On the other hand, as the histories of the League Covenant, Universal Declaration on Human Rights, and Havana Charter on the International Trade Organization suggest, the United States recoiled from adhering to the far-reaching obligations of those multilateral treaties. This pattern has persisted to this day. Surveying the post–Cold War making of international law, Krisch finds a United States that continues to lead in fostering treaty negotiations; but he also finds an increased tendency on its part to opt out of the resulting treaties, usually by refusing to ratify them. The International Criminal Court (ICC), the Comprehensive Nuclear Test Ban Treaty (CTBT), the amended Convention on the Law of the Sea, the Kyoto Protocol, and the Convention on Biological Diversity are cases in point. For

Krisch, this pattern of behavior, which has become slightly more marked since the end of the Cold War, suggests a substantial cleavage between the U.S. role in making international law (which creates obligations for other states) and its willingness to abide by it. Krisch's analysis hones in on two themes, one explicit and one implicit, that will recur throughout this book. The first is a tendency by the United States, especially since 1990, to "establish strong legal rules for other states" while seeking for itself the right to be "exempt from or even . . . above" these rules. The second and implicit theme is that this tendency has become more marked as the United States has grown more powerful. These themes will also be found and elaborated upon in many of the following chapters.

The International Criminal Court. Georg Nolte's chapter on the ICC provides a fascinating behind-the-scenes analysis of how the United States came to reject the "most important treaty in . . . general public international law since the Law of the Sea Convention of 1982." Nolte argues that U.S. behavior during and after the negotiations was unilateral in two senses. Opting out the Rome Statutes was merely "a passive form of unilateralism"; more troubling was its "active unilateralism" in pursuit of "its own vision" of the ICC against the adopted Statute "with the purpose of modifying or reinterpreting important aspects of the statute." For Nolte, this riding roughshod over the expressed objections of the international community reveals a United States bent on remaining "beside" and even "above" the law. What pains Nolte about U.S. behavior is that most of the delegations in Rome "had bent over backward to accommodate the United States" in recognition of its special superpower position. Nolte also believes that supporting the Rome Statute would have advanced broader U.S. national interests by encouraging the prevention and punishment of international crimes, ensuring U.S. freedom of action for humanitarian operations, and reinforcing the global leadership role of the United States. In the final analysis, Nolte attributes U.S. rejection of the ICC to the domestic political situation in the United States, including congressional refusal to let a non-U.S. court try U.S. citizens, as well as to U.S. perceptions of the country's special role in international affairs and attendant concerns that the ICC might be used against the United States for political reasons. Nolte finds those concerns as unconvincing as they are alarming; the United States, it seems to him, sought recognition (in the Rome Statute) as the world's policeman while demanding legal immunity from a functioning ICC. This U.S. arrogation of a special position for itself, combined with its refusal to compromise in Rome, was instrumental in persuading the other states—such as France and Russia, which also had reservations—to support the ICC "in reaction to what they consider excessive unilateral behavior" on the part of the United States.

Human rights. Rosemary Foot finds that U.S. participation in the international human rights regime has improved since the end of the Cold War, but domestic political considerations continue to make its attitude and adherence to these regimes "qualified." The fact that the United States is willing to participate in the multilateral human rights regime can be seen in its ratification of the Genocide Convention (1989), the International Covenant on Civil and Political Rights (ICCPR, 1992), and the Convention on the Elimination of All Forms of Racial Discrimination (1994). But even in these cases the Senate insisted on including significant reservations, understandings, and declarations that qualified the U.S. commitment to the regimes. Moreover, Foot reminds us, the United States remains outside of the International Covenant on Economic, Social, and Cultural Rights, the Convention on the Rights of the Child, the Convention on the Elimination of Discrimination Against Women, and protocol one of the ICCPR. Thus, compared to its European allies, the United States retains a propensity to opt out of a significant number of human rights regimes. Foot attributes this tendency to U.S. feelings of exceptionalism, the separation of powers central to the federal structure of the U.S. political system, and concerns that hostile actors may seek to use the multilateral system as a weapon to attack the United States, the sole remaining global power. She concludes her chapter by suggesting that the selective participation by the United States in the international human rights regime comes at a cost to U.S. reputation while undermining the credibility of the country's external human rights policy.

Transnational crime. Monica Serrano's analysis of U.S. drug policy characterizes the advent of the drug certification process in 1986 as the "crescendo" of U.S. unilateral action, especially toward its Latin American neighbors, the primary source of drugs entering the United States. For Serrano, what is notable about U.S. drug diplomacy is not only that the United States was unilateral in acting alone; the United States was also intent on using "forceful persuasion and coercion" to get its way even within multilateral settings. The strands of U.S. policy that seem especially unilateral and counterproductive in Serrano's view are U.S. insistence on the "supply control" solution, its unwillingness to consider alternative solutions to its drug problem within multilateral fora, and the swerving-off toward the patently unilateral track of the drug certification process. Serrano attributes this veering-off and the securitization of U.S. drug diplomacy from the mid-1980s to U.S. domestic political forces.

The certification process required the president to certify annually that drug-producing and transit countries were cooperating fully with the U.S. government to stem the flow of drugs into the United States. Those that failed the certification process, such as Colombia, would be denied bilateral aid and face a negative U.S. vote for loans from the international financial institutions. Serrano argues that certification was ineffectual, singled out smaller states such as Colombia for discriminatory treatment (while Mexico, through which 70 percent of the cocaine aimed at the U.S. market passes, was routinely certified), and proved to be a serious irritant in U.S.–Latin American relations. Certification temporarily ceased in 2001, as efforts within the Organization of American States for an alternative regional drug control regime gathered force. Serrano concludes by arguing that both the regional and global drug control regimes still need to free themselves from the influence of the supply paradigm and embrace a more balanced consumption-supply paradigm.

Part 2: Peace and Security

The United States and the United Nations. Kishore Mahbubani's chapter on the U.S.-UN relationship makes the case for a strong United Nations and argues that recent developments demonstrate that U.S. interests are better served by strengthening the United Nations rather than weakening it. Mahbubani suggests that even though the General Assembly may have passed resolutions that displeased the United States, these recommendations were nonbinding and seldom hurt the country. Within the Security Council and in functional organizations—where things really count—the United States has held great sway, and more often than not the international community has bent over backward to accommodate U.S. wishes. This notion of the international community's willingness to accommodate the United States out of respect for its power and preferences is echoed in many of the chapters in this book (not least those by Malone and Krisch). Given this reality, Mahbubani laments the largely successful U.S. efforts over the last twenty years to weaken the United Nations. He argues that in this increasingly interdependent world, the United States can better serve its interests by working alongside the representatives of the earth's other 6 billion inhabitants and that the United Nations is the only organization through which such cooperation can be effected. As the events of September 11, 2001, and its aftermath indicate, a strong United Nations will be one that serves U.S. interests, whether the task is one of forging a global consensus to combat terrorism or providing a mechanism to rebuild failed states like Afghanistan.

Peacekeeping. Ramesh Thakur's analysis of U.S. policy toward international peacekeeping finds a more subtle mix of multilateral-unilateral tendencies on the part of the United States. He begins by questioning the dichotomy between unilateralism and multilateralism, and he argues that the United States switches between the two approaches according to circumstances. Thakur's overall assessment, however, is that the United States remained essentially multilateral for much of the 1990s. For Thakur, Washington's multilateral approach can be seen from the way it relied on the United Nations to legitimize and mobilize world opinion in favor of peacekeeping and on NATO to carry out, militarily, peace operations in Europe. Thakur also observes that in the case of non-UN peace operations, the United States would reject a prior Security Council resolution "as a *mandatory* requirement for the use of military force overseas." For him, this suggests an "unresolved" dilemma for the United States, a dilemma that is also discussed in the Krisch, Nolte, and Foot chapters: on one hand, the "instilling of the principle of multilateralism as the world order norm," and, on the other, the attempt to exempt itself "from the same principle because of the . . . belief in exceptionalism, in its identity as a virtuous power."

Use of force. Ekaterina Stepanova agrees with Thakur that Washington is acting multilaterally when it uses the United Nations to legitimize actions involving the use of force, but she considers the use of NATO military power without UN Security Council sanction as more akin to unilateralism than multilateralism. Thus, she regards U.S. efforts to forge the ad hoc multilateral Coalition to oust Iraqi forces from Kuwait in 1990–1991 as a good benchmark for genuine multilateralism. The involvement of the Security Council was what gave Operation Desert Storm its multilateral identity and legitimacy, although the sheer number of countries participating actively in the Coalition (more than two dozen) also contributed to both aims. In Kosovo, however, the United States acted unilaterally—even though it acted in concert with NATO to bomb Yugoslavia—because it chose to bypass the Security Council when it became clear that Russia and China would not sanction the use of force against Yugoslavia. Stepanova's analysis leads her to the conclusion that the U.S.-NATO 1999 air campaign against Yugoslavia was an act of "unilateral multilateralism." She concludes that this approach to the use of force was insufficiently sensitive to the security worries of several major U.S. interlocutors such as Russia and China (and, one might add, India).

Nuclear policy. Like Thakur and Stepanova, Qingguo Jia sees the United States as adopting a mix of unilateral and multilateral strategies in its approach to nuclear issues. On issues requiring the cooperation of the international community, the United States relied on multilateralism to realize its objectives, as in the renewal of the NPT, the negotiation of the CTBT, and the strengthening of the Missile Technology Control Regime. On other issues, such as nationwide missile defense and achieving full-spectrum dominance in war, the United States felt it had to proceed regardless of international reactions. Focusing his analysis on the George W. Bush administration's repudiation of the ABM Treaty in order to proceed with the development of missile defense, Jia critiques what he regards as a U.S.

insistence on "absolute security" that pays little heed to existing treaties and international sentiments. Jia sees the latter as a consequence of three factors: U.S. status as the sole superpower; U.S. perception of rogue states and rising powers as the new security challenges; and an impulse to impose liberal U.S. values on illiberal states. Like virtually all the other authors, Jia also emphasizes the increasingly interdependent nature of the world and its security problems; in such a world, he concludes, the United States has a unique role to play in charting the path of multilateral cooperation.

Nonproliferation. U.S. ambivalence about multilateral approaches to control nuclear weapons is not limited to the pursuit of national missile defense. As Kanti Bajpai observes, reluctance to accept the constraints binding on other countries and insistence on special privileges has also been apparent in U.S. policies toward the NPT and particularly the CTBT. The difference in U.S. approaches to these two treaties is instructive, however. The United States was a major force behind the initial negotiation of the NPT and its subsequent extension during review conferences in 1995 and 2000, in large part because the NPT is a more unequal treaty that grants the United States differentiated privileges as a nuclear power. Moreover, the United States has made little progress in its NPT commitment to work toward complete nuclear disarmament. In the case of the CTBT, the U.S. Senate rejected a more universalistic treaty to preserve its freedom of action to test nuclear weapons. Bajpai's comparison of U.S. behavior on the NPT and the CTBT leads him to the conclusion that "on nonproliferation . . . the U.S. preference is to be unilateralist at the limit."

Part 3: Economics and the Environment

Multilateral trade and the World Trade Organization. In his chapter on U.S. trade policy, Per Wijkman detects a dual-track approach by the United States since the 1980s. U.S. trade policy has been characterized by "unilateral protectionism" as well as "multilateral liberalism." The result has been, as Wijkman puts it colorfully, "unilateral freewheeling within a multilateral system" that has "created confusion abroad." However, Wijkman provides a key to sort out this confusion by identifying and analyzing the conditions under which unilateral protectionism or multilateral liberalism gains the upper hand. A weak executive branch, strong protectionist sentiments in Congress, and international perceptions of a declining United States create the conditions that foster unilateral U.S. restrictions of free trade, whereas a strong executive branch, a pliable Congress, and international perceptions of a resurgent United States are conducive to free trade and U.S. support for multilateral trading rules. Wijkman sees the former set of conditions as characterizing the last years of Ronald Reagan's administration and the first few years of Bill Clinton's—hence the unilateralist and protectionist policies of the late 1980s and early 1990s, whereas the latter conditions seem to have returned in the mid-1990s and are continuing into the initial years of George W. Bush's administration. The best indication of this is U.S. willingness to live with the World Trade Organization.

International monetary coordination. Toyoo Gyohten emphasizes the hegemonic role of the United States in the world economy in general and in the global financial arena in particular. Overwhelming U.S. strength in the global financial arena means that there are fewer coequals to consult or negotiate with; moreover, U.S. policymakers and businessmen are so confident of the superiority of the U.S. model that they see their forceful leadership in international finance as natural and self-evidently beneficial. For Gyohten, this go-it-alone approach has had deleterious effects in areas such as the management of international capital flows, the stability of exchange rates, and the independence of the International Monetary Fund.

The Environment. Lucas Assunção argues that while the United States has oscillated between multilateral and unilateral approaches in dealing with climate change, it has become more prone to unilateralism since the late 1980s. Assunção suggests that this trend toward unilateralism is a result of the U.S. desire to protect its domestic economic and trade interests. As the largest emitter of greenhouse gases, the United States would incur the highest costs in cutting down emissions as mandated by the Kyoto Protocol (although it could also exploit its technological edge by developing the means across a broad range of economic activities to combat climate change, thereby creating and strengthening a new source of prosperity for the United States). Unilateral "economic self-defense," as indicated by the U.S. refusal to sign the Kyoto Protocol, has been the preferred strategy. Assunção finds this stance shortsighted, coming as it does from the country that had "played a leading role in setting standards and advancing the science of climate change." It seems that as the science became more certain and the costs to the United States became clearer, the United States decided to opt out in favor of its economic self-defense.

Part 4: Regional Perspectives

Latin America. Although Latin America has lived, and continues to live, under the hegemonic shadow of its northern neighbor, Gelson Fonseca finds a regional environment in which it will be increasingly difficult for the United States to act unilaterally. Contrasting the propensity of the United States during the 1980s to protect its interests via unilateral, non-legitimized military interventions in Central America with its willingness to countenance a UN-mediated settlement to the civil war in El Salvador, Fonseca argues that democratization, combined with a less permissive international context, gives the United States less opportunity to pursue unilateral military solutions. As he puts it, to act unilaterally one must now argue that one is defending "inestimable values" and that a multilateral solution is impossible because of institutional paralysis and incapacity to react quickly in grave crises. Thus, Fonseca concludes that the United States has shown a general preference for multilateral approaches, but when the stakes are sufficiently high, it is not averse to acting unilaterally (as in Iraq in recent years or in the past in Latin America). Fonseca argues that U.S. unilateralism tends to have negative systemic consequences, and he concludes the chapter by providing pointers on how developing countries can mitigate it while strengthening U.S. multilateralism.

Africa. Unlike Latin America, Africa's foremost concern about post–Cold War U.S. foreign policy is that the United States may consider the region strategically unimportant and therefore neglect it. Christopher Landsberg's analysis of the U.S. role in the African Crisis Response Initiative (ACRI) and African Growth and Opportunity Act (AGOA) shows that the United States is aware of the importance of its continued involvement in the security and economic growth of the region. However, the nonconsultative way in which the United States has gone about promoting ACRI and AGOA evinces a unilateral streak that irritates the region's leaders, makes it difficult for its principal ally (South Africa) to advance those initiatives, and, in the end, raises questions about U.S. intentions. Landsberg's essay also points to two interesting developments: First, the perceived unilateral U.S. approach to the Lockerbie incident (i.e., the imposition of sanctions against Libya—later multilateralized in part through the UN Security Council) and the Palestinian issue have enhanced South Africa's role as the "counterunilateralism" power in Africa, as exemplified by Nelson Mandela's success in pressing, through multilateral channels, for the lifting of sanctions against Libya, and South Africa's recent call for a more multilateral peace process in the Middle East.[5] Second, as the region embarks on multilateral regional initiatives such as the Millennium Africa Recovery/Renaissance Plan, the extent and manner of U.S. involvement will indicate whether the United States is committed to advancing African interests multilaterally.[6]

The United States and NATO. U.S.-NATO interactions in the post–Cold War period can be divided into three phases, according to Sophia Clément. From the early to the mid-1990s (specifically, the signing of the Dayton peace agreement), the United States favored unilateralism by default, in part because NATO was unprepared for the conflicts in the former Yugoslavia. After 1995, Clément senses a United States that gave precedence to multilateral cooperation as it coordinated its policies on Kosovo with its NATO allies. Since September 11, 2001, however, the United States has chosen unilateral military action in its war against terrorism, although it has also re- lied on a mix of bilateral and multilateral measures to obtain the cooperation of friends and allies in functional areas such as intelligence and the moni- toring of financial flows. Like Thakur's chapter on the United States and peacekeeping, Clément also eschews a simple unilateralism-multilateralism dichotomy; each of the phases contain a nuanced description of the interplay between unilateralism, bilateralism, and multilateralism. Clément concludes her analysis by suggesting that unilateralism is not a viable long-term ap- proach in the war against terrorism, and she provides some pointers on what an optimal form of multilateralism might involve.

The Asia-Pacific. In marked contrast to the transatlantic security relationship, which has been founded on the multilateral NATO alliance, U.S. policy to- ward the Asia-Pacific region has long been based on bilateral relationships between the United States and key actors. As Andy Mack explains in his chapter, the unilateralism-multilateralism dichotomy appears to be less helpful as an approach to understanding U.S. relations with the region. Mack examines the sources and motivations behind the historical U.S. pref- erence for bilateralism and documents Washington's more recent use of "à la carte multilateralism" to adapt to the changing Asia-Pacific security en- vironment. Contrary to predictions by "realist" scholars, he notes, the United States did not disengage after the end of the Cold War but rather redoubled its involvement as the guarantor of Asia-Pacific security. Mack examines the reasons for this pattern, focusing particularly on Northeast Asia, the most volatile potential flashpoint and the location of the most creative regional multilateral initiative, the Korean Energy Development Organization.

Envoi

These findings support those of the earlier companion book insofar as U.S. ambivalence toward multilateralism is concerned. However, our chapter au- thors make clear that in the last decade the United States has been pursu- ing increasingly unilateral strategies across a wide range of issues. What explains this growing U.S. preference for unilateralism? This question is es- pecially relevant in light of the earlier book's thesis that the nature of the new international challenges makes them less susceptible to unilateral U.S. solutions.

Although factors specific to each of the issue areas are important in ex- plaining the U.S. approach, the contributors in this book point to several common underlying factors.[7] One of the most obvious recurring factors is the condition of unipolarity, in which the United States possesses far greater power resources than any of its allies and adversaries. Few of our chapter

authors are surprised by the desire of a hegemon to foster bargaining outcomes favorable to itself or its conception of what is good for the international community. Thus, when the United States partakes actively in multilateral activities—in the negotiations over the ICC and climate change, for
example—but then rejects outcomes that may cramp its sovereign style or are
inimical to its economic interests, it can get away with this kind of unilateral
behavior. Although the power equation explains this in part, U.S. interlocutors have also become used to the pleadings of successive U.S. administrations that their constitutional situation (specifically, the strength of Congress
in policy formulation) makes it a special case. They may be irritated by U.S.
exceptionalism, but they tolerate it on many issues. On other questions,
where the cost to them of U.S. exceptionalism is high (e.g., potentially, on
climate change), frustration and resistance are greater, even among close allies such as the European Union (EU) member countries and Canada.

Congress's prerogatives in ratifying treaties, regulating commerce, and
controlling the purse strings all bear importantly on the U.S. ability to act
multilaterally. Related to this are of course issues of domestic politics.
George W. Bush, for example, was strikingly candid about the reasons for
the U.S. refusal to sign the Kyoto Protocol: the economic costs for domestic growth and hence the international competitive position of the United
States were deemed unacceptable. When Brazilian President Fernando Hen-
rique Cardoso criticized the United States for imposing tariffs on imported
steel in March 2002 on the grounds that it went against the thrust of the
planned Free Trade Area of the Americas, U.S. Trade Representative Robert
Zoellick was equally frank about the rationale behind the tariffs: domestic
political reasons. (Zoellick's cabinet colleague, Treasury Secretary Paul
O'Neill, went even farther, according to a *New York Times* report of an ostensibly off-the-record talk to the Council on Foreign Relations: he disagreed with the tariff decision and believed it would be self-defeating because "the move would cost more jobs in the United States than it would
save," but he obviously lost the argument on domestic political grounds.)[8]

Inextricable from issues of political structure is the conception and domestic appeal of U.S. exceptionalism—the widely held belief in the United
States that its values and institutions are the best yet devised, the conviction
that the world needs to adapt itself to American ways rather than vice versa.
More deeply, U.S. exceptionalism can be seen as a widely held conviction
among Americans that the United States, by virtue of its unique attributes,
has a special destiny among nations. The U.S. belief in a national mission
at the international level is an important impulse for its unilateral action.
In February 1998, Secretary of State Madeleine Albright drew tellingly on
this tradition before a domestic audience. U.S. global leadership was indispensable, she argued, because "we stand tall and we see further than other
countries into the future."[9] Such views, so couched, have naturally grated
on other countries. However, all of the contributors to this book would

likely accept that the United States retains certain core "systemic" responsibilities for international order and stability.

Yet the United States is not the sole country possessing an exceptionalist view of itself and its role in the world. France, for instance, may represent an even more striking case of the phenomenon, particularly with regard to cultural policy. Yet as the evolution of its African policy in the 1990s demonstrated, an exceptionalist France (unlike the United States) may no longer have the means or the will to act unilaterally in former spheres of influence. French approaches also suggest that the alternative to great-power unilateralism may not be multilateralism; it can also be inaction (cloaked in diplomatic rhetoric and often underpowered policy initiatives).

One difference between France the United States is that whereas the former has historically fostered several geographically defined spheres of influence, the latter's sphere of influence remains global. The United States is the only country in such a position in the early twenty-first century. In the words of Egypt's Nabil Elaraby, one of the leading recent ambassadors on the UN Security Council, the United States is not so much the last remaining superpower as the "supreme power" of the age.[10] It is not only the country's global reach but also its widely perceived global responsibility (even more sharply advocated by other countries than within the United States) that tripped up the initially doctrinaire George W. Bush administration in early 2001.

However, the United States is clearly not insensitive to the views of others. The drastically revised and improved terms of reference for military tribunals established to try detainees in Guantanamo Bay, Cuba, announced by Washington in mid-March 2002, demonstrated that international criticism by allies on the ground in Afghanistan had elicited a significant and broadly positive response from Washington.

What have been the consequences of U.S. unilateralism in the post–Cold War era? In a couple of areas, U.S. unilateralism may have made a positive contribution. Implicit in Ramesh Thakur's chapter, for example, is the argument that the United States, in bypassing the Security Council and using NATO to intervene in the Kosovo conflict, advanced the worthy cause of saving the lives of Kosovar Albanians.

In general, however, U.S. unilateralism—especially the decision by the United States not to join regimes that it has a role in negotiating (e.g., the ICC, the Kyoto Protocol)—weakens the particular institution and foreign perceptions of the common good. The U.S. decision to opt out of an international institution also tends to damage its reputation as well as undermine the capacity of allied governments to sell to their own publics the idea of partnership with the United States in controversial ventures. (This was the case for U.K. Prime Minister Tony Blair, who came under heavy domestic bipartisan fire in early 2002 for his staunch support of U.S. objectives in Iraq at a time when the United States seemed indifferent to the value of

U.K. support, e.g., by slapping punitive tariffs on EU, including British, steel exports to the United States.)

A variant of how unilateral behavior can undermine one's reputation relates to U.S. approaches to Latin America and Africa. A priori, the hegemonic status of the United States makes many observers in those two regions suspicious of U.S. intentions. U.S. inconsistency, as well as coercive and nonconsultative behavior, makes it even more difficult for many to trust the United States, even when the latter's intentions are benign. In areas such as nuclear policy, the use of force, the United Nations, climate change, international crime, human rights, and the ICC, all the authors agree that the particular multilateral regime is dealt a serious, though not necessarily fatal, blow when the United States opts out of the agreement. The contributors agree that a more multilateral U.S. approach to global and regional challenges will better serve the international community as well as U.S. interests. Thus, Thakur's analysis of peacekeeping shows that a United States more deeply engaged with the United Nations is able to get more done. Similarly, Gelson Fonseca advocates an Inter-American future that moves away from the frequent U.S. unilateral military interventions of the past to a more multilateral approach that is more likely to serve long-term U.S. interests

Few serious international analysts question the need for U.S. leadership on a broad range of international issues, but some U.S. assumptions underlying the exercise of such leadership have been sharply contested, not least in the fields of human rights and global environmental stewardship (where the U.S. public has often seen itself as being in the lead). In the weeks immediately following the September 11, 2001, attacks on the World Trade Center and the Pentagon, U.S. foreign policy seemed to take a 180-degree turn, newly emphasizing the value of allies and concerted action with partners, but as time passes this increasingly looks like a tactical adjustment rather than a strategic reorientation.

Strong international cooperation on terrorism seems unlikely to endure unless the George W. Bush administration also shows greater sensitivity to the views of allies on such issues as climate change, international criminal courts and tribunals, and defense issues other than terrorism. It is in this context that the contributors assay inquiries into non-U.S. perceptions of the U.S. approaches to multilateralism in recent years.

Notes

The editors would like to express their heartfelt thanks to Shepard Forman, Stewart Patrick, the contributors, and the Center on International Cooperation, New York University, for their support and encouragement, without which this project would not have been possible.

1. *The Independent,* December 14, 2001, p. 3. The fact that Cornwell is positively disposed toward the United States can be seen in his comment, "I'm disturbed by all this hostility to America," with reference to the treatment of prisoners at Guantanamo Bay. Weekend Review, *The Independent,* January 26, 2002, p. 4.

2. Stewart Patrick and Shepard Forman, eds., *Multilateralism and U.S. Foreign Policy.*

3. John Gerard Ruggie, ed., *Multilateralism Matters,* p. 11. See also Stewart Patrick, "Multilateralism and Its Discontents: The Causes and Consequences of U.S. Ambivalence."

4. Ruggie, *Multilateralism Matters,* p. 12.

5. This latter development has been facilitated by the African National Congress's steady move away from unqualified support for the tactics of the Palestinian National Authority (PNA) and a more evenhanded policy toward all parties to the conflict. For example, South Africa strongly advised PNA Chair Yasir Arafat against proceeding with a Unilateral Declaration of Independence, even after the failure of the 2000 Camp David summit.

6. The presence of President Mbeki of South Africa, alongside President Obasanjo of Nigeria and several other African leaders, at the G8 Summit in Genoa in July 2001 to advocate support for the MAP indicates a certain openness among all G8 members to such proposals, in principle, although the principal champions of giving priority to African issues within the G8 have been the United Kingdom and Canada.

7. Cf. Stewart Patrick, "Multilateralism and Its Discontents," pp. 7–10.

8. *New York Times,* March 16, 2002.

9. From an interview with Secretary of State Madeleine Albright on NBC-TV's "The Today Show" with Matt Lauer, Columbus, Ohio, February 19, 1998.

10. Interview with David Malone, New York, January 1996. Mr. Elaraby has since been elected to the International Court of Justice in The Hague.

2

A Decade of U.S. Unilateralism?

David M. Malone

THIS CHAPTER PROVIDES A *TOUR D'HORIZON* OF U.S. FOREIGN POLICY IN THE twentieth century, with special emphasis on the 1990s and after. It posits the defense of U.S. sovereignty as a defining principle of U.S. foreign policy and analyzes some uses to which the United States has put multilateralism in recent years. It then outlines how the makers of U.S. foreign policy navigated between these two concepts during the twentieth century. The chapter places particular emphasis on U.S. attitudes toward the United Nations, an institution that the United States played the key role in creating.

Sovereignty and the United States

U.S. attitudes toward sovereignty have been both sharply defined and differentiated. For policymakers in Washington, the protection of national sovereignty has generally implied that U.S. norms, standards, and laws should take precedence over foreign or internationally promoted ones. This approach has both favored internal autonomy and indirectly encouraged external freedom of action. Just as in U.S. domestic governance, where state and local prerogatives are often seen as conflicting with (and superior to) those of Washington, so at the international level, many in the United States see their own national government as locked in constant struggle with foreign iniquities and error. This attitudinal cast has favored assertive U.S. efforts to encourage—and even impose—its own values and practices on the international community through the construction of U.S.-dominated multilateral institutions. At the same time, it has made consistent U.S. compliance with the decisions of these institutions controversial domestically. Indeed, as the institutional cultures of several international organizations have drifted away from preferred U.S. models, Washington has often been reluctant to continue engaging with them.[1]

Like the inhabitants of some other countries, Americans tend to view their own sovereignty as paramount, that of others as peripheral. Within its own hemisphere, certainly, the United States throughout its history has successfully asserted its sovereignty largely unchallenged while it also, through skillful norm-building during the twentieth century, helped to define the content of the sovereignty of others—without necessarily internalizing norms it has expected others to adopt completely.

Even where U.S.-inspired norms have come to be broadly accepted at the international level—as is the case, for example, with norms concerning war crimes and human rights violations—the United States has not always been prepared to craft or support new doctrines binding on itself. While recognizing that international law cannot, through slavish respect for sovereignty, be allowed to shield delinquent governments from being held to international account for their crimes, Washington has generally been extremely reluctant to promote approaches that could systematically expose domestic U.S. practices to international scrutiny. The ambivalent U.S. position was best summed up by President Bill Clinton in his remarks to the UN Millennium Summit of September 6, 2000:

> Today, there are fewer wars between nations, but more wars within nations. Internal wars—often driven by ethnic and religious differences—took five million lives in the 1990s, the vast majority innocent victims. This trend presents us with a stark, collective challenge. We must respect sovereignty and territorial integrity. But whether it is diplomacy, sanctions, or collective force, we must find ways to protect *people* as well as *borders*.[2]

Republican attitudes, in Congress and elsewhere, were unambiguous on this matter during the 1990s: U.S. sovereignty was vital, and international bodies could not be encouraged to challenge it (although international arbitration was accepted in a number of fields, not least trade through the World Trade Organization and processes under the North American Free Trade Agreement).[3] The chairman of the Senate Foreign Relations Committee, Jesse Helms, in an unprecedented address to the UN Security Council on January 20, 2000, laid down a clear marker:

> If the United Nations respects the sovereign rights of the American people, and serves them as an effective tool of diplomacy, it will earn and deserve their respect and support. But a United Nations that seeks to impose its presumed authority on the American people, without their consent, begs for confrontation and—I want to be candid with you—eventual U.S. withdrawal.[4]

The argument by Helms and others (largely shared also by U.S. courts) has been that international law takes no precedence over domestic U.S. legislation and, indeed, is relevant only to the extent that it is fully reflected in the latter.

Given such congressional sensitivity about foreign oversight of—or intervention into—U.S. legislative, judicial, or administrative processes, the Clinton administration, like many other governments, adopted a case-by-case approach to the Security Council's incursions into the sovereignty of UN member states, generally avoiding assertions of an abstract "right" or "duty" to intervene in situations of grave humanitarian crisis. Where convenient in terms of U.S. interests, or strongly compelling in terms of international humanitarian law, the administration was prepared to champion, or at least support, the violation of state sovereignty.[5] However, its positions in the UN Security Council have never been characterized by a systemic approach to the interpretation of international law, clearly for fear that others might one day use such positions to hold U.S. sovereign behavior to account. This has been most clearly evident in debates over international criminal law. The United States championed the creation of ad hoc international criminal tribunals for the former Yugoslavia and Rwanda, under the authority of the Security Council, but it has viewed with deep suspicion the idea of an international criminal court that could hold American citizens internationally responsible for their actions.

Multilateralism

Interaction between the United States and other countries at the United Nations, and in other multilateral fora such as the North Atlantic Treaty Organization (NATO), can help Washington both to define and to realize its own international strategies. This was clearly the case with respect to Haiti in 1993 and 1994, when the United Nations provided a mechanism for sharing the burden, an imprimatur of legitimacy, and an eventual exit strategy for the U.S.-led intervention.[6] Nevertheless, given U.S. ambivalence about the constraints accompanying multilateral approaches, especially in matters of security as opposed to economics, the process of working out the relationship between the United States and multilateral organs has often been painful. It has been particularly fraught in cases where the views of the United States within these organizations have diverged sharply from those of allied and friendly governments. Some U.S. partners, including Canada and the United Kingdom, view multilateralism as an important goal in itself, whereas the United States mostly views multilateral approaches as instrumental, useful only insofar as they advance its own narrow interests.

The U.S. policy toward Bosnia-Herzegovina provides a case in point. During 1992–1995, the United States caviled from the sidelines, contributing to the notorious ineffectiveness of UN decisions. The fighting came to an end in late 1995, only when the United States chose to exercise strong and decisive leadership, most notably at Dayton, Ohio, where Washington allowed its European allies virtually no voice—as related with some asperity by the senior U.K. delegate there.[7] (In fact, the United States might have averted several critical problems in the implementation of the Dayton accords had it made some use of European experience.) Subsequently, the United States proved willing to lead innovative, NATO-organized enforcement operations in the Balkans, including the Intervention Force and the Stabilization Force in Bosnia and the Kosovo Force in Kosovo. These effective multilateral approaches, succeeding ineffective ones undermined by the United States itself, were largely brokered by Washington to serve U.S. interests.[8]

Not only do multilateral approaches help shape U.S. policies, particularly in the economic sphere, where several international financial crises have been successfully managed by the Group of Seven (G7) treasuries with Washington in the lead; but in the political field, they also help induce support by allies and compliance by adversaries. Indeed, as Oleg Levitin notes, multilateral engagement with Russia has provided Moscow with an opportunity to narrow cleavages among Western allies, providing opportunities to associate Russia progressively with Western policy preferences, as was ultimately the case in Kosovo.[9]

In international relations, there is not only safety but also legitimacy in numbers, as noted by the British scholar of the laws of war Sir Adam Roberts.[10] While providing no legal authorization of NATO action, a Security Council vote on March 26, 1999, rejecting (by a 12:3 vote) a Russian effort to mandate a halt to the bombing certainly undermined Moscow's position.[11]

Furthermore, even though the bulk of the military forces deployed in the war over Kosovo in 1999 were U.S. forces, the United States was in a much better position to negotiate a final settlement to the crisis because it had the cooperation of Russia and its NATO partners. Conversely, the defection of most U.S. allies from the U.S.-British strategy of seeking to contain Iraq and its capacity to produce weapons of mass destruction has been damaging, undermining the prospects that U.S. policy will be successful.[12]

Thus, in multilateral forums, the United States does not constantly yield to its allies and partners. More frequently—and unsurprisingly, given its sheer weight in international relations—it successfully coaxes them into supporting U.S. strategies in support of mutual interests. This has been very much the history of international trade negotiations since World War II, a pattern fostered, no doubt, by wide acceptance of the positive-sum nature of commercial liberalization.

A flashpoint in relations between the United States and its allies has been Washington's strong inclination to resort to sanctions against adversaries, often unilaterally. Particularly objectionable to the European Union (EU) and Canada has been the passage of extraterritorial measures like the 1996 Helms-Burton legislation (the Libertad Act) regarding Cuba, which targets foreign companies and individuals doing business with that country. U.S. unilateral economic sanctions against Cuba were increasingly condemned by the

UN General Assembly as the 1990s proceeded, recently netting 151 votes in favor, eight abstentions, and only two votes (by Israel and the United States) against.[13] Subsequent unilateral U.S. sanctions against Libya and Iran, though mitigated to some extent by the Clinton administration, fueled the sense that Congress wished to impose its will throughout the world while upholding U.S. sovereignty as its highest value. [14]

More generally, a U.S. preference for punitive approaches (short of military engagement), as opposed to inducement-based strategies, struck many allies as pathological, although the Security Council generally supported U.S. policy in this area.[15] However, differences eventually came to a head in the years 1998–2001 over the UN-imposed sanctions regime against Iraq with its humanitarian (and commercial) repercussions.[16] Washington argued that Saddam Hussein's regime was responsible for the humanitarian plight of Iraqis due to misallocation of available resources, but this cut little ice with a General Assembly membership and UN Secretariat increasingly hostile to a policy that appeared to be producing perverse results.[17]

In early 2001, the United States and Britain began responding to heavy international pressure with significant proposals that would in fact (if not in theory) significantly relax the sanctions regime. But U.S. and U.K. air operations against Iraq, stepped up since late 1998, continued to display limited effectiveness while remaining unpopular with international opinion.[18]

In sum, until the U.S. military response to the attacks of September 11, 2001, the favored coercive instruments of the United States by decade's end were sanctions (Iraq) and bombing (the former Yugoslavia). Neither instrument risked heavy casualties, at least for U.S. forces. Although NATO's strategy (which was essentially Washington's) in the former Yugoslavia proved effective over time, with Slobodan Milosevic ultimately overthrown by popular a uprising, U.S. policy before September 2001 generated a widespread perception abroad that the United States was a risk-averse bully.

In the late twentieth century, the United States was also fast losing the confidence of its closest allies that it would respond to international crises appropriately:

> One of the reasons the Europeans are so eager to organize their own rapid reaction force is that they are no longer convinced that they can count on agreeing with the United States on what is to be defended by the allies, where and when. They worry both about Washington refusing to respond to what they discern as threats, and Washington rushing unilaterally into conflict and dragging them in.[19]

This perception was qualified among European populations (if not among all European intellectuals) by the energetic and impressive U.S. response to September 11. Still, it is deeply rooted and may grow back.

Some History

U.S. foreign policy–making has long been influenced by the country's early experiences: by its struggle to free itself from its colonial master, by the self-reliance that served it so well in this uncertain endeavor, but also by the limited and tactical alliances it forged to that end. Suspicion of formal agreements easily betrayed and the obligations imposed by treaties have been deeply ingrained in the United States since 1776. To this day, the most quietly telling argument against a treaty-based international system in the corridors of Washington is that rogues ignore treaty provisions while only fools respect them. This mistrust of international entanglements helps explain why the framers of the U.S. Constitution divided treaty-making powers between the executive and legislative branches, which could be reliably expected to tangle over serious treaty undertakings. Although the United States has entered a variety of tactically useful treaties throughout its history, unilateral policies, such as the Monroe Doctrine, have served the United States equally well. Indeed, some of the most positive U.S. contributions to international relations, such as the Marshall Plan, have been advanced unilaterally.[20] The former Israeli diplomat Abba Eban, commenting on the long-standing U.S. view of itself as morally superior to other powers, depicts the belief in U.S. exceptionalism as a delusion:

> The truth is, no one outside America has ever taken the theory of American exceptionalism seriously. The theory rests on the assumption that America has an anticolonialist lineage. But the difference between ravaging populations and conquering vast territories within a continent, and conquering them in colonial fashion by sending armies overseas, has never struck non-Americans as a moral distinction.[21]

U.S. impulses have been paradoxical, even when not strictly contradictory: On the one hand, throughout the twentieth century the United States sought to shape (when not actually creating) multilateral architecture on a broad range of issues; on the other, it often either stayed out of the ensuing organizations or worked, intentionally or unwittingly, to undermine them. The most notable example occurred soon after World War I when the U.S. Senate, in a bout of isolationism, refused to accede to the Covenant of the League of Nations, thereby condemning the League, the creation of U.S. President Woodrow Wilson, to ineffectiveness. It was the sheer power of the United States on the global stage after 1900 that allowed it to determine the success or failure of many multilateral initiatives.

U.S. approaches toward the United Nations—itself largely a U.S. project, created at San Francisco in 1945—provide insight into the evolution of U.S. attitudes toward global issues and international organizations. No country played a greater role in designing and building global aspirations for the United Nations than did the United States. In the early years of UN deliberations, the United States could readily muster a majority of members to support its views. At the outset, it was the Soviet Union, the strategic adversary of the United States, that found itself most often on the defensive. Indeed, until October 13, 1956, all but two of the seventy-eight vetoes in the UN Security Council were cast by Moscow.[22]

Western domination of the UN General Assembly began to be challenged in the immediate postcolonial period of the early 1960s, with the emergence of apartheid in Rhodesia and South Africa as a key international issue that rallied the mushrooming nonaligned movement. Likewise, the question of Palestine became a growing bone of contention, with large numbers of newly independent countries supporting Arab positions and with the United States increasingly relying on its veto to protect Israel from binding Security Council resolutions that Washington considered unbalanced or injurious. Overcharged rhetoric, temporarily ascendant Arab diplomacy, and mismanagement by Western powers led to an infamous resolution by the UN General Assembly equating Zionism with racism on November 10, 1975.[23] The United States received the adoption of this resolution with dismay and fury. U.S. Permanent Representative to the United Nations Daniel Patrick Moynihan complained eloquently of double standards. The resolution would have profound and lasting consequences in discrediting the United Nations with the U.S. public and political leadership. By contrast, its repeal in 1991, supported by a strong majority of UN members and (thanks to a sustained U.S. diplomatic campaign) essentially unopposed by most Arab countries, passed largely unnoticed. The damage had been done.[24]

Changing demographics within the General Assembly similarly encouraged the developing countries, joined by sympathetic Western states, to press for a new international economic order (NIEO), which foresaw greater redistribution of wealth from industrialized to developing countries through regulation and the intermediation of the UN system. The 1970s witnessed intense negotiations on specifics of a proposed global economic "new deal," culminating with the Cancun Summit of 1981, the communiqué of which held some promise for further progress. In fact, the NIEO was soon dead, killed off by "Ronald Thatcherism."[25] A faint echo of this international psychodrama was the hideously misguided new international information order (NIIO) advocated at the United Nations Educational, Scientific, and Cultural Organization (UNESCO) in the 1980s, which many journalists around the world saw as little more than a license for censorship to be exercised by governments and international institutions. The NIIO, along with notorious UNESCO mismanagement, incited the United States (along with the United Kingdom and Singapore) to leave the organization.

The end of the Cold War led to a shift in U.S. thinking with respect to the United Nations. During that bipolar struggle, U.S. foreign policy priorities had been determined by the military and political needs of the United States and its allies. In the 1990s, values battled with interests in the hearts and minds of Washington policymakers (as they had during Jimmy Carter's administration, 1977–1981). Nowhere did this dichotomy in U.S. policy find its expression more than at the United Nations, which many in the United States viewed as a useful vehicle for the propagation of U.S. values. Positions and views crossed party lines to a significant, even surprising, degree. It was President George H. W. Bush, a Republican, who in 1992 advocated and pulled together a sizeable international coalition to rescue from starvation the inhabitants of Somalia, a country where the United States had few material interests. His Democratic successor, Bill Clinton, conducted an election campaign in 1992 that laid the foundations for a short-lived "assertive multilateralism." Once in office, however, his administration signally failed to live up internationally to the values he and his party promoted domestically, most notably in doing nothing to stop genocide in Rwanda in 1994.

President Clinton, in an address to the UN General Assembly on September 21, 1999, hedged his bets on the question of humanitarian intervention, making clear that the humanitarian impulse would continue to influence U.S. policy but would also be balanced against other factors:

> I know that some will be troubled that the United States cannot respond to every humanitarian catastrophe in the world. We cannot do everything everywhere. But simply because we have different interests in different parts of the world does not mean we can be indifferent to the destruction of innocents in any part of the world.[26]

Nowhere did the humanitarian imperative find more radically innovative expression than in the field of international criminal law. Indeed, the 1990s may be remembered in part for the creation of the ad hoc International Criminal Tribunal for the Former Yugoslavia (ICTY) in 1993 and the ad hoc International Criminal Tribunal for Rwanda (ICTR) in 1994, designed to bring to justice those responsible for war crimes, crimes against humanity, and genocide.[27] These tribunals were championed by then U.S. Permanent Representative to the United Nations Madeleine Albright. The creation of the ICTY provided, inter alia, an outlet for U.S. frustrations over the apparent impunity accorded to perpetrators and, perhaps, over the ineffectiveness of U.S. Balkan policy during the early 1990s. Albright also pressed hard for the creation of the ICTR, possibly out of concern over consistency and possibly over a sense of responsibility for Washington's reluctance to authorize reinforcement of the United Nations Mission in Rwanda. This early, constructive support for both tribunals only heightened the disappointment of many international observers when the United States chose to oppose the establishment of the International Criminal Court (ICC), a reaction only partly mitigated by President Clinton's last-gasp decision that the United States should sign the Rome Statue in December 2000. (As pointed out by Vesselin Popovski, the United States could soon be grappling with difficult policy problems vis-à-vis a newly created ICC.[28] If the ICC were to indict Osama bin Laden, or other terrorists threatening the United States, for instance, would Washington refuse to cooperate? From this perspective, more worrisome than U.S. nonparticipation in the ICC are efforts by some in the Senate to preclude any U.S. cooperation with this body.)

A valuable benefit of multilateral forums, and one that is often overlooked, is the opportunity they can provide for bilateral dialogue between hostile powers. During the 1990s, for example, the United Nations provided a venue for dialogue between the United States and North Korea. This mechanism is quite nonthreatening, as it requires mutual consent for activation. Beyond this benefit, multilateral initiatives can be used to signal changes in national policies that may have significant repercussions for a country's bilateral relations. Arguably, this could be the case with Iranian President Mohammed Khatami's advocacy of a "dialogue of civilizations" through UN intermediation; such a process could yet lead, indirectly, to moderation of U.S. views of Iran as a rogue state, with potential benefits all around.[29] Likewise, Iran and the United States might have exploited their participation in the UN's 6+2 support group of negotiations on Afghanistan as cover for efforts to achieve a rapprochement (although neither side seemed, as of 2002, to have used that group for this purpose).

There is a strong sense internationally that even though the United States can choose not to play multilaterally on a variety of issues, thus damaging prospects for successful international action, it cannot be allowed to derail joint action by others when the stakes are deemed important. This was the clear message emerging from the multilateral negotiations in Bonn and Marrakesh in 2001 concerning the implementation of the Kyoto Protocol to combat climate change, which took place after the United States had essentially withdrawn from negotiations. Although there is general recognition that a multilateral climate change regime cannot work optimally without U.S. participation, allies and other partners have concluded that they can no longer afford to wait or make further concessions to U.S. reservations. (It may be worth noting that George W. Bush administration's stance on climate change, which caters to industrial interests, is also unpopular among broad swaths of U.S. public opinion.) U.S. diplomatic blocking power, though significant, is thus not complete.

Contemporary U.S. Attitudes

The conflict between values and interests as impulses in U.S. foreign policy, particularly on issues of military intervention, continued to hold sway in the 2000 presidential election campaign. During a debate in February 2000, a leading Republican candidate, Governor George W. Bush of Texas, indicated that he would not commit U.S. troops to avert another Rwanda-type genocide;

his challenger, Senator John McCain of Arizona, indicated that he might wish the United States to intervene under such a dire scenario.[30] Democratic challenger Bill Bradley took a contrarian tack and advocated greater cooperation with other countries on humanitarian crises through multilateral forums such as the United Nations.[31] Fellow Democrat Al Gore was widely suspected of being a closet UN supporter on the basis of his extensive involvement in environmental issues both as vice president and previously as a senator, but he had little good to say about the United Nations on the campaign trail. Prominent advisers to the Republican front-runner, Bush, saw some uses for the United Nations, but only when convenient for the United States and in support of U.S. interests, narrowly defined:

> Using American forces as the world's "911" will degrade capabilities, bog soldiers down in peacekeeping roles, and fuel concern among great powers that the United States has decided to enforce notions of "limited sovereignty" worldwide in the name of humanitarianism. This overly broad definition of America's national interest is bound to backfire as others arrogate the same authority to themselves. Or we will find ourselves looking to the United Nations to sanction the use of American military power in these cases, implying that we will do so even when our vital interests are involved, which would be a mistake.[32]
>
> Republicans judge international agreements and institutions as means to achieve ends, not as forms of political therapy. Agreements and institutions can facilitate bargaining, recognize common interests, and resolve differences cooperatively. But international law, unlike domestic law, merely codifies an already agreed-upon cooperation. Even mechanisms will need negotiations in order to work, and international law not backed by power cannot cope with dangerous people and states. Every issue need not be dealt with multilaterally.[33]

One should not read too much into these policy platforms, which are, after all, statements of campaign rhetoric. Neither should one view Republicans as innately hostile to the United Nations, or Democrats as firm friends of multilateralism. It was George H. W. Bush in 1990, after all, who sought to reverse the Iraqi annexation of Kuwait by working through the United Nations, and it was that Republican president, ably assisted by Secretary of State James Baker, who built the impressive international Coalition mandated by the Security Council to this end.[34] By contrast, Clinton and his team proved extremely volatile and unreliable patrons and allies for the United Nations.

The United States today is clearly not isolationist. Its economic interests, for one thing, are global. Accordingly, whatever their stated preferences, successive U.S. administrations aimed aggressively to contain financial crises in Mexico, Brazil, Russia, and several Asian countries in order to avoid contagion and the threats to its own prosperity, which itself is highly dependent on international markets in an increasingly globalized world. The more hands-off, even tough-love approach of the Bush administration to the economic policy implosion in Argentina in December 2001 may signal a change of tack. This may be helpful, systemically, if it can underscore the responsibility of political leaders for the success of their policies—and also the responsibility of international banks and businesses for their own lending and investment decisions, without the safety net of assured international bailouts. However, the more emollient attitude of Washington at a time of economic crisis in Turkey earlier in the same year, induced by similar local economic mismanagement, suggested that the administration would continue to tend carefully to valuable geostrategic assets—whatever its overall policy preferences.

Overall, the United States has exercised strong international leadership within the International Monetary Fund, World Bank, and the G7 forum of finance ministers and central bank governors to protect international financial markets from major systemic upheavals (although U.S. ideology and modus operandi can grate on partners, as clearly suggested in Chapter 13 by Toyoo Gyohten, perhaps Japan's most experienced actor on the stage of international economic relations).

The Clinton Track Record

The record of the Clinton administration on multilateralism was very much one of hopes unfulfilled (and often unpursued), with one significant exception: the North American Free Trade Agreement, U.S. ratification of which was perhaps Clinton's greatest foreign policy achievement. There were other successes in the multilateral arena, including Senate ratification of the Uruguay Round trade agreements, including the creation of the World Trade Organization, and Senate acceptance of NATO expansion. And having retreated from Madeleine Albright's early espousal of "assertive multilateralism" following U.S. military casualties in Somalia and the U.S. failure to meaningfully address genocide in Rwanda (by effectively blocking action on the issue within the UN Security Council), the administration nevertheless maintained a flirtation with a number of other important multilateral initiatives during the late 1990s, including a convention banning the use of antipersonnel landmines and negotiations toward a statute for an international criminal court. Nevertheless, the administration failed to promote these initiatives, in part due to hostility in the Pentagon, and essentially blamed the ensuing hostile U.S. stance on Congress.

The Clinton administration also fumbled its handling of the Comprehensive Nuclear Test Ban Treaty (CTBT). Signed by 160 countries, the CTBT was dealt a near-fatal blow when the U.S. Senate, where a two-thirds majority is needed for ratification, rejected it by a 51–48 vote in October 1999. The Senate's action did not result from an in-depth review of the CTBT's merits from the perspective of U.S. national interests. Rather, a bold legislative ambush by Republicans, compounded by sloppy legislative management in the Clinton administration, left the White House unprepared, with insufficient time for the intensive lobbying generally preceding major treaty ratification votes.

The dominant international perception of the Clinton record in foreign policy, particularly on multilateral issues, was one of disappointment. On the one hand, President Clinton frequently advocated multilateral causes, seemed eager to support the United Nations (short of expending political capital with Congress), and appeared genuinely engaged in the key diplomatic issues of his day. On the other, having been tripped up by the U.S. military nearly immediately following his assumption of power in Washington over the controversial issue of gays in the military, he never subsequently seemed willing to confront the Pentagon or its allies in Congress until all other options failed (as they ultimately did in Haiti and Bosnia). International opinion was dismayed in October 1993 when he blamed the United Nations for the deaths of U.S. Army Rangers, who had in fact been deployed on a U.S.-controlled mission about which the United Nations knew nothing. Clinton's approximate sense of the truth was apparent in international relations even before it surfaced in the domestic sphere. The disappointment arose particularly from a sense that this singularly talented political operative, a fast and keen learner on international affairs, never lived up to his potential. His last-gasp signature of the Rome Statute of the International Criminal Court merely drew attention to his lack of gumption in not signing it earlier (if he believed in it at all). Ultimately, the Clinton administration, so successful in the management of domestic economic policy, was seen internationally as a reluctant, inconsistent sheriff prone to damaging half-measures.[35]

A significant problem for the Clinton administration, and one it handled poorly, was a push by the Republican majorities in the Senate and the House of Representatives for a greater congressional role in shaping U.S. foreign policy. Jesse Helms, chair of the Senate Foreign Relations Committee from 1994 to 2001, directed a highly effective campaign to impose reform and restructuring not only on the U.S. State Department, the U.S. Agency for International Development, and the Arms Control and Disarmament Agency but also on the United Nations, seeking to micromanage a myriad of aspects of UN structure, budgeting, and practice. The administration protested but assented. Although this was part of a broader pattern of administration submission to congressional demands, it left Washington on increasingly tenuous grounds with other UN member states, as shrill complaints from even key UN allies over nonpayment of U.S. dues to the organization made clear.

> Critics point to the hypocrisy of the United States on the world stage.
> America seeks UN endorsement when convenient but is slow to pay its

dues; America practices legal abortion at home but denies funds to organizations that do the same abroad. . . . The president has a favored policy
but is powerless to make Congress follow it.[36]

The Early George W. Bush Administration

The George W. Bush administration came to power under the misapprehen-
sion that a sentimental Clinton administration had undermined U.S. interests in order to accommodate multilateral institutions. In advancing a new
approach, the style evolved more than did the substance. In pursuing missile defense more aggressively, and by insisting that the largely redundant
bilateral Anti-Ballistic Missile (ABM) Treaty be formally junked rather
than overtaken by new treaties, Bush obscured the fact that missile defense
had been tested, however tentatively, under the Clinton administration and
that the latter had kept options open on the matter. In rejecting outright the
1997 Kyoto Protocol to the 1992 United Nations Framework Convention
on Climate Change, Bush once again obscured how little the Clinton team
had done to give it effect. However, with these bold strokes and rhetoric
throughout the administration, with the exception of Secretary of State
Colin Powell, seemingly hostile to a treaty-based system of international relations, Bush telegraphed that he would pursue assertive unilateralism. This
go-it-alone posture raised many hackles abroad, contributing to U.S. defeats for reelection to the UN Commission on Human Rights and the UN
Narcotics Control Board in May 2001. These, in turn, led to a predictable
but overwrought outpouring of invective in Congress, although the administration reacted steadily.

However, the administration's suspicion of many treaties continued,
with a case-by-case review soon codified by the State Department's policy
planning director, Richard Haass, as "multilateralism *à la carte*."[37] In July
2001, the administration withdrew from negotiations on the protocol addressing verification of the Biological and Toxin Weapons Convention, declaring that the proposed instrument would not deter other nations, although
the United States continued to support the treaty itself.[38] (Information soon
emerged in the media that the United States was actively engaged in forms
of biological weapons testing.) The negotiations toward this protocol,
which were nearing completion after six-and-a-half years of intense discussions, promptly collapsed. "Washington's allies reacted with dismay and
confusion. . . . Diplomats said the move would reinforce criticism of unilateral U.S. actions."[39] Meanwhile, at the UN conference seeking to curtail
illegal trafficking in small arms, the United States "managed to create unanimity" against its insistence on its right to sell weapons to nonstate actors
and its refusal to allow a mention of children in the related UN Plan of
Action.[40] The White House adopted the intriguing approach that friendly

personal ties between President Bush and European leaders were all that mattered: "It doesn't matter whether the leaders agree with him or not on the issues. He has very good, warm relations throughout."[41] Perhaps European leaders were too oblique in expressing to Bush in person their reservations over Washington's approach, although on Kyoto EU leaders could not have been much more clear.

Interpretations of Washington's approach in Europe and elsewhere singled out U.S. exceptionalism as highly objectionable. "On a number of questions, Washington says it isn't changing policy. But it doesn't want to accept commitments that would put the United States on an equal level of policy obligation with other states. . . . [The United States] cannot seek to exempt itself."[42]

European unhappiness with the United States during this period focused not only on perceived U.S. global irresponsibility and economic selfishness in rejecting the Kyoto Protocol but also on growing perceptions of U.S. normative deviancy centered on the death penalty, most egregiously the execution of mentally retarded convicts. In a poll conducted in mid-2001, Europeans expressed disapproval of Bush foreign policy in proportions triple to approval. In Britain, France, and Germany, those polled also overwhelmingly opined that Bush made decisions based entirely on U.S. interests rather than taking into account European concerns.[43] One expert opined: "The strength of opinion holds across borders and across age groups. If the President wants allied support on anything, he's got his work cut out for him."[44] A leading German editor, Josef Joffe, noted that these opinions reflected "an underlying reality which is hard to deny": President Bush was a unilateralist. He noted that the president was very different from his father, who "was careful in keeping his international ducks lined up. There was a guy who knew that he represented Mr. Big, but who understood that Mr. Big needed allies for legitimacy."[45] The administration's threat to unilaterally abrogate the ABM Treaty binding the United States and Russia provoked even harsher European responses.

Many U.S. students of international relations, unconvinced by actual progress toward a genuine European Union, meaningful also in the defense sphere, chafed at European pretensions to global or even alliance leadership. In particular, acerbic Americans wondered why the EU required fifteen UN votes to help defeat the United States for bodies on which they felt it belonged by right. Although the manners of the Bush administration with respect to consultation of allies over missile defense improved notably over its first few months, suggesting it could learn on the job, the tone of U.S. rhetoric remained tough on many issues, whereas the substance of its message was often contradictory (particularly when involving Defense Secretary Donald Rumsfeld, on one side, and Secretary of State Powell on the other).

Many in the European policy community were alarmed by the swift deterioration in the climate of the transatlantic relationship while being much less cowed by differences than they might have been during the Cold War. The early preference of President Bush for emphasizing hemispheric relations and the ill-disguised search by some in the administration for new adversaries in Asia had the potential to shift international relations, but they were not perceived abroad as of mid-2001 as (yet) fundamentally altering it. However, the more belligerent U.S. tone was seen as unpalatable, unnecessary, and possibly likely to produce destabilizing consequences. At home, Democratic legislators in Congress were sharply critical of the Bush administration's tone and of its unilateral policy thrust. But they were accused by some hostile commentators of playing to European galleries.[46]

The World After September 11, 2001

The September 11, 2001, terrorist attacks on the World Trade Center and the Pentagon appeared to open a new chapter in relations between the United States and its partners, most visible at the United Nations. The day after the attacks, the Security Council adopted, at the initiative of France, a strong resolution condemning the attacks, terming them a threat to international peace and security and to referring the inherent right to self-defense.[47] Some days later, the Security Council adopted, under UN Charter Chapter VII, a U.S. text stigmatizing the harboring of terrorists and setting out detailed measures member states were mandated to implement to prevent financing of terrorism from within their borders.[48] The Security Council established a committee to monitor implementation of the resolution's manifold provisions.

The United States did work to preclude any language that might constrain its ability to strike back at terrorists or states harboring them wherever they might be. Furthermore, in pursuing its military campaign against the Al-Qaida network and the Taliban regime, the United States, through a hub-and-spoke strategy, ensured that it alone made the key decisions, drawing on allies and other coalition partners individually as their contributions were required for intelligence, military, or diplomatic purposes. It thus marginalized the decisionmaking role of NATO allies and regional partners.[49] In late November 2001, the United States clashed publicly with the United Kingdom, which had championed the deployment to Afghanistan of international peacekeepers to establish security for the delivery of humanitarian assistance and perhaps to help a transitional Afghan government to take root. Washington argued that its military objectives had to take priority over everything else.[50] The manner in which it managed this campaign stands in contrast to the Kosovo air campaign, which it conducted through the NATO Council and NATO military headquarters—an experience that many in Washington had found cumbersome. Echoing U.S. and U.K. diplomatic lobbying at the United Nations for "smart sanctions" against Iraq, one could describe the U.S. approach as one of "smart unilateralism," providing for an apparently multilateral "coalition profile" but without the aggravation of committee decisionmaking. The allies did not complain publicly. They understood that no government, in the absence of a crushing response to the attacks on the Pentagon and World Trade Center, would be free from risk of similar attacks. Thus, in the security sphere they were content to allow Washington call the tune of the international diplomatic minuet, if still somewhat concerned over its intention, reiterated by President Bush in December 2001, to withdraw from the ABM Treaty linking it with Russia.

In spite of agreement in the U.S. Senate to confirm a new Permanent Representative to the United Nations (John Negroponte's nomination had been held up for many months) and its action to repay most U.S. arrears to the United Nations, it was not clear that anything basic in the U.S. approach had changed. The United States stuck to its guns in opposing a protocol to establish a verification regime for the Biological and Toxin Weapons Convention, continued to reject the Kyoto Protocol, most recently at negotiations in Morocco, and worked to undermine implementation of the International Criminal Court statute.[51] Thus, it was too early to predict whether the international struggle against terrorism would infuse Washington with a more multilateral spirit. To many, it seemed clear that U.S. multilateral engagement on the issue of counterterrorism alone would not, as a practical matter, work for long.[52] Partners would look for some United States "give" on matters of importance to them to recognize Washington's "take" on counterterrorism, even though, obviously, Americans would frown on any formal linkage. Yet Washington as well as many Americans seemed to feel, at the outset of 2002, that the United States needed to rely mostly on itself for its defense and that foreigners by and large understood although did not welcome this.

With the military defeat of the Taliban, achieved impressively by mid-November 2001, it became possible internationally to discuss several propositions.[53] First, military firepower matters. So far did U.S. capacities outstrip those of even its best-equipped allies that NATO capabilities proved irrelevant in the Afghan military campaign. Allies helped with diplomatic support, intelligence, and action against suspected terrorists or terrorist sympathizers within their own borders. But they had little to offer militarily. Second, from Washington's perspective, complete control of military decisionmaking worked far better than the consensus decisionmaking on which it and other allies relied during the air campaign over Kosovo and Serbia in 1999. NATO's political unity was critical in staring down Moscow at that time, and a less efficient command format was then well worth some irritation among military brass in Washington. But it was not necessary in the Afghanistan theater (and may never be again). Third, key allies are decisively weakened diplomatically when they have nothing much to offer militarily. For years, successive U.S. administrations had pleaded with leading European and other allies to increase their military spending, enhance their capabilities, and rationalize their defense industries. As efforts within the EU to create an EU-wide, rapidly deployable military force had become bogged down (as has so much else in Brussels) in wrangling, technological and other gaps between U.S. and European weaponry increasingly became unbridgeable. Consequently, by mid-November 2001, in the absence of any significant military contribution to the coalition effort in Afghanistan, it proved impossible for U.S. allies to prevail in their argument that an international peacekeeping force needed to be deployed in the parts of Afghanistan newly freed of the Taliban until the U.S. Central Command in Tampa, Florida, calling the military shots, was ready. Thus, even passively the United States retains significant diplomatic blocking power in the security sphere (if not always, as seen above, in the economic and social spheres).[54] Europeans were still mulling over these stark developments as this book went to print.

The crisis did bring about a significant modification in tone of the Bush administration's rhetoric toward Moscow and Beijing. Although the cooperation of NATO allies with Washington in its hour of need can never have been greatly in doubt, diplomatic and intelligence support from Moscow, freely offered, has allowed President Vladimir Putin to reposition his country diplomatically, netting him a vastly enhanced relationship with NATO. Beijing demonstrated to the United States that its diplomatic support, in the UN Security Council and well beyond, carried real value. This dispelled dyspeptic talk of "strategic adversaries" in Washington, as well as the earlier sour approach of the Bush administration to the governments of several major non-NATO countries.

Conclusion

This brief examination of trends in the Bush and Clinton administrations and international reaction thereto begs the question as to what foreign governments and experts might, on balance, prefer. The inconsistent, often two-faced multilateralism on offer from the Clinton administration stands in sharp contrast to the frank unilateralism of the Bush government. On this, the jury in mid-2002 is still out. Washington's essentially unilateral campaign against Al-Qaida and the Taliban has benefited most governments. Its skill in sustaining a political coalition broadly in support of its military goals is widely admired and has engendered in some quarters the perhaps naive hope that greater willingness to engage multilaterally on other issues may ensue. The real tests are yet to come on trade, climate change, arms control, and implementation of international criminal justice. The events of September 11 and the decisive reaction thereto of Washington have inhibited foreign governments as they have fallen silent. They have little sense of what is to come in relations with the United States in coming years.

Notes

1. In some cases, it is hard to fault Washington for walking away from institutions it had once supported. UNESCO, latterly a self-sustaining, bloated bureaucracy with few meaningful programs had, by the late 1970s, developed an alarming penchant for unnecessary international regulation, disastrously finding its ultimate expression in the media censorship–tinged proposals for a New International Information Order. Although it is more sensibly oriented and managed today, its credibility remains largely shattered in Washington.

2. www.un.org/millennium/webcast/statements/usa.htm.

3. A few Republican voices, often seen as mavericks within the party, such as Indiana Senator Richard Lugar, bucked this trend but did not dent it.

4. Barbara Crossette, "Helms, in Visit to UN, Offers Harsh Message," *New York Times,* January 21, 2000.

5. In justifying its own military interventions entailing the sovereignty of other states, conducted singly or multilaterally, the United States has traditionally preferred to rely on arguments of self-defense. The removal of General Manuel Noriega from the helm in Panama is one such example. However, the United States has allowed itself to be persuaded by purely humanitarian considerations of the need for international intervention, leading a large international force into Somalia in late 1992 to save the country from famine and agreeing to support in the UN Security Council a French-led intervention (Opération Turquoise) into southwestern Rwanda in 1994.

6. See Malone, *Decision-Making in the UN Security Council,* pp. 69–164.

7 See Neville-Jones, "Dayton, IFOR, and Alliance Relations in Bosnia," pp. 48–53.

8 For a discussion of how U.S. priorities shaped the Dayton accords and subsequent difficulties in implementing it, see Cousens and Cater, *Toward Peace in Bosnia.*

9. See Levitin, "Inside Moscow's Kosovo Muddle," p. 139.

10. See Roberts, "NATO's 'Humanitarian War' over Kosovo," pp. 106–109, esp. p. 107.

11. Ibid., p. 105.

12. See Malone "Goodbye UNSCOM: A Sorry Tale in US-UN Relations," pp. 393–411.

13. See General Assembly Resolution A/Res/54/21 of November 9, 1999. U.S. legislation imposing severe sanctions on foreign companies and foreign subsidiaries of U.S. companies investing in Cuba were also strongly resisted by the European Union and Canada.

14. The legislation in question was the Cuban Liberty and Democratic Solidarity Act (the so-called Helms-Burton bill) signed into law by President Clinton of March 12, 1996, and the Iran and Libya Sanctions Act signed by Clinton on August 5, 1996.

15. For a recent discussion of sanctions and the increasing use of targeted sanctions, see Drezner, *The Sanctions Paradox.* Also see Cortright and Lopez, *The Sanctions Decade.*

16. See Malone, "Iraq: No Easy Response to 'The Greatest Threat,'" pp. 236–245.

17. See Jim Wurst, "Security Council Faces Iraqi Inspections and Sanctions Issues," *Inter-Press-Service (IPS) Terra,* April 14, 2000, www.ipsdailyjournal.org. See also the hard-hitting paragraphs on sanctions in the UN Secretary-General's *Millennium Report* of April 3, 2000, at www.un.org/millennium/sg/report.

18. See Malone, "Goodbye UNSCOM."

19. Flora Lewis, "US Military Policy Ought to be Getting an Airing," *International Herald Tribune*, September 15, 2000. See also United Nations, *Report of the Panel on United Nations Peace Operations* (A/55/305-S/2000/809), August 21, 2000.

20. Interestingly, though, Washington ensured that the actual European Recovery Plan that emerged from Marshal's initiative took a multilateral form, in the hopes of stimulating European integration.

21. Eban, "The UN Idea Revisited," p. 42.

22. The text vetoed by France on the Indonesian question can be found in UN Document S/513 of August 25,1947, and that vetoed by China in S/3502 of December 13, 1955. France joined Russia in vetoing a resolution on the Spanish question on June 26, 1946 (the text can be found in *UN Yearbook 1946,* p. 350). The countries possessing vetoes under the terms of the UN Charter are China (Taiwan until 1971, the People's Republic of China since then), France, the Russian Federation (which succeeded to the Soviet Union veto unchallenged in December 1991), the United Kingdom, and the United States.

23. General Assembly Resolution 3379 of November 10, 1975.

24. General Assembly Resolution A/46/86 of December 16, 1991.

25. The term "Ronald Thatcherism," describing the free-market philosophy and activism of Margaret Thatcher, the British prime minister (1979–1991), and Ronald Reagan, the U.S. president (1981–1989), was to my knowledge coined by Sylvia Ostry, head of economics at the OECD and subsequently a senior Canadian trade and economic negotiator.

26. See "Remarks by the President to the 54th Session of the UN General Assembly," The White House (Office of the Spokesman), www.state.gov.

27. See Security Council Resolutions 808 and 827 (1993) on the former Yugoslav tribunal and Security Council Resolution 955 (1994) on Rwanda.

28. See Popovski, "International Criminal Court," pp. 416–417.

29. See Roshandel, "Iran's Foreign and Security Policies," pp. 110–113.

30. For a cogent analysis of the debate and its implications, see an op-ed piece by Michael Ignatieff, "The Next President's Duty to Intervene," *New York Times,* February 13, 2000.

31. See "Foreign Policy Town Meeting," November 29, 1999, Fletcher School of Law and Diplomacy, Tufts University, www.billbradley.com. The issue came up in response to a question on criteria for U.S. responses to humanitarian crises.

32. Rice, "Promoting the National Interest," p. 54.

33. Zoellick, "A Republican Foreign Policy," p. 69.

34. James Baker subsequently served the UN as Kofi Annan's Special Envoy on the Western Sahara issue.

35. For an examination of some of the challenges underpinning the unique role of the United States in world politics, see Haass, *The Reluctant Sheriff.*

36. Mallaby, "The Bullied Pulpit," p. 7.

37. See Thom Shanker, "White House Says the US Is Not a Loner, Just Choosy," *New York Times,* July 31, 2001.

38. See Richard Wolffe and Frances Williams, "US Says Bio-Warfare Deal is Unworkable," *Financial Times,* July 26, 2001.

39. See Frances Williams and Richard Wolffe, "Allies React with Dismay," *Financial Times*, July 26, 2001.

40. Authors' translation. See Afsané Bassir, "La Conférence de l'ONU sur les Armes: égères S'acheve sur un Échec Complet," *Le Monde,* July 22–23, 2001.

41. White House Spokesman Ari Fleischer, quoted in Judy Dempsey and Richard Wolffe, "Differences of Style," *Financial Times,* July 27, 2001.

42. See Flora Lewis, "The US Is Turning Its Back on Any Global Rules," *International Herald Tribune,* July 14, 2001.

43. Pew Research Center survey conducted in August 2001 with the *International Herald Tribune* and the Council on Foreign Relations. See www.iht.com.

44. Samuel P. Wells, head of West European Studies, Woodrow Wilson Center, Washington, quoted in Adam Clymer, "Surveys Find European Public Critical of Bush Policies," *New York Times,* August 16, 2001.

45. Ibid.

46. See Lawrence F. Kaplan, "On Foreign Policy, Democrats Court European Voters," *Wall Street Journal,* August 16, 2001.

47. SCR 1368 of September 12, 2001.

48. SCR 1373 of September 18, 2001.

49. Confidential interviews with senior UN diplomats.

50. Michael R. Gordon, "US and UK at Odds Over Use and Timing of Peacekeeping Troops," *New York Times,* December 2, 2001.

51. So far, the administration's position on climate change has been influenced neither by mounting evidence originating with the UN and other sources that the last decade has been the warmest by far since records have been kept, nor, more significantly, by the domestic unpopularity of its stance. See "This Year Was Second Hottest, Confirming Trend, UN Says," *New York Times,* December 19, 2001.

52. See David M. Malone, "How to Wage a Diplomatic War," *Toronto Globe and Mail,* September 19, 2001.

53. See David M. Malone, "Uncle Sam's Coalition of One," *Toronto Globe and Mail,* December 11, 2001.

54. This was also demonstrated when Canada offered to lead a coalition of countries into Eastern Zaire in late 1996 to provide urgently needed security for humanitarian assistance efforts. A lack of enthusiasm in the Pentagon, privately shared in London, proved sufficient to torpedo the effort, with tragic results on the ground.

PART I

THE RULE OF LAW

3

Weak as Constraint, Strong as Tool: The Place of International Law in U.S. Foreign Policy

Nico Krisch

LAW AND POWER HAVE ALWAYS COEXISTED IN AN UNEASY RELATIONSHIP. THE powerful have appreciated law as an instrument for governing others, for lending legitimacy to the exercise of power, for rationalizing this exercise, and for creating stable expectations as to the behavior of those governed. However, the powerful have also regarded law with skepticism because it provides a shield for the weak by not only authorizing the exercise of power but also limiting it, because it urges rational justifications and restricts arbitrariness, and because its formality is relatively resistant to change. If the exercise of power is thus supported but also limited by the form of the legal instrument, law itself, too, is both shaped by power and acts as a restraint on it. It reflects the realities of power in its content and structure, but it also imposes certain limits, the most important of them probably being its equal application to all its subjects. Law and power thus mutually influence each other, in both a reinforcing and a weakening way.

International law has long occupied a unique position in this respect. Its nonhierarchical character has made it less amenable as a tool for the exercise of power, as it does not allow for unilateral lawmaking and requires the equal application of the law to the states creating it.[1] However, its small range, imprecise content, and lack of enforcement tools have made it less harmful to powerful states and have rendered possible significant inequality in its definition and application. Indeed, "the demands that international law [has made] on states [have been] on the whole so light that its rules in general [have been] fairly well observed."[2] Moreover, except for the vague rules of customary law, it has historically consisted mainly of bilateral treaties that can be shaped according to the power relations of its parties; and the lack of universality has weakened the pull toward equality that characterizes domestic law to a high degree. Thus, international law has been of lesser use but has also caused lesser harm to the powerful than law in the domestic order. Indeed, its limiting force was so weak that it even allowed for an exercise of power so blatant as that of the Concert of Europe in the nineteenth century. Inequalities of power were considered outside the international legal system.[3]

These particularities of international law, however, have been subject to gradual change, altering the relationship of international law and power. Contemporary international law increasingly consists of lawlike treaties, aspiring to universal application and thus pulling toward greater equality. Its rules have become both more precise and better enforced, and it now poses greater limits on the powerful, too. Except for the hierarchical mode of its creation, international law increasingly resembles domestic law, rendering its use as an instrument of power more difficult.

Given this background, it is hardly surprising that the United States exhibits significant ambivalence toward international legal rules, an ambivalence possibly greater than that shown by earlier great powers. Although this ambivalence has old roots, I argue in this chapter that it has become more marked since the United States rose to the status of the world's sole superpower. Even as the United States has remained very active in the development and enforcement of international law, paradoxically it has in many areas sought to avoid its own subjection to such law. Moreover, U.S. policy has had a significant impact on the structure of international law, as the United States has attempted to transform its superior power position into legal rules and to make the rules less harmful to its own interests. To this end, it has devised means to counter tendencies toward equality and stability of international legal norms. As a result, the United States has emerged as a leading obstacle to those phenomena that characterize "modern" international law, notably universal treaties and strong enforcement mechanisms.

Ambivalence toward international law, however, does not necessarily signify hostility toward multilateralism. Certainly, international legal rules are usually an expression of a multilateral (or at least bilateral) approach; but they are only one particular form of multilateralism, characterized by high formality and strong commitments.[4] States that are wary of international law may prefer, and thus rely more heavily on, alternative forms of multilateral action.

At the same time, international law is not always the multilateral form par excellence that it seems to be. Its structure is, in principle, still dominated by the rule that states may do whatever is not prohibited; thus, international law contains a presumption in favor of the legality of unilateral action, at least if it remains within the confines of a state's jurisdiction.[5] While not endorsing unilateralism, neither does it condemn it in the absence of a specific rule to the contrary. Thus, every attempt by a state to weaken an existing rule or to prevent a more stringent rule from developing can be regarded as a defense of the freedom to act unilaterally; whether directed at a new rule of international law or the preservation of an old one, it remains in this sense a multilateral endeavor.

Moreover, international rules can be the result of processes initiated by action that seems to be purely unilateral. New rules of customary international law sometimes evolve because some states start to break old rules and try to replace them with others; this has happened, for example, with the assertion of the coastal states' rights to the continental shelf following the Truman Proclamation.[6] Similarly, new treaties often result from unilateral action: for example, in 1967, the bombing by Great Britain of the *Torrey Canyon* tanker to prevent an oil spill led to the adoption of the Intervention Convention two years later.[7] And the "aggressive unilateralism" of the United States with respect to trade practices and intellectual property rights since the mid-1980s helped prod other states to engage in the Uruguay Round of trade negotiations under the General Agreement of Tariffs and Trade (GATT) and eventually to create the World Trade Organization (WTO) in 1994.[8] Thus, international law and unilateralism are often closely intertwined.

More often, however, the creation of new international law serves as a tool of multilateral action, and it is on this function that I focus. This chapter describes the ways in which the United States uses international law as a tool of multilateralism and seeks to shape international law according to its own wishes. The discussion may help clarify the factors that make law appear as a useful or dangerous tool for powerful states. To that end, I confine myself to a descriptive analysis of the creation of new law and the modification of existing rules, rather than analyzing U.S. compliance with existing rules. Such an analysis could certainly provide further insights into the place of multilateralism in U.S. foreign policy, but its main focus would be on the effect of legal norms, rather than their usefulness as a foreign policy tool.[9] Furthermore, this chapter is primarily descriptive, examining the uses the United States makes of international law. By and large, it refrains from offering hypotheses to explain U.S. action, which likely involves a complex mixture of systemic, cultural, and political factors. Hopefully, this chapter will offer a useful framework for future explanatory investigations.

A Mixed Tradition: The United States and International Law Until the End of the Cold War

U.S. ambivalence toward international law is not a recent phenomenon; the country's attitude has long been one of mixed feelings. Initially, when the United States was still a comparatively weak state, it regarded international law with much sympathy, as reflected, for example, in the constitutional assertion that treaties are the "supreme Law of the Land."[10] In *The Federalist,* the observance of international law was regarded as an essential means for securing peace, and indeed it was argued that a closer union of the American states was needed to ensure this observance.[11] In the early years of the republic, international law was held in high esteem, and in 1793 Chief Justice John Jay could declare that the "peace, prosperity and reputation of the United States, will always greatly depend on their fidelity to their engagements."[12] Accordingly, U.S. courts applied international law carefully, as in the piracy cases of the 1810s and 1820s.[13] These early commitments left strong traces in U.S. law, and the Supreme Court's finding in the 1900 *Paquete Habana* case that "international law is part of our law" remains, in principle, valid.[14]

Despite this generally positive attitude toward existing international law, however, the United States was from the beginning cautious about entering into new treaty obligations. Accordingly, the Constitution contains, as a special hurdle, the requirement of a two-thirds majority for treaty ratification in the Senate. The nineteenth century also saw tendencies to restrict the domestic impact of international law. These were reflected in the development and more frequent use of the later-in-time rule, which allowed statutes to deprive earlier treaty provisions of their force in internal law, and in the rise of the concept of non–self-executing treaties—that is, treaties that required further action by Congress in order to take effect in U.S. law.[15] By removing such treaties from the jurisdiction of the courts, the U.S. government secured a freer hand in pursuing foreign policy in areas regulated by international law. Compliance with international law could no longer be enforced by judicial means, and governmental deviation from treaties became easier. Moreover, the United States was always ready to deny international legal limitations to the pursuit of its core national interests. It did so, for example, by insisting that it alone was competent to assess whether recourse to self-defense was justified. To this effect, the United States made a reservation to the Kellogg-Briand Pact of 1928. Similar positions resurfaced during the Cuban missile crisis of 1962 and with respect to U.S. involvement in Nicaragua in the 1980s.[16]

Paradoxically, in view of these tendencies, the United States has long been a driving force behind the development of international law, especially after the U.S. rise to major-power status. The three most important treaties of the first half of the twentieth century—the Covenant of the League of Nations, the Kellogg-Briand Pact, and the United Nations Charter—drew heavily on U.S. initiatives, as did many later treaties, such as the Non-Proliferation Treaty and the Human Rights Covenants. But the histories of the League Covenant, the Universal Declaration on Human Rights, the Havana Charter on the International Trade Organization, and the Human Rights Covenants also reflect an ever-present reluctance by the United States to subscribe to far-reaching international obligations, especially if they are coupled with strong institutional arrangements.[17]

This is, of course, due in part to the supermajority required by the U.S. Constitution for Senate ratification, a requirement that originally flowed mainly from the wish to remain outside European power struggles and their violent excesses. This wish was most famously reflected in George Washington's warning against "entangling alliances" in his Farewell Address.[18] But the requirement for a two-thirds majority in the Senate can also be traced back to the specific concerns of federalism, in this case to a desire to protect small groups of states against a majority of the others.[19] This constitutional requirement is unique among industrialized democracies, and it is certainly responsible not only for the United States's greater unease with treaties compared to other countries but also for its greater reluctance to use treaties as compared to other forms of multilateral cooperation.[20]

From the earliest years of the U.S. republic onward, but most effectively since World War II, U.S. presidents have sought to circumvent this rule by distinguishing treaties from executive agreements, which are concluded either with prior authorization by a simple majority of both houses of Congress or on the basis of the president's own executive powers.[21] More than 90 percent of U.S. treaties now take this form,[22] but the Senate has always insisted that the most important be concluded as "treaties," with the main exception being trade agreements like GATT, the treaty on the WTO, and the North American Free Trade Agreement (all concluded as executive agreements).[23] Moreover, multilateral agreements are more often concluded as treaties than are bilateral ones.[24] For such treaties to be ratified, broad domestic consensus and bipartisan support is necessary, and any treaty arousing controversy is likely to fail. As a result, in the United States it is hardly possible for one administration to subscribe to a treaty obligation in order to bind its successor to a certain policy—a strategy governments in other countries often pursue in entering into international agreements.[25]

Continued Ambivalence: The United States and International Law After the Cold War

Since the end of the Cold War, the U.S. attitude toward international law has continued to be characterized by ambivalence, and many elements of its earlier behavior have reappeared. However, some of these characteristics are more marked, and changes have occurred in the issue areas affected by U.S. skepticism toward legal regulation.

Developing and Evading International Law: The Conclusion of Treaties

During the early 1990s, the United States played an important role in several new initiatives to strengthen the international legal order, particularly in the field of arms control. Early on, the United States took the lead in international progress toward a Comprehensive Nuclear Test Ban Treaty (CTBT), the extension of the Non-Proliferation Treaty, the Chemical Weapons Convention, and the treaty to ban landmines (the Ottawa Convention).[26] Similarly, U.S.

initiative was crucial to the process leading to the adoption of the Rome Statute of the International Criminal Court (ICC), as well as to the reform of the world trade system through the Uruguay Round and the creation of the WTO.[27] In the latter case, success was, somewhat paradoxically, achieved in part through the "aggressive unilateralism" of the United States since the mid-1980s.[28]

In some of these fields, however, the United States was surprised by the dynamics generated by its own initiative, and it found itself unable to control the outcome of the processes that it had set in motion. Once unleashed, the forces driving toward the ICC and the Ottawa Convention began, in the eyes of U.S. officials, to resemble the sorcerer's apprentice. This helps account for the stark contrast between the strong role of the United States in fostering treaty negotiations and its opposition to the eventual outcome. Apart from the ICC and the Ottawa Convention, the United States also declined to ratify the CTBT, the amended Convention on the Law of the Sea, the Kyoto Protocol, and the Convention on Biological Diversity (and the ensuing Protocol on Biosafety) despite the country's strong, often dominating impact on the negotiations of each of these instruments. This evidence points to a substantial disjunction between U.S. influence over the development of international law (and thus the obligations of other states) and U.S. unwillingness to accept obligations flowing from it. In other words, the United States appears more comfortable in the position of a legislator than as a subject of international law.

It is not immediately clear whether these findings reflect an exceptional, or even a recently increased, U.S. reluctance to subscribe to treaties in general, as is often assumed. To try to answer this question, it may help to examine the U.S. attitude toward treaties that have found widespread acceptance among other states. (For treaties with only a limited number of parties, in contrast, U.S. abstention would not appear as exceptional.)[29] If one examines the list of treaties deposited with the UN Secretary-General to which more than half of the states of the world (i.e., more than ninety-five states) are parties, one finds the United States to be somewhat exceptional, particularly when compared to other powerful states and its allies. Of the thirty-eight treaties under consideration, the United States is a party to twenty-four, or 63 percent. By way of comparison, other states have, on average, ratified 76 percent of these treaties, with an average of 147 parties per treaty. However, China and Canada have ratified thirty-two of them; Russia, France, and Japan, thirty-five each; the United Kingdom, thirty-six; and Italy and Germany, thirty-seven. On average, the seven other members of the Group of Eight (G8) are parties to 93 percent of these treaties, far more than the United States.

At first sight it seems as if U.S. reluctance to accept these treaties has increased since 1990. For treaties concluded between 1945 and 1989, the United States became a party to twenty-one out of thirty-two cases (66 percent); since 1990, it has done so in only three cases out of six (50 percent).[30] If one includes treaties during the year 1989, the ratio decreases to 38 percent.[31] And of the three other conventions negotiated during the 1990s that are not yet in force but have attracted signatures from more than half of the world's states, the United States has already rejected two of them.[32] (This does not even count the Kyoto Protocol, with its eighty-four signatures.)

Yet this increase appears less significant if one considers the typical delay in U.S. ratification of international conventions. Out of the thirty-two treaties between 1945 and 1989, the United States ratified only eight in the decade in which they were concluded, and the average time needed for ratification was almost ten years. In previous decades, in other words, the United States was in no hurry to ratify such treaties quickly. Indeed, only one-third of them were ratified within five years after conclusion and less than half within ten years.[33] Much of this delay was always caused by the need to wait for a favorable composition in the Senate, especially in the area of human rights.[34] In any event, the figures show that the current U.S. hesitation is far from unprecedented. In sum, one can hardly conclude that the United States has become more reluctant to enter multilateral treaties after the end of the Cold War. The degree of U.S. reluctance has always been relatively high, and it has not significantly grown since 1990. Moreover, the figures show that the United States still uses multilateral treaties to an important degree; by no means has it entirely opted out of the process of international lawmaking.

The main phenomenon that needs to be explained is why the United States remains far more reluctant to accept multilateral treaties than other states, particularly other powerful states and especially its European allies. The latter have subscribed to almost all "global" conventions since 1945 and have set the pace for, and kept pace with, the expansion and strengthening of the international legal order during that period. The fact that the United States lags behind might thus reflect either a greater U.S. reluctance to accept international treaties or an increased willingness on the part of European and other states to develop international law at a high speed.[35] In this light, the transformation of international law and of international politics might be more decisive than actual changes in U.S. attitudes.

Selective Uses of International Law: Some Issue Areas

If quantitative changes are difficult to discern, some change can be observed in the fields of law affected by U.S. reticence. During the Cold War, the United States developed a pattern of refusal primarily with respect to human rights treaties. This reached its peak with discussions on the Bricker Amendment to the U.S. Constitution, designed to render impossible U.S. accession to the UN Human Rights Covenants.[36] In other areas, nonparticipation in universally accepted agreements remained rather sporadic, as with the Havana Charter on trade or the Convention on the Law of the Sea. In recent times, however, other fields, such as the environment or arms control, have been affected by general U.S. skepticism as well.

Fields of reluctance: human rights, environment, arms control. With respect to human rights, the particular reluctance just mentioned largely persisted in the 1990s. The United States is still not a party to the Covenant on Economic, Social, and Cultural Rights; to the Protocols to the Geneva Conventions; to the Convention on Discrimination Against Women; to the Convention on the Rights of the Child; and to the American Convention on Human Rights. It has pledged not to become a party to the Rome Statute of the ICC. And although since the mid-1980s it has ratified the Genocide Convention, the International Covenant on Civil and Political Rights (ICCPR), the Convention Against Torture, and the Convention on Racial Discrimination, it has attached significant reservations that have met with serious criticism by the UN Human Rights Committee and objections by other, mainly Western European, governments.[37]

In environmental matters, the United States had long been a leading actor in international negotiations, but it became less active under Ronald Reagan's administration and recovered only slightly in successive years.[38] In addition, the Senate reversed its initial support of an active stance in international environmental policy in the 1990s.[39] This development reflected changes in domestic environmental policy;[40] as a result, the United States was in the 1990s much more reluctant to sign and ratify international conventions, especially with respect to treaties of a broader range. Many conventions with a somewhat limited scope—as, for example, those pertaining to migratory birds, plants, and fisheries issues, among them the Straddling Stocks Convention—were approved, and in October 2000 the United States ratified the Convention Against Desertification. But significant concerns were raised over many other far-reaching multilateral agreements, like the Basel Convention on Hazardous Wastes, the UN Framework Convention on Climate Change (UNFCCC), the Kyoto Protocol, and the Convention on Biological Diversity. Some of these concerns, mainly with respect to the instruments on climate change, were directed at the preciseness of the provisions; both the executive branch and the Senate sought to ensure that no legally binding targets and timetables were established.[41] On other treaties, namely the Basel Convention, the Protocol on Environmental Protection of Antarctica, and also the UNFCCC, the Senate objected in particular to the prohibition on reservations.[42]

Similar tendencies were observable in the field of arms control. The United States had, despite some ambivalence, subscribed to or even initiated the most important arms control treaties during the Cold War, such as test ban treaties, the Non-Proliferation Treaty, and the Biological and Toxin

Weapons Convention (BWC). At the same time, the United States did not ratify until 1990 the Threshold Test Ban Treaty of 1974, out of concerns about verification. Beginning in the mid-1980s, this generally reluctant attitude increased significantly, especially in the Senate. Although the United States finally ratified most bilateral agreements, such as the Intermediate-Range Nuclear Forces Treaty[43] and both treaties under the Strategic Arms Reductions Talks (START I and II),[44] it did so only with numerous conditions set by the Senate.[45] The same held true for the Conventional Forces in Europe (CFE) Treaty and the CFE Flank Agreement and, to a lesser extent, for the Open Skies Treaty. Even greater concerns were raised over the Chemical Weapons Convention, which the Senate only consented to with twenty-eight conditions, and which was ratified by the United States with such far-reaching reservations that its effectiveness is doubtful. Later implementation has only aggravated these doubts.[46] Toward the end of the 1990s, U.S. reluctance to subscribe to new multilateral arms control arrangements grew again, with the rejection of the CTBT in the Senate and the refusal to sign the Ottawa Convention on landmines.

By 2001, the administration of George W. Bush exhibited significant skepticism toward a number of arms control treaties, taking a negative stance toward the draft protocol to the BWC[47] and adopting a restrictive stance toward the proposed Convention on Small Arms.[48] Likewise, the U.S. position on missile defense challenged the ABM Treaty of 1972, and Washington made only vague proposals for a replacing "framework," leaving unclear whether this framework was supposed to be of a legal nature.[49] In the area of arms control, it seemed that the United States, perceiving itself as dominant in both military and intelligence terms, had come to essentially deny the value of legal regulation.

Fields of engagement: trade, investment, and legal assistance. One area in which treaties clearly are of greater importance for the United States is trade. Since its rejection of the Havana Charter, the United States has increasingly worked toward legal regulation of international trade, and it has especially urged the reform of the GATT, with its expansion through the General Agreement on Trade in Services (GATS) and the Trade-Related Intellectual Property (TRIPS) Agreement as well as its institutionalization in the WTO.[50] More recently, the United States has urged the creation of a Free Trade Area of the Americas, which is to follow the wide-ranging regional market liberalization under NAFTA.[51]

A similarly positive stance toward legal instruments prevails with respect to other economic issues. Following European states, in 1981 the United States began to conclude Bilateral Investment Treaties (BITs). Although approximately a dozen of these were concluded in the 1980s, their number rose sharply in the 1990s, during which thirty-three were concluded.[52] The United States has also urged the conclusion of the Multilateral

Agreement on Investment in the framework of the Organization for Economic Cooperation and Development (OECD), albeit without success.[53] Likewise, it has continued to enter into tax treaties with other countries, concluding or renegotiating twenty-two such treaties since January 1993.[54]

In matters of legal assistance, the United States has always maintained a dense net of extradition treaties, but it has begun to conclude broader treaties on mutual legal assistance as well. These are bilateral in nature and are directed at obtaining evidence needed for criminal cases and at promoting cooperation among law-enforcement authorities. Since the first such treaty entered into force in 1977, twenty-four have followed, with a great number of new treaties being concluded in the late 1990s.[55] Similarly, the United States has actively supported the UN Convention on Transnational Organized Crime, which mainly contains provisions on mutual legal assistance.[56]

Just a matter of issues? Thus, while United States has shown a continuing (human rights) or growing (environment, arms control) skepticism toward certain new treaties, its practice has been very different in areas related to economic regulation (trade, intellectual property, investment, taxes) and crime control. These latter areas, though, are particularly apt for legal regulation: Legal assistance in criminal prosecutions involves highly formalized interactions between courts and law-enforcement authorities, which in domestic law are governed by very precise rules; legal assistance, like extradition, thus also calls for legal regulation if effected beyond borders. Similarly, trade and investment are characterized by great numbers of transnational interactions, and stable and precise rules reduce both intergovernmental transaction costs and private risk premiums.[57] Domestically, trade agreements create fewer difficulties than other treaties, as they can often be concluded as executive agreements and thus do not require a two-thirds majority in the Senate.[58] On an international level, moreover, the United States no longer enjoys a position of unchallenged predominance in trade, as Japan and the European Union have gained considerable weight. Under these circumstances, the United States may find multilateral cooperation and legal regulation to be more desirable than unilateral measures, as the latter will often face strong resistance and have results that are hard to predict. A balance of power has often been regarded as indispensable for—or at least favorable to—a significant role for international law.[59]

If strong U.S. reliance on international law can be explained in part by the specificities of these issue areas, the same holds true for the areas in which the United States has shown reluctance. With respect to the environment, as noted above, the change in U.S. foreign policy mirrors changes in domestic policy; on both levels, the United States has become less active in environmental protection. And the reluctance in arms control parallels a particularly predominant position of the U.S. military; this issue area is even farther away than others from a balance of power. As a domestic matter, the

Senate has also asserted its role more vigorously in arms control than in other fields.[60] Moreover, in all three fields (human rights, environment, and arms control), treaties establish, albeit to different degrees, objective regimes rather than mutual relations of exchange. States gain from these regimes in a less immediate way than they do from exchange treaties, merely profiting from the public good provided by the regime. This good might, however, be provided regardless of the participation of a specific state if other states are willing to establish the regime anyway. Even without U.S. participation, for example, global warming will be reduced if states ratify the Kyoto Protocol. Similarly, the pernicious effects of landmines will be diminished if most states subscribe to a ban on landmines. Likewise, war criminals will be brought to trial when the ICC statute enters into force for a sufficient number of states.[61] In these cases, the United States can, to some degree, remain a free-rider. Incentives for joining these treaties are therefore low and consist mainly in gains to the country's reputation, which might be considered too limited to justify significant policy changes and compromises with other countries.[62]

The situation is different when free-riding is impossible because of the specificities of the regime (e.g., as for the CTBT). A state that considers the public good provided by the regime desirable will adhere to such a treaty if it cannot provide for the beneficial effects by less costly unilateral action. But if unilateral measures also appear capable of ensuring the good, as seems to be the case for the United States in security issues, or if the good appears less desirable than for most other states, as is the case for the United States in environmental matters, incentives for joining a treaty are low. Of course, this does not apply when treaties, especially in the environmental field, not only provide a public good but also create a level playing field for industries. Thus, the United States was proactive in international negotiations on the protection of the ozone layer, as a mere domestic prohibition on ozone-depleting substances would have put its own industry at a disadvantage.[63]

Both reliance on and reluctance toward treaties are thus, to some degree, explicable by characteristics of the policy areas in question. In this regard, there is little ground for a finding that the United States is in general hostile to international law. However, the specific attributes of the issue areas do not tell the whole story; the shape of the treaty regime seems equally important, in that the United States tends to be most opposed to those treaties that establish objective regimes, that is, those that resemble laws rather than contracts.

Guarantor but Not Subject: The Enforcement of International Law

If the U.S. role in the progressive development of international law has been described as markedly ambivalent, the same holds true for its role in the enforcement of the law. In the 1990s, the United States contributed significantly to stronger enforcement mechanisms in many areas of international law, most notably in the adoption of the WTO dispute settlement mechanism.[64] It also took the initiative for the creation of a strong monitoring system in the Chemical Weapons Convention, and it has been instrumental in creating the ad hoc international criminal tribunals for the former Yugoslavia and Rwanda as well as in beginning the negotiations on the permanent International Criminal Court.[65] Moreover, in the area of peace and security, the United States helped during the 1990s to transform the UN Security Council into a tool for law enforcement, so that Security Council sanctions can now often be characterized as countermeasures against violations of international law.[66]

The United States has also created various unilateral tools for the enforcement of international law. Among these are the extensive use of unilateral economic sanctions, which are often applied with the specific aim of ensuring observance of international legal standards, for example, in the areas of human rights and the environment.[67] Moreover, the United States justified extraterritorial sanctions against Libya in part on the need to enforce resolutions of the UN Security Council.[68] Similarly, U.S. courts have become an increasingly important arena for the enforcement of international law. Through the Alien Tort Claims Act, which was revived by courts in 1980 and later supplemented by the Torture Victims Protection Act, individual victims of breaches of international law have been empowered to seek compensation before U.S. courts. And with the restriction of sovereign immunity for states deemed to be sponsors of terrorism, domestic courts have become available even for suits against governments.[69] Moreover, in several areas the United States has introduced certification schemes to measure other countries' compliance with both international and domestic norms. Noncertification often leads to severe disadvantages for the states concerned, particularly with respect to market access or aid.[70] Finally, on several occasions the United States has used force unilaterally in order to bring other states into compliance with international law, most notably in the cases of Kosovo and Iraq.[71] Through all these measures, the United States has laid claim to be the guarantor of international law, the enforcement arm of the international community. This claim, however, has not gone unopposed. Especially in cases of the use of force, many states have criticized the U.S. assumption of this role as being "in flagrant disregard of the United Nations Charter."[72]

Despite its strong efforts in the enforcement of international law, the United States has shown a marked reluctance to accept mechanisms of supervision and enforcement potentially applicable against itself. It has accepted such a mechanism in the WTO, and it has shown compliance with the findings of the relevant dispute settlement bodies, albeit with a resistance similar to that of the EU. And even though it has accepted an enforcement mechanism for NAFTA antidumping and investment disputes, it has agreed to no strong enforcement in other areas covered by the agreement.[73] Moreover, the United States has sought to protect its citizens from potential action by the ICC through attempts to limit the court's jurisdiction,[74] and it has made reservations and enacted hurdles in domestic law with respect to the supervisory mechanism of the Chemical Weapons Convention.[75] Similarly, it concluded in summer 2001 that the draft verification protocol to the BWC was flawed, arguing that the envisaged monitoring mechanism was too weak toward other states and too strong toward U.S. industry. U.S. officials even argued that monitoring would be better if performed by Western intelligence services.[76]

In a similar vein, the United States has chosen not to allow individual petitions to the Human Rights Committee, as provided for by the Optional Protocol to the ICCPR, which is now accepted by ninety-eight states. Likewise, it has not signed the Optional Protocol to the Convention on the Elimination of All Discrimination Against Women, adopted in 1999, which provides for a procedure of individual petitions. Again with respect to human rights instruments, the United States has made reservations to clauses establishing the jurisdiction of the International Court of Justice (ICJ) for the settlement of disputes.[77] And it has defied the ICJ by disregarding provisional measures in the *Breard* and *LaGrand* cases involving instances of capital punishment in violation of the Vienna Convention on Consular Relations.[78] Thus, the U.S. record with respect to enforcement is mixed—and asymmetrical: it supports strong enforcement against others, little against itself. In this regard, U.S. behavior corresponds to general observations on the particular reluctance of powerful states to delegate power to international actors.[79]

Maintaining a Primitive Order:
The U.S. Quest for Flexibility and Fragmentation
in International Law

International law has often been shaped more by the structural demands of the United States than by the latter's outright retreat. This is particularly visible in the phenomenon just discussed: oftentimes, the reluctance of the United States to accept strong enforcement mechanisms has not led to U.S. rejection of a specific legal instrument but rather to its reformulation according to U.S. demands. This specific reluctance, as shall be demonstrated in the following part of this chapter, is part of a general U.S. tendency to maintain international law in its traditional state—in a primitive state, characterized mainly by indeterminate primary rules, few and weak institutions for lawmaking and enforcement, and a strong fragmentation without a defining center.

Indeterminacy and fragmentation have characterized the international legal system for most of its existence. Until the mid–twentieth century, universal international law consisted mainly of customary rules whose content was not susceptible to precise restatement and that therefore hardly posed limitations to state action. Most other rules of international law were contained in bilateral treaties, so that each state had a very different set of rights and obligations. Accordingly, international law's legal character has again and again been drawn into doubt.[80] Contemporary international law has, to some degree, overcome this condition and has taken on many characteristics of domestic legal systems. Its content is now defined largely by treaties aspiring to universal application, embodying far more precise provisions than would be conceivable in customary law. Moreover, the last decades have witnessed an unprecedented surge in institutions for the enforcement of international law, with, for example, the creation of the international criminal tribunals, the International Tribunal for the Law of the Sea, the WTO panels, and many new monitoring mechanisms in treaties on arms control, the environment, and human rights.

This increased maturity of the international legal system must leave powerful states somewhat uneasy. In many cases, they have the option of inducing the compliance of other states by their own means and therefore gain little by new international enforcement mechanisms. Moreover, their own behavior may become more visibly restrained by international norms, making evasion more difficult. Furthermore, change in the content of norms is hindered by their greater precision and more formal mechanisms of amendment. In general, states that are still rising in power tend to regard existing norms as inadequate constraints. Consequently, it does not come as a surprise that the United States, which enjoys a predominant position in the international system and perceives itself as still rising, opposes many characteristics of this "modern" international law. In response, it has developed several means of maintaining international law in its traditional shape, some of which shall be outlined in the following paragraphs.

Maintaining and Increasing the Flexibility of International Law

The most obvious reflection of this general tendency to maintain the flexibility of international law is certainly the U.S. reluctance to subscribe to supervisory mechanisms or to accede to treaties that have such mechanisms at their core, such as the Rome Statute of the ICC. Several examples of this reluctance have already been analyzed above. The determination to avoid such international supervision has been most pointedly expressed by the then chairman of the Senate Foreign Relations Committee, Jesse Helms, in his speech to the UN Security Council in early 2000: "No UN institution— not the Security Council, not the Yugoslav tribunal, not a future ICC—is competent to judge the foreign policy and national security decisions of the United States."[81] As a result of U.S. negotiation strategies, other states needed to compromise on or even drop strong enforcement mechanisms in several cases, including in the design of the ICC and the additional protocol to the BWC.

The United States is not only reluctant to agree to international mechanisms of supervision and enforcement but also, as has already been noted, does not entrust this task to its domestic judicial branch, either. Through the doctrine of non–self-executing treaties, most international agreements now fail to produce effects in U.S. domestic law; such effects instead depend on prior legislative action. Thus, in most cases domestic courts are barred from examining the precise content of a treaty, and the other branches of government retain some freedom in the interpretation of and compliance with international obligations of the United States.

In a further attempt to increase the flexibility of certain norms and to make them more malleable in their application, the United States has several times had recourse to arguments based on the "interests of the international community." In the U.S. view, these interests have led to changes in the basic normative structure of international law, as became most evident in the discussion on the legality of the NATO action in Kosovo, in the contention that the interest in the protection of human rights had gained such a status in international law as to draw into question the strict limitations the United Nations Charter posed on the use of force for humanitarian purposes. Put simply, the interests of the international community as a whole superseded the interests of individual states in the protection of their sovereignty, and the United States, together with its NATO allies, could act as the guarantor of those community interests. The United States has made similar arguments to justify continued military action against Iraq after the end of the Gulf War. In 1991–1992, it invoked the necessity of protecting the civilian population to justify the establishment, with the United Kingdom and France, of no-fly zones in northern and southern Iraq. And for its air strikes against Iraq at the end of 1998, the United States referred to the need for prevention of further aggression. In both cases, the United States depicted its actions as furthering community objectives by citing UN Security Council resolutions that had determined, though without authorizing military action, that Iraqi behavior posed a threat to international peace and security.[82] In a similar vein, President George W. Bush claimed that the U.S. military response to the terrorist attacks of September 2001 was supported by the "collective will of the world."[83]

Community objectives have also been invoked to permit increased flexibility in the application of fundamental rules with respect to state immunity. In order to justify the restrictions through the Foreign Sovereign Immunities Act, U.S. courts referred to such overarching principles:

> As . . . the terrorist is the modern era's *hosti humani generis* [*sic*]—an enemy of all mankind, this court concludes that fair play and substantial justice is well served by the exercise of jurisdiction over foreign state sponsors of terrorism which cause personal injury to or the death of United States nationals.[84]

Just as other Western countries have made such arguments to restrict the immunity of former heads of states, so here the United States cited the rise of human rights as a value of the international community to justify changes in the basic rules of international law.[85]

Certainly in all these instances, international lawyers have argued seriously over the validity of these arguments. In many of them, a strong case can be made in favor of the U.S. interpretation. Nevertheless, one should not lose sight of the fact that the greater flexibility of international rules that accompanies reference to such structural changes in international law serves an important interest of powerful states: It weakens the normative force of existing legal limitations and allows for greater freedom in the exercise of power. It also weakens the role of the process of lawmaking and shifts emphasis to the results to be achieved; in so doing, it increases disregard for the strictures of equality prevailing in formal international lawmaking. As a result, redefinitions of fundamental rules may come to reflect more closely than previous rules the current distribution of power.

Maintaining the Fragmentation of International Law: Contracts Instead of Laws

While international law moves toward more lawlike treaties, aspiring to universal application and embodying equal rules for every state, the United States places greater emphasis on more traditional, contractlike treaties and thereby seeks to maintain the fragmented structure of the international legal order. This has been noted already with respect to the issue areas most affected by U.S. skepticism, which were all characterized by a predominance of objective regimes rather than relationships of mutual exchange. It is equally visible in the relatively strong U.S. reliance on bilateral treaties. As has been pointed out above, the United States favors legal regulation not only in trade but also in matters of investment, taxes, and legal assistance. In these latter areas, though, bilateral treaties dominate, and few universal treaties exist. A plausible reason for this preference is that bilateral negotiations are far more likely to be influenced by the superior power of one party than are multilateral negotiations, in which other states can unite against a dominant one.[86] *Divide et impera!* has always been a convenient mode of governing.

The United States seems to privilege such bilateral treaties on the domestic level as well. They are almost the only instruments to be granted self-executing character and thus to be enforceable in U.S. courts. Since the end of World War II, this status has been conferred mainly on Treaties of Friendship, Commerce, and Navigation. Bilateral Investment Treaties (BIT) approach this model in providing for the enforcement in domestic courts of international arbitral awards sought by private parties.[87] Both these categories (like chapter 11 of NAFTA, whose enforcement mechanism resembles that of the BITs) are primarily concerned with investment, an area in which the strict enforcement of treaty rules would most seem to benefit U.S. investors abroad, as the United States already adheres to similar domestic rules. These specific benefits, coupled with the minimal risk of enforcement against itself, seem to have led the United States to grant these bilateral treaties a privileged status in domestic law.

Building a Strong Legal Order:
International Law Subject to U.S. Law

The United States seeks to maintain international law in its traditional shape as far as it is itself subject to the law, but it appears intent on building a strong legal order for other states. As has been noted above, in both lawmaking and law enforcement the United States has been a very active force, and its activism has mostly ended only where creation or application of the law against itself was in question. This has been analyzed in greater depth already for the enforcement of international law. In this respect, the United States has appeared to be a guarantor rather than a subject of international norms: It seeks to ensure other states' respect for such norms by urging strong enforcement mechanisms and using various unilateral means, but it consistently resists monitoring and enforcement against itself. The more extreme measures in this regard, such as extraterritorial sanctions, have drawn significant criticism from international organizations and third states, which have declared such measures to be "unacceptable," violations of international law, and an example of "bully" behavior.[88] As will be shown in the following section, similar observations might be made on the asymmetry of U.S. foreign policy concerning the creation of law. The resulting pattern is characterized by high inequality and, eventually, by a subjection of international law to U.S. law. Alongside U.S. law, international law appears merely as an additional way of regulating the behavior of other states.

Creating Law for Other

Abstention from treaties. As regards lawmaking, the most striking aspect of U.S. practice has already been analyzed: the assumption of a dominant role in negotiations on new international legal instruments without eventually ratifying such treaties. Examples include the Rome Statute of the ICC, the

Kyoto Protocol, and the Ottawa Convention banning landmines. In all these cases, the United States helped create law for others but not for itself. A similar recent example is that of the Biosafety Protocol to the Convention on Biological Diversity (CBD). As the United States had not become a party to the CBD, it was formally not entitled to participate in the negotiations on the protocol. Endowed only with observer status in the negotiations, it was nevertheless part of the important Miami Group and able to exert strong influence on the resulting agreement, as reflected, for example, in provisions on the scope of the agreement, on the role of the precautionary principle, and on the protocol's relationship with other treaties.[89] Likewise, without an intention to eventually ratify the ICC statute, the United States nevertheless signed it at the last minute in order to be able to influence its further development.[90]

However, the option of negotiating but not acceding to a treaty is viable only if the respective treaty is not dependent on U.S. participation. When U.S. accession is necessary, as in the case of the CTBT, it is impossible to create differential obligations in this way.[91] Moreover, in some instances mere abstention may not secure freedom from the effects of a treaty. For example, the jurisdiction of the ICC will extend to U.S. citizens even if the United States is not a party to the statute—a result that the United States worked hard, but failed, to prevent.[92]

In any event, U.S. abstention from important treaties nowadays requires, in the view of many states, some justification by the United States. In this respect, international perceptions of global responsibility and expectations of U.S. engagement have significantly changed. This is, for example, reflected in the EU's reaction to the U.S. rejection of the Kyoto Protocol in early 2001, which the Union deemed "not acceptable" and as a failure to meet U.S. "responsibilities in a common effort."[93] As the French foreign minister put it, the United States, due to the scope of the problem and its own high greenhouse gas emissions, could not simply stay away and say, *Je m'en lave les mains* (I wash my hands of the matter).[94] The conclusion of treaties on many issues of global importance is now regarded as the norm, and deviation from these must be justified. The United States, however, apparently continues to take the opposite perspective.

Privileges in legal instruments. Where mere abstention is not sufficient to reach its aims, the United States often seeks to exempt itself from the law by introducing differential obligations into the treaties themselves. Paradigmatic cases include the United Nations Charter, in the case of the UN Security Council; the Non-Proliferation Treaty; and the founding articles of the Bretton Woods institutions. Differential rights and obligations are, however, particularly suspect to most states, and they are more and more difficult to achieve in universal, multilateral agreements. Thus, the U.S. attempt to secure a paramount role for the Security Council in the work of the ICC failed, as it would have effectively transferred its veto power in the council to the court as well.[95] Likewise, the United States was unable to achieve recognition of its particular rights in the Ottawa Convention. The United States had sought to remove the prohibition on reservations and to except its mines in Korea from the ban, but both attempts eventually failed.[96]

Reservations. A third strategy for effecting a set of obligations different from other parties to a treaty is to make reservations upon ratification. To the dismay of many observers, the United States has made use of this instrument with respect to most important new conventions, and where reservations are excluded—as in the ICC statute and the Ottawa Convention—it has often preferred not to become a party. So essential have reservations become to U.S. foreign policy that the Senate has even urged the president to reject in treaty negotiations any provision excluding them.[97] Indeed, U.S. reservations are often so extensive that they change treaty obligations significantly, and other states, especially those in Western Europe, have consequently questioned their admissibility. Sweden voiced particularly strong criticism with respect to the International Covenant on Civil and Political Rights:

> The reservations made by the United States of America include both reservations to essential and non-derogable provisions, and general references to national legislation. Reservations of this nature contribute to undermining the basis of international treaty law.[98]

Even the UN Human Rights Committee, responsible for overseeing the implementation of the ICCPR, stated that it "regrets the extent of the State party's reservations, declarations and understandings" and expressed its view that some of them were "incompatible with the object and purpose of the Covenant."[99]

Privileged lawmaking procedures. Some fora enable the creation of international law that does not apply to the states participating in its creation. This is the case, for example, in the UN Security Council, which the United States increasingly uses for lawmaking, as with the establishment of the International Criminal Tribunal for the Former Yugoslavia (ICTY) and for Rwanda.[100] Unlike the ICC, these tribunals seemed to avoid the problems of potential application to U.S. citizens. However, once it became evident that the ICTY could also judge on NATO action during the war in Kosovo, the United States reacted with indignation. The further the possibilities of the Security Council to enact regulations in such fields as arms control, diamond markets, and so on, the greater becomes the control of the veto powers over these acts; the more such regulation is shifted to the Security Council, the more the permanent members can prevent measures from being applied to themselves. Likewise, the United States is able to use the World Bank and the International Monetary Fund to create law for others by way of conditioning aid, and the more these institutions become central to the definition of these conditions, and thus to the standards to be fulfilled by developing countries, the more the United States can undertake law-making without being bound itself. In a similar vein, the G8 and the OECD increasingly produce standards to be observed by nonmembers. The Multi-lateral Agreement on Investment in the OECD framework was one example that failed; others, such as the rules on money laundering, have indeed led third states to abide by them.[101] In these instances, the multilateral form is used for essentially unilateral action, and law is, formally or informally, created for other states.

Unilateral lawmaking. Probably the broadest results in lawmaking for other states are achieved through the means least connected with international law: through domestic law. Domestic law cannot formally bind other states, and because of international legal constraints it cannot provide for the ap-plication of force against them to make them abide by a norm. Therefore, it can reach a similar result only through less formal means, most notably the withdrawal of privileges such as access to markets or military and eco-nomic aid. With respect to the former, the most famous instrument has cer-tainly been Section 301 of the Trade Act of 1974, which allows for retalia-tory sanctions in cases of unfair trade practices, and, in particular, Special 301, which is deemed to secure the protection of intellectual property rights abroad. As these provisions are not limited to the enforcement of existing obligations, they have enabled the U.S. executive to set new rules, and other states have often chosen to abide by them.[102] Similarly, the United States has set and enforced environmental standards through trade sanc-tions, in particular with a view to protecting dolphins and sea turtles.[103] The establishment of rules in this context does not occur informally and in se-cret but through very transparent procedures. The wide-ranging mechanism of presidential certifications for other states' behavior is the most evident example. Through the certification mechanism, the United States defines desirable behavior in areas as diverse as abortion, arms control, environ-ment, human rights, narcotics, and terrorism.[104] Although in some of these areas certification requirements largely follow international rules,[105] in oth-ers, especially with respect to narcotics, the mechanism has relied on rules that exceed by far those internationally agreed upon, and many states, in particular in Latin America, have been forced to adapt their laws accord-ingly, although some have expressed severe criticism over the U.S. certifi-cation policy.[106] However, the different unilateral measures of the United States have produced a whole set of new rules that in some areas, such as intellectual property, have eventually been transformed into international law according to the U.S. domestic model.

The Supremacy of the U.S. Constitution

As has been noted before, the United States has not only helped to build a legal order it is not subject to, and it has not only enforced law without allowing enforcement against itself; in most cases it also accepts new treaties only if they merely mirror U.S. domestic law. It has, for example, made declarations to this effect with respect to certain crucial provisions of the Covenant on Civil and Political Rights[107] and the Convention Against Torture,[108] and the extent of U.S. reservations to the covenants has led the UN Human Rights Committee to state it "believes that, taken together, [the reservations] intended to ensure that the United States has accepted what is already law of the United States."[109] The United States has achieved a similar result in the negotiations on the recently ratified International Labor Organization Convention,[110] has largely exported its drug control laws to Latin America,[111] and does not accept any treaty on small arms that would require changes in its domestic law concerning the possession of guns.[112] Another striking example is the recent OECD Convention on Bribery of Foreign Public Officials, which is modeled on U.S. domestic law and was strongly supported by the United States just because of its wish to spread its own law globally.[113]

Given such extensive evidence of the U.S. tendency to subject international law to its control, one can hardly avoid the impression that the United States, as some critics of U.S. trade practices put it, has set itself up "as judge, jury and executioner, all wrapped up in one."[114] In other words, in the U.S. view international law is subject to U.S. governmental powers and subject specifically to the U.S. Constitution.[115] This claim has been most actively defended by the former chairman of the Senate Foreign Relations Committee, Jesse Helms,[116] who has even succeeded in introducing a standard condition in Senate resolutions on treaties, stating that nothing in the respective treaty "requires or authorizes legislation or other action by the United States of America that is prohibited by the Constitution of the United States as interpreted by the United States."[117] Such a condition, first formulated with respect to the Genocide Convention in 1986, has in varying forms been used for different treaties in the first half of the 1990s and, since 1997, has become a routine formula. Although such reservations are not usually included in the instruments of ratification themselves, the president typically sends special notes to this effect to the depositary.[118]

This procedure is chosen with a view to avoiding the impression of a reservation that, in the opinion of U.S. senators, could allow other parties to invoke it on a reciprocal basis as a means of limiting their own obligations.[119] In effect, while the United States subjects international law to its constitution, other states may not subject it to theirs. Since its first use, however, this kind of reservation has elicited severe international criticism, and states have referred to the established principle that provisions of national law cannot be invoked as a justification for failure to perform treaty obligations. Some states, like Portugal and Sweden, have gone so far as to declare that the U.S. practice "undermine[d] basic principles of international law," and even the United Kingdom has formally objected to it.[120]

The Road Ahead:
U.S. Interests in a Strong International Legal Order

The United States is driving in two different though not incompatible directions. Insofar as it is subject to international law, it seeks to maintain it in a primitive state, too weak to constitute real constraints on the pursuit of the U.S. national interest. And it seeks to establish strong legal rules for other states, through international or domestic processes, remaining itself exempt from or even, as far as possible, above the law. Except for specific areas such as international trade, the United States hardly accepts meaningful constraints on its action apart from its own constitution. In the hierarchy of norms, the U.S. Constitution is uppermost, and international law is merely part of subordinate foreign-relations law.

From the perspective of international law, this is no desirable state of affairs. U.S. attempts to evade new constraints and international supervision have severely hampered the development of international law. As is arguable, the human rights regime has in general not suffered from the abstention of the United States;[121] even if that is so, other areas of international law have been severely affected, most notably the field of arms control, with the CTBT effectively blocked, the Chemical Weapons Convention weakened, the ABM Treaty cancelled, and the draft protocol to the Biological Weapons Convention rejected. But also in environmental law, the U.S. abstention from the CBD and the Kyoto Protocol impede the establishment of effective new regimes. And the Rome Statute of the ICC contains several restrictive provisions, inserted to make it acceptable to the United States. Taken together, this performance threatens to overshadow the many positive contributions that the United States has made to international law in recent years. International law could be significantly strengthened if the United States decided to return to its processes as a more equal participant.

From the perspective of the United States, however, the potential gains of greater engagement with international law are less obvious. It is not immediately clear why the United States should accept compromises that would not be required if it pursued its policy unilaterally or in fora other than those of international law. It is even less clear in areas where U.S. preferences differ substantially from those of other states: The United States may be mistaken in its decision not to accord priority to the problem of climate change, but the refusal to ratify a treaty demanding such a priority is only a consequence of this mistake and not unreasonable as such. Participation in international negotiations and agreements does not represent a value in itself. However, when international instruments reflect U.S. policy preferences vis-à-vis other states—as they often do (e.g., in the area of arms control)—careful analysis is needed on whether unilateral action can render similar results or whether even the short-term interests of the United States demand adherence to the treaty.

Even the United States itself recognizes the value of *legal* regulation of international relations, as the description of its attempts to create and enforce law by unilateral means has shown. It is not ready to renounce law as an instrument, because law stabilizes expectations and reduces the costs of later negotiation and of the enforcement of certain policies. Thus, the question is whether it is in the U.S. interest to accept the more egalitarian processes of international law instead of using unilateral, hierarchical legal instruments. Although it is impossible to enter into a comprehensive discussion of the general value of international law in this chapter, I shall outline at least some arguments in favor of such an acceptance.

First, a stronger use of international law could help stabilize the current predominant position of the United States. If the United States now concludes treaties with other states that reflect its superior negotiating power (even if not to the degree the United States would wish), U.S. preferences can shape international relations in a longer perspective, as change in international law is slower and more difficult than political change.[122] It is worthwhile noting that past great powers similarly influenced the international legal order to such a degree that it is possible to divide the history of international law into epochs dominated by these powers—epochs that have left many traces in contemporary law.[123]

Second, even if U.S. power continues to increase and this argument therefore appears to be less appealing, the United States can gain from stronger reliance on international law because the law can help legitimize its current exercise of power. Unilateralism in international politics is always regarded suspiciously by other states, and it is quite probable that perceptions of "imperialism" or "bully hegemony" will lead to stronger reactions by other states in the long run. Already now, some states show greater unity. Although it remains to be seen whether in the case of Russia and China this greater unity is only symbolic, other instances, such as the strong stance of the like-minded states in the ICC, indicate a more substantive regrouping in the face of U.S. predominance.[124] Similarly, the accelerated integration of the EU can be regarded as caused in part by the desire to counterbalance the United States. If the United States were able to channel its power into the more egalitarian process of international law, it could gain much more legitimacy for its exercise of power and significantly reduce the short- and long-term costs of its policies. This has been recognized in the aftermath of the terrorist attacks against the United States in September

2001, and the U.S. president has not only sought to build an international ad hoc coalition but also taken steps to bolster the international legal regime against terrorism, in particular by transmitting conventions against terrorism to the Senate in order to proceed with ratification. Multilateralism is certainly valued more highly by the U.S. administration since the attacks,[125] but reluctance still prevails in many areas, as enduring U.S. opposition to the ICC and to the additional protocol to the BWC shows.[126]

Third, it is highly questionable whether the United States will in fact be able to pursue its strategy of subjecting international law in the future. In the past, it might have been possible to exert significant influence on the content of international agreements and then not subscribe to them. Repeating this in the future is likely to be more difficult—as the United States discovered in the case of the ICC statute after a certain point. As one observer to the ICC negotiations notes:

> Increasingly, the other delegations felt that it would be better to stop giving in to the United States; they believed that the United States would never be satisfied with the concessions it got and ultimately would never sign the treaty for completely unrelated domestic political reasons.[127]

Similarly, the use of reservations in order to secure a privileged position has become increasingly difficult as other states become wary of this strategy and seek to foreclose the possibility of reservations to new treaties entirely, as in the ICC statute and the Ottawa Convention. And discontent with U.S. behavior might backfire in unexpected circumstances—as with the loss of the seat in the Commission for Human Rights, or the suit brought and vigorously defended by Germany in the *LaGrand* case. In general, these effects are likely to undermine the U.S. capacity for leadership, which to a large degree is based on reputation, credibility, and persuasiveness—not only on brute power.[128] Moreover, as the United States discovered in its failure to achieve desired goals in the climate change and the landmine negotiations, leadership can be barred by too great a difference in opinion between the leader and those to be led.[129] Compromise may thus be necessary to maintain the momentum to lead. The United States may be forced to choose between engagement, leadership, and control, on the one hand, and free-riding, isolation, and a loss of influence on the other.

Finally, a stronger reliance on international law seems not to be precluded—as some have argued—by a specific American political identity— that is, by the clash between a vision of popular self-government and external rules that restrict U.S. action and cannot be amended by the United States alone.[130] Similar political theories prevail in many other countries, but those countries cannot afford to turn to unilateral action—their power is not sufficient to subject others to their self-government. Therefore, if they wish to achieve goals beyond their borders, they must seek cooperation and accept compromise. Even the Swiss population, whose preferences often closely resemble those of U.S. politicians, increasingly recognizes the need for international agreements and organizations. Thus, if specific political identity is a factor in the U.S. tendencies described in this chapter, it does not appear to be the decisive one. Neither does it seem to be a conclusive objection to international law and international institutions: Through the process of ratification, international agreements are rooted in domestic political processes; they are one form of self-government, that is, cooperative self-government. International institutions are not immutable but susceptible to transformation into entities more receptive to questions of transparency, accountability, and participation. Moreover, even European states, with their long and bloody history of nationalism, have come to recognize the value of cooperation and have subjected themselves to supranational bodies. They have finally accepted that self-government and international cooperation are mutually supportive rather than inimical.[131]

Conclusion

From its earliest days, the United States has been ambivalent about international law, and it has been especially reluctant to accept new obligations. Somewhat paradoxically, however, it has always been a driving force behind new developments in international law; without U.S. initiative, many important international legal instruments would never have been conceivable. Since the end of the Cold War, this ambivalence has persisted, but it has become slightly more marked. Even while the United States has been very active in instigating negotiations on new instruments, it has been increasingly reluctant to subscribe to new obligations and especially to subject itself to new mechanisms of supervision. It has thereby defied attempts to render international law more similar to domestic legal orders, to grant it greater effectiveness, and to "constitutionalize" it. To this end, it has sought to secure inequality in international law and to retain the flexibility that had traditionally characterized international rules. Its quest for inequality has even led to results that reflect hierarchical elements in international law— international law as subject to the U.S. Constitution.

These observations are not surprising considering that international law has long been acceptable to great powers simply because of its indeterminacy and its openness to inequality. These characteristics have made international law a useful tool for the powerful: Despite the lack of hierarchical processes of lawmaking, the powerful could establish rules beneficial to themselves; and they could profit from the lack of clarity of rules equally applicable to all. It is only natural that a great power would oppose developments that tend to deprive it of these benefits while giving little in return.

Yet even though the return might seem marginal in material respects, it might be far greater in idealist terms. An invigorated international legal order could achieve what people, and most notably Americans, have long fought for: the rule of law. And it is yet to be shown why law should take such a supreme place within a state but only a very restricted one outside.

Notes

This chapter has greatly benefited from comments by Georg Nolte, Maya Steinitz, Michael Byers, Stewart Patrick, and the participants in the roundtable discussion at NYU Law School in September 2001.

1. On the inherent restraints of customary international law on the exercise of power, see Byers, *Custom, Power, and the Power of Rules.*

2. Brierly, *Law of Nations,* p. 74.

3. Cf., e.g., Oppenheim, *International Law*, pp. 162–164.

4. On the specificities of the use of law in international politics, see the special issue on "Legalization and World Politics," *International Organization* 54, no. 3 (2000).

5. See Permanent Court of International Justice, Lotus, Series A, No. 10 (1927), 18; but for more recent tendencies to revise this basic rule, see Spiermann, "Lotus," pp. 131–152.

6. See International Court of Justice, North Sea Continental Shelf, *ICJ Reports* 1969, pp. 32–33, para. 47.

7. International Convention Relating to Intervention in High Seas in Cases of Oil Pollution Casualties, reproduced in *International Legal Materials* 8 (1969), 466; see M'Gonigle and Zacher, *Pollution,* pp. 143–199. On other examples of unilateralism in environmental lawmaking, see Bodansky, "What's So Bad About Unilateral Action," pp. 343–346.

8. See Elliott and Hufbauer, "Ambivalent Multilateralism."

9. For tentative assessments of U.S. compliance with treaties and international law, see Vagts, "Taking Treaties Less Seriously" and "The United States and Its Treaties"; and Forsythe, *Politics of International Law.* For general studies of the reasons for compliance of states with international law, see Arend, "Do Legal Rules Matter?"; Kingsbury, "The Concept of Compliance"; Koh, "Why Do Nations Obey International Law?"; see also Henkin, *How Nations Behave;* Franck, *The Power of Legitimacy.*

10. U.S. Constitution, art. VI.

11. Federalist No. III, in Madison, Hamilton, and Jay, *The Federalist Papers,* p. 95.

12. Trial of Gideon Henfield, United States Circuit Court for the Pennsylvania District, 1793, reprinted in Franck and Glennon, *Foreign Relations and National Security Law,* p. 110.

13. See White, "Piracy Cases."

14. 175 U.S. 677 (1900), p. 700.

15. See Henkin, *Foreign Affairs and the United States Constitution,* pp. 198–204, 209–211; Vagts, "The United States and Its Treaties," pp. 313–322.

16. See Schachter, "Self-Defense and the Rule of Law," pp. 260–263.

17. On U.S. attitudes to international organizations, especially to the UN, in the last eighty years, see Luck, *Mixed Messages.*

18. See Franck and Glennon, *Foreign Relations and National Security Law,* p. 276.

19. See Bemis, *Diplomatic History of the United States*, pp. 79–80.

20. For examples of Senate rejection of treaties, see Henkin, *Foreign Affairs and the United States Constitution*, pp. 178–179.

21. See Franck and Glennon, *Foreign Relations and National Security Law*, pp. 281–289; Henkin, *Foreign Affairs and the United States Constitution*, pp. 215–228. For a discussion of the transformation of the constitutional status of the congressional-executive agreement, see Ackerman and Golove, "Is NAFTA Constitutional?"

22. See *Treaties and Other International Agreements*, p. 39.

23. See Ackerman and Golove, "Is NAFTA Constitutional?"; Spiro, "Treaties, Executive Agreements, and Constitutional Method," pp. 993–1003.

24. See *Treaties and Other International Agreements*, p. 42.

25. See Moravcsik, "Origins of Human Rights Regimes"; Kahler, "Causes and Consequences of Legalization," pp. 663, 669.

26. See Graham and LaVera, "The Cost of U.S. Unilateralism to the Nuclear Nonproliferation Regime"; Smithson, "The Chemical Weapons Convention"; Malanczuk, "International Criminal Court and Landmines."

27. See Nolte, "International Criminal Court"; Elliott and Hufbauer, "Ambivalent Multilateralism."

28. See Elliott and Hufbauer, "Ambivalent Multilateralism."

29. Although this will be true in general, there are some treaties whose limited number of parties is due to U.S. abstention.

30. Of these treaties, the United States ratified the Climate Change Convention, the Chemical Weapons Convention, and the Convention on Desertification. It did not ratify the Convention on Biological Diversity, the Agreement on Part XI of the Convention on the Law of the Sea (it has not ratified the Convention either), and the Convention on the Ban on Landmines.

31. The United States has not ratified the Convention on the Rights of the Child and the Basel Convention on Hazardous Wastes, both concluded in 2001.

32. The CTBT, the ICC statute, and the UN Convention on Transnational Organized Crime. (As above, the analysis is restricted to treaties deposited with the UN Secretary-General.)

33. All data in this paragraph from United Nations, Status of Multilateral Treaties Deposited with the Secretary-General, http://untreaty.un.org/ENGLISH/bible/ englishinternetbible/bible.asp (August 3, 2001).

34. See Moravcsik, "Why Is U.S. Human Rights Policy so Unilateralist?"

35. I am grateful to José Alvarez for drawing my attention to this point.

36. See Moravcsik, "Why Is U.S. Human Rights Policy so Unilateralist?"; Foot, "Credibility at Stake."

37. See the Human Rights Committee's Final Observations on the U.S. report, UN Doc. CCPR/C/79/Add.50 of April 7, 1995, especially No. 14, as well as reactions by other states to the U.S. reservations, http://untreaty.un.org/ENGLISH/bible/ englishinternetbible/partI/chapterIV/chapterIV.asp (October 8, 2001). See also Schabas, "Spare the RUD or Spoil the Treaty," pp. 112–115.

38. See Harris, "International Environmental Affairs," pp. 4–17.

39. See *Treaties and Other International Agreements*, p. 274.

40. See Harris, "International Environmental Affairs," pp. 5–6.

41. See Betsill, "The United States and the Evolution of International Climate Change Norms," pp. 209–210; *Treaties and Other International Agreements*, p. 276.

42. See *Treaties and Other International Agreements*, pp. 274–276.

43. Intermediate-Range Nuclear Forces Treaty of December 8, 1987.

44. Treaties on the Reduction and Limitation of Strategic Offensive Arms of July 31, 1991, and January 3, 1993.

45. See *Treaties and Other International Agreements*, pp. 254–255, 258–261.

46. See Smithson, "The Chemical Weapons Convention."

47. See Graham and LaVera, "The Cost of U.S. Unilateralism to the Nuclear Nonproliferation Regime"; Malanczuk, "International Criminal Court and Landmines"; Olson, "U.S. Rejects New Accord."

48. See "Nations Agree to Limit Sales of Illicit Arms."

49. See Gordon, "Bush's Missile Plan."

50. See Elliott and Hufbauer, "Ambivalent Multilateralism"; Wijkman, "US Trade Policy."

51. Sanger, "Bush Links Trade with Democracy."

52. See *Treaties and Other International Agreements*, pp. 266–269.

53. See Canner, "The Multilateral Agreement on Investment," pp. 677–679.

54. See *Treaties and Other International Agreements*, p. 270.

55. See *Treaties and Other International Agreements*, pp. 282–285.

56. See Guymon, "Combating Transnational Organized Crime," p. 98; for the convention, adopted on December 15, 2000, see *International Legal Materials* 40 (2001), p. 335.

57. See Abbott, "NAFTA and the Legalization of World Politics."

58. See note above.

59. See, e.g., Oppenheim, *International Law*, pp. 73–74.

60. See Ackerman and Golove, "Is NAFTA Constitutional?" p. 903.

61. See also Moravcsik, "Why Is U.S. Human Rights Policy so Unilateralist?" arguing that U.S. abstention from human rights instruments has little effect on other states' adherence to them. For a different view, see Foot, "Credibility at Stake."

62. Such considerations, mainly pertaining to leadership, have apparently played the major role in U.S. ratification of human rights conventions in the beginning of the 1990s, in particular of the CCPR. See Cerna, "The United States and the American Convention on Human Rights," pp. 100–103.

63. See Sitaraman, "Evolution of the Ozone Regime," pp. 116–124.

64. See Elliott and Hufbauer, "Ambivalent Multilateralism."

65. See Smithson, "The Chemical Weapons Convention"; Bassiouni, "From Versailles to Rwanda"; Nolte, "International Criminal Court."

66. See Gowlland-Debbas, "Functions of the United Nations Security Council."

67. See, e.g., Cleveland, "Norm Internalization and U.S. Economic Sanctions"; DeSombre, "Environmental Sanctions."

68. For the statement of the respective aim in the D'Amato Act, see *International Legal Materials* 35 (1996), p. 1275. On the weak basis of this justification, see Stern, "Vers la mondialisation juridique?" p. 996.

69. See Stephens and Ratner, *International Human Rights Litigation in U.S. Courts;* Rosen, "Alien Tort Claims Act and Foreign Sovereign Immunities Act"; Baletsa, "The Cost of Closure"; Caplan, "The Constitution and Jurisdiction over Foreign States."

70. See Chinen, "Presidential Certifications"; Serrano, "The US and Transnational Crime."

71. See Krisch, "Unilateral Enforcement of the Collective Will."

72. See ibid., pp. 67–68, 77, 83–85.

73. Abbott, "NAFTA and the Legalization of World Politics," pp. 536–539.

74. Nolte, "International Criminal Court"; Malanczuk, "International Criminal Court and Landmines," p. 80.

75. Smithson, "The Chemical Weapons Convention."

76. See Gordon, "Germ Warfare Talks Open"; Busse, "Und wieder sind die Amerikaner die bösen Buben."

77. See Henkin, "U.S. Ratification of Human Rights Conventions," pp. 344–345.

78. See Addo, "Vienna Convention"; Oellers-Frahm, "Pacta sunt servanda."

79. See Abbott and Snidal, "Hard and Soft Law," pp. 448–449; see also Kahler, "Causes and Consequences of Legalization," pp. 665–666.

80. See only Austin, *The Province of Jurisprudence Determined,* pp. 142, 201; Hart, *The Concept of Law,* pp. 213–237.

81. Address to the Security Council, January 20, 2000, available at http://www.senate.gov/~helms/FedGov/UNSpeech/body_unspeech.html (August 7, 2001).

82. See Krisch, "Unilateral Enforcement of the Collective Will."

83. See the text of his speech, *New York Times*, October 8, 2001.

84. *Flatow v. Islamic Republic of Iran*, F. Supp. 999, 1, 23 (D.D.C. 1998).

85. See, in particular, the first decision of the U.K. House of Lords, *International Legal Materials* 37 (1998), pp. 1302, 1333. For further information and the defense of a similar position, see Bianchi, "Immunity Versus Human Rights."

86. See also Abbott and Snidal, "Hard and Soft Law," p. 449, note 68. On the specific reasons for the conclusion of bilateral investment treaties, see Guzman, "Why LDCs Sign Treaties That Hurt Them."

87. Alvarez, "Do Liberal States Behave Better?" pp. 195–198.

88. See Mastanduno, "Extraterritorial Sanctions."

89. See Falkner, "Regulating Biotech Trade."

90. See the statement of President Clinton, *New York Times,* January 1, 2001. For similar considerations upon the ratification of human rights instruments in the beginning of the 1990s, see Cerna, "The United States and the American Convention on Human Rights," pp. 101–103.

91. In order to enter into force, the CTBT requires the ratification of all potential nuclear weapon states, including the United States. See article XIV of the treaty.

92. See Nolte, "The International Criminal Court."

93. See the EU press release IP/01/821 of June 12, 2001; and the Declaration of Heads of State and Government of the EU on climate change of July 16, 2001, available at www.eu2001.be (October 6, 2001).

94. See the interview of the French foreign minister with several French TV and radio stations in Washington, March 27, 2001, available at www.diplomatie.fr/actual/dossiers/visiteus2001.html (October 6, 2001).

95. See Nolte, "The International Criminal Court."

96. See Malanczuk, "International Criminal Court and Landmines," pp. 84–85.

97. See *Treaties and Other International Agreements,* pp. 274–276.

98. Available at http://untreaty.un.org/ENGLISH/bible/englishinternetbible/partI/chapterIV/treaty5.asp (October 6, 2001).

99. See note above.

100. See Frowein and Krisch, "Introduction to Chapter VII."

101. See Simmons, "International Efforts Against Money Laundering."

102. See Puckett and Reynolds, "Rules, Sanctions, and Enforcement Under Section 301."

103. See DeSombre, "Environmental Sanctions." On the restrictions flowing from the GATT, see Trebilcock and Howse, *The Regulation of International Trade,* pp. 406–420.

104. See the survey in Chinen, "Presidential Certifications," pp. 297–306.

105. See Cleveland, "Norm Internalization and U.S. Economic Sanctions," pp. 70–73.

106. See Serrano, "The US and Transnational Crime."

107. See http://untreaty.un.org/ENGLISH/bible/englishinternetbible/partI/chapterIV/treaty5.asp, United States reservations (3) and (5).

108. See http://untreaty.un.org/ENGLISH/bible/englishinternetbible/partI/chapterIV/treaty12.asp, United States reservation (1) (September 28, 2001).

109. UN Doc. CCPR/C/79/Add.50 (1995).

110. See *Treaties and Other International Agreements,* pp. 289–290.

111. See Serrano, "The US and Transnational Crime."

112. See Crossette, "Effort by U.N. to Cut Traffic in Arms."

113. See Murphy, "United States Practice," pp. 489–490.

114. See the references in Elliott and Hufbauer, "Ambivalent Multilateralism."

115. See also Foot, "Credibility at Stake."

116. "No treaty or law can ever supersede the one document that all Americans hold sacred: The U.S. Constitution.," Address to the UN Security Council, January 20, 2001, at http://www.senate.gov/~helms/FedGov/UNSpeech/unspeech.html (September 28, 2001). For similar examples, see Luck, *Mixed Messages,* pp. 68–75.

117. See *Treaties and Other International Agreements,* p. 131.

118. See, for example, the note on the Convention against Torture, at http://untreaty.un.org/ENGLISH/bible/englishinternetbible/partI/chapterIV/treaty12.asp, note 11 (September 28, 2001).

119. See *Treaties and Other International Agreements,* pp. 131–136.

120. See, e.g., the responses of Norway and the U.K. to U.S. reservations to the Genocide Convention and the responses of Portugal and Sweden to the U.S. reservations to the Covenant on Civil and Political Rights, at http://untreaty.un.org/ENGLISH/bible/englishinternetbible/partI/chapterIV/treaty1.asp; http://untreaty.un.org/ENGLISH/bible/englishinternetbible/partI/chapterIV/treaty5.asp (October 6, 2001).

121. See Moravcsik, "Why Is U.S. Human Rights Policy so Unilateralist?"; but see also Foot, "Credibility at Stake."

122. See also Byers, "International Law and the American National Interest," p. 260.

123. See Grewe, *Epochen der Völkerrechtsgeschichte.*

124. See Tyler, "Russia and China Sign 'Friendship' Pact." After the terrorist attacks of September 11, 2001, however, Russia and the United States are coming closer again. See Wines, "NATO Plan Offers Russia Equal Voice."

125. See the speech of Richard N. Haass, Director of the Policy Planning Staff, November 14, 2001, "Multilateralism for a Global Era," at http://www.state.gov/s/ct/index.cfm?docid=6134 (December 5, 2001).

126. See, e.g., Olson, "U.S. Calls for Global Action."

127. Bassiouni, "Negotiating the Treaty of Rome," p. 457.

128. See Ikenberry, "Multilateralism and U.S. Grand Strategy"; Foot, "Credibility at Stake."

129. See Missbach, "Regulation Theory and Climate Change Policy," pp. 147–149; Betsill, "The United States and the Evolution of International Climate Change Norms," p. 221; Lawson et al., "The Ottawa Process," p. 179.

130. See Rabkin, *Why Sovereignty Matters;* and the discussions in Kahn, "Speaking Law to Power"; Luck, *Mixed Messages,* pp. 68–75; Spiro, "The New Sovereigntists."

131. See Moravcsik, "Conservative Idealism and International Institutions."

4

The United States and
the International Criminal Court

Georg Nolte

THE ROME STATUTE OF 1998,[1] WHICH ESTABLISHED THE INTERNATIONAL CRIMinal Court (ICC), can be seen as the most important treaty in general public international law since the 1982 Law of the Sea Convention.[2] The United States played a key role in the negotiations of the statute. The decision by 120 states in August 1998 to adopt the final text of the statute over the opposition of the United States (as well as China, Israel, and four other states) can be interpreted as the most serious diplomatic defeat United States has suffered since the end of the Cold War.[3]

The ICC and the Debate over U.S. Unilateralism

At first glance, the ICC issue seems to be a prime example of the debate over U.S. unilateralism. However, it does not fit neatly into the unilateralism-multilateralism paradigm. The ultimate isolation of the United States was not due to an adverse position toward the ICC project as such. After all, China and certain other countries exhibited an even less constructive attitude in Rome than did the United States.[4] Beginning in the early 1990s, when the project of an international criminal court reappeared on the political agenda, the United States had expressed its support.[5] As in the case of the Ottawa Convention banning antipersonnel mines, the United States initially adopted a multilateral approach only to find that its negotiating partners were prepared to go farther than it was.[6] It may therefore appear unfair to classify U.S. resistance to the ICC statute as a form of unilateralism. In principle, there is nothing objectionable to a state not adhering to a treaty that it considers unacceptable.

In the case of the ICC, however, it is the treaty's subject matter that brings U.S. action into the context of the unilateralism debate. Today, it is practically undisputed among states that the creation of the permanent International Criminal Court was desirable and even necessary.[7] Apart from the general restrictions on sovereignty that the ICC entails, the creation of such a court does not directly affect typical forms of national interests, in particular economic interests. Much more than the Ottawa Convention or the Convention on the Law of the Sea, the ICC statute is a piece of international legislation whose significance lies very much in the symbolic sphere and whose effects are mostly indirect.[8] Its significance extends beyond the institutionalization of international criminal responsibility for individuals: It touches on the kind of world order that is perceived to exist. It was the decision to reject an almost universally agreed-upon project, without invoking generally accepted countervailing national interests, that made the rejectionist attitude of the United States appear as a form of unilateralism.[9]

A merely rejectionist attitude, however, is only a passive form of unilateralism. Unilateralism also encompasses the active pursuit of a goal in spite of the resistance of most others. Again, in this sense, the U.S. position toward the ICC can be seen as unilateral. The United States has pursued its own vision of the ICC, and it has announced its intention to pursue this goal either against the adopted statute or with the purpose of modifying or reinterpreting important aspects of the statute.[10] Thus, in a sense, the United States has proclaimed its intention to pursue a different type of world order, namely, a world order that leaves more room for unilateralism.

Depending on one's point of view, the issue of the ICC is either comparatively unimportant or comparatively important for the general debate on U.S. unilateralism. On the one hand, the question of U.S. participation is certainly important if the ICC is to become a successful institution.[11] On the other hand, the U.S. decision on this matter will not directly and immediately affect any tangible aspects of U.S. power. It is also unlikely that other states will retaliate against the United States for its lack of cooperation on the ICC statute by refusing to cooperate with the United States in other areas of interest. In that sense, the ICC issue is self-contained and comparatively insignificant. Because of its symbolic dimension, however, the ICC issue can significantly affect perceptions regarding the fundamental relationship between the United States and much of the rest of the world. These perceptions may have long-term implications for the global role of the United States.

The U.S. Role in the ICC Negotiations

To assess the degree of U.S. unilateralism in the ICC context, one must first examine the most important issues that arose during the negotiations. Unfortunately, no records were kept at the mostly informal meetings prior to and in Rome.[12] The diplomatic conference itself lasted five weeks. When it opened, it was generally felt that the ad hoc and preparatory committees had done valuable work but that they had not resolved key issues.[13] Before the conference had opened, the United States had not formulated a clear and comprehensive position.[14] Therefore, there were expectations that certain U.S. demands were merely negotiating positions that would be dropped at a later stage.[15] Other states had also made specific demands,[16] but no state openly doubted the desirability of the ICC as an objective.[17] Thus, the conference opened with cautious optimism.

Primary and Secondary Issues

Every conference has its own dynamic. In Rome, the conference increasingly focused on U.S. objections to proposals by a group of approximately sixty so-called like-minded states.[18] This final polarization, although it was not unforeseeable, was neither an inevitable outcome of the negotiations nor a product of radically unilateral behavior on the part of the United States.

Many other states had their own demands, the rejection of which might plausibly have provoked their ultimate refusal to sign the treaty.[19] This is true, for example, of the demand made by many states that the statute include and define the crime of aggression, the demand by India that nuclear weapons be inserted into the list of prohibited weapons, the demand by Arab and Caribbean states that the death penalty be permitted as a possible sanction, and, finally, the demand by a number of states to incorporate a list of specific treaty crimes such as drug-trafficking, terrorism, and others. It was not due to U.S. unilateralism that such demands were not accepted. The statute would have been unacceptable to all nuclear states (and many of their allies) had nuclear weapons been prohibited.[20] Similarly, it would have been unacceptable to most NATO states if aggression had been defined in any but the most restrictive terms.[21] Likewise, it would have also been unacceptable to most of the like-minded states had it included the death penalty.[22] Lastly, it would have been unacceptable to many states to include certain treaty crimes.[23]

It is therefore not surprising that such issues were dropped or merely cosmetically accommodated by the conference bureau in the final phase of the Rome conference. It is noteworthy, however, that most states that had vigorously supported these proposals either ultimately voted to adopt the draft treaty or abstained. Perhaps this can best be explained by the need most states felt to take a position on the main question: the issues separating the like-minded states and the United States.

The Independence of the Court

The ICC's independence from individual states represented the main topic of debate at the conference. If domestic laws were to serve as a standard, the presumption would have been to favor a strong and independent court with broad jurisdiction. The distinctive nature of the international system, however, required some departure from national models. There were valid arguments to be made both in favor of and against the court's independence. It was legitimate for a state to demand that the functions of the Security Council not be undermined by the new court, that safeguards should exist, so that only the most serious crimes of international concern be tried, that prosecutions not be politically biased, and, finally, that the court should not jeopardize national systems of jurisdiction.[24] When the United States voiced these concerns, they were taken seriously, and hard efforts were made to accommodate them.[25] Indeed, U.S. objections not only were based on domestic or unilateralist considerations but also expressed a legitimate general interest in building an institution that realistically fit into the international system as it stood.[26] Still, the more the Rome conference progressed, the more it appeared to most other delegations that the U.S. position not only represented the search for a more realistic alternative but also implied the assertion of a unique and unilateral role of the United States in the international system, including a demand to legalize this assertion. The perceived U.S. demand to remain beside or even above the law ultimately hardened the stance of the like-minded states and won many other states over to their conceptions. Cherif Bassiouni, the chairman of the drafting committee, later wrote:

> Most delegations, especially those from the like-minded States, had bent over backward to accommodate the United States. For example the articles dealing with procedure and with the definition of crimes were substantially as the United States wanted. When the delegations began to grapple with such issues as the I.C.C.'s jurisdiction and the independent role of the Prosecutor, the U.S. delegation, which had previously secured broad concessions on many points, adopted an unyielding position. Many delegations were dismayed by this display of diplomatic inflexibility, which was widely interpreted as another sign of U.S. intransigence and as a weakness in the U.S. negotiating approach. The U.S. response failed to alleviate these concerns, thus confirming the delegates' negative judgment.[27]

The Role of the UN Security Council

The ultimate isolation of the United States would not have come about if the permanent members of the United Nations Security Council had insisted on an exclusive prerogative to refer cases or situations to the court. This possibility was excluded at the outset, as the very point of creating the permanent International Criminal Court was to provide a mechanism that went beyond the monopoly of the Security Council and the selective, ad hoc nature of the tribunals it had created in the past.[28] It was therefore generally accepted at the outset that the ICC statute would provide for the right of individual states to refer cases or situations to the court.[29]

The Independent Prosecutor

The controversial issues concerned whether states could be expected to use their right to refer cases or situations to the court and under what preconditions the court would be able to exercise its jurisdiction. Experience with interstate complaint procedures in human rights treaties has shown that states are reluctant to use this instrument against other states, as it is considered rather confrontational.[30] The more politically powerful a state is, the less other states are inclined to jeopardize bilateral relations by directing a referral against it. A system that only permits referrals by individual states can be expected, de facto, to suppress referrals against the most powerful states. Such a system might have provided the United States with a certain de facto immunity from the jurisdiction of the court.[31] To avoid a regime in which the court would distribute justice selectively, many states favored the idea of an independent prosecutor.[32] The United States, believing that an independent prosecutor would increase the likelihood that investigations might be conducted against its own nationals, long opposed its establishment.[33]

Its stance on this issue helped to identify the United States, in the eyes of many, as a state whose primary concern was to minimize risk to itself, even at the expense of an independent and impartial court. It is true that the creation of an independent prosecutor creates the risk of prejudicial action or political insensitivity (raising the danger, for example, of jeopardizing peace processes).[34] Still, most states, including three permanent members of the Security Council, ultimately concluded that this risk was acceptable, with the safeguard that no investigation begin without authorization by a pretrial chamber.[35] Because many states were willing to accept the risks of creating a prosecutor with an independent right to initiate proceedings, it was clear that the United States must have had specific reasons for refusing the statute.

The Preconditions for the Exercise of Jurisdiction

The establishment of an independent prosecutor was not sufficient to ensure that the court would work independently and impartially. Negotiations therefore culminated in discussions about the preconditions for the exercise of jurisdiction by the court.[36] If jurisdiction depended exclusively on the consent of the state whose nationals were alleged to have committed a crime, as the United States demanded, the powers of an independent prosecutor would have been quite limited.[37] If, however, the principle of universal jurisdiction applied, the prosecutor might investigate any situation, even if it occurred on the territory of a nonstate party.[38] The principle of universal jurisdiction was originally upheld by Germany,[39] a leading member of the like-minded group.[40] It was on this question of the preconditions of jurisdiction that ultimately no compromise could be found. The like-minded states first moved away from the German position to support a South Korean proposal, backed by roughly three-quarters of the participating states, that would have made the exercise of jurisdiction contingent on the consent of either the territorial state, the national state, the guardian state, or the victim state.[41] Because the South Korean proposal, in its practical effects, came very close to the principle of universal jurisdiction, the United States was not alone in rejecting it. Two other permanent members of the Security Council, China and France, supported the U.S. position.

In order to accommodate objections to the South Korean proposal, the conference bureau ultimately proposed that jurisdiction require the consent of either the national state of the accused or the territorial state of the crime.[42] The United States, however, remained inflexible. To justify its position, the United States[43] (and a number of commentators[44]) invoked the generally accepted rule that a treaty cannot be binding on nontreaty partners (article 34 of the Vienna Convention of the Law of Treaties). According to the United States, this rule excludes the consent of the territorial state as a basis for the exercise of ICC jurisdiction against nationals of a state that is not a party to the statute.[45]

Although sophisticated arguments have been put forward to justify the original U.S. position, it can be comparatively easily refuted.[46] It is undisputed that the state where the crime has been committed has criminal jurisdiction over foreign nationals, including jurisdiction over international crimes.[47] The only question, therefore, is whether the territorial state may transfer this power to an international institution without the consent of the national state of the accused. So far, there may have been no precedents for such a transferal.[48] Still, if there are specific dangers of abuse, no convincing reasons exist why states should not be able to pool and transfer their criminal jurisdiction to an international institution, just as they have transferred various other state powers to international institutions.[49] For example, European states have transferred their power to regulate competition matters to the Commission of the European Union (EU). That commission issues punitive orders to U.S. companies that act within its jurisdiction. This practice has not been questioned. It is difficult to see why EU member states should not be able to fully transfer their criminal jurisdiction to the Union. And if the Union can create a true international criminal court, why should a larger group of states not be able to do so?[50] Perhaps in recognition of the weakness of its argument, the United States stopped making it during follow-up negotiations to the Rome conference. The United States has, however, continued to oppose the jurisdictional regime. Thus, at least politically, the jurisdictional regime has remained the main bone of contention for the United States.

In Rome, before the final decision of the delegates, the United States tabled a motion to make the consent of the national state of the accused the exclusive precondition of jurisdiction.[51] The rejection of this motion constituted a breakthrough for the diplomatic conference.[52] Cherif Bassiouni describes the situation:

> Although the United States had rejected the proposed compromise package, the other delegations were growing weary of what they perceived as the U.S. delegation's lack of negotiating flexibility and subtlety. Increasingly, the other delegations felt that it would be better to stop giving in to the United States; they believed that the United States would never be satisfied with the concessions it got and ultimately would never sign the Treaty for completely unrelated domestic political reasons. The other delegations therefore decided to go ahead with [the] proposed compromise package rather than to have it unravel due to last minute U.S. demands.[53]

Underlying Issues for the United States and the Other States

Bassiouni's words describe the mood of the delegates. His description does not, however, fully explain why compromise was impossible. Three main factors were critical: the domestic political situation in the United States, the perception of the United States of its own role in world affairs, and the fundamental interest of most other states not to accommodate U.S. concerns beyond a certain point.

The U.S. domestic political situation. It is well known that the former chairman of the Foreign Relations Committee of the U.S. Senate, Jesse Helms (R–North Carolina), threatened, even before the Rome conference, that the statute would be "dead on arrival" in the Senate if it created a court that could try U.S. citizens.[54] According to informed observers, this position was increasingly supported by the U.S. Defense Department, which sought to protect its military personnel against the risk of politically biased prosecutions.[55] It is widely assumed that the State Department was more inclined to compromise.[56] Such domestic disagreements are not unusual in the United States. The world has grown accustomed to what some perceive as a good cop–bad cop game and what this means for international negotiations.

The effects of this domestic political situation have made themselves felt more strongly in the ICC context than in other political situations. Due to bureaucratic infighting and to signals from the Senate, the United States was slow to develop a negotiating position.[57] This created a false impression that the U.S. delegation possessed significant bargaining space. This turned out to be an illusion, confirming the ultimate U.S. inability to agree to a compromise in the decisive final phase of the conference.[58] It is thus not surprising that other states felt misled by U.S. representatives.

Internal disagreements within the U.S. government, however, did not constitute the core of the problem. After all, the other delegations knew about the structural basis of U.S. foreign policy, namely, that it is driven, often incoherently, by various domestic forces. They could have taken this into account. The question remains whether the Rome conference would have led to a substantially different result had the United States announced from the outset its insistence that the exercise of jurisdiction require the agreement of the national state of the accused, no matter how many safeguards were built into the system. In all probability, other states would still have had to decide whether to establish a court that might over time become acceptable to a sovereignty-minded U.S. Senate or, alternatively, to create an institution that would work without the United States and its support in the foreseeable future. The closing move in the negotiating process was probably motivated by precisely this consideration: the final package represented a last attempt to appeal to U.S. interests, as the bureau substantially reduced even further the preconditions for the exercise of the court jurisdiction. This change was also designed to preserve the ICC statute as a debatable treaty within the context of U.S. domestic politics.[59]

In sum, the U.S. delegation may have created false expectations in Rome in the hopes of receiving at some point workable instructions from the State Department—instructions that never came through. Although these false impressions might have been grounds for legitimate international resentment, they were only a marginal issue in and of themselves. Still, it was significant that the court emerged as an institution that was not dependent on U.S. domestic politics.[60] In the aftermath of the Rome conference, other states successfully resisted U.S. pressure to reinterpret or supplement the wording and spirit of the treaty.[61] It is now up to the United States either to accept or to reject the treaty as it stands. The decision by other states not to yield to U.S. demands also has wider implications for the future U.S. role in international affairs, as it challenges conventional assumptions that the creation of an important international institution cannot work without U.S. participation.[62] If these assumptions were indeed true, the United States should be able to dictate the rules of international regimes that it regards as dispensable, such as the ICC.

The terrorist attacks on the World Trade Center and the Pentagon on September 11, 2001, the worldwide reaction to those events, and the Bush administration's decision to support an anti-ICC bill, the American Servicemembers Protection Act of 2001, provide serious challenges both for the international community, as it seeks to move forward on the ICC without U.S. participation, and for a United States, which is increasingly aware that it depends on international cooperation to secure critical national objectives.

Perceptions of the U.S. role in international affairs. A second factor that sheds light on the U.S. position toward the ICC is the perception held by U.S. leaders of their country's role in international affairs. David Scheffer, the head of the U.S. delegation in Rome, defended the U.S. position by asserting: "The United States has special responsibilities and special exposure to political controversy over our action." In Scheffer's words, "We are called upon to act, sometimes at great risk, far more than any other nation. This is a reality in the international system."[63]

Such a statement must be alarming for other states. It is certainly true that the United States has a special responsibility as a permanent member of the UN Security Council. This cannot be what Scheffer has in mind, however, because the United States shares this responsibility with the four other permanent members, three of whom accept the Rome Statute. What Scheffer's statement refers to is a *unique* responsibility that the United States assumes for itself as the world's only superpower. Whether one agrees with this political assertion or not, there are indications that the United States has currently assumed the role of world policeman.[64] Nevertheless, other states cannot but reject regimes that appear to legalize this self-appointed U.S. role. It is one thing to accept U.S. leadership in a particular situation, but it is yet another to accept that the United States should, by virtue of its role as the world's policeman, enjoy a legally supported de facto immunity from a functioning ICC. This position is not a product of resentment in Europe and elsewhere, as is sometimes assumed in the United States.[65] Instead, it is a principled approach that the United States would immediately adopt if, for instance, China were to increase its influence and develop into the predominant global power.

U.S. officials, however, do not always base their arguments on the sweeping level of the Scheffer statement. More often, they note that the United States is in a unique position because its military is stationed around the globe and that it would be inhibited in performing what is widely agreed to be a beneficial role if it were subjected to the risk of unfounded prosecutions by the ICC.[66] Framed in such terms, the argument is less absolute and can therefore be interpreted as a reasonable statement justifying more limited exemptions on the basis of the country's assumed status as the single superpower. The like-minded states, understanding U.S. concerns about the possible exposure of its military, accepted a number of provisions that had the effect of substantially reducing the risk to the United States.[67] The most important modification of rules were procedural reinforcements of the complementarity mechanism, according to which the ICC may exercise jurisdiction only if the national state of the accused is either unwilling or genuinely unable to carry out the investigation or the prosecution (article 19 of the ICC statute). Other examples included the control of the independent prosecutor by a pretrial chamber (article 15[3]) and the guarantee that bilateral status-of-forces agreements prevail over the duty to surrender suspects to the ICC (article 98). These limitations on the scope of the ICC statute, and the powers contained therein, were accepted primarily in response to U.S. insistence on protection against inappropriate action by the ICC.

International lawyers continue to debate whether these safeguards are sufficient and whether they can be accepted by the United States without compromising its self-perceived role in international affairs.[68] Without entering the legal minutiae of this debate, it is widely agreed that the chances of U.S. actions or citizens being subject to ICC investigation are rather remote under the current rules.[69] I am not, however, persuaded by those ICC proponents who argue that the risk is practically nonexistent. Plausible hypothetical situations can be conjectured that might result in the investigation of cases against one or more U.S. citizens by ICC institutions. Marcella David, in an article for the *Michigan Journal of International Law,* has argued that "if interpreted strictly, the shield of complementarity jurisdiction may prove thin: a persuasive challenge to the impartiality of American domestic proceedings could be made."[70] She cites past investigative practices into questionable military activities, including the My Lai massacre. It is true that as long as the crime of aggression is not defined, prosecution for that particular offense is excluded. War crimes, however, are another matter; they remain a serious possibility in almost all international armed conflicts. Under the statute, it is a war crime to "intentionally launch an attack in the knowledge that such an attack will cause incidental loss of life or injury to civilians, or . . . which would clearly be excessive in relation to the concrete and direct overall military advantage anticipated." Allegations of such crimes are easily raised in armed conflicts. As long as essential information on pertinent events is largely under exclusive U.S. control, it is legitimate for the prosecutor first to conduct inquiries by utilizing his or her own authority to investigate other sources.

It should be kept in mind that it was precisely this consideration that led the like-minded states to insist on the territoriality principle as a precondition for the exercise of jurisdiction. This would provide the court with a sufficient degree of independence and establish the credibility of the ICC as an impartial institution.[71] Such credibility would have been lost had the like-minded states accepted that the ICC could exercise jurisdiction only with the agreement of the national state of the accused. Such a rule would have transformed the character of the court. It was therefore a bare necessity for the like-minded states to refuse this ultimate accommodation of the United States if they wanted to preserve the essence of their project.

Conduct of Negotiations by the United States

Any description of the role of the United States in the ICC negotiations would remain incomplete if it did not address U.S. conduct during the negotiations. As mentioned above, U.S. negotiators were slow to present a clear position, which may have led to false expectations in some quarters. There were clear indications, however, that the United States was not prepared to compromise much. According to some diplomats, the United States adopted a duplicitous position during the Rome negotiations: Specifically, it publicly affirmed its general support for the project, but in reality it worked against the ICC behind the scenes. The United States brought various forms of pressure to bear to undermine the determination of other states to build an independent court. This pressure can be illustrated by one incident, which has been related by several sources.[72] In the final phase of the conference, when the question of the preconditions for the jurisdiction of the court had become the main point, the U.S. secretary of defense indicated to his German counterpart that the United States might be forced to withdraw its forces from Germany if Germany continued to press for a broader base of jurisdiction than the consent of the national state of the accused. Given the fundamental political importance of the presence of U.S. troops for Germany, for Europe, but also for the United States itself, such words obviously went beyond customary negotiating tactics.

Assessing National Interests

Taking matters as they stand today, what are the policy implications for the United States and for other states? What are the advantages and disadvantages for the United States of continuing to resist the ICC statute? And what are the implications of U.S. abstention or opposition for other states and for the international system as a whole? In the United States, the preferred language in which to argue about the implications of U.S. nonparticipation in the ICC regime is to talk in terms of national interest, which is widely considered the only language acceptable to important domestic groups. The implication is that purely altruistic or abstract international interests will not suffice to garner U.S. support. Voices exhibiting this type of attitude have shown themselves to be unmoved by appeals in favor of the precedence of international values. Although the resulting limits placed on a possible dialogue must not bring an end to the discussion, they do force the participants in the ICC debate to translate and reassess all relevant considerations in terms of national interests, both for the United States and other countries.

Defining the national interest, obviously, is not an easy task. Its definition depends to a certain extent on the perception of the interested. But perceptions of national interest may be broadened by persuasion. European national governments, for example, have been persuaded that their national interest lies not in preserving self-sufficiency and autonomy but in fostering mutual cooperation and dependency. National interest is ultimately a question of the range of acceptable considerations. It is therefore, perhaps, most useful to distinguish between core national interests and national interests in the broader sense. Core national interests are those that concern the immediate security of the national territory and its citizens, as well as the realization of the state's critical short-term policy options. National interests in the broader sense are those that affect the well-being and status of a state or its citizens in important but less immediate ways. Of course, this dichotomy does not imply a value judgment about the normative status of either concept.

Core U.S. National Interests

The ICC debate appears to touch on four main categories of core U.S. national interests.

Protection from illegitimate prosecution. The first core U.S. national interest is to protect U.S. citizens from illegitimate prosecution, that is, prosecution by a jurisdiction that is inherently unfair or inappropriate.[73] It is undisputed that other states can, under certain conditions, prosecute U.S. citizens for international crimes.[74] It can therefore hardly be maintained that the ICC as an institution is inherently unfair or inappropriate. The main question is whether the ICC guarantees a sufficiently high standard of individual rights for the accused. It is undisputed that the statute conforms to all available international human rights standards. It is disputed, however, whether the ICC statute provides the accused with the same rights as those guaranteed under the U.S. Constitution. The sponsors of the American Servicemembers Protection Act assert that the prohibition against self-incrimination, the right to cross-examine a witness, and the right to trial by jury are not guaranteed. These assertions are demonstrably untrue for the prohibition against self-incrimination (Article 67[1][g] of the ICC statute) and the right to cross-examine adverse witnesses (Article 67 [1][e]). The Fifth Amendment of the U.S. Constitution guarantees trial by jury, but not to service members.[75] It is therefore quite obvious that the legal objections with which the sponsors justify their bill are pretexts for their general opposition to the ICC and U.S. participation in it. It should be noted, however, that even if the ICC statute were not to guarantee the same rights as those provided under the U.S. Constitution, the United States cannot, and should not, insist on exactly the same level of rights protection. After all, U.S. citizens standing trial before the criminal courts of other states can only expect to be tried on the basis of the law of the state concerned, as far as this law conforms with international human rights standards.

Freedom of action or military operations in self-defense. The second core U.S. national interest is to preserve freedom of action for military operations that in the eyes of the U.S. government serve the purpose of self-defense.[76] Given the state of international law on the use of force, it is possible to argue that some of the recent U.S. military operations constituted aggression or even involved war crimes and that they would therefore be subject, in principle, to the jurisdiction of the ICC.[77] Again, for the time being aggression is not defined and therefore not punishable. The report of the prosecutor of the International Criminal Tribunal for the Former Yugoslavia

(ICTY) on the conduct of the bombing campaign against Yugoslavia suggests that international organs will not behave in an unduly activist fashion.[78] It is always possible, however, that an individual U.S. soldier or a particular unit may commit a war crime. Although it cannot constitute a U.S. national interest that the perpetrator of a war crime remains unpunished, U.S. national interests could be affected if the perpetrator were prosecuted by an international criminal court in a way that would cause embarrassment to the United States as a state. Yet the embarrassment that is caused by an actual war crime will come about whether or not the perpetrator is prosecuted by a U.S. or an international court. Still, it is theoretically not excluded that a biased international institution might use a questionable case to stage a mock trial against the United States. However, the self-interest of the international institution in preserving its own existence should preclude such a contingency.

Even if the United States does not become a party to the ICC statute, its actions will be measured against the standards that the court is developing. In addition, the United States runs a certain risk, when undertaking military operations, that its personnel will be subjected to international prosecution on the basis of a referral by the state in which the purported crimes have been committed. This risk, however, appears to be rather low given the numerous preconditions that have been included in the statute, due mainly to U.S. demands.[79]

Preservation of sovereignty and constitutional structures. The third core U.S. national interest is to preserve the nation's sovereignty and underlying constitutional structures and values. This interest has been a major concern in domestic U.S. politics, and it has been voiced on several occasions in congressional circles.[80] Some authors indeed assert that the ICC statute contradicts the U.S. understanding of constitutionalism.[81] This assertion takes different forms. Its most extreme version denies the binding nature of international law, because this law does not derive from a popularly elected legislature.[82] Similar to other constitutions, however, the U.S. Constitution, in the Supremacy Clause (Article VI, section 2), recognizes the legally binding nature of international treaties. The fact that the U.S. Congress, like many legislatures in other states, has the power to annul the domestic legal effect of treaties by subsequent legislation is an entirely different issue.[83]

Another constitutionalist argument against the ICC statute challenges the allegedly unaccountable position of the prosecutor and the judges of the future ICC.[84] Upon closer inspection, this argument is equally unconvincing. Most international organizations in which the United States participates consist of unaccountable officials. The UN Secretary-General, the judges at the International Court of Justice, and the members of the Inter-American Commission of Human Rights are all unaccountable in the sense that they do not derive their position from a popularly elected organ (but from nomination by a government and agreement by other governments) and cannot be removed simply by a decision of a popularly elected executive. This is not a deficiency inherent in international law (which the U.S. Constitution accepts and which the United States has agreed to in numerous cases); it is also a normal feature in U.S. constitutional law. The U.S. Supreme Court has accepted, to a larger extent than permitted under many European constitutions, that certain agencies are independent of direct executive control in order to ensure that they function effectively and that they are not restricted by special interests.[85] This is precisely the reason why the prosecutor under the ICC statute has been conceived as an independent entity. As in the United States, the main check under the ICC statute against prosecutorial abuse is vested in the judiciary. The judges are subject to a nomination procedure that requires a measure of support from the various constituencies (different states), a procedure that can be regarded as comparable to the requirement of a two-thirds majority in the U.S. Senate.

These considerations suggest that the real objection to the ICC is based not on sovereignty and constitutional law, or even constitutional values, but on the perceived legitimacy of the constituency. It may indeed be hard for the United States to swallow the possibility (to take a provocative example) that an Iranian judge might pass judgment over U.S. service personnel. The United States has, however, previously accepted (in the U.S.-Iranian Claims Tribunal) that an Iranian judge, with only one neutral judge sitting beside an American judge, can pass judgment over the claims of U.S. citizens. Obviously, there is an important difference between a civil procedure and a criminal trial. But there is also an important difference between a court in which judges from rogue or terrorist states will certainly remain a small minority and a tribunal in which such judges are only one vote away from pushing through their agenda. If the United States seriously fears that a majority of the ICC judges will be driven by anti-U.S. sentiments—as some have interpreted the experience of the Nicaragua judgment of the International Court of Justice—then the United States would have to conclude that the frequently invoked international community does not exist. In that case, the United States should not conceive of itself as a leading nation that is followed by the majority of states but should instead only purport to be a great power that selectively imposes its will on others.

Recognition of U.S. leadership. The fourth core U.S. national interest is to preserve international recognition of the country's leadership role. This role not only enables the United States to take the lead in altruistic projects for the benefit of humankind but also facilitates the safeguarding of core national interests.[86] If the United States continues to remain outside the ICC project, which has become a symbol of the international community's self-perception, its reputation as a persuasive leader of the world community will probably suffer in the long run.[87]

This prospect should not be underestimated. The need to build coalitions in the U.S.-led war on terrorism, particularly in the wake of September 11, suggests that legitimacy is decisive for the capacity to safeguard core national interests. The U.S. decision about whether or not to participate in the ICC is not a onetime technical issue that will quickly be forgotten. It is true that nonparticipation by the United States will not have an immediate effect in any particular context. Still, once the court begins operations, the question of U.S. support will become a topic of frequent debate. Opponents of the United States will regularly have a plausible argument against U.S. foreign policy. Depending on the importance that one accords to credible moral claims in international relations, the diminished moral high ground of U.S. foreign policy could have practical effects in the long run. The possible impact of credible propaganda directed against the United States, in the name of the international community, may slowly undermine the U.S. national interest to preserve its recognized leadership role.

In sum, it appears that the ICC regime will have a significant effect on core national U.S. interests, but this will take place only indirectly and over a longer period of time.

Broad U.S. National Interests

U.S. interests include more than core national concerns, such as the immediate safeguarding of national territory, the well-being of its citizens, and important short-term policy options. They also carry over into broader international issues, the most important of which are identified below.

Prevention and punishment of international crimes. The first international concern that engages a broader U.S. national interest is the prevention and punishment of international crimes. This interest is undisputed in principle, and the debate is merely about the means, not about the end itself. Clearly, nonparticipation by the United States in the ICC regime will weaken the court's overall ability to deter international crime.[88] This may lead to more demands for U.S. intervention and involvement in such situations.

Freedom of action for humanitarian operations. The second concern engaging a broader U.S. national interest is to preserve freedom of action for humanitarian interventions by the United States and its allies. This national interest is part of a time-honored U.S. commitment to helping secure basic human rights worldwide.[89] Whether or not the United States chooses to participate in the ICC regime, it will need to take account of its allies' concerns when undertaking, for example, a Kosovo-type operation in the future. Assuming that its allies equally reject the prospect of a prosecution of their nationals by the ICC, the United States will have to decide whether it wants to act alone or accommodate its allies' concerns about the initiation and the conduct of operations. Even if the United States is prepared to act alone, its nationals will be subject to the principle of territorial jurisdiction, which carries with it certain risks due to international responsibility.[90] NATO states knew, or should have known, that the ICTY had jurisdiction over their actions with respect to Kosovo. The actual exercise of this jurisdiction, however, appeared remote at the time.

No abuse by others. The U.S. interest in preserving freedom of action to defend basic human rights worldwide conflicts with a third broader U.S. national interest: ensuring that other states do not abusively avail themselves of such a freedom. To ensure against such abuse, it is in the U.S. interest to insist on the primary responsibility of the UN Security Council for the maintenance of international peace and security. Whether or not the United States joins the ICC regime, the Security Council's role will undergo modification.[91] When international crimes arise, other members of the Security Council will press for a referral of the situation to the ICC. At that point it will be difficult for the United States to justify its veto (and general opposition to the ICC) while simultaneously claiming that it would like to protect U.S. citizens. It will therefore be increasingly difficult for the United States to pressure other states into establishing ad hoc tribunals, like the ICTY, instead of employing the ICC.

Preservation of recognized leadership role. The fourth broad U.S. national interest is to preserve the country's recognized leadership role in order to build a stable and conducive international system and to further liberal and democratic values worldwide. Although this interest is also undisputed in principle, the means by which the United States goes about it remains controversial. U.S. nonparticipation in the ICC risks transforming the international role of the United States from that of a credible, universalistic leader to a mere leader of a self-interested alliance. Yet the U.S. decision about whether to join the ICC regime is not likely to affect the furtherance of liberal and democratic values worldwide. Many countries around the world adopt these values already, without looking to the United States as a primary role model. Should the United States refuse to join the ICC regime, this will reinforce the impression that the process of liberalization and democratization that is taking place around the world is, indeed, not a by-product of U.S. hegemony.

Other States' Motives and National Interests

It is difficult to apply the dichotomy between core and broad national interests of the United States to the national interests of other states that are involved in the creation of the ICC. These states obviously have very diverse national interests and perspectives as well. It is not necessary, however, to go into much detail here, as the focus is on U.S. unilateralism.

The point of departure should be the driving force behind the actions of the like-minded states. As observers have noted, most of those states share a common feature: a relatively recent totalitarian or authoritarian past.[92] This is true for many of the Latin American, African, and European states that formed the core of the like-minded group in Rome. It is especially true for my homeland, Germany, which played a leading role within this coalition.[93] One possible critique of the like-minded states was that they were attempting to overcompensate for their own historical legacies.

Yet overcompensation cannot explain why countries like the United Kingdom, the Netherlands, Belgium, the Scandinavian countries, Canada, Australia, and New Zealand also joined in with this group. Some might argue that these countries, due to the pressure of nongovernmental organizations, decided to pursue an ethical foreign policy, leaving the morally difficult aspects of maintaining international peace and security to more important powers, in particular the United States. This argument, however, cannot explain why states like France and Russia ultimately joined the ranks of those who agreed to the ICC statute. France and Russia have certainly had their totalitarian, or otherwise difficult, pasts, but this factor was not a main driving force behind their positions.

Another possible explanation for why so many states ultimately agreed on the statute is fear of violent conflicts and the general interest in deterring them. It is possible that the great majority of states, including France and Russia but not the United States, fear secessionism or other violent forms of intra- or interstate conflict. However, this consideration would not necessarily push a government in the direction of favoring a strong ICC. On the contrary, it might be more likely to make states wary of becoming implicated one day by such a court.

Still another important factor common to almost all states was a shared sentiment that the time was ripe to institutionalize ad hoc procedures. Adding to this sentiment was a reinvigorated sense of the importance of international justice, particularly in the aftermath of conflicts in the former Yugoslavia and in Rwanda.[94] Although this reinvigorated international sense of justice provided an important driving force for the negotiations, it cannot by itself explain the degree of consensus that appeared in the final stages of negotiation.

In the end, the consensus in Rome appears to have been in large part a reaction against the U.S. negotiating position. It was, after all, U.S. concerns that increasingly became the focus of the negotiations. No other state could completely identify with the U.S. position at Rome, as the United States sought to influence the treaty so as to conform to its self-perceived special position. France and Russia, too, had initially displayed a rather reserved attitude toward the ICC project, by virtue of their status as permanent members of the Security Council and their self-perception as guardians of certain regions.[95] They could have easily shared an interest in joining the United States in its adverse position toward the ICC. Instead, France and Russia chose to support the ICC, most likely in reaction to what they consider excessive unilateral U.S. behavior.

Even if the U.S. negotiating position was not the decisive factor prompting the great majority of states to coalesce behind the final draft, it certainly helped to motivate a significant number of states to press for the independent permanent International Criminal Court as an alternative to the repeated creation of ad hoc tribunals by the UN Security Council. The ad hoc nature of these tribunals was perceived as being incompatible with the requirements of equal treatment and impartiality that courts must satisfy in systems operating under the rule of law.[96] In addition, many states perceived such tribunals as setting a trend that overextended the role of the Security Council.[97] Many states questioned whether the Security Council should continue to play a quasi-judicial or a quasi-legislative role, as it had in the Lockerbie case.[98] At the same time, there was growing concern that the Security Council might not procure the necessary agreement to establish new tribunals in the future. It was under these circumstances that a diplomatic conference was convened, in which many states sought a nonselective and principled legal basis for the extension of international criminal justice. The statute would have defeated this main purpose had it guaranteed immunity to certain states and their citizens. If the International Criminal Court is to extend justice equally and remain credible as an institution, other states had no other choice but to reject attempts by the United States to remain above the law.[99]

Conclusion

To conclude, it may be useful to raise a few questions and speculate on the answers.

Is the ICC issue a good example of U.S. unilateralism? The answer should probably be yes. From a formal standpoint, the United States merely defended the right of every state to reach an international agreement that encroaches as little as possible on its own self-perceived interests. In a substantive sense, however, the United States acted in a specific unilateralist fashion in attempting to impose a particular solution onto the great majority of states and by refusing to sign (and later to ratify) the Rome Statute. More important, in its public justification, the United States went one step farther by generally asserting a unilateralist role in world affairs for itself.

Is the reaction of the other states in any way significant beyond the ICC context? The answer is also probably yes. The ICC regime is certainly a special issue of debate. It concerns an intangible issue, and it is not easily foreseeable whose interests will be specifically affected by its operations. During the course of the negotiations, however, it became clear that a more general issue was at stake: the role of the United States in international affairs. From that perspective, the decision by other states to adopt the statute can be interpreted as a signal of their determination to oppose what they perceived as excessive U.S. unilateralism. The Rome conference has shown that such a signal can be at least partly successful. This experience may in the future serve as a model. It will certainly be much more difficult to build a united front against the United States in areas where more tangible interests are at stake, such as in the area of climate change. Still, during the Rome negotiations many states were subjected to strong bilateral U.S. pressure. Ultimately, they found that international solidarity permitted them to deliver a message against excessive U.S. unilateralism.

What lessons will states draw from the ICC experience? The danger is that the United States and the other states will draw opposite lessons from the affair. U.S. commentators have criticized the U.S. government for being too slow to formulate its position clearly and for missing an opportunity to influence decisively the momentum toward a strong and independent court. If this analysis is correct, the most plausible lesson for the United States is to formulate its opposition earlier and more forcefully. Other states, by contrast, remember the Rome conference as a continual concession to U.S. demands, which ultimately did not yield the desired results, that is, U.S. participation. They are more likely to draw the opposite conclusion: that one should not make too many concessions to the United States and that one should move earlier toward the creation of international regimes without the participation of the United States.

Was the conflict in Rome inevitable? Again, probably yes. Although the ICC project as such rests on almost universal consensus, the effort to put it into practice has raised unresolved questions about the role of the United States in world affairs. As long as other states insist that the ICC is credible only if no state can ensure the immunity of its citizens, and as long as the United States, de jure or de facto, insists on exactly the opposite demand for itself, it is hard to see a solution. It is not impossible that the other states will one day drop their demands, reasoning that a weak ICC with U.S. support is stronger than a strong ICC without it. As long as those states perceive the underlying issue as U.S. insistence on remaining above the law, however, such a policy change is very unlikely to occur. In fact, the negotiations after Rome have shown that the other states have remained determined to preserve the Rome rules intact.[100] Despite President Bill Clinton's decision to sign the Rome Statute at the eleventh hour in December 2000, the likelihood of a policy change in the United States appears to be equally remote, particularly after September 11 and the ensuing decision by the administration of George W. Bush to support the American Servicemembers Protection Act.

Finally, what are the prospects for a resolution of the ICC dispute and its underlying concerns? One danger is that the ICC issue will remain linked to questions of the political identity of various participants, in particular those in the United States. As long the United States does not perceive ratification of the Rome Statute as a core national interest, the resolution of the issue will depend entirely on U.S. domestic policy. Isolationists and parochialists in the United States are likely to change their position probably only in response to a loss of relative U.S. power. Moralistic internationalists, by contrast, will continue to be dissatisfied by the comparatively weak institution built in Rome. The U.S. public, finally, will probably have many occasions to witness the practical working of the International Criminal Court. The public's judgments could contribute to a developing sense of international community, perhaps leading eventually to what professor Thomas Franck has called a "pull to compliance."[101] The current U.S. attitude toward the ICC, therefore, may not be fatal to the institution. The court should have a chance to convince the U.S. public that it is compatible with a U.S. leadership role and that joining this regime is even an important element of legitimate U.S. leadership. This, however, presupposes that the United States will be, for the time being, a good neighbor of the court.

Notes

I would like to thank Claus Kress, Roy Lee, John Washburn, and Andreas Zimmermann for their comments. I would also like to thank Seyda Dilek Emek and Julie Harris for their significant and enthusiastic help with research and language aspects of the draft. Errors and misconceptions are mine.

1. Rome Statute of the International Criminal Court of July 17, 1998, UN Doc. A/CONF. 183/9; 37 I.L.M. 999 (1998); See also Bassiouni, *The Statute of the I.C.C.*

2. United Nations Convention on the Law of the Sea of December 10, 1982, 21 I.L.M. 1261 (1982).

3. The vote was unrecorded; for more details on this point, see Dicker, "Issues Facing the International Criminal Court's Preparatory Commission," p. 471.

4. Bassiouni, "Negotiating the Treaty of Rome on the Establishment of an I.C.C.," p. 449, note 49.

5. Barrett, "Ratify or Reject: Examining the U.S. Opposition to the I.C.C.," pp. 89–91.

6. U.N. Convention on the Prohibition of the Use, Stockpiling, Production, and Transfer of Anti-Personnel Mines and Their Destruction of September 18, 1997, 36 ILM 1507 (1997).

7. Kaul, "Towards a Permanent I.C.C., Some Observations of a Negotiator," p. 169.

8. See the speech by M. Cherif Bassiouni, chairman of the drafting committee of the conference, at the ceremony in Rome on July 18, 1998, in: Bassiouni, "Negotiating the Treaty of Rome," pp. 468 ff.

9. King and Theofrastous, "From Nuremberg to Rome," p. 50, note 9, and p. 105; Wedgwood, "Fiddling in Rome," p. 20; Zwanenburg, "Peacekeepers Under Fire?" p. 125.

10. David, "Grotius Repudiated," p. 337; Dicker, "Preparatory Commission," p. 473; Malanczuk, "The I.C.C. and Landmines," p. 84.

11. Wedgwood, "Ithaca Package," p. 537; Malanczuk, "The I.C.C. and Landmines," p. 89.

12. Lee, "Foreword," in *The International Criminal Court: The Making of the Rome Statute,* p. vii.

13. On the state of the negotiations before Rome, see Kaul, "Towards a Permanent I.C.C.," pp. 169 ff.; for the positions during Rome: Kirsch and Holmes, "The Birth of the I.C.C.," pp. 4–7; Bassiouni, "Negotiating the Treaty of Rome," p. 444, note 5.

14. David, "Grotius Repudiated," p. 337.

15. King and Theofrastous, "From Nuremberg to Rome," pp. 78 ff.

16. See Bassiouni, "Negotiating the Treaty of Rome," pp. 443 ff.

17. Kaul, "Towards a Permanent I.C.C.," p. 172.

18. Kirsch and Holmes, "The Birth of the I.C.C.," p. 10; Kaul, "Towards a Permanent I.C.C.," p. 172; Bassiouni, "Negotiating the Treaty of Rome," p. 445, note 51; Arsanjani, *The Rome Statute,* p. 23.

19. Details in Kirsch and Holmes, "The Rome Conference on an I.C.C.," pp. 3–5; Malanczuk, "The I.C.C. and Landmines," p. 80.; Farhan Faq/Interpress Service (IPS), "Alliances Cut Through North-South Divide," *Terra Viva,* June 22, 1998, http://www.ips.org/icc/tv220602.

20. Kirsch and Holmes, "The Rome Conference on an I.C.C.," pp. 10 ff.

21. V. Hebel and Robinson, "Crimes Within the Jurisdiction of the Court," pp. 85 ff.; "Non-Aligned Nations Target Nukes," Farhan Faq/Interpress Service (IPS), *Terra Viva,* June 26, 1998, http://www.ips.org/icc/tv260601.

22. "Trinidad in a Spot over Death Penalty," *Terra Viva,* June 26, 1998, http://www.ips.org/icc/tv260602 and from July 1, 1998, "Killing the Death Penalty," http://www.ips.org/icc/tv010702.

23. See "Cuba: Make Economic Blockades 'Crimes Against Humanity,'" *Terra Viva,* June 25, 1998, http://www.ips.org/icc/tv250601.

24. See "US Lays Down its Cards," *Terra Viva,* July 10, 1998, http://www.ips.org/icc/tv100702.

25. See, e.g., Kirsch and Holmes, "Towards a Permanent I.C.C.," pp. 28–35.

26. Wedgwood, "Fiddling in Rome," p. 20; Barrett, "U.S. Opposition to the I.C.C.," p. 84.

27. Bassiouni, "Negotiating the Treaty of Rome," p. 457.

28. McCormack and Simpson, eds., *The Law of War Crimes,* pp. 236 et seq.; Wedgwood, "The International Criminal Court: An American View," p. 96; David, "Grotius Repudiated," p. 351; Barrett, "U.S. Opposition to the I.C.C.," p. 88.

29. Wilmshurst, "Jurisdiction of the Court," p. 134.

30. Nolte and Oeter, "Inter-State Applications," pp. 152 ff.

31. Zwanenburg, "Peace Without Justice?" p. 6; David, "Grotius Repudiated," p. 409; Malanczuk, "The I.C.C. and Landmines," p. 83.

32. It is true that the idea of an independent prosecutor was not part of the original conceptions for an ICC. Indeed, the International Law Commission, in its 1994 draft, had not included a right of the prosecutor to initiate proceedings independently, assuming that states would not be prepared to assume this risk "at the present stage of development of the international legal system." During the preparations for the Rome conference, however, a majority view emerged among states that only a right of the prosecutor to initiate proceedings proprio motu would ensure that the ICC would not adjudicate on a selective basis. For the relation concerning the UN Council and the ICC, see Wilmshurst, "Jurisdiction of the Court," p. 134.

33. Barrett, "U.S. Opposition to the I.C.C.," pp. 96 et seq.; Zwanenburg, "Peacekeepers Under Fire?" p. 136.

34. Rubin, "The International Criminal Court," pp. 153–165.

35. Barrett, "U.S. Opposition to the I.C.C.," p. 97.

36. Kirsch and Holmes, "Towards a Permanent I.C.C.," p. 27.

37. See ibid., p. 10.

38. Hafner, Boon, Rubesame, and Huston, "A Response to the American View," pp. 116 ff.

39. Kirsch and Holmes, "The Rome Conference on an I.C.C.," pp. 8 ff.

40. For the "LMG," see v. Hebel and Robinson, "Crimes Within the Jurisdiction of the Court," pp. 85 ff.; "Non-Aligned Nations Target Nukes," *Terra Viva,* June 26, 1998, http://www.ips.org/icc/tv260601. The leading states are listed in Washburn, "International Lawmaking," p. 368.

41. Hafner, Boon, Rubesame, and Huston, "A Response to the American View," p. 116.

42. King and Theofrastous, "From Nuremberg to Rome," p. 88; see also Wedgwood, "The International Criminal Court: An American View," pp. 100 et seq.

43. Scheffer, "U.S. Policy and the I.C.C.," pp. 532 ff.

44. Rubin, "Challenging the Conventional Wisdom: Another View of the International Criminal Court," p. 794; Wedgwood, "The International Criminal Court: An American View," p. 100; and Barrett, "U.S. Opposition to the I.C.C.," p. 102.

45. Scheffer, "International Criminal Court," pp. 12 ff.

46. Morris, "High Crimes and Misconceptions," pp. 26–52; but see Scharf, "The ICC's Jurisdiction over the Nationals of Non-Party States," pp. 110–116.

47. Scheffer, "U.S. Policy and the I.C.C.," p. 532.

48. Morris, "High Crimes and Misconceptions," p. 44.

49. Hafner, Boon, Rubesame, and Huston, "A Response to the American View," p. 117, note 51, and p. 123; but see Morris, "High Crimes and Misconceptions," pp. 45–47; and Wedgwood, "The International Criminal Court: An American View," p. 100.

50. Hafner, Boon, Rubesame, and Huston, "A Response to the American View," p. 123.

51. See Washburn, "The Negotiation of Rome Statute for the I.C.C.," p. 372; Bassiouni, "Negotiating the Treaty of Rome," p. 458.

52. Kirsch and Holmes, "Towards a Permanent I.C.C.," p. 10.

53. Bassiouni, "Negotiating the Treaty of Rome," p. 457.

54. See King and Theofrastous, "From Nuremberg to Rome," pp. 79, 81.

55. *Neue Zürcher Zeitung* (international edition), January 3, 2001, p. 2; King and Theofrastous, "From Nuremberg to Rome," pp. 63, 79–81, 95.

56. Wedgwood, "Fiddling in Rome," pp. 20, 24.

57. Washburn, "The Negotiation of Rome Statute for the I.C.C.," p. 373; Wedgwood, "Fiddling in Rome," pp. 20, 24.

58. Wedgwood, "Fiddling in Rome," pp. 20, 24.

59. "Canada Floats Compromise," *Terra Viva* (1998), http://www.ips.org/icc/tv070702.

60. Malanczuk, "The I.C.C. and Landmines," pp. 83 and 89 et seq.; Kirsch, "Keynote Address," p. 439.

61. Kaul, "The Continuing Struggle," pp. 21–46; Dicker, "Issues facing the International Criminal Court's Preparatory Commission," pp. 473 et seq.

62. Washburn, "The Negotiation of Rome Statute for the I.C.C.," pp. 374 ff.

63. Scheffer, "The U.S. and the International Criminal Court," p. 12.

64. David, "Grotius Repudiated," p. 409, offers further references.

65. Malanczuk, "The I.C.C. and Landmines," p. 83.

66. Wedgwood, "The International Criminal Court: An American View," p. 102.

67. King and Theofrastous, "From Nuremberg to Rome," p. 95; Wedgwood, "Fiddling in Rome," p. 22.

68. Wedgwood, "Fiddling in Rome," p. 23.

69. Zwanenburg, "From Nuremberg to Rome," pp. 132.

70. David, "Grotius Repudiated," p. 387.

71. Kirsch, "Keynote Address," p. 439.

72. King and Theofrastous, "From Nuremberg to Rome," p. 82; "USA Threatens Germany Because of the I.C.C.," *Reuters,* July 14, 1998.

73. Wedgwood, "The U.S. and the I.C.C.: Achieving a Wider Consensus through the 'Ithaca Package,'" p. 538.

74. See Scheffer, "U.S. Policy and the I.C.C.," pp. 532 ff.

75. Leigh, "The United States and the Statute of Rome," p. 130 ff.

76. David, "Grotius Repudiated," pp. 344, note 19; pp. 345, 390 et seq.

77. Wedgwood, "The International Criminal Court: An American View," p. 82, and "The U.S. and the I.C.C.," p. 538.

78. ICTY, Prosecutor's Report on the NATO Bombing Campaign, Final Report to the Prosecutor by the Committee Established to Review the NATO Bombing Campaign Against the Federal Republic of Yugoslavia, June 8, 2000, 39 ILM 1257 (2000).

79. David, "Grotius Repudiated," p. 408.

80. McNerny, "The International Criminal Court," pp. 181–191.

81. Bolton, "Weaknesses of the International Criminal Court," pp. 167–180, esp. p. 169.

82. Ibid., pp. 171–173.

83. See Tribe, *American Constitutional Law,* vol. 1, pp. 643–646.

84. Bolton, "Weaknesses of the International Criminal Court," pp. 173–175.

85. Tribe, *American Constitutional Law,* vol. 1, pp. 643–646.

86. Malanczuk, "The I.C.C. and Landmines," p. 82.

87. Ibid., pp. 89 ff.

88. Wedgwood, " The U.S. and the I.C.C.," p. 537; Malanczuk, "The I.C.C. and Landmines," p. 89.

89. Malanczuk, "The I.C.C. and Landmines," p. 88.

90. David, "Grotius Repudiated," p. 404.

91. Wedgwood, "The International Criminal Court: An American View," pp. 97 ff.

92. Kirsch and Holmes, "Towards a Permanent I.C.C.," p. 8.

93. Washburn, "The Negotiation of Rome Statute for the I.C.C.," pp. 368 ff.

94. Wedgwood, "The International Criminal Court: An American View," p. 94.

95. See in this context Kaul, "Towards a Permanent I.C.C."

96. Kirsch and Holmes, "The Birth of the I.C.C.," p. 4; David, "Grotius Repudiated," p. 351.

97. See for details McCormack and Simpson, *The Law of War Crimes,* pp. 236 ff.; Wedgwood, "The International Criminal Court: An American View," p. 96; David, "Grotius Repudiated," p. 351; Barrett, "U.S. Opposition to the I.C.C.," p. 88.

98. Nolte, "The Limits of the Security Council's Powers," pp. 317–320.

99. Dicker, "Issues facing the International Criminal Court's Preparatory Commission," p. 475.

100. Kaul, "The Continuing Struggle," pp. 21–46.

101. Thomas Franck, *The Power of Legitimacy Among Nations.*

5

Credibility at Stake: Domestic Supremacy in U.S. Human Rights Policy

Rosemary Foot

THE U.S. FAILURE TO RATIFY CERTAIN OF THE CORE TREATIES ASSOCIATED WITH the international human rights regime, and to introduce reservations when ratifying others, has made the United States the focus of criticism from allies and adversaries alike. At first glance, such behavior seems puzzling given the attention that successive U.S. administrations have given to the development and projection of a human rights dimension in their foreign policies. Unilateralist action in this issue area opens up the United States to charges of being hypocritical and inconsistent, thereby undermining the force of its arguments in the global arena in support of better human rights protections. In sum, it damages the U.S. reputation, undermines the credibility of its externally directed human rights policies, and diminishes the effectiveness of those policies.

This chapter focuses on U.S. participation in the international human rights regime, with the aim of exploring those linkages between reputation, credibility, and policy outcomes. It sets out to explain two interrelated forms of behavior: First, the modest U.S. record of involvement in multilateral human rights efforts overall; and second, the qualified—though somewhat improved—nature of U.S. participation in the post–Cold War era. I argue that a reputation for consistency and credibility is a critical source of state strength in the human rights field (as it is in other policy areas such as security) and that the absence of such a reputation carries significant costs for the effective promotion of policy goals. I also show that the qualified U.S. involvement in the global human rights regime has separated the United States from its democratic allies and weakened the message that such like-minded states have attempted to promote internationally. Moreover, U.S. unilateralism has diminished the ability of the United States to shape the future evolution of the global human rights regime, a position starkly illustrated by the U.S. failure in May 2001 to win reelection to the United Nations Commission on Human Rights (UNCHR).

There are two main ways of thinking about unilateralism and multilateralism with respect to the human rights policy of states. First, governments can sign and ratify international covenants, which implies an acceptance of multilateral international supervision of domestic practices. Second, they can project a human rights policy externally as one dimension of their foreign policy. Both cases, entail—or present an opportunity for—collaboration with others of like mind. Unilateral behavior in the first instance implies a refusal to join other countries in ratifying the major human rights treaties and thus to submit domestic practices to a degree of international review. In the second case, unilateral or multilateral action is a foreign policy choice, subject to the usual range of domestic and external constraints.[1]

There are a number of compelling reasons to believe that multilateral frameworks are likely to be less costly and more effective than unilateral action in promoting a global human rights regime. Multilateral cooperation helps to legitimize, universalize, and thereby strengthen both the rights regime and foreign policies that might otherwise appear to have been advanced to satisfy the narrower political interests of an individual state. Where an external human rights policy is concerned, verbal and material sanctions are likely to be far more effective when promoted multilaterally rather than unilaterally. Similarly, a collective approach shields individual governments from certain forms of retribution that target states might contemplate undertaking.

The decision by a state to opt out of signing or ratifying an internationally negotiated human rights convention is perceived to strike at the heart of the global human rights regime. Although the costs to an individual state may be more diffuse in this instance, as compared with those outlined in reference to an external policy, unilateralist behavior is typically seen internationally as a strong disservice to the hard-won progress that has been made in this issue area, damaging the reputation of the state in question. Moreover, if a nation claims that internationally agreed-upon rights conventions are irrelevant to its own domestic circumstances, it may undermine the credibility of its own external human rights policy. Lacking authority to marshal the collective will of the international community, it may need to rely more heavily on coercive measures to secure human rights goals in other countries. Such measures typically have negative consequences for both parties in contention.

Despite the manifest advantages of multilateral engagement in the field of human rights, the U.S. record of adherence to human rights treaties since 1948 has indeed been circumspect. Although the United States improved its performance in the 1990s, to this day it stands outside a number of important treaties, most notably the International Covenant on Economic, Social, and Cultural Rights (ICESCR), the Convention on the Rights of the Child (CRC), and the Convention on the Elimination of Discrimination

Against Women (CEDAW). It has not signed the optional protocol of the International Covenant on Civil and Political Rights (ICCPR), which allows for individual petition, and it remains unwilling to give special protection to convicted felons under the age of eighteen. The United States is one of only six countries that executes persons convicted for acts committed before the age of eighteen, placing it in the company of Iran, Nigeria, Pakistan, Saudi Arabia, and Yemen. Likewise, it stands alongside Somalia as the only country not to have ratified the CRC. Beyond such core treaties, the United States took a separate path toward several major human rights initiatives during the late 1990s. In August 1998, for example, it resisted adoption of the Rome Statute of the International Criminal Court (ICC). Although Bill Clinton signed the statute as one of his final acts as president, joining the 120 states that had reached agreement at Rome in 1998, the United States has now "unsigned" the ICC treaty (see Chapter 4 by George Nolte). Similarly, in the case of the Ottawa Convention and the curtailment of the use of child soldiers, the United States has also been obstructive. In the latter case, it lobbied for six years until January 2000 to maintain a domestic provision allowing for enlistment of those under the age of eighteen. The United States has also resisted some regional human rights arrangements, declining to ratify the hemispheric American Convention on Human Rights even though all Spanish-speaking states (except Cuba) and Portuguese-speaking Brazil have done so.

Moreover, when it has ratified human rights conventions, the United States has generally insisted on attaching various reservations, understandings, and declarations (RUDs). Such actions have themselves attracted adverse comment from the domestic and international human rights communities, as well as from U.S. allies.[2] In sum, while the United States has a well-developed external human rights policy, its uneven level of participation in the multilateral human rights regime stands in marked contrast to the behavior of its major democratic partners and often aligns the United States with unsavory foreign regimes, as noted above.

Yet one should note that matters—at least on the surface—do seem to have improved since the late 1980s, as symbolized by U.S. ratification of the Genocide Convention in 1989, the ICCPR in 1992, as well as the Convention Against Torture (CAT) and the Convention on the Elimination of All Forms of Racial Discrimination (CERD) in 1994. These actions would seem to indicate some diminution in the general level of hostility toward the international human rights regime and even a reluctant acceptance that participation in multilateral frameworks does require some modest international supervision of domestic practices. However, domestic opposition to—and constraints on—U.S. participation in international multilateral human rights conventions remain strong, creating major obstacles to full involvement in multilateral frameworks.

This U.S. suspicion of the international human rights regime was marked throughout the second half of the twentieth century. It manifested itself soon after the successful completion of Eleanor Roosevelt's stalwart efforts on behalf of the 1948 Universal Declaration of Human Rights (UDHR). The same year that the UN General Assembly adopted both the UDHR and the Genocide Convention, it became obvious that the U.S. Senate was likely to reject any human rights treaty. These attitudes were expressed most concretely in the debate over the Bricker Amendment, a series of proposals that would limit the power of the executive—and increase that of the Senate— to ratify treaties.[3] A proposed constitutional amendment—backed by a powerful coalition of states' rights advocates, civil rights opponents, and cold warriors—was narrowly defeated only after Dwight Eisenhower's administration promised not to adhere to the human rights treaties being created pursuant to UDHR principles.[4] U.S. Secretary of State John Foster Dulles justified this position in a letter to the head of the U.S. delegation to the UN Commission on Human Rights. He claimed that the covenants being drafted at the United Nations established standards lower than those in place in a number of countries; that covenants were not necessarily the best way of promoting human rights; and that there had to be broader acceptance of human rights goals before one moved to the codification of standards.[5] The conservative underpinnings of the U.S. national position were stated more explicitly in the arguments advanced by the powerful American Bar Association (ABA). The ABA claimed that an international bill of rights would threaten the separate lawmaking powers of individual U.S. states; introduce a universal right to asylum that undermined U.S. immigration and naturalization laws; provide the federal government with powers to enact civil rights legislation; and undermine U.S. values by expanding economic and social (as opposed to civil and political) rights.[6]

For more than two decades, the United States continued to remain apart from the international human rights regime—with a few exceptions such as ratifying the Slavery Convention and the Geneva Conventions on the laws of war. Not until Jimmy Carter's administration did a U.S. president seek Senate consent for the ratification of the two major international human rights covenants, which had come into force in 1976 after attracting the requisite number of signatures. Carter failed in his quest for Senate approval. This may seem surprising, at first glance, because the 1970s were an era of great congressional activism in the human rights field. But the focus of that activism was ensuring an activist U.S. human rights policy abroad, rather than participating in a multilateral regime in which all signatories were potential subjects of investigation. Moreover, the congressional human rights legislation that did pass during these years required only a simple majority to be enacted, unlike the international treaties themselves, which require the support of two-thirds of the Senate.

With the Senate made up disproportionately of representatives from southern, midwestern, and western states, who were frequently hostile to treaties perceived as attacking values they held dear, that two-thirds majority proved extremely hard to build.[7] However, the United States has still not ratified the ICESCR, CRC, or CEDAW.

Explaining U.S. Behavior

The discussion so far hints at a number of factors that are at the root of this wariness toward the international human rights regime: a sense of the superiority of the U.S. political and constitutional system; a concern to protect the federal structure and the separation of powers; the politicized and partisan nature of the human rights debate, aided and abetted by structural conditions that give the veto power to conservative forces in the U.S. Senate; and a fear of special targeting because of the global power and presence of the United States.

U.S. Superiority and Domestic Supremacy

The international regime has held little appeal for a country that has long seen itself as a beacon of human rights—rights that are enshrined in a revered document (the U.S. Constitution) that protects various personal freedoms and guarantees judicial independence. Jack Donnelly has probably put this in its pithiest form in noting that "most Americans apparently believe that 'human rights' problems exist only in places that must be reached by flying over large bodies of salt water."[8] Indeed, many perceive a U.S. duty, as Woodrow Wilson declared, "to show the way to the nations of the world how they shall walk in the paths of liberty." As Edward Luck observes, the foreign policy of the United States has long reflected a sense of U.S. exceptionalism,

> an assumption that its national values and practices are universally valid
> and its policy positions are moral and proper, not just expedient; a strong
> tendency to look inward, to domestic political considerations and
> processes, when determining how to act in international forums, in some
> cases coupled with a willingness to adopt national legislation that contra-
> dicts the rules and responsibilities imposed by international arrangements;
> and a belief by national policy makers and legislators that they have other
> options for pursuing their nation's interests and that acting through multi-
> lateral institutions is only an option, not an obligation.[9]

This sense of exceptionalism is reinforced by a dominant legal tradition in the United States that subordinates international law to national law.

Despite a history that encompasses genocide (against the American Indian), slavery, and racial and gender discrimination, comparatively few U.S. citizens appear to believe that there are any improvements in the lives of individuals that could be effected by full adherence to the two main international covenants.

These features of U.S. political culture help account for the particular virulence of U.S. opposition to the ICESCR. The U.S. failure to ratify this covenant is often explained by the opposition of conservatives who are convinced that its acceptance would introduce socialist principles into the United States through the backdoor and would be thus destructive of the American way of life. During the Cold War, U.S. opposition to the treaty was reinforced by the covenant's association with the definition of "rights" favored by the Soviet bloc and other socialist states, not with understandings that reflected the values primarily associated with the Western world. Despite an official public commitment to the indivisibility of all human rights—articulated strongly at the 1993 World Conference on Human Rights held in Vienna—many U.S. commentators do not consider economic, social, and cultural rights to be real rights. Rather, they are objectives for which individuals should strive in a land of opportunity without state involvement. As the U.S. representative to the UNCHR put it in 1992, a perspective that few others at that meeting would reinforce, it was not that the U.S. government did not consider the principles enshrined in the ICESCR to be unimportant but rather subordinate; that is, "political and civil rights were the foundation on which the economic and social welfare of the individual should be constructed."[10]

Such exceptionalist concerns have not informed the behavior of the major European allies of the United States. From the beginning of the European project, multilateralism in the human rights area has been the prevalent mode of operation for the Western European states. As early as 1950, the European Convention for the Protection of Human Rights and Fundamental Freedoms was available for signature and ratification, and both the European Human Rights Commission and the European Court of Human Rights were granted strong monitoring and decisionmaking powers. Between 1953 and 1973, virtually all Western European states had accepted that individuals could file complaints and had awarded jurisdiction to the European Court of Human Rights in these matters. The European Human Rights Commission and Court of Human Rights subsequently became very active, receiving thousands of complaints each year.[11] According to Ian Brownlie, the work of the commission and court has had "important consequences" in Europe, helping states elaborate the provisions in the convention and exposing anomalies in the national systems of law, "with the result in some cases that the relevant national legislation has been changed for the better."[12] Most European states have also paid serious attention to the promotion of social and economic rights, a commitment reaffirmed strongly when the European Union expanded its human rights program in 1998.[13]

The regional equivalent to the European Convention is the American Convention on Human Rights, which entered into force in 1978. As noted earlier, all Spanish-speaking states (except for Cuba), as well as Brazil, have ratified that convention, subjecting themselves to the compulsory jurisdiction of the Inter-American Court. President Carter signed the American Convention on Human Rights in 1977, but despite signals that it would be ratified during President Bill Clinton's term of office, that did not happen. This has proven a source of resentment to other parties to the convention, given that its terms are in general the same as those protected in the ICCPR and that U.S. policy in the hemisphere since the end of the Cold War has been publicly based on the explicit promotion of human rights and democracy.[14]

To this day, many conservatives in the United States strongly resist the prospect that the U.S. Constitution might become subordinate to international treaty law and the possibility that the international covenants might award new and sweeping powers to the federal government to the detriment of states' rights. In response to these fears, the U.S. government often declares that human rights conventions are non–self-executing, that is, judges cannot appeal to international human rights standards as a way of judging human rights conditions inside the United States.[15] This represents a key conservative demand. Thus, Senator Jesse Helms, during the debate over ratification of the ICCPR in 1992, suggested adding the clause: "The Covenant does not require any legislation or other action prohibited by the Constitution."[16] He made this type of argument even more bluntly nearly a decade later, with reference to international treaties generally. In a statement before the UN Security Council in January 2000, Helms explained:

> When the United States joins a treaty organization, it holds no legal authority over us. We abide by our treaty obligations because they are the domestic law of our land, and because our elected leaders have judged that the agreement serves our national interest. But no treaty or law can ever supersede the one document that all Americans hold sacred: the U.S. Constitution.[17]

This argument for domestic supremacy has inevitably affected the U.S. approach to the idea of a standing international criminal court able to prosecute war crimes and crimes against humanity. The preference of conservative forces in the Senate (concerned as always about international review of U.S. practices) as well as of defense officials at the Pentagon (fearful about the prosecution of U.S. military personnel for actions undertaken in the course of duty abroad) has been for a court that can function only with the consent of the state of the nationality of the accused. The U.S. effort to build a coalition in support of the U.S. stance has apparently included crude reminders of allies' dependence on security provided by the United States.[18] During his term of office, President Clinton chose for political reasons not to mount a campaign to overcome domestic resistance to the ICC. George W. Bush is even less likely to do so, as his sympathies lie closer to those held by the ICC's U.S. opponents.

U.S. Policy After the Cold War

Despite this continuing wariness toward the multilateral human rights regime, the end of the Cold War has brought some change in U.S. behavior. This suggests that the structure of the international system may have constrained U.S. adherence to the human rights regime during the bipolar struggle and that the end of that conflict has diminished U.S. concerns about the domestic consequence of treaty ratification. Not only has the record of U.S. ratifications improved considerably since 1990; the United States has also implemented certain treaty requirements, including subjecting itself to international scrutiny of domestic practices. Ratification of the ICCPR, for example, requires parties to submit a report on compliance to the UN Human Rights Committee, and the U.S. government produced such a report in 1994. Similarly, the United States has lodged reports to both the CAT and the CERD. Three UN special rapporteurs have visited the United States to investigate racial discrimination, women's rights, and extrajudicial executions.

This shift in the U.S. stance is connected to two main changes in the international system during the late 1980s. During the Cold War, the human rights discourse was treated—within both ideological camps—as a weapon to be wielded against the enemy, regardless of the mismatch between claims and performance. Today, the human rights debate is less politicized, the voting coalitions at the UNCHR have become somewhat more fluid, and the visibility of the UNCHR and its various associated offices has risen. Ambassador Harry G. Barnes notes that the United States faces additional pressures in this less politicized era:

> During the Cold War we could easily compare ourselves with the Soviet Union, knowing such a comparison was to our advantage. Now we must learn to measure ourselves against our proclaimed ideals of human rights, including democratic freedoms. These ideals are part of the International Bill of Human Rights. We should not fear such measurement.[19]

The United States has not always embraced the sort of introspection that Barnes was advocating, however. In seeking Senate ratification of the ICCPR in 1992, President George H. W. Bush emphasized various sorts of political gains that would accrue to the United States. Bush seized on the ending of the Cold War as offering "great opportunities for the forces of democracy and the rule of law throughout the world." He claimed that the

United States had a "special responsibility to assist those in other countries who are now working to make the transition to pluralist democracies"; that the covenant codified "the essential freedoms people must enjoy in a democratic society"; that the ability to influence the development of human rights principles would be enhanced after ratification; and that the United States would gain an additional tool for the promotion of human rights in "many problem countries around the world." Clearly, the only human rights issues of concern to the U.S. administration were those across large bodies of salt water. Nevertheless, ratification represented an irrevocable step in the direction of multilateralizing U.S. human rights policy.

Yet this greater degree of participation in the international human rights regime should not be seen as representing a fundamental shift in U.S. behavior. The advent of the post–Cold War era, the heightened role of the UNCHR, and the assumption that participation in the rights regime would assist the external human rights policy of the United States have not been sufficient to still the voices of domestic critics of international treaties or to render U.S. administrations enthusiastic participants in them. In 1998, the UN Special Rapporteur on Extrajudicial, Summary, or Arbitrary Execution produced a report critical of the widespread use of the death penalty in the United States, suggesting that it was possibly racially discriminatory in its application and that local judges, as elected officials, might not be independent. The report incensed not only Jesse Helms, Republican chair of the Senate Foreign Relations Committee and a longtime critic of human rights treaties, but also the U.S. representative to the UN in Geneva, who described it as "severely flawed" and predicted that it would "collect a lot of dust."[20] In addition, the United States has been persistently late in submitting compliance reports that are required by parties to certain treaties. In the case of the CAT, it took the U.S. government four years to submit its first report; in the case of the CERD, five years.[21]

The United States stands virtually alone—bar Somalia—in failing to ratify the CRC, despite Clinton's signature of the convention in February 1995. Helms has described the treaty as a "pernicious document," and Alan Keyes, during his quest for the Republican presidential nomination in 1996, called the CRC "the most explicit assault on the authority of parents and the integrity of the family we have ever seen. We absolutely never should ratify it."[22]

Moreover, even where the United States has ratified human rights treaties, ratification has typically been contingent on RUDs introduced in order either to obtain Senate agreement or because they fit with the views that prevailed in the executive branch. This heavy reliance on RUDs shows that concerns with domestic law tend to predominate over ideas embodied in the internationally negotiated agreements. Ratification of the ICCPR was contingent on five reservations, together with various understandings and declarations. Likewise, U.S. ratification of CERD in 1994 was subject to three reservations, because the convention called for a broader governmental regulation of private conduct than that outlined in the U.S. Constitution. As the U.S. government explained, "Individual privacy and freedom from governmental interference in private conduct . . . are . . . recognized as among the fundamental values which shape our free and democratic society." In a similar vein, when the United States ratified the CAT, it redefined torture to include only forms of conduct prohibited under the U.S. Constitution. As usual, it also declared the treaty to be non–self-executing.[23]

A poor statutory civil rights record until the mid-1960s may have imposed some constraints on U.S. ratification of human rights treaties in the first decades after World War II, and the Cold War itself may have led security interests to define and limit the degree to which human rights could become a U.S. foreign policy concern, thereby damaging the authority of the international human rights regime. Both these factors, however, have by now been removed as constraints on U.S. participation. The main explanations for U.S. behavior, then, derive from an unwillingness to subordinate domestic law to international standards, to tinker with the balance between federal and local powers, or to regard the human rights treaties as particularly relevant to the betterment of U.S. domestic conditions.

Andrew Moravcsik has argued that for an established democracy this position has a certain logic: by replacing successfully functioning domestic laws with binding obligations, a government may risk undermining the domestic democracy the state has long enjoyed.[24] This argument, though generally persuasive, when applied to the United States underplays the extent to which antidemocratic forces—in the guise of segregationists—long prevented U.S. ratification of the major human rights treaties. Elsewhere, Moravcsik usefully extends his argument to suggest that four forces are responsible for the country's ambivalent and unilateralist human rights policy. These include, besides the stability of its democracy, its geopolitical power, ideological conservatism, and political decentralization.[25] More problematic is Moravcsik's contention that the U.S. failure to participate fully in the human rights regime entails few costs either to itself or to the regime. I suggest otherwise in the next section. I focus first on the resources that the United States has devoted to the promotion of a human rights dimension in its foreign policy. Subsequently, I show how its own failure fully to participate dissipates these efforts and undercuts the credibility and force of its arguments.

The United States as Leading Norm Entrepreneur

The United States, since the early 1970s, has been especially active in projecting an external human rights policy.[26] A great deal of time, energy, and resources have been put into this effort, beginning with a series of initiatives emanating from the U.S. Congress in the 1970s. These developments have been attributed to the increased activism of the civil rights movement, the character and outcome of the Vietnam War, and the amoral aspects of the behavior within Richard Nixon's administration (whether expressed through the Watergate break-ins or through its realpolitik approach toward foreign policy). Congressional reaction to the unsavory elements of U.S. foreign policy and to the poor relationship between the executive and legislative branches prompted congressional hearings. Chaired by Representative Donald Fraser, these hearings resulted in significant bureaucratic and legislative changes. New amendments to the Foreign Assistance Act required the denial of military or economic aid to any government that grossly violated the human rights of its people. The Harkin Amendment, attached to the International Development and Food Assistance Act in 1975, similarly sought to deny economic aid to those deemed to be gross violators of human rights. In 1976, the International Security and Arms Export Control Act called for similar denials of aid and for the U.S. government to formulate programs designed to promote human rights. Similar legislative restraints were also placed on U.S. executive directors operating within the International Monetary Fund and World Bank. The major bureaucratic changes of the period came with the creation of the State Department's Bureau of Human Rights and Humanitarian Affairs, which was eventually obliged to prepare human rights reports on all members of the United Nations. This annual report has become a huge document of more than 1,000 pages, the compilation of which involves many U.S. officials in embassies abroad and in Washington, D.C.

In 1976, the Democratic nominee for the U.S. presidency, Jimmy Carter, picked up on this new attention to human rights concerns, basing his campaign partly on a call for the United States to "set a standard within the community of nations of courage, compassion, integrity, and dedication to basic human rights and freedoms."[27] With the advent of his administration, the post of human rights coordinator was upgraded to assistant secretary level, and by 1979 the original staff of two had increased to twenty-nine. The Carter administration also established a special interagency group, which included representatives from the State, Treasury, Defense, Agriculture, Commerce, and Labor Departments; the National Security Council; the Export-Import Bank; and the U.S. Agency for International Development. This group was to help ensure that administration policy complied with congressional directives in the human rights area.

During the Ronald Reagan era the administration initially sought to downgrade the place of human rights in foreign policymaking but soon found that Congress was restive over this decision. Reagan's first nominee for the post of assistant secretary for human rights was rejected because of his known antipathy for introducing human rights considerations into policymaking beyond relations with the Soviet bloc. The second nominee, Eliot

Abrams, survived the confirmation process and promised to inject human rights concerns into policymaking. According to a leaked confidential memorandum of October 1981, from Abrams to the U.S. secretary of state, the Reagan administration chose to take human rights more seriously in order to avoid the disruption of other important foreign policy initiatives— an interesting indication of the extent to which attention to human rights had become embedded in the policy process.[28]

During the Clinton administration, which championed human rights as a central component of its foreign policy, the Bureau of Human Rights became the Bureau of Democracy, Human Rights, and Labor (DRL), which served somewhat to increase its resources and prominence.[29] In December 1998, the president signed an executive order charging all executive branch departments to make themselves aware of U.S. human rights obligations. An interagency working group on human rights treaties was also created at the same time. Externally, the U.S. administration lobbied hard in the UN General Assembly for the creation of the post of UN High Commissioner for Human Rights and promoted the notion of the universality and indivisibility of rights at the 1993 Vienna Conference on Human Rights.

Leaving aside questions about the ultimate effectiveness or consistency of U.S. human rights policies abroad, the resources devoted to rights promotion clearly increased steadily over the years. There was, too, a deepening of the structures that pertain to human rights promotion. Bodies such as the DRL or (in Congress) a standing House subcommittee with a mandate to examine human rights matters on a regular basis have become embedded in the government. The annual human rights report has become a fixture, and over time its consistency, accuracy, and comprehensiveness have all improved. Accordingly, accurate and unbiased human rights reporting has become "an intrinsically important goal for many key actors" involved in the policy process.[30] Such embeddedness will ensure that the promotion of an external human rights policy continues to be part of U.S. foreign policy, whatever the complexion of the administration in power.

The Costs of U.S. Unilateralism

The promotion of a human rights policy is especially complex for powerful states that have interests around the globe and relationships with a wide range of countries. As Kathryn Sikkink reminds us, human rights necessarily have to be balanced against a variety of other policy considerations, policies that are less intrusive than human rights and that generate less resistance on the part of the target state.[31] Yet the United States, as a result of its unilateralist policy on treaty adherence, has reduced the potential effectiveness of its human rights policy and of the international regime itself.

The reduced effectiveness of U.S. policy occurs because it weakens the persuasiveness of U.S. arguments. Except for certain specific and unusual circumstances, an external human rights policy rarely relies on the use or threat of material sanctions. More frequently, governments must rely on processes of argument, exposition, and persuasion. These are "the characteristic method[s] by which international regimes seek to induce compliance . . . the principal engines of this process."[32] In such circumstances, consistency and credibility are critical ingredients to the effectiveness of a state's arguments.

Those U.S. officials charged with promoting human rights abroad have regularly alluded to the costs that U.S. unilateralism impose in this issue area. Charles Yost, a former U.S. ambassador to the United Nations, claimed in 1979 during the unsuccessful U.S. ratification debate for the ICCPR that there were "few failures or omissions on our part which have done more to undermine American credibility internationally than this one." He went on:

> Whenever an American delegate at an international conference, or an American Ambassador making representations on behalf of our Government, raises a question of human rights, . . . the response is very likely to be this: If you attach so much importance to human rights, why have you not even ratified the United Nations' conventions and covenants on this subject? Why have you not taken the steps necessary to enable you to sit upon and participate in the work of the United Nations Human Rights [Committee]?

In his view, the U.S. case for denouncing human rights violators like the Soviet Union, Cuba, Vietnam, Argentina, Chile, and others was seriously damaged because of U.S. resistance to joining in the international enforcement effort.[33]

Twenty years later, Harold Hongju Koh, Clinton's assistant secretary for human rights, expressed similar dismay at the U.S. failure to ratify the ICESCR and CEDAW, among other such treaties. Speaking before the U.S. Institute of Peace in March 1999, he referred to the administration's intention to press hard to bring about "the long delayed, embarrassingly delayed," ratification of the CEDAW, as well as of the need for the country formally to recognize that all rights are "universal, indivisible, interdependent, and interrelated." Koh went on: "We need to take freedom from poverty, for example, and treat it not just as an economic right but as something connected deeply to political repression. We need to understand that the right to organize means little without the right to food."[34]

Alongside this critical self-awareness of U.S. officials closely associated with human rights protection has come serious criticism from international bodies, such as the UN Human Rights Committee, about the frequent U.S. use of reservations upon ratification. Two years after the Vienna Declaration and Plan of Action of 1993 had called for states to reduce the number of reservations to human rights covenants, the UN Human Rights Committee adopted the following statement with respect to RUDs that the

United States had attached to its ratification of the ICCPR: "The Committee regrets the extent of the State party's reservations, declarations and understandings to the Covenant. It believes that, taken together, they intended to ensure that the United States has accepted what is already the law of the United States." The committee recorded its particular concern at U.S. reservations to article 6, paragraph 5 (prohibiting use of the death sentence for those who had committed crimes below the age of eighteen) and article 7 of the covenant (no one shall be subjected to torture or to cruel, inhuman, or degrading treatment or punishment), "which it believes to be incompatible with the object and purpose of the Covenant."[35] Critical statements such as these can only have diminished the authority and credibility of U.S. human rights officials in their dealings with abusive states. For example, it must have rung somewhat hollow for both Harold Koh and his interlocutors when he urged Chinese officials in January 1999 to ensure the "earliest possible ratification" of the ICCPR and for Beijing "to apply consistently and universally to all Chinese citizens the fundamental principles embodied in those instruments."[36]

The reservation to ICCPR article 6 has also separated the United States from its democratic allies and, on occasion, complicated their joint endeavors to promote human rights abroad.[37] European allies of the United States have been supportive of the adoption of a second optional protocol to the ICCPR that would outlaw the death penalty. In 1999, Germany, on behalf of the European Union, submitted an anti–death penalty resolution to the UNCHR, intended to prevent "the execution of minors, of the mentally ill, . . . and extradition to countries where the death penalty is in force." At the start of the UNCHR session that year, a number of U.S. allies used their opening statements to emphasize opposition to the death penalty. Although the United States was not mentioned by name in the EU resolution, it was clearly a target. At the same meeting, Amnesty International representatives excoriated the United States for ignoring a worldwide trend toward a moratorium on executions.[38]

Such instances suggest that U.S. resistance to international human rights instruments carries costs to the country's international image: weakening its identity as a leader among its democratic allies, reducing its authority in the issue area, and requiring that more coercive means be used to make an external human rights policy effective. More direct costs to a U.S. policy decision were made plain in 1997, when the United States decided that it had to ensure the introduction of a resolution critical of China's human rights record at the annual meeting of the UNCHR in order to keep the pressure on China to sign the two international covenants. The United States persuaded Denmark to introduce the resolution, but the actual drafting process created enormous problems because Washington would not support an additional Danish clause that condemned use of the death penalty and wanted to weaken sections dealing with social rights. Things got even worse for the United States later in the session when Italy and forty-four cosponsors introduced a resolution to bolster the Human Rights Committee's interpretation of ICCPR article 6. That interpretation reads: "all measures of abolition [of the death penalty] should be considered as progress in the enjoyment of the right to life." The resolution as a whole carried 27-11-14, the United States on the opposing side along with Algeria, Bangladesh, Bhutan, China, Egypt, Indonesia, Japan, Malaysia, Pakistan, and South Korea.[39] In May 2001, the United States was voted off the UNCHR. This occurred partly because of the George W. Bush administration's delay in getting its UN delegate confirmed and failure to lobby to retain its seat. But it also reflected a widening gulf between Washington and its allies over a range of human rights concerns. In the spring 2001 session, for example, the United States stood virtually alone in failing to support resolutions on lower cost access to drugs to combat HIV/AIDS, the right to food, the condemnation of disappearances, as well as the moratorium on executions.[40]

Beyond increasing divisions between the United States and its democratic allies, the weaknesses in America's multilateralist human rights policy have damaged its ability to promote human rights within "problem countries"—the avowed aim of the first Bush administration back in 1992. With respect to China, for example, the United States has devoted much time and attention since the Tiananmen Square bloodshed of June 1989 to pressuring Beijing to improve its human rights record. The U.S. State Department's annual *Country Report on Human Rights Practices* has a large China section that gives detailed attention to evidence of abuse and evaluations of legal reforms undertaken in that country. The two U.S.-China summits of the Clinton era, in Washington in October 1997 and in Beijing in June 1998, included agreements in the human rights area. The communiqué signed on the conclusion of Jiang Zemin's visit in 1997 committed the two countries to an exchange of legal experts and legal materials, U.S. help with the training of Chinese judges and lawyers, and the restarting of a bilateral human rights dialogue. The Clinton administration's so-called rule-of-law initiative, headed by presidential special adviser Paul Gewirtz, reinforced the administration's attention to China's human rights stance, as did its efforts to pass resolutions critical of China's record at annual meetings of the UNCHR.

Undoubtedly, U.S. efforts in this area have helped to push China toward signing the two international covenants.[41] Nevertheless, Beijing has become adept at drawing attention to the shortcoming in the U.S. record itself on multilateral treaties (not to mention flaws in the system of rights protection inside the United States), thereby weakening the force of U.S. policy both with the Chinese domestic audience and with the Chinese government. Chinese domestic reformers, so crucial to the advancement of the country's human rights protections, reflect on the publicity their government gives to

U.S. unilateralist behavior and therefore often dismiss U.S. human rights pressure on China as being politically biased rather than based on moral conviction. U.S. behavior undermines the work of domestic groups pressing for legal reform in the human rights area and contributes to the growth of an angry Chinese nationalism that blocks the human rights messages that the United States has been attempting directly to promote in the country.

Countless articles and statements from Chinese scholars and officials point to the inconsistency between U.S. demands on China and the patchy U.S. record of compliance. In January 1999, during a bilateral dialogue with Chinese officials on human rights matters, Koh urged China to ratify as quickly as possible the ICCPR, which Beijing signed in October 1998.[42] Given the U.S. position, however, he could not put equal stress on speedy ratification of the ICESCR, which China had signed a year earlier than the ICCPR.[43] Unsurprisingly, the Chinese frequently respond that it took the United States fifteen years to ratify the ICCPR and that it has yet to ratify the ICESCR. Beijing has also accused U.S. politicians of double standards, as the matter of delayed ratification has not been a particularly contentious matter in the United States. China, too, frequently notes that the United States has joined fewer international human rights treaties than any other major country, including China. Neither is the United States prone to self-reflection on its own record, according to Beijing (many other governments agree), even though there are examples of inadequate protection of rights. Finally, in its harsh criticism of NATO action in Kosovo—and of the general claim that the action was legitimate on the grounds that widespread violation of human rights required the transcendence of state sovereignty in favor of the protection of those subject to abuse—China has pointed to the U.S. claim that its own domestic law is superior to international law.[44] Chinese officials frequently make these points to their home audience, as well as at the United Nations, influencing how others advance their own arguments and the wider discourse on human rights.

To some degree, these points are part of the ongoing political battle over human rights between the United States and states such as China and Cuba. But they have a broader impact for a human rights regime that already gives governments that wish to avoid its prescriptions considerable room for maneuver. Failure to ratify the core human rights treaties not only undermines the policy aims of the United States but also, as L. Henkin has put it, "undermines a half century of effort to establish international human rights standards as international law."[45] The U.S. use of RUDs provides a negative example to other countries of how to exploit the treaties to minimize their domestic impacts. Chinese officials' perusal of these treaties and their domestic consequences has involved an examination of practices elsewhere, with the United States operating as an important benchmark.[46]

Finally, the international image of the United States itself also suffers when domestic legislation is given precedence over international commitments and when U.S. laws (e.g., Helms-Burton) are applied extraterritorially.

This smoothly shifts the international perception of the United States from "benign hegemon" to "insufferable bully."[47] Even close allies feel moved to voice their objections: as the British ambassador to the United Nations put it in 1997: "American exceptionalism cannot mean being the exception to the laws everyone else has to obey."[48]

Conclusion and Recommendations

The separation of powers in the treaty-making area and the requirements for a two-thirds majority for treaty acceptance are powerful explanations for the unilateralist U.S. stance in the human rights field: all administrations—Republican and Democrat—either have strived to stay in step with domestic opponents of the international human rights regime or have been faced with the need to compromise their objectives as a result of these domestic constraints. However, beyond these partisan, mainly conservative critics, located predominantly in Congress, there is a powerful tradition of U.S. exceptionalism that fosters the belief that U.S. domestic arrangements for the protection of human rights are superior to those mechanisms at the international level and that others would do well to emulate the U.S. experience. Otherwise, nonadherence to these treaties would have generated a higher level of controversy in the United States than has been the case. Thus, even without the presence of conservative senators such as Jesse Helms, it seems probable that the United States still would have issued various RUDs on signature of the core human rights treaties, thereby ensuring the supremacy of domestic constitutional law over international arrangements.

The costs of this unilateral tendency are both diffuse, in terms of U.S. reputation and image, and direct, in terms of diluting the credibility of the message the United States has sought to send through its promotion of an external human rights policy. In the period immediately after World War II until 1948, the United States was a powerful force in the creative development of the human rights regime. But at the beginning of the twenty-first century, when that regime is experiencing a further wave of expansion, the United States appears less the creator and more as a major obstructive force, particularly where human rights law threatens to impinge on U.S. domestic practices. This has become particularly noticeable at a time when its major European allies have been developing a more elaborate internal and external human rights policy of their own, one that for a variety of historical and cultural reasons is based on a broader definition of human rights than that used in the United States.

Although Washington has devoted significant resources in both the executive and legislative branches to promote human rights abroad, its external image as a norm entrepreneur is decidedly mixed because of its reluctance to allow its own domestic behavior to be subject to international scrutiny. This has given additional weapons to those governments that are resistant to some of the core principles in the international human rights regime, and it has provided them with examples of how best to exploit the room for maneuver within it. For a country that regularly proclaims that widespread adherence to human rights protections and democratic practices benefits U.S. national security as well as global peace and security, the policy seems remarkably shortsighted. But evidence of a widespread debate in the United States about removing some of the RUDs introduced at the time of treaty ratification, or for adherence to the ICESCR, CRC, or CEDAW, or for the benefits of staying more closely in step with its democratic partners in this issue area, seems to be lacking.

Ideally, such a debate should take place now in order to develop the perception that the United States stands fully behind the idea of the universality and indivisibility of human rights. Fuller adherence to the human rights regime would also move the United States closer not only to its democratic allies but also to democratizing countries, thus harmonizing and strengthening the human rights message. The UNCHR has proven an important forum for the advancement of human rights, especially since the 1980s, with growing attention to facets of abuse such as torture, arbitrary detention, disappearances, and the like, together with the creation of special rapporteurs and the post of UN High Commissioner for Human Rights. Washington needs to make the effort to regain its seat on the UNCHR and then to take it seriously as a negotiating forum, one that does help advance the cause of human rights. This suggests engaging in the debate about the removal of reservations to existing treaties, participating in the creation of new legislation that advances human dignity, and working to gain the agreement of like-minded others. Broad-based coalitions of support for human rights resolutions do have an impact on those so criticized, as studies of target states such as Argentina in the 1970s and 1980s and China in the 1990s have shown.[49] Effective and early lobbying to build these coalitions is essential to enhance the power of human rights norms, but so is the decision to lead by example and provide tangible support for the international legislation that has been steadily created.

With respect to the U.S. failure to adhere fully to major pieces of international human rights legislation and in recognition of the caution of its legislators, as others have suggested, the United States could experiment with the idea of introducing a sunset clause for reservations introduced on signature of human rights treaties. Such reservations would terminate automatically unless the Senate determined otherwise, thereby placing on Senators the onus of demonstrating that the reservations were necessary and had indeed played a vital role in preventing any undermining of the American way of life.[50]

In the absence of actions such as these, the United States will continue to hobble an external policy that has become a permanent, although not always primary, feature of its foreign relations. Many in the United States will also continue to refrain from examining more closely their belief that the country is as near-perfect a societal model as we are ever likely to encounter—not a healthy state of affairs for any society.

Notes

1. Kathryn Sikkink explains distinctions similar to these in "The Power of Principled Ideas," pp. 142–143.

2. The Dutch, for example, challenged the RUDs introduced on ratification of the ICCPR as being in violation of international law. See Forsythe, "US Foreign Policy and Human Rights," p. 28.

3. On the human rights issue in particular, Senator Bricker stated: "My purpose in offering this resolution is to bury the so-called Covenant on Human Rights so deep that no one holding high public office will ever dare to attempt its resurrection." Quoted in Henkin, "U.S. Ratification of Human Rights Conventions," p. 349. For a detailed discussion of this debate see Kaufman, *Human Rights Treaties and the Senate,* esp. chap. 4.

4. Sikkink, "The Power of Principled Ideas," p. 150.

5. Steiner and Alston, *International Human Rights in Context,* pp. 753–754.

6. Evans, *U.S. Hegemony and the Project of Universal Human Rights,* pp. 108–109.

7. These points are made in Kaufman, *Human Rights Treaties,* and Moravcsik, "Why Is U.S. Human Rights Policy so Unilateralist?"

8. Donnelly, *Universal Human Rights in Theory and Practice,* p. 268, note 9.

9. Luck, "American Exceptionalism and International Organization," p. 4.

10. Summary record of the thirteenth meeting, forty-eighth session of the UNCHR, February 5, 1992, E/CN.4/1992/SR.13, p. 8.

11. Sikkink, "The Power of Principled Ideas," pp. 148–149, 154.

12. Brownlie, *Basic Documents on Human Rights,* p. 326.

13. See "Leading by Example: A Human Rights Agenda for the European Union for the Year 2000," in Alston, ed., *The EU and Human Rights,* annex.

14. Cerna, "The United States and the American Convention on Human Rights," pp. 94–109.

15. For a critical evaluation of the effects of U.S. attachment of reservations, understandings, and declarations to human rights conventions, see Henkin, "U.S. Ratification of Human Rights Conventions," pp. 341–350.

16. Cerna, "The United States and the American Convention on Human Rights," p. 98.

17. Address by Senator Jesse Helms, Chairman, U.S. Senate Committee on Foreign Relations, Before the United Nations Security Council, January 20, 2000. Archived at www.usinfo.state.gov/regional/af/unmonth/t0012005.htm.

18. Dorsey, "U.S. Foreign Policy and the Human Rights Movement," p. 186, *Human Rights Watch 1999,* p. 470. Officials from the Defense Department even went so far as to lobby military attachés from embassies in Washington, including those from states that had made recent transitions to civilian rule and whose militaries had been responsible for widespread human rights violations. In addition, U.S. allies such as Germany and South Korea were pointedly reminded about the value of the presence of U.S. troop deployments in their own countries. Ibid.

19. Ambassador Harry G. Barnes, Jr., "Preface," p. ix.

20. Senator Helms wrote to the U.S. ambassador to the United Nations, Bill Richardson, querying whether the Special Rapporteur had not in fact mistaken the

United States for another country. See Tessitore and Woolfson, *A Global Agenda* (1998–1999), pp. 174–175; Luck, *Mixed Messages*, p. 126.

21. *Human Rights Watch World Report 2001*, p. 427.

22. *Human Rights Watch World Report 1998*, p. 387; Luck, *Mixed Messages*, pp. 124–125.

23. Schabas, "Spare the RUD or Spoil the Treaty," pp. 112–115; Steiner and Alston, *International Human Rights*, pp. 777–778; *Human Rights Watch 2001*, p. 427.

24. Moravcsik, "The Origins of Human Rights Regimes," pp. 217–252.

25. Moravcsik, "Why Is U.S. Human Rights Policy so Unilateralist?" As can be seen, I find Moravcsik's argument with respect to the factors shaping U.S. attitudes toward the human rights regime to be persuasive.

26. See Forsythe, "Human Rights and U.S. Foreign Policy: Two Levels, Two Worlds," pp. 111–130, for a survey from Carter to Clinton.

27. Mower Jr., *Human Rights and American Foreign Policy*, p. 15.

28. Ibid., pp. 82–83.

29. See, for example, the presidential statement, *A National Security Strategy for a New Century*, December 1999, which noted that U.S. strategy had three main objectives: to enhance U.S. security, to bolster its prosperity, and to promote democracy and human rights abroad; p. iii.

30. Neufville, "Human Rights Reporting as a Policy Tool," p. 682.

31. Sikkink, "The Power of Principled Ideas," p. 143.

32. Chayes and Handler Chayes, *The New Sovereignty*, pp. 25–26.

33. Yost is quoted in Steiner and Alston, *International Human Rights in Context*, pp. 758–759.

34. Koh, "Promoting Human Rights in the Pursuit of Peace," pp. 13–14.

35. Quoted in Schabas, "Spare the RUD or Spoil the Treaty," p. 111. See also Schabas's "Invalid Reservations to the International Covenant on Civil and Political Rights," where he states (at page 10): "The Committee's conclusion that the U.S. reservations to articles 6, paragraph 5 and 7 of the Covenant are invalid is supported by recognized sources of international law, including legal scholarship, case law and state practice."

36. Koh, "On-the-Record Briefing on U.S.-China Human Rights Dialogue," p. 1.

37. U.S. reservations to articles 6 and 7 of the ICCPR led eleven European state parties formally to object. Schabas, "Invalid Reservations," p. 7.

38. *International Herald Tribune*, March 29, 1999.

39. See Tessitore and Woolfson, eds., *A Global Agenda* (1997–1998), pp. 196–197.

40. See among many other reports, Koh, "America Gets a Wake-Up Call on Human Rights," *International Herald Tribune*, May 9, 2001.

41. For a fuller discussion, see Foot, *Rights Beyond Borders*.

42. Koh, "On-the-Record Briefing."

43. China subsequently ratified the ICESCR in March 2001.

44. For a variety of sources that pertain to these points, see *Foreign Broadcast Information Service (FBIS)*, Daily Report, China, 94–110, June 8, 1994; *Beijing Review*, March 13–19, 1995, and October 21–27, 1996; BBC *Summary of World Broadcasts*, Asia-Pacific, FE/3166/S1/5, March 4, 1998, FE/3481 G/4, March 12, 1999, FE/3526 G/1, May 5, 1999, FE/3535 G/7, May 15, 1999, FE/4084, March 2, 2001. A *Beijing Review* article of March 22–28, 1999 (page 49), for example, noted that when the United States joined the ICCPR in 1992, and the CAT in 1994, it stated that "it would only implement the two within the limits of its own laws, which makes joining meaningless."

45. Henkin, "US Ratifications of Human Rights Conventions," p. 349.

46. Private discussion with Chinese scholar, Beijing, September 1999. Koh, in his "On-the-Record Briefing," January 13, 1999, recalled in response to subsequent questioning that Chinese officials had "raised . . . the style in which we have ratified our international human rights conventions" (page 3).

47. Heisbourg, "American Hegemony?" p. 9.

48. Quoted in Luck, *Mixed Messages,* p. 15.

49. Flood, "U.S. Human Rights Initiatives Concerning Argentina"; Flood, "Human Rights, UN Institutions, and the United States"; Kent, "China and the International Human Rights Regime."

50. The sunset clause is mentioned in Barnes, "Preface," p. x.

6

Unilateralism, Multilateralism, and U.S. Drug Diplomacy in Latin America

Mónica Serrano

THE 1990S WITNESSED THE CLIMAX OF A CENTURY-LONG U.S. POLICY OF UNI-lateralism in the international control of narcotics, one that had started with a U.S. campaign for a global prohibition norm against drugs. Today, at the beginning of the twenty-first century, multilateral mechanisms of global governance appear to be on the rise in the area of illegal drugs as in other spheres. In response to an increase in drug-trafficking and transnational criminality, global institutions of crime control have emerged as "major developments in the world legal order."[1] In 1997, the Organization of American States (OAS) adopted its new Anti-Drug Strategy based on a renewed commitment to respect both the sovereignty and the territorial jurisdiction of member states. More recently, in December 2000, the United Nations Convention Against Transnational Organized Crime was signed. Yet the dawn of new multilateral efforts to control illicit drugs and transnational crime is occurring even as the sun has yet to set on the United States's own long-standing unilateral drug diplomacy.

In this chapter I examine the evolution of U.S. drug diplomacy within the framework of the international drug regime.[2] In the first section I consider the role of the United States in laying the foundations for this multilateral regime and shaping its subsequent evolution. I then identify the main factors that have obstructed the functioning of the regime and explore the crescendo of U.S. unilateralism during the 1990s. In the third section I delve into the politics of the certification process in Latin America. My aim in this chapter is not only to illustrate this unilateral shift within the multilateral drug regime but also to examine the contradictions between the drug prohibition norm, on the one hand, and the functioning of the global regulatory framework on the other. I analyze the consequences of U.S. drug diplomacy both for Latin American republics and the hegemonic power itself. In the final section I explore the links between the international drug control regime and the more recently established regional framework against transnational crime. I suggest more promising multilateral avenues are available to Washington and Latin American states in their shared efforts to tackle the drug problem.

Like other contributors in this book, I depict unilateralism and multilateralism not as clear polar opposites but as ends of a continuum. Moreover, it may be useful to think of unilateralism itself as spanning a spectrum, from decisions to opt out or act alone (at one end) to the ability—through forceful persuasion and coercion—to set the agenda in a multilateral framework (at the other). Leaving aside the question of opting out, a critical issue in the multilateral drug control regime has been the extent to which the United States has sought to maintain the ascendancy of the supply control paradigm.[3] Any overview of U.S. drug diplomacy also needs to take account of the complex mix of historical, bureaucratic, and personal factors behind U.S. policy.

U.S. Drug Diplomacy
and the International Drug Control Regime

The United States has been at the forefront of a war on drugs for more than a century. It has attempted to suppress and prohibit the consumption and trade of drugs that inhabited, during the nineteenth century, an ambiguous zone of semimedicalized tolerance and represented an important commodity in the global market place.

China's fateful experience with opium addiction in the nineteenth century, along with rising concern about the potential impact of the drug on public morals, prompted moral entrepreneurs in Britain and the United States to call for an end to the opium trade. Accordingly, in the early twentieth century, formal restrictions gradually came to replace informal patterns of control and regulation in both countries. Given the close relationship between demand, supply, and regulation, this impetus for the control of illicit drugs inevitably expressed itself in the international arena as well. In 1909, the United States sponsored the first international meeting, in Shanghai, to consider drugs as a matter of global concern. The extreme prohibitionist views adopted at this conference reflected the thesis first pursued in Washington by the two zealous prohibitionists Bishop Henry Brent and Hamilton Wright.[4]

The conference failed to persuade the main opium-producing countries to reduce their production; it also failed to secure agreement among countries with large pharmaceutical companies (including Germany, Switzerland, and the Netherlands) on such limitations. The U.S. government, and in particular Henry Brent, were undeterred. On the contrary, momentum quickly built for the internationalization of the drug prohibition norm. During 1909–1911, a conference at The Hague widened the scope of regulation by requiring signatories to enact domestic legislation aimed at controlling the manufacture and distribution of opium, heroin, cocaine, and other stimulants.[5]

The outbreak of World War I not only interrupted this process but also brought into clearer focus the international component of the drug control equation. Efforts to control illicit drugs within the United States were undermined by lax and uneven enforcement elsewhere. It thus became clear that the success of both domestic and global control efforts was ultimately dependent upon the commitment of the great majority of states to the enforcement of common standards. Notwithstanding the reluctance manifested by producing and manufacturing states toward the Opium Convention signed at the Hague in 1912, London and Washington insisted on the inclusion in the Paris peace agreements of a clause requiring the ratification of that treaty. This paved the way to the Opium Convention's entry into force in 1919–1921.[6] By 1923, the League of Nations's bureaucratic interest in an expansive drug control regime and the single-minded pursuit by the United States of drug diplomacy had moved the world definitively toward the supply control paradigm. This step took the regime irreversibly away from alternative approaches more in tune with social and medical realities.[7]

More than anywhere else, it was this new emphasis on compulsory international controls, as opposed to national regulatory frameworks, that shaped the global prohibition regime. Washington's participation in drug control negotiations, led as it was by moralistic U.S. advocates of uncompromising goals, left an indelible mark in the form of an irreversible bias in favor of policies to control drug supply.[8] For example, the provisions of a subsequent treaty, the 1925 Agreement Concerning the Suppression of the Manufacture of, Internal Trade in, and Use of Prepared Opium, included the creation of the Permanent Central Opium Board (PCOB; a U.S. initiative); a system of import and export certificates; restrictions on the trade in coca leaves and marijuana; and controls on processed drugs. As a practical matter, the actual implementation of these provisions would reflect the various and often contradictory interests at play in the drug control scene, including domestic bureaucracies, international agencies, the rising medical profession, competing pharmaceutical companies, producing countries, and others.

The 1931 Conference on the Limitation of the Manufacture of Narcotic Drugs further deepened the divide between the licit drug market and the illicit drug trade. This convention set out to bring legitimate drug production into line with legitimate medical and scientific needs, and it was an important step in the regulation of the licit market. Yet the shift toward formal prohibition and conventional restrictions increasingly encouraged clandestine production and illicit marketing while pushing nonmedical drug use underground. In the period between 1931 and 1939, U.S. drug diplomacy sealed the fate of the drug control regime. On the one hand, Harry Anslinger, commissioner of the U.S. Federal Bureau of Narcotics (FBN), increasingly relied on the international drug control regime to stave off domestic bureaucratic pressures that were building up to a reorganization of the federal drug control apparatus, targeted in particular at the FBN.[9] On the other hand, the decision, at U.S. request, to locate the PCOB and the Drug Supervisory Body (DSB) in the United States gave a small but powerful U.S. clique of drug control advocates a unique opportunity to retailor the multilateral regulatory framework to an orthodox supply control strategy.[10]

The imminence of world war during the 1930s not only subordinated drug control concerns to wider economic and strategic considerations but also enabled Harry Anslinger to pursue the radical supply control agenda through "unilateral action" and in "ways not possible in peacetime."[11] Anslinger cajoled states to adhere to the 1912 Opium Convention and the 1931 Limitation Convention and to submit statistics to the PCOB and the DSB. As the United States amassed and exercised control over licit drug stockpiles in wartime, it gained leverage to compel adherence to the multilateral control regime. Subsequently, the transfer of the League of Nations's drug control institutions to the United Nations in 1946 enabled this same U.S. clique to seize control of the newly established UN Commission on Narcotic Drugs and its sister agency, the Division on Narcotic Drugs. This allowed Anslinger and his followers to suppress all opposition to the doctrine of supply control and, most important, to rule over the UN drug control agenda.[12]

Notwithstanding these and other achievements (e.g., preeminently, the negotiation of the 1948 Synthetic Narcotics Protocol), it soon became clear that by stimulating the expansion of agricultural production and manufactured drugs the war had helped to fuel a growing illicit drug market.[13] Moreover, as had been the case in the course of hostilities, the advent of the Cold War forced drug control reformers to accommodate to the realities of pressing economic and security considerations.

Efforts to consolidate the eight existing multilateral treaties into a single convention and to tighten restrictions to control production started in 1948. Yet Anslinger's plans were temporarily brought to a halt, first by the open consideration of an international monopoly to control opium—modeled along the lines of the atomic regulatory framework—and subsequently by the negotiation of the 1953 Opium Protocol.[14]

In the middle and late 1950s, European powers gradually recovered their capacity to resist orthodox measures aimed at controlling the supply of drugs. As a campaign against the 1953 Opium Protocol and in favor of a single convention developed, physicians, academics, and lawyers laid siege to the clique around Anslinger. This temporarily weakened U.S. control over the multilateral drug control agenda, tilting the balance in favor of new and more eclectic approaches to the drug problem. First, producing countries like India, Iran, and (subsequently) Afghanistan, by arguing that production control was ultimately dependent on financial support, established a link between programs to control supply and foreign financial and technical aid. In the early 1960s, aid became a permanent feature of drug control diplomacy. Second, events like Turkey's deviation from agreed ceilings, along with the reality that newly independent states had little or no control over portions of their territories, drew attention to the difficulties of effective monitoring and compliance. Finally, as mass coca production began to make inroads in Latin America and elsewhere, Cold War considerations hindered U.S. efforts to control production at the source.[15]

In 1961, as the United Nations brought together the existing multilateral instruments into the Single Convention on Narcotic Drugs, the global drug prohibition regime was further consolidated. Although the supply-side paradigm remained firmly in place, differing worldviews affected the balance between priorities and approaches. The negotiation of the 1961 convention was accompanied by wide disagreements over the form and scope of regulation. Producing states favored a weak treaty, whereas concerns about securing ratification prompted Britain to oppose controls on cultivation. U.S. participation (in the absence of Anslinger) lacked clear direction.[16] In the end, marijuana producers were given a twenty-five-year grace period to comply while opposition from various industrialized countries protected synthetic drugs from encroaching prohibition.

The Single Convention and U.S. preferences soon came into open conflict. In the spring of 1962, Anslinger (who had returned) effectively attempted a coup against the UN convention, persuading the State Department to denounce it and compelling Greece to ratify the 1953 Opium Protocol. However, the overwhelming backing of eighty-two delegates for the Single Convention in autumn of 1962, combined with the lack of international support for the Opium Protocol, led Washington to reconsider and, in 1967, to adhere to the UN convention.[17]

The 1970s witnessed an unprecedented surge in both narcotics trafficking and in consumption of illicit and psychotropic drugs, particularly in the United States. The gradual widening of the drug control debate to include issues of prevention and treatment, and the negotiation of the 1971 UN Convention on Psychotropic Substances, highlighted multilateral concern with the drug emergency.[18] Under these new conditions, Washington's drug diplomacy acquired new momentum. This momentum did sweep up multilateral endeavors but was still deeply propelled by unilateral thinking. President Richard Nixon declared war on drugs in the early 1970s, breathing new life into U.S. efforts for strong multilateral drug control. As the new war targeted old external enemies—narcotics and heroin in particular—Washington renewed its campaign to toughen the 1961 Single Convention. These efforts resulted in a 1972 protocol, which amended the previous convention and marked yet another victory of the supply paradigm on the multilateral battlefield.

This new U.S. war on drugs, however, had implications that went far beyond multilateral efforts. The unilateral impulse also marched down bilateral paths, as the United States deployed considerable pressures on countries like Turkey and Mexico.[19] Whether Washington behaved unilaterally in a multilateral framework, or favored bilateral coercion, observers became increasingly aware of the bridge linking domestic U.S. politics and U.S. drug diplomacy.[20] From 1974 to 1988, a global explosion of production, trafficking, and consumption took place. As cocaine consumption in the United States became chic and reached epidemic proportions, partly as a result of tighter controls on synthetic drugs, the U.S. emphasis on prohibition became ever more pronounced.

A shift in drug control rhetoric, which now acknowledged the demand side of the equation, was indeed welcomed and led to encouraging, if ephemeral, changes in drug policies within the United States.[21] However, at the multilateral level, the U.S.-defined drug control regime clung to the fixed assumption that controlling supply should remain the priority. Moreover, this supply-focused regime was reinforced in the decades that followed by the adoption of a language of war. Indeed, throughout the 1980s, U.S. drug control policies became increasingly "securitized," so that by 1986 the drug crisis had become defined as a threat to U.S. national security.[22]

By this time, the compounded effect of the explosion of drug use and the securitization of antinarcotic policies tilted the balance in U.S. drug policy hopelessly in favor of military responses at the expense of approaches focusing on demand. The paramount objective became the strengthening of enforcement capabilities—aimed at eradicating capacities, disrupting distribution networks, increasing interdiction levels, and, ultimately, defoliating supply at the very source.

Two distinct but related factors accounted for this increased reliance on the language of war. The first was the growing perception within the U.S. security establishment of evolving links between drug-traffickers and revolutionary organizations. The second was the domestic political capital to be gained from rhetorical denunciations of the link between drugs and crime and the practical need to respond to the public demand for increased military action, itself awakened by the language of war. Politicians and the media, more than public concerns, propelled the armed campaign against drugs.[23]

For half a century, the evolving prohibition policies of the United States had neglected the relationship between control and criminality, continuing to work on the assumption that the repression of the drug trade would result in drug scarcity, higher prices, and declining purity of drugs. Throughout these decades supply supporters continued to believe that once the right norms were in place, international cooperation and/or effective diplomatic pressure would drain excess supply, leading to the eradication, once and for all, of drug abuse. Results on the ground, however, diametrically contradicted such hopes. As the United States intensified its war on drugs and coerced governments into military responses, trafficking and smuggling routes constantly relocated. Seizures continued to increase, consumption to linger, and prices to fall, but nevertheless drug prices remained sufficiently competitive to lure drug-traffickers toward the U.S. market. In Latin America, underground economies mushroomed, and relatively small and stable illicit drug markets gave way to large, violent, and chaotic criminal economies.[24]

As the 1980s drew to a close, voices in favor of reforming the multilateral drug control regime appeared to gain prominence internationally. Mounting pressures on the United Nations were a symptom of the worldwide recognition of the need to tackle this problem. The 1987 UN Conference on Drug Abuse and Illicit Traffic and the associated document ("Comprehensive Multidisciplinary Outline of Future Activities in Drug Control") marked an important stage in this multilateral endeavor. For the first time, drug prevention and addict treatment received equal attention with prevalent supply-side control measures.

However, this multilateral impetus did not last long, given the difficulty of balancing the interests of producing and consumer countries. Unilateral impulses again gathered force in the United States, rattled by a violent explosion in the consumption of crack cocaine. These impulses translated into a supply-side inertia in multilateral drug control efforts. Two were its main manifestations. The first was a failure to translate the incessant search for new concepts and policies to tackle the drug problem into viable alternatives to supply-side policies. Indeed, the apparent rhetorical shift of focus toward demand did not produce practical effects in the form of new approaches to international drug control.

The second signal was the revalidation of the punitive supply control regime in the 1988 UN Convention Against Illicit Traffic in Narcotic Drugs and Psychotropic Substances. As with its predecessors, the new instrument both revealed the "entrenched nature of the supply side paradigm" and aided the trend toward widening the contours of criminalization, even as current efforts were plainly failing to deliver the expected results.[25] The new multilateral convention committed signatories to share law-enforcement information, to provide mutual legal assistance, and to extradite individuals charged with drug law offenses. It renewed and redoubled previous commitments to eradicate and interdict drugs and to seize drug-related assets, and it broadened the scope of criminalization to include both money laundering and the movement of precursors and essential chemicals. The commitments and obligations contracted by the parties to this convention closely reflected the hierarchical power of developed consumer countries, most notably the United States.[26]

The logic at work in U.S. drug diplomacy became particularly clear with the setting up of the U.S. certification process. Since its introduction in 1986, the certification ritual has represented a sharp acceleration of the pace and scope of unilateralism in U.S. foreign drug policies. It is to the growing difficulties brought about by U.S. unilateral behavior, and to the greater awareness of the limits of repressive prohibitionist policies, that we must now turn.

The Politics of the Certification Process

Ronald Reagan's declaration of war against drugs in the summer of 1986 represented more than a serious setback for the drug policy reform movement in the United States; it also had serious repercussions abroad. That same year, the U.S. Congress amended the Foreign Assistance Act to require the president to certify whether or not drug-producing countries and transit countries were fully cooperating with antinarcotic efforts.

As the certification process evolved over nearly two decades, the unilateral turn in U.S. drug diplomacy became increasingly stark. Concomitantly, the weight of domestic political dynamics in determining the course of U.S. foreign drug policies became ever more pronounced. Indeed, the logic of internal U.S. politics now steered U.S. drug diplomacy away from multilateralism. The activation of political and bureaucratic interests, the growing media attention to drug problems, the qualitative weight of small but powerful constituencies, and changes in relations between the legislative and executive branches all encouraged this shift in Washington's foreign drug policy.

The introduction of the certification process by the U.S. Senate in 1986 was triggered, to a considerable extent, by rising domestic concerns generated by the murder in Mexico of Enrique Camarena, for the most part an undercover Drug Enforcement Administration (DEA) agent in 1985.[27] The certification mechanism was also intended to ensure that successive U.S. administrations gave sufficient attention to foreign drug control.[28] As public concern with crime and drugs mounted, Congress played an increasingly important role in U.S. drug diplomacy, and tensions built up in executive-legislative relations. Decisionmaking in foreign drug policy became hostage to voters' concerns. The resulting drug policy took the form of a measure tailored to suit domestic consumption and to appease an agitated U.S. audience; it was not necessarily conducive to effective international drug control.

From 1986 until its temporary halt at the turn of the century, the certification process was the main instrument of U.S. leverage over drug-affected states.[29] Indeed, under the certification process the United States has conditioned bilateral relations with an entire group of countries on progress in the arena of drug control. However, as the record in Latin America and elsewhere makes clear, certification has evolved into a powerful instrument serving a wider variety of foreign policy goals beyond drug control per se. Through the 1980s and 1990s, the certification process became the vehicle by which numerous U.S. agencies and institutions increasingly became involved in U.S. drug control diplomacy.[30]

In what is perhaps a conciliatory multilateral gesture, the criteria for certification applies to those countries that "have cooperated fully with the U.S., or taken adequate steps on their own, to achieve full compliance with the goals and objectives of the UN Convention." Thus, through the certification mechanism, the United States appears to claim a "custodial" role as the self-appointed guarantor of norms and standards accepted or imposed on the international community.[31] Such rhetoric notwithstanding, the degree to which certification has become embedded in the wider and more complex context of U.S. domestic politics and foreign policy making helps one understand the inconsistencies and apparent double standards that have accompanied its implementation.

Since its inception, the certification mechanism has developed into a thorny issue in relations between the United States and countries affected by drug-trafficking. The poison that certification has injected into bilateral relations is particularly strong in Latin America. Relations between the United States and drug-affected Latin American states soured in 1995, when Colombia, Bolivia, and Peru were "conditionally certified," and hit a new low point one year later, when Colombia was decertified.

The annual U.S. certification process increased the vulnerability of drug-affected states to U.S. sanctions. These include the cancellation of 50 percent of bilateral aid (with the exception of some humanitarian aid); a negative U.S. vote for loan concessions in international financial institutions; and the denial of access to Export-Import Bank credits for U.S. exporters selling to decertified countries. Equally significant has been the impact of the certification ritual upon political stability in drug-affected countries.

Since its inception, the certification process has been strongly criticized as discriminatory and ineffectual. Nowhere have the costs of this unilateral policy been more evident than in the downward spiral of the Colombian state. Although it could be argued that mounting pressures did force Colombian authorities to take drug issues more seriously, the overall results of Colombia's three-year decertification appear highly unfortunate. Despite rising U.S. pressure, designed to punish the administration of Ernesto Samper for financing his 1994 campaign with drug money from the Cali cartel, the Colombian president remained in power for the whole of his term. Although it is true that the Samper administration showed greater willingness to cooperate throughout these years, decertification produced counterproductive results on various fronts, most notably in the weakening of the Colombian state and the shot in the arm given to the Colombian guerrillas as coca cultivation boomed. The Colombian experience showed too clearly how decertification reduced Washington's ability to bolster counterdrug cooperation and hence induce the desired policy changes in drug-driven countries. This reality led an inspector general of the State Department to accept publicly in 1996 that "the certification process has had limited success in improving counter-narcotic performance overseas."[32]

Double standards have also become apparent in the U.S. application of certification policies. Despite clear evidence that Mexico had become the main corridor for more than 70 percent of the cocaine aimed for the U.S. market, Mexico continued to be certified. Such unevenhandedness in U.S. policies toward drug-affected countries has been the Achilles' heel of certification. Strategic considerations of the moment have plainly tainted the process. Although countries that have been the object of specific U.S. security concerns seldom escaped the fallout of certification, it became increasingly clear that the effectiveness of antinarcotic efforts was not the only criterion upon which certification decisions would depend. Countries of major importance for U.S. interests, such as China, Taiwan, Panama, Brazil, and indeed Mexico, have usually been certified. According to one view, Bill Clinton's administration chose to decertify Colombia in 1996 based on the belief that it would make possible Mexico's full certification by the U.S. Congress. Exceptions have also been contemplated on the basis of political considerations. In 1996, for instance, Paraguay and Peru received special treatment to preserve a fragile transition to democracy and to avoid disrupting the peace process with Ecuador, respectively.[33]

As certification moved to center stage in U.S.–Latin American relations, the scope for disagreement grew. In March 1997, in the context of the second meeting of experts of the Rio Group, Mexican President Ernesto Zedillo, backed by a solid domestic consensus, made public his opposition to the U.S. certification policy. Similarly, during the regional meeting of foreign ministers held in Paraguay in May of that year, Latin American representatives discussed possible alternatives to the certification process, widely regarded as an illegitimate unilateral mechanism.

From a Latin American viewpoint, a particularly distressing feature of the unilateral certification process has been the militarization of U.S. antinarcotic policies. Clearly, since the mid-1980s, the definition by the U.S. government of the drug problem as a security issue has paved the way for the internationalization of costly military responses. The disappointing and even perverse effects of initial U.S. policies, which had remained under the control of civilian law enforcement, led to an ever-increasing emphasis on the role of force. However, as the diminishing returns of earlier policies became manifest, the response was not a shift from this emphasis but precisely an escalation of military-style responses.[34]

Equally important was the fact that the securitization of antinarcotic policies provided new grounds for foreign intervention. The vulnerability of states to intervention has indeed increased, as first became clear with the deployment of U.S. troops to Bolivia in 1986 and the unprecedented military and police (i.e., DEA) presence—without congressional approval—stationed in that country under the government of Victor Paz Estenssoro (1985–1989). This was followed by the invasion of Panama in 1989 and by the incursion of U.S. warships into the Colombian Caribbean in January 1990.[35] The militarization of drug control policies not only endangers democratic rule and sovereign state institutions (in countries other than Panama) but also has important regional security implications. These range from violent resistance against antinarcotic policies to shifts in regional military balances as a result of arms transfers originally aimed at strengthening the capabilities of states besieged by drug-traffickers.

Although initially the arrest of a few notable criminal figures suggested some measure of success, the lack of clear military objectives in U.S. policy raised serious questions about the wisdom of enlisting the armed forces and offering military responses to a singularly elusive threat. The lack of clear or feasible military missions, in other words, involves the risk of falling into the trap of sterile escalation. An ambiguous sense of purpose creates the danger of setting goals in terms of seizures, eradication results, arrests, and destroyed facilities—of confusing the mission with statistical results that may look impressive but are always abstracted.

Like other forms of coercive diplomacy, the prohibition norm assumes that the enemy can be identified and punished, given sufficient motivation and appropriate tools. However, it is the mobility and anonymity of drug-trafficking and other forms of transnational organized crime, it has been persuasively argued, that make such "trans-state actors essentially non-coercible."[36] Is there a conclusive way of winning a war against an enemy that lacks a "center of gravity" against which the use of force can be directed—an enemy that behaves like a mercury globule?

The lack of standard criteria to assess the efforts deployed by different countries, the questions raised by the trend toward militarization, and the distortion of certifications by the dynamics of U.S. domestic politics—these have become the main targets of mounting criticism outside the United States. However, in spite of the deficiencies in its current approach and the presence of more impartial alternatives, such as the annual report of the UN International Narcotics Control Board, the balance in the United States has not yet swung against the certification process or even against the general policy of supply control. Although General Barry MacCaffrey, the previous U.S. drug czar, acknowledged many of the flaws present in the certification process, the supply control paradigm is likely to remain in place, largely because U.S. politicians, including the president, have much to lose by appearing soft on the drug issue. The persistence along this course of action can perhaps best be explained by the semiautonomous politics of policy-making. Increasing social costs—in terms of a mushrooming prison population, health epidemics, and an encroachment upon civil liberties—have not been sufficient to impel a change of policy within and beyond the

United States. For politicians driven by the requirements of reelection, the price for abandoning this crusade seems much higher than the cost of reforming this set of policies.[37] Unilateralism in U.S. drug diplomacy thus needs to be understood as a phenomenon possessing many layers of motivation arising from within the U.S. political system.

A Regional Drug Control Regime?

Concurrently with the U.S. certification process, efforts have begun within the OAS to push forward an alternative drug control route. Among the main avenues that have been explored, two deserve special attention: first, efforts to bring illicit arms trafficking under control; and second, steps to find an alternative regional framework to the certification process.

In relation to arms trafficking, it is true that in the aftermath of pacification, pockets of illegal arms were indeed found in Central America. However, the explosion of arms trafficking has long been seen as the direct offspring of the narcotics market. Flows of arms have accompanied drug-trafficking routes, but the north-south direction of these flows has been preponderant. Under the pressure of states like Mexico and Colombia, both the OAS and Washington itself were encouraged to address this increasingly complex problem.[38]

Likewise, as the 1980s drew to a close, efforts to build an alternative regional drug control regime moved forward. In 1986, the Inter-American Drug Abuse Control Commission (CICAD) was created during the Specialized Conference on Traffic in Narcotic Drugs held in Rio de Janeiro. The long-term goal of the new agency was the elimination of the illicit traffic in, and abuse of, drugs. By the beginning of the 1990s, hopes of change paved the way for rising expectations about the possibility of multilateral cooperation.[39] During the 1994 Miami Summit of the Americas, such hopes seemed to materialize as a new principle of shared responsibility and reciprocity in the control of drugs emerged.[40] Yet despite the OAS General Assembly's adoption a few years later of the Anti-Drug Strategy in the Hemisphere and the introduction at the 1998 Santiago Summit of the Multilateral Evaluation Mechanism, many of the methods chosen were in fact practically modeled on the certification example, with the only exception being measures on prevention and treatment.[41]

Moreover, the financial difficulties encountered by these OAS drug control institutions highlight the lukewarm commitment of the hemisphere's states to a viable regional alternative. Frustrated by the weak Latin American response to its efforts to set up a hemispheric network of drug information centers, CICAD turned to the EU instead.[42]

An additional important consideration is the apparent incapacity, or lack of imagination, of Latin American republics to generate new ideas and approaches to the drug problem. The accumulated inertia of U.S. drug control policies, and the leverage Washington has amassed through the certification process, have led individual countries and now the region as a whole to pursue institutional drug control policies according to the orthodox supply paradigm. Even if one could argue that these regional initiatives have placed certain limits on the unilateral certification process, they seem unlikely to produce tangible results.

Thus, notwithstanding the costs incurred by supply policies, just as the reformist wave has so far failed to make an impact on domestic policy-making in the United States, so on the multilateral regional front Latin American initiatives have not succeeded in transcending the old paradigm. As long as the drug problem continues to be seen as deeply embedded in a criminal framework, punishment at home and abroad is likely to continue as the only "appropriate response."[43]

Conclusion

The gradual change in official U.S. discourse on the drug problem has yet to produce an equivalent policy shift. Washington has continued to rely on what one could call a body-count strategy to measure success at home and abroad. As in Vietnam, success has been measured according to quantifiable variables that may tell little about progress in the "war."[44] Certification proceeded in the belief that it would compel governments to devote much-needed attention to drug-trafficking, violence, and corruption that indeed threatened the long-standing economic and political stability of their countries.

However, the central question may not be the efficacy of policies to control supply (including certification) but rather the degree to which anti-narcotic policies have themselves exacerbated chronic instability in source states.

The prohibition norm has served up a veritable feast of dilemmas. Yet because this norm is unlikely to be revoked anytime soon, it might be more productive to engage in lateral thinking than in the search for clear-cut solutions. It is increasingly clear that the United States, by enforcing the global drug prohibition norm, has forced drug-driven states on one horn of the dilemma, itself on the other. States like Colombia and Mexico have borne the costs of repressive U.S. policies beginning after 1986; the longer it takes for those policies *not* to work, the more likely it is that the United States will also have to contemplate paying costs. As long as the United States fails to wean itself from the fiction of prohibition—the fiction that the drug problem will fade by controlling production at the source—the chances of genuine, as opposed to enforced, multilateralism will also continue to fade.

The real dilemma specific to the United States is unilateralism by default, that is, a situation where multilateralism is not an option given the chronic institutional weakness of the states that should be cooperative actors. (Colombia is a clear case.) A charitable interpretation might judge the certification process in this light. But even here, the problem is not only that cooperation may be a forced donation reluctantly received but also that cooperation itself may be a sign of a state—and a policy—in crisis. Given the weakness of states penetrated by drug-trafficking and other forms of transnational organized crime, neither unilateralism nor even multilateralism may succeed until the states themselves are strengthened.[45]

If the weakness of the cooperative state is one gigantic stumbling block to multilateralism in international drug control efforts, another is the incommensurability of perspectives about whose drug problem it really is. Even when the United States seeks multilateral cooperation, it is often perceived as a unilateral actor, seeking to export its own domestic problems. At the same time, naturally, U.S. awareness of such perceptions abroad provide another incentive for the country to seek to impose its own preferences or to go it alone. Mutual incomprehension is invidious for both sides. Although it is true that the drug prohibition regime is now underpinned by an elaborate institutional structure, it is impossible to deny the fundamental difficulty that lies at the heart of the regime. This is the persistent tension between adherence to the norm and its implementation.[46] Above and beyond conflicting perspectives, there may well be a unanimous impulse to support the norm. The practical difficulty of multilateralism, however, is that even though unanimity may be forthcoming in principle, there may come a point when internal and external costs rise so high that states become persuaded that it is in their interest to bail out of the consensus. Failing to cooperate is thus again a matter of perception. Depending on how you hear it, "We'd love to help, we really would . . ." can signal either good faith or default—or a messy combination of both.

Notwithstanding this difficulty, the *transnational* dimension of drug trafficking and other associated forms of transnational crime is by now common knowledge. The need for some form of cooperation among states is overwhelming. Thus, although prohibitionist and repressive policies have generated little except cynicism and disillusionment outside the United States, what we need to see now is the coming together of some of the ideas developed over a decade's worth of frustration with the ascendancy of supply-side policies—ideas that opponents of the certification process, as mentioned, have themselves been remiss in promoting.

Washington historically has engaged the rest of the world community, trying to persuade and mobilize it in its crusade against the drug problem. It is precisely this historical effort at persuasion that complicates the characterization of U.S. drug diplomacy as a purely unilateral force. However, as disagreements about the means to the desired end sharpen, U.S. efforts to cajole other states into its own vision of the drug problem readily became exercises in force majeure. In an ideal future world, the United States would have to relinquish its monopoly on its own perspective on fixes to the drug problem and allow itself to become at least persuadable vis-à-vis other (i.e., European) perspectives. As of today, we have two competing versions of what multilateralism might mean. From the orthodoxy of the supply paradigm, it will continue to mean as many actors as possible to subscribe as regiments in an army whose generals will remain mostly American. The alternative version of multilateralism would involve an open exchange of explanations and answers to the drug problem aimed at bringing into harmony and proportion the demand and supply sides of the drug equation. It would entail a drug control regime free both of the vicissitudes of U.S. domestic politics and of the inertia of the supply control paradigm, that is, a regime at least equally committed to the heterodoxy of prevention and treatment. In a quiet way, these views, strengthened by an increasing recognition of the costs incurred by prohibitionist policies, are finally, and publicly, entering the equation. The solution to the dilemmas of unilateralism will thus be found in more lateral thinking on all sides.

Notes

The author would like to thank the editors and Stewart Patrick for their valuable comments on an earlier version of this chapter.

1. McDonald, "The Globalisation of Criminology," p. 10.

2. The drug problem encompasses various nuclei of phenomena that can be grouped around four sources: initiation, dependence, distribution, and production. To the extent that different dimensions of the problem have different sources, particular policies do not always have the desired effect across the spectrum. Both the negative interactions and policy trade-offs become clear as we unpack and examine these categories. Thus, for example, more stringent enforcement may reduce drug use while exacerbating related crime and health problems. And tighter interdiction may increase drug seizures while raising the demand for drug exports and aggravating, in turn, source country difficulties. See MacCoun and Reuter, "Drug Control," pp. 215–217.

3. In the course of one century, U.S. participation in building, developing, and implementing the drug control regime has oscillated between the more clearly multilateral prophetic or missionary role and practices that go beyond "custodial" responsibilities and more openly gravitate toward unilateralism. This is the case of the controversial certification process, in which the weight of internal constituencies and considerations has been clearer. Reisman, "The United States and International Institutions."

4. Brent and Wright represented the U.S. government in the Shanghai conference. As main architects of the drug prohibition regime, Brent (appointed in 1911 as State Department adviser on international narcotic matters) and Hamilton Wright found inspiration in a previous Sino-British agreement that enabled China to significantly cut down opium production between 1908 and 1910. Overlooking many of the fundamental flaws in this strategy—most notably, the sharp increase in smuggling,

the rise of Persia and Turkey as new players in the market, and the proclivity of addicts to switch between substances and drugs—U.S. policymakers settled for a policy of controlling supply under the illusion that by eliminating excess supply the drug problem would be solved. The 1907 Ten Year Agreement and the idea that drug control was essentially a matter of political will became the axioms upon which the drug regime was built. See Reisman, "The U.S. and International Institutions," p. 66; McAllister, *Drug Diplomacy* pp. 24–29 and 39; Jensen and Gerber, "The Social Construction of Drug Problems: An Historical Overview," pp. 6–7.

5. In the United States, the Harrison Narcotics Act, enacted in 1914 to comply with the recently acquired international obligations, became the basis for regulating narcotics for nearly five decades. In the 1920s, comparable domestic legislation was introduced in Britain and other European countries. However, conversion to formal drug laws did not always entail harmonization in terms of implementation. The implementation of prohibition laws has varied significantly, reflecting wider national concerns and goals. For an analysis of the criminalization of narcotic drugs within the U.S. jurisdiction, see Jensen and Gerber, "The Social Construction of Drug Problems," pp. 6–11; see also Stares, *Global Habit,* p. 18; McAllister *Drug Diplomacy,* pp. 35, 64; MacCoun and Reuter, "Drug Control," pp. 212, 225.

6. As Turkey and Germany were forced to comply in order to conclude peace, the requirement of near universal ratification was finally satisfied. McAllister, *Drug Diplomacy,* p. 37.

7. Like their predecessors, Rupert Blue and Stephen G. Porter, the U.S. representatives to drug control negotiations in the interwar period, advocated inflexible supply control measures. The British government, pro-League organizations in the United States, and international bureaucrats all hoped that drug negotiations would entice the United States to engage in the international arena and, through its example, help propel arms control negotiations. Washington's participation brought to the multilateral framework not only the uncompromising attitude that has ever since characterized U.S. drug diplomacy but also the undeniable link with domestic politics. Porter, U.S. drug czar during the 1920s, was among the first to hold intransigent positions in international forums in order to build domestic political capital at home. McAllister, *Drug Diplomacy,* p. 55.

8. The literature on this theme is extensive; see, among others, McAllister, *Drug Diplomacy*; Nadelmann, *Cops Across Borders*; and Jensen and Gerber, "The Social Construction of Drug Problems."

9. The Anslinger campaign can be seen as having aimed at the Americanization of antidrug policies around the world. It was a campaign with two main fronts: the promotion of international police cooperation, and the inclusion within the 1931 Convention on the Limitation of the Manufacture of Narcotic Drugs of an article requiring signatories to establish a national agency modeled on the FBN. McAllister, *Drug Diplomacy,* pp. 107–108.

10. Despite overwhelming evidence to the contrary, this group of policymakers, headed by Anslinger and Colonel Sharman, continued to see demand as a mere function of supply. The shift to a mandatory international drug control regime was based on two main pillars: the international accounting system established by the Permanent Central Board, and the regulations laid down by the 1936 Convention for the Suppression of the Illicit Traffic in Dangerous Drugs. These regulations included many provisions still in force today, namely, severe penalties for taking part in the drug market, extradition of traffickers, and so on. Although forty-two governments participated in this conference, only twenty-six, excluding the United States, signed the convention. Stares *Global Habit,* pp. 17–20; McAllister, *Drug Diplomacy,* pp. 100–139, 150.

11. McAllister, *Drug Diplomacy,* p. 144.

12. As McAllister suggests, the rise of an international group of drug experts and the survival of successful drug agencies closed the door to alternative views. As the postwar institutional framework was laid down, supply control policies again took precedence. Hence drug enforcement was increasingly considered as a police and administrative matter. See McAllister, *Drug Diplomacy*, pp. 133, 153–160.

13. The contradictory policies pursued by the United States during the war illustrated how the interaction of political, economic, bureaucratic, and medical considerations resulted in a perplexing drug problem. In the context of war, Anslinger sought to limit and reduce agricultural production in Latin America and Asia while considering a regional scheme—embracing Puerto Rico, Canada, Mexico, and the United States—to cultivate hemp and opium. The U.S. drug commissioner also presided over the largest ever stockpile of licit opium.

14. The protocol, the result of a French initiative that received Anslinger's blessing, sought to establish controls over raw opium production. Parties to the treaty agreed to buy opium solely from those producers recognized by the agreement (Bulgaria, Greece, India, Iran, Turkey, Yugoslavia, and the Soviet Union). China's bid to join the licit market was the key factor underlying the producers' readiness to agree on market share. McAllister, *Drug Diplomacy,* pp. 172–182.

15. This was undoubtedly the case of Bolivia, where Cuban traffickers first built a coca processing base in the 1950s and drug diplomacy became increasingly trapped in the vicissitudes of anticommunism. Despite the fact that the links between the Bolivian government (most notably the army) and drug traffickers expanded through the 1960s and well into the 1970s, U.S. drug diplomacy not only overlooked but indeed tolerated this partnership, which helped fund anticommunist campaigns and anti-Castro opponents. See McAllister, *Drug Diplomacy,* pp. 193–200; Gamarra, "The United States and Bolivia," pp. 182–184; Gamarra, "Transnational Criminal Organizations in Bolivia," pp. 173–174; Serrano and Toro, "From Drug-Trafficking to Transnational Organized Crime."

16. Such apparent lack of direction can also be explained in terms of the changes taking place within the United States and, in particular, the rise of the reformist movement calling for a change in the punitive approach. During the first White House Conference on Narcotics and Drug Abuse held in Washington in 1962, scientists and reformers moved toward the conclusion that current drug control policies were exacerbating rather than ameliorating drug problems. Jensen and Gerber, "The Social Construction of the Drug Problem," pp. 12–13.

17. McAllister, *Drug Diplomacy*, pp. 206–218.

18. This convention brought synthetic drugs into the confines of prohibition. Although during the negotiations manufacturing countries and pharmaceutical companies objected to stringent controls, the pressures exerted by the "strict control coalition" (Soviet bloc and Scandinavian countries) and the UN Secretariat gradually closed many of the treaty's loopholes. Stares, *Global Habit*, pp. 26–27; McAllister, *Drug Diplomacy,* pp. 224–234.

19. Under the impact of the U.S.-led Operation Interception, the Mexican government was compelled to launch a forceful eradication campaign. The 1970 Operation Condor was underpinned by intelligence-sharing, the development of highly specialized police corps, close cooperation with the U.S. Drug Enforcement Administration (DEA), as well as finely tuned rotations of police and military forces. Its much publicized success proved short-lived and was accompanied by counterproductive effects, the most important of which were the cartelization of the drug market and the strengthening of criminal organizations. Toro, *Mexico's "War" on Drugs*, p. 27, and Sharpe, "The Military, the Drug War, and Democracy," p. 78.

20. By emphasizing the link between crime and drugs, Nixon sought to build domestic political support. Although the link between crime and drugs is to a large extent the result of prohibition, politicians in the United States and elsewhere have profited considerably by denouncing it. On Nixon, see McAllister, *Drug Diplomacy*, p. 235, and Jensen and Gerber, "The Social Construction of the Drug Problem," p. 13.

21. In the United States, the passage of the Comprehensive Drug Abuse Prevention and Control Act of 1970 and the National Commission on Marijuana and Drug Abuse Report of 1972 marked important victories for the reformist movement. Although the report's recommendation to decriminalize marijuana had been rejected by the Nixon administration, the casuistic approach adopted by states along with reduced penalties for first-time possession of marijuana significantly reduced the prison populations. Jensen and Gerber, "The Social Construction of Drug Problems," p. 13; Nadelmann, "Commonsense Drug Policy," pp. 121–122.

22. In 1986, the National Security Decision Directive 221 (NSDD-221) defined drug-trafficking as a national security threat. This trend was further reinforced, three years later, by the State Department's 1989 International Narcotics Control Strategy. Such securitization of antinarcotic policies was partly motivated by evidence pointing to links between drug trafficking and revolutionary movements. See Doyle, "The Militarization of the Drug War in Mexico," p. 85.

23. See Jensen and Gerber, "The Social Construction of Drug Problems," pp. 16–19, for an analysis of the forces at play at the moment in which Reagan declared war on drugs in 1986.

24. Serrano and Toro, "From Drug-Trafficking to Transnational Organized Crime."

25. McAllister, *Drug Diplomacy*, p. 125.

26. Between 1989 and 1995, new measures were introduced to tighten the international drug control regime. These followed the lines set up by the 1988 UN convention and included initiatives to control the diversion of chemical precursors and to suppress money laundering. In 1989, the G7 agreed to establish the Financial Action Task Force to address this growing problem. This was followed by the creation of the Chemical Action Task Force in the early 1990s. Stares, *Global Habit*, pp. 36, 45.

27. From the 1980s, the DEA abandoned police cooperation in Latin America and emerged as an extraterritorial security force. Benefiting from the drug scare in the United States, the DEA increasingly sought to escalate pressure on drug-affected states and the extraterritorial enforcement of U.S. drug laws. The decision of the U.S. Supreme Court in the early 1990s in *United States v. Alvarez Machain* (authorizing the kidnapping of foreign nationals by U.S. police) marked a turning point in the extraterritorial reach of the U.S. judicial and security arms. Toro, "The Internationalization of Police," pp. 633–634, 637.

28. According to Jensen and Gerber, the 1986 drug war was in fact at odds with consumption patterns. Having peaked in the late 1970s, drug-use patterns followed a decreasing trend throughout the early 1980s. In their sociological analysis, bureaucratic and political actors triggered a media avalanche and "constructed" a social emergency that was followed by policies that further exacerbated the drug problem. Jensen and Gerber, "The Social Construction of Drug Problems," pp. 16–17; Nadelmann, "Common Sense Drug Policy," pp. 112–114; Reisman, "The United States and International Institutions," pp. 76–77; and Joyce, "Packaging Drugs," p. 214.

29. The decision to suspend the certification process for three years originated in legislation introduced in spring 2001 by a bipartisan group of senators including

Christopher Dodd, Charles Hagel, and Lincoln Chaffee. Although this measure was intended to allow for the consideration of multilateral alternatives based on the understanding of shared responsibilities, it proceeded on the assumption that the certification process would be amended and released from its most "insulting aspects" but not entirely abolished.

30. Joyce, "Packaging Drugs," pp. 207–210.

31. Quoted in ibid., p. 211; see also Reisman, "The United States and International Institutions," pp. 71–75.

32. A similar analysis applies to the effects of the pressures exerted on Mexico in the mid-1990s. Before leaving Mexico, James Jones, U.S. ambassador, described the U.S. strategy for fighting drug trafficking as a total failure and called attention to the risk of repeating the Colombian path in Mexico. These declarations were reported in *Reforma*, May 5, 1997. See also Oxford Analytica, "Latin America Daily Brief," March 4, 1997, and August 31, 1999, and the Latin American Programme, "Drug Certification and US Policy in Latin America," Woodrow Wilson Center for Scholars, April 1998.

33. Serrano, "Transnational Crime in the Western Hemisphere," pp. 102–103; Joyce, "Packaging Drugs," pp. 212–215.

34. Under the pressure of the Reagan and Bush administrations, governments across the world were pushed to conceive of drug control in terms of combat. Thus, as they sought to strengthen capabilities by enlisting the armed forces, the term "drug war" won its notorious currency. Joyce, "Conclusion," pp. 193–194.

35. Gamarra, "The United States and Bolivia," pp. 191–192; Steiner, "Hooked on Drugs," p. 163.

36. For the view that military responses may not offer the best solution to the drug threat and may "ultimately exacerbate the very problem [they try] to solve," see Sharpe 1994, p. 81; Lepgold 1998.

37. See Domínguez, "US–Latin American Relations." A change in policy has only been contemplated by U.S. authorities, including Barry McCaffrey, in the context of an unthinkable "success of international anti-narcotic cooperation" in the future.

38. This was indeed the aspiration of the Inter-American Convention Against the Illicit Manufacturing of and Trafficking of Firearms, Ammunitions, Explosives, and Other Related Materials signed in 1997. This instrument entered into force on July 1, 1998, after ten of the thirty-two countries that had signed the convention deposited instruments of ratification. Similarly, the decision of the Clinton administration to implement supply-control regulations in the small arms trade in the region symbolizes an important shift in the share of obligations and responsibilities in the multilateral drug control framework. Granada, "The OAS and Transnational Organized Crime"; Serrano and Toro, "From Drug-Trafficking to Transnational Organized Crime."

39. In June 1990, the OAS adopted the Declaration and Program of Action of Ixtapa, a twenty-point plan of action that set CICAD priorities.

40. As the metaphors of pandemic and disease, of balloon and push-down pop-up effects, became well established at the turn of the twenty-first century, the U.S. government was finally forced to accept that "the lines demarcating source, transit and consuming nations have become blurred as drug abuse and drug-related social harms [have] become a shared problem," National Drug Control Strategy, prepared by the Network of Reform Group, 1999.

41. Countries are expected to provide information on national plans and strategies; prevention and treatment; reduction of drug production; law enforcement measures; and an overall estimate of the cost of the drug problem. There are four main planks of this strategy: the strengthening of antidrug plans; prevention and

treatment; the reduction of drug production and improved law enforcement; as well as the control of money laundering and the illegal misuse of chemical precursors. The Multilateral Evaluation Mechanism (MEM) aspires to evaluate and reinforce unilateral and collective efforts by requesting member states to develop their national and multilateral efforts. The ultimate goal is to secure the implementation of an antidrug strategy that aspires to respect the sovereignty and territorial jurisdiction of member states. The MEM is thus intended to monitor individual and collective efforts in the hemisphere. Granada, "The OAS and Transnational Organized Crime."

42. Joyce, "Packaging Drugs," p. 221.

43. MacCoun and Reuter, "Drug Control," p. 234.

44. In Vietnam, a body-count strategy, which placed the emphasis on a few counted bodies, remained in place until the arrival of General Abrams, when the focus shifted to efforts aimed at breaking the enemy's system. Thompson, *Defeating Communist Insurgency.*

45. Experiences across the spectrum show that relatively strong governments can indeed choose between viable and cost-effective punitive policies (Norway and Sweden) or quietly opt out by maintaining their grip on implementation. This is the course followed by Britain's decision in 2001 to downgrade cannabis. See MacCoun and Reuter, "Drug Control," pp. 224–231; Nadelmann, "Commonsense Drug Policy."

46. As Lepgold points out, these characteristics "strongly favour the target of coercion rather than the coercer." Lepgold, "Hypothesis on Vulnerability," p. 132.

PART 2

PEACE AND SECURITY

7

The United Nations
and the United States:
An Indispensable Partnership

Kishore Mahbubani

IN SEPTEMBER 2000, ON THE EVE OF THE MILLENNIUM SUMMIT, I WROTE THE following passage in a volume of essays edited by the permanent representative of India to the United Nations:

> Daily, the forces of globalisation are generating greater and greater interdependence. Actions in one corner of the world can affect a distant corner relatively quickly. Most people living outside the U.S. can feel and understand the impact of globalisation: they feel a loss of autonomy each day. Most Americans do not feel this, or not yet. They live in one of the most powerful countries seen in the history of man. Sheer power and two huge oceans make Americans unaware of how the world is changing. The great paradox here is that the world's most open society is among the least well informed on the inevitable impact of global changes. A tidal wave of change is already on its way to American shores.[1]

Rereading this paragraph after September 11, 2001, it is clear that the tidal wave of change has reached U.S. shores. The events of that day were a great tragedy, and the entire world joined the United States in condemning the attacks. But the attacks also clearly demonstrated that we have truly shrunk and become a small, interdependent globe.

The key challenge of the twenty-first century will be to manage this shrinking globe as the forces of globalization generate growing interdependence day after day after day. The need for multilateral institutions and processes will grow in tandem. But multilateralism will succeed only if the great powers, and especially the United States, support it.

Throughout most of the twentieth century, as the United States progressively expanded its power relative to every other state, it treated multilateral institutions with either benign neglect or deliberate constraints. It was no accident that the League of Nations disappeared. At various moments in the late twentieth century, when U.S. power saw little use for the United Nations, it, too, faced many precarious moments. The entire organization could have disappeared into the dustbin of history, much like the League of Nations. Fortunately, today UN survival is not in doubt. But it may only survive in its present, crippled form: accepted as part of the international furniture but hobbled carefully to avoid giving it a major role. The least likely possibility is that the United Nations will emerge as a dynamic multilateral institution whose historical moment has finally arrived: fulfilling its potential to cope with the new interdependent and interconnected world generated by globalization.

In this chapter I argue that after September 11 it may serve U.S. national interests to strengthen rather than weaken the UN. Virtually every other state has accepted the fact that the world needs stronger multilateral institutions and processes. However, given the enormous and overarching power of the United States, multilateralism cannot survive or develop in the twenty-first century without U.S. support. No appeal to universal ideals or principles will convince the U.S. body politic to support multilateralism. Only an appeal to national self-interest will do so. This is what I will attempt to do.[2]

The chapter has three sections: a brief historical description of the processes and events that led to the development of a weakened United Nations; an analysis of the causes and consequences of U.S. behavior; and some prescriptions that could strengthen multilateralism as well as enhance U.S. national interests.

A History of U.S.-UN Relations

The history of the U.S.-UN relationship is long and complex.[3] In recent years, the main issues have been ostensibly financial. Since the mid-1980s, from the days of Ronald Reagan's administration, the United States held back paying its assessed UN dues, leading to arrears totaling some $1.7 billion by the end of 2000. The primary reason the United States gave for this withholding was that the UN had become a fat and bloated bureaucracy that needed to be reformed. Undoubtedly, some of these criticisms were justified. But a small personal anecdote may help to explain why some apparently useless UN institutions survive.

In the mid-1980s, I was a member of the Group of 18 high-level experts set up to reform the UN. One of our key goals was to trim the fat from the organization. It wasn't easy. We found that every UN institution had some key stakeholder pressing for its retention. Finally, after much effort, we discovered what we thought was a moribund UN Committee on Taxation. All of us agreed that this was not a natural field for UN expertise, and we agreed to shut it down. At the eleventh hour, just as we were about to finalize the report, the U.S. expert entered the room. Sheepishly, he said that the U.S. Treasury saw great value in preserving the UN Committee on Taxation. So we did.

This is a minor anecdote, but it illustrates that the UN has tried to be sensitive, rather than insensitive, to U.S. concerns. Most Americans will be surprised, perhaps even shocked, by this statement. Some will remember the raging debates in the UN General Assembly, especially in the 1970s and 1980s, when it seemed to produce a string of anti-U.S. resolutions. Two of the most famous were, first, the resolution equating Zionism with racism (and this was probably the organization's lowest moment), and second, the resolution calling for a new international economic order. At least two U.S. ambassadors to the UN, Daniel Patrick Moynihan and Jeanne Kirkpatrick, became famous as U.S. representatives who could say no to the UN.

It is true that the U.S.-UN relationship has had its share of difficulties. But any discussion of the UN role needs to be based on conceptual clarity. The UN is not a single unit, but a family of institutions. Some are completely independent, such as the International Labor Organization (ILO) and the World Health Organization (WHO). Some are related to and dependent on it, like the United Nations Development Program (UNDP) and the United Nations Children's Fund (UNICEF). But at the core, three principal organs play critically different roles: the Security Council, the General Assembly, and the Secretariat.

The Security Council represents the aristocracy. Within it, the permanent five members (the United States, Russia, China, the United Kingdom, and France) exercise tremendous powers, both formally and informally. As the United Nations Charter confers upon the Security Council "primary responsibility for peace and security," it is the only body that authoritatively deals with vital issues of war and peace. Decisions of the Council, taken by fifteen members, are binding on all 189 UN member states.

The UN General Assembly represents the masses. All 189 member states, in an affirmation of the principle of sovereign equality, have an equal vote in the General Assembly. But the decisions of the Assembly are not binding, even though most are adopted by consensus. At best, they are recommendations.

Finally, there is the UN Secretariat. Technically, it is only the implementing arm of the UN. It is accountable to the Assembly in theory, but in practice it pays greater heed to the views of the Council (which has a decisive say in the appointment of the Secretary-General). The Secretary-General does have a capacity to launch independent initiatives and act as a moral force. The personal prestige and stature of the individual Secretary-General does matter, as demonstrated by the current Secretary-General, Kofi Annan.

Most of the troubles that the United States has had with the UN have been with the General Assembly, which has produced resolutions causing the United States discomfort. But none of these resolutions has had the power to hurt the United States, as they have been at best (or worst) recommendations, not decisions. But both the Secretariat (including the Secretary-General) and the UN Security Council have been sensitive and responsive to U.S. concerns. Only one recent Secretary-General, Boutros-Ghali, was perceived to be taking stances independent of the United States. His term was not renewed because of a U.S. veto.

It is vital to mention here that the General Assembly has also been critical of other major powers besides the United States. In the 1980s, especially during Cuba's chairmanship of the Non-Aligned Movement, it was generally assumed that the General Assembly, with its third world majority, would naturally take pro-Soviet positions during the Cold War. But the General Assembly was equally critical of the Soviet invasion of Afghanistan and the Soviet-supported Vietnamese invasion of Cambodia. The United States cheered when this happened. Speaking in the UN General Assembly in 1985, on the occasion of the fortieth anniversary of the UN, Margaret Thatcher, then the British prime minister, said, "When we ask about shortcomings we should start by looking at ourselves. The United Nations is only a mirror held up to our own uneven, untidy and divided world. If we do not like what we see there is no point in cursing the mirror, we had better start by reforming ourselves."

Unfortunately, despite the efforts of those like Mrs. Thatcher, public opinion in the United States turned increasingly against the UN throughout the 1980s, especially in the Republican administrations that were traditionally less sympathetic to the UN. These U.S.-UN frictions became more acute when the Cold War ended. With the end of the Soviet Union, the United States no longer needed a friendly United Nations for anti-Soviet causes. Attacking the organization carried no costs for the United States. There was a brief interlude of harmony, especially in the immediate aftermath of the Gulf War since the United Nations had played a constructive role in helping to build the allied coalition and legitimize the war. This harmony did not last long. In additon, the problem of withheld dues was never resolved.

It is therefore not surprising that U.S. efforts to control or constrain the UN increased in pace through the 1990s. This happened even though a generally pro-UN and sympathetic Democratic administration was in place under Bill Clinton from 1993 to 2000. U.S. withholdings increased significantly. Consequently, the United States came perilously close to losing its vote in the General Assembly, which (if it had indeed happened) could have led to a repetition of the League of Nations experience, with the United States renouncing membership in the world body. This might be seen as another of history's interesting might-have-beens. But if it had indeed occurred, it would have left the United States at a tremendous disadvantage in the battle against terrorism that has been the focus of U.S. foreign policy since September 11, 2001.

By the dawn of the twenty-first century, the U.S.-UN financial crisis had crested. Thanks to dynamic U.S. diplomacy under the leadership of Richard Holbrooke, U.S. ambassador to the UN, the United States succeeded in lowering its annual UN assessments. Under the new formula, the less rich agreed to pay more to allow the richest country in the world to pay less than what it would have paid if the same rule applied to all states. A deal was reached between the United States and the other 188 member states in December 2000 to resolve the financial crisis. However, the final payments under this deal were made only after September 11, 2001, a telling indication of the real considerations that drive U.S.-UN relations.

Causes and Consequence of U.S. Actions

In the 1980s and 1990s, when the U.S. media reported on the U.S.-UN relationship, nearly all of the focus was on these financial troubles. The debate was, of course, complex. But the public impression was that the United States was doing essentially the right thing in withholding its assessed dues to the UN as an effort to discipline a bloated international bureaucracy. There was also a perception that the United States had been overtaxed.[4]

The sad part of this debate was that the real issue at stake in the controversy—which concerned power—never broke the surface. Some forty years ago, the last activist UN Secretary-General, Dag Hammarskjöld, attempted to forge a new role for the UN as an international conscience and an independent global actor. Ever since that time, the world's major powers have tacitly agreed that, whatever their differences, they were all better off with a less independent and more compliant United Nations. Hence, for several decades the UN has been relegated to a peripheral rather than a central role in international affairs. It was instructed to steer clear of many important and vital international issues, such as the Vietnam War and (after some initial involvement) the Middle East peace process, even though the UN Charter explicitly mandates the Security Council with the "primary responsibility for the maintenance of international peace and security." The big, silent conspiracy that has surrounded the UN since its creation is a tacit understanding among all major powers (including both the Soviet Union and the United States during the Cold War) that they were better off with a weaker institution. For most of its existence, the UN has been crippled—not by accident, but by design.

The difficulty in substantiating these arguments is that no major power, not even an open society like the United States, has fully admitted its real agenda vis-à-vis the UN. The complex U.S. political process makes it even harder to arrive at simple explanations.

Since about 1980, no power has done as much damage to the United Nations as the United States. Much of this damage has resulted from an irrational and angry U.S. reaction to the third world domination of the agenda of the UN General Assembly and other multilateral fora in the 1970s and early 1980s. But when the third world domination ended, the U.S. attacks against the UN continued, often in an incoherent form. As Gene Lyons has noted, "The United States has been seemingly obsessed with reforming UN management and dealing with overloaded bureaucracies, overlapping programs, and unaudited finances—not without reason but without equally expounding on where the world is going and how the UN fits in."[5]

Neither an ostensibly bloated bureaucracy nor an apparent waste of funds can explain the growing negative agenda that the United States has had toward the UN. It costs the international community only about $1 billion a year—an infinitesimal fraction of global gross national product.

It does not seem rational for a major power like the United States to expend so much energy or risk so much political capital in a simple dispute over a tiny sum of money. Accordingly, deeper considerations must be driving such policies. The United States is, ultimately, a rational actor in world politics. And it would be rational for any major power to try to minimize external constraints on its freedom of action generated by multilateral institutions and processes. Many other nation-states, of course, wish that they had such an option, but few have the power to defy the will of the international community.

From the origins of the interstate system, no strong power has allowed itself to be subject to rules set by weaker nations—unless those rules benefit it also. The United States has clearly been the most benign great power in the history of mankind. It is reasonable to assume that any other nation with the enormous relative power of the United States would probably have behaved far worse. But it is rational for great powers to walk away from multilateral constraint. As the United States is a complex society that prides itself as being based on the rule of law, domestic debates about the acceptability of such constraints on U.S. power are conducted in sophisticated language: unilateralism versus multilateralism; à la carte multilateralism versus constructive multilateralism. But these sophisticated terms disguise realities as much as they explain them. The only way to understand the policies of any country is to look squarely at the deeds. And U.S. deeds on the UN have spoken loudly and clearly.

A case can be made, if a brave senior U.S. figure is prepared to do so, that in the post–September 11 world, the time has come for a radical rethinking of U.S. strategy toward the UN. To a surprising degree for an open society, U.S. thinking on international issues easily slips into a rut. The United Nations is no exception. As I wrote prior to the events of September 11:

> The current overwhelming power and geographic isolation [of the United States] are at best a temporary dam holding back the inevitable impact of globalisation on American society. And when the dam is breached, Americans will regret the fact that they did not use the window of opportunity available to them (when they were clearly and overwhelmingly powerful relative to the rest of the world) to strengthen the UN to help deal with the small interdependent world emerging. Of course, many Americans firmly believe that they will be so powerful forever. History teaches us otherwise.[6]

Time for New U.S. Thinking on the UN

What makes the absence of new thinking even more surprising is that the case for a stronger institution is as simple as it is obvious. U.S. technology has changed the world. Distance has disappeared. The world has shrunk to a global village. Every village needs a village council. The United Nations represents the only real village council we have. There is no other.

Perhaps another simple analogy could help to explain to the U.S. public why an effective institution serves U.S. interests. Americans, like anyone else, understand the need for traffic rules. Without such rules, highways and interchanges would not function: traffic could not move safely if we were to drive on both sides of the road. With globalization, new global highways are being opened daily, literally and metaphorically. The traffic of people, money, ideas, goods, and the like around the world is going to increase at an exponential pace. What would happen if we destroyed or weakened the only organization (or, more accurately in the case of the UN, the only family of organizations) capable of providing the viable setting required for formulating larger global rules?

Thus far, a few Americans have begun seeing the impact of interdependence in a few areas. They now understand the risk that the Ebola virus in Africa may reach U.S. shores overnight. Viruses do not need passports. They do not respect borders. And neither do environmental disasters. Americans have not experienced a Chernobyl-like nuclear disaster yet. But they are beginning to understand that climate change can also affect them. In the world of finance, where the United States now appears to reign supreme, the Asian financial crisis of 1997–1998 proved that a crisis emerging in a distant Southeast Asian country, Thailand, could eventually ripple into U.S. stock markets via Korea, Russia, and Brazil. This was a healthy scare. It has made senior U.S. finance officials more aware of global interdependence than their counterparts in other areas. It would be a pity if similar scares and disasters were necessary to open the eyes of other U.S. officials.

After September 11, the reality of global interdependence should have become still clearer for Americans. As the UN Secretary-General said on December 10, 2001, when he received the Nobel Prize,

> If today, after the horror of 11 September, we see better, and we see further—we will realize that humanity is indivisible. New threats make no distinction between races, nations or regions. A new insecurity has entered every mind, regardless of wealth or status. A deeper awareness of the bonds that bind us all—in pain as in prosperity—has gripped young and old.

No one can foretell the future in specific terms. We all know that technology will change the future of the globe, particularly given the explosive and exponential growth of new technology that we experience now. But we can begin to prepare for the future in more general terms, just as one can predict floods in the Ganges River six months after heavy snowfall in the Himalayas. Today we know that the heavy snowfall of new technology has descended upon the globe. The floods of change are coming. This much we can be certain about. It is strange, therefore, not to begin preparing for it.

The UN Role

But what can the UN do to help cope with the impending floods? How can a fragile, much-ravaged institution be a leader in global change? After all, it has stumbled in its response to crises in small countries like Rwanda and Bosnia. How can the UN realistically take on major global burdens? These are fair questions.

Each of the different units in the UN family can make unique contributions to our efforts to adapt to an increasingly interdependent world. A few examples may help clarify the picture. First, norm-setting will become an increasingly important role for the UN. As the world changes, new norms will have to be created, both for the multilateral architecture as well as multilateral processes of the world. The creation of norms, if they are to be accepted in practice, has to be a consensual exercise (which almost by definition makes it a painful exercise). The conversion of these norms into binding legal obligations has to be done in the context of the UN. All new global norms—in the Law of the Sea, in environmental conventions, in the Ottawa Convention abolishing landmines, in the statute of the International Criminal Court—have been created either under the aegis of the UN General Assembly or in global conferences that are offshoots of the General Assembly (e.g., the summits at Rio, Cairo, Copenhagen, and Beijing during the 1990s). Without this norm-setting function of the General Assembly (or its equivalent), the world would be left paralyzed with its old norms. Indeed, global advances that respect human rights have been made possible only because of their legitimization by UN processes. This was true before September 11. The events of that day made global agreement on norm-setting institutions more critical than ever.

Second, to deal with specific crises that emerge from time to time and engage global attention (e.g., East Timor, Kosovo, Sierra Leone), the world has to agree on a process of burden-sharing. Some disputes are now resolved primarily outside the UN (e.g., Kosovo). But eventually, these need to be brought under the UN umbrella to gain international legitimacy. Not all countries can get involved in all disputes. Geography, political interests, treaty relationships, and cultural links help determine which countries will take the lead in solving particular conflicts. For example, both history and geography, as well as strong U.S. support, led to Australia's leadership role in East Timor. But Australia could not have intervened on its own without the legitimizing role of the Security Council and the participation of other countries from the region. Each new UN peacekeeping operation that is created also means that the world as a whole, rather than merely the countries of the relevant region, is taking responsibility for a specific problem. Until the Security Council got involved in Sierra Leone, for example, the Economic Community of West African States Monitoring Group (ECOMOG) had to pay all the bills. After the UN took over, all its member states contributed to the expenses. All these decisions can be made only by the UN Security Council. In similar fashion, only the Security Council could quickly and promptly legitimize multilateral responses to the events of September 11, as well as make it mandatory for countries to comply with antiterrorism resolutions.

The Secretary-General, for his part, can provide essential moral and intellectual leadership in the resolution of global challenges. It is surely an amazing fact that on this planet of 6 billion human beings only one person appears to symbolize the collective interests of all humanity. Therefore, when he speaks, he can draw global attention to global concerns in a way that virtually no one else can. The current Secretary-General, Kofi Annan, has been relatively bold in suggesting new ideas. In response to the crises in Bosnia, Rwanda, and Kosovo, he has suggested, for example, that the international community has a duty to undertake humanitarian intervention within sovereign states if massive human rights violations occur. This is a bold idea. No other global leader has had the courage to make this case. He was equally bold when he spelled out the key challenges that the world faced in his Nobel address of December 10, 2001.

These three examples help to illustrate the constructive role the UN can play in coping with the new world. None of these functions can be performed easily by others. The Group of Seven (G7; now G8 with Russia) leaders, for example, sometimes make crucial decisions on key global issues. They can move financial markets with their decisions (e.g., the Plaza accords), but in the real world, they have no means either to impose their views on other nation-states (without the legal authority of the Security Council) or to have these viewed as legitimate by the international community (without the General Assembly's endorsement). Within any modern society, the rich have no authority to make decisions for the whole society. Neither can the G7 speak on behalf of the international community. Only the UN or its Secretary-General has the institutional and moral legitimacy to do so. President Clinton himself told the UN General Assembly in September 1999 that the UN was an "indispensable" institution. His UN ambassador, Holbrooke, has also made a similar point: "The U.S. has only three choices regarding the UN. It can leave the UN as it is and eventually its weakness will undermine its potential effectiveness. It can abandon it and yield to the far right's constant flirtation with destroying the UN. Or it can proceed from the understanding that the UN is flawed but nonetheless indispensable to our national interest and therefore make it more effective."[7]

Working with the World Population

But there is another indispensable element that cannot be ignored in preparing the world for a new future: the wishes of the 6 billion people who inhabit the planet. Americans tend to make a natural assumption that what is good for the United States is naturally good for the world (perhaps an extension of the old adage that what was good for General Motors was good for the United States). There is, however, a great diversity of needs, interests, and aspirations among the 6 billion. The great challenge that the world faces is that of harmonizing and balancing the needs and interests of so many people on a shrinking planet.

It is only natural that there should be differences in the needs and interests of the rich and the poor. The poor wish to put priority on economic development. By contrast, the rich have a vested interest in the status quo. Hence, for example, the United States and most other developed countries have a vital interest in preventing the spread of weapons of mass destruction, especially the new generation of chemical and biological weapons. Conventions to restrict their development have been negotiated and adopted through the General Assembly process, clumsy and slow though it may be. But the only real way to prevent their proliferation is by creating a global consensus where all the countries feel that they have a common stake in global peace and prosperity. To have such a stake, each society—no matter how rich or poor, small or large—must feel that it is a stakeholder in a global community.

Effective participation in UN processes helps to convert all nations into stakeholders. Both psychologically and materially, all nations must feel that they have a say in the management of the globe. Just as democracy elicits the commitment of the citizen to respect the results of elections and the subsequent decisions of the elected government, a vote in the UN delivers a similar commitment from the nation-state. These processes do not work perfectly, either nationally or internationally, but the crucial role that the UN plays in making stakeholders out of each nation is neither well understood nor appreciated.

Possessing the world's largest economy and the greatest range of global interests, the United States is indeed the single biggest beneficiary of the stabilizing role that the UN plays. Ed Luck has put this point across succinctly:

> The United States has a fundamental interest in the United Nations as an institution because it has an unquestionable stake in international law, order and stability. However imperfectly the UN performs this function, the world body is, on balance, a net contributor to a more orderly, predictable, norm-abiding and hence stable world.[8]

This statement is simple and commonsensical. Yet few Americans, especially politicians, are able to grasp it or see it. The reason is simple. They have been blinded by stories in the media on how anti-U.S. the UN General Assembly has become. This was especially true during the 1970s. In that decade, there was a close alliance between Arabs and Africans to work together to secure strong majorities against apartheid rule in South Africa and Israeli occupation of Arab lands. The United States was often implicitly and explicitly criticized in these resolutions. It then became fashionable for Americans to rail against the tyranny of the majority in the General Assembly. This in turn sparked a decade of UN-bashing in the U.S. Congress, which advanced increasingly absurd demands that the UN meet certain conditions before the United States would release its legally assessed funding.

The great paradox here, which few Americans have grasped, is that the demonstrated independence of the General Assembly from U.S. domination—while not serving some short-term American interests—does indeed serve long-term U.S. interests. Were the General Assembly to be perceived as a compliant U.S. instrument, it would quickly lose the respect, trust, and commitment of the 5.75 billion people who live outside the United States. The more independent the General Assembly is seen to be, the more confidence the people of the world will have in it—and the greater their commitment will be to the larger norm-generating activities of the Assembly. The greater their commitment to these norms, the more U.S. interests will be served. It may be useful to recall what Adlai E. Stevenson said in a 1963 Senate testimony about the United Nations:

> The United States does not own or control the United Nations. It is not a wing of the State Department. We are no more and no less than the most influential of the 110 members. If we were less, we would be failing to exert the influence of freedom's leaders; if we were more, we would destroy the effectiveness of the United Nations, which depends precisely on the fact that it is not an arm of the United States or of any other government, but a truly international organization, no better or worse than the agreements which can be reached by the controlling majorities of its members.[9]

The failure of U.S. policymakers (especially those in Congress) to understand this paradox has led them on a futile course of trying, to use a crude analogy, to squeeze both ends of a tube of toothpaste. If you squeeze both the top and bottom ends, no toothpaste will come out. With sufficient pressure, the tube will eventually break. The same could happen to the UN if the United States continues to squeeze both ends—that is, to try to make the UN appear compliant to U.S. interests and yet try to make it an effective instrument to manage larger global interests.

Instead of railing against the UN each time the General Assembly or (rarely) the Security Council demonstrates its independence of U.S. wishes or demands, U.S. policymakers should quietly cheer on the UN's efforts. The United States need have no real fear that the UN, without the current U.S. Congress's sword of Damocles hanging over it, will turn fundamentally anti-U.S. This cannot happen for a simple reason: most of the world shares the fundamental U.S. interest, as Ed Luck says, in international law, order, and stability.

Occasionally, short-term U.S. interests may not necessarily be in the interest of the rest of the globe or in long-term U.S. interests. A particularly egregious example may make the point clearly. Americans have become accustomed to low gasoline prices. They object when the prices increase. Yet if other countries matched U.S. levels of per capita gasoline consumption, the whole world would be in deep trouble, in both the economic and environmental fields. For the long-term interests of the globe (including those of the United States), the international community should urge the United States to increase its gasoline prices and rationalize its consumption patterns. Of course, if anyone were to suggest this now, many Americans would protest in public, but thoughtful Americans would also agree in private.

There are many other such areas where U.S. policies do not necessarily serve either global or long-term U.S. interests. The Senate's rejection of the Comprehensive Nuclear Test Ban Treaty in October 1999 was a disaster. Even the closest European allies of the United States said so. If the United States, as the world's leading status quo power, walks away from treaty obligations, it is only opening the door for others to do the same.

Swallowing Paradoxes

U.S. policymakers are not used to thinking in terms of paradoxes. The U.S. worldview, which seems to be deeply rooted in old myths, tends to see the world in terms of black and white. Throughout their history, Americans fought well when the enemies that they had to cope with could be portrayed in a clear and simple way: the scalp-hunters (Native Americans), the dark forces of slavery, the Nazi reign of terror, or the red menace. For the United States to be galvanized into action, the enemy had to be clear and demonized.

For a while, the UN came close to being demonized, but either through luck or through hidden sources of wisdom it managed to escape such a fate. It was a shrewd move by UN Ambassador Holbrooke to invite Senator Jesse Helms to attend and address the august chambers of the UN Security Council in January 2000. When Senator Helms did this, and when he persuaded Kofi Annan to take pictures with his family (and subsequently even invited Annan to address his alma mater in North Carolina), he lost the capacity to demonize the UN.

But the real challenge U.S. policymakers will face if they want to deal effectively with the UN is to resist the temptation to characterize the world body in black-and-white terms. The minds of U.S. policymakers will have to learn to handle paradoxes and contradictions in trying to formulate coherent, long-term strategies toward the UN.

A few examples might help to explain this point. U.S. technology is slowly but inexorably creating a global community where global interests will have to be both understood and dealt with. But the only global organization available to manage global interests is the United Nations, which, despite the preambular words of the UN Charter, does not defend the common global interests of mankind but instead acts as a clearinghouse for the varied interests of 191 member states. The Secretary-General captured this new challenge succinctly in his Millennium Report:

> Here, however, is the crux of our problem today: while the post-war multi-lateral system made it possible for the new globalization to emerge and flourish, globalization, in turn, has progressively rendered its designs antiquated. Simply put, our post-war institutions were built for an inter-*national* world, but we now live in a *global* world. Responding effectively to this shift is the core institutional challenge for world leaders today.[10]

It is conceivable that leaders and diplomats working to defend their national interests may end up inadvertently boosting global interests. But the record so far shows that most diplomats find it difficult to reconcile national with global interests.

A current fashion among U.S. (and some other Western) intellectuals is to assert that where selfish government officials have failed to protect common global concerns, the representatives of civil society and nongovernmental organizations (NGOs) can act as a better conscience of mankind. In theory, this may be so. But the battle of Seattle at the 1999 WTO conference showed that NGOs and other elements of civil society are no less prisoners of their sectoral interests than are the UN member states. The NGOs may find it easy to claim the moral high ground, because in the U.S. scheme of things nongovernmental representatives believe they represent the public good and the welfare of average Americans better than government representatives do. But as demonstrated in Seattle, most third world representatives were mystified by the claims of Western-based NGOs, which have little connection to, or understanding of, the needs of the billions who live outside the developed world, to speak on behalf of the world's poor.

Altruism is a guise that has been worn by many in history but has been rarely implemented in practice. In real life, governments, business corporations, and NGOs have one fundamental thing in common: Each seeks to defend its own interests (even if they believe that their interests best represent those of mankind). The U.S. government may have a strong case for defending the patent interests of large pharmaceutical companies, but one cannot deny that this can also effectively lead to depriving the poor of medicine and the loss of millions of lives. This point came through loud and clear in the UN Security Council debate on AIDS in January 2000. Fortunately, the U.S. delegation took a more enlightened view of this issue at the WTO ministerial meeting at Doha in November 2001. Similarly, Greenpeace may feel that it is doing mankind a favor by saving whales from Japanese whalers. But the list of endangered species is a long one. Why pick on Japan and not some other country? Who should make such a decision and how?

The point of all these examples is a simple one. The world is being driven inexorably into a single global community. A simple enlightened policy for the world to adopt at this stage would be to put into place— ahead of time—the right multilateral processes and institutions required to manage the world to come. After September 11, the global community should accept this principle as plain common sense. The largest stakeholder in this single global community is the United States. Only the United States can provide the leadership that this single global community needs.

Notes

Kishore Mahbubani is currently the permanent representative of Singapore to the United Nations. These are his personal views and should not be taken as a reflection of the views of the government of Singapore.

1. Mahbubani, "UN: Sunrise or Sunset Organization in the 21st Century?" p. 37.

2. It may seem strange to U.S. readers that a diplomat from Singapore would argue in terms of U.S. national interests. The simple reality is that without the United States neither the UN nor any multilateral institution can survive. Hence, it serves the national interests of other states if the United States can be persuaded that its national interests favor a strong UN.

3. Several books spell out this complexity well. The best recent volume is Edward Luck's *Mixed Messages*. Boutros Boutros-Ghali, former UN Secretary-General, in *Unvanquished: A U.S.-UN Saga,* provides a unique perspective of a man who felt injured by the United States. I cannot attempt to do a fair summary in only a few paragraphs.

4. For a critique of U.S. resistance to funding the UN during the 1980s, the key arguments of which remain valid today, see Kishore Mahbubani, "U.S. Doesn't Bear Excessive Share of UN Costs," *Wall Street Journal*, October 30, 1986.

5. Lyons, "The UN and American Politics," p. 501.

6. Mahbubani, "UN: Sunrise or Sunset Organization in the 21st Century?" p. 37.

7. Quoted in Carola Hoyos, "U.S. Signal Sought on UN Stance," *Financial Times,* February 13, 2001.

8. Maynes and Williamson, *U.S. Foreign Policy and the United Nations System*, p. 32.

9. Cited in Luck, ed., *Mixed Messages,* p. 20.

10. Report of the Secretary-General on the Millennium Assembly entitled "We the Peoples: The Role of the United Nations in the Twenty-First Century," March 27, 2000.

8

UN Peace Operations and
U.S. Unilateralism and Multilateralism

Ramesh Thakur

IN THIS CHAPTER I WILL EXAMINE THE COMPETING IMPERATIVES BETWEEN UNI-
lateralism and multilateralism in U.S. policy with respect to UN peace operations and the balance struck between them since the mid-1980s. The
United Nations has the primary responsibility to maintain international
peace and security and is structured to discharge this responsibility in a
multipolar world where the major powers have permanent membership of
the key collective security decisionmaking body, namely, the UN Security
Council (UNSC). The emergence of the United States as the sole superpower after the end of the Cold War distorted the structural balance in the
UN schema. The ending of the Cold War also shifted the balance away
from interstate warfare to internal armed conflicts. The question for the decisionmakers in Washington often became that of determining whether U.S.
security and political interests were better served by engaging with the distant and possibly inconsequential conflicts unilaterally, through UN peace
operations, or not at all; and whether the consequences of this choice on the
authority and capacity of the United Nations to keep the peace would have
any rebound effects on the United States itself.

At the same time, with the end of the Cold War, the number of peace
operations multiplied even as their nature changed quite significantly. The
cardinal distinction between collective security and traditional peacekeeping lay in their reliance on force and consent respectively. During the Cold
War, UN peacekeeping forces were interposed between warring parties and
used to forestall major-power confrontations across global fault lines. They
had no military objectives, were barred from active combat, were located
between rather than in opposition to hostile elements, and were required to
negotiate rather than to fight.

The number of peacekeeping operations increased dramatically after
the end of the Cold War as the UN was placed at center stage in efforts to
resolve outstanding conflicts. However, the multiplication of missions was
not always accompanied by coherent policy or integrated military and

political responses. The scope and complexity of their tasks expanded greatly, to embrace such additional responsibilities as organizing and monitoring elections (Namibia, Cambodia), peace enforcement (Somalia), and administration (East Timor).[1] In Bosnia and Haiti, UN peacekeeping was authorized by the UN Security Council but undertaken by a single power or ad hoc multilateral coalitions. The UN itself took back responsibility for traditional, consensual peacekeeping once the situation had stabilized.[2] In East Timor a UN-authorized multinational force was prepared for combat, if necessary, and was given the mandate, troops, equipment, and robust rules of engagement required for such a mission. However, the military operation was but the prelude to a de facto UN administration that engaged in state-making for a transitional period.

When the expanded and proliferating missions encountered problems, the "crisis of expectations" of the late 1980s and early 1990s in turn gave way to a crisis of confidence-cum-credibility in UN peacekeeping in the late 1990s, and member states began to limit their military, political, and financial exposure.[3] Yet the need for UN peacekeeping has remained and will continue. Although the causes of conflict are many, the fact of conflict remains a constant feature of international affairs. The challenge lies in the gap between the continuing demand for international peacekeeping, on the one hand, and the declining confidence in its effectiveness and efficiency and diminishing financial support for it on the other.

The UN Security Council is the proper locus for authorizing and legitimizing the creation, deployment, and use of military force under international auspices. But it is singularly ill-suited to take charge of the command and control of fighting forces. The UN's own panel on peacekeeping concluded that "the United Nations does not wage war."[4] Accordingly, the burden of responsibility for international military engagement typically falls on the United States, which as the world's most powerful country often can make the biggest difference. If the UN is the font of legitimate international authority, the United States has unparalleled capacity for the maintenance of international peace and security. The U.S. military budget is greater even than that of all other NATO members combined, accounting for more than 60 percent of NATO's total budget.[5] Reflecting this dominance, three-quarters of all military aircraft deployed by NATO in the air war in Kosovo in 1999 were U.S. aircraft.

What is the optimal mode of articulation between the United Nations, as the authoritative custodian of international peace and world order, and the United States, as its de facto underwriter? For many U.S. decisionmakers, it is difficult to understand why those countries that do not contribute a fair share of the military burden should be given any determinative role in deciding on the deployment of U.S. military forces. In 1992, Richard Cheney, then–defense secretary in the administration of George H. W. Bush (and elected vice president under George W. Bush in 2000), remarked that critics of the United States should remember that world order was maintained by the United States, not the UN. As William Pfaff notes, the statement reflected two dominant U.S. views. First, given its history of isolationism, the United States did not seek such a role but accepted the responsibility (flowing from its power) thrust upon it after World War II. Second, the United States is uniquely qualified to be the sole superpower because it is a virtuous power.[6]

One of the main reasons for the U.S. rejection of the League of Nations after World War I was fear of an automatic requirement to use military force as decided by the League. The symbolic shift of the world organization's headquarters from Geneva to New York after World War II did not lessen the innate U.S. suspicion of overseas entanglements at others' behest. For defeated and pariah states like Japan and Germany after World War II, UN peacekeeping was helpful in the 1990s in providing the legitimizing framework of multilateralism for hesitant and tentative participation of their military units in overseas missions. The United States, by contrast, has not needed international organizations as a vehicle and imprimatur of reintegration into the community of nations. As Sarah Sewell notes, the UN remains a lightning rod for many U.S. concerns about distracting entanglements of U.S. forces overseas.[7] The Congress was careful to enunciate that decisions by the UNSC could not encroach upon the internal constitutional distribution of warmaking power in the United States.

Operation Desert Storm, launched in 1991 to expel Iraqi troops from Kuwait, generated unwarranted and unsustainable optimism about the centrality of the UN in the new world order, as well as about the degree to which the United States was prepared to place its military power at the disposal of the United Nations. This idealism was ephemeral because it was based on a unique confluence of circumstances that had produced a fortuitous conjunction of national U.S. and international interests. President George H. W. Bush left office on a cautiously optimistic note with regard to U.S.-UN relations in the realm of international peace operations. The initial naive enthusiasm of the succeeding administration under Bill Clinton, which assumed office committed to enlarging U.S. involvement in expanding UN peace operations, quickly faded in the face of hard realities, notably the complexities of external intervention in civil wars. Presidents Bush and Clinton both grappled with five interlinked and challenging questions, that is, when and how Washington should: (1) offer political support to UN missions; (2) provide military assistance to them; (3) participate in possible combat operations through them; (4) enhance the peacekeeping credentials of the UN; and (5) opt for military action outside the UN framework.

These five policy dilemmas, I will argue in this chapter, suggest that the division between unilateralism and multilateralism in U.S. foreign policy with respect to international peacekeeping is a false dichotomy. The relationship is dynamic, not static, and multifaceted, not unidimensional. The

United States remained essentially multilateral throughout the 1990s. Significant signs of unilateralism surfaced only in 2001, after President George W. Bush took office, with respect to a raft of issues from the Kyoto Protocol on climate change to arms control treaties to the International Criminal Court. But what did change over the course of the 1990s was the centrality of the UN in the U.S. scheme of multilateralism. Learning from experience in a world no longer divided by the Cold War blocs yet facing messy internal conflicts, Washington progressively divided its multilateral impulse between the UN—as the global mobilizing and legitimizing organization—and NATO—as the strategic enforcement arm for peace operations in Europe. Outside Europe, Washington progressively retrenched from direct participation—but not necessarily all forms of involvement—in UN peacekeeping; the answers to some of the five issues outlined above could still be in the affirmative.

I substantiate this argument in a brief overview of peacekeeping during the Cold War, followed by more extensive examinations of the formative U.S. peacekeeping experiences in Somalia and the Balkans. During the 1990s, the United States faced difficult choices about acting through the alternative multilateral frameworks of the UN, NATO, or ad hoc military alliances. By the end of the century, international peacekeeping tended to be channeled through the UN, armed military action through NATO or coalitions of the willing, and diplomatic efforts through the EU or other regional organizations. I argue that multilateralism remains important to U.S. foreign policy and that the U.S. remains the pivot of multilateral action in the maintenance of international peace and security. I conclude, finally, with nine propositions regarding the theory and practice of U.S. multilateralism with regard to UN peacekeeping.

The United States and Traditional Peacekeeping

During the Cold War the United States was not among the ranks of the major UN peacekeepers. The core mission of the U.S. military was considered to be the defense of the United States at home and abroad; its core task was war-fighting; ancillary tasks like disaster relief operations could be accepted on an ad hoc basis; but peacekeeping was a distraction and carried the baggage of too many unnecessary complications, with the potential to infect and undermine the core task of waging and winning wars. That is, U.S. political support in the UNSC was necessary and generally forthcoming; its specialized technical support was irreplaceable and welcome; and its financial support was substantial and unmatched. But the United States neither wanted to be—nor was it wanted as—a UN peacekeeper.

During the Cold War, the main imperative for traditional peacekeeping was to forestall the competitive intrusion of the two rival power blocs in areas where neither had vital interests engaged. It permitted superpower disengagement before conflict could arise. As a general rule, therefore, military participation by the five permanent members (P-5) of the Security Council, and certainly of the United States and the Soviet Union, in the traditional UN peacekeeping operations (PKOs) was generally excluded. Traditional PKOs advanced stability in particular theaters while the major powers were diplomatically engaged (or not) in efforts to resolve the underlying conflict. Peacekeepers from non-P-5 nations took responsibility for the first part of the equation while P-5 diplomats engaged in the second part. The thin blue line was used to contain and quarantine essentially local conflicts. At the same time, PKOs were based on three tiers of consent: from the local conflict parties and host governments, which agreed to the stationing of foreign troops under the UN insignia; from the Security Council, which set up each mission by a mandating resolution; and from other states, which contributed soldier-peacekeepers on a voluntary basis.

By definition, therefore, the United States as a P-5 member had to consent to the establishment of any peacekeeping mission; it was able to protect its national interests by avoiding direct military entanglement in conflicts without major significance; and the stability maintained by PKOs reinforced its role as the underwriter of world order. Because the P-5 were not in fact required to underwrite world order militarily (as had been the expectation when the UN system was created), they were instead asked to assume a disproportionately large share of the financial burdens of UN peacekeeping. Other major powers bore a fair share, and poor countries assumed a disproportionately low share. Washington willingly acquiesced in this set of agreements and arrangements. Whereas the U.S. financial contribution to the UN's regular budget was capped at 25 percent, its assessed share of UN peacekeeping bills has been 30.4 percent.[8]

Thus, the UN's universal-multilateral forum provided a useful conduit for minimizing and constraining the risks of international engagement in a bloc-divided world. The first substantial UN peacekeeping operation was launched in the Middle East in 1956, as a means of extricating two U.S. allies, Britain and France, from a reckless military adventure strongly opposed by Washington. In Congo in 1960, a robust UN peacekeeping mission largely furthered U.S. goals and interests. The Cyprus operation in 1964, at the request and with the participation of loyal ally Britain, was a useful means of keeping NATO members Greece and Turkey from each other's throats. The principle of UN peacekeeping therefore continued to receive diffuse U.S. support until the mid-1960s.

U.S. disillusionment began to set in after 1967, when UN Secretary-General U Thant acquiesced to Egypt's request for the withdrawal of the UN Emergency Force (UNEF-I) from the Middle East in 1967, providing a curtain-raiser to the Six Day War. U.S. dissatisfaction was deepened by the perceived rise of anti-Americanism and anti-Zionism within the UN (and in the UN Educational, Scientific, and Cultural Organization, from which Washington withdrew in disgust in 1984), which had been captured, in U.S. eyes, by radical third world countries determined to pursue a fundamentally illiberal agenda. Nevertheless, Washington returned to the UN instrument of peacekeeping after the Yom Kippur War of 1973, approving the establishment of UNEF-II. Another traditional mission was established in southern Lebanon in 1978 with full U.S. backing.

Post–Cold War Optimism

During the Cold War, in sum, U.S. policy ranged from supporting the establishment of some UN peacekeeping missions, paying for them, and providing technical and logistical help to them; being indifferent and hostile to other international peace operations; to taking the lead in organizing extra-UN operations like the Multinational Force and Observers in the Sinai and the Multinational Force in Beirut. The breadth and depth of U.S. involvement with UN and other multilateral peace missions increased dramatically during the closing days of the Cold War, as the number and complexity of such missions rose.

With the end of the Cold War, given the new role accorded to the UN in George H. W. Bush's conception of the new world order, it was entirely appropriate for the administration to support the British call, at the UNSC summit in January 1992, for Secretary-General Boutros Boutros-Ghali to prepare a position paper on how the UN could play a more enhanced and effective role in maintaining international peace. The report, *An Agenda for Peace,* was presented in July.[9] The Bush I administration also initiated a parallel review in Washington of ways and means by which the United States could help the UN execute an expanded security role.[10] The outcome of the review formed part of the president's address to the UN General Assembly on September 21, 1992.[11] Bush described the maintenance of peace, the prevention of proliferation of weapons of mass destruction, and the global spread of market-based prosperity as the three challenges facing the international community. Enhancement of the UN's peacekeeping capabilities was necessary for meeting the first of these challenges. As part of the international response, the United States was prepared to introduce a peacekeeping curriculum in U.S. military schools; to train combat, engineering, and logistical units for international peacekeeping duties; and to open U.S. military bases for multinational training and field exercises.

There was intense disagreement in Washington over whether the U.S. military should actually participate in UN peacekeeping operations. There were those who argued, especially in the State Department and the National Security Council, that peacekeeping was integral to the new security architecture and that U.S. participation would be helpful to the UN and important to the United States in cementing its post–Cold War leadership role. To that end, the United States could train and equip a dedicated peacekeeping brigade for standby call-up duty by the UN. Others, especially in the military and the Department of Defense, regarded UN peacekeeping as a threat to the mission clarity of the task-oriented U.S. military and insisted that U.S. contributions should be limited to unique capabilities like lift, command and control, and intelligence.[12] Ground troops and equipment could come from other sources. Neither was the military hierarchy prepared to accept U.S. troops serving under the operational command of UN officers. Although the generally more skeptical approach to U.S. military participation in UN peacekeeping prevailed, this cautious interaction was nonetheless encased in a somewhat more sympathetic stance toward UN peacekeeping than had been the case during the Cold War.

The end of the Cold War simultaneously enhanced the potential for more UN peacekeeping and made U.S. participation in them more problematical.[13] The abatement of the Soviet threat removed the rationale for the containment doctrine that had underpinned an unprecedented engagement of the United States with the international order. U.S. foreign policy objectives privileged domestic over international concerns even more in structuring the decision incentives of the administration and Congress. The absence of a clear and present danger from the Soviet menace made it more difficult to justify the dispatch of U.S. military personnel to risky foreign conflicts. Moreover, between the end of the Bush administration and the end of the Clinton administration eight years later, optimism about the new world order had yielded to widespread pessimism about a new world disorder.

The end of the Cold War removed the overlay of superpower rivalry from many local conflicts and left the United States as the principal, and sometimes the only, significant player in the field of international diplomacy. Some local conflicts spun out of control as the pace of their internal dynamics intensified. Others saw a muting of conflict intensity and the achievement of peace accords with the assistance of the international community. As peacekeeping expanded, the goals of the missions changed from monitoring cease-fires to facilitating political transitions from chaos and conflict to order and stability. UN peacekeeping missions were used in Namibia, Cambodia, and other places to legitimize the transition from Cold War conflicts to post–Cold War stability and to reintegrate those countries into the international community. The United States subscribed to both of these broad goals and could not have achieved either of them on its own. Given the demands that such growing ambitious missions placed on human, technical, logistical, and financial resources, the UN would have been hard-pressed to achieve anything lasting without active U.S. support and participation in planning and conducting elections, seconding electoral and human rights observers and specialists, protecting and resettling refugees, providing airlift and other logistical capability, transmitting helpful intelligence, paying the bills, and so forth. When the United States brought the full weight of its power, influence, and capabilities to bear on behalf of multidimensional UN missions, many local belligerents concluded that the costs of compliance with UN peacekeeping (including defeat in UN-run elections) were preferable to those of noncompliance.

Thus, later-generation peacekeeping missions required deeper engagement both by the UN and by the United States, as its most influential member, in nation-building and peacebuilding tasks like creating structures of governance and administration alongside military functions like disarmament and demobilization of combatants. Among the lessons that were quickly and painfully learned were the risks of mission creep, that is, the danger that mandates and tasks would expand well beyond the original, limited functions. The presence of many inter- and nongovernmental organizations with overlapping and competing functions and agendas added to the complexity, untidiness, and risks of these operations. Mission creep and the lack of credible exit strategies were crucial to the steady erosion of U.S. support for UN peacekeeping operations. The fear of mounting public and congressional opposition heightened the risk aversion of U.S. administrations; but increased U.S. casualty aversion—as it became widely known— merely added to the danger that U.S. personnel would be deliberately targeted by hostile elements determined to wreck a peacekeeping mission by severing its weakest link—ironically, the strongest member state of the UN. For UN peacekeepers intervening in civil wars where there was no peace to keep, the dilemma appeared intractable: They could neither move forward into an unwinnable war, nor stay put taking casualties for no purpose, nor withdraw without substantial setbacks for UN peacekeeping and for the foreign policy interests of the major troop providers.

Multilateralism at Its Peak

Events in Europe and Africa tested the limits of the new complex peace support operations and the division of labor between the United States and the UN.

The UN Protection Force

The European setting was the Balkans, that graveyard of outside intervention. The initial U.S. response, under the administration of George H. W. Bush, was to treat the Balkans essentially as Europe's problem. Washington was prepared, as a P-5 member, to support humanitarian peacekeeping by the UN, to provide relief supplies for delivery by UN peacekeepers, and to provide financial and logistical support for the operation, but it insisted on limiting U.S. military and diplomatic exposure by handing over responsibility to the Europeans and the UN.

The escalating crisis in the Balkans in the 1990s had its roots in the inability of Marshal Tito's successors to pursue policies that would keep Yugoslavia united in the changed circumstances of the post–Cold War period. As the republic disintegrated, Washington faced conflicting pressures, from different quarters, to support Yugoslav territorial integrity, recognize the independence of newly formed countries seceding from the former republic, champion the principle of multiethnicity, prevent systematic and pervasive violations of human rights, and resist any hint of embarking down the slippery slope of military intervention. The effort to maintain a delicate balance between different NATO members, which possessed competing interests in the Balkans, was fraught with difficulty. Yet another complicating factor was the U.S. effort to draw Russia into some sort of partnership for the peace and prosperity of Europe—and to avoid antagonizing it in its geopolitical backyard.

By 1992, NATO troops were already deployed in the Balkans, but their role was limited to monitoring compliance with UNSC resolutions. The UN Protection Force in the former Yugoslavia (UNPROFOR) was established by UNSC Resolution 743 on February 21, 1992.[14] Its initial mandate for Croatia was soon extended to Bosnia-Herzegovina and Macedonia. It would be impossible, even for the most committed UN apologist, to describe UNPROFOR's record in keeping the peace as a glittering success. But the mission did provide uninterrupted delivery of humanitarian relief supplies to many in desperate circumstances, even during the worst years of 1992–1995.[15] Washington supported the establishment of the UN force and offered logistical and transport assistance to alleviate humanitarian suffering, but it would not contemplate any U.S. military personnel serving in the UN force. Given the bloody history of the Balkans, the complexity of the conflict, and the rugged, inhospitable topography, Washington effectively regarded the conflict as a no-win quagmire. Even congressional exhortations took the form of asking the administration to urge more forceful UN (not U.S.) action. As the scale of the atrocities being committed became clearer, the domestic clamor for more U.S. involvement grew, but the administration's response remained restricted to substantial financial support, transport, and logistical assistance for the UN to airlift relief supplies to Sarajevo. In-theater military risks were transferred wholly to the UN.

The UN Operation in Somalia

In the Horn of Africa, the level of U.S. cooperative involvement with UN peacekeeping did grow rapidly, substantially, and disastrously. Ironically, both in Bosnia and Somalia the argument of U.S. exceptionalism, used effectively by the Bush I administration in mobilizing domestic as well as global support for the multinational operation in the Persian Gulf in 1990–1991, was marshaled by critics of the administration's passivity in the face of evil in Europe and tragedy in Africa. These critics recalled and reiterated the argument that

U.S leadership—military, moral, diplomatic, and financial—was essential to catalyze the world into doing whatever was necessary. Intimidated by the difficulties in Bosnia, the administration responded to pressures to act in Somalia on the basis of the adage that it should if it could.

A humanitarian emergency in Somalia in 1991 precipitated a crisis of state authority in 1992, bringing forth many calls for active involvement by the international community. UN Secretary-General Boutros Boutros-Ghali favored the dispatch of fifty unarmed military observers and an additional 500 infantry peacekeepers to provide a secure environment for the delivery of humanitarian relief to the beleaguered Somali population. Washington, however, was concerned about congressional opposition to the escalating costs of UN peace operations, in the context of the large missions in Cambodia and the former Yugoslavia. The Security Council adopted a resolution authorizing the immediate deployment of military observers and deployment of the infantry force as soon as possible. As the situation in Somalia deteriorated rapidly, the administration faced intensified interventionist pressures from Congress, humanitarian relief organizations, and the media.[16] By the time of President Bush's address to the General Assembly on September 21, Boutros-Ghali's rebuke to the Security Council for its preoccupation with the "rich man's war" in the Balkans—to the neglect of more deadly conflicts and crises in Africa (with implicit undertones of prejudice based on skin color)—had become a staple of international reporting and African complaints.

The public debate over the appropriate U.S. response to the unfolding crisis in Somalia was mirrored in internal administration discussions. The State Department, especially its Africa Bureau, was more responsive to public sentiment for greater U.S. involvement in relief and rescue efforts. The Department of Defense and the Pentagon were more concerned with limiting U.S. exposure to uncontrollable events.[17] The complexity and intractability of the conflict made the latter skeptical about the clarity of the objectives and the exit point of any operation, as well as sensitive to the dangers of mission creep and open-ended commitments to an ill-defined nation-building mission. In August 1992, following the UNSC approval of July 27, the United States agreed to airlift relief supplies and 500 Pakistani peacekeepers (already authorized in April) to Somalia. But by this time the situation on the ground had worsened, and toward the end of August the Security Council authorized the deployment of another 3,000 peacekeeping troops.

In the context of no improvement on the ground in the Balkans and Somalia, calls for greater U.S. commitment to both theaters, and the president's promise of enhanced interaction with UN peacekeeping, Washington concluded that a military operation was more "doable" in Somalia than in Bosnia. The Bush administration therefore agreed to commit U.S. troops to create a secure environment in Somalia for the delivery of relief supplies to those most in need. But in a concession to the skepticism in the Defense

Department and in the Joint Chiefs of Staff, the White House decided that this military operation would remain under U.S. control. Although authorized by the UNSC (Resolution 794 of December 3, 1992), it would remain separate and independent from the ongoing UN operation. It would have a defined endpoint and an exit strategy, with the mission being handed off to the UN once a secure environment for humanitarian relief operations had been established.

This was the mandate for the UN-authorized and U.S.-led Unified Task Force (UNITAF). It embodied a low-risk and low-cost concept of U.S.-UN cooperation in multinational peace operations, in which the risks, burdens, and costs would be shared between the United States and the UN on the basis of comparative ability. The United States would first secure the environment by military means in a time-bound mission, and then, in early 1993, hand over responsibility for nation-building and restoring political stability to the UN. The advantage for the United States was that the Pentagon retained complete command and control over its troops and operated under more robust rules of engagement than normal in UN peacekeeping missions. The disadvantages were that the relationship with the UN Operation in Somalia (UNOSOM I) was fuzzy and that the task of disarming Somalia's warring factions was not clearly assigned to either party. The justification for the U.S. commitment to Somalia, spelled out by President Bush in an address to the nation on December 4, 1992, was that U.S. engagement was indispensable to the resolution of some of the world's crises, that the United States could not resolve them on its own, and that U.S. involvement was often the catalyst for the involvement of the broader community of nations.

The failure to specify the nature and extent of U.S. participation in the follow-up UN operation (UNOSOM II) would in time contribute to wrecking the mission and poison the relationship between the United States and the UN for the duration of Boutros-Ghali's tenure as Secretary-General.[18] UN peacekeeping rests on a conjunction of interests in overseeing peace. That consensus has difficulty surviving any effort to transform the mission into *keeping* the peace by force. Force cannot be used effectively without the participation of major powers. The international consensus collapses because the use of force by great powers is inseparable from calculations of national interest. As U.S. decisionmakers internalized this reality in the 1990s, they progressively shifted the task of peace enforcement from the UN to NATO while retaining the UN framework as a useful venue for legitimizing multilateral enforcement operations.

At the end of 1992, the UN framework appeared to provide the United States with the means to avoid the destiny of becoming a hyperpower, engaged and entangled everywhere. Success in the Gulf War, during which the United States had used the UN to mobilize the international community to U.S. strategic ends, generated a sense of triumphalism and produced the rhetoric of the "indispensable" power. Some in the Bush administration had already worried about the potential pitfalls of relying on the UNSC as the sole legitimizing agency for international enforcement action. This might carry risks in unforeseeable future contingencies, they feared, by leaving the United States vulnerable to the interests, actions, and coalition-forming (or action-blocking) "spoiler" behavior of others.

The start of the Clinton presidency, however, was a time of great euphoria about pursuing U.S. interests and promoting U.S. values through the UN system. The international organization could provide an established cooperative framework and legitimating authority to realize U.S. foreign policy objectives. Madeleine Albright, speaking as Clinton's UN ambassador, argued in 1993 that the end of the Cold War had placed the UN at the center of the effort to guide and safeguard a chaotic world and that engagement with the UN would give the United States an opportunity to help set the rules of the game for the emerging order and promote the UN as the repository of those rules.[19] Accordingly, the United States should adopt a policy of "assertive multilateralism," implying not only multilateral engagement but also U.S. leadership within collective organizations in order to infuse them with U.S. values and ideology. The desire to work through the UN would also advance the administration's goal of concentrating policy energy on the domestic economy: in effect, the UN would provide the Clinton administration with the means to purchase a leveraged buyout of unilateral U.S. responsibility for world order.

The initial Clinton stance toward peacekeeping itself was outlined in Presidential Review Directive 13 (PRD-13), which was designed to bolster the capabilities and efficiency of UN peacekeeping. In mid-1993, the administration was interested in various proposals, including setting up a planning cell and a twenty-four-hour operations center in the UN Department of Peacekeeping Operations (DPKO); standardizing the training, doctrine, and rules of engagement for UN peacekeepers; identifying force capabilities that could be made available to the UN at short notice; and reforming the financing and management of UN PKOs. Concomitantly, U.S. support for specific missions would be made conditional on the presence of concrete U.S. interests, the nature of international participation in the mission, the adequacy of human and financial means for success, and the level of domestic U.S. support. In July 1993, Washington signaled its willingness, though not without misgivings within the Pentagon, to contribute combat units under the operational control of a UN commander (while insisting that overall command remain with the U.S. president in accordance with the U.S. Constitution).

The Retreat from Multilateralism

However, under charges of handing over control of the U.S. national security agenda to the United Nations, weakening the ability of the United States to defend its own interests, and entangling the country in UN-led actions, the Clinton administration steadily retreated from early positions.

Somalia

The concept of a ready reaction force, for example, was watered down, first to on-call ready units and then to a database of combat capabilities that could be loaned to the UN under the right circumstances. These transformations in the administration's philosophy toward UN peacekeeping were not unrelated to the rapidly evolving situations on the ground in Somalia and Bosnia. Boutros-Ghali continued to call for the United States to expand and extend its involvement in UNOSOM II, as the follow-up operation to UNITAF, on the grounds that only the United States had the requisite military capacity.[20] When the UN seemed to stall on reassuming responsibility for Somalia unless the factions were disarmed—on the grounds that armed factions would impede the delivery of humanitarian relief—Washington agreed to provide a 1,150-member Quick Reaction Force and an additional 3,000 logistical personnel in order to facilitate the transition from UNITAF to UNOSOM II (which occurred on May 4, 1993). This allowed Washington to claim mission success with respect to UNITAF—a claim that was politically important in the context of subsequent U.S. efforts—largely successful—to pin blame for UNOSOM II's failures solely on the UN.

UNOSOM II, established by Security Council Resolution 814 of March 26, 1993, had a complex mandate to accomplish a mishmash of humanitarian, disarmament, and state-building objectives throughout all of Somalia. Most crucially, and without precedent in the annals of UN peacekeeping, the operation was established under the enforcement provisions of chapter VII of the UN Charter. The significance of this fact was not apparent to the U.S. political and journalistic establishment at the time. Arguably, Resolution 814, which the United States played a key role in drafting, reflected the view of a new, inexperienced administration on the appropriate UN role in the new world order—not U.S. interests in the new world disorder. Madeleine Albright, the new ambassador to the UN, had no previous government experience, and many members of the new foreign policy team were still awaiting Senate confirmation in March 1993. Their collective naïveté was dispelled within a few months.

The command-and-control relationship between U.S. troops and UNOSOM II was fuzzy, to say the least. This was the farthest that the United States had ever—and has ever—gone in working under UN command. But contrary to conventional wisdom, in fact, the U.S. troops never took operational orders from UN Force Commander Lieutenant General Cevik Bir of Turkey. Instead, the logistics unit was under the operational command of U.S. Major General Thomas M. Montgomery, who served under the command and control of the U.S. Central Command (CENTCOM); the Quick Reaction Force was under direct CENTCOM command.

In addition, the civilian head of UNOSOM II was U.S. Admiral Jonathan Howe, appointed at Washington's request.

These complicated command-and-control arrangements created confusion and generated mutual suspicion and anger in the field, and they were simply unworkable once crisis struck. On June 6, 1993, a day after a group of Pakistani peacekeepers had been killed, the UN Security Council authorized "all necessary measures" to deal with their attackers. U.S. forces took part in the ensuing operations. The administration justified these actions as necessary both to prevent a return to lawlessness that would jeopardize the humanitarian relief operation, as well as to safeguard the credibility of the UN as a collective security organization in the post–Cold War world. But the heightened U.S. military involvement turned U.S. soldiers into targets for retaliatory attacks, and four were killed in a landmine explosion in August. These casualties in turn awakened congressional and media interest in—and questioning of—U.S. involvement in a conflict devoid of vital interests for the United States. Another 400 U.S. soldiers were dispatched, but these special forces troops were to serve directly under CENTCOM command, not even under General Montgomery, let alone the UNOSOM force commander. In October 1993, they launched, without prior UN knowledge or approval, a raid on a suspected hideout of Somali warlord General Mohamed Farah Aideed. On October 3, eighteen U.S. Rangers were killed—the largest single combat casualty for the U.S. military since Vietnam—and one dead American soldier was paraded through the streets of Mogadishu by the very people that Americans had supposedly risked their lives to help. The decision to remove U.S. troops from UNOSOM, after a suitable grace period for the sake of appearances, was made in Washington without any encumbering consultations with the UN. The announcement of a U.S. withdrawal by the end of March 1994, and of a scaling-down of the operation to focus solely on humanitarian delivery, forestalled congressional calls for an immediate end to the U.S. participation in the Somalia mission.

The footage of the incidents, broadcast repeatedly throughout the world, sapped any remaining U.S. resolve to stay the course in Somalia. More important for current purposes, the administration, sensitive to the charge of having ceded control of U.S. foreign policy to the UN, did little to discourage Congress, the press, and the public from attributing blame to the world organization.[21] An impression was left to fester that the operation had been ordered, directed, and controlled by the UN and that the fiasco was the result of the UN's institutional incapacity to fight wars and keep the peace. When President Clinton announced on October 6, 1993, that an additional 1,700 soldiers were being sent to Somalia to protect the troops already there, he made a point of emphasizing that they would be under direct U.S. command—as if this had not already been the case. The alienation of responsibility from the United States to the UN helped to shore up the administration's crumbling credibility in domestic politics—but only at the expense of lasting damage to U.S.-UN relations.

Besides testing the feasibility of the UN's peace-enforcement machinery, UNOSOM II committed the prestige of the United States as the world's only superpower. The unwillingness of the United States to devote significant resources to ensure a successful resolution of the crisis and the U.S. readiness to retreat quickly after a setback suggested, to many, significant limits to U.S. strength and determination and the credibility of U.S. commitments. It thus harmed broader U.S. national interests in its domino effect of eroding the authority of the United States as a world leader.

Doctrinal Disengagement

U.S.-UN relations also got caught up in domestic debates over the size and composition of the U.S. foreign policy budget. Specifically, the political agenda of reducing the U.S. fiscal deficit happened to coincide with ballooning UN peacekeeping bills as the number and size of missions grew in the early 1990s. In the congressional elections of November 1994, the Republican Party gained control of both houses for the first time in four decades. Deeply suspicious of international entanglements in general and the UN in particular, they launched sharp political attacks against the already fraying fabric of U.S.-UN relations. The Clinton administration, in deep domestic trouble on a variety of fronts, concluded that little was to be gained by investing scarce political capital in arguing the case for the UN within a domestic political spectrum in which the institution commands few votes in Congress or among citizens.

The tragedy in Somalia in October 1993 and calls for active U.S. involvement in the worsening humanitarian situation in the Balkans eroded domestic support for placing U.S. combat units under UN command. A new Washington consensus emerged concerning modern peace operations: that the complexity of their tasks was beyond the institutional capacity of the UN to manage; that they were too dynamic and fluid for rigid criteria and guidelines to be of much practical use; that their relationship to U.S. political and security interests was unclear; and that they relied on a degree of international consensus that the UN system was too divisive and fractured to provide. The administration—its hands full simply trying to maintain sufficient political and public consensus at home—had little energy or will left to worry about a UN that was blamed for having drawn the United States into misadventures in Somalia where no vital U.S. interests were engaged. By the time that Clinton addressed the UN General Assembly on September 27, 1993, therefore, he spoke more of the limits to multilateralism in shaping U.S. foreign policy than its potential for externalizing the costs while internalizing the benefits of international engagement.

On peacekeeping, the administration now made a distinction between offering political support and making military contributions. Henceforth,

U.S. support would be contingent on a clear threat to international peace and security caused by aggression, humanitarian crisis, or the violent overthrow of a democratic government; clear objectives and scope for the proposed peacekeeping mission; agreed cessation of hostilities by all parties to the conflict; adequate financial and human resources; and an exit strategy. As for U.S. participation, the country's comparative advantage lay in specialized areas like logistics, training, intelligence, communications, and transportation (air- and sealift capability). When the drawn-out review of U.S. policy toward UN peacekeeping was finally completed and signed in May 1994, as PDD-25, the emphasis was far more on making UN peacekeeping efficient, cost-effective, and selective ("It will be easier for the U.S. to say Yes if the UN learns when to say No") than on enthusiastic U.S. participation in UN peacekeeping.[22] From this moment on, U.S. emphasis shifted from ensuring the effectiveness of peace operations to considerations of fiscal responsibility and exit strategies in determining the level of U.S. support for and involvement in the operations.

PDD-25, conceived originally as an effort to strengthen peacekeeping, in fact marked a significant retreat from the 1993 doctrine of assertive multilateralism and the start of the effort to distance Washington from the UN. The utility of the organization as a tool of U.S. foreign policy was seen as suspect, because of doubts about its leadership and managerial qualities and a noncompliant membership. The U.S. national interest was reinterpreted to preserve a working legislative-executive relationship as a prerequisite for an effective U.S. role in world affairs, even if it came at the expense of a supportive role for the United Nations. The most immediate and tragic price was to be paid by almost 1 million Rwandans, when the United States in general, and Ambassador Albright in particular, rejected calls for a modestly expanded UN operation to defeat, contain, or avert the genocidal killings.

In turn, the conviction grew in the UN community that the United States was becoming an irresponsible member state, prone to making illegal and unreasonable demands on the organization in return for less than full financial support. It is worth making the point that the U.S. public, for its part, favored channeling U.S. overseas military action through the UN. Thus, in 1992, 87 percent of Americans supported the commitment of U.S. military troops only as part of UN operations, 73 percent supported action with other allies, and those prepared to support unilateral U.S. action dropped to 62 percent.[23] In the light of such figures, there is merit to the assertion that the Clinton administration's decision to distance the United States from the UN was less a response to public hostility than an attempt to preempt political opponents from making peacekeeping a damaging issue in the internecine domestic squabbles between a Democratic White House and a Republican Congress.[24]

The Balkans

As the Somalia intervention turned to disaster in the second half of 1993, Washington found it expedient not to allay the gathering impression that the major policy decisions leading to the debacle in Somalia were the fault of the UN, as well as that U.S. troops killed in Mogadishu had been under the operational command of the UN (which had thus implicitly failed to assure the safety of U.S. soldiers). The United States found it similarly expedient not to dispel the illusion that a passive UNSC was preventing a more active U.S. engagement in Bosnia.

Bill Clinton had pressed George Bush hard on Bosnia during the election campaign in 1992, and he entered office believing it to be the most urgent foreign policy issue. But the complexity of the conflict and the limited nature of U.S. interests engaged there convinced the new administration to stay essentially within the parameters of the previous administration's policy: to mitigate the humanitarian crisis and contain the Bosnian conflict without getting the United States directly involved in another Vietnam. Washington had to perform a juggling act in managing intra-NATO relations, engagement with a precarious Russia, and political relationships with the UN. These competing pressures led progressively to an increasing complementarity-cum-partnership between the legitimizing and authorizing agency of the UNSC and the enforcement machinery of NATO. As the situation on the ground in Bosnia worsened, the UN-NATO relationship came under increasing strain. The final leg of Washington's strategy—the significance of which would grow beyond all expectation over the course of the decade—was to establish, through the UNSC, an international war crimes tribunal for the former Yugoslavia.

Washington, NATO, and the UN could neither contain the Bosnian conflict nor end the humanitarian catastrophe. Calls grew more insistent in Congress and in the press for Washington to do something, including ending the arms embargo, which was disproportionate in its impact on the Muslims. But a unilateral lifting of the UN-imposed embargo would complicate efforts to maintain the increasingly fraying international coalition behind sanctions on Iraq, as well as undermine the authority of the UNSC more broadly. As the Serbs grew ever bolder in challenging UN-imposed limitations on their activity, the UN and NATO worked out so-called dual-key military arrangements, whereby the Special Representative of the Secretary-General could authorize NATO air strikes against designated targets. This neither intimidated, deterred, nor defeated the Serbs' territorial ambitions and their increasingly brazen atrocities. By the time reports of ethnic cleansing could no longer be credibly denied, and Serb troops were engaged in massacring civilians who had sought shelter in UN safe areas that had been overrun by Serb troops, leading NATO members began in 1995 to contemplate pulling out of the increasingly ineffectual UNPROFOR. At this point Washington faced the choice between increasing its direct exposure in the Balkan conflict or witnessing a fatal erosion of NATO's authority and credibility as the guarantor of European peace in the post–Cold War Europe, ensuring the defeat of UN peacekeeping in the Balkans, and suffering a loss of U.S. credibility as both an alliance and global leader. Washington ensured that the authority to launch air strikes was progressively detached from the UN, assumed directly by NATO and used more forcefully and effectively, while the UN mission was scaled down to humanitarian and traditional peacekeeping activities. In addition, the United States led diplomatic negotiations outside the UN framework, culminating in the Dayton accords of November 1995.

One item of unfinished business at Dayton was Kosovo. One lesson of the Balkans in the 1990s was that NATO, by virtue of its political solidarity and military cohesion, offered a more congenial multilateral framework than the UNSC for decisive and effective action against President Slobodan Milosevic. In the early 1990s, the UN framework had enabled Washington to disclaim responsibility for the tragedy in the Balkans. But the scale of the tragedy had magnified to such an extent that it threatened to destabilize the entire region, destroy the credibility of NATO, and diminish the authority of the UN. Sickened by Milosevic's record of brutality and evasions and deceit in dealings with the Europeans and the UN, the United States in 1999 decided to lead a humanitarian intervention in Kosovo through the multilateral framework of NATO—without prior UNSC authorization.[25]

With regard to the implications of the war in Kosovo for the U.S.-UN relationship, several different lines of argument are possible.[26] The first is the simple claim that NATO's action violated both the UN Charter and the terms of the 1949 Treaty of Washington in attacking a sovereign state that had not committed aggression against any outside country. A second, opposing line of argument contends that even though NATO's war was not explicitly authorized by the UN, it was an implicit evolution from earlier UN resolutions, and certainly not prohibited by any UN resolution. A third response is that if Milosevic had been allowed to get away with his murderous campaign of ethnic cleansing, the net result would have been a fundamental erosion of the idealistic base on which the UN structure rests. Yet a fourth strand is that while NATO made war it still needed the UN to help secure the peace. Finally, it can be argued that the sequence of events shows that the real center of international political and economic gravity has shifted from the UNSC to the G8 countries plus China. The latter forum, not the Security Council, was the one in which the critical negotiations were held and the crucial compromises and decisions made.

By 1999, Somalia and Rwanda had become metaphors in U.S. political discourse for the failures of the United Nations as an international organization, and this perception helped Washington rally support for military action in Kosovo outside the UN framework. Yet the United States bore significant responsibility for both of these earlier disasters, both through acts of commission in Somalia—where U.S. troops went on a hunt for General Aideed like cowboys beyond UN control—and of omission in Rwanda— where the U.S. refusal to get involved in, or even support, any enforcement action (at whatever level) in Africa stymied any possibility of timely action by the Security Council. Africa continues to play a marginal role in U.S. foreign policy in general and U.S. peacekeeping policy in particular. Although many human rights organizations were bitterly critical of the U.S. complicity in the scandalous lack of action by the international community in Rwanda, not one member of Congress called for U.S. action there.[27] Indeed, U.S. officials went to extraordinary lengths to avoid using the word "genocide" to describe the events in Rwanda in order to avoid generating public pressure to do something.

Since 1999, stung by criticisms of double standards with regard to differential reactions to the humanitarian crises of the Balkans and African hotspots, Washington has been prepared to offer political support, in the form of affirmative votes, for starting up new missions in Africa, such as between Ethiopia and Eritrea. But the United States is still not prepared to commit U.S. military personnel to these missions, preferring instead to regionalize African peacekeeping through train-and-equip programs. Not surprisingly, other Western countries have followed the U.S. lead, despite the clear demonstration in Sierra Leone of just what a difference even one Western country (in that case, the United Kingdom) can make by providing professional troops and determined leadership. The lack of U.S. political, logistical, financial, and military support for UN peacekeeping makes complex peace operations more costly and prone to failure and therefore leads other countries to try also to limit their exposure to such risky operations. Non-U.S. involvement and backing thus have a negative multiplier effect on UN peacekeeping.

Relative Gains and Costs
of Unilateralism and Multilateralism

At times U.S. power and international authority can be disconnected, as occurred in the Multinational Force in Beirut in the early 1980s[28] and in the international control commissions in Indochina in the 1950s.[29] At other times, force and authority can work in tandem. Using the metaphor in its exact sense, the UN can lead and the United States can support, which is the preferred U.S. model today with respect to peacekeeping duties in Africa; or Washington can lead and the UN can support, as in Korea in the 1950s, the Gulf War in 1991, and peacekeeping efforts in the Balkans today. When faced with a clear and compelling danger, the UN does have the capacity to respond quickly to urgent security requirements. After the terrorist attacks of September 11, 2001, condemnation by the UN Secretary-General was immediate. In addition, within forty-eight hours the Security Council and the General Assembly had also condemned the attacks and voted to take action against those responsible and any states that aided, supported, or harbored them.

The United States, more than any other country, shaped the normative architecture and multilateral machinery for the maintenance of international peace and security that emerged after World War II. In the series of conferences and negotiating sessions that established the United Nations, culminating at San Francisco in 1945, smaller states secured some concessions to their interests; but the essential machinery was still designed by and for the major powers, especially the United States, the United Kingdom, and the Soviet Union. In the postwar years, the UN system became an important forum and instrument for externalizing U.S. values and virtues like democracy, human rights, the rule of law, and the market economy and embedding them in international institutions.

Neither has the United States had any peer competitor in operating and driving the multilateral machinery for the maintenance of international peace and security. Thus, the United Nations was simultaneously the embodiment of the virtues of globalism and the instrument through which collective action could be authorized and implemented. The very fact of veto power available to the United States and the other four permanent members of the UNSC symbolizes a compromise in the UN Charter between national and global interests because the veto clause was inserted to ensure that the organization would never construct a global interest in conflict with the national interest of any one of the P-5. Thus, the veto is a reconciling instrument designed to ensure that any global interest forged by the UN is in harmony with the common national interests of the five most important members.

The UN helps to mute the costs and spread the risks of the terms of international engagement. It provides a means of mediating the choice between isolationism (disengagement from the world) and unilateralism (going it alone); between inaction (refusing to be a cop) and intervention (being the world's only cop). In the 1990s, the UN forum enabled successive U.S. administrations "both to legitimate interventions and to spread the burden to a wider group of countries."[30] But in order to maximize these benefits, the United States will need to instill in others, as well as itself embrace, the principle of multilateralism as a norm in its own right: states must do X because the United Nations has called for X, and good states do what the United Nations asks them to do. The promotion of multilateralism and globalism can thus become foreign policy goals in themselves.

The alienation and institutionalization of fundamental U.S. value preferences within the UN would greatly reduce the compliance and transaction costs of pursuing U.S. national interests directly and without the mediating framework of global multilateral machinery. In just such a manner, the language Washington used in 1990–1991 to classify Iraq as a major threat to international peace (as distinct from U.S. material interests) emphasized the danger of Iraq's action to the system of codified order (the so-called new world order) whose basic tenets were being challenged and defied. An international consensus was forged and maintained, and U.S. national interests were subsumed within that international consensus. Moreover, being the virtuous power, the United States, and no one else, had both the moral standing and the material capacity to provide international leadership and galvanize the UN into action. In the future, Washington may also have an indirect interest in supporting UN peace operations, in that they may be of more direct interest to other countries whose support the United States will need on unrelated issues: political horse-trading is integral to UN policymaking.

Peacekeeping is but one item on the full menu of the multilateral meal. Cherry-picking, or forum-shopping, with regard to multilateralism risks generating normative inconsistency (different applications of the same norm) and incoherence (incompatibility between cognate norms). Many foreign observers perceive sole superpower status as encouraging the United States to try to set the rules of globalization; choose some parts (trade liberalization) and reject others (globalized decisionmaking); lecture others on the rule of law while refusing to accept international criminal jurisdiction; promote the rhetoric of pluralism and diversity when the world is concerned about the concentration of multimedia power in a few U.S. hands; and so on.[31] Double standards have also become a pressing concern. For example, if it is right to engage in humanitarian intervention in Kosovo, then why not also in Rwanda, Chechnya, and the Democratic Republic of Congo? If NATO can intervene militarily in Kosovo without Security Council authorization, then why cannot Russia in Chechnya? Such questions provoke normative contestation: those who are unhappy with an existing norm begin to question its validity or point to U.S. rejection of one norm as justification for their own rejection of another norm. Over time, extensive contestation over specific norms risks chipping away at the foundations of the global normative architecture—the collapse of which would be more damaging to the national interests of the United States than those of any other country in the world.

In some regimes and instruments, U.S. interests, as defined by the incumbent administration, are subordinated to others' conceptions of the global interest, for example, with respect to proscribing antipersonnel landmines, controlling toxic emissions, and institutionalizing processes of international criminal justice in a new world court. In that case, the real question for Washington is never simply whether to reject the particular regime with which it disagrees. Rather, the question becomes How much damage will rejecting any one particular multilateral regime do to other multilateral regimes, to the principle of multilateralism, and boomerang badly on U.S. national interests? The United States has substantial political, security, and economic interests in delegitimizing the use of force in world affairs and constructing firebreaks around violent conflicts so that they are localized and low-level. It cannot promote the accountability of individual soldiers and political leaders to international norms, law, and courts and tribunals if it demands ironclad guarantees that Americans will never be prosecuted in international forums.

My argument parallels that of John Ikenberry in his important book *After Victory*: that U.S. power is made more acceptable, and its exercise more palatable, when it is institutionalized. As the sole superpower, the United States should seek neither to dominate everyone else nor to abandon international engagement but to transform its favorable power position into a durable order that commands the allegiance of others. Subjecting power preponderance to institutional restraints helps to give the new order "constitutional" characteristics that makes the order acceptable to the broader community as a whole and therefore more stable and enduring.[32] As Ikenberry puts it, "The institutional model of order building is based on a potential bargain between unequal states. . . . The leading state wants to reduce compliance costs and weaker states want to reduce their costs of security protection—or the costs they would incur trying to protect their interests against the actions of a dominating lead state."[33]

Peace operations constitute a continuum of international responses to disorder and poverty. They permit Washington to choose its preferred mode of articulation between international/UN responses and U.S. engagement on a spectrum of the level (low or intense) and geographical theater (differentiating in particular between Europe and Africa) of international involvement. At the end of the spectrum, if the UN is unable or unwilling to acquit itself of the responsibility to protect victims of genocide, ethnic cleansing, or other egregious humanitarian atrocities, Washington can forge multilateral coalitions of the willing to lead military interventions to stop the atrocities.

It is also worth noting that some of the core criticisms leveled at UN peacekeeping by Washington have been addressed by the UN Panel on Peacekeeping Operations. That panel, which issued its report in August 2000, concluded that political neutrality has too often degenerated into military timidity and the abdication of the duty to protect civilians. Impartial peacekeeping should not automatically translate into moral equivalence among parties to the conflict on the ground. In some cases, local parties consist not of moral equals but aggressors and victims.[34] The report admonishes the UN Secretariat not to "apply best-case planning assumptions to situations where the local actors have historically exhibited worst-case behaviour."[35] The panel reinforces the importance of a UN-authorized force under the active leadership of a significant military power. For even though the UNSC can validate the legitimacy of a peace support operation, the UN does not have enough professionally trained and equipped troops and police forces of its own. Successful operations that need robust mandates might still have to depend on coalitions of the able, willing, and duly authorized.

Conclusion

The United States is the world's indispensable power, and the United Nations is the world's indispensable institution. The UN has unmatched legitimacy and authority, on the one hand, and convening and mobilizing power on the other. Peacekeeping draws on the UN's authority as the organ of the international community and helps to muster political will on the part of member states. Peace operations enlarge the spectrum of capabilities available to the international community to respond to threats of chaos in the periphery. Participation in such operations symbolizes solidarity and encapsulates shared responsibility. But the UN does not have its own military and police forces. The DPKO is understaffed and underresourced. It manages a number and range of military missions and personnel around the world with resources and under conditions that the Pentagon would find simply intolerable and unacceptable. A multinational coalition of allies can offer a more credible and efficient military force when robust action is needed and warranted. The UN would be hard-pressed to achieve anything of note without active U.S. engagement, let alone against its vital interests and determined opposition.

The benefits of UN peacekeeping to the United States, although uneven, are considerable. For decades, UN peace operations have served U.S. security interests from the Middle East to southern Africa, Central America, Southeast Asia, and Haiti. By their very nature, peacekeeping operations cannot produce conclusive results either on the battlefield—they are peace operations, after all, not war—or around the negotiating table—they are military deployments, not diplomatic talks. Criticisms leveled at UN peace operations can be fundamentally misconceived, intentionally ill conceived, grossly exaggerated, or designed to deflect criticisms from the failures of U.S. administrations.[36]

Conversely, the disengagement of the United States from UN peacekeeping has had a spillover effect, eroding partially the legitimacy of UN operations and therefore the effectiveness of the UN as the primary manager of international security. In turn this has reduced U.S. leverage in spreading the burden of providing international security and lessening the demands and expectations on the United States to take up the slack. At the same time, scapegoating the UN has produced a backlash among other nations and so reduced the ability of the United States to use the UN in pursuit of U.S. goals, where the interests of the two do coincide.

Because the world is essentially anarchical, it is fundamentally insecure, characterized by strategic uncertainty and complexity because of too many actors with multiple goals and interests and variable capabilities and convictions. Collective action embedded in international institutions that mirror mainly U.S. value preferences and interests enhances predictability, reduces uncertainty, and cuts the transaction costs of international action in the pursuit of U.S. foreign policy. America-first nationalists like Senator Jesse Helms are skeptical of the value of the UN to U.S. foreign policy, viewing it more as a constraint. Why should U.S. power be harnessed to the goals of others? Multilateralism implies bargaining and accommodation, and compromise is integral to such multilateral negotiation. But U.S. power and assets are such that Washington does not need to compromise on core values and interests. Liberal institutionalists, in contrast, believe that multilateral organizations can externalize such bedrock U.S. values as respect for the rule of law, due process, and human rights. Multilateralism—the coordination of relations among several states in accordance with certain principles[37] (such as sovereign equality)—rests on assumptions of the indivisibility of the benefits of collective public goods like peace (as well as international telecommunications, transportation, and so on) and diffuse reciprocity (whereby collective action arrangements confer an equivalence of benefits, not on every issue and every occasion, but in aggregate and over time).[38]

The discussion in this chapter permits nine concluding propositions about the unilateralism-multilateralism debate. First, the power, wealth, and politics of the United States are too deeply intertwined with the crosscurrents of international affairs for disengagement to be a credible or sustainable policy posture for the world's only superpower. In their insular innocence—and, in the views of some, in their in-your-face exceptionalism—Americans long embraced the illusion of security behind supposedly impregnable lines of continental defense.[39] The terrorist attacks of September 11, 2001, proved the vulnerability of the U.S. homeland to quarrels rooted in complex conflicts in distant lands. The hope of outsiders is that the event will change the United States; their fear is that Americans might conclude that September 11 changed the world.

Second, if isolationism is not an option in today's globally interconnected world, unilateralism cannot be the strategy of choice either. Like the two world wars, the war against global terrorism is one from which the United States can neither stay disengaged nor win on its own; neither is it a war that can be won without full U.S. engagement.[40] A world in which every country retreated into unilateralism would not provide a better guarantee of U.S. national security, now and for the foreseeable future, than multilateral regimes. The most authoritative forum for constructing an effective antiterrorism regime, like other global regimes, is the UN.

Third, exceptionalism is also deeply flawed. Washington cannot construct a world in which all others have to obey universal norms and rules while the United States can opt out whenever, as often, and for as long as it likes on global norms with respect to nuclear tests, landmines, international criminal prosecution, climate change, and other regimes—what Richard Haass, director of the Policy Planning Unit at the State Department, calls "à la carte multilateralism"[41] and what some others privately call, even more insultingly, "disposable multilateralism."

Fourth, because peacekeeping is likely to remain the instrument of choice by the UN for engaging with the characteristic types of conflicts in the contemporary world, the U.S. approach to peace operations will continue to define the nature of the U.S. engagement with the UN. Perceptions of U.S. disengagement will in turn erode the U.S. ability to harness UN legitimacy to causes and battles that may be more important to the United States than peacekeeping in messy conflicts in faraway countries whose names can neither be pronounced nor remembered by U.S. voters and members of Congress.

Fifth, because the United States, in addition to being the pivotal P-5 member in the UNSC, will also remain the main financial underwriter of the costs of UN peacekeeping, it will continue to exercise unmatched influence on the establishment, mandate, nature, size, and termination of UN peace operations. At the same time, the level of informed interest about the UN is so low in the U.S. body politic that any administration will always be able to distance itself from spectacular failures of UN peacekeeping.

Sixth, the overarching U.S. policy goal with respect to UN peace operations is to make them efficient, cost-effective, and selective. Part of the last point includes leaving war-fighting—peace enforcement—to multinational coalitions acting under UN authority. Part of the efficiency drive includes a campaign to increase the professional military capabilities of the DPKO at the expense of such other units like the Department of Public Information that, in Washington's view, are bloated and top-heavy.

Seventh, U.S. participation in chapter VII operations under direct UN command can almost certainly be ruled out in the foreseeable future. The contribution of U.S. infantry troops to UN peace operations under chapter VI, with no (or little) likelihood of fighting, can be contemplated but are highly unlikely. U.S. participation in UN peace operations, whose creation and continuation require U.S. consent, is likely therefore to remain limited to the provision of unique capabilities like transportation, communications, and logistics units and skills, as well as bearing the main burden of the costs of the operations.

Eighth, UN peace operations are only one of many foreign policy tools available to the United States, others being multilateral action through standing alliances like NATO, or an ad hoc multinational coalition as in the Gulf War, or even unilateral U.S. action if the interests involved are sufficiently vital to the United States.

Finally, in the case of non-UN operations, the United States would *prefer* to obtain the legitimating approbation of the UN if possible, in the form of enabling UNSC resolutions authorizing the operations. But the United States is most unlikely to accept a prior UNSC resolution as a *mandatory* requirement for the use of military force overseas. The problematic element in this comes from the equally compelling U.S. interest in promoting the norm of the UN being the only collective legitimator of international military action when the United States and NATO are not involved. Washington thus faces an unresolved and irreconcilable dilemma between instilling the principle of multilateralism as the world order norm and exempting itself from the same principle because of the sustaining and enduring belief in exceptionalism in its identity as the virtuous power.

Notes

1. See Thakur and Schnabel, "Cascading Generations of Peacekeeping."
2. For an analysis of the issues surrounding such a division of labor, see Malone, *Decision-Making in the UN Security Council.*
3. The phrase is taken from Thakur and Thayer, eds., *A Crisis of Expectations.*
4. *Report of the Panel on United Nations Peace Operations,* para. 53.
5. International Institute for Strategic Studies, *The Military Balance, 1999–2000,* p. 37.
6. Pfaff, "Europe Is Unqualified for the World Role It Seeks."
7. Sewell, "Multilateral Peace Operations," manuscript p. 26.
8. Given U.S. financial arrears, both figures must be treated as hypothetical shares of the U.S. contribution to the UN's finances.
9. Boutros-Ghali, *An Agenda for Peace.*
10. See Daalder, "Knowing When to Say No."
11. George H. W. Bush, *Address to the United Nations General Assembly,* September 21, 1992.
12. It is worth recalling that the secretary of defense at the time was Dick Cheney, and the chairman of the Joint Chiefs of Staff was Colin Powell. The two were to become, respectively, vice president and secretary of state in the administration of George W. Bush in 2001.
13. See Durch, "Keeping the Peace," pp. 15–16.
14. See Lamb, "The UN Protection Force in Former Yugoslavia."
15. Rose, "The Bosnia Experience."
16. The thesis of the so-called CNN factor holds that the U.S. government can be propelled into foreign adventures on the basis of active but selective attention to particular crises by the main U.S. media. The case of Somalia, like those of others, shows that the relationship between the selective attention devoted to foreign events by public authorities and the media is more nuanced and mutually reinforcing: the media will cover stories where U.S. personnel are involved more than other stories. But the prospect of U.S. involvement increases if the U.S. media cover a foreign crisis in a big way. Thus, Mohamed Sahnoun, the Special Representative of the Secretary-General for Somalia at the time, actively courted the major Western media in 1992 in order to focus the minds of the principal policymakers on Somalia. Private discussions, 2001.
17. One of the best accounts of the U.S. story with respect to Somalia is by ambassadors John Hirsch and Robert Oakley, *Somalia and Operation Restore Hope.* See also Bolton, "Wrong Turn in Somalia."

18. For analyses of the Somalia failure as a peacekeeping operation see, in addition to Hirsch and Oakley and Bolton, Durch, "Introduction to Anarchy"; Makinda, *Seeking Peace from Chaos;* Patman, "The UN Operation in Somalia"; and Thakur, "From Peacekeeping to Peace Enforcement."

19. In an address to the Council on Foreign Relations, New York, June 11, 1993; quoted in Dodds, "The Role of Multilateralism and the UN in Post–Cold War U.S. Foreign Policy," chap. 7.

20. Boutros-Ghali, *Unvanquished,* pp. 59–60.

21. One of the most influential op-ed articles of the time was former UN Ambassador Jeanne Kirkpatrick's "Where Is Our Foreign Policy?"

22. For a study of PDD-25, see MacKinnon, *The Evolution of US Peacekeeping Policy Under Clinton.*

23. Figures cited in Glennon, "Accountability in the Use of Force."

24. The two competing hypotheses are explored and evaluated in MacKinnon, *The Evolution of US Peacekeeping Policy Under Clinton.*

25. For a comprehensive account of that intervention, see Schnabel and Thakur, eds., *Kosovo and the Challenge of Humanitarian Intervention.*

26. See Thakur, "A Future Role for the U.N."

27. MacKinnon, *Evolution of US Peacekeeping Policy Under Clinton,* p. 108.

28. See Thakur, *International Peacekeeping in Lebanon.*

29. See Thakur, *Peacekeeping in Vietnam.*

30. Blechman, "Emerging from the Intervention Dilemma."

31. See, for example, Bowring, "Bush's America is Developing an Image Problem."

32. Ikenberry, *After Victory,* pp. 4, 6.

33. Ibid., p. 258.

34. *Report of the Panel on United Nations Peace Operations,* para. 50.

35. Ibid., para. 51.

36. See, for example, the systematic rebuttal of persistent U.S. criticisms of UN peace operations by a former New Zealand secretary of defense who is anything but anti-U.S., having been pilloried in the second half of the 1980s in his home country for having been too pro-U.S.; McLean, "Peace Operations and Common Sense," pp. 321–332.

37. Ruggie, "Multilateralism," pp. 8–11.

38. Keohane, "Reciprocity in International Relations."

39. For the importance of the sense of exceptionalism in U.S. foreign policy, see Huntington, "American Ideals Versus American Institutions."

40. See Thakur and van Ginkel, "An International Perspective on Global Terrorism."

41. Quoted in Shanker, "Bush's Way: 'A la Carte' Approach to Treaties."

9

The Unilateral and Multilateral Use of Force by the United States

Ekaterina Stepanova

A DECADE AFTER THE UNITED STATES SUCCESSFULLY ORGANIZED THE BROAD, ad hoc, multilateral Coalition against Iraq in Operation Desert Storm, the issue of the U.S. use of force in the post–Cold War era has come full circle. After a series of controversial and limited unilateral strikes against various rogue states, most often Iraq, and an even more controversial NATO air campaign against the Federal Republic of Yugoslavia, the United States has suddenly found itself supported by most of the rest of the world in building a coalition to mount a massive retaliation campaign in response to unprecedented terrorist attacks on the territory of the United States itself.

Observers have cited many parallels between Desert Storm and the more recent U.S. campaign of retaliation, including broad international and almost unanimous domestic support and a U.S. readiness to use massive force to defend vital national interests. Nevertheless, significant differences make the analogy somewhat misleading. Whereas Desert Storm involved a huge buildup of troops and heavy weapons, the first massive use of force by the United States in the twenty-first century is bound to rely both on more sophisticated technology and on smaller, mobile units and to come as a more focused, measured, and—most important—longer-term response. In addition to direct military action, the U.S. government must consider a variety of intelligence, economic, and diplomatic actions to disrupt terrorist networks and, possibly, the governments that support or tolerate them. In the words of U.S. Secretary of Defense Donald Rumsfeld, "It will take a long, sustained effort" to fight global terrorism, what President George W. Bush has called a new kind of war against a shadowy, stateless enemy.[1]

The radically new nature and scale of the terrorist threat helps to explain why the U.S. military response has departed from the manner in which the United States used force in the 1990s. Rather than an act of clear-cut aggression by a third world regime against a neighboring state thousands miles away from New York City and Washington, D.C., the world witnessed a massive, well-coordinated terrorist attack in the very heart of the Western world, the product of a secretive planning process that is extremely hard to confirm by indisputable evidence. In addition, the massive loss of life has given the United States the legitimacy to practice self-defense, as implied in UN Security Council Resolution 1368 of September 12, 2001.

It is not only the attack on the U.S. homeland that distinguishes the U.S. military operations of 2001 and thereafter from those conducted in 1991. Between them stand ten years of U.S. experience in the use of force in different regions of the world. In this sense, the U.S. military retaliation for September 11 offers a test of whether Washington has gleaned any relevant lessons from its post–Cold War experience. Perhaps the main lesson since 1991 is that security is indivisible and that international support, cooperation, and legitimacy are essential for any effective use of force by the United States. Yet throughout the 1990s, multilateralism in the use of force was the exception rather than the rule in U.S. policy, stimulating criticism from much of the rest of the world, especially from non-Western countries. Not surprisingly, much of that criticism came from the main successor state to the country's Cold War communist foe—Russia.

Why should post-Soviet Russia—a regional power focused on solving its own domestic (primarily social and economic) problems and confronted by local instability along its own periphery—be concerned about whether and when the United States chooses to use force unilaterally or multilaterally? Although retaining a nuclear potential second only to that of the United States, Russia can no longer afford politically to use force outside its own territory—whether unilaterally or even as part of a U.S.-led multilateral military coalition. So why should one be concerned with Russia's views on the matter?

In fact, a view from Russia is important for several reasons. First, Russia has been the most outspoken and persistent international critic of the U.S. use of force, especially since the mid-1990s. Moscow, certainly, has not always been alone in this undertaking. But as one U.S. diplomat said, referring to the case of Iraq, while "France and China are holding out as well, it's the Russians that are the problem."[2] Second, of Russia's residual power, the one that has counted the most since the end of the Cold War, and which underpins Moscow's claim to a continuing international role, is its military potential. In this context, it is not surprising that Russia has employed the few remaining international levers still at its disposal to make its views known in cases that involve the use of force, such as Iraq and Yugoslavia.[3] Third, since 1991 military force has been used or threatened mainly against anti-Western regimes, the so-called rogue states, with which Russia traditionally enjoyed close ties. Whether deliberately or unintentionally, a certain division of labor has arisen between the United States and Russia: frequently, Washington (or Brussels in Europe) has threatened military force while Moscow has touted prospects for peace. This arrangement has sometimes worked to mutual benefit, as in the case of the NATO-led war in

Kosovo, when Russian diplomatic intervention was required to end the quagmire for both NATO and Belgrade. Russia has certainly not been the only international actor to play the role of good cop. The United Nations, for instance, has done so on a global scale, and the Organization for Security and Cooperation in Europe (OSCE), the European Union, and neutral European states have done so in Europe and in other regions. But a combination of factors—including Russia's general reluctance to sanction the unconstrained use of force to settle international disputes, its traditional ties to many rogue states, its ability to talk both to the West and the latter's harshest opponents, a decades-long international experience, and its substantial representation in major international organizations—has given Moscow a unique opportunity to assume this mediating role while also tying it closer to the bad cop of the West.

Finally, in the post–Cold War years, no other country has undergone changes as deep and profound as Russia. Although this adaptation has been a painful process, it has arguably made Russia more favorably disposed than the United States to adjust to current international realities. As the sole remaining superpower, the United States has not had to change its behavior much and has proved slow to grasp the real security challenges of the twenty-first century, as demonstrated by the September 2001 events.

The Unilateral Use of Force Against Iraq

There is no doubt that the role of military force changed significantly with the end of the Cold War. It was not that force became less relevant in absolute terms. (Despite Russian hopes, for example, the 1999 war between NATO and Yugoslavia over Kosovo showed the continued importance of military instruments in world politics). What has changed, however, is the balance between military and nonmilitary instruments of power: the use of force has become merely one of many instruments in achieving strategic goals. As the case of Iraq demonstrates, it is now impossible to focus on the use of force per se without considering the wider context of policy instruments, including economic sanctions, international legal mechanisms, political and diplomatic levers, and so on. Another significant change is that in the post–Cold War world the unilateral use of force seems to have become an exception rather than the rule. Specifically, it has been used in most cases only by the United States—the only power that can fully *afford,* both politically and militarily, to conduct unilateral military actions outside its own territory. The mere fact that almost no other state can afford to take such actions has reduced the risk (suggested by some observers) that U.S. unilateralism may stimulate unilateral actions by other states.[4]

Retaining the capability to apply force unilaterally and demonstrating periodically the willingness to use it remains a cornerstone of the U.S. military strategy. For the United States, unilateralism in the use of force is first and foremost an essential element and a compelling demonstration of U.S. strategic independence and global leadership. Given U.S. military superiority and the significant technological gap that exists between the United States and even its closest Western allies, the U.S. political-military leadership often views unilateralism as a technical prerequisite for effective command and control of military action. More important, in a world more complex than the bipolarity of the Cold War, the political interests of countries tend to be diverse and fragmented, even within the Western community of nations. For the United States, even partial accommodation to these interests, which is essential for any multilateral cooperation, presents a number of serious political, military, and technical constraints in the use of force.

Throughout the first post–Cold War decade, the United States not only retained the capability to use force unilaterally but also resorted to unilateral military actions, particularly in the Middle East. The case of Iraq demonstrates most vividly the general trends in the unilateral use of force by the United States during the 1990s.

To begin with, unilateral military options of the 1990s remained strictly conventional and were bound to be limited in scope, intensity, and duration, as demonstrated by U.S. air strikes against Iraq. Unilateral military actions came mainly in the form of preventive and punitive actions, surgical air strikes, rescue efforts, and other limited operations that were mostly short-term (although they could be repeated regularly, as in the case of Iraq). In this regard, the four-night Operation Desert Fox (December 1998) was an exception rather than the rule; more typical were shorter and less intensive unilateral military actions, such as operations Northern Watch and Southern Watch over the no-fly zones in Iraq or the U.S. cruise missile strikes against Sudan and Afghanistan (August 1998).

In addition, the unilateral use of force by the United States was highly selective. While unilateral military actions were mainly conducted or threatened against semi-isolated backlash states or statelets (Iraq, North Korea, the Bosnian Serbs, etc.), even the designation of rogue-state status did not automatically imply that unilateral military action would be politically acceptable or forthcoming. The United States launched no strikes on Iran or Cuba during this period, for instance. Although the U.S. military strategy explicitly linked unilateral military actions to vital U.S. interests, use of the unilateral military option depended on a case-by-case analysis of the particular balance of threats, interests, and goals (military, economic, and political).[5]

As a rule, during the 1990s the threats alleged to be presented by states subject to unilateral attack by the United States were described in terms that were questionable at best and frequently abstract, such as Iraq's remaining weapons potential. The military goals also tended to be vague: A typical justification, made by President Bill Clinton to defend a cruise missile attack against Iraq in 1996, referred to the need to "increase America's ability to prevent future acts of violence and aggression."[6] Stated objectives, moreover, normally had little relation to the concrete justification for the air strikes. This was especially evident in the case of Southern Watch and Northern Watch, created to police the United States's self-proclaimed air exclusion zones in northern and southern Iraq. As part of this low-key but active military campaign against Iraq, focused almost exclusively on challenges to the no-fly zones from Iraqi planes and on antiaircraft batteries, U.S. missiles and bombs slowly degraded Saddam's 1970s-era antiaircraft capabilities.[7] Although the short-term military goal of methodically destroying Iraqi air defenses appeared definable and achievable, it did not seem to be conclusively linked to any larger political objective in Iraq. As John Hillen of the Center for Strategic and International Studies has put it, "Using the destruction of anti-aircraft batteries in Iraq to measure the success of our policy may be as irrelevant as using body counts to measure the success of American strategy in Vietnam."[8]

This does not mean, of course, that the United States did not have wider military interests in the region. One of these concerns was to maintain a significant military presence in the oil-rich Persian Gulf, and the most effective way to justify such a presence at current levels was to keep the situation around Iraq tense but under control. The U.S. Air Force also needed a place to train regularly in combatlike situations. On a more imaginative note, some observers have speculated about U.S. plans to establish a more or less permanent intelligence presence in Iraqi Kurdistan. But all this does not change the main conclusion about U.S. policy: Paradoxically, and contrary to the official U.S. position throughout the decade, it was the absence of an imminent military threat to the United States and of the actual necessity of a decisive military action that had in fact become one of the chief prerequisites for the unilateral use of force by the United States.

Let us carefully suggest that the United States was more inclined to use military force unilaterally in cases where U.S. economic interests were directly affected. For instance, if we examine economic aspects of U.S. unilateral attacks against Iraq, it is clear that Washington was ready to use all means, including military force, to prevent Baghdad from regaining full control of Iraq's oil revenues and from restoring Iraq's position as one of the leading oil exporters. At the same time, in a situation where even the possibility of military action in the Persian Gulf would affect the world oil markets, U.S. air strikes against Iraq have become a convenient noneconomic instrument to regulate oil prices.

On the one hand, U.S. air strikes, which would lead to short-term increases in oil prices, could, if necessary, be used in concert with other measures to relieve the world market of surplus oil. The first day of Operation Desert Fox, for instance, witnessed a sharp increase in oil prices, followed on the next day by the slump of prices to the precrisis level. Another increase in prices occurred in February–April 1999, when U.S. strikes seriously damaged an Iraqi export oil pipe, forcing Iraq to cut its oil exports in half. Other cases of the link between military action and oil-price fluctuations could be cited. In the world market for oil and petroleum products, the Iraqi factor has proven more important than, say, news about the increased oil reserves in the United States. Among other things, U.S. strikes against Iraq, conducted from U.S. bases in Saudi Arabia and Kuwait, have helped to keep relations between Iraq and its regional neighbors strained—which, in turn, has prevented the strengthening of the Organization of Petroleum Exporting Countries (OPEC). The anti-OPEC message of U.S. unilateral strikes against Iraq was demonstrated, for instance, by the synchronization of a new round of U.S. and British air strikes with visits to Baghdad of the presidents of two leading OPEC nations, Venezuela and Indonesia, in August 2000.

On the other hand, there were also objective and subjective economic reasons for keeping the duration and scale of unilateral U.S. attacks as limited as possible. Carefully measured U.S. air strikes, of more or less predictable intensity and duration, were partly counterbalanced by the UN sanctions and the UN Oil for Food quota system regulating Iraqi oil export and thus could not significantly alter world oil markets. According to assessments made by the Japanese Research Institute on Energy and Economy, limited air strikes against Iraq could not result in the stable increase of oil prices, something that could happen only in the case of an escalated and protracted conflict in the Persian Gulf involving Iran, Syria, and other states.[9] Given the relatively high level of oil prices by the end of the 1990s, the United States was unlikely to launch larger-scale military action against Iraq, which could lead to even higher prices and cause more serious damage to Iraq's oil infrastructure. U.S. intentions to undermine that infrastructure in order to cut state income from oil exported as part of Oil for Food should not be exaggerated. Operations with Iraqi oil, traded for two-thirds of average world prices, are very profitable: While publicly ostracizing Saddam's regime, the United States was one of the main importers of the Iraqi oil, with Russian firms serving as intermediaries for Mobil, Exxon, and Valero Energy. According to some assessments, the United States consumed 40 percent of the oil exported under the Oil for Food program. Since 1998, Iraq has been the fifth-largest exporter of crude oil to the United States.

Apart from economic motivations, the U.S. decisions on the use force against Iraq have largely been about politics—and primarily about preserving U.S. prestige, both domestically and internationally. Domestically, U.S. administrations used unilateral air strikes against Iraq as a flexible political instrument that could be tied to particular domestic events and to solve short-term political goals at home, even when such actions were ill-timed internationally. One might place in this category the Clinton administration's decision to strike Iraq on the eve of the House impeachment vote in December 1998, despite the start of Ramadan. Similarly, the February 2001 strikes against Iraq—the most intensive since 1998—were meant to demonstrate the resolve of the George W. Bush administration, at the time when the Arab-Israeli crisis was worsening. U.S. unilateral military actions also carried political symbolism internationally. The United States justified these strikes in ideological and moral terms, demonizing Saddam as a personification of the world evil, a suppressor of his own people, and a mastermind of covert plans to acquire, develop, and use weapons of mass destruction. The attacks were apparently intended to have a demonstrative effect for the UN and the rest of the world. The United States used the strikes as an instrument of political pressure almost every time the UN Security Council met to discuss the Iraqi problem, especially on the issue of sanctions. For example, the bombing raids were synchronized with the start of Security Council discussions on the possible lifting of sanctions against Iraq (December 1998) and the prospects for renewal of dialogue between the UN and Iraq (February 2001). The strikes were also meant to put regional powers, such as Russia, in their place, being carefully timed, for instance, to create the "appropriate" context for the Russian Foreign Minister Igor Ivanov's visit to Baghdad, or for U.S. Secretary of State Madeleine Albright's visit to Moscow at the time of the Cairo summit of the Arab League (January 1999).

Although they served short-term domestic political purposes, U.S. unilateral strikes were, to put it mildly, of limited effectiveness in advancing any longer-term U.S. foreign policy interests, let alone progress regarding Iraq. The limited strikes against Iraq have not helped to change the government in Baghdad or to secure the implementation of the will of the international community. Continued attacks only proved that the general U.S. policy toward Iraq reached deadlock and was governed by the logic that bombing is better than nothing. Moreover, U.S. unilateralism was often counterproductive: The United States, supported by Great Britain, insisted that only the credible threat and use of military force would secure Iraqi compliance with UN Security Council Resolutions; in fact, it only stimulated Baghdad's intransigence. The most intensive of the U.S. attacks, Operation Desert Fox, led to Iraq's refusal to abide by the conditions of its capitulation after the 1991 Persian Gulf War. As a result, the UN inspections regime, imperfect as it was, collapsed. It took an entire year to get a new UN resolution reestablishing a much-weakened inspection organization. As of this writing, there is still no reasonable prospect of reestablishing a vigorous inspection and monitoring regime in Iraq. By contrast, the attacks allowed Iraq to exploit its image as a victim of aggression rather than as an aggressor. It was no longer isolated internationally, especially in the Arab world, and used the oil lever and favorable oil prices to push its own political interests effectively.

This political deadlock largely resulted from a lack of international legitimacy for U.S. actions against Iraq. The illegal character of U.S. unilateral military actions has been made apparent in other parts of the world, such as the August 1998 strikes against sites in Afghanistan and Sudan, when the United States launched cruise missile attacks in retaliation for terrorist bombings of its embassies in Kenya and Tanzania, without consultations with the UN, other international organizations, or even U.S. allies. It was in the case of Iraq, however, that U.S. violations of international law became chronic.

The United States asserted that the U.S. aircraft monitoring the situation in two no-fly zones in northern and southern Iraq, which the United States had unilaterally set up after the Gulf War, were entitled to protect themselves from attack by destroying antiaircraft installations. However, neither the highly contentious right to anticipatory self-defense (protective retaliation), nor even a direct breach by Baghdad of the cease-fire resolution (No. 687 of 1991), could automatically justify unilateral attacks conducted against Iraq's military and occasionally civilian infrastructures. Although the UN Security Council distinguishes between the chapter VII enforcement resolutions and the authority to enforce them militarily, the United States and the United Kingdom have selectively appointed themselves the executors of the will of the international community. One cannot help contrasting Washington's enthusiasm to secure full and unconditional implementation of the Security Council resolutions on Iraq—which have in fact been effectively enforced to a large extent—with the U.S. defiance of numerous Council resolutions regarding, for instance, the Jewish settlements by Israel in the occupied Palestinian and Syrian territories.

Even as it assumed the prerogatives of the UN Security Council by unilaterally attacking Iraq, the United States used its diplomatic influence to block various UN political initiatives to lessen international tensions over Iraq, from Council resolutions to statements by the Secretary General that were to be approved by consensus. On the one hand, U.S. pressure helped marginalize the role of the UN Security Council in addressing the Iraqi crisis: for instance, during Operation Desert Fox in December 1998, the Council was not able to mount a single viable initiative to end the crisis. Afterward, the Council's role was largely limited to discussing the Oil for Food program. Humanitarian issues remained the only link between the UN and Baghdad. On the other hand, U.S. unilateralism definitively undermined the already weak consensus in the Security Council for maintaining sanctions against Iraq and reinforced already deep international divisions over how to deal with Baghdad. As a result, the aura of the U.S. victory in the Gulf War evaporated. The United States could no longer count on UN political support on the issue of Iraq, and the reactions even from NATO allies (with the usual exception of Britain) ranged from muted, qualified support to disquiet and concern. Even France, which initially supported the creation of the two no-fly zones over Iraq and once flew air strikes alongside U.S. and British warplanes, expressed incomprehension and discomfort over the raids. In this situation, if the United States chose to undertake military action, unilateralism was the only option at its disposal. It was clear from numerous crises related to Iraq that U.S. policy toward the Gulf could not be based on reliance on any European ally other than Britain, on other coalition partners from outside the Gulf, or on major Gulf states like Saudi Arabia unless there was a clear, unambiguous danger to a Gulf state. In contrast to the experience in Operation Desert Storm, no country except Kuwait was ready even to provide financial assistance during Desert Fox.

While the United States could rely on no states to support its unilateral military actions against Iraq, few governments were willing to object openly to U.S. air strikes given Baghdad's track record and semi-isolation. Of these governments, Moscow has been the most active, repeatedly disagreeing with the United States about the need to use force against Iraq. The peak of Russian criticism came in December 1998 following a string of U.S. and British air strikes officially aimed at liquidating Iraq's challenge of the two no-fly zones. Moscow condemned U.S. policy in an unusually harsh manner, marking the first time it had recalled its ambassadors from the United States and the United Kingdom since the Cold War.

Russia's persistent opposition to U.S. air strikes combined a set of general concerns about the effect of such unilateral military actions on the role and image of the UN Security Council with the reluctant recognition that Russia's own leverage at the UN was limited. Long before Kosovo, the case of Iraq had vividly demonstrated Moscow's inability to win Security Council approval for decisions unless Russia was supported by permanent Western members, particularly by the United States. Russia could still try to tie U.S. hands by blocking particular resolutions on Iraq and other issues, but only in the context of a serious disagreement among the Council's members. The right of veto at the UN Security Council, a privilege closely guarded by Russia, could be effective only as long as the United States and its Western allies needed a Council approval for a resolution. But the veto per se could not prevent the United States from taking unilateral military actions against Iraq or help moderate the sanctions regime against Baghdad. The experiences of 1998–1999 showed that Moscow could still block a UN Security Council decision—something that further discouraged the United States from taking this body seriously—but under no circumstance could it push its own initiative through the Council against U.S. opposition.

At the same time, it has to be acknowledged that Russian perceptions about the motivations of U.S. unilateralism were often based on threat assessments dating from the Cold War. Moscow often underestimated the burden on the United States of being the world's sole remaining superpower, and the increased responsibility for international security and stability that this implied, while perceiving Russia as the primary target of U.S. policies. Although much of this attitude could be attributed to Russia's painful transition process—from a global leader to Eurasian regional power—it was not completely ungrounded in current events. After all, Russia confronted the controversial process of NATO's inertial enlargement eastward. This enlargement proceeded despite its irrelevance to the real security threats confronting the United States and its Western allies, as has become clear in the light of the 1999 Kosovo war, the subsequent conflict in Macedonia, and especially the September 2001 terrorist attacks.

On a brighter side, the unilateral use of force by the United States throughout the 1990s gave Moscow an excellent pretext to criticize Washington harshly without damaging bilateral relations seriously—a task that has become particularly important in the rapidly deteriorating general context of U.S.-Russia relations in the late 1990s (with disagreements over Kosovo, Chechnya, and the U.S. plans to deploy nationwide ballistic missile defenses). Russian criticism of U.S. unilateralism in general, and the use of force in particular, although largely innocuous and toothless in practical terms, nevertheless brought Russia certain political and propaganda benefits. So even though U.S. unilateralism in Iraq and elsewhere violated international law and carried many negative international consequences, it also presented Moscow with an excellent opportunity to promote its own political agenda, to improve its international image, and (occasionally) even to seize international diplomatic initiative on Iraq—something that Russian Prime Minister Yevgeni Primakov did in February 1998.

Overall, the limited U.S. unilateral attacks against Iraq, which raised a number of Russian concerns about U.S. unilateralism and were shared by a wider group of states, complicated Moscow's relations with Washington much less than did the larger military action undertaken by the United States within the framework of NATO in 1999. Although Russia is fully aware of the fact that the United States retains the potential for selective unilateral military interventions in regions of key strategic importance, Moscow has been most disturbed by the way the United States has sought to reconcile its readiness to use such force with the participation in a multilateral military bloc—NATO.

Narrow Multilateralism in the Use of Force Against Yugoslavia

U.S. military strategy, stressing consistently that the United States must possess the capability to act unilaterally, strongly emphasizes coalition operations as essential to protecting and promoting U.S. interests. Such operations can be conducted either by an ad hoc coalition of the willing or in cooperation with regionally based security forces. U.S. involvement in the former Yugoslavia, particularly in the Kosovo crisis, demonstrates that NATO has become Washington's first instrument of choice when the United States wants to be engaged militarily, at least in Europe and adjacent areas.

There are many technical problems associated with multilateral military actions: Multilateralism slows down the use of force and, in this sense, is not a force multiplier; it also exacerbates the problem of optimal division of labor between participants. In addition, in cases that involve (or might involve) large-scale combat, multilateral coalition is not just supportive of, but often relies on, the exclusive military capabilities of the United States, which gives Washington one more argument for keeping the unilateral option open. Nevertheless, throughout the 1990s the single remaining global superpower increasingly needed multilateral support and participation in the use of force for at least two sets of reasons: economic (financial) and political (the issue of legitimacy).

Unilateral military actions are certainly expensive, even for the United States: by some counts, the seventy-hour Operation Desert Fox cost up to $500 million apart from the regular expenses of projecting power overseas. For the first eight years after 1991, the cost of the U.S. military actions against Iraq exceeded $50 billion. Given significant U.S. defense budget cuts throughout the 1990s, there were compelling financial justifications for taking a multilateral approach to the use of force. At the same time, suggestions that the United States lacked not only the will but also the resources to lead the post–Cold War world (stated most memorably in the 1993 Tarnoff Doctrine) proved to be an exaggeration.[10] The impact of financial considerations in choices between unilateral and multilateral options would depend on the intensity and scale of the operation, as the massive use of force requires greater financial resources than limited air strikes.

For the United States, the financial issue was less important than the capacity of multilateralism to help legitimize the use of force. In the early 1990s, after the peaceful end of the Cold War and the victory of the multilateral anti-Iraq Coalition in the Persian Gulf, many in the United States and worldwide were caught by political euphoria about the possibility of relying on major international organizations, and particularly the United Nations, to legitimize the use of force. Even within the U.S. political class, the concept of the new world order generated ideas about the promise and viability of multilateral involvement in local and regional conflicts in place of unilateral actions. In the summer of 1993, National Security Council staff member Morton Halperin argued that the United States should use force to defend its interests only with prior multilateral approval by the United Nations. He also called on the United States to relinquish unilateral military involvement in regional crises and to view the 1991 victory in the Gulf as primarily the result of successful coalition-building.[11] Initially, the Clinton administration was heavily influenced by the idea that the end of the Cold War would finally permit the United Nations to provide a workable system of global collective security. This was reflected in the administration's concept of assertive multilateralism, which suggested that the United States would work primarily through the UN to contain various problems around the globe, as well as initial U.S. support for Secretary-General Boutros Boutros-Ghali's call for a more ambitious UN agenda and the decision to elevate the country's UN ambassador to cabinet rank.[12]

However, as the contours of the post–Cold War world became clearer and as a number of UN-sponsored interventions in regional crises were apparently failing (e.g., in Bosnia), the general U.S. attitude toward the UN, as well as Washington's perception of the UN's capacity to use or authorize force, gradually changed from cooperation to distrust. This deterioration in relations, which included conflict over the need for UN reform and U.S. financial arrears, coupled with the erosion of once almost certain consensus at the UN Security Council as a result of strained or deteriorating relations with the Council's non-Western permanent members (Russia and China), limited the U.S. ability to use these international mechanisms to legitimize military actions. By the mid-1990s, the Clinton administration had begun to retreat from broad multilateralism, not only as a result of the changing international environment but also for reasons of domestic policy. Once the Republicans won control of Congress, the strategy of assertive multilateralism was no longer sustainable politically. The idea that U.S. military interventions would be conducted only if mandated by the UN and that U.S. forces would operate under the aegis of the UN, was gradually abandoned. Thus, the administration was once again confronted with the problem of how to win political legitimization of U.S. military actions, preferably outside of the UN framework, and it had to review its earlier policy on the use of force by making clear that the United States would henceforth take multilateral or unilateral action on a case-by-case basis.

This free-hands concept—formulated by Richard Haass, a top National Security Council official in the George H. W. Bush administration, among others—did not imply that there was no need for any kind of wider international legitimization of the U.S. use of force or that there was no need for effective burden-sharing. Rather, it put an emphasis on so-called narrow multilateralism, a more traditional approach of enlisting existing alliance relationships, such as NATO structures in Europe, while not excluding the option of building informal coalitions in the rest of the world, if necessary, and always keeping unilateral options open for special cases. This concept fully applied to the U.S. military involvement in Bosnia. Although the United States was capable of striking the Bosnian Serbs' positions unilaterally in 1994 and 1995, it tried to secure the maximum international cover for this operation.

In the case of Kosovo, by 1998 the Clinton administration had become convinced that only superior military force would alter Belgrade's behavior. But Washington ruled out unilateral military strikes against Yugoslavia as early as April of that year. If any military action were to be taken, it would have to be done in concert with NATO. Although the UN Security Council had voted in September 1998 to demand both a halt to the indiscriminate attacks against civilian populations in Kosovo and the withdrawal of Serb security forces engaged in attacks, not all of the UN Security Council members shared the view that military strikes were needed to punish Yugoslavia for noncompliance. Although any new resolution authorizing NATO to enforce compliance with these demands faced a near-certain Russian and a possible Chinese veto, the United States (in contrast to some of its European allies) insisted that the UN authorization would be welcome but not necessary for NATO to act "on its own in matters of European security." The threshold was crossed in October 1998, when NATO member states finally agreed to threaten military action against Yugoslavia to obtain compliance with the Security Council demands—yet without requesting prior Council approval. As a natural progression, in early 1999 Washington openly bypassed the Security Council altogether, dealing a major blow to the UN's credibility, anointing NATO instead as both the legitimator and implementer of military action. According to the Clinton administration, this major blow to the UN's credibility was simply recognition of the reality that the alternatives (either unilateral U.S. intervention or a UN Security Council–sanctioned intervention) would be difficult to sustain.

This raises a more general question of how closely the U.S. choice to operate through narrow NATO multilateralism was tied to the perceived need for some international legitimacy—and indeed raises a question about the very nature of international legitimacy in the post–Cold War world. For the United States, the UN Security Council and the UN Secretariat had both proved themselves incapable of using force competently, as demonstrated by the failed operation in Bosnia. Neither could the Council and Secretariat be counted on simply to rubber-stamp either unilateral or multilateral military actions conducted or led by the United States, especially in cases of intrastate conflicts. This reluctance, a veritable paralysis on the use of force, undermined the main, if not the only, resource that Washington needed from the UN: unquestionable international legitimacy. Facing possible obstruction at the UN, the United States started to search for a capable framework that might provide the desired multilateral cover for unleashing military force in the name of the international community, with fewer constraints on U.S. policy. In this context, NATO, the international body in which U.S. influence is greatest, appeared as the only multilateral force that could undertake military actions as well as bridge the gap between international legality and legitimacy.

All this became possible provided that with the end of East-West confrontation NATO's highly developed military capabilities were no longer inherently suspect as narrowly self-interested but rather were expected to operate in the service of broader global interests. At a time when there appeared to be no traditional, systemic threat to NATO countries or to European stability, NATO found itself considering military responses in crises—like Bosnia or Kosovo—that did not directly affect allied territory but could have implications for wider national or humanitarian interests of member-states. In the case of Kosovo, NATO allies decided to use military force even though the Article 5 collective defense commitment was not at stake. The United States in particular, as a global power with global interests, argued that NATO must deal with threats to the common interests of its members, wherever these threats arise, and prepare for the full spectrum of missions—ranging from peace support to regional collective defense operations within and beyond Europe.

Of all the issues relating to the threat and use of force by NATO that have divided the allies, none have been as contentious as the so-called mandate question: Under what authority or on which legal basis, other than a collective defense contingency, can NATO threaten or use military force? In theory, NATO may embark on non–Article 5 missions without the consent of governments involved only if its actions enjoy the authorization of the UN Security Council. The advocates of a legalistic perspective within NATO, championed by many European allies and especially France, believed that NATO should not act in this type of situation without an explicit mandate or authorization from the United Nations or the OSCE. The most critical reason for U.S. opposition to this legalistic perspective is that limiting NATO to actions approved by the Security Council would subject the alliance to a veto by two states (Russia and China) that do not share many of the values and interests that unite NATO members.

According to this logic, a mere consensus among serious countries— that is, countries with democratic governments—confers sufficient legitimacy for the use of force by a narrow multilateral group of states. In justifying its policy in Kosovo, the Clinton administration argued that if nineteen democracies deem the threat or use of force necessary to right a specific wrong, then that fact in and of itself provides sufficient justification and legitimacy for the use of force. Ironically, this thesis was shared by liberal internationalists as well as radical conservatives such as Jesse Helms, who argued that the United Nations had no power to grant or decline legitimacy to actions that were inherently legitimate, such as the NATO military campaign against Yugoslavia.[13]

This values-based approach alone explains why the U.S. model of legitimizing the use of force will never become universally accepted. Countries as different as Russia and China do not share some of the values of the Western world and have a different position on many international issues. In contrast to most Western states, for instance, both Russia and China are not happy with the precedent that NATO, or other organizations, or groupings of states have the right to intervene in the internal affairs of sovereign states. Depending on the circumstances, either Russia or both Russia and China would use their veto in the Security Council to prevent forceful NATO action in a situation similar to that in Kosovo. The United States and some of its Western allies simply cannot accept the reality that if a certain action is opposed by leading non-Western governments like Russia and China (sometimes joined by India), there are grounds for wondering whether the proposed action is politically biased and legally questionable on a global scale. The will of the so-called international community in this context becomes nothing more than a euphemism for the will of the Western community—a group of nations that might share some common values, and that might be the most advanced economically, but cannot pretend to pose as the world's sole voice.

Throughout the 1990s, much was said about the UN Security Council's inadequacy and particular inability to react promptly to the new challenges to international security and to authorize use of force. Yet this international body, however imperfect, remains by far the closest to representing the plethora of the world's views. The Security Council stands in stark contrast to suggested narrower multilateral alternatives, most of which represent either the Western community of nations (NATO) or the community of postindustrialized highly developed nations (the Group of Seven). It must be mentioned that neither Russia nor China believe that the post–World War II arrangements are fully adequate to current international realities. But the way out of the current impasse, these two countries believe, is through considering the ways of gradually and carefully reforming the main bodies of the United Nations, especially the Security Council, so that they are better suited to the post–Cold War environment, rather than through unilateral violations of international law, even if they are undertaken by a multilateral Western alliance. The process of de facto adaptation of the UN structures, including the Security Council, to the post–Cold War environment has already started. In order to make the UN-sanctioned use of force more effective, for example, a system is being created in which the Council authorizes military actions, which are then placed under the effective control of a state or a regional group of states.

Instead of searching for a compromise solution, however, the United States, in order to overcome the opposition to its Kosovo policy by two non-Western permanent members of the UN Security Council, turned to NATO, a security institution viewed at least by one of the Council's permanent members (Russia) as presenting a serious military threat to its own security. A typical something-has-to-be-done-now NATO counterargument was that the UN was not capable of effective crisis management and that NATO's war against Yugoslavia was illegal but justified because basic humanitarian requirements were violated in Kosovo. The humanitarian argument, however, does not sound very convincing, as it should stem from certain general humanitarian principles—such as political neutrality and proportionality of assistance—that were violated by NATO during the Kosovo emergency. One could also point out the selective nature of Western humanitarianism, which rarely transforms into military actions in more distant regions of the world that are less strategically or politically important for the West.

Was NATO's 1999 intervention in Yugoslavia unilateral or multilateral (i.e., collective)? There is no question that the use of force by a multilateral alliance can be as illegitimate as a unilateral military action. Although the UN Charter prohibition on intervention, even for humanitarian ends, is addressed to individual states, what is prohibited to a single state does not become permissible to several states acting together. As opposed to individual states or regional organizations such as NATO, the UN Security Council can authorize military action in response to threats to peace that fall short of an actual or imminent armed attack. Regardless of the U.S.-sponsored, de facto erosion of the UN Security Council's unique authority to sanction the use of force, de jure intervention by several states remains unilateral unless authorized by the Security Council. In this context, the NATO 1999 air campaign against Yugoslavia could be defined as a test for NATO's new strategic credo of unilateral multilateralism: Force was massively employed by multilateral military alliance outside its borders without the UN authorization, that is, unilaterally. The U.S. readiness to use force unilaterally, if necessary, coupled with U.S. preference for NATO in cases that require multilateral use of force, led the U.S. leadership to argue, essentially, that NATO had the right to use force whenever the interests of its members so required.

Although U.S. unilateral military actions undertaken throughout the 1990s certainly contributed to the weakening of the UN's authority to serve as a single clearinghouse for the use of force in the post–Cold War world, it was NATO's 1999 decision to launch a military campaign against Yugoslavia that fundamentally undermined that authority. This was facilitated by the UN Security Council's after-the-fact confirmation of the results of NATO intervention—an act that not only partly ratified NATO's unilateral action but also created an important precedent. From now on, in most controversial cases, the United States, confident that the Security Council will acquiesce in its decisions to intervene, no longer needs to seek advance authorization by the Council, which would be subject to veto. Rather, the United States can proceed with military action unilaterally or in the framework of NATO and challenge the Security Council afterward to terminate the action, secure in the knowledge that any such resolution can always be blocked by the United States, backed by its allies among the Council's permanent members.

Conclusion

The essence of U.S. unilateral interventionism in the post–Cold War period has been the ability to exercise surgical and demonstrative projection of military power. This policy has been fully consistent with a limited-objectives school of thought in the United States on the use of force. This school has advocated U.S. involvement in affairs of another state or international organization aimed at changing their behavior or character by using a variety of instruments—from information campaigns and economic sanctions to the use of military force.[14] The military substance of recent U.S. unilateral military actions, usually limited in scope and highly selective, has been secondary to their political and demonstrative effects.

Although typical unilateral military actions by the United States during the 1990s, such as repeated air strikes against Iraq, were clearly problematic from the perspective of international law and could have disastrous economic effects on the target country, Russia did not view these as either directly threatening militarily or as portending radical challenges to regional balances of forces. This helps to explain the measured nature of Moscow's reaction to the U.S. bombings of Iraq on February 16, 2001, despite the facts that they were not limited to the no-fly zones and also targeted sites near Baghdad, as well as Moscow's efforts to pressure the UN Security Council to ease the sanctions regime imposed on Baghdad rather than restart a useless argument over routine U.S. air strikes against Iraq.

For Russia, it was NATO's narrow multilateral unilateralism, exercised during the 1999 military campaign against Yugoslavia, that appeared to be a far more dangerous phenomenon than the limited military actions the United States had unilaterally undertaken throughout the 1990s. Russia's basic concerns about NATO's out-of-area military actions in the so-called Euro-Atlantic region were that these actions did not have to be limited in scope or intensity; were conducted by a regional political-military bloc that had its own long-term military and strategic agenda that did not take into account Russia's security concerns and interests in Europe; and created an illusion of international legitimacy despite the absolute lack of it.

The inadequate and illegal character of NATO multilateralism makes it all the more pressing to find an optimal form of a multilateral, UN-mandated action in the use of military force, with participation by—or preferably under the leadership of—the United States. The post–Cold War experience suggests that widespread international concerns about U.S. unilateralism and specific Russian concerns about NATO-type unilateral multilateralism can only be addressed when the United States conducts a military operation as part of an ad hoc multinational coalition of the willing in response to a clear threat to international security and in accordance with UN decisions. Although this form of multilateralism is the most restrictive politically, it entails far fewer costs and risks and, more important, seems to be the only one to promise a genuine resolution of the crises that might require the use of outside force. The paradox of the post–Cold War world has been that such cases, combining a clear and unambiguous threat to both general international security and vital U.S. security interests and amenable to this optimal form of multilateral cooperation, have been exceptional.

The twenty-first century, however, has immediately brought about new security challenges that seem to be far more critical and real for the United States than the risks posed by abstract post–Cold War threats of fragmentation and instability or by a repetition of the Cold War in the shape of a rising China or a militarily resurgent Russia. The massive, asymmetric, nonconventional attack against the United States on its own territory undertaken on September 11, 2001—as well as all potential future attacks of this kind—require an unprecedented military response. Although international relations theorists will certainly make their own conclusions about what the September 11 attacks mean for the entire world system, it is clear that this tragic chain of events marks a start of a new era for international security, perhaps even an end of the so-called post–Cold War period. No longer is the territory of the world's only superpower, as well as the rest of the Western world, immune from a massive asymmetric attacks against its territory and citizens—attacks that are far more serious and much greater in scale than a typical terrorist act of the 1990s.

In sharp contrast to the international reaction to numerous instances of the use of force by the United States throughout the 1990s, there has been little questioning of the legitimate right of the United States to respond militarily to attacks against its own citizens on its own territory; neither has the U.S. response drawn complaints about U.S. unilateralism even from frequent critics such as Russia or China. On the contrary, Russia, which views terrorism by Islamic extremists as a grave threat to its own security and to the security of its southern neighbors in the Commonwealth of Independent States and has a counterterrorist record of its own, has been supportive of harsh U.S. measures taken against those responsible for the attacks—provided that the culprits are identified correctly. This attitude proves once again that the main concern of the non-Western world in general and of Russia in particular has not been about U.S. unilateralism per se, which is to a certain extent a natural extension of the surplus of power the United States has enjoyed. More worrisome was the specific U.S. pattern of unilateralism in the use of force during the 1990s aimed at responding militarily to actions that did not present any direct military threat to the United States itself. Such a unilateralist approach made some observers even within the United States talk about the rogue superpower. The new international consensus is based on a recognition that any state has a right to defend itself and its people directly—whether it chooses to act unilaterally or multilaterally.

At the same time, the demonstrative effect of the September 11 attacks for anti-U.S. and anti-Western forces throughout the world could hardly be underestimated. Moreover, the attacks have demonstrated that U.S. post–Cold War policy on the use of force, described above, has in turn become an object of manipulation by forces hostile to the United States. It is a certainty of U.S. military retaliation, after all, that the perpetrators of the September 11 attacks undoubtedly counted on. The massive military retaliation launched by the United States against hard-to-verify targets in Muslim-dominated regions of the world may, in fact, have been the attackers' primary goal. Also, it has to be recognized that while the scale of the attacks and the number of victims was unprecedented, the choice of the United States as a target has surprised no one—whether observers attributed the choice of the United States as a target to its leading position in the civilized world or, perhaps less obviously, as one of the long-term costs of U.S. unilateralism.

In this context, any disproportionate and inaccurate U.S. military action against appointed culprit states, particularly one with the potential of seriously destabilizing states under attack and in adjacent regions, could have created more security problems than it was meant to solve by stimulating a backlash in the form of aggressive acts from forces hostile to the United States and by leading to the erosion of the wide international consensus currently in favor of the United States. So even though U.S. unilateralism is unlikely to be openly disputed, as the case for self-defense could be easily justified, the longer-term need to counter international terrorism more than ever requires multilateral solutions that are not to be limited to the use of military force.

The high levels of worldwide compassion for the U.S. people and international support for the U.S. military reaction to the September 11 attacks could not have lasted for long if the retaliation campaign had not been based on existing international law and explicitly sanctioned by the supreme international authority, which in contrast to other cases was not hard to acquire this time. Not surprisingly, when it comes to the framework for building a wide international coalition in support of the United States, it is the UN Security Council that is most often cited as the key institution to be called upon.[15] Apart from international legal obligations, this time a direct resort to the UN authority would make concrete practical sense for the United States, making it easier for many states, especially those in the Muslim world that fear the repercussions of adopting a pro-U.S. policy, to justify—domestically and internationally—their support even for the toughest U.S. actions. Yet the George W. Bush administration, though recognizing the need for a broad international support, has continued to downplay the roles of the UN in general and of the UN Security Council in particular. A possible explanation might be that the idea of assembling a broad and deep coalition, mandated by the UN Security Council, seemed to be working against the drive within the U.S. administration, already known for its unilateralist bent, for a broad and deep military response that would deal with states viewed by the United States as sponsors and agents of terrorism.[16]

Only time will tell whether this approach, formulated in the spirit of unilateralism and fully embodied in the newly emerged Bush Doctrine—"Either you are with us, or you are with the terrorists"—will survive unmodified. In a longer-term perspective, however, the world cannot afford to see its leader, the United States, become another Israel—a fortress state whose active and effective unilateral counterterrorist measures are largely irrelevant to the underlying problems that fuel terrorism in the Middle East and in other parts of the world.

Notes

1. Cited in Ricks, Kamran, and Moore, "US Speeds Preparation for Conflict," *Washington Post,* September 20, 2001.

2. A senior U.S. government official speaking on September 21, 1999 (see Iraq chronology, http://usinfo.state.gov/regional/nea/gulfsec/irqchr13.htm).

3. Other fields where Russia's position still counts include arms control and disarmament (primarily in the context of weapons of mass destruction) and oil and gas exports.

4. Israel's unilateral military strikes against Lebanon and against targets on the territory, controlled by the Palestinian Authority, constitute one of the exceptions.

5. As stated, for instance, in the 1997 *Quadrennial Defense Review:* "When the interests at stake are vital—that is, they are of broad, overriding importance to the survival, security, and vitality of the United States—we should do whatever it takes to defend them, including, when necessary, the unilateral use of military power."

6. CNN, "U.S. Launches 2nd Attack Against Iraq," September 3, 1996, www.CNN.com/WORLD/9606/03/iraq.wrap/.

7. Such as illumination of U.S. and British planes by an Iraqi radar or even the very presence of Iraqi installations that might be used to detect and target these planes.

8. "U.S. Policy Towards Iraq," Statement by Dr. John Hillen, Senior Fellow in Political-Military Studies, Center for Strategic and International Studies, before the Committee on Armed Services of the U.S. House of Representatives, March 10, 1999.

9. *Business Oil,* December 28, 1998.

10. Named after Peter Tarnoff, then undersecretary for political affairs at the U.S. Department of State.

11. Halperin, "Guaranteeing Democracy," p. 120.

12. See Albright, "Use of Force in Post–Cold War World."

13. Helms, "American Sovereignty and the UN," p. 31.

14. For more detail on the "limited objectives" school (as opposed to the "all or nothing" school) arguments, see, for instance, Aspin, "The Use and Usefulness of Military Forces in the Post–Cold War, Post-Soviet World," and "Aspin's Formula for U.S. Defense," p. 82 ff.

15. For the most consistent argument, see Halperin, "Dodging Security."

16. In security matters, this is most obviously manifested by the administration's determination to proceed with the U.S. missile defense program, despite objections from Western allies as well as from leading non-Western powers, such as Russia and China, and regardless of the potential impact on strategic security and stability, as well as arms control.

10

In Search of Absolute Security: U.S. Nuclear Policy

Qingguo Jia

Since the end of the Cold War, the U.S. government has been trying to improve its security through a proactive nuclear policy. In doing so, it has found the international community supportive of its efforts on some issues, such as the extension of the Nuclear Non-Proliferation Treaty (NPT), the conclusion of the Comprehensive Nuclear Test Ban Treaty (CTBT), and the strengthening of the Missile Technology Control Regime (MTCR). Meanwhile, it has also discovered that the international community is opposed to its efforts on some other issues, such as development and deployment of a nationwide missile defense, especially when it comes at the expense of the Anti-Ballistic Missile (ABM) Treaty. However, instead of deferring to the preference of the international community on the dissenting issues, the United States tends to pursue its own preferences, as it has on the question of missile defense. Such an approach demonstrates that the United States is willing to take a multilateral approach on security questions only when other states go along with its policy preferences. If they do not, it is more willing to go its own way. As the George W. Bush administration demonstrated in its recent decision to withdraw from the ABM Treaty, even the terrorist attacks against the United States on September 11, 2001, have not significantly changed this tendency in U.S. behavior, at least for the time being. During the post–Cold War era, the United States has been continuously pulled between multilateral and unilateral forces. At the turn of the twenty-first century, it appears that unilateralism is the prevalent tendency in U.S. nuclear policy.

Admittedly, the United States has only done what any other country would have done, that is, to look after its own interests. However, the United States is not just another country. It is the world's sole superpower, and whatever it does is likely to have a tremendous impact on world affairs. In this context, single-minded efforts to seek absolute security on the part of the United States serve only to alienate U.S. allies and make other countries potential adversaries. Such an approach is unlikely to make the United

States more secure, precisely because it promises to make the rest of the world less secure. If the United States wishes to maintain its leadership as well as to promote its interests in the world, it must help construct a set of effective institutional security arrangements that will enhance the security of the world as well as that of the United States.

Changes in U.S. Nuclear Policy
Since the End of the Cold War

Since the end of the Cold War, U.S. nuclear policy has experienced some changes as well as continuities. Although the United States continues to maintain superiority in nuclear weapons as a cornerstone of its security strategy, it has made some important changes to its nuclear policy over time. To begin with, it has changed its nuclear weapon targeting policy. During the Cold War, the United States targeted its nuclear weapons at the Soviet Union and Eastern European countries. Since the end of the bipolar conflict, it has shifted its nuclear targets from the former Soviet bloc countries to other states and expanded the scope and number of countries that are potential nuclear targets. In a 1992 report by the U.S. Strategic Air Command for the Department of Defense, the proposed list of potential nuclear targets included not only some countries of the former Soviet Union but also some developing countries that possessed or might possess nuclear weapons, such as Libya, Pakistan, India, Iran, Syria, and China. Bill Clinton's administration approved the proposed list. Although the United States may not be targeting countries such as Russia and China today, it can easily do so in a matter of minutes should it feel necessary.[1]

Second, since the early 1990s the United States has redoubled its efforts to attain overwhelming military superiority in any conceivable war. In his message preceding the *Report of the Quadrennial Defense Review* in May 1997, U.S. Secretary of Defense William S. Cohen wrote: "Joint Vision 2010 describes four new operational concepts. Together, they promise significant advantages in any operation or environment, something we call 'full spectrum dominance.'" He continued: "New operational concepts and organizational arrangements will enable our joint forces to achieve new levels of effectiveness across the range of conflict scenarios. We want our men and women to be the masters of any situation. In combat, we do not want a fair fight—we want capabilities that will give us a decisive advantage." Conceivably, what Secretary Cohen refers to as "full spectrum dominance" might logically include dominance in nuclear capabilities, and the "decisive advantage" would also imply a decisive advantage in nuclear capabilities.

Third, the United States not only strives for absolute superiority in nuclear weapons but also aspires to absolute security in missile defense. Following the end of the Cold War, the United States gradually gave up Ronald

Reagan's ambitious and unattainable Strategic Defense Initiative. However, instead of dropping the idea of Fortress America, during the administration of George Bush the elder it began to develop ballistic missile defense (BMD) systems. Since that time, the U.S. government has devoted increasing resources to the development of nationwide missile defense and theater missile defense (TMD) systems. On January 20, 1999, Defense Secretary Cohen announced that the United States would step up development of the BMD programs, and for this purpose he lodged a formal request for additional appropriations of $6.6 billion from Congress. The secretary's plan envisioned that the United States would spend a total of $10.5 billion on this program in the following six years. And that is on top of the $4 billion that President Clinton had requested for the same program in the previous year. In March 1999, the U.S. Congress passed legislation to the effect that the United States would promptly deploy the system if the proposed tests were successful.[2]

Fourth, in its search of absolute security, the U.S. government has demonstrated that it is ready to ignore international treaties as well as international opposition in the event that it fails to obtain agreement from concerned parties to revise these conventions in the direction that the United States desires. That is the way Washington has dealt with the ABM Treaty, concluded between the Soviet Union and the United States in 1972. The treaty has been widely regarded by the international community as a force for international strategic stability. It clearly forbids BMD programs such as National Missile Defense (or NMD, the moniker used by the Clinton administration and since dropped in favor of the more generic nationwide missile defense, or simply missile defense). Accordingly, the United States demanded that Russia, the successor to the Soviet Union, agree to revise the ABM Treaty. Under U.S. pressures, Russia agreed in 1997 to revise the treaty in a way that would allow the United States to develop a limited version of NMD.[3] However, as time has passed, the United States became increasingly dissatisfied with the revised treaty, which it sees as an obstacle to building an expanded version of BMD. Consequently, in 2001 the administration of George W. Bush demanded that Russia agree to revise the ABM Treaty again. When Russia refused, the United States threatened that it would abrogate the treaty.[4] On December 12, 2001, the Bush administration did so, formally announcing that the United States would unilaterally withdraw from the ABM Treaty.[5]

Finally, since the end of the Cold War the United States has redoubled its efforts to promote international regimes for nonproliferation, for the control of missile technology, and for a global ban on nuclear tests. For these purposes, it has tried to secure compliance from the Russian government by providing aid and technical assistance to ensure that Russian nuclear and missile technologies stay at home. It has also tried to get the Chinese government to join the renewed NPT, the CTBT, and the MTCR through a combination of inducements and pressures. Similarly, it imposed various sanctions against India and Pakistan in the wake of their respective tests of nuclear weapons in 1998. It even went out of its way to trade two light water nuclear power plants for the North Korean government's commitment not to develop its own nuclear programs.[6] Finally, it has repeatedly used force in Iraq to destroy what it believes to be the latter's nuclear, biological, and chemical weapons facilities. Through these and other measures, the United States has tried to prevent, or at least to slow down, the pace of global proliferation of nuclear and missile technologies.

Dynamics for Change

The unilateralist tendency of post–Cold War U.S. nuclear policy is primarily a product of the interaction among the following factors: (1) the role of the United States as the sole superpower; (2) perceived international challenges to U.S. security; and (3) U.S. domestic political considerations.

The U.S. as the Sole Superpower

The collapse of the Soviet Union in the early 1990s left the United States as the only superpower in the world. As such, it has overwhelming political, economic, and military capabilities that no other country in the world can come close to matching. Moreover, the U.S. economy experienced an unprecedented period of growth in the 1990s, further consolidating its superpower status. Over time the United States acquired new and qualitatively far more advanced military technologies, as demonstrated during the Gulf War and the Kosovo crisis. While sustained economic growth allowed the United States to keep up its high—and, in the eyes of many other countries, lavish and wasteful—defense spending, the revolution in military technologies has opened the possibilities of guaranteed U.S. victory in international war with minimal or even no loss of U.S. lives. Consequently, the United States finds itself more capable of meeting its traditional security needs than at any time in its history.[7]

Against this background, at least to some Americans, U.S. allies are no longer indispensable for national security, in contrast to the old days of the Cold War. In fact, in an age when the United States has abundant resources, and when the primary sources of threat to the United States come from the so-called rogue states and terrorists, the role of the allies has appeared increasingly irrelevant. Unlike during the Cold War, when the Soviet threat appeared to be omnipresent and when U.S. resources often seemed overstretched, the United States can now afford to defend itself alone. In addition, Europe and Japan have suffered from slow economic growth or stagnation and are less willing to share responsibilities for international security responsibilities. Furthermore, there is little the United States can expect from the Europeans or the Japanese to prevent North Korea from firing a missile at the United States or to stop a terrorist group from placing a bomb somewhere in the United States. Finally, the United States has been frustrated with the demonstrated inability of its allies even to help themselves. In the eyes of many Americans, Japan is crippled by its pacific constitution (ironically a handiwork of an American, General Douglas MacArthur, at the end of World War II),[8] and Europe is paralyzed because of its inaction-driven policymaking process and its lack of unity and courage—as shown during the Balkan crises in the 1990s.[9]

Just as the United States can (and at times must) do without its allies in defense matters, it also finds less reason to depend on other countries for its security. During the Cold War, when the United States attempted to contain the Soviet Union, it sought to rally support from a large number of the neutral countries to enhance the strength of the Western camp. This resulted in sizable U.S. foreign aid programs to third world countries. Following the disintegration of the Sino-Soviet alliance in the late 1960s, moreover, the United States sought a rapprochement with China in the early 1970s and made much effort to cultivate friendly relations with China afterward. It even tried to reach a modus vivendi with the Soviet Union to avert a nuclear war. This latter effort eventually gave rise to a number of security arrangements, including the ABM Treaty, between the two countries.

At the beginning of the twenty-first century, however, Americans are less inclined to see cooperation from other countries as necessary for U.S. national security. Now that the United States enjoys vast advantages in military capabilities, including that in weapons of mass destruction (WMD), it finds fewer and fewer incentives to accommodate these countries' concerns and interests. In fact, increasingly one finds the United States determined to ignore opposition from such countries, as well as from its allies, in U.S. foreign policy, including efforts to push for ballistic missile defense systems.

In international relations, military security cooperation serves two purposes for any given country. One is to make up for a deficiency in its military capabilities; the other is to reduce the cost of maintaining sufficient security. Both objectives require a state to make use of outside resources through military alliance and to offer concessions to allies to secure their cooperation. As the only superpower in the world, with a long period of rapid expansion in the economy and no serious global rivals, the United States has sufficient military capabilities to deal with any kind of threat and can afford to bear the cost of maintaining such capabilities alone. Accordingly, as far as the United States is concerned, international security cooperation is no longer a question of necessity but one of desirability.

It is true that the United States still endeavors to maintain its Cold War military alliances and at times even talks about strengthening those alliances. It is true that the United States still provides aid to some developing countries. It is also true that the United States still wants to engage the countries that it classifies as potential adversaries. However, the United States does this out of considerations other than necessity. In other words, it has been doing these things because it chooses to rather than because it has to. Support for U.S. policy from allies and other countries is appreciated. Cooperation from potential adversaries is also welcome. However, such support or cooperation is no longer allowed to dictate or even influence U.S. policies. Today the United States believes that it can afford to do what it believes to be in its best interests—regardless of what other countries may feel or how they may react.

Perceived New Security Challenges

If its sole superpower status makes it unnecessary for the United States to prioritize international security cooperation, its perception of new security challenges has enhanced its conviction that it should do what it needs to do to respond to these threats. In general, since the end of the Cold War U.S. assessments of international security challenges have changed fundamentally. When the Soviet Union was the most important threat, the United States adopted a whole range of political, economic, and military measures to cope with it. Among other things, it sought to enhance its military alliance with its allies, developed strategic cooperation with China, and reached an understanding with the Soviet Union on ways to prevent confrontation from escalating into a full-scale nuclear war. In so doing, it tried to show respect for its allies, showed significant tolerance for differences with other major states (notably China), and reluctantly accepted the Soviet capability to destroy the United States in exchange for Moscow's cooperation in the management of the nuclear threat—as in the ABM Treaty. Despite occasional outbursts of domestic isolationist or unilateralist sentiments in the United States, the U.S. government largely adhered to this approach toward international security.[10]

With the end of the Cold War, as pointed out, the Soviet threat basically disappeared, at least in its previous form.[11] However, to an increasing number of U.S. foreign policy makers and shapers, the dissolution of the Soviet Union has not resulted in greater security for the United States. Instead, it confronts different, and perhaps more threatening, security challenges, particularly from so-called rogue and transitional states.

In his announcement that his administration would deploy missile defense, President Bush claimed, "Unlike the Cold War, today's most urgent threat stems not from thousands of ballistic missiles in the Soviet hands, but from a small number of missiles in the hands of these states—states for whom terror and blackmail are a way of life."[12] In a similar vein, former U.S. Secretary of Defense William Cohen takes the view that international terrorism has replaced the Soviet Union as the target of U.S. global strategy.[13]

To the U.S. government, rogue states are those states that are recalcitrant and illegitimate. They attack the basic values of Western democracy from the outside. They cooperate with sponsors of terrorism and adopt non-traditional means of terror. Their behavior negatively affects the interests of the United States and those of the international community at large. Unlike normal states, they do not conform to international norms and pay no attention to normal means of persuasion.[14] They include such countries as North Korea, Iran, Iraq, Libya, Sudan, Cuba, and Serbia.[15]

And despite the backwardness of rogue states, the U.S. government also finds that the rogues' life expectancy is longer than one might expect. Moreover, their influence grows as the negative impact of globalization increasingly affects international society. More alarming, the number of rogue states is predicted to grow, posing a greater threat to other countries, especially the United States. Although rogue states may have diverse ideologies and goals, their common objective to change the status quo, with force if necessary, binds them together. Even when they do not directly threaten the United States, they pose threats to neighboring countries, many of which are U.S. friends and allies or control resources that Western societies need.[16]

The threat posed by rogue states will become even more serious to the degree that they can acquire WMD. They can use these weapons to deter international intervention, even when they use force against their neighboring states. Without such unconventional weapons, they would probably pose little direct threat to U.S. military forces given the unsurpassable U.S. lead in nuclear and conventional capabilities. However, rogue states can pose an asymmetric threat to the United States by using indirect but effective means to challenge U.S. military capability. These include striking at soft targets such as U.S. civilians and civilian installations. Such a strategy may prevent the United States from employing its troops under some circumstances—or at least from doing so effectively.[17]

The U.S. government also believes that the threat posed by rogue states has been further enhanced by the acceleration of proliferation of WMD in the world. According to a U.S. study by the National Defense University, as the cost of making WMD lowers, it has become easier for states and sub-state organizations to acquire such weapons. Moreover, international market mechanisms have made it increasingly difficult to trace and prevent proliferation of WMD and their delivery systems. Consequently, more and more countries have acquired WMD. One study suggests that at least twenty-four states already possess or have acquired the capacity to produce such weapons. Although international nonproliferation efforts have slowed WMD proliferation, it nevertheless continues.[18]

In addition to the immediate security challenges to national security posed by rogue states and terrorist groups, the United States perceives security challenges emanating from the so-called transitional states, including India, Russia, and, especially in the longer term, China. According to the above-cited National Defense University study, these three countries are not rogue states, but they nevertheless pose serious security challenges to the United States. India and Pakistan, for example, are locked in a nuclear arms race that has been changing the regional security contours of South Asia. China and Russia, meanwhile, have been suppliers of advanced missile and nuclear weapon parts and technologies to Pakistan and Iran.

Moreover, China, Russia, and India are all going through serious and fundamental political and economic transformations. As a result of these transformations, for example, the Russian government's control of its society has been weakened and its defense industry has become increasingly corrupt. This in turn has contributed to proliferation of WMD. Internal political weaknesses in Russia, India, and China, coupled with possible political breakdowns in the event of economic and political failures, also pose serious threats to the security of other countries.[19] This situation is all the more threatening to U.S. security because all three countries have nuclear weapons and either possess or will possess long-range missiles capable of delivering WMD against the United States.

Finally, an increasing number of U.S. policymakers believe that the United States must meet the challenge posed by rising powers. China poses a serious security threat in this regard, because it not only has the potential to break down politically but also may manage to wade through its transition and emerge as a superpower comparable to the United States itself. These U.S. observers note that since the late 1970s the Chinese economy has been expanding at an astonishing speed. As a result of this expansion, China is already a strong regional power with some global influence. If the current development trend is sustained, China's economy will reach the size of Japan's and then that of the United States in the not-too-distant future, and China's power and influence will grow in proportion.

According to realist theories of international relations, the interests of the established powers and those of the rising ones inevitably collide, and conflicts between them are unavoidable. The well-known American realist John Mearsheimer writes: "If China's economy continues growing at a robust pace," this "would eventually enable it to become a potential regional hegemon." "Like all previous potential hegemons," he continues, "China would be strongly inclined to translate its potential influence into reality, and all of its rivals, including the United States, would encircle it to try to keep it from expanding."[20] The sentiment also finds expression in the U.S. Defense Department's newly released *Quadrennial Defense Review Report,* which states: "Although the United States will not face a peer competitor in the near future, the potential exists for regional powers to develop sufficient capabilities to threaten stability in regions critical to U.S. interests."[21]

The U.S. government has decided that it must seek new ways to deal with these and other security challenges. Among other things, the United States has determined to step up its efforts to strengthen the nonproliferation regimes and, at the same time, to construct a shield that can effectively foil any attempts to use WMD against the United States or blackmail it in any way.

As the U.S. government becomes increasingly concerned with the new security threats, it has come to the belief that with the revolution in military technologies it is possible for the United States not only to win international wars with increasing certainty but also to shield itself from potential ballistic missile attacks. In the words of Lieutenant General Ronald Kadish, director of the Ballistic Missile Defense Organization,

> Intercepting a ballistic missile in space is a tough technical and management challenge—tough science and tough engineering—and has been ever since ballistic missiles were invented. But it is not impossible. We are now on the threshold of acquiring and deploying missile defenses, not just conducting research. We are, in fact, crossing over from rhetoric to reality, from scientific theory to engineering fact to deployed systems.[22]

The U.S. concern with new security threats, coupled with this faith in the feasibility of the missile defense, underlines the George W. Bush administration's determination to push for such a system. In a speech on the administration's decision to deploy missile defense, President Bush said that times had changed and that old security arrangements had become obsolete: "No treaty that prevents us from addressing today's threats, that prohibits us from pursuing promising technology to defend ourselves, our friends and our allies is in our interests or the interests of world peace." And this includes especially the 1972 ABM Treaty signed with the Soviet Union. "This treaty does not recognize the present or point us to the future. It enshrines the past," Bush said. The president advocated a "clear and clean break from the past" on this issue.[23]

Perceiving that the United States was pushing for defense programs, many countries, including U.S. allies, have been deeply concerned. They believe that the ABM Treaty, however flawed it may be, has served the world well by maintaining international strategic stability. Accordingly, it is dangerous to throw it away. They have been worried that U.S. efforts to develop missile defense programs, especially at the expense of the ABM Treaty, would start a new international arms race and thus undermine global strategic stability. They thus tried hard to dissuade the Bush administration from continuing with such programs. However, the administration believes that the new security threats are serious enough that it has no choice but to proceed with the missile defense programs, with or without international support.

U.S. Politics

If the sole superpower status and security perceptions of the United States provide the U.S. government with the necessary rationale for the adoption of a more unilateralist approach to foreign policy, U.S. domestic politics has further encouraged it to do so. The widespread perception of a U.S. victory in the Cold War has deepened the U.S. conviction in the superiority of liberal democracy and the free market and encouraged a U.S. determination to spread this gospel to those parts of the world that do not yet embrace this political and economic system. Perceiving a valuable opportunity to advance their careers, many U.S. politicians have raised their voices in urging the U.S. government to take tougher measures against those countries that are reluctant or refuse to adopt liberal democratic practices for a variety of reasons. These politicians argue that the United States has a moral obligation to take global leadership on this issue. Allies, likewise, have a moral obligation to follow the U.S. lead. If they do not, the United States should not let their petty considerations stand in the way. This pattern emerges clearly in U.S. efforts to push for resolutions condemning China's human rights record at the annual UN Human Rights Commission meetings in Geneva. During the early 1990s, the United States persuaded other Western countries to introduce such a resolution. Earlier last year, failing to secure their support, the United States introduced such a resolution alone.

The ideological impulse of U.S. society during the post–Cold War era has led the United States to push for freedom and democracy as part of its foreign affairs agenda. Such efforts have in turn generated strong reactions from various states. For example, Malaysia and Singapore have advocated an alternative to Western liberalism based on Asian values. Russia and China, similarly, have expressed their opposition to international intervention in their domestic affairs. On the human rights question, various states voted the United States out of the UN Human Rights Commission in Geneva in May 2001. Even Western allies openly differ with the heavy-handed U.S. approach in advancing their shared values. These and other reactions have in turn generated frustration among some in the U.S. public and led them to intensify pressure on their government to take a harder and, if necessary, unilateralist line on this issue.

Ironically, this U.S. ideological bent has been accompanied by a decreased U.S. willingness to spare resources to deal with international problems. On the question of foreign aid, for example, Americans have suffered what some call "aid fatigue." As one U.S. politician writes, "If one were to conduct a national opinion survey to discover which federal program a stressed-out Middle America most wanted to abolish, the runaway winner would be: foreign aid."[24] In a 1999 editorial on this issue, the *New York Times* wrote,

> Foreign aid is not among Washington's most popular causes. But it happens to be one of the more effective investments in long-term global security that America can make. Yet Congress now proposes to cut some $2 billion from President Clinton's already modest $14.6 billion foreign aid

request for next year, much of it from crucial crisis prevention programs. When the foreign aid bill goes to a House-Senate conference committee next month, the Republican Congressional leadership should work to reverse these shortsighted cuts. What cannot be restored then should be included in a supplemental foreign aid bill later this fall.[25]

Whereas the U.S. Congress is poised to reduce its appropriations for foreign aid, it has taken an opposite position on defense spending. In fact, in recent years Congress has gone out of its way to pressure administrations, whether Republican or Democratic, to spend more on defense. And this has been going on for a few years. In 1998, with the U.S. budget in surplus, Congress began to call for more military spending:

With the end of the fiscal year . . . fast approaching, members of Congress are anxious to return to their districts for some last minute election year campaigning. But they still have not passed most funding measures for Fiscal Year 1999. . . , including the Pentagon's budget, which many members—amid increasingly vocal concerns about the readiness of U.S. combat forces, the need to find $1.9 billion to fund the continued U.S. presence in Bosnia, and a desire on the part of Congress to find funds to address the government's "Year 2000" computer problem—are seeking to increase.[26]

Two years later, one heard a similar story:

As members of the House and Senate Budget Committees begin their work on the annual budget resolution, congressional "hawks" are already putting pressure on their colleagues to boost funding for the Pentagon. The budget resolution sets the annual spending levels for the annual congressional funding bills, including the "topline" for the military.[27]

The congressional approach appears to reflect three primary concerns. One is related to parochial, selfish political interests. Put simply, congressmen want to spend money on voters, especially those in their own districts, in the form of defense spending, rather than on foreign strangers in the form of foreign aid. Local expenditures are more likely than foreign aid to bring them political reward in future elections. Another concern is more fundamental: Americans are frustrated with efforts to promote international security with more refined means such as aid and diplomacy, as opposed to the use or threat of more coercive means like sanctions or military power. Many appear to consider the outside world so corrupt and beyond redemption that it is not amenable to refined approaches like aid and diplomacy. Accordingly, one hears frequent condemnations of U.S. aid programs and diplomatic endeavors. In reaction, successive administrations since the end of the Cold War have found themselves highly defensive when they came to request appropriation for aid and diplomacy.

The third concern relates to the way international threats have been depicted in U.S. politics since the Cold War ended. In the eyes of any non-American, it is obvious that the United States is much more secure since the downfall of the Soviet Union, which made it the only superpower in the world, much stronger in almost every way than any other major state. Americans, however, do not appear to share this perception. Instead, one has heard many clamoring about successive international threats of one sort or another. First, there were sensational speculations about the possibility of Russians losing control of their nuclear weapons. Then there was talk of the chilling scenario that terrorists or rogue states might possess WMD. After that, some loudly predicted a coming conflict with China.[28] In view of such threats, the U.S. public should not let down its guard and blindly enjoy the peace dividend but rather keep alert and, moreover, prepare well in advance to confront such ominous security challenges. And the best way to do this is to develop various new defense mechanisms, especially ballistic defense systems, in addition to the vastly superior offensive weapons the United States already has.

These tendencies of U.S. domestic politics—a push to be proactive in promoting human rights and democracy, less interested in aid and diplomacy, and more generous with defense spending—have contributed to the development of a more unilateralist U.S. approach to world affairs. In this context, politically speaking, a nuclear policy that aims at absolute security of the United States is both correct and rewarding for the incumbent administration.

Where To?

The previous analysis has argued that the status of the United States as the sole superpower, the nature of U.S. threat perception, and domestic political preferences within the United States have been responsible for a unilateralist tendency in U.S. foreign policy in general and in nuclear policy in particular. If this finding is accurate, future U.S. nuclear policy is likely to reflect the evolution of these factors. A preliminary analysis has resulted in a mixed picture, with both continuities and changes. On the side of continuities, given the vast gap in power between itself and other countries, the United States is likely to remain the sole superpower for the foreseeable future. It is likely to be capable of defending itself without the help of its allies—let alone other countries—for some time to come. The United States is also likely to continue to attach greater importance to the new security threats from rogue states and transitional states and to take necessary security measures irrespective of the views of the international community. And finally, U.S. domestic politics is also likely to continue to favor the unilateralist approach, as it has done throughout its history, except during certain crisis periods—such as the latter part of the two world wars and the Cold War.

Other factors might encourage change, rather than stasis, in U.S. policy. First, after many years of strong economic growth, the U.S. economy went into a recession. Although many remained confident that it would recover, it could last longer than expected, and it is unlikely that the U.S. economy will regain the high level of sustained growth it enjoyed during the better part of the 1990s. This means that the United States may have to spend more on welfare and other domestic needs and less on military defense—especially for such high price tag projects like missile defense. Following the terrorist attacks against the United States on September 11, 2001, the U.S. government has devoted an increasing amount of resources to homeland security. This is likely to continue given the persistence of terrorist threats. This also implies fewer resources for traditional military security in the days to come.

Moreover, after September 11 the threat perception of the U.S. public has also undergone some subtle changes. Previously, as the United States talked about international terrorism and rogue states, it increasingly focused its attention on coping with the potential threat from the so-called rising states, especially China. Now it finds that threats from the so-called failing states and the international terrorism associated with them deserve more attention. Given the enormous power gap between rising states and the United States, it is inconceivable how such states can pose a serious security threat to the United States.

Rogue states and international terrorist groups, however, present true threats to the United States. Although they may be weak in terms of power, they do not have much to lose and may not even share the interests-maximizing mentality of an average state. And as the September 11 attacks demonstrated, rogue states have the potential to cause great harm to life and the American way of life.

Finally, since September 11 U.S. domestic political preferences have also been undergoing some changes. Although still favoring strong military defense, more and more citizens have come to realize that to cope effectively with the threat of international terrorism the United States cannot afford to rely simply on traditional military defense measures. This is especially true with missile defense. Although they accept that missile defense systems may help increase U.S. security, they also recognize the limits of its utility. Accordingly, one hears important U.S. politicians openly differing from the Bush administration on the question of missile defense. They argue that the United States cannot afford to spend so much on a program that deals only with the least likely form of terrorist threat.

Since September 11, the United States has made many efforts to build an international coalition against terrorism. Among other things, it has conducted extensive consultation with its allies, dropped sanctions against

India and Pakistan imposed after they tested their respective nuclear devices, and tried to improve relations with China. On top of all this, President Bush went to Shanghai to attend the Asia-Pacific Economic Cooperation Summit shortly after September 11, at a time when the United States was consumed with fear about recent anthrax outbreaks. Many of these efforts would have invoked strong domestic criticisms had they happened before the September 11 attacks. Instead, the administration's critics have remained largely silent.

These and other changes have some subtle but broad implications for the unilateralist tendency in U.S. nuclear policy. To begin with, given a sluggish economy the United States may have to reconcile a more modest defense budget and may see more reason to make use of external resources (e.g., cooperation from its allies) to enhance security. Second, after September 11, given that the most serious threat came from the failing states and terrorism associated with them, the United States found it both desirable and necessary to build an international antiterrorism coalition. This is because although the United States is prepared to deal with rising states by itself, it is not able to respond alone against faceless and often stateless terrorism. Finally, as domestic political preferences shift against ambitious and expensive missile defense programs, the U.S. government may also need to rely more than before on international resources to enhance U.S. security. All this appears to favor a more multilateral U.S. approach to security. True, the George W. Bush administration has announced the decision to abrogate the ABM Treaty. However, with fewer resources, an altered threat perception, and a changed domestic mood, it may have to adopt a different approach toward nuclear security, one that gives more attention to multilateral cooperation than it did previously.

Conclusion

The world at the beginning of the twenty-first century is much different compared to a century ago. Never before has the world been as integrated as it is now, and never before have the interests of nation-states been so interdependent, both in terms of welfare and in terms of security. Confronted with an increasing number of international problems, nation-states can either try to deal with them individually or they can work together. They took the former approach at the beginning of the twentieth century, and they ended up with economic disasters and two world wars. To get a different outcome today, it is crucial for them to take the latter. For international peace and prosperity, there is no alternative to international cooperation.

As the world's sole superpower, the United States has a unique role to play in shaping national choices and, for that matter, world history. It can lead the world to prosperity and security through international cooperation.

It can also mislead the world with a beggar-thy-neighbor approach toward international affairs. Because no country has as extensive interests throughout the world, no country benefits from international cooperation more than the United States. It is thus in the best interests of the United States to assume leadership in international cooperation.

In the area of nuclear policy, the United States can get by with lowering its posture and treating other countries as equal and respectful partners united in the common cause of global peace and stability. In international relations, trust builds up common ground and facilitates cooperation, whereas mistrust undermines them both. The United States must work with the world's major states to enhance the enforcement of existing international security regimes such as the NPT, CTBT, MTCR, and so on and negotiate new ones to minimize nuclear threats. Finally, it can work with the major states to strengthen the UN, especially the Security Council, with an aim to make that organization a genuine guardian of peace for all countries. If these can be done, both the United States and the rest of the world would become much safer.

All this, of course, will come at a price: The United States will need to accept international responsibilities and obligations. It will need to observe treaties, rules, and procedures. It will need to respect other countries' views and interests. Meanwhile, it may not have the same kind of freedom and flexibility it once had to address some of its own security concerns. However, the price of the alternative is much higher. In security affairs, a unilateralist approach begets mistrust and fear in other countries. No matter how many and how advanced the weapons the United States may possess, it will not feel secure if it finds itself in a world of mistrust and fear. Therefore, the price for international cooperation is one worth paying. And if other countries are willing to pay the price, why not the United States?

Notes

1. Wang Zhongchun and Wen Zhonghua, *Busan de he yinyun* (Undispelled cloud of nuclear weapons), p. 222.

2. Ibid., pp. 230–231.

3. Zhu Feng, "Meiguo dandao daodan fangyu jihua yu emei guanxi" (U.S. BMD program and Russo-American relations), paper delivered at the conference on the BMD in Fudan University, Shanghai, December 20–21, 2000, pp. 1–5.

4. Ibid., pp. 5–16; Wang and Wen, *Busan de he yinyun,* p. 231.

5. http://news.xinhuanet.com/world/2001–12/14/content_162394.htm.

6. Gu Guoliang, "Kelindun zhengfu duichao zhengce: he yu daodan wenti" (Clinton administration's Korea policy: nuclear and missile questions), pp. 43–44.

7. Here, traditional security needs are those to cope with military attacks or threats posed by other states for power, interests, or ideological ambitions, as distinguished from new security needs such as those to cope with terrorist and suicidal attacks from individuals, groups, or states for venting frustration and/or making some kind of statement.

8. The Gulf War, in which Japan made no military contributions, reinforced this view in many U.S. minds. See Funabashi, *Alliance Adrift*, pp. 288–289.

9. Meiguo guofang daxue guojia zhanlue yanjiusuo (Institute of National Strategic Studies of the U.S. National Defense University), *Qingli fenluan de shijia: meiguo kuashiji quanqiu zhanlue pinggu* (Priorities for a turbulent world: strategic assessment), translated by Lin Dong et al. (Beijing: National Defense University Press, 2000), p. 167.

10. The most disturbing case is the Strategic Defense Initiative launched by the Reagan administration.

11. See the book by Ashton Carter, former U.S. assistant defense secretary, and William Perry, former U.S. defense secretary, *Ashdun kate he weilianmu peili, Yu-fangxing fangyu: yixiang meiguo xin anquan zhanlue* (Preventive defense: a new security strategy for America), translated by Hu Liping and Yang Yunqin (Shanghai: Shanghai Renmin Publishing House), p. 11.

12. Ron Fournier, "Bush Commits U.S. to Missile Defense," May 1, 2001, http://dailynews.yahoo.com/h/ap/20010501/ts/bush_defense.html.

13. *Qingli fenluan de shijie,* p. 415.

14. Ibid., p. 413.

15. Ibid., p. 43.

16. Ibid., pp. 410–412.

17. Ibid., pp. 413–415.

18. Ibid., pp. 414–415, 511.

19. Ibid., pp. 401–403.

20. John Mearsheimer, "The Future Of the American Pacifier."

21. Department of Defense, *Quadrennial Defense Review Report,* September 30, 2001, p. 4.

22. "Revolutionary Technology Development Requires Patience," *Backgrounder,* 01–05a, March 23, 2001, issued by the Public Affairs Section, Embassy of the United States of America, p. 2.

23. http://dailynews.yahoo.com/h/ap/20010501/ts/bush_defense.html.

24. Patrick J. Buchanan, "Foreign Aid: Ever with Us," December 21, 1994, http://www.thecore.com/~gib/foreign_aid.html.

25. "Congressional Myopia on Foreign Aid," *New York Times* editorial, August 24, 1999, http://www.globalpolicy.org/socecon/ffd/oda-us99.htm.

26. Christopher Hellman, "Pressure Growing to Boost Pentagon Spending," *Weekly Defense Monitor* 2, no. 37 (September 17, 1998), http://www.cdi.org/weekly/1998/Issue37/#3.

27. Christopher Hellman, "Congressional Leaders Looking to Increase Pentagon Budget," *Weekly Defense Monitor* 4, no. 9 (March 3, 2000), http://www.cdi.org/weekly/2000/issue09.html#2.

28. Lichade Boensitan and Luosi Mangluo (Richard Bernstein and Ross Munro), *Jijiang daolai de meizhong chongtu* (The coming conflict with China) (Beijing: Xinhua Publishing House, 1997).

11

U.S. Nonproliferation Policy After the Cold War

Kanti Bajpai

IF THE UNITED STATES ACTS UNILATERALLY RATHER THAN MULTILATERALLY IN international relations, then this should be most evident in areas related to national security. Nonproliferation policy is a key component of U.S. national security policy. Is the U.S. approach to nonproliferation after the Cold War unilateralist or multilateralist?

A good part of U.S. nonproliferation policy is unilateralist. For example, the United States has passed legislation against proliferation and, most important, the spread of nuclear weapons. Other U.S. nonproliferation options include the unilateral use of force to prevent countries, other than China, France, Russia, and the United Kingdom, from acquiring nuclear weapons. However, there is also a multilateralist component to U.S. nonproliferation policy. The most important multilateral instrument is the Nuclear Non-Proliferation Treaty (NPT). Until 2001, when President George W. Bush came into office, it appeared that a second vital multilateral instrumentality for the United States would be the Comprehensive Nuclear Test Ban Treaty (CTBT). The United States was the first country to sign the CTBT when it was opened for signature in 1996. In addition to the NPT and CTBT, the United States is party to a number of understandings with other countries designed to prevent the spread of dual-use technologies. These include, most importantly, the Nuclear Suppliers' Group (NSG) and the Missile Technology Control Regime (MTCR).

This chapter analyzes U.S. thinking and U.S. policies toward the NPT and CTBT, arguably the two most important multilateral efforts to control the spread of nuclear weapons. It focuses on the NPT review conferences of 1995 and 2000 and the CTBT negotiations and debates from 1994 to 1996. All things being equal, one might have expected U.S. nonproliferation policies to shift in a unilateral direction following the end of the Cold War, which left the United States as the greatest power on earth. I suggest that the United States was ambivalent about multilateralism in this period. Ultimately, the United States stuck with the more unequal treaty, the NPT, whereas it opted out of the more universalistic treaty, the CTBT. I attribute U.S. interest in multilateralism to the fact that even though the United States is the world's most powerful country, it is not omnipotent and cannot hope to do everything by itself. I also suggest that the U.S. decisionmaking system has a culture of multilateralism in security affairs, which encourages the country to explore the possibility of negotiating universalistic norms and rules to regulate the use and instruments of force. U.S. policymakers have justified U.S. ambivalence about multilateralism—such as insistence on retaining a differentiated system of norms and rules in the NPT—not simply in terms of narrow national interest but also in terms of the indispensability of U.S. military power for international security. In the case of the CTBT, the United States opted out of the treaty mostly for domestic political reasons. With the arrival of the George W. Bush administration, we have seen a sharpening of U.S. discomfort with multilateralism. The multilateral "moment" in U.S. policy in the immediate aftermath of the events of September 11, 2001, seems to be giving way to a more unilateralist thrust in policy.

How would we recognize unilateralism and multilateralism in U.S. nonproliferation policy? One way of answering this question is by distinguishing between ends and means, interests and instruments, motives and behaviors. In the most generic terms, policies of unilateralism and multilateralism differ in terms of ends/interests/motives, on the one hand, and means/instruments/behavior, on the other.

In a unilateralist conception, the ends of policy are narrowly self-regarding, and national interest is reckoned in terms of short-run gains and losses. By contrast, in a multilateralist conception, the ends of policy are defined more broadly to take account of others' concerns as well—the concerns of allies, of antagonists and rivals, even of the international system as a whole. Multilateralism does not mean the abdication of national interest. Rather it implies "indivisibility"—that is, the connectedness or interdependence—of national and international goals, of parochial and cosmopolitan interests and aims.[1] In the multilateralist view, the motives of states are neither purely selfish nor purely altruistic. In addition, the calculus of gains and losses is not necessarily immediate. States are quite properly worried about national interest in the short run, but they are able to sacrifice freedom of action in the present for more or less equivalent future returns, even if those returns are in another realm of policy. Put differently, multilateralism implies what scholars of international relations call "diffuse reciprocity"—a readiness to cooperate on the grounds that the benefits of cooperation will balance out in the long run.[2]

The unilateralist and multilateralist conceptions of policy differ also in respect to the means of policy. In a unilateralist conception, national goals and interests are protected and advanced by differentiated rules and norms.

Unilateralism accepts that, depending on the circumstances, there can be different strokes for different folks. In a multilateralist conception, by contrast, states pursue a general and nondiscriminatory set of norms and rules.[3] Multilateralism is universalistic; it does not admit exceptions. It should be added that unilateralism, in the everyday language of diplomacy, also connotes a willingness to use coercion, even force, to attain one's ends. Multilateralism, by contrast, is suggestive of negotiated solutions.

We will be sensitive to these markers of unilateralism and multilateralism in analyzing U.S. involvement in the NPT and CTBT after the Cold War and will ask two central sets of questions. First, what were U.S. interests and motives? Did the United States have a short-term or long-term view of its interests, and was it narrowly self-regarding or more cosmopolitan in its view of these two negotiations? Second, what was the nature of U.S. behavior and actions in the negotiations? Did the United States work toward a differentiated or a generalized set of rules, and, if so, did it use coercive tactics in these negotiations, or was it willing to bargain and accommodate?

This chapter has been organized into four sections. In the first, I describe U.S. policies toward the NPT and CTBT in terms of U.S. interests and motivations, U.S. behavior during the negotiations, and the outcomes of the negotiations. The second section addresses the causes of U.S. behavior in order to better understand them. In the third section, I take stock of the consequences of U.S. actions. And finally, I ask what an optimal form of U.S. multilateral behavior in arms control and nonproliferation would look like.

The United States and the NPT

The United States was one of the original movers behind the NPT back in 1966. It was by no means the only force behind the treaty. The Soviet Union was an enthusiastic cosponsor of multilateral nonproliferation efforts. Indeed, we forget that such unlikely countries as India were originally also supporters of the idea of a nonproliferation treaty.[4] The United States was thus a prime mover, but by no means was it the sole one.

It had always been U.S. policy to limit the proliferation of nuclear weapons. During World War II, the United States was not keen on sharing nuclear research and technology. It was highly secretive about the Manhattan Project even with its closest ally, Great Britain, as well as with its more distant ally, the Soviet Union.[5] U.S. concerns about proliferation persisted after the war. From the Acheson-Lillienthal and Baruch plans to the Atoms for Peace proposal, U.S. efforts to control the spread of nuclear weapons capability were clear enough. The culmination of these efforts was the NPT in 1968.

Negotiating the NPT, 1966–1970

The NPT negotiations were set in motion in 1966 by a United Nations resolution cosponsored by the United States. Although discussions leading up to the treaty were multilateral, the focus of U.S. policy was on cutting a deal with the Soviet Union. The two countries negotiated bilaterally and brought a draft text before the international community on August 24, 1967.[6] In response to international criticism that the treaty would limit horizontal proliferation but do little to constrain vertical proliferation, Washington and Moscow agreed to insert an article obliging them to pursue seriously the cause of nuclear disarmament. They also agreed, along with other powers with the capacity to produce nuclear reactors, to make nuclear technology available to other countries for research, medicinal, and energy purposes, provided various safeguards were observed. The amended treaty was put up for signature in 1968 and entered into force in 1970, by which time ninety-seven countries had signed and forty-seven had ratified it. By 1975, 111 states had signed the treaty.[7] Among those who refused to sign were Argentina, Brazil, China, Cuba, France, India, Israel, Pakistan, and South Africa. From 1970 onward, the treaty came up for revision every five years.

Washington's aim in sponsoring the treaty was to prevent horizontal proliferation. By 1968, there were already five nuclear weapon powers, and the United States feared that this number could go as high as twenty over the next two decades.[8] Non-U.S. commentators perceive in the U.S. nonproliferation "crusade" of the 1960s a unilateralist motive, namely, a concern with U.S. security and status. Clearly, the safety and security of the U.S. public were crucial factors in U.S. nonproliferation thinking. However, U.S. analysts and decisionmakers also argued that proliferation would have deleterious consequences for the broader international system. The spread of nuclear weapons could well destabilize the so-called central balance between the United States (and its allies) and the Soviets, increasing the risks of generalized nuclear war. The spread of nuclear weapons might destabilize particular regions, threatening U.S. allies and other states.[9]

Neither was the United States the only country to worry about the impact of proliferation for its own narrow national security interests. The Soviets by 1958 had refused to help the Chinese with their nuclear program.[10] Similarly, the British were concerned about potential nuclear threats from countries besides the Soviet Union, particularly Germany, and they saw nonproliferation as a means to forestall an even more complex global nuclear game and to protect their interests in distant regions where the rise of local nuclear powers might affect those interests.[11] As far as unilateralism of motives or intentions goes, then, the United States was no more selfish than the two other nuclear powers that opposed proliferation.[12]

What about U.S. actions during the nonproliferation negotiations? Did the United States use coercive tactics to get its way in the NPT parleys?

There is little doubt that U.S. diplomats applied pressures, including threats and inducements, on delegations from the third world and key allies like Germany and Japan to secure the requisite support in the UN for the treaty vote.[13] However, the United States was not the only coercive power. The Soviets used their influence bluntly on Eastern European as well as third world countries. Britain also lobbied hard for the treaty.

Finally, was the outcome of the NPT negotiations not simply a reflection of U.S. preferences? In fact, although Washington was satisfied with the NPT that resulted, it was the United States that was forced to accommodate in three areas. First, it was forced to agree under article VI that it would make progress with other nuclear weapon states toward nuclear disarmament. Second, by article IV, the United States and other nuclear powers agreed to provide nuclear technology, with appropriate safeguards, to those countries that had given up the right to produce nuclear weapons. Third, outside of the NPT, the United States was forced to commit itself to extending its nuclear umbrella ever more explicitly to countries that might be the object of nuclear threats.[14] Washington's commitment to coupling its security with both Germany and Japan and to a nuclear first-use policy must be understood in this light.

Were these real concessions on the part of the United States? Article VI obliged the nuclear powers to pursue disarmament, but it contained no means of enforcing that obligation. Accordingly, critics have argued that the United States and other nuclear powers did not concede anything of substance, whereas the rest of the signatories gave up the right to develop nuclear weapons. The treaty is therefore discriminatory, establishing unequal rights and obligations between nuclear and nonnuclear parties. However, I would note three things. First, given that not all countries had nuclear weapons, the treaty perforce had to have a differentiated structure of rules. Second, the promise to pursue disarmament seriously in return for nonproliferation by the other signatories indicates that there was a measure of reciprocity built into the treaty. Washington was obliged to shift its position from rejection of any obligation to disarm to public acceptance that it would try "in good faith" to do so (article VI). Third, there was no time limit for disarmament, so the resulting normative pressures on the United States and other nuclear powers to disarm should not be completely discounted.

With respect to article IV, the nuclear powers, including the United States, have done much to make nuclear technology available to other countries. They have not only trained nuclear scientists and technicians but also transferred nuclear reactors and fuel to nonnuclear countries interested in acquiring research and power facilities. Although the United States and other nuclear weapons states might have transferred nuclear technology to others on a bilateral basis, either in deference to an alliance relationship or for commercial purposes, the treaty and subsequent policy under the International Atomic Energy Agency (IAEA) made it obligatory for them to provide such technology to *any state* that requested it as long as recipients were willing to abide by international safeguards.

Lastly, the United States, along with Great Britain and the Soviet Union, stated publicly that as members of the UN Security Council they would come to the aid of any nonnuclear signatory of the NPT that was threatened by nuclear weapons. This represented a compact with reciprocal obligations: in return for remaining nonnuclear, these countries (including Germany and Japan) would be protected by the United States and the other nuclear powers.

It should be remembered that the overwhelming majority of states favored the adoption of a nonproliferation treaty. Some did so not because they feared arm-twisting by the United States and the other nuclear powers but rather because they wanted to prevent regional neighbors from pursuing nuclear weapons and threatening their survival.[15] Some states could not match the technical sophistication of their neighbors and would have been hard-pressed to build the bomb. Others doubted that nuclear weapons would bring about stable mutual deterrence in their region. And others had no interest in nuclear weapons but thought that a treaty on nonproliferation might constrain, if not reverse, the nuclear arms race and prevent the global catastrophe of nuclear war.[16] In short, the NPT represented the preferences not only of the United States but also scores of other states. As the above discussion makes clear, the U.S. role in the NPT during 1966–1970 was hardly as unilateralist as is sometimes thought.

The NPT Review of 1995

After the Cold War, there was considerable optimism about the international community's capacity to stem both vertical and horizontal proliferation. A number of developments encouraged this view. The United States and its allies, as well as Russia and the former Soviet republics, cut their nuclear weapons stocks drastically, agreed to a moratorium on testing, and halted the production of fissile material. A number of holdouts joined the nonproliferation treaty, including China, France, and South Africa. Argentina and Brazil jointly renounced their quest for nuclear weapons and indicated that they might join the NPT. The former Soviet republics agreed to give up the nuclear weapons currently on their territory and to send them back to Russia. In 1993, negotiations began within the Conference on Disarmament (CD) in Geneva on a comprehensive test ban.

It was in this context, in 1995, that the signatories to the NPT met to carry out a five-year review of the treaty. Twenty-five years from the treaty's entry-into-force, the signatories had to face a number of issues. The most crucial was whether or not to extend the treaty indefinitely. There were various alternatives to a permanent extension. One option was to extend the treaty for another twenty-five-year period in a so-called rolling extension. Another was to extend it for only five years, whereupon its extension would again be considered.[17] The United States favored an indefinite and unconditional extension, arguing that discrete time periods and conditions would damage the treaty's credibility and encourage unrealistic expectations about what could be achieved, thereby preventing the achievement of concrete, progressive steps toward nonproliferation and disarmament.[18] U.S. motivations were little different from those that had guided its original NPT policy back in 1966–1968. If there was a difference, it was in U.S. estimations of the potential sources of proliferation, which had shifted from the specter of a nuclear-armed Germany and Japan to India, Pakistan, and a number of so-called rogue states.[19]

Firsthand accounts, including a series of interviews with diplomats conducted by Susan Welsh of the Monterey Institute for International Studies, show clearly that the United States used coercive tactics, including both threats and inducements, during the 1995 review conference. According to the Indonesian Permanent Representative to the UN: "The U.S. delegation really worked on this indefinite extension, targeting many members of the NAM [Non-Aligned Movement], from one and a half years ago until the last minute."[20] In the opinion of Ambassador Miguel Marin Bosch of Mexico, U.S. policy also constrained what the conference was able to achieve: "I personally think that we could have gotten more [in the conference]. In my view [the inability to gain more was due to] a) the divided non-aligned . . . and b) the situation that we are living everyday in this building [i.e. the UN]. . . . It is a unipolar 1946 world—there is only one superpower."[21] Bosch claimed that the United States "insinuated" that there was a link between indefinite extension and the continuation of U.S. obligations to nonnuclear NPT signatories under article IV, namely, access to U.S. technology in the nuclear field.[22] The Venezuelan ambassador, Adolfo Taylhardat, felt so strongly about U.S. tactics that he eventually resigned when his government agreed, under U.S. pressure, to cosponsor the resolution on indefinite extension. Earlier in the conference, Taylhardat tried to push for a middle way between those who wanted an unconditional and indefinite extension and those who wanted a conditional and short-term one. His proposal was to extend the treaty for twenty-five years or a series of fixed-period rolling extensions. As Taylhardat concluded: "There are many ways of exerting pressure, especially when countries are going through difficult times, and most of the developing countries are going through difficult times, including my own."[23] Regarding the role of the NAM, he responded: "It is not that the NAM *is* fractured. It has *been* fractured. . . . External factors have fractured the non-aligned."[24] An Iranian diplomat present at the conference similarly noted, "A lot of pressures, . . . promises and sometimes threats, . . . were put on non-aligned countries . . . by certain nuclear weapon states, in particular the United States. . . . Had members of the non-aligned had the opportunity to express themselves freely on the issue of extension, they would have decided otherwise, I am sure."[25]

However, it was not just the United States that applied undue pressure. The other nuclear weapons states also did so, as did various countries from the European Union. Several smaller Western countries felt the brunt of this pressure. As the Indonesian ambassador concluded, "What I feel as very disturbing is how they [i.e., all the nuclear weapon states] have reached majority for indefinite extension. It is simply by the use of pressure tactics against smaller countries."[26]

Evidently, there were also unwelcome pressures from the NAM countries. As the Canadian ambassador for disarmament described it:

> Of course pressure was applied regarding the decision on extension— powerful countries often exert pressure over important issues. . . . However, the argument that *unfair* pressure tactics, threats, or bribes ruled the day does not hold up well. Indeed such pressure would in many cases have been counterproductive and could not have achieved the goal. (italics added)

He went on to note that the majority of states found themselves pressured between two forces: the nuclear weapon states as well as the Non-Aligned Movement.[27]

In the end, the conference adopted by consensus an indefinite extension of the treaty. Some critics have inferred from this outcome that the United States got its way and that this is another sign of U.S. unilateralism.[28] On the contrary, one can argue that as in 1968 there was a significant degree of consensus between the nuclear and nonnuclear powers. Before the conference even began, seventy countries out of the 176 had already indicated publicly that they supported indefinite extension, only nineteen short of the simple majority required to carry the day. The United States estimated that a majority of states were in favor of a permanent extension and that a snowball effect would bring in most of the rest. According to one estimate, by the end of the plenary session, one week into the conference, 103 countries would support an indefinite extension, twenty-three were against, twenty-eight were leaning yes, twelve were leaning no, and only eleven remained undecided. Thus, early in the conference 130 or so states were already inclined to permanent extension.[29]

There is little doubt that the United States and the nuclear weapon powers exerted pressures on the smaller and weaker countries, but the nuclear powers had to give ground in order to get an indefinite extension. The conference thus ended with consensus on two other issues: (1) the Decision on Principles and Objectives for Nuclear Non-Proliferation and Disarmament; and (2) a strengthening of the review process. The former contained three key items. First, it obliged the NPT signatories to complete the CTBT negotiations no later than 1996. Second, it urged them to commence negotiations on, and conclude as early as possible, the proposed Fissile Material Cut-Off Treaty (FMCT). Third, it asked the nuclear weapon states to get more serious about disarmament.[30] Although the third item was explicitly directed at the nuclear weapon states, the first two also required rather more from the United States and the other nuclear powers than it did of other countries. Few countries had any interest in testing or stockpiling weapons-grade fissile material, and not many had the capacity to do so either: the call for accelerated progress toward a CTBT and an FMCT was therefore largely directed at the nuclear weapon states.

In the buildup to the review conference, the United States had taken other propitiatory actions. These included, most importantly, President Bill Clinton's decision to give up the U.S. demand for a ten-year easy-exit clause from the CTBT, which would have allowed Washington to pull out from the test ban after a decade. Another helpful U.S. move, intended to jog the discussions at the NPT review, was to withdraw 200 tons of fissile material from the U.S. stockpile. Yet another useful decision was Senate ratification of START II, hurried along in order to strengthen the case for indefinite extension of the NPT. Finally, prior to the NPT review, the United States indicated that it would accept stronger language on nuclear disarmament and would support nuclear weapon–free zones in the Pacific and Caribbean.[31] In terms of outcomes, therefore, the record is mixed, as it was in 1968. The United States achieved its major objective—indefinite extension—but this objective was one that was widely shared. Moreover, Washington was forced to make some concessions to get what it wanted. These were not as momentous as the ones it had granted in 1968, but they were not innocuous.

The NPT Review of 2000

Although the NPT review of 2000 was less dramatic than the 1995 conference, it was an important milestone. The intervening years were witness to a number of events that seemed to challenge the NPT head-on, and there was a widespread view that the conference would fail. Key challenges to the nonproliferation regime included the Indian and Pakistani nuclear tests of May 1998, the NPT violations by Iraq and North Korea, the growing anger among Arabs over Israel's unfettered nuclear capabilities, the glacial pace of disarmament efforts by the nuclear weapon states, the U.S. Senate's rejection of the CTBT, the stalled START process, and the growing support in the United States for nationwide missile defense.

In the end, however, 155 states present at the conference adopted by consensus a final document and a five-year program of action. The highlights of these agreements included the consensus on an "unequivocal undertaking by the nuclear-weapon states to accomplish the total elimination of their nuclear arsenals," an early entry into force of the CTBT, prompt negotiations on an FMCT, further unilateral efforts to reduce nuclear arsenals, greater transparency on nuclear capabilities, the reduction of nonstrategic weapons, concrete measures to further reduce the operational status of nuclear weapons, steps to diminish the role of nuclear weapons in security policy, and the involvement of all five nuclear weapon states in nuclear reductions and disarmament efforts.

With the 1995 conference behind it, the United States was less ambitious about the 2000 conference. The primary U.S. motivations were to ensure that the treaty did not decay in the face of the Indian and Pakistani tests and the Senate's rejection of the CTBT and that no serious strictures were passed against itself and the other nuclear weapon states on the issue of article VI obligations. The United States wanted to ensure that the South Asian tests were criticized and that the conference acknowledged its record on article VI and other provisions.[32]

In contrast to the 1995 conference, U.S. tactics at the 2000 conference were generally low-key. Without a burning agenda, the U.S. delegation kept a low profile and was slow to show its negotiating hand, preferring to allow others to argue their cases first. There was little sign of the coercive, crusading diplomacy featured in 1995, when Washington made no secret of its determination to get an indefinite extension of the NPT. Another possibility is that the United States expected the conference to fail because of the contradictions among the nuclear weapon states and among the wider membership and thus moderated the tempo and intensity of its effort.[33] In the 2000 review, other players took a far more active role in shaping negotiations. This included most prominently the New Agenda Coalition (NAC), a mix of states from different continents and groupings, including from the West. Among the nuclear weapon states, Great Britain and France were very active and were not always in agreement with the United States. Russia, especially at the beginning, with its surprise preconference ratification of START II and the CTBT, helped shape the direction and pace of the discussions. The nonaligned states were not a factor this time around and played second fiddle to the NAC.[34]

U.S. preferences were reflected in the outcome of the conference, but once again the United States had to compromise. Moreover, it is not easy to judge whether the United States prevailed. On the one hand, the NPT did not collapse under the weight of the challenges of the preceding five years, and the conference did not accept a time-bound plan for the elimination of nuclear weapons. Neither of these was a serious possibility, however, and not only because of U.S. opposition to them. As in 1995, the majority of states were solidly behind the treaty and anxious to avoid any serious disruptions.

A finer reading of the outcome indicates that the United States both got and gave at the conference. An official U.S. press release issued at the conference lists the following conclusions as highlights of the 2000 consensus: the continuing role of the NPT in preventing the spread of nuclear weapons; continued pressure to gain universal adherence to the NPT; rejection of any special status for India and Pakistan after their nuclear tests; strengthening of IAEA safeguards; enhancements of nuclear export controls; further steps on nuclear disarmament with an emphasis on the entry into force of the CTBT, immediate commencement of the FMCT talks, further reductions under the START process, and the preservation and strengthening of the ABM Treaty; increasing transparency of nuclear weapons capabilities; support for the irreversibility of nuclear reductions; the deactivation of nuclear forces consistent with military stability; and a reaffirmation of the unequivocal commitment of the nuclear weapon states to the total elimination of nuclear weapons.[35] Seen from Washington, the primary achievements of the conference were in the area of nonproliferation rather than disarmament.

An authoritative assessment by the Acronym Institute interprets the outcome rather differently, emphasizing the disarmament aspects of the consensus. Rebecca Johnson regards the principal achievement of the conference to be the historic, "unequivocal commitment" by nuclear weapon states to nuclear elimination. In her view, the various measures involving nonnuclear weapon states were secondary. By agreeing to stronger language on disarmament, the United States and the other nuclear weapon states certainly gave some ground, committing themselves to increase unilateral efforts to reduce nuclear arsenals, provide greater transparency about their nuclear weapon capabilities, further deactivate the operational status of nuclear weapons, and reduce the role played by nuclear weapons in security.[36] These were all significant concessions.

In 2000, the major objective of the United States was to ensure that the NPT hung together, in the aftermath of the South Asian nuclear tests and the CTBT debacle at home, and to avoid strictures regarding the disarmament of nuclear weapon states. The fact that the NPT hung together was not due to U.S. efforts alone. It resulted from the shared belief of both nuclear and nonnuclear states that the survival of the treaty would bring them security benefits. The United States managed to avoid strictures on disarmament in the consensus document, but the unequivocal commitment to disarmament was accepted in recognition that the record could be better. This understanding—that more could and should be done—was also the basis for other recommendations on unilateral measures of nuclear reductions, on the irreversibility of arms control, on measures to reduce nuclear risks and dangers, and on greater transparency, among other issues.

Do these recommendations matter at all? Do they cost the United States and other nuclear weapon states anything? Public promises, however hedged and watered down they may be, are not irrelevant. Even the United States is not above recognizing both the normative and practical importance of keeping promises. International covenants should be kept because there is moral value in keeping covenants freely arrived at. As a practical matter, the reputational value of making an effort to keep to covenants freely arrived at is a good investment for the future. States, however powerful, that cannot be trusted to keep their word will find life in international anarchy much more costly.

The United States and the CTBT

One of the most important items on the U.S. and global nonproliferation agenda has long been the Comprehensive Nuclear Test Ban Treaty. The checkered career of the test ban through the Cold War years finally seemed to be at an end in 1994, when the international community began negotiations on a treaty. In 1996, what President Clinton called "the longest-sought, hardest-fought prize in arms control history" was at hand when the treaty was opened for signature over the objections of India, the only hold-out state in the Conference on Disarmament.[37] The United States was a central player in the test-ban negotiations and devoted considerable diplomatic time and effort to produce the treaty. Senate rejection of the treaty in October 2000, and the Bush administration's allergy to a test ban, may be the end of the saga, which provides another important test case of U.S. unilateralism in nonproliferation.

The CTBT essentially bans nuclear weapons tests or any other peaceful nuclear explosion. Although the term "explosion" is not defined by the treaty, the permanent five members of the UN Security Council have agreed among themselves that it will exclude subcritical, hydronuclear, and computer-simulated tests. The treaty creates the Comprehensive Nuclear Test Ban Organization (CTBTO), to be based in Vienna, consisting of the Conference of States Parties, which meets once a year; an executive council, composed of fifty-one rotating members drawn from all continents and that meets on short notice as needed; and a technical secretariat, including the International Data Center, responsible for day-to-day management. Decisions are taken by majority vote on procedural questions and by consensus on substantive matters.

Verification, of course, is vital to the credibility of the treaty. Under its terms, four verification systems are to be used: consultations and clarifications sought from parties to the treaty; the International Monitoring System, consisting of seismological sensors, radionuclide sensors, hydroacoustic sensors, and infrasound; on-site inspections; and confidence-building measures. If any state party to the treaty suspects another country of having conducted or preparing to conduct a test, it is expected first to seek consultation and clarification from that country. Three principles are to guide verification: that it be undertaken by the least intrusive method; that it be conducted in a cost-effective manner; and that it show due regard for the confidentiality of any information gathered. On-site inspections are considered the most intrusive method of verification. Countries are obliged not to make mischievous or frivolous demands to the CTBTO for inspections.

Any demand for inspections must be considered by the CTBTO and, when authorized, be undertaken according to a very stringent method. At least thirty affirmative votes in the fifty-one-member executive council are necessary for an inspection. All states that are party to the treaty can be inspected. These states have the right to have their own representatives accompany the inspection team and to reply to the inspectors' report. Inspections are defined by duration (no longer than sixty days maximum, extendable by another seventy days maximum), facilities, and area of visit. Finally, the CTBT also relies on national technical means—a country's own sources of information (e.g., satellite intelligence)—to gather information regarding nuclear testing.

The CTBT will enter into force when the forty-four states that possess a nuclear power and/or research reactor accede to it. In acceding to the treaty, parties cannot enter any reservations to its articles and annexes. They may enter reservations on its protocols. The annexes include the list of states from which the executive council will be drawn and the forty-four states whose accession is required for the treaty's entry into force. Once the treaty enters into force, noncompliance by a party is to be addressed by suspension of membership rights and privileges, multilateral sanctions, and other collective mechanisms, such as recourse to the United Nations. The treaty is of unlimited duration, but reviews of it are to be carried out every ten years after its entry into force. In addition, any party to the treaty may propose amendments, to be considered by an amendment conference and adopted by a majority vote of members plus no negative vote by any party. Any party can withdraw from the treaty with six months' notice by citing extraordinary events affecting the supreme national interest.

Negotiating the CTBT

U.S. motivations in pursuing a multilateral test-ban treaty were to build on the possibilities that had opened up after the end of the Cold War. A test ban would be part of an effort to shut the door on proliferation. A state that could not test would find it that much harder to build a reliable nuclear arsenal and, in that measure, would be deterred from trying to do so. A world with fewer nuclear weapon states would be a safer place for the United States: the fewer nuclear-armed powers, the less threats to the U.S. homeland. It would also be safer for U.S. allies, as a number of possible proliferators were their potential enemies. Indeed, a world with fewer nuclear-armed states would be safer for everyone. The breakup of the Soviet Union, which created new nuclear powers, created an added incentive to move toward a test ban. The arguments for nonproliferation were familiar enough: all had been used during the NPT debates of the 1960s and were used again in the 1995 NPT review conference. The United States was not alone in these concerns. The other nuclear weapon states reasoned similarly, as did most NPT signatories. For most states, regional security concerns and the fear of nuclear proliferation in one's own neighborhood proved far more compelling than abstract arguments about equity or about the need to link the CTBT to a time-bound plan for disarmament, as India insisted.

During the three-year negotiations within the CD, U.S. tactics included a mixture of coercion and accommodation. The United States made a unilateral decision to seek a zero-yield test ban, effectively dragging the other nuclear weapon powers in its wake.[38] Great Britain's discomfort with a zero-yield treaty was ignored, as were its requests for additional tests at U.S. facilities. But London eventually agreed to a zero-yield test ban a month after President Clinton announced the U.S. determination to seek such a limit.[39] Likewise, the United States ignored French discomfort with zero yield. As a result, Paris decided to conduct a series of tests even as the negotiations at Geneva were in progress. Here the United States ultimately proved accommodative, promising the French access to U.S. test data in return for France's agreement to a zero-yield ban.[40] Russia and China eventually came around to zero yield as well. The Chinese "did a France," testing their way to a zero-yield position.[41]

On the issue of verification, too, the United States and the other nuclear weapon states resorted to coercive bargaining. Washington, for its part, was determined to get an on-site inspection provision. Although Great Britain, France, and Russia were in substantial agreement, China was not. During the negotiations, the United States threatened to walk out of negotiations altogether in order to force the issue with China.[42] Whereas the United States wanted a red-light approach to on-site inspections, whereby in the initial phase an inspection would go forward unless stopped by a negative vote of the executive council, the Chinese favored a green-light approach, whereby an inspection could occur only if three-quarters of the executive council agreed to it. The United States argued that the on-site inspection issue was a potential treaty-breaker and that it could not sell a weak verification structure to domestic U.S. opinion.[43] However, the tactic was only partly successful. Beijing accepted the need for on-site inspections but stuck to its guns on the regime governing them. To demonstrate their resolve, the Chinese continued to test during the negotiations. When they had completed their tests, they made concessions.[44]

The eventual compromise on verification gave the Chinese quite a lot of what they wanted. The United States diluted its stand to a green-light position with the proviso that a simple majority of those present and voting in the executive council could authorize an inspection. The Chinese opposed this and finally got agreement that a three-fifths majority would suffice.[45] The final text also acceded to another Chinese demand, namely, that newer forms of verification could be added to the treaty if and when they became available, including electromagnetic-pulse monitoring and satellite monitoring, two technologies for which China had argued and that had not found favor with the other nuclear weapon states.[46]

The outcome of the CTBT negotiations was certainly consistent with the primary U.S. goal of enacting a test ban. However, the United States, despite its power, was forced to settle for a treaty that made various concessions to the other nuclear states and to larger international opinion in the three crucial areas of scope, verification, and entry into force. The original U.S. position on scope was that the threshold should be set not at zero yield but rather at 1.8 kilograms. In addition, Washington had initially insisted on a ten-year easy-exit option in the treaty. In the end, it relinquished both of these initial positions.[47] The United States succeeded in obtaining its objective of a strong verification regime with a layered system of verification, including provisions for on-site inspections. Yet the compromises with China on the on-site inspections regime showed the limits of U.S. power. On the issue of the treaty's entry into force, the United States had favored a simple formula, namely, signature and ratification by the five nuclear weapon states. Here, Washington lost out to Great Britain, Russia, and China with, as it turned out, negative effect in that India found in the entry into force formula a clinching reason to reject the treaty.[48]

The United States was the first country to sign the CTBT, on September 24, 1996. The other four nuclear powers appended their signatures on the same day. On April 6, 1998, Great Britain and France simultaneously ratified the treaty. Russia ratified it on June 30, 2000. China has yet to ratify it. On October 13, 1999, after a twelve-day debate, the U.S. Senate voted to reject the treaty. The world was confounded. The United States had led the campaign for a test ban in 1993 and yet had found it impossible to ratify it and thus assist its entry into force.

U.S. Domestic Politics and Opting Out of the CTBT

Why did the U.S. Senate fail to ratify a truly multilateral treaty governing nuclear weapons, one that had been so tortuously negotiated over a three-year period? More than anything else, domestic politics defeated the treaty's chances in the U.S. Senate. The overwhelming evidence is that a combination of partisan politics, the Clinton administration's mismanagement of the ratification process, widespread misinformation and misunderstanding of treaty provisions and of the role of nuclear testing, and doubts about the utility of the treaty in dealing with the challenge of proliferation doomed its prospects in the Senate.

First of all, deeply partisan politics, between Republicans and Democrats in Congress and between Republican senators and the White House, cast an enormous shadow over the ratification process. The political animosity, particularly between senior Republican senators led by Trent Lott and Jesse Helms, on the one hand, and the Clinton administration, on the other hand, ensured that the treaty was hostage to politics to an unprecedented degree.[49] The president had transmitted the treaty to the Senate for ratification in September 1997. A year later, the Senate Foreign Relations

Committee, under the chairmanship of Helms, had not held a single formal hearing on the treaty.[50] On January 21, 1998, Helms wrote to Clinton stating that the committee would discuss the CTBT only after the president forwarded for Senate consideration the protocols to the ABM Treaty and the Kyoto Protocol to the UN Convention on Climate Change. Helms in any case warned the president that the CTBT was "very low on the Committee's list of priorities" and concluded that the CTBT "has no chance of entering into force for a decade or more."[51] By linking Senate action on the CTBT to the ABM Treaty protocols, Helms evidently wanted to stall the CTBT, ensure that he laid the groundwork for the abrogation of the ABM Treaty so that missile defense could go forward, and make it appear that the administration was responsible for the lack of progress in nuclear-related policy-making. The Clinton administration had held back on transmitting the ABM protocols to encourage Russia to ratify START II, a fact well known to Helms and the Republican Party leadership.[52] The procedural hurdles that Lott and Helms erected ensured that there were barely twelve days to debate the treaty and to lobby for its passage. Even some Republican senators recognized that the treaty had been ill-served by the time limitation imposed on the deliberations.[53]

In suggesting that the Helms-Lott strategy was marked by partisanship, I should note that in contrast to the Republican leadership's oppositional stand the treaty enjoyed wide-ranging support in the United States. Four former chairmen of the Joint Chiefs of Staff—John Shalikashvili, Colin Powell, William Crowe, and David Jones—publicly endorsed it. In addition, the directors of the three major nuclear weapons laboratories declared that the newly formed Stockpile Stewardship program would "enable us to maintain America's nuclear deterrent without nuclear testing"; the American Association for the Advancement of Science also added its voice of support.[54] The treaty also found powerful support among the U.S. public, regardless of party affiliation. Roughly 70 percent of those polled, whether Republicans, Democrats, or independents, wanted the treaty approved. Historically, since the first nationwide polls conducted in 1957, eleven separate polls have indicated support levels for a test ban ranging from 61 percent to 85 percent.[55]

The second factor that hurt the treaty's chances was the Clinton administration's mismanagement of the ratification process. Even though the administration sought and received the support of the former joint chiefs, the directors of the weapons laboratories, and NATO allies, it was unable "to build upon the strong base of expert and public support . . . and take the case for the treaty directly to the Senate."[56] In effect, the White House simply did not state its case as aggressively and expansively as it should have. By the time the administration got serious about mobilizing support in the Senate, particularly among those who remained undecided on their vote, and about countering the anti-CTBT arguments of opponents, it was too late.

Part of the problem was the administration's hope that the Russian Duma (parliament) would ratify START II in time for President Clinton to forward the treaty to Helms. This did not happen. The ratification effort was complicated by a number of contemporaneous domestic and international preoccupations that, while unrelated to the CTBT, consumed the administration's energies. Domestically, the top concern was the impeachment process then under way against President Clinton. The revelations of Chinese spying on U.S. nuclear installations also occupied a good deal of time. Internationally, the challenge of NATO expansion, which also had to be piloted through the Senate, and the bombing of Yugoslavia were major distractions to the CTBT ratification process.[57]

Third, misinformation and misunderstanding about the treaty and its provisions, as well as about the role of nuclear testing, played a significant role in its defeat on the floor of the Senate. Ignorance, misrepresentation, and misjudgments of the treaty's scope and verification provisions were difficult to counter in the paltry twelve-day debate. In terms of scope, treaty critics charged that a test ban of indefinite duration was contrary to U.S. national interests. The Republican Policy Committee of the Senate, for example, noted that "no Republican administration has ever sought a zero-yield test ban, let alone one of unlimited duration."[58] Allied to this criticism was the argument that, contrary to the expectations of the laboratories and of the Clinton administration, the Stockpile Stewardship program being proposed by the White House as an alternative to testing would not be effective for at least ten years.[59] The Republican Policy Committee argued that the "diagnostic tools" of the program were not proven, that the National Ignition Facility was at least two years behind completion, and that by 2005 U.S. weapons would not have been tested for thirteen years.[60]

In what way was this line of criticism misleading? On the matter of indefinite duration, critics ignored the fact that during the CTBT negotiations the U.S. attempt to get agreement on a ten-year easy-exit option had excited more international opposition than any other U.S. stand. To tamper with this element of the CTBT would most likely lead to retaliatory defections by the other major signatories that had also made concessions along the way. The net result could be an unraveling of the agreement altogether. In any case, the United States, like all other signatories, could always pull out of the pact by using the supreme-national-interest clause, a point that the Clinton administration avowed in Safeguard F of the safeguards list it had proposed to the Senate in signing the treaty.[61]

As for the Stockpile Stewardship program, its core safety and reliability element was already operational. Its core element is not tests but "an extensive stockpile surveillance, disassembly, and component inspection program based on valid statistical random sampling techniques"; based on this program, any limited-life components that have deteriorated may be replaced and remanufactured, including the nuclear warhead "primary."[62] The

Stockpile Stewardship program was therefore already effective in detecting safety and reliability problems as well as carrying out remedial action. The program's more advanced techniques, such as the National Ignition Facility and the Accelerated Strategic Computing Initiative, though "useful," were not "essential" and were in part related to the effort by the laboratories to "maximize their annual congressional budget appropriations."[63]

Misinformation and misunderstanding extended to the issue of verification as well. Some critics argued that by insisting on a zero-yield treaty the Clinton administration had made it possible for countries to cheat without fear of detection. According to this argument, the treaty would not prevent cheating by China and Russia, in particular, which were believed to have the expertise to carry out low-yield tests that would be impossible to detect. Given that the United States, as a democratic country, would not cheat, its two major nuclear rivals would therefore gain an advantage from the test ban. Indeed, they might succeed in narrowing the gap in nuclear capabilities by conducting clandestine tests, whereas the United States was unable to test.[64] Critics also charged that the verification provisions were not enforceable and that it was not clear how the verification systems proposed by the treaty would add anything substantial to existing U.S. verification instruments.[65]

These criticisms of the treaty's verification provisions were also misleading. Although cheating is always a possibility in arms control, and verification is a constant challenge, the question is, How much verification is enough? The CTBT's verification structure—the International Monitoring System and on-site inspections, plus national intelligence and civilian seismic networks—are capable of detecting nuclear tests of a kiloton or lower. Tests below that limit, as well as hydronuclear tests, probably can escape detection. However, low-level tests of this magnitude have little utility in the development of new weapons.[66]

In regard to enforceability, this issue represents a challenge for any treaty, given the decentralized nature of world politics. However, it should be noted that the CTBT does address noncompliance by a signatory, providing three measures against violators: suspension of membership rights and privileges, sanctions, and other collective mechanisms, including action to be determined by the UN. Where justified and/or feasible, responses to violations might include the collective use of force. If so, it is unclear what additional measures could reasonably be included by way of enforcement provisions.

Do the CTBT's verification systems add anything to U.S. capabilities? Although U.S. resources are rather extensive, the International Monitoring Facility—consisting of a worldwide network of seismological sensors, radionuclide sensors, hydroacoustic sensors, and infrasound instruments as well as the provisions for on-site inspections in the CTBT—do indeed add significantly to the U.S. ability to detect unauthorized explosions and activities.

Behind much of the criticism on both scope and verification were misapprehensions about the role of testing. Some critics maintained that a fairly extensive, high-yield testing program was necessary to ensure the safety and reliability of the U.S. arsenal, as well as to upgrade older weapons and develop new weapons to deal with emerging threats.[67] Other critics wanted at least low-yield tests to be permitted. Thus, Richard Perle, an adviser to former President Ronald Reagan, claimed, "low-yield testing that carries no negative environmental effects should not be regarded as an evil."[68] In a longer debate on the merits and demerits of the treaty, and in a less-charged and rancorous political atmosphere, a number of replies to these charges might have found more serious consideration, at least among the more internationalist Republican senators who might have swung the Senate tally the other way.

Given the opportunity for a more prolonged and cool-headed debate, a number of other responses might have been made with greater effect. We have already noted that testing is not central to maintaining the safety and reliability of the weapons stockpile. As Thomas Graham, Jr., and Damien LaVera have pointed out, the United States "is better prepared than any other nation to maintain its arsenal without testing."[69] It should be added that fears about the safety and reliability of the U.S. arsenal and the role of testing were almost certainly greatly exaggerated by critics. As Darryl Kimball notes, "The current arsenal is 'safe' in that it meets modern 'one-point' safety standards against accidental nuclear detonation, and the benefits of marginal safety improvements have not been proven to outweigh the costs."[70] Kimball also notes that of 830 defects found in stockpiles from 1958 to 1993, "less than 1 percent were 'discovered' in nuclear tests," and they were related to stockpiled items that had entered service before 1970. Also, only one out of 387 tests since 1970 has helped to diagnose an "age-related flaw" in a weapon.[71] Testing may also not be required for upgrading existing warhead designs.[72] Still, testing is almost certainly required for new warhead design. Does the United States require a new generation of nuclear weapons? This depends on the perceptions of U.S. policymakers. At some point in the future, U.S. decisionmakers might judge that circumstances warrant new warheads. In that case, the United States, like any other signatory, may invoke the supreme-national-interest clause, allowing it to escape the treaty and resume testing.

Finally, the Senate vote was influenced by doubts about the utility of the CTBT in curbing nonproliferation, its primary goal. At least four arguments were used to suggest that the treaty might not be effective. Some argued that the May 1998 nuclear tests of India and Pakistan demonstrated that a test ban would not necessarily prevent proliferation. Indeed, Senator Lott argued that the treaty had in fact pushed India into testing. Both Lott and Helms doubted that the CTBT could help curb proliferation in South Asia.[73] A second argument was that the NPT already implied a test ban, and therefore the CTBT added very little to nonproliferation efforts.[74] Third, there were those who suggested that no treaty, not even the CTBT, would deter states that were convinced they needed to test; regional circumstances, rather than U.S. tests, would determine the testing decisions of others.[75] Far more important than U.S. testing, critics argued, was U.S. "ambiguity" about when and where it would use nuclear weapons; ultimately, this was a more powerful constraint on the decisions of threshold nuclear states to test or acquire nuclear weapons.[76] Fourth, critics such as the Republican National Committee suggested that in any case it was no longer necessary to test in order to possess a workable nuclear device.[77] None of these arguments were trivial or easily dismissed. However, given the shortage of time allotted for debate, the Senate was unable to discuss such portentous matters with the kind of attention and rigor that was required.

Explaining U.S. Behavior

Why does the United States, the preeminent world power, bother with multilateralism on nonproliferation issues? Two broad explanations exist: material and normative. First, even with its massive, unrivalled military and economic resources, the United States cannot do everything by itself. Second, there exists a culture of multilateralism in the U.S. diplomatic tradition that predisposes it to enter into such negotiations. Why, conversely, does the United States end up being ambivalent about multilateralism? Why did it decline to enter arguably the most important universalistic arms control treaty ever negotiated? We suggest three answers. The first is that the United States remains unconvinced that the technical limitations in verifying ambitious arms control and disarmament agreements can be overcome in the foreseeable future. The second is that the country has a tendency to regard its own national security as more or less coterminous with its broader role in providing security for others. There is a real sense in which Americans believe that they are an exceptional and indispensable power and that what is good for the United States is good for everyone in security matters. Skeptics in other countries may see this as unilateralism, but Americans see it as a kind of cosmopolitanism. The third answer is that domestic politics at critical junctures can matter, as in the case of the CTBT.

First, even though the United States has been the preeminent power since World War II (some would argue even earlier), it cannot do everything by itself. Even if one does not take an alarmist view of the number of possible nuclear proliferators, several countries clearly have the potential capabilities and motivations to go nuclear. No single state, no matter how powerful, can monitor and constrain these countries by itself. It must necessarily be a joint enterprise involving many countries. From Washington's point of view, there is in addition the possibility that one or more of the nuclear weapon states might transfer nuclear weapons or technologies to a potential proliferator. The United States has always been suspicious of Russia and China in this regard. Neither state is altogether vulnerable to U.S. pressures. The only way of ensuring that both countries cooperate on nonproliferation is by persuading them to agree to a common structure of norms and practices.

Second, the United States has a culture of multilateralism that predisposes it to at least explore the possibility of constructing multilateral processes and agreements. This is true even in the security and, specifically, the nonproliferation realms. The arms control agreements of the 1920s, the Acheson-Lillienthal and Baruch plans for the control of nuclear materials, the Partial Test Ban Treaty, the Outer Space Treaty, and the Seabed Treaty—all these are multilateral agreements in the military-nuclear realm. A combination of "ideals and self interest" has long informed U.S. choices and behavior.[78] The more agreements it has signed, the more a culture of multilateralism has grown, in the sense that the United States is willing to enter into real and protracted negotiations to develop a shared set of rules and conventions governing security choices.

Having entered into multilateral negotiations in various cases, why has the United States either adopted an ambivalent approach to these or, at the limit, opted out of agreements? In the case of the NPT, the United States has insisted that it is not possible for the nuclear weapon states to get rid of their nuclear arsenals altogether. At the same time, Washington has argued that it is essential to stop others from going nuclear. The United States is not alone in adopting such a two-track policy: All the nuclear powers hold this view. The United States has borne the brunt of international criticism about the purportedly discriminatory nature of the NPT, but the other nuclear weapon states are no less insistent on maintaining an unequal structure. U.S. policy in the case of the NPT is probably best described as minilateral: The United States is attentive to the need for a common set of rules and obligations among the nuclear weapon states that are different from the rules and obligations governing the behavior of the rest of the world.

U.S. policymakers make two basic arguments to justify the differentiation between the nuclear and nonnuclear powers and, more specifically, between the United States and all other powers. First, they argue that it is not technically feasible for the nuclear weapon states to disarm. Given that nuclear weapons cannot be disinvented, and given the physical and political limits on verification, it is simply not possible to ensure that every single nuclear device will be destroyed.[79] This is especially the case because many current or putative nuclear powers are untrustworthy. Such authoritarian states face no internal pressures to be transparent and accountable, whereas the United States, which is an open society, must honor its word because of domestic political scrutiny and a tradition of public accountability.

Second, even if it were technically and administratively feasible to dismantle the nuclear arsenals of the five nuclear weapon states, this would not at present be desirable for U.S. national security and the security of the broader international system. From a narrow national security perspective, the United States needs nuclear weapons to deter attacks on its homeland and to protect nonnuclear allies from attack. Because of its unmatched strength and, consequently, its larger interests and responsibilities, the United States is a natural target for more threats. It therefore has a greater right to nuclear weapons and other forms of defense.[80] From a broader systemic perspective, nuclear deterrence is a crucial element of military stability between the major powers, in particular between the United States, Russia, and China. Nuclear weapons in the hands of the United States and its allies are also vital for dealing with so-called rogue states in order to deter them from attacking the United States, its allies, and others and, if need be, to compel them to behave in particular ways.[81] In sum, the United States does not see its privileged possession of nuclear weapons as being only in its narrow national interest. The U.S. arsenal serves more cosmopolitan purposes as well.[82]

In the case of the CTBT, the ambivalent multilateralism of the United States ended with the George W. Bush administration's announcement that it would not seek ratification of the treaty before the U.S. Senate. It should be remembered that in signing the treaty in 1996, and then in sending it up for ratification, the United States had suggested that it was willing to commit itself to a truly universal arms control treaty. What went wrong? Clearly, domestic politics played a crucial role in wrecking the treaty. Partisan (and highly personalized) politics, led by a small section of the Republican leadership in the Senate, combined with the White House's mismanagement of the ratification process, prevented a serious, rigorous debate on the provisions of the treaty and its implications for nonproliferation. The treaty's opponents argued that a test ban was neither feasible nor desirable: The United States could not maintain the safety and reliability of its arsenals or its nuclear superiority without a testing program; the verification system of the treaty might not be up to the challenge of monitoring and deterring others; and the CTBT was neither a necessary nor a sufficient condition of further nonproliferation. These were not all unreasonable objections, but they could have been answered if a small, powerful coterie of Republican senators had not made a thorough debate on the treaty virtually impossible. In the end, the United States "opted out" of this multilateral agreement.

When President Clinton departed the political stage, there was some hope that the next administration, whether Democratic or Republican, might resurrect the CTBT and once again ask the Senate to ratify it. It soon became clear, however, that the successor Bush administration would have nothing to do with a test ban. The administration based its hostility to the

CTBT on the argument that the United States may need to resume testing to ensure the safety and reliability of its nuclear arsenal. Beyond that, the Republican Party is in no mood to reverse itself on a treaty that it has so publicly denounced. Conservative strategic analysts continue to contend that the CTBT's nonproliferation rationale is no longer valid. Given that India and Pakistan tested in 1998, the treaty has little remaining utility. In any case, the NPT, which has been extended indefinitely, in effect implies a permanent test ban, making the CTBT largely redundant. Not surprisingly, General Shalikashvili's report on the CTBT, commissioned by the Clinton administration, which made a number of sober recommendations on how to reinvigorate support for the treaty, has been rather unceremoniously ignored by the new administration.[83]

The Bush administration has gone even farther. Along with its announcement, in December 2001, that it is withdrawing from the ABM Treaty, it has suggested that the United States may no longer be interested in negotiating tortuous arms control agreements. It will instead resort to unilateral actions, such as one-sided cuts in strategic nuclear forces, and/or it will rely on case-by-case bilateral agreements when and where necessary.[84] The U.S. position seems to rest on the judgment that there is not much more to be achieved in terms of the control of nuclear, biological, and chemical weapons.[85] With the indefinite extension of the NPT, the implementation of the Chemical Weapons Convention, the unworkability of a more comprehensive verification scheme to give effect to the Biological and Toxin Weapons Convention, the setting aside of the ABM Treaty, and unilateral cuts in strategic weapons by the United States, there is little else that can or needs to be done. In this view, neither rogue states (or states of concern) nor various regional situations (the Middle East, South Asia, and North Korea) are susceptible to multilateral schemes and are better dealt with, if at all, on an individual, customized basis.

The Consequences of Ambivalent Multilateralism

What have been the consequences of U.S. actions in the NPT review conferences and the CTBT negotiations? This is not an easy question to answer. The real long-term consequences may simply not be known or understood for years, if not decades. The assessments of the major powers about U.S. behavior can only be guessed at or inferred from rather sketchy evidence. However, we would hazard at least three thoughts here.

First, the indefinite extension of the NPT and the conclusion of the CTBT negotiations caused considerable unease in India, which in turn culminated in New Delhi's decision to conduct a series of nuclear tests in May 1998. Although the Indian government was rather subdued in its public reaction to the NPT review conference and to the indefinite extension of the treaty in 1995, in private Indian leaders saw the extension as having been orchestrated by the United States. They were dismayed over the collapse of unity among the nonaligned countries, which they had counted on to oppose the United States and other nuclear powers more effectively. India feared that the United States, armed with the indefinite extension of the NPT, would intensify efforts to get New Delhi to accede to the treaty or to roll back its nuclear program in some other way.[86]

India's analysis of the NPT extension in all probability fed into its decisionmaking on the CTBT and, later, on whether or not to test. New Delhi was convinced that the test-ban negotiations were primarily aimed at entrapping India.[87] Therefore, India's efforts turned increasingly toward finding a way out of the treaty without assuming the role of treaty-wrecker. Faced with an indefinite extension of the NPT and then, in 1996, with the CTBT, Indian leaders calculated that the nonproliferation noose was drawing tighter and that the only way out was to test and confront the international community with a fait accompli.[88] This was by no means the only factor in India's decision to test, but it was a factor.

At the very least, the extension of the NPT and the opening of the CTBT for signature, both over India's objections, were used by the Indian government to suggest that India's tests were a legitimate response to an increasingly unfair regime. The Indian tests, of course, led Pakistan to test, and so one could argue that one of the consequences of U.S. insistence on an indefinite extension of the NPT and the conclusion of the CTBT was to push those two countries over the nuclear edge, on which they had been teetering for about a decade. In all likelihood, both countries would have tested at some point anyway, but certainly the two agreements and the way they were portrayed—the result of U.S. "bullying"—hastened the chain of events.

Second, the U.S. decision to opt out of the CTBT cleared the way for Washington's most recent move, namely, notification of its withdrawal from the ABM Treaty. Unilateralism is apparently producing more unilateralism, and this is worrying U.S. allies as well. The Bush administration seems to have concluded that as there were few if any discernible political costs associated with U.S. rejection of the CTBT, the ABM can probably be torn up in the same manner. The administration has also rejected a number of other multilateral agreements since it came to office.

The growing U.S. tendency to opt out of multilateral agreements is causing some indignation even among U.S. allies. Virtually all the closest allies—the British, French, Germans, and Japanese—have criticized the United States in public for one unilateral decision or another. In addition, though the attacks of September 11, 2001, stifled differences with Washington, there is discomfort brewing with respect to the war on terrorism. U.S. suggestions that Iraq may be the next target of U.S. military actions have not gone down well with European allies.[89] And the Bush administration's treatment of Taliban and Al-Qaida prisoners at Guantanamo Bay,

Cuba, has led even the usually congenial British to protest.[90] President Bush's reference to Iran, Iraq, and North Korea as an "axis of evil" in his 2002 State of the Union address has been disquieting to Britain and France.[91] Russia, even as it engages the new administration, is exploring the possibilities of closer relations with China and India. Although an India-China-Russia axis is unlikely, all three powers have noted the increasing unilateralism of U.S. behavior, and all three, along with the French, talk openly about "multipolarity" as a more desirable state of international relations.[92] All in all, recent U.S. behavior, combined with earlier instances such as the rejection of the CTBT, may drive a wedge between the United States and particularly its European allies, with profound implications for world politics.

Third, the decisions by the United States to opt out of the CTBT and to withdraw from the ABM Treaty may well signal the end of the post–Cold War era of multilateralism—or even minilateralism—in arms control. With the United States failing to ratify the CTBT, there is no prospect that India and Pakistan will sign it. The treaty therefore cannot enter into force. The CD is demoralized and stalled. The U.S. decision on the CTBT, combined with the petering-out of discussions on the FMCT and Washington's determination to press ahead with missile defense, have raised serious questions about the future role of the CD in nuclear matters.

What Kind of Multilateralism in Arms Control and Nonproliferation?

What should the United States do to revive multilateralism in the area of arms control and particularly nonproliferation? Here, we can distinguish between an ideal conception of U.S. multilateralism and a more realistic optimal conception.

Ideally, the United States would begin to address its article VI obligations under the NPT immediately. In doing so, it might even agree to strive for or bind itself to a deadline for complete nuclear disarmament based on multilateral discussions involving the other nuclear powers as well as the rest of the international community, preferably in an institutional setting such as the CD in Geneva. In addition, the United States would immediately ratify the CTBT and release its complete share of funding for the CTBTO, which implements the verification and other functions of the treaty. As a way of signaling its renewed multilateral intentions, it would reverse its unilateral decision on missile defense, revive its participation in the fissile-ban talks, and restate its commitment to oppose the militarization of outer space. Even as it moved toward the achievement of a multilateral agreement on nuclear disarmament, it would engage Russia in the next generation of strategic weapons reductions. It would state as its aim the reduction of strategic nuclear forces to a minimum, perhaps as low as 150 weapons, in preparation for the final difficult step of complete disarmament.

Finally, the United States would speedily sign and/or ratify the protocol to the Biological Weapons Convention, the Ottawa Convention, and the convention on the spread of small arms. In doing this, it would acknowledge that arms control is indivisible, that progress in one area is linked to progress in others, that rules and obligations between signatories must be symmetrical, and that covenants between signatories must be arrived at free of coercion.

Needless to say, this ideal conception of U.S. multilateralism in arms control and nonproliferation bears little resemblance to current realities. Accordingly, it may make sense to outline the optimal U.S. stance that would be plausible under today's circumstances. Even this more pragmatic scenario would nevertheless represent a challenge to the current state of U.S. thinking and practice. In this optimal conception, the United States, first, would agree to the creation of a subcommittee within the CD to begin work on a study of complete nuclear disarmament. The United States would not necessarily commit itself to accepting the recommendations of the study or even to participating in the study, but it would have the right to nominate members to the committee. Second, the United States would make strategic arms talks with Russia a priority and would commit itself to uninterrupted bilateral negotiations in this matter. Third, the Bush administration would announce its intention to forward the CTBT once again to the Senate for its advice and consent. It would in the meantime take into account the report and recommendations of General Shalikashvili and work with the Senate leadership of the Republican and Democratic parties to give the treaty a fair and rigorous hearing. It would ensure that U.S. contributions to the CTBTO, if they have been remiss, are immediately fulfilled. Fourth, the United States would substantially slow down its research and development and testing of missile defense and would simultaneously begin minilateral discussions on defensive systems with concerned allies, friends, neutrals, and rivals. Finally, it would sincerely revisit the various arms control treaties it has so recently rejected, namely, those pertaining to biological weapons, landmines, and small arms. It would, by embarking on this rather different course from the present, propose that after September 11 all countries must work against the common scourge of large-scale violence, be it from terrorist attacks or nuclear weapons, and make clear that the United States is prepared to play a leadership role in bringing the world community together in finding multilateral solutions to multilateral problems.

Conclusion

The United States has been an ambivalent multilateralist on nonproliferation issues. It has initiated and participated actively in negotiating generalized norms and rules in a nonproliferation treaty as well as a test-ban treaty. In the case of the NPT, it has been a minilateralist: It has accepted a common set of norms and rules for itself and the four other original nuclear powers, but it has insisted on the continuation of a differentiated set of norms and rules for all other members of the treaty. In the case of the CTBT, U.S. policy has gone through two phases: a multilateralist phase followed most recently by a unilateralist one. Having accepted a test-ban treaty that contained a common set of rights and obligations, it has subsequently withdrawn from the agreement altogether. Thus, the United States has been ambivalent in two ways: ambivalent in the NPT on the question of universalist, nondiscriminatory rights and obligations; and ambivalent in the CTBT on the question of its own participation in a universalist, nondiscriminatory pact, fluctuating between acceptance of common rights and obligations and rejection of such a structure. On the one hand, the United States recognizes the benefits of multilateralism even for the greatest power on earth. On the other hand, domestic political partisanship, as well as genuine differences over the utility of multilateralism in specific cases, particularly in a unipolar world, account for the fluctuating fortunes of multilateralism in U.S. thought and practice.

It is striking that the United States has chosen to remain within the NPT, which is built on a differentiated set of rights and obligations, and has opted out of the CTBT, which is the more genuinely universalist treaty. This suggests that on nonproliferation—a core area of national and international security—the U.S. preference is to be unilateralist at the limit. At best, as in the NPT, it is minilateralist in the sense that it accepts the four other nuclear powers' special rights and obligations. Although it would be easy to conclude that U.S. insistence is based on a hard view of national security, this is not the whole story. Americans genuinely seem to believe that their security is important to international security. The United States, as the indispensable power, must be granted special rights and obligations in order for it to carry out its more cosmopolitan functions. The victory of George W. Bush in the presidential elections of November 2000 and the events of September 2001 and beyond are pointing to a growing unilateralism in the security posture of the United States. This is perhaps one of the most consequential senses in which the world has changed.

Notes

1. Ruggie, "Multilateralism: The Anatomy of an Institution," p. 11.
2. Ibid., p. 11.
3. Ibid., pp. 12–13.
4. Blacker and Duffy, *International Arms Control,* p. 153, on the role of Ireland and other small countries in pushing for a nonproliferation treaty. India was one of the original nonaligned countries to cosponsor a UN General Assembly resolution on the guidelines for a nonproliferation treaty. See Mirchandani, *India's Nuclear Dilemma,* pp. 122, 128–129.

5. See Herkin, *The Winning Weapon,* p. 36, on President Harry Truman's decision to deny nuclear secrets to U.S. allies. See also pp. 61–66, on the U.S. reluctance to share information and ideas with Britain. On General Leslie Groves's fears of the dangers of disseminating nuclear knowledge and materials to U.S. allies, see pp. 97–150. See also Sherwin, *A World Destroyed,* pp. 67–140.

6. Blacker and Duffy, *International Arms Control,* p. 156.

7. Ibid., p. 158.

8. President John F. Kennedy in 1963 stated: "I am haunted by the feeling that by 1970 . . . there may be ten nuclear powers instead of five, and by 1975, 15 or 20." Quoted in Keeny, "The NPT: A Global Success Story," p. 4.

9. See the interview with Lawrence Scheinman, assistant director, Arms Control and Disarmament Agency (ACDA), in "Delegate Perspectives in the 1995 NPT Review and Extension Conference: A Series of Interviews Conducted by Susan B. Welsh," *The Non-Proliferation Review* 2, no. 3 (Spring–Summer 1995), p. 16, http://cns.miis.edu/index.htm.

10. The Soviet Union was particularly worried about Germany and Japan going nuclear or getting access to nuclear weapons. See Keeny, "NPT: A Global Success Story," p. 4.

11. British concerns are noted in Oliver, *Kennedy, Macmillan, and the Nuclear Test Ban Debate, 1961–1963,* p. 7.

12. France and China were more equivocal, at least in public, in the early years: Both refused to sign the NPT and stayed aloof from the global nonproliferation campaign of the original nuclear powers.

13. Keeny, "NPT: A Global Success Story," p. 4.

14. Shortly after the NPT was opened for signature, the United States, United Kingdom, and Soviet Union agreed that as Security Council members they would respond to nuclear threats against the nonnuclear NPT states. See Blacker and Duffy, *International Arms Control,* p. 158.

15. Keeny, "NPT: A Global Success Story," pp. 3–4.

16. Ibid., p. 4.

17. On the various options, see Bunn and Rhinelander, "Extending the NPT," pp. 8–10.

18. Davis, "The End of the Beginning or the Beginning of the End?" p. 37, refers to U.S. opposition to conditionalities and time limits on the NPT extension.

19. Klare, *Rogue States and Nuclear Outlaws,* pp. 16–24.

20. "Delegate Perspectives on the 1995 NPT Review and Extension Conference," p. 6.

21. Ibid., p. 7.

22. Ibid., p. 8.

23. Ibid., p. 10.

24. Ibid., p. 10.

25. Ibid., p. 13.

26. Ibid., p. 6.

27. Ibid., p. 5.

28. Indian critics in particular argued that the United States railroaded the international community and in particular the third world countries into going along with its preferences.

29. BASIC Papers, *US Policy Leading into the NPT Conference,* p. 1, and BASIC Publications, *NPT Plenary in Review,* p. 1, http://www.basicint.org/nptcon95.htm.

30. "Principles and Objectives for Nuclear Non-Proliferation and Disarmament," NPT/CONF.1995/32/DEC.2, and "Strengthening the Review Process for the

Treaty," NPT/CONF.1995/32/DEC.1. See U.S. State Department website at http://www.state.gov/index.htm.cfm.

31. BASIC Papers, *US Policy Leading into the NPT Conference,* pp. 3–4.

32. We rely here for this account of the negotiations on Johnson, "The NPT Review," http://www.thebulletin.org/issues/yearindex.html, and Johnson, "The 2000 NPT Review Conference," http://www.acronym.org.uk/46npt.htm.

33. On U.S. expectations and the United States's low-key approach at the conference, for the most part, see the various reports penned by Johnson, in particular "Nuclear Disarmament Priorities," p. 1, http://www.acronym.org.uk/npt9.htm, and "Midnight Oil on Troubled Waters," p. 2, http://www.acronym.org.uk/npt14.htm, and "The NPT Review: Disaster Averted," p. 5.

34. On the role of the New Agenda Coalition, see Johnson, "The 2000 NPT Review Conference," p. 13, and on Russia, p. 2.

35. U.S. Department of State, "2000 NPT Review Conference Achieves an 'Historic Consensus,'" *Fact Sheet Released by the Bureau of Nonproliferation,* July 1, 2000, http://www.state.gov/www/global/arms/bureaunp.html.

36. See Johnson, "The 2000 NPT Review Conference," pp. 11–12.

37. Quoted in Kimball, "What Went Wrong," p. 3.

38. On the U.S. decision to go for a zero-yield test ban, see Manish, "Negotiating the Comprehensive Test Ban Treaty, 1994–1996," pp. 80–86. We use this study extensively to reconstruct some of the key negotiating moments and issues.

39. Manish, "Negotiating the Comprehensive Test Ban Treaty," p. 85.

40. Ibid., pp. 79–80.

41. Ibid., p. 97.

42. Ibid., p. 125.

43. Ibid.

44. Ibid., p. 126.

45. Ibid., pp. 125–127.

46. Ibid., p. 118.

47. Ibid., pp. 67–69.

48. On the British, Russian, and Chinese views of entry into force, see ibid., pp. 134–151.

49. Graham and LaVera, "Nuclear Weapons," p. 232.

50. Kimball, "Holding the CTBT Hostage in the Senate," p. 1, http://www.armscontrol.org/ACT/junjul98/abjj98.htm.

51. Ibid., p. 2.

52. Ibid.

53. Senators Hagel and Lugar complained publicly about the shortage of time to debate the CTBT. See Kimball, "What Went Wrong," p. 5.

54. Kimball, "Holding the CTBT Hostage in the Senate," p. 2.

55. Ibid., p. 4.

56. Kimball, "What Went Wrong," p. 3.

57. Ibid., pp. 3–4.

58. U.S. Senate Republican Policy Committee, "Comprehensive Test Ban Treaty Jeopardizes U.S. Nuclear Deterrent," October 5, 1999, http://www.senate.gov/~rpc/releases/1999/df100599.htm.

59. Ibid., p. 3.

60. Ibid.

61. Graham and LaVera, "Nuclear Weapons," p. 233. For the text of the safeguards, see "Comprehensive Test Ban Safeguards," September 22, 1997, http://www.state.gov/index.cfm.

62. This was a point made to the Senate Committee by the scientist Richard Garwin. See Kimball, "What Went Wrong," pp. 5–6.

63. Ibid., p. 6.

64. Graham and LaVera, "Nuclear Weapons," pp. 231–232.

65. Ibid., p. 232.

66. Kimball, "What Went Wrong," pp. 6–7.

67. Republican Policy Committee, "Comprehensive Test Ban Treaty Jeopardizes U.S. Nuclear Deterrent," pp. 1–2. The committee argued that it was particularly important to test for safety given that the last U.S. test had been carried out in 1992. It also argued that because the size and diversity of the U.S. arsenal was declining, any safety or reliability problems assumed even greater importance.

68. Quoted in Kimball, "What Went Wrong," p. 9.

69. Graham and LaVera, "Nuclear Weapons," p. 232.

70. Kimball, "What Went Wrong," p. 5.

71. Ibid.

72. Graham and LaVera, "Nuclear Weapons," p. 232. The authors note that without carrying out tests the W-61 "warhead package" has been already modified to give it earth-penetrating capabilities.

73. Kimball, "Holding the CTBT Hostage in the Senate," p. 3.

74. Graham and LaVera, "Nuclear Weapons," p. 232.

75. Republican Policy Committee, "Comprehensive Test Ban Treaty Jeopardizes U.S. Nuclear Deterrent," p. 4.

76. Graham and LaVera, "Nuclear Weapons," p. 232.

77. Republican Policy Committee, "Comprehensive Test Ban Treaty Jeopardizes U.S. Nuclear Deterrent," pp. 1 and 3–4.

78. For a history of idealist and pragmatist trends in U.S. foreign policy, see Osgood, *Ideals and Self Interest in American Foreign Policy.*

79. See the interview with Ambassador Thomas Graham of the United States, Special Representative of the President for Arms Control and Disarmament: "Ambassador Graham on US Policy and the Non-Proliferation Treaty," *Basic Papers,* no. 44 (April 14, 1995), www.basicint.org/frmain.htm.

80. See Graham and LaVera, "Nuclear Policy," p. 226–227.

81. Cambone and Garrity, "The Future of US Nuclear Policy," pp. 76–78, for why the United States must remain a nuclear power.

82. This point is also made by Graham and LaVera, "Nuclear Weapons," p. 226–227.

83. Shalikashvili, "Report on the Findings and Recommendations Concerning the Comprehensive Test Ban Treaty," pp. 18–28.

84. Kerrey and Hartung, "Towards a New Nuclear Posture," p. 5, on the Bush administration's interest in making unilateral cuts in U.S. strategic weapons and its lack of interest in tortuous arms control negotiations.

85. See "Ambassador Graham on US Policy and the Non-Proliferation Treaty."

86. See Subrahmanyam, "Nuclear India in Global Politics," p. 25, and Percovich, *India's Nuclear Bomb,* pp. 360–361.

87. Brahma Chellaney, "Nuclear Deterrent Posture," p. 165.

88. Perkovich, *India's Nuclear Bomb,* pp. 361 and 376.

89. Julian Borger, "US Split With Allies Grows: Hawks and Doves Clash Over Iraq," *Guardian Unlimited,* Special Reports, February 15, 2002, http://www.guardian.co.uk/bush/story 0, 7369, 650601, 00.html.

90. "More Arrivals at Camp X-Ray," *CBS News,* February 12, 2002, http://www.cbsnews.com/now/story/0, 1597, 326146–412, 00.shtml.

91. David E. Sanger, "Allies Hear Sour Notes in 'Axis of Evil' Chorus," *New York Times,* February 17, 2002, http://www.nytimes.com/2002/02/17/international/asia/17ALLI.html.

92. On the latest Russian move to encourage the idea of a India-China-Russia triangle and the reservations of both India and China, see "China Against Axis With India, Russia," *Times of India,* February 8, 2002, http://www.timesofindia.com/articleshow.asp?art_id=393076&sType=1.

PART 3

THE INTERNATIONAL
POLITICAL ECONOMY

12

U.S. Trade Policy:
Alternative Tacks or Parallel Tracks?

Per Magnus Wijkman

THE VAGARIES OF U.S. TRADE POLICY—CHANGING TACK FROM UNILATERAL protectionism to multilateral liberalism and back—often give rise to confusion and criticism abroad. Since the late 1970s, the United States has pursued two tracks in parallel: protectionism and liberal trade. A weak executive branch, strong protectionist sentiments in Congress, and declining U.S. influence abroad have resulted in a pattern of unilateral freewheeling within a multilateral system. This has cast doubt about where the United States is heading. Today, George W. Bush's administration is returning U.S. trade policy to its historical mainstream: multilateral liberalism. This reflects the coincidence of three factors: the transformation of the Republican Party during the last decades of the twentieth century into the champion of free trade; the reemergence of a strong executive branch with its own majority in Congress; and a strengthened capability for U.S. leadership abroad. This coincidence, together with recognition that the United States no longer can go it alone in trade, creates favorable prospects for a liberal and responsible U.S. trade policy that serves both the nation and the world.

In this chapter I view unilateral and multilateral tendencies in U.S. trade policy in light of three determining factors. The first is the balance of power between the legislative and executive branches. The U.S. Constitution gives Congress the right to regulate commerce with foreign nations, but since the 1930s Congress has delegated to the executive branch, more or less conditionally, the power to negotiate international trade agreements. The balance of power and the coincidence of views between these two branches have been crucial for the formulation of trade policy. By nature, the president tends to lean toward liberalism regardless of party. Ideally, he defends the welfare of the nation as a whole, weighing the benefits of any trade proposal to particular groups or regions against the costs that it may bring to others, bearing in mind that the nation as a whole gains from trade. By nature, Congress tends to lean toward protectionism, regardless of party.

Each member of Congress represents a relatively small district. He responds to the concerns of local interests, bearing in mind that costs and benefits from trade are unevenly distributed. Thus, a congressman responds to local demands, whereas the president trades off competing interests within a larger constituency. Recurrent executive branch initiatives to launch new negotiating rounds tend to be necessary to offset the inherent protectionist tendencies of Congress. Critical factors in the success of these rounds are the effectiveness of the United States Trade Representative (USTR), the role of the International Trade Commission (ITC), and the political clout of the chairs of the House Ways and Means Committee and the Senate Committee on Finance.

The second factor concerns the relative strengths of protectionists and liberal traders in Congress. In earlier decades, these tendencies were closely associated with the country's two main political parties. Republicans and business interests were inclined to protectionism, whereas Democrats, agricultural interests, and labor—in the days of the domestic trusts—were inclined to liberal trade. Gradually, these inclinations changed and are now reversed. Republicans and business interests are the main proponents of free trade, as U.S. corporations invest and trade internationally, whereas protectionist sentiments dominate trade-union members, who represent the rank-and-file of the Democratic Party. Laborers outnumber management interests at the polls, boding ill for freer trade when labor turns protectionist. Until the mid-1970s, a bipartisan coalition of those advocating freer trade, Republicans and Democrats, held a majority in the House of Representatives.

The third factor determining policy is the willingness and the ability of the U.S. government to exercise leadership abroad on international trade. For most of the twentieth century, the prevailing sense in the United States was that the country was a model for the world. But this attitude translated into U.S. leadership of the multilateral system (rather than withdrawal from it) only when combined with U.S. predominance on the global stage *and* appreciation that the rest of the world exercised a strong influence on the United States. When the United States is only one of several major traders, it can legitimately ask why it—and not others—should temper its national interests by assuming prime responsibility for the stability of the system. At critical moments in history, a combination of U.S. ideals and the country's pivotal role have led it to assume this responsibility.

The relative strengths of these competing forces have changed over time, and the complex interaction of political checks and balances has shaped U.S. trade policy. The process is difficult for the foreign observer to understand, and the outcome is difficult to predict. Continuity in policy formation suffers. In spite of these confounding vagaries, multilateral liberalism remains the mainstream of U.S. trade policy.

The Legacy of the Interwar Period

On November 8, 2001, Robert B. Zoellick, the United States Trade Representative, stated:

> The world economy of about a century ago held out the promise of great technological change, trade flows and economic integration similar to the forecasts of today. But the world's leading trading nations chose the wrong course, and it took the second half of the century to overcome the disastrous mistakes of the first fifty years.[1]

U.S. attitudes toward multilateral trade organizations have been influenced by a few key policy choices. Two have been particularly influential: the decisions to opt for isolationism in 1919 and for protectionism in the 1920s. These experiences contributed decisively to the swing to multilateral liberalism that dominated U.S. trade policy in the immediate decades after World War II. They form an important backdrop to today's return to that mainstream.

The Internationalist Vision

President Woodrow Wilson (who held office from 1913 until 1921) was the foremost U.S. exponent of multilateralism. Wilson saw free trade as a powerful force for international comity. As the newly elected Democratic president, he had dramatically lowered U.S. tariff rates in 1913.[2] He advocated multilateral agreements to assure freedom of the seas, advance free trade, and promote peace. He held that the moral power of the United States— emerging as the leading industrial and agricultural nation—could influence world affairs. Characteristically American, he was convinced that an enlightened electorate, wielding power at the polls, was the ultimate arbiter of national affairs. Democracy, decency, and dialogue could create the good society abroad as well as at home. This constituted an American vision, one that would inspire the rest of the world and illuminate the rest of the century.

In the short term, however, Wilson misjudged the spirit of his times. Commanding Democratic majorities in both houses of Congress in his first term, he lost his House majority in 1916 and his Senate majority in 1918 (see Figure 12.1). Subsequently, the Senate rejected U.S. participation in the League of Nations and Wilson's messianic "politics of morality" following World War I. U.S. voters confirmed this rejection at the polls in 1920, electing a Republican president.[3] Rather than project the values of U.S. exceptionalism internationally, the country withdrew into isolationism and the false sense of security that it provided.[4] The rejection of internationalism echoed through the remainder of the twentieth century and caused continuing concern among U.S. allies about the credibility of any president's commitment to multilateralism.

Three successive Republican presidents between 1921 and 1933, each commanding Republican majorities in both the House and the Senate, reversed Wilson's low tariff policy with a vengeance (see Figure 12.1). Under the slogan of the "New Nationalism," the Warren Harding, Calvin Coolidge, and Herbert Hoover administrations gave industry greater tariff protection than it had ever received previously. The Fordney-McCumber and Smoot-Hawley acts increased tariff rates on industrial and agricultural goods alike.[5] However, most agricultural interests were strongly in favor of freer trade.[6] If foreigners were to buy more U.S. agricultural goods, they had to be able to sell more industrial goods to the United States. Reducing the industrial tariff was not an option to achieve this, as Harding's businessman's cabinet was committed to industrial protection.[7] As Coolidge famously put it, "The business of America is business."

Republican attempts during the 1920s to foster a "return to normalcy" through protectionism resulted ultimately in trade wars, as other countries retaliated to Smoot-Hawley by increasing their own tariffs. International trade contracted and incomes fell in a vicious circle that prolonged and spread the Great Depression of the 1930s. At the depth of this crisis, in November 1932, Americans voted overwhelmingly for Democratic presidential candidate Franklin D. Roosevelt and for a Democratic House and Senate. It took the Great Depression to drive home to the U.S. body politic the costs of protectionism and isolationism. Only after learning the lessons the hard way did it opt for trade liberalization. This formative experience continues to shape U.S. policies today.

Figure 12.1 Representation by Party in the House and in the Senate

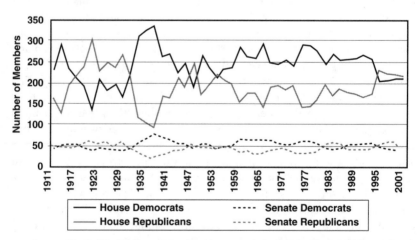

Source: *The Political Science Reference Almanac* website, www.polisci.com/almanac/legis/polidivs.htm.

Figure 12.1 Con't.

Period	President & Party		Majority House	Senate	House Dem.	Rep.	Senate Dem.	Rep.
1911	William Taft	Rep.		X	228	162	42	49
1913	Woodrow Wilson	Dem.	X	X	290	127	51	44
1915			X	X	231	193	53	42
1917				X	210	216	53	42
1919					191	237	47	48
1921	Warren Harding	Rep.	X	X	132	300	37	59
1923	Calvin Coolidge	Rep.	X	X	207	225	43	51
1925			X	X	183	247	40	54
1927			X	X	195	237	47	48
1929	Herbert Hoover	Rep.	X	X	163	267	39	56
1931			X	X	216	218	47	48
1933	Franklin Roosevelt	Dem.	X	X	313	117	59	36
1935			X	X	322	103	69	25
1937			X	X	333	89	75	17
1939			X	X	262	169	69	23
1941			X	X	267	162	66	28
1943			X	X	222	209	57	38
1945	Harry Truman	Dem.	X	X	243	190	57	38
1947					188	246	45	51
1949			X	X	263	171	54	42
1951			X	X	234	199	48	47
1953	Dwight Eisenhower	Rep.	X	X	213	221	46	48
1955					232	203	48	47
1957					234	201	49	47
1959					283	153	64	34
1961	John Kennedy	Dem.	X	X	262	175	64	36
1963	Lyndon Johnson	Dem.	X	X	258	176	67	33
1965			X	X	295	140	68	32
1967			X	X	248	187	64	36
1969	Richard Nixon	Rep.			243	192	58	42
1971					255	180	54	44
1973	Gerald Ford 1974	Rep.			242	192	56	42
1975					291	144	61	37
1977	James Carter	Dem.	X	X	292	143	61	38
1979			X	X	277	158	58	41
1981	Ronald Reagan	Rep.		X	243	192	46	53
1983				X	268	167	46	54
1985				X	253	182	47	53
1987					258	177	54	46
1989	George H.W. Bush	Rep.			260	175	55	45
1991					267	167	56	44
1993	William Clinton	Dem.	X	X	258	176	57	43
1995					204	230	48	52
1997					207	226	45	55
1999					211	223	45	55
2001	George W. Bush	Rep.	X		212	221	50	50

Source: An "X" indicates that the party of the president has a majority in House or Senate.

The Golden Period of Multilateral Liberalism

In an increasingly integrated world, a major power can remain isolationist only at its peril. World War II made a majority of Americans realize that trade policy was also foreign policy. Revolutions in transport and communications technologies were making "One World" out of national economies.[8] Isolationism was no longer an option. As a major power, the United States had to shoulder the main responsibility for maintaining world peace or be drawn into world wars. The domestic U.S. debate over nationalism versus internationalism receded, to be replaced by a debate over whether the United States should take a unilateral or multilateral tack in the international economy. From 1933 to 1969, except for two brief periods (1947–1949 and 1953–1955), Democrats controlled both the House and the Senate (see Figure 12.1) Throughout most of this period, even when Republican Dwight Eisenhower occupied the White House, Democrats formulated postwar trade policies with Republican support except for the critical years at the start of the Cold War.

At the outset, the United States took the multilateral tack, and a period of U.S. leadership followed, inspired by U.S. exceptionalism. It was based on the trade polices of the New Deal. Cordell Hull, Roosevelt's secretary of state from 1933 to 1944, enacted a policy of trade liberalization based on reciprocity: opening the U.S. market in exchange for the opening of foreign markets. Hull had been a strong supporter of Wilson and of the League of Nations.[9] His experience as a Democratic congressman during World War I had deeply influenced his view of trade policy and foreign policy:

> But toward 1916, I embraced the philosophy I carried throughout my twelve years as Secretary of State, into numerous speeches and statements addressed to this country and to the world. From then on, to me, unhampered trade dovetailed with peace; high tariffs, trade barriers, and unfair economic competition, with war.[10]

The Reciprocal Trade Agreements Act (RTAA), adopted by the Democratic Congress in 1934, had given the president authority to negotiate bilaterally with any country on product-by-product tariff reductions. These reductions were then "multilateralized" to other countries through the most-favored-nation principle.

Through Cordell Hull the multilateralism of Woodrow Wilson belatedly triumphed. Early in World War II, Hull set up a task force to design multilateral postwar economic institutions. The United States emerged from the war as the unchallenged economic, military, and moral power in the Western world. As the leader of the free world, it assumed responsibility for the global trading system. The proposed International Trade Organization (ITO) contained a comprehensive set of trade rules and a mechanism for liberalizing trade based on the RTAA, but with bilateral negotiations replaced by multilateral ones. The rules gave countries within the system nondiscriminatory access to each other's markets. Those outside the system had a strong incentive to join and gain access to the benefits. To join, they would eventually have to improve access to their own markets, creating a virtuous cycle of liberalization.

From 1947 to 1948, with the Cold War under way, President Harry Truman faced a Republican-controlled House and Senate that limited his powers and balked at the ITO proposals.[11] Congress circumscribed liberalization by requiring that all U.S. trade agreements include a safeguard provision, to be administered by the then International Tariff Commission (ITC), and it fought against authorizing the president to negotiate tariff reductions in the General Agreement on Tariffs and Trade (GATT) rounds. The rest of the world once again feared the prospect of a Democratic executive too weak to sell multilateral solutions to Congress and a Congress too prone to accommodate protectionist interests. And like the League of Nations, the ITO, which President Truman had abandoned in the Senate, was not ratified by the United States.[12] Republicans in Congress continued their opposition to the RTAA into the 1950s.

Nevertheless, the messianic spirit of U.S. exceptionalism that had prevailed at the end of the war produced a multilateral system under strong but enlightened U.S. leadership. The United States did not use its considerable market size to negotiate "equivalent" concessions from each smaller trading partner.[13] It bore most of the public good costs of providing a multilateral regime, allowing other countries to free-ride on the tariff reductions it negotiated with a few others, which were then multilateralized to third countries. It initiated most of the eight negotiating rounds in the GATT, and after thirty years tariff rates on industrial products in the United States (and in several other industrial countries) were negligible on average (see Table 12.1). The dramatic reductions in tariff rates negotiated in the Kennedy Round meant that nontariff measures replaced tariffs as the most important barrier to trade. These barriers were dealt with in the next two rounds. In effect, Truman and his successors achieved the basic aim of Woodrow Wilson and Cordell Hull: to avoid major wars in the future by setting up a multilateral system that secured the U.S. system of free enterprise, democracy, and openness in a large part of the world. The communist planned economies were excluded from the multilateral system throughout most of the Cold War, but eventually that was to change.[14]

Unilateral Freewheeling Within a Multilateral System

In his statement before the Committee on Finance of the U.S. Senate on January 30, 2001, USTR Robert B. Zoellick stated, "I will not hesitate to use the full power of U.S. law to defend American business and workers against unfair trading practices." Experience lends the words an ominous ring.

Table 12.1 GATT Negotiating Rounds and Trade Liberalization in U.S.

Round	Average Cut in all Duties	Remaining Duties as a Proportion of 1930 Tariffs	Subjects Covered	Countries Participating
1934–1937, Pre-GATT	32.2	66.8		
First Round, Geneva, 1947	21.1	52.7	Tariffs	23
Second Round, Annecy, 1949	1.9	50.7	Tariffs	13
Round, Torquay, 1950–1951	3.0	50.1	Tariffs	38
Fourth Round, Geneva, 1955–1956	3.5	48.9	Tariffs	26
Dillon Round, Geneva, 1961–1962	2.4	47.7	Tariffs	26
Kennedy Round Geneva, 1964–1967	36.0	30.5	Tariffs and antidumping measures	62
Tokyo Round, Geneva, 1974–1979	29.6	21.2	Tariffs, nontariff measures, framework agreements	102
Uruguay Round, Geneva, 1986–1994	51.7	10.2	Tariffs, nontariff measures, rules, services, intellectual property, dispute settlement, textiles agriculture, creation of WTO.	123

Sources: Philipe Lavergne, "The Political Economy of U.S. Tariffs," Ph.D. thesis, University of Toronto (1981), reproduced by Robert Baldwin, "The Changing Nature of U.S. Trade Policy Since World War II," and Hanspeter Tschäni and Ossi Tuusvuori, *Principles and Elements of Free Trade Relations,* p. 26. The update for the Uruguay Round is from WTO.

When Richard Nixon assumed the presidency in 1969, Republicans were to occupy the White House until 1993, except for four years. Throughout the entire period, Democrats controlled the House. They also controlled the Senate, except for six years (1981–1987) under Ronald Reagan's presidency (see Figure 12.1). The four-year presidency of Jimmy Carter (1977–1981) brought little change in terms of trade policy, preoccupied as it was with the negotiations mandated by the Trade Act of 1974. The period 1969–1993 was marked by two major negotiating rounds to liberalize trade (Tokyo and Uruguay) but also by a number of unilateral U.S. measures to correct a perceived lack of reciprocity. This simultaneous pursuit of multilateral and unilateral tracks endowed U.S. trade policy during the period with a Jekyll and Hyde quality. This split personality reflected four important changes in the policy environment.

First, U.S. protectionist sentiments had grown strongly, especially in the Democratic Party, following the major tariff cuts agreed upon in the Kennedy Round. A key indicator of this was the imposition of import quotas on textiles and footwear, promised by Nixon in his 1968 election campaign, applauded by the AFL-CIO, and passed by the House in 1970 (as the so-called Mills legislation).[15] Trade union opposition to freer trade was reflected in increasing skepticism also among Democratic representatives. Whereas Republicans voted overwhelmingly for the Trade Reform Act of 1974 in the House, more Democrats voted against it than for it (see Figure

12.2; see also Figure 12.3 for the Senate picture). During the last three decades of the twentieth century, the percentage of Democrats in the House that voted for liberal trade bills fell continuously, hovering at times around only 20 percent. Republicans increasingly supported free trade, in part

Figure 12.2 Free Trade Sentiments in the House

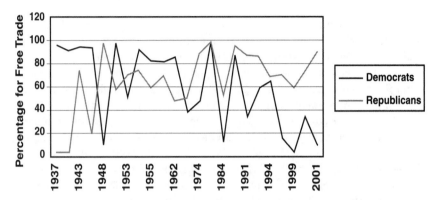

Source to 1994: Hiscox, Michael J. *International Organization,* 53, 4 (Autumn 1999).
Source from 1994: The Congress website, www.congress.gov.
Note: Trade sentiment is measured by the votes cast in the House and in the Senate respectively on major pieces of trade legislation. A vote for liberalization of trade or against a protectionist measure is counted as a vote favoring free trade. The votes are on the following legislation: Reciprocal Trade Agreements Act 1934, 37, 40, 43, 45, 48, 49, 53, 54, 55, 58; Trade Expansion Act 1962; "Miles Bill" 1970; Trade Reform Act 1974; Trade Agreements Act 1979; Trade Remedies Act 1984; Canada-U.S. Free Trade Act 1988; Fast Track Authority 1991, 93, 98; Uruguay Round Agreement 1994; Steel Import Quota 1999; China Permanent Normal Relations 2000, and Trade Promotion Authority 2001.

Figure 12.3 Free Trade Sentiments in the Senate

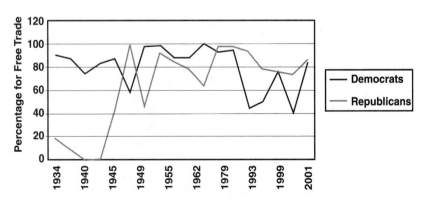

See Source and Note for Figure 12.2 above.

under the influence of supply-side economics that transfused the party under Reagan.

Second, domestic political power shifted from the executive branch to Congress. President Nixon, relatively uninterested in economic affairs, allowed a protectionist Congress to lead in trade policy during his first term. The power of Congress grew following his forced resignation in 1974 and remained strong into the 1990s with the unsuccessful attempts to impeach Bill Clinton.

Third, the United States lost its unquestioned economic, political, and moral leadership in the world. Under the strains of financing the Vietnam War, the Nixon administration unilaterally abandoned the Bretton Woods system of pegged exchange rates and imposed a 10 percent surcharge on imports. Meanwhile, a united Europe, following U.S. assistance, postwar recovery, and progressive integration, came to rival the United States as the world's leading trading nation. The completion of decolonization, symbolized by U.S. withdrawal from Vietnam in 1975, spread political power more evenly around the globe and generally reduced U.S. political influence. In the United Nations, the United States found itself opposing developing countries' demands for a new international economic order, symbolized by the deep-seabed mining regime of the UN Law of the Sea Conference.[16]

Finally, the United States had increasing difficulty projecting its positive values internationally. At home, racial discrimination and poverty, violence, and political assassinations combined with support for dictatorships abroad to suggest that an ugly American now inhabited the city on the hill.

This combination—protectionist Democrats in Congress with no loyalty to the president, a strong Congress and a weak presidency, and a United States with insufficient moral stature to lead the multilateral system—complicated U.S. trade policy. Nevertheless, the executive branch succeeded in negotiating an agreement in the Tokyo Round (containing a number of codes on nontariff barriers to trade), which was overwhelmingly approved in both Houses in 1979 (see Figure 12.2). To achieve this, the executive branch had had to make use of quotas and orderly marketing arrangements for a number of products. Quotas were imposed on textiles through the Multi-Fiber Agreement of 1973, and the executive negotiated orderly marketing arrangements with Korea and Taiwan for shoes and with Japan on color TV sets in 1977. It also introduced a system of reference prices to limit steel imports in 1977.[17] Buffeted by dramatic swings in the value of the U.S. dollar in the 1970s and 1980s, and hence in the competitiveness of U.S. firms, administrations pursued U.S. trade interests by unilateral protectionist measures that often conflicted with the requirements of the multilateral system.

The Nixon and Reagan administrations made extensive use of three types of measures: unilateral measures to limit imports deemed by the United States to constitute unfair trade; unilateral actions to free U.S. exports from "unjustifiable, unreasonable, or discriminatory foreign trade practices"; and bilateral trade agreements. All measures were based on extensive U.S. legislation.[18] This aggressive use of U.S. laws to administer protectionism placed the commitment of the United States to multilateralism in question.

Applying U.S. law to protect U.S. business—which continues to this day—arouses major concerns abroad, because it often contravenes GATT/WTO rules. Hence, while the above statement by the current United States Trade Representative, Robert Zoellick, may read well in the Senate, it has an ominous ring to it abroad. Zoellick, of course, could hardly have said otherwise, but he might instead have said nothing. The following three measures, in particular, have aroused widespread resentment abroad, seriously eroding the credibility of the U.S. commitment to multilateralism.

Unilateral Pursuit of Fair Trade: Import Protection

Abroad, heavy criticism has been directed against the use of U.S. laws designed to remedy the damage caused by unfair competition (i.e., by dumping and subsidies). In 1916, when President Wilson proposed an antidumping act, it was intended to deflect protectionist pressures in Congress. In the 1970s and 1980s, antidumping was a common means to accommodate protectionist pressures. It was often designed to suit a particular interest group, was seldom in conformity with GATT rules, and was applied in such a way that foreign competitors were often prevented from benefiting from due process of law. Available almost on demand to petitioners, subject to arbitrary administrative procedures, and expensive for the defendant to combat, antidumping action became the foremost recourse of well-organized industries in search of protection from foreign competition.

Between 1980 and 1999, the United States used such procedures a total of 633 times. This represents about 24 percent of the antidumping actions initiated by all GATT signatories during that period.[19] Recently, other countries have increased their use of these measures, with the EU in 1999 initiating almost twice as many antidumping investigations as the United States. However, the United States still leads with 27 percent of the number of antidumping measures in force notified to the WTO; the EU is second with 17 percent.[20]

Tailor-made protectionism. The domestic steel and pork industries illustrate the influence of specific industry groups on drafting U.S. trade laws. Since the late 1960s, the U.S. steel industry has benefited from a series of antidumping, countervailing duty, and gray-zone measures.[21] In the 1970s, it lobbied the government to expand the definition of dumping to include selling in the U.S. market at prices below average cost (instead of the fair value price). Pricing below average costs can be rational and legitimate in any industry, and it is especially common in industries, like steel, that suffer from excess capacity and large fixed costs. In spite of this, an amendment to the antidumping law in 1974 adopted the "below-cost" definition of dumping.[22] As a result, antidumping measures can be used against cheap imports in general and are not limited to cases of predatory pricing.

Similarly, the pork industry in 1984 requested that the ITC initiate an action concerning live swine and pork processing in Canada. U.S. producers alleged that Canadian producers were unfairly subsidized. Because the ITC could not determine that this was the case under existing U.S. law, Congress altered how it assessed unfair subsidies under the Tariff Act of 1930.[23] Even so, the investigation did not find that pork processing was subsidized (under the new subsidy definition), only that live swine was. The U.S. pork industry was unhappy and took action, seeking a legislative remedy from Congress. As a result,

> In 1988 the U.S. passed the Omnibus Trade and Competitiveness Act, which included a clause (written we are told, by counsel for the U.S. pork interests) essentially directing the ITC to find injury from "upstream subsidies," such as those for Canadian hogs, for a downstream product, such as pork.[24]

Legal harassment. Foreign exporters (especially in smaller countries) complain that it is difficult to make full use of the due process ostensibly provided by U.S. trade remedy laws, even if the laws are in conformity with GATT. The costs of posting bond (to cover a possible adverse-injury ruling) and the expenses and time-consuming nature of legal procedures in the United States can discourage a firm from pursuing its rights under the law, even if it feels its prospects of winning are good.[25] Previously, these costs inclined smaller companies to settle out of court, by agreeing to a voluntary export restraint, which they usually found more profitable than abstaining from exporting altogether or accepting terms decided by the United States. The WTO now prohibits the use of such gray-zone measures, forcing smaller foreign firms to accept U.S. terms.

WTO legality. The WTO antidumping agreement of 1994, while allowing governments to protect firms from legitimate instances of unfair competition, establishes procedures for determining whether an industry is suffering from serious injury or the threat thereof and whether this is due to dumping. A number of WTO panels have ruled that application of U.S. legislation is not in conformity with this agreement.[26] Thus, the below-cost definition in the U.S. antidumping legislation as amended in 1974 is inconsistent with the WTO. Aspects of the 1916 antidumping law are inconsistent with WTO rules. Several U.S. methods of calculating the dumping margin have been disallowed. Similarly, WTO panels have found U.S. countervailing duty measures to be inconsistent with the Agreement on Subsidies and Countervailing Measures. For instance, WTO has disallowed the U.S. procedure to apply countervailing duties against companies that once received a subsidy after they had been privatized. WTO panels have found elements of U.S. safeguards measures (section 201) to be inconsistent with WTO rules. A number of panel rulings will be necessary to identify inconsistencies between U.S. legislation and WTO rules. How quickly the United States adjusts its legislation in the light of these rulings will determine the credibility of the U.S. commitment to the WTO.

As long as GATT discipline was lax, the U.S. government tended to provide protection when major industries requested it, even if in contravention of GATT rules. Those demanding protection are often vocal and well organized. The costs of protection, in contrast, are spread over a large segment of society and unlikely to lead to complaints. Foreign exporters do not vote and can be disregarded if their capacity to retaliate is small. This problem is not limited to the United States. Trade remedy laws—often modeled on U.S. laws—have spread to other countries. It will take time for the WTO dispute settlement mechanism to bring national rules and procedures into conformity with the WTO, on a case-by-case basis.

Unilateral Opening of Foreign Markets: Export Promotion

Both the Nixon and the Reagan administrations introduced unilateral measures widely criticized abroad. The amended section 301 of the Trade Reform Act of 1974 was designed to open markets abroad in a most innovative way. The traditional GATT procedure is to open markets through negotiations, based on extending reciprocal benefits. The innovation in the amendments of section 301 (special 301, super 301 [1988]) was to force U.S. trading partners to open their markets unilaterally (i.e., without reciprocity by the United States) or face unilaterally determined retaliatory measures.

The procedures left the administration little discretion about whether or not to act. Based on annual reports of foreign practices to be drawn up by the USTR, the government was mandated to propose actions against countries found to employ "unjustifiable, unreasonable, or discriminatory foreign trade practices which burden or restrict U.S. commerce."[27] In particular the legislation was aimed at Japan, which was viewed as protecting its domestic market by inscrutable means. Individual firms could petition the government to take action. Congress drafted this legislation with the explicit aim of forcing countries to undertake measures that would guarantee U.S. firms "effective" market access. Underlying the amendment of section 301 lay a feeling that the tariff reductions negotiated by the United States in the early postwar period had not been appropriately reciprocated and that market access was imbalanced. At the risk of being perceived as backtracking on its commitments, the Reagan administration now decided to correct this imbalance.

Foreign critics of the section 301 amendments held that the United States had contravened GATT by taking unsanctioned unilateral retaliatory actions; that the United States had set aside the principle of reciprocity by requiring unilateral concessions; and that the United States had violated the most-favored-nation principle by gaining market access only for itself and not generally for all countries. In short, they held that section 301 allowed the United States to bully the weak and feel justified in doing so.

Some have argued that the executive branch had more noble aims than Congress. Section 301, in this view, was a strategic instrument used to force GATT signatories to improve discipline, in particular concerning the protection of intellectual property rights (super 301), and to initiate a new round of GATT negotiations.[28] This view attributes an impressive capacity for strategic rationality to the political system. More likely, the objective of Congress was simply to pry open markets, and the executive branch used the crowbar provided by Congress.

Nevertheless, super 301 may coincidentally have helped the administration achieve its own targets: to agree on a new GATT round, to include intellectual property in the multilateral rules system, and to improve enforcement of the multilateral system's rules. The price the United States paid for these gains was to accept the WTO, which effectively prohibited further use of section 301, hoisting Congress on its own petard. Through article 23 of the WTO's dispute settlement understanding (DSU), the United States foreswore the use of section 301, committing itself to use the multilateral DSU procedures first. If used today in contradiction to article 23, section 301 would not be considered to conform to WTO rules. Thus, the WTO put an end to aggressive unilateralism. Whether achieved by design or by accident, the outcome was welcomed abroad.

Bilateral FTAs: Double-Header or Exit Option? In the 1980s, the Reagan administration announced a dramatic policy reversal: it declared that it was prepared to sign bilateral free trade agreements (FTAs) with other countries.[29] Many abroad feared that the United States was veering away from the multilateral track. Since that time, the United States has signed agreements with Israel (1985), with Canada (Canada-U.S. Free Trade Agreement, 1987), with Canada and Mexico (the North American Free Trade Agreement, 1993), and with Jordan (2001). The United States is currently negotiating a Free Trade of the Americas Area (FTAA), to be concluded by 2005 and encompassing every nation of the hemisphere except Cuba. In addition, it has started negotiations with Chile and Singapore. The administration of George W. Bush is considering negotiating additional FTAs, in particular with countries in Asia, within the framework of the Asia-Pacific Economic Cooperation (APEC) forum.

This "competition in liberalization" by whatever means—unilateral, bilateral, or multilateral—is not necessarily harmful to the multilateral trading system. It is often pointed out, especially in Europe, that regional FTAs are not in contradiction to global liberalization and can actually speed it up.[30] During the 1960s and 1970s, trade liberalization among the industrial countries moved faster on a regional basis, and this actually speeded up multilateral liberalization.[31] The creation and successive enlargements of the EU discriminated against outside countries. Consequently, the United States took the lead in initiating successive GATT rounds aimed at lowering the common external tariff (and thereby the internal preferential margin) of the EU. Through GATT, the tariff reductions that the United States and the EU negotiated with each other were extended to all other members via the most-favored-nation principle. Thus, global liberalization resulted from the close interplay of regional and multilateral approaches.

In the 1980s, the United States found it difficult to interest others in a new multilateral round. It put the shoe on the other foot and took to the regional track itself, creating preferential margins in North America that other countries were interested in reducing. The United States pursued regional FTAs in the Americas for political reasons, to further prosperity and stability in its two great neighbors. Canada and Mexico share long land borders with the United States, and economic or political disorders in either country could easily spill over the border. Similarly, the proposed FTAA can be seen as a means to encourage elected governments in the wider hemisphere to get their financial houses in better order and to lock in economic reforms. Granting preferential access to the U.S. market is one means to reward such progress.

Bilateral FTAs are cause for concern because they can complicate the international trading system and reduce the stimulus for new GATT rounds. FTAs can be either offensive or defensive.[32] Offensive FTAs use a country's bargaining strength to create a preferential margin for its goods in another market. The EU is the hub of an extensive network of FTAs (with Eastern European and Mediterranean Basin countries). The political motivation behind these is strong and similar to that behind the planned FTAA between the United States and its hemispheric neighbors. Defensive FTAs protect market shares in response to an FTA by an important competitor in a key market.

The preferred way to reduce preferential margins is GATT negotiations rather than defensive FTAs, as the tariff reductions are then multilateralized to other WTO members. However, the EU has sought to counter NAFTA by negotiating its own FTA with Mexico (July 2000), with tariff reductions by Mexico benefiting only the EU.[33] Similarly, the United States may defend its competitive position in the Mercosur market, following the EU's FTA with those countries, by contemplating its own FTAs with Mercosur countries. Jordan, meanwhile, has sought to capture a competitive edge vis-à-vis Israel in the U.S. political as well as economic markets by signing its own FTA with the United States. If the APEC countries do embark on regional integration, including FTAs with the United States, it is likely that the EU will negotiate FTAs with APEC countries to defend its market shares.

The result of this process is the emergence of crisscrossing networks of bilateral FTAs, raising the transaction costs to businessmen of conducting foreign trade. This will be especially damaging to small and medium-sized firms. Business decisions about what country to produce goods in and where to export them will require intimate knowledge of a maze of country-specific trade agreements. This would undercut the WTO and destroy the "public-good" character of the multilateral trade system.

It is premature to regard NAFTA, the proposed FTAA, or even APEC as signals that the United States is taking a regional exit from the multilateral highway. The emergence of regional trading blocs does not signal a division of the world economy. Each bloc needs the others and has strong incentives to remain open.[34] This is especially true for the United States. The combined markets of the rest of the Americas are too small for the United States to make even the FTAA hemispheric option an alternative to multilateral liberalization on a global scale.[35] Regional trade areas, together with multilateral liberalization, have in the past constituted a "double-header" to the great benefit of the smaller countries in the global trade system. The United States has signed fewer FTAs than the European Union and focused on regional agreements. Its reaction to the creation of FTAs by others has been to initiate global liberalization through GATT rather than additional preferential agreements. The result is what USTR Zoellick calls "regionalism with a global goal."[36] Hopefully, the United States will continued to avoid the temptation to pursue bilateral, nonregional FTAs. As a global trader, the United States has a greater interest in pursuing global rather than preferential liberalization. Therefore, U.S. preferential agreements are likely to remain part of a double header, rather than an exit from the multilateral system.

Learning to Live with the WTO, If Not to Love It

Again, USTR Robert B. Zoellick provides a good introduction to our discussion. On June 29, 2001, he stated, "Our challenge at the dawn of the 21st century is to learn from the mistakes of the 20th century so we do not repeat them."[37]

The end of the Cold War posed major challenges to the multilateral trading system, challenges that the Clinton presidency was not prepared to meet. An apparent advocate of so-called assertive multilateralism, the president lacked support from his party and the pollsters on trade issues, and he was in bitter conflict with Congress over other matters during the latter part of his presidency. Deferring to political convenience rather than to conviction, he presided over a policy characterized, like those of several predecessors, by strong unilateral and protectionist aspects.

Most Democrats in Congress opposed concluding NAFTA, launching the FTAA, normalizing trade relations with China, and admitting it to the WTO. These positions all reflected the concerns of their trade-union constituents of protecting jobs from low-wage competition. In contrast, Congress supported the use of unilateral trade sanctions (such as the Iran-Libya Sanctions Act of 1996 and others against Iraq, India, and Pakistan), as well as attempts to extend U.S. labor and environmental standards to other countries through unilateral trade measures. An action widely criticized abroad, especially by the closest U.S. allies, was the passage of the Helms-Burton legislation in 1996.[38] This measure, which reflected the charged domestic politics of an election year, tightened trade embargoes of varying severity that the United States had imposed on Cuba since 1962. Most controversially, it adopted the principle of extraterritoriality (ostensibly designed to protect private property rights in Cuba). The legislation's title III allows U.S. citizens to take legal action against non-U.S. citizens who "traffic" in property confiscated by the Castro regime. Title IV "bars the granting of U.S. entry visas to corporate officers, agents, or shareholders with a controlling interest in firms that traffic in expropriated property."[39]

Trade embargoes are ineffective if not universally subscribed to, and no U.S. allies subscribed to the U.S. embargo on Cuba. Hence, Helms-Burton aimed to establish a so-called secondary embargo, penalizing other countries that traded with Cuba. Ironically, the United States had objected vigorously when the Arab League countries blacklisted U.S. firms that traded with Israel (a secondary embargo) in an attempt to make their embargo on trade with Israel more effective. The extraterritorial application of U.S. laws through Helms-Burton added insult to injury for U.S. allies by exposing any foreign businessman dealing with Cuban companies (most of which had once been confiscated) to a civil suit by any former Cuban owner who had since become a U.S. citizen.[40] In addition, foreign management and shareholders of such companies (and even their spouses and children) were denied entry visas to the United States.

The major U.S. allies, including Australia, Canada, Israel, Mexico, and the countries of the EU, had significant investments in Cuba and were directly exposed to titles III and IV of Helms-Burton. They objected to such extraterritorial applications of U.S. law, designed to force them to adhere to policies they did not share, and passed laws making it illegal for their companies to obey Helms-Burton–type laws. Thus, the Cuba embargo became a major issue of contention between the United States and its allies, creating a lose-lose situation for commercial interests. Recognizing that the measure was counterproductive, Clinton temporarily waived the implementation of title III every six months.[41]

Another unilateral and protectionist measure indicative of the mood of Congress during Clinton's second term is the so-called Byrd Amendment. Senator Robert Byrd (D–West Virginia) proposed an act approved by Congress in October 2000 that earmarked the revenues collected from antidumping duties and distributed them to petitioners for antidumping relief.[42] This act increased the incentives for U.S. companies to request antidumping measures by providing double protection, a subsidy to them financed by a tax on their competitors. The act is incompatible with the WTO. The Clinton administration opposed but did not veto it.

Thanks to Republican votes, liberal trade policy initiatives nevertheless were passed in Congress during the 1990s. NAFTA was approved in 1993, even though most Democrats in both houses voted against it. Implementation of the Uruguay Round (including accession to the WTO) was agreed on with strong support from both parties in 1994. Bill Clinton could claim little credit for either initiative, as both had been negotiated by his predecessor, George H. W. Bush, but deserves credit for their skillful passage through Congress. Clinton convened the first forum for APEC in 1993 in Seattle, and the four following summits agreed in principle to liberalize trade and investment in the region. With the WTO increasingly up and running, Clinton found it difficult to get APEC to go anywhere fast, especially following the Asian crisis in 1997–1998. From 1995 until 2001, with Republicans in control of both houses and with increasingly antagonistic relations between the president and Congress, the administration's trade initiatives concerning APEC, FTAA, and a new WTO round were effectively dead. The president failed in his attempts to obtain trade promotion authority (TPA) in both 1997 and 1998. In the trade field, Clinton had quickly become a lame duck strutting in borrowed feathers.

The Clinton presidency's major trade achievement was to help the United States learn how to live with the WTO, if not to love it.[43] Although growing global interdependence favors multilateral institutions in the trade field, it took fifty years for the United States to accept much of what Republicans had once found difficult to accept in the ITO: an international organization, a comprehensive system of binding rules, an effective mechanism for international dispute settlement, and decisionmaking based on "one-country, one-vote." U.S. hesitations left it to the European Union to champion the WTO. The EU made acceptance of the WTO a precondition for concluding the Uruguay Round.[44] The United States was more interested in the results of the round itself: better access to protected agricultural markets abroad, incorporation of trade in services, protection of intellectual property rights, and the discipline of trade-related investment measures.[45] Congress accepted the WTO only after inserting a notice clause.[46] The United States was no longer prepared to pay the price of leading the system, but it found that a multilateral regime could protect its interests better than unilateral measures. Accordingly, the Clinton administration participated actively in the WTO work program that followed the Uruguay Round, including completing the negotiations on telecommunications and financial services. The positive experiences of these first years contributed to Democrats and Republicans alike voting overwhelmingly in 2000 not to withdraw from the WTO.

Initial U.S. reluctance to accept the WTO raised concerns abroad and at home that centered on three factors. Could the United States control the

WTO agenda and the decisionmaking process? Would dispute settlement based on retaliation favor the stronger members? Would the United States be able to justify protectionist measures by reference to its concerns for labor standards and environmental issues? Decisionmakers in the United States feared that the answer to each of these questions would be no, those abroad that it would be yes. If the former, would future U.S. administrations, once they discovered the full implications of WTO membership, backtrack from commitments made by predecessors? This possibility surfaced in statements such as those by Senator Robert Dole (R–Kansas), who argued in the mid-1990s that the United States should withdraw from the WTO if three consecutive rulings in the dispute settlement mechanism went against it. It was nourished by Congress's capacity to vote every five years on withdrawal from the WTO. The contribution of the Clinton administration was to prove that both foreign and U.S. fears were in fact exaggerated. The experiences of the WTO's first five years showed that the outcome lay between U.S. and foreign concerns. Although the jury is still out on how the necessary adjustments will ultimately be accepted at home, the first five years laid a promising basis for expanded multilateral cooperation.

Maintaining U.S. Influence in Decisionmaking

The United States has long dominated the agenda and decisionmaking in global trade policy. This was partly because an informal management system ran the GATT and an assertive country could play a lead role. The formal management system was unwieldy, consisting of a "committee of the whole," a vestige from the founding era when the number of members was a "manageable" twenty-three.[47] Governance by a "general assembly" that contains a larger number of parties can easily become a Polish parliament.[48] In such situations, decisionmaking usually devolves to informal "kitchen cabinets" or "inner circles."[49] In the GATT these took the form of so-called Green Room meetings, or informal gatherings, to which a chairman invited only those countries in his committee showing an active interest in an issue.[50] The United States and the EU, prime movers in the WTO, were always present at Green Room meetings. Together with a small number of other active countries, they effectively managed the GATT.[51]

The major countries also exercise control through the WTO budget. Although voting is based on the principle of "one-country, one-vote," decisionmaking by consensus is the rule.[52] Consensus decisionmaking supplies any mini-state with a veto—and any large country as well. Backed with its veto, a large country effectively controls the budget of the WTO. Ambassadors in Geneva claim that the WTO is a "member-driven organization," with a secretariat that does the bidding of its members. But problems arise because some members drive the organization more than others, due to larger contributions to the budget. The EU and the United States contribute

42 percent and 16 percent, respectively, of the WTO annual budget.[53] They control its size and its composition. The WTO's budget in 2001 was $82 million and its staff was 552.[54] This is modest compared to the Organization for Economic Cooperation and Development (OECD), with an annual budget of $200 million and a staff of 1,850; the International Monetary Fund, with an annual budget of $638 million and a staff of 1,900 (regular and contractual); and the World Bank, with a budget of $789 million in 2000 and a staff of 8,000 in Washington.

An understaffed WTO secretariat means that smaller countries suffer while larger countries, with highly professional staffs, can manage on their own. Understaffing affects two areas in particular. The legal division included in 2000 about ten people. The DSU has dramatically increased the need for legal opinions, and this division researches and writes, albeit often at excessive length, the draft opinions for the DSU panels. The shortage of legal staff makes it increasingly difficult for the WTO to meet its deadlines in the dispute settlement process. Ambassadors of larger countries often claim that a larger legal division would lead to excessive legalism. But their reluctance can also reflect a preference to downsize this crucial activity and be freer to negotiate settlements of disputes themselves.

The second area to suffer is the research division, which employed about eight people and a temporary director in 2000. This seriously constrains the secretariat's ability to present policy proposals. Ambassadors have argued in the budget committee against increased funding for the research division with the words: We do not expect the secretariat to take any initiatives. The larger members appear happy with a "pencil sharpening" secretariat, that is, one that performs secretarial tasks and does not question the established order. For instance, efforts by the research division to deal with antidumping issues have not been welcomed.

The Seattle debacle of October 1999 forced the WTO to make special efforts to improve its decisionmaking processes. The WTO secretariat is now more transparent. Open meetings in the General Council are more frequent and the developing countries better represented. Proposals have been made to rationalize decisionmaking by creating an executive board representing significantly fewer members.[55] If enacted, this will reduce the influence of the major trading nations in the decisionmaking process compared to informal Green Room governance.

More active participation by members besides the United States is inevitable. China's accession introduces a new major player. EU enlargement and the adoption of the euro will further increase the EU's influence in the WTO. All this will reduce the effective influence of the United States, which will find it more difficult to have its way. More skillful diplomacy—partnership rather than unilateral leadership—will be required in the future if the United States is to achieve its objectives.

A reduced U.S. role in decisionmaking combined with a high U.S. contribution to the WTO budget may lead some to criticize U.S. membership in the WTO. However, U.S. influence, though less today than in the past, will still be greater when exercised from within the WTO than from without. The interdependence inherent in trade makes it far more costly for the United States to leave the WTO than to leave UNESCO. Rather than leave the WTO if things do not go its way, the United States is likely to stay and make the most of its ability to control the organization.

Dispute Settlement Is Not Rule Enforcement

Enforcement of rules was notoriously lax in the GATT.[56] In the 1980s, the United States joined smaller countries in calling for improved enforcement. A key motivation was that the European Community had emerged in the 1970s as a commercial power equivalent to the United States. If the United States could enforce EU compliance in the future no better than the EU had been able to enforce U.S. compliance in the past, it faced a problem.[57]

The Understanding on Rules and Procedures Governing the Settlement of Disputes (i.e., the DSU), negotiated as part of the WTO, provides two important improvements relative to the GATT. First, panel rulings are automatically adopted unless there is a consensus to reject them. This effectively ensures that panel rulings are adopted.[58] Second, there is a tight timetable for the conciliation and panel procedure. From the moment a dispute is brought before the WTO, it is supposed to take a maximum of nine months before a preliminary decision is made, thereby eliminating procrastination.[59] There is also a verification process to ensure that compliance has occurred.

The WTO is not a supranational organization, and the DSU does not enforce rules in a judicial process. Instead the WTO relies on the GATT principle of enforcement through retaliation, granting the right for an aggrieved country to withdraw previously granted benefits. The DSU allows the parties to reach a mutually acceptable solution to a dispute, which may very well deviate from the rules. Retaliation is an effective enforcement mechanism between countries of roughly equal size.[60] Between large and small countries, it is likely to lead to asymmetric enforcement. Small countries will comply with a ruling to avoid retaliation by a large country, whereas large countries are unlikely to comply with a ruling simply to avoid retaliation by a small country if implementation threatens to create political difficulties at home.

The United States has lived up to the WTO rules and regulations and complied with rulings in a timely manner. It has had a number of significant outcomes in its favor, such as the banana case and beef hormones, but also a number against it, most recently the foreign sales tax case. The United States shows an active interest and belief in the WTO system, as indicated by the number of cases it is involved in as a plaintiff. From the creation of the WTO through April 20, 2001, the United States has been the plaintiff in fifty-seven cases and the defendant in forty-nine out of a total of

228 cases (i.e., it has been involved in 46.5 percent of all WTO cases).[61] Looking at cases where the United States was the plaintiff, it received favorable outcomes in twenty-nine of thirty-four occasions, and fourteen of those were resolved without resorting to the full dispute settlement process. In those cases where the United States was the defendant, twelve of the resolved twenty-six cases were solved outside the dispute settlement mechanism. The United States had a favorable ruling in one case and an unfavorable ruling in thirteen.[62] Not all trading nations have lived up to the rulings that have gone against them. Examples include the continuing complaints against Canada by the United States in dairy products, against the EU by the United States over beef hormones, and against Brazil by Canada over aircraft subsidies.

The DSU has gained credibility and experience in dispute settlement. It has contributed markedly to improving compliance with WTO rules. The cases brought before it are complex, however, and recently the mechanism has been unable to meet the time frames that were set out at its inception to guarantee a timely resolution to disputes. Both the WTO secretariat and smaller nations are finding the expense of going through the process increasingly burdensome as the agreements expand and the ability to bring complaints forward under a number of sections increases. The WTO needs increased budgetary resources to handle the requirements of the DSU, its core activity. Until now the larger trading nations have not responded to proposals for an increased budget. How the United States responds both to panel rulings and to the need to increase resources of the WTO secretariat for dispute settlement will reveal the strength of its commitment to the multilateral system.

Dealing with Nontrade Issues

Attempts by the United States and the EU to improve labor and environmental standards in other countries through trade policy measures were the major reason for the collapse of the Seattle ministerial meeting. The trade field had witnessed a sharp rise in the activism and influence of nonindustry NGOs in the United States, where an open system of governance allows citizens and interest groups to have a significant say and to shape government decisions. These interest groups saw trade policy as a means to pursue nontrade objectives, giving rise to a number of so-called trade-related issues.[63] They lobbied the government about their concerns, whether environmental protection, labor rights, promotion of democracy and civil society, human rights, or health objectives. Trade policy measures can be a powerful instrument to further nontrade interests, as the prospect of losing market access is a strong incentive for foreign firms to ensure that products they wish to export conform to desired labor or environmental standards. Whereas NGOs in developed countries applaud the enforcement of such standards, developing countries call it blackmail, seeing it as a way to disguise protectionist measures in a cloak of good intentions.

Recent proposals have suggested that the United States should apply trade sanctions against countries that fail to apply U.S. laws or standards concerning labor and environmental conditions. For instance, the proposed Steel Revitalization Act of 2000 would require foreign companies to disclose information on pollution emissions and wage levels in the exporting country, with the implication that the United States might limit imports if it deems that appropriate levels have been breached. Proposals have also been advanced in the United States to impose fines on foreign countries that do not live up to their own environmental and labor standards. In this case, it is not the imposition of U.S. standards on others that is objectionable but rather that the United States unilaterally assumes the authority to monitor and enforce the laws of other countries. A protectionist purpose can be suspected when the United States decides on its own, rather than jointly, to impose standards (whether national or foreign) on others. To include environmental, labor, and human rights concerns in trade agreements could easily legitimize a new source of protectionism by industrialized nations.[64] Were this to be possible, self-interested industries and labor groups bent on improving their competitive position would quickly partner up with well-meaning and idealistic NGOs, forming bootlegger-Baptist coalitions.

The WTO has taken a commendably clear stand to prevent a country from imposing domestic standards on foreign producers. In a prejudicial case in 1991, Mexico complained to the GATT that the United States had embargoed the import from Mexico of tuna caught in purse seine nets.[65] The GATT panel upheld Mexico's complaint, confirming the rights of Mexico to trade in the product and declaring as irrelevant in this context the process by which the product was produced. Furthermore, the panel ruled that the United States was not justified in attempting to enforce U.S. legislation on Mexicans (a form of extraterritoriality).[66] The distinction between product and process is necessary to prevent special and specious interests in developed countries from using issues like environmental protection or prevention of child labor as arguments to justify restrictive trade actions. This potential conflict with influential U.S. pressure groups complicates the administration's trade policy task.

A New Beginning: Back to Basics?

In his statement before the U.S. Senate Committee on Finance on January 30, 2001, USTR Robert B. Zoellick said, "Given the size of the U.S. economy—and the reach, creativity, and influence of our private sector—we should be and can be shaping the rules of the international economic system for the new century." Thus the United States should work within the multilateral system.

The assumption of the presidency by George W. Bush, in January 2001, ended the trade policy paralysis that had afflicted the Clinton White House. With Republicans in control of both the executive and legislative branches (at least for the time being), preconditions existed for reestablishing strong U.S. leadership in global trade (see Figure 12.1, p. 254).[67] The presidency was stronger than it had been for a decade. The House was inclined toward liberal trade more than during the previous decades of Democratic majorities. The United States enjoyed unparalleled geopolitical power after the dissolution of the Soviet Union. Its economy was the subject of envy, following the revolution in information and communications technologies and a record economic boom. Finally, the United States had regained moral leadership through decades of successful legal enforcement of civil rights at home and a successful military intervention to protect human rights in Kosovo. The country stood tall as the defender of values such as democracy, pluralism, and tolerance.

The Bush administration moved quickly to return trade policy to the U.S. mainstream of multilateral liberalism. It argued that liberal trade was in the nation's economic interest and advocated a new WTO negotiating round. It saw economic engagement—not isolationism—as the best way to avoid U.S. entanglement in foreign wars. It claimed that issues concerning labor and environmental standards should be addressed in appropriate multilateral forums, such as the ILO and the secretariats of international environmental organizations. It did not shirk from accepting that U.S. power implies a special international responsibility and that this responsibility is global. It opted for multilateral solutions and overcame fringes in the Republican Party that wished to go it alone or to withdraw into isolationism.

The attack on the World Trade Center and on the Pentagon on September 11, 2001, strengthened the hand of Republicans who, like USTR Robert Zoellick, appreciated the need for multilateral solutions and believed that the most efficient way to exercise U.S. leadership in a multilateral context was to be an active team player. Prior to the WTO ministerial meeting in Qatar in October 2001, Zoellick sought out common ground with the EU and, together with it, exercised leadership.[68] At home, the administration attempted to accommodate the concerns of Democratic politicians about jobs by considering safeguards and adjustment assistance to noncompetitive industries. In November 2001, Bush obtained trade promotion authority from the House by a margin of one vote. This confirmed that the House now supported, albeit by the slimmest possible margin, multilateral liberalism. The Bush administration had regained the momentum for global liberalization lost during the Clinton years.

The Revival of the Wilson-Hull Legacy

USTR Zoellick often emphasizes the historical context that shapes today's policies. The trade policies and rhetoric of the Bush administration carry on the tradition of Woodrow Wilson and Cordell Hull. Bush aligns himself with these two figures in emphasizing that trade can change societies positively. At the start of the Cold War, Republicans had been keen to contain communism and to exclude the communist countries from the benefits of unhindered trade. After the collapse of the Soviet Union and the global extension of the market economy, this adversarial context faded. Today, George W. Bush holds that "when we promote open trade, we are promoting political freedom. Societies that open to commerce across their borders will open to democracy within their borders."[69] This is consistent with the attitude of Cordell Hull and constitutes the motivation for Republican initiatives and support for establishing normal trade relations with China (1980) and Russia (1992). The embargo on Cuba increasingly appears as an anomaly dictated by Florida politics.

Acceptance of multilateralism is easier for the Bush administration in the trade field than in other fields. Unlike protectionism, which is eminently unilateral, trade liberalization requires a multilateral system. Multilateral trade systems have traditionally been limited in scope, providing a framework for negotiations about market access and for defining trade rules, procedures that do not infringe upon U.S. sovereignty. Indeed, the U.S. negotiating framework (the RTAA of 1934) was adopted as a multilateral procedure. No longer the undisputed commercial hegemon, the United States lacks the ability to go it alone that it once had in trade and may still have in other areas. The EU has surpassed the United States as a commercial power, so it makes sense for the United States to limit its freedom of action through multilateral accords in return for other countries accepting the same limitations.

Common rules are decided by consensus, and rule observance follows not from judicial procedures but from dispute settlement based on the right of retaliation. To opt out of such a consensual system would allow others to define rules, which ultimately would affect U.S. interests. The implications of this can be seen in the field of competition policy. In the absence of international rules, U.S. companies are increasingly influenced by EU competition policy, especially concerning mergers and acquisitions. A common set of comprehensive rules and procedures benefits U.S. businessmen and consumers.

U.S. views still carry a special weight in the multilateral trade system, despite the rise of other countries and blocs that have begun to compete with it economically. The one-country, one-vote principle applies in the WTO, but the United States is not merely one country among others. It remains a major importer and exporter, as well as a major contributor to the WTO budget, and its vote comes with a veto. The Bush administration has signaled that it is prepared to play by the WTO rules, accommodate others' priorities in exchange for accommodation of its own, refrain from bullying, buying, or bashing the opposition, and lead in partnership with others to defend systemic interests. This should allow the United States to continue to exercise a disproportionate influence in the multilateral trading system.

Domestic Adjustments to Trade

Establishing credibility abroad for the U.S. commitment to the new round also presupposes overcoming opposition in Congress to trade liberalization. This opposition is fueled by the concerns of both management and trade unions that production, jobs, and pension rights will be threatened by cheaper imports (e.g., steel, textiles and apparel, dairy products, citrus, sugar). The Bush administration is not facing a new situation. Most U.S. administrations have had to deal with the fears of noncompetitive industries prior to a negotiating round. Traditionally, they have done so by using escape clauses and adjustment assistance.

President John F. Kennedy, for example, advanced the Trade Adjustment Assistance (TAA) programs for workers and firms to ensure passage of the Trade Expansion Act (1962). Labor found it insufficient, however, and the House significantly eased the eligibility criteria for adjustment assistance in the Trade Reform Act of 1974 to win support from Democratic representatives prior to the Tokyo Round.[70] The emphasis of such programs tended to be on compensation for lost income rather than job training. The Bush and Reagan administrations attempted to abolish TAA, but Congress refused to budge. The TAA program was amended as part of the Omnibus Budget Reconciliation Act of 1993; this added the NAFTA TAA program in response to labor's concerns.

Adjustment assistance is significantly cheaper than protectionism, especially quotas, and it is often necessary to obtain political acceptance for trade liberalization.[71] It has two components: buying reasonable time to adjust, and facilitating the process of adjustment itself. Safeguard measures provide the time to adjust while adjustment assistance provides the means to adjust by assisting unskilled workers, elderly employees, and employees in regions with weak labor markets to retrain, retire, or relocate.

Prior to both the Kennedy Round and the Tokyo Round, U.S. administrations attempted to make safeguard protection (e.g., section 201 of the 1974 trade law) easier to obtain as an alternative to antidumping measures. However, until the last three years of the Clinton administration, industry seldom requested safeguard actions, as such protection is temporary, whereas other trade remedies can be renewed more easily.[72] The Bush administration appears to be signaling its intention to encourage use of safeguard measures rather than antidumping measures.

In 2001, Congress passed the Steel Revitalization Act, which proposed quotas to limit increases in imports of unfinished steel.[73] The imposition of quotas would be unacceptable under WTO and initiate a major trade conflict with the EU and other trading partners, especially given the significant support that the U.S. steel industry has long received through antidumping measures and countervailing duties. The Bush administration's response to head off the Steel Revitalization Act was promising, though the outcome remains to be seen. In June 2001, the president requested the ITC to determine under section 201 whether steel imports seriously injured or threatened seriously to injury the industry. In December, the ITC ruled that this was the case and proposed a number of remedies, involving tariffs, tariff quotas, and tariff-rate quotas. In March 2002, the president had to make a determination as to which, if any, remedies to apply. This coincided with the Senate's vote on trade promotion authority, and because steel may influence swing votes, the president's determination on steel safeguards may prove decisive for his obtaining TPA. The one-vote majority for TPA in the House no doubt included assurances by the administration to the 104 representatives in the House from steel districts.

Given global overcapacity in the steel industry, the president was required to propose measures in March 2002 that involved a reduction of steel capacity in the United States, protected the pension and health benefits of retired steel workers whose former employers are filing for bankruptcy, assisted laid-off steel workers to adjust to new jobs, and, finally, granted companies a grace period in which to carry out necessary structural adjustments. The executive branch may well propose a package of safeguard measures providing temporary increased tariff protection to the industry, guarantees of pension and health insurance rights to workers in steel companies making the necessary structural adjustments, and adjustment assistance to laid-off workers.[74] The president should enact these measures as part of a multilateral program in the OECD to reduce steel capacity internationally.

The steel industry attracts special attention because of previous protection, political clout, and timing of the current crisis, but it is not unique. Other industries, such as textiles and apparel, and some agricultural products are in the same situation.[75] Hence, policies providing both time and assistance for U.S. producers to adjust to the effects of trade liberalization will have to play a role in the president's approach prior to the new trade round.

Conclusion

USTR Robert Zoellick also provides the segue to the concluding section:

> At the dawn of this new century, we again have a choice of ideas. Which ones will triumph—those of fear, destruction and dwindling dreams, or those of humankind's untapped potential, its aspirations and the creative energy of free people seeking better lives? . . . We can build on the momentum of the past fifty years, championing ideas that led to opportunity and growth, and setting a course of increased peace and prosperity for the world, not just for a year or two, but for decades to come.[76]

The United States is the largest open trading nation in the world. Once again, it subscribes to the belief of Wilson and Hull that trade policy is a central part of foreign policy for a major power. Multilateral arrangements are necessary for liberalization, because of economic interdependence through trade, but superfluous for protectionism. A free-trading United States naturally advocates multilateralism, whereas protectionism led to isolationism.

U.S. trade policies have varied over time, changing tacks from multilateral liberalism to unilateral protectionism and back. These swings are determined by an intricate interplay among the executive and legislative branches, the protectionist and liberal sentiments of the major political parties, their control of the different branches of government, and the capability of the U.S. government to exercise global leadership. During the immediate post–World War II period, U.S. values were sufficiently strong to persuade others to follow when the United States led. During the following decades, U.S. commercial strength diminished and its leadership capability weakened. Protectionist pressures grew stronger in Congress and increasingly pitted the United States against other countries and against the multilateral system itself. U.S. national interests took precedence over responsibility for the stability of the trading system. The U.S. commitment to multilateralism was called into question, weakening the multilateral organization itself.

Today, the United States has ceased the unilateral freewheeling within the multilateral system that characterized the 1970s and 1980s. It appears to be returning to the multilateral tack, although the outcome is not yet clear. The end of the Cold War and the near worldwide triumph of market-economy principles have changed the international scene. The return to power of a Republican Party championing free trade has changed the domestic scene. A truly global organization, the WTO has greatly increased value for a global trader like the United States. The reduced commercial weight of the United States in the WTO today precludes the option of going it alone. The United States started the difficult process of learning to live with the WTO during the Clinton administration. The WTO placed greater demands on U.S. diplomacy than the GATT had. Congress, trade unions, and NGOs will have to accept reduced scope for extraterritorial application of U.S. laws and bring domestic legislation into conformity with WTO rules and procedures. Congress should repeal the Helms-Burton legislation, the Byrd Amendment, and the Anti-Dumping Act of 1916. It will have to revise antidumping and countervailing duty laws, the FSC tax provisions, and make adequate use of escape clauses and adjustment assistance. It will have to strengthen the capacity of the ILO to ensure fulfillment of core labor standards, improve the resources of the WTO, especially for dispute settlement, and refrain from using trade measures to enforce labor and environment standards in other countries. Much remains to be done by the Bush administration, and its task is not made easier by the concerns evidenced by Congress in granting Bush trade promotion authority. Nevertheless, prospects are good that the Bush administration will succeed, especially if it can recapture a protrade Republican majority in Congress after the 2002 congressional elections.

Robert Zoellick has expressed the hope that the FTAA will inaugurate "a second American century—but this time a century for all of the Americas."[77] The new negotiating round of the WTO is more powerful than that. It can herald the century of the common man, for the common people of all the nations are the primary beneficiaries of freer trade. At the moment, it looks as though USTR Zoellick, by returning U.S. trade policy to the multilateral tack, is doing his best not to let them down.

Notes

The author thanks Michael Leigh for untiring research assistance and Anders Ahnlid, Richard Blackhurst, Emil Ems, Rosemary Foot, Gary Clyde Hufbauer, Thorvaldur Gylfason, Peter Kleen, Mikael Lindström, Patrick Messerlin, Håkan Nordström, Göran Norén, and Stewart Patrick for comments.

1. USTR Robert B. Zoellick, "Five U.S. Reasons for Liberalizing Trade." *International Herald Tribune*, November 8, 2001, p. 17.

2. Wilson reduced the high Republican tariff of 1909. After the outbreak of World War I, he deflected pressure in Congress to raise tariff rates by proposing the Anti-Dumping Act of 1916. Together with the Federal Reserve Act (1913), the antitrust laws, and the establishment of the Federal Trade Commission (1914), the tariff legislation of 1913 constituted the heart of Wilson's "New Freedom" program. Blum, *Woodrow Wilson and the Politics of Morality,* chap. 4.

3. Wilson took his League of Nations proposal to the people in a desperate attempt to overcome the opposition of Henry Cabot Lodge, Republican majority leader in the Senate and chairman of the Foreign Relations Committee. The United States remained outside the League of Nations, did not ratify the Treaty of Versailles, and concluded a separate peace with Germany. Under the Versailles Treaty, France, Italy, and the United Kingdom exacted reparations from Germany. These contributed to the turmoil that preceded World War II. See Blum, *Woodrow Wilson,* chap. 9.

4. The mood of U.S. exceptionalism was well expressed in the influential midwestern journal *Wallaces' Farmer.* An editorial in 1922 held that the United States was "the only really worth while nation of the world today. . . . The more we see of European affairs [a quagmire of crookedness . . . devious diplomacy and warfare . . .] the more we like the idea of being in a position to keep away from Europe as much as possible." The writer was later to become a consistent exponent of internationalism. Quoted from Walker, *Henry A. Wallace and American Foreign Policy,* p. 13.

5. The Fordney-McCumber bill, passed by Congress in November 1922, introduced the highest tariff schedule to date in U.S. history and was raised further when President Herbert Hoover signed the Smoot-Hawley Tariff Act in June 1930. Most farmers suffered from higher tariffs because U.S. agriculture was a net exporter of most goods and a user of protected industrial inputs.

6. During World War I, the Midwest had cultivated more land and produced more output per acre than ever before. Agricultural exports to Europe were threatened by the termination of U.S. government loans to Europe in 1920 and high industrial tariffs in the United States.

7. The secretary of agriculture spoke in vain for improved access for agriculture to foreign markets and reluctantly endorsed proposals such as the NcNarry-Haugen

bill, vetoed by both Coolidge and Hoover, to dump surplus U.S. agricultural production on foreign markets.

8. Wendell L. Wilkie, the Republican candidate for president in 1940, popularized this slogan—so common today—in his book *One World* in 1943.

9. As a congressman from Tennessee in 1914, Hull drafted the first U.S. income tax bill, necessitated by Wilson's low tariff policy. In 1945, he received the Nobel Prize for his contribution to establishing the United Nations, as had Wilson in 1921 for the League of Nations.

10. Cordell Hull, *Memoirs,* p. 81.

11. The mood swing presaging the Cold War started before World War II ended. In 1944, Thomas E. Dewey replaced the internationalist Wilkie as the Republican candidate, and on the Democratic ticket Harry S Truman replaced Vice President Henry A. Wallace, the Democrats' main internationalist.

12. The GATT replaced it, but due to contention between the Republican Congress and the Democratic president, it was never formally approved as an executive agreement but only "provisionally applied." Robert E. Baldwin, in Baldwin and Krueger, *The Structure and Evolution of Recent U.S. Trade Policy,* p. 10.

13. In fact, during the first GATT rounds the United States granted disproportionately favorable concessions to the European countries for political reasons. This was to lead later to U.S. resentment over unbalanced terms of market access.

14. Most-favored-nation treatment was suspended for the communist countries in 1951 and 1952 (except Yugoslavia, and Poland in 1962), making the high Smooth-Hawley tariff rates applicable to them.

15. The bill was made unnecessary by a voluntary export restraint agreement negotiated with Japan. Destler, *Making Foreign Economic Policy,* pp. 197–200.

16. See Wijkman, "Managing the Global Commons."

17. Destler, *Making Foreign Economic Policy,* p. 200.

18. The laws in question are the antidumping laws of 1916 and 1920, the Tariff Act of 1930, and section 1317 of the Omnibus Trade and Competitiveness Act of 1988 (the Trade Act of 1974 as amended). Bhagwati, *The World Trading System at Risk,* coined the phrase "aggressive unilateralism"; see chap. 4 and app. 4.

19. Martin et al., "Countervailing and Antidumping Actions," p. 319.

20. WTO Annual Report 2000.

21. "About a third of all antidumping cases launched in the United States between 1980 and 1995 were steel cases. Steel imports from nearly every country are now subject to one or more antidumping or countervailing duty actions." Hufbauer and Goodrich, "Steel: Big Problems, Better Solutions."

22. Senator Russell Long, chairman of the Senate Finance Committee, introduced this amendment to the antidumping law in the 1974 trade bill following the failure by the Department of the Treasury to apply the "below cost" criterion in an antidumping petition. The GATT antidumping code of 1978 was similarly understood by the EU, the United States, Canada, and Australia to refer to sales below cost although this wording does not appear in the text of the code. Finger, ed., *Antidumping: How It Works and Who Gets Hurt,* p. 29.

23. "This challenged its own 'general availability' criterion for assessing subsidies, leading to the perception in Canada (and in other countries that suffered the changing U.S. definitions) that, as 'prosecutor, judge and jury', the U.S. was prepared to meet its trade protection objectives as legally as its laws permitted it to." Martin et al., "Countervailing and Antidumping Actions," p. 326.

24. In 1988, Congress amended the Tariff Act of 1930 by adding Section 771B. "In the case of an agricultural product processed from a raw agricultural product in which (1) the demand for the prior stage product is substantially dependent on the

demand for the latter stage product, and (2) the processing operation adds only limited value to the raw commodity, subsidies found to be provided to either producers or processors of the product shall be deemed to be provided with respect to the manufacture, production, or exportation of the processed product." Martin et al., "Countervailing and Antidumping Actions," p. 321.

25. "It is also required under the laws to make the exporters post security in the form of a bond, cash deposit or some other appropriate security for each subsequent importation of the product in question. These securities are based upon a preliminary estimate of what the Department of Commerce believes the extent of injury to be. There is nothing in the laws to prevent the U.S. from establishing penalty levels that fundamentally prevent imports and hence, protect the domestic industry not from unfair competition, but from international competition period." Martin et al., "Countervailing and Antidumping Actions," p. 323.

26. See Leibowitz, "Safety Valve or Flash Point?"

27. Section 301 of the 1974 Trade Act, as amended (19. U.S.C. sec. 2411).

28. Robert Hudec has argued that disobedience of the law is justified when the law is imperfect. And Gary Hufbauer has argued that it occasionally is necessary to "break the crockery" in order to achieve progress. Although true as a general statement, this may in this case be a rationalization after the deed. Hudec, "Section 301: Beyond Good and Evil" in Bhagwati and Patrick, eds., *Aggressive Unilateralism: America's 301 Trade Policy and the World Trading System.* Elliott and Hufbauer, "Ambivalent Multilateralism and the Emerging Backlash: The WTO and the IMF."

29. The GATT allows regional liberalization on certain conditions (article XXIV). These conditions have not been rigorously enforced, which could be problematic for the future if FTAs expand dramatically.

30. As Herbert Simon put it, regionalism "creates some intermediate organization and structure to the international economic system. The international economy is overwhelmingly vast, and the number of nations is correspondingly large. This system has become too large to deal with on an undifferentiated basis. There is a need to 'decompose' the system in order to manage it effectively, and regionalism presents a kind of 'parts-within-parts' decomposition which is recommended by analysts who study complex systems." Simon, " The Architecture of Complexity," pp. 84–118.

31. Not all countries are at the same level of development. Neighbors often share history, culture, needs, and values, which make bilateral or regional agreements easier and faster to achieve than multilateral ones.

32. "America's place in the world is going to be determined by trade alliances in the next ten years the way military alliances determined our place in the past." Congressman John Tanner quoted by Zoellick, "A Time to Choose: Trade and the American Nation," June 29, 2001.

33. This is because NAFTA is a free trade area rather than a customs union and Mexico is the high-tariff country.

34. Lawrence shows that Japan, the EU, and the United States are all global traders. They may all find benefits in regional agreements, but they need the world outside the region far too much to cut themselves off from it. "In sum, the importance of extra-regional trade to nations all over the world means that no region is in a position to sever, or even significantly curtail, its trade ties with the rest of the world by forming closed blocks." Lawrence, *International Political Economy: Perspectives on Global Power and Wealth.* "Emerging Regional Arrangements," pp. 407–414.

35. "These countries [Canada, Mexico] even with all of Latin America constituted too small a share of world trade to make a regional free trade area preferable

to a significant, even if disappointing, Geneva package." Odell and Eichengreen, "The United States, the ITO, and the WTO," p. 183.

36. Zoellick, "Republican Foreign Policy," p. 72.

37. Zoellick, "A Time to Choose: Trade and the American Nation."

38. The Cuban Liberty and Democratic Solidarity Act (the Libertad Act). See Mastanduno, "Managing 'Hyper-Unilateralism.'"

39. See Groombridge, "Missing the Target: The Failure of the Helms-Burton Act."

40. This right to take legal action applies to a U.S. citizen who has property that was once confiscated in any country, not just in Cuba.

41. The executive branch was against the Helms-Burton Act, but President Clinton signed it into law in March 1996 following the shooting down by Cuba of the plane of a Cuban exile group in February.

42. The Continued Dumping and Subsidy Offset Act. See Leibowitz, *Safety Valve or Flash Point?*

43. The felicitous phrase is from Noland, "Learning to Love the WTO."

44. One EU trade practitioner noted that the main contribution of the United States was to change the name from Multilateral Trade Organization to World Trade Organization.

45. The inclusion of services and trade related intellectual property rights in the WTO was at the insistence—Bhagwati uses the word "bullying"—of the United States and against the opposition of the developing countries.

46. Congress has the right to vote on leaving the WTO every fifth year.

47. Any member could attend the WTO's various decisionmaking bodies. Most important of these is the General Council, consisting of the permanent representatives (ambassadors), which takes day-to-day management decisions. The General Council reigns over a maze of councils, committees, and working groups attended by government representatives. Major policy decisions are taken at the ministerial conference held every second year.

48. Jeffrey Schott: "The WTO will likely suffer from slow and cumbersome policy making and management—an organization with more than 120 member countries cannot be run by a 'committee of the whole.' Mass management simply does not lend itself to operational efficiency or serious policy discussion." WTO, *Trading into the Future*, p. 61. The expression "Polish parliament" derives from the fact that in seventeenth-century Poland all members of the noble estate were allowed to attend the meetings of parliament. Other countries applied the principle of representative assembly, each noble family being represented by its head.

49. A classical alternative, management entrenchment (i.e., informal empowerment of the secretariat), is not an alternative here due to the strong control that a few major trade powers exercise over the GATT/WTO.

50. Originally convened in the Green Room in the GATT building on rue de Lausanne in Geneva, these informal meetings have assumed that name.

51. One-third of the members in the WTO have no representation in Geneva, and most have a staff in Geneva that is too small to follow the maze of WTO activities effectively. As a result, only a few developing countries—such as Brazil, Egypt, Mexico (until joining NAFTA), India, and (recently) Pakistan—have played an active role in the GATT/WTO process. Even Japan has been surprisingly passive. This has allowed other, larger countries to control decisionmaking in the WTO. To offset this, some smaller countries have formed groups to advance their common interests. A coalition of eighteen developed and developing agricultural exporters has formed the Cairns Group. The ASEAN countries have started to speak as a group in the WTO. Traditionally, the European Free Trade Area (EFTA) countries have

consulted prior to WTO meetings. A number other OECD countries have formed their own grouping ("the dirty dozen"). The United States has played a dominant role in the past but is increasingly constrained by emerging coalitions of like-minded states.

52. Only in a limited number of specified cases are decisions taken by qualified majority voting: interpretation or amendment of the multilateral trade agreements, waiver of a member's obligations, and admission of a new member. Unlike the IMF and the World Bank, the WTO does not weight a country's votes by country size or by its financial contribution—decisionmaking procedures that the United States as a major player might prefer.

53. Annual contributions are based on each country's share of world trade. In the case of the EU, this includes intraunion foreign trade.

54. One WTO official noted that its total budget is about equivalent to the travel budget of the World Bank.

55. Executive boards manage the IMF and World Bank. In the early 1970s, the Group of 18 proposed an executive body but this proposal died in house. It is periodically revived. Schott and Jayashree, "Decision-making in the WTO."

56. Any country involved in a trade dispute could block the adoption of a GATT panel report that went against it (common agreement required). In the case of noncompliance, the contracting parties could allow for retaliation if a country did not comply with a panel ruling.

57. The United States had the worst compliance record of any country to panel judgments. Hudec, *Enforcing International Trade Law.* See Wijkman, *Informal Systemic Change in the GATT,* for the stresses that the GATT was subject to in its last years.

58. Decisions are automatically binding on all signatories, and though there is an appeal process, the inability to block resolution gives the decisions stature of international law. It is up to the aggrieved party to encourage compliance by "retaliation."

59. The ambitious time frames established for resolving disputes contribute to promoting liberalized trade. Formal negotiations between the disputing parties have only sixty days to be completed before the complainants can request a panel and that panel is to be formed within thirty days. Finally that panel is to bring forth a judgment within six months of being convened—all of which adds up to a total of nine months to produce a preliminary resolution. Davey, "The WTO Dispute Settlement System."

60. Disputes between large countries can wreck havoc in the international trading system. The congressional requirement that the president retaliates by using the carousel method (alternating retaliation between countries) illustrates this. By creating uncertainty about where retaliation will strike next, the carousel method raises the costs of dispute settlement excessively. It is currently subject to a panel investigation in the WTO.

61. This ignores cases where the United States is a third party interested in the outcome.

62. www.USTR.gov.

63. Bhagwati, a longstanding critic of this linkage, pointedly refers to these issues as "trade-unrelated issues." See Bhagwati, "After Seattle: Free Trade and the WTO."

64. Das, "Debacle at Seattle," p. 193.

65. The United States requires that countries exporting tuna to the United States prove that they catch tuna in conformity with the U.S. Marine Mammal Protection Act. This act requires foreign exporters to prove to U.S. authorities that they meet the dolphin protection standards of the act, which forbid the use of purse seine nets, a source of entrapment for dolphins.

66. The panel decision was taken under the GATT procedures but was in fact never adopted. The United States effectively vetoed the panel report, and Mexico and the United States reached a settlement out of court. This veto would not be possible under the WTO dispute settlement procedures, an indication of the stronger rule compliance that it will provide.

67. The fact that the Senate was evenly divided was less important because it normally is more liberal and multilaterally inclined than the House.

68. Pascal Lamy and Robert B. Zoellick, "In the Next Round," *Washington Post,* July 17, 2001.

69. Quoted by Zoellick, "Five U.S. Reasons for Liberalizing Trade," *International Herald Tribune,* November 8, 2001, p. 17. Bush does not appear to apply this principle to Cuba.

70. Destler, *The Making of Foreign Economic Policy,* p. 156.

71. Hufbauer and Goodrich have estimated the cost of quotas to be U.S.$800,000 per job saved in steel by the Steel Revitalization Act. This is about ten times the average wage, including fringe benefits. The excessive cost explains why quotas are proscribed.

72. Producers of wheat gluten, steel wire rod, welded line pipe, and lamb meat requested and received safeguard measures at the end of the Clinton administration.

73. The Steel Revitalization Act of 2001 (H.R. 8708 and S. 957) is based on the Visclosky steel quota bill (H.R. 975) passed in the House in March but defeated in the Senate in June 2001.

74. Hufbauer and Goodrich present such a proposal in *Time for a Grand Bargain in Steel?*

75. U.S. agricultural products, which could be seriously affected by reduced protection in a new round are sugar, rice, cotton, dairy products, and lamb meat. For the case of sugar, see Groombridge, "America's Bittersweet Sugar Policy."

76. Robert B. Zoellick, "Five U.S. Reasons for Liberalizing Trade."

77. "Free Trade and the Hemispheric Hope," remarks to the Council of the Americas, p. 8.

13

The United States in
the Global Financial Arena

Toyoo Gyohten

THE END OF THE COLD WAR REFLECTED, IN ECONOMIC TERMS, THE TRIUMPH OF
the market over the centrally planned economy. Although the collapse of
the Soviet empire came at the end of a period of gradual deterioration
caused by many factors, the coup de grace was the inability of the Soviet
economy to cope with the new global economic environment that began to
emerge in the 1980s.

The Triumph of U.S.-Style Capitalism

The new international environment was the product of an irreversible trend
toward globalization and of revolutions in information and communications
technologies. As competition became global, no individual, corporation, or
government could succeed without winning in the global marketplace. Simultaneously, the introduction of a universal, efficient, and inexpensive
means of communication enabled millions of taxpayers, consumers, employees, and shareholders to access key financial information instanta-
neously. As the result, information could no longer be monopolized by
those in power. The market—an aggregate of all economic agents—became
the ultimate arbiter, scrutinizing and rewarding (or punishing) the performance of government policymakers and corporate CEOs alike. To satisfy the
market, governments as well as corporations had to persuade the market
that they were competent players, willing to be transparent in and accountable for their actions.

The information technology (IT) revolution had far-reaching implications for economic activity, stimulating huge gains in labor productivity
among other things. Thanks to the enormously enhanced capability of com-
puters, enlarged transmission capacity, and the rising global use of internet
services, the processes of planning, designing, and manufacturing goods,
managing inventories, marketing, and all other facets of economic activity

were made more efficient. The centrally planned economy, unable to adapt to these fundamental changes because of its inherent rigidity, thus lost the battle.

The U.S. economy was best positioned to capture the opportunity provided by globalization and the IT revolution. The U.S. tradition of a free and competitive market, risk-taking entrepreneurship, and market-friendly government policies all supported the quick adaptation of the U.S. economy to the new environment, helping to make it the most efficient, competitive, and powerful in the global marketplace.

The benefits of globalization and IT revolution were most conspicuous in the financial services industry. Following the oil price crises in the 1970s, global capital flows began to increase rapidly. This trend was encouraged and accelerated by factors such as the large global trade imbalance, the expansion of corporations' cross-border activities, and the accumulation of private financial assets (mainly as a result of aging populations in industrialized economies). The massive and rapid transnational flow of capital became the dominant force in the global economic scene. Naturally, the financial services industry, which acts as the major intermediary for capital flows, was given the best opportunity to capture the benefit.

Advances in IT, meanwhile, have opened vast new horizons for the financial services industry, which has been able to developed new products and services. The financial services industry, in a sense, has transformed itself into a computer industry. The technology of financial engineering became the most important ingredient of financial services.

The U.S. financial services industry has successfully established itself as the indisputable leader in the global market. This supremacy resulted from a fierce sense of competition among U.S. companies, as well as the ample human and technological resources companies possessed. Thus, the U.S. economy, led by its financial services industry, became the most competitive and dynamic economy on the globe by the 1990s. In the post–Cold War world economy, the U.S. economy has played an almost hegemonic role. The U.S. standard of corporate governance, characterized by key principles of competition, efficiency, and shareholder value, has become the global standard. All other economies are forced, to some degree, to emulate the American way.

The predominant role of the United States has been the most outstanding feature of the world economy in the post–Cold War period. It is quite natural that in parallel with the expansion of U.S. power came an expansion of global concern regarding how the United States should play its dominant role. The fortune of the world economy, after all, is very much dependent on U.S. policies and behavior.

It is certainly arguable that the strength of U.S. hegemony in the international financial arena (and the fact that the rest of the world has basically accepted the validity of that hegemony) has contributed to the stable development of the world economy by providing a common framework of activity for all players. However, the problem has been that the United States, as hegemon, has not always tried consciously to balance and harmonize its own interests with those of others countries. U.S. shortsightedness was the result of a few factors. First, the United States made the naive assumption that anything that was good for itself should be good for others as well. The second factor results from the structure of the U.S. decisionmaking process. In its domestic economic management, the U.S. government is constantly faced with the conflicting interests of businesses and of consumers. The challenge for the economics policy maker is how to strike the best balance between the two while achieving the greatest benefit for the national economy as a whole.

In international economic policy management, however, the consumer has much less interest in what the government does. Thus, business interests tend to prevail. This is particularly the case in a country like the United States, where the influence of big business over the government is relatively great. As a result, U.S. international economic policy is prone to support and protect the interests of U.S. business—and notably of the U.S. financial industry, which is today the most globalized, aggressive, and competitive in the world. The U.S. financial industry's quest to maximize its global business opportunities coincides with the U.S. government's aspiration to export worldwide a U.S. model of the market economy based upon free competition.

This is the clashing point between unilateralism and multilateralism. The U.S. policy in the international financial arena is fundamentally motivated by the national interest. What complicates matters is the fact that Americans do not view their unilateralism as something incompatible with multilateralism. Just as they strongly believe in the value of their market system and business model, so they believe their unilateralism is in perfect harmony with the idea of multilateralism. Indeed, if we look at the end result, we cannot deny that in many instances their naivete is warranted. Many companies, industries, and economies have recorded remarkable success by consciously emulating the U.S. model. What was good for the United States was good for others.

Nonetheless, U.S. unilateralism in the global financial arena, no matter how bona fide it might be, has sometimes been implemented without due regard to the actualities and the needs of other economies. In some situations, U.S. unilateralism has run counter to the multilateral benefit. There are three areas where U.S. unilateralism has not been compatible with multilateralism: (1) in the management of international capital flows; (2) in the stability of exchange rates of currencies; and (3) in the role of international financial institutions, particularly the International Monetary Fund (IMF).

Management of International Capital Flows

The expansion of international capital flows has been nothing short of phenomenal. First, the volume of financial resources moving across national borders everyday is more than fifty times the volume of transaction in goods and services. The world today is a huge whirlpool of money. This development was prompted first by the accumulation of investment capital. Investors in pension, mutual, and hedge funds, seeking higher returns on their money, move increasing sums of capital internationally through portfolio investment and currency speculation. Second, corporations, particularly big multinationals, have expanded their activities globally by way of foreign direct investment and cross-border mergers and acquisitions. U.S. corporations and funds, armed with strong resource bases and high competitiveness, are undoubtedly the dominant players in international capital movement.

In order to enlarge the market, U.S. corporations, investment banks, and institutional investors pressured other economies, particularly emerging and small economies, to open up their capital market for foreign participation. U.S. corporations, often with the encouragement and endorsement of official U.S. policy, persuaded foreign governments that opening capital markets would facilitate the inflow of productive foreign capital into the economy, thereby stimulating economic development and improving efficiency. In most cases the recipient countries accepted U.S. advice and opened their capital markets, sometimes willingly but sometimes reluctantly. As events transpired, liberalization of capital controls did encourage vigorous foreign investment and stimulate economic activity in many countries. In other cases, however, ill-managed capital liberalization created currency crises and caused serious economic dislocation. Tragedies of this kind happened in a number of small and emerging economies, notably in Asia and Latin America.

When the Asian financial crisis erupted in Thailand in 1997, it spread quickly to other East Asian economies. The contagion also hit Russia and Brazil and, eventually, Wall Street itself. Numerous analyses have already been made of the causes and development of the crisis, and the subject is outside the scope of this chapter. However, one thing is clear: The crisis was triggered by massive international capital flow. It was, in fact, a capital account crisis—quite different from classical crises, traditionally caused by a deterioration in a country's current account position. In most of the crisis-hit countries, macroeconomic fundamentals such as current account, fiscal balance, and inflation were not in a state of desperate deterioration. The crisis resulted from a massive inflow and then rapid withdrawal of capital, resulting in an uncontrollable fluctuation of the exchange rate, a serious dislocation of resources, and a steep deterioration in social welfare characterized by massive suffering.

Although one might be tempted to treat the Asian crisis as an unexpected natural calamity, the crisis-hit economies themselves had serious vulnerabilities that made them unable to prevent and cope with the crisis. At least three of these weaknesses should be highlighted. The first, apparent in many of these economies, was a weak financial system, including a poor balance sheet and the faulty supervision of the country's banks. The second was an inappropriate speed and sequencing for capital liberalization. And the third was an ill-designed exchange-rate arrangement. In hindsight, it is clear that many banks in crisis-hit countries were poorly and unsoundly managed. Most of their assets were composed of bad loans, and bank management often colluded with politicians. There was little transparency and accountability. The central banks and other supervisory apparatuses were not functioning properly. Banks were not independent from political influence, and there was no strict rule of law or regulations. Capital liberalization was implemented without clear assessment of internal and external situations: More often than not, it was motivated by a desire to attract foreign capital quickly. One technique to do so was the hasty establishment of an offshore market. Foreign direct investment flourished, thanks to inexpensive labor. But when there was no real transfer of skills and technologies, and when there was little effort made to develop broadly based supporting industries, it became apparent that foreign investment would not contribute to indigenous economic development.

In addition, inflexible exchange rate arrangements, such as the dollar-peg system, proved to be a dangerous proposition in a changeable environment. The dollar-peg system was certainly able to attract large amounts of volatile foreign capital. But when the tide reversed, the inevitable result was an unsustainable loss of foreign reserves. All too often, the system collapses, and the currency suffered an unjustifiably large depreciation—thus causing lasting damage to the country's economy.

Clearly, crisis-hit countries must bear most of the responsibility for their failures. However, are those foreigners who preached the benefits of globalization to developing countries and urged the latter to open their capital markets totally immune from responsibility? When foreigners were pressing liberalization, did they have an accurate assessment of the real situation in those countries, and did they offer advice about the prerequisites for successful globalization? Indeed, the governments and private businesses of developed countries, particularly the United States, along with official international financial institutions, have a responsibility to these developing nations. These foreigners acclaimed globalization and liberalization, but they failed to provide developing countries with the requisite tools to achieve the real benefit from either. In this respect, then, the responsibility of the United States is the greatest, because the United States has played by far the most important role in championing the global crusade.

The opposing argument would be that necessary reforms in developing countries, such as the strengthening of the banking sector, would never have happened without the pressure of market forces; therefore, the opening of capital markets, even if painful, was a necessary bitter pill for many emerging economies. And though a bitter pill was necessary in some cases, those who provided it were not motivated by the genuine desire to improve the welfare of the emerging economy. In most cases, they were driven by the prospect of expanding market and increasing profit. It was an act of sheer greed. The bottom line is that there are often conflicts between the national interests of emerging economies and the private business interests of developed economies.

The best approach for both emerging and established economic interests should be a joint effort, whereby the emerging economy expedites its own internal reform and the private businesses of developed countries exercise prudence with due consideration for the stable development of the emerging economy. It is encouraging that, in the international effort to rebuild the global financial architecture, there has been a broad consensus on the need to tighten the supervision of speculative hedge funds, to contain the disturbing activity of offshore financial centers, and to support the proper sequencing of capital liberalization. For this supervision to have the necessary impact, private businesses must cooperate fully. If they do not, it is the responsibility of their authorities to enforce appropriate public regulation. The United States, as the biggest beneficiary of the stable growth of international financial markets, should take an active, leading role in the effort to accomplish the joint endeavor.

There is a widely held suspicion that the United States is reluctant to implement these measures in a compulsory fashion, being preoccupied with the desire to protect the interests of its financial institutions. If that is accurate, then the United States needs to moderate its unilateral posture. By approaching the issue with a greater spirit of multilateralism and by paying greater attention to the condition of vulnerable economies, Washington could greatly assuage such suspicions.

Exchange-Rate Stability

Under the Bretton Woods monetary regime, which was maintained for a quarter-century after World War II, the global economy enjoyed a period of remarkable stability in exchange rates among major currencies. All major countries committed to maintaining a fixed rate between their currency and the U.S. dollar, the value of which was in turn guaranteed by its free convertibility into gold at the fixed price of $35 per troy ounce. In other words, international economic activities were freed from exchange-rate risk. Under this favorable environment, world trade and investment expanded, and the world economy on the whole achieved remarkable development. In retrospect, the success of the Bretton Woods regime was made possible by the value of the U.S. dollar, which in turn was supported by the overwhelming relative strength of the U.S. economy vis-à-vis the economies of other major countries. Therefore, when the relative supremacy of the U.S. economy was eroded, the Bretton Woods regime was bound to collapse. The demise was prompted by a number of factors, including the greater relative growth of other major economies, the progressive overvaluation of the U.S. dollar, and the damage inflicted upon the U.S. economy by the Vietnam War.

In 1973, the United States suspended the dollar's convertibility into gold, and major currencies abandoned their parity with the dollar. The global monetary regime entered the age of floating exchange rates. It should be noted that although the value of the dollar was no longer guaranteed by its convertibility into gold at a fixed price, the dollar continued to play the role of the key currency in the system. In other words, the world financial market continued to operate under a de facto dollar standard. The big difference from the earlier Bretton Woods regime was the recurrent, wild fluctuation of the dollar's exchange rate in the marketplace, which made stable expansion of international trade and investment more illusory and costly and, more often than not, caused the misallocation of economic resources.

The advanced economies made repeated efforts, both bilaterally and multilaterally, to restore an adequate degree of stability and predictability by eliminating excessive volatility and by preventing the prolonged misalignment of exchange rates. Monetary authorities of major currency countries conducted joint interventions into the global currency market. They also tried to coordinate their domestic macroeconomic policies so that the market would not be tempted to speculate on the divergent economic performance. On a different front, the countries of continental Europe launched a historic endeavor to eliminate the risk and the cost of exchange between their respective currencies. They ultimately triumphed in this endeavor by introducing a single European currency, the euro, at the beginning of 1999. Nevertheless, volatility persisted in the exchange rate between the U.S. dollar and other major currencies. The situation was aggravated by rapid increases in the speed and volume of international capital flows.

Earlier, when international capital flows were relatively small compared to the volume of trade in goods and services, the main factor determining exchange rates was a country's relative current account balance. At that time, there was a certain degree of predictability in the movement of exchange rates. However, trouble started when capital flows began to overwhelm the volume of current account transactions, because the bulk of capital movement was not predictable. Large and rapid capital movements could be triggered by sudden changes of market sentiment, which in turn were caused by all sorts of information, expectations, and speculative motives—not all of which were accurate or valid indicators of economic performance. To make the situation more uncontrollable, there emerged a strong tendency among market players to succumb to a herd mentality, out of fear of missing the bandwagon. When a critical mass of market players falls victim to this mentality, the vector in the market, no matter how irrational it might be, can transform the movement into a self-fulfilling prophecy. Economic actors are forced to run in the same direction until they crash.

In sum, in today's currency market, which is dominated by capital movement, exchange rates are much more susceptible to irrational, violent fluctuations. This poses a dilemma for policymakers. Although the situation calls for greater effort to restore stability, achieving that goal has become extremely difficult.

In any effort to influence the currency market, two principles are fundamental and must be borne in mind. First, because an exchange rate is a relationship between two currencies, there must always be close cooperation between the two issuing countries. Efforts made by a single country alone will not produce real effect. Second, because we are dealing with a market, or the aggregate judgment of millions of individual players, we cannot possibly achieve the goal unless we succeed in changing their perceptions. We must admit that the market is right in most cases. When the majority of market participants are inclined to sell a currency, they do so because they detect something wrong with it. Wolves will not approach unless they smell blood. Thus, the fundamental problem of the issuing country's economy needs to be rectified; market intervention alone cannot solve the problem.

However, the market can also err. The market is often driven by the aforementioned herd mentality, which is not vindicated by fundamental economic fact. Most of the so-called overshooting of exchange rates occurs in such circumstances. To prevent reduce the risk of overshooting, currency authorities must send a clear and strong message to the market participants, telling them that the market is wrong. The message can take the form of a massive and concerted intervention in the market or a strong and convincing statement. It will work as a bucketful of cold water thrown over a drunken head.

So far in this chapter I have discussed the exchange rate between major countries, because it is relevant not only to their respective economies but also to the stability of the international financial market. Indeed, the stability of the exchange rate between major currencies is of critical importance for many smaller economies, which are vulnerable to this volatility. The 1997 East Asian crisis provided clear evidence of the importance of exchange-rate stability.

Before the crisis, many East Asian currencies were pegged to the U.S. dollar, although in reality their international economic activities were diversified between the dollar zone and the Japanese yen zone. The steady weakening of the dollar vis-à-vis the yen until 1995, and the dollar's strong recovery thereafter, brought about an unintended shift in the price-competitiveness of those East Asian countries and distorted their economic policies, thus enhancing their vulnerability to volatile international capital flow. When they abandoned the dollar-peg policy, under the ferocious attack of currency speculators, the value of their currencies plummeted to levels far below those justified by economic fundamentals. It was a clear case of overshooting.

Since the onset of the floating exchange rate system, many attempts have been made to reduce volatility in the exchange rates between major currencies, but none of them have succeeded, and no international agreement for that purpose exists today. The reason for the failure is obvious. There has never been a common understanding among major countries. When clear cases of overshooting have occurred, the countries concerned have conducted joint market interventions on an ad hoc basis. Some of these interventions have succeeded, but others have failed. An overall agreement on the framework of cooperation has not been established, because countries continue to hold different views on the desirability of stable exchange rates, although even critics from time to time have admitted the detriment of volatility. The United States has been the country most reluctant to commit to international cooperation on exchange rates. This reluctance is not without reason. The U.S. dollar is de facto the international key currency, and the United States carries out most of its international transactions in its own currency. Compared with other countries, the United States must contend with a relatively low level of exchange risk. Also, there is a lingering view in the United States that exchange rates can and should be used as a tool of economic diplomacy. When faced with the need to address its huge trade deficit, the United States pressured its trading partners to increase their purchases of U.S. goods and services, using the threat of a dollar devaluation if they do not comply. The tactic of talking the dollar down has been employed intentionally. In recent years, the United States has maintained a strong dollar policy, because a strong dollar is indispensable for the steady inflow of foreign capital to finance its large current account deficit. Also, there is a strong ideological predisposition in the United States that contends that the market should be left as free as possible. According to this view, the market is always the best judge.

However, experience shows that exchange rates do overshoot and misalignment does happen, and both hurt the economy. Accordingly, there is a legitimate and persuasive case to be made for a workable framework of international cooperation that has the capacity to prevent overshooting and to rectify misalignment. The lack of U.S. leadership in creating a more stable international exchange rate system is regrettable. It is obvious that without a strong U.S. commitment, international cooperation on this issue will be impossible. In contrast, if the U. S. decides to take the lead, the EU and Japan will certainly cooperate. The purpose of such international cooperation would not be to maintain exchange rates at unrealistic levels, something the market would find unacceptable. Rather, its purpose would be to prevent the market from irrationally overshooting and to try to keep the exchange rate within a range acceptable to the rational judgment of the market.

The United States should recognize that the exchange rate is a matter of global concern and that there is no unilateral solution to exchange rate instability. The stability of exchange rates is only achievable through multilateral agreement and cooperation. The firm commitment of the United States to the principle of multilateralism is the key to success.

The Role of the IMF

When the IMF was created in 1945 as the cornerstone of the Bretton Woods regime, its mission was clear: It was to uphold stable parity among currencies based upon the dollar-gold standard. To assist member countries in meeting their obligations, the IMF was empowered to provide them with short-term financing in the event of short-term balance-of-payments crises. The IMF's mission was accomplished successfully, and the parity system was maintained for a quarter-century. However, when the Bretton Woods regime collapsed in 1973, the parity system was virtually abandoned. Accordingly, the IMF lost its original mission.

In hindsight, the international community should have tried to redefine the IMF's mission, reorganizing it so that it could have played a proper role in the age of floating exchange rates. Instead, the international community wasted time trying vainly to fix the broken regime with some alterations. As they were fumbling with this repair work, the world economy was hit by oil-price crises and recurrent currency turmoil. The international financial situation seemed to have become unstable and unpredictable, and the world was preoccupied with addressing immediate problems. The IMF's major shareholders lost interest in the fundamental reform of the IMF and instead started to use it as an adaptable lending facility. The bureaucracy of the IMF was not necessarily unhappy about this. The lending activity of the IMF was diversified and expanded from narrowly defined balance-of-payment financing to large-scale budgetary support and a variety of supports for long-term structural reform. The demarcation line between the World Bank and the IMF became blurred. The IMF became an all-purpose rescue team. To many observers, it appeared that the United States, as the largest shareholder and the country with veto power, was using the IMF as an agent to pursue its own global strategy. The IMF was criticized on occasion for incorrectly diagnosing the economic problems of borrowers and for offering prescriptions that were inappropriate to their situations.

There is no question that the world economic scene has changed greatly since the Bretton Woods days. There are many more countries, both large and small, that are in the process of developing or restructuring. Private institutions have become much more important than official institutions in international capital flows. The nature of financial crises are more diverse now, and crises have become more frequent and contagions more severe. In other words, the world economy today is much more complicated than before. There is a serious need for the international community to be prepared to cope with various troubles in an efficient and well-coordinated fashion. We need a set of multilateral financial institutions, each of which should be provided with a clearly defined objective, efficient management, and adequate resources. In this way, the IMF should act as the guardian of the stability of the global financial market. The mainstay of its role should be the prevention and management of financial crises. In order to carry out such a role, the IMF should be assigned to conduct surveillance of macroeconomic policies, to coordinate international cooperation to improve exchange-rate stability, and to provide short-term financing to countries on the verge of crisis. This financing needs to be bolstered by regional, governmental, or private sources.

As I said earlier, the IMF has often been criticized for its incompetence and inadequacy. However, the crux of the issue has not been the IMF itself but the lack of serious involvement by the home governments of major shareholders in the function of the IMF. Some of these countries have been preoccupied with manipulating the selection of the managing director in a very opaque way while being unwilling to supervise closely the activity of the IMF bureaucracy. In this respect, the responsibility of the United States, as the IMF's largest shareholder, is naturally the greatest. The policy of the United States toward the IMF has not always been unified. In many instances, Washington has been seen as trying to use the IMF as a tool to accomplish its narrow economic and political aims. There are many people around the world who believe that the United States is more supportive of generous IMF assistance to Latin America and other areas, which carry great strategic importance to the United States. Yet in 1997, in the aftermath of the Asian crisis, when some Asian countries plotted to circumvent the IMF by creating an Asian Monetary Fund, the United States objected strongly. At the same time, there is a strong group of IMF critics in the United States, particularly in the Congress, who argue that the IMF is not functioning well for the interest of U.S. taxpayers. This is disturbing, because the IMF is an international institution designed to serve the purpose of global welfare rather than the specific interests of any one nation, no matter how powerful. The guiding principle of the IMF is one of shared responsibility among all members. Accordingly, its activity is supposed to be undertaken with this global perspective, and not simply the national interest, in mind. It is essential that the U.S. government, including its executive and legislative branches, fully acknowledge the global value of the institution. U.S. policy toward the IMF should be firmly based upon multilateralism, not on unilateralism.

Conclusion:
The Role of the United States in International Finance

As I argued at the outset, the United States now enjoys almost a hegemonic status in the global economy. If one considers the vast resources it owns, particularly the unchallenged competitiveness of its financial services industry, it is likely that the predominance of the United States in international finance will continue for the foreseeable future. However, one should not overlook that there are also risks in the U.S. economy. The most serious one is the shortage of savings, which is reflected in the huge current account deficit. One implication is that the country needs a large, constant inflow of outside capital to finance this shortage. Any disruption in this flow will inflict serious damage on the U.S. economy. In other words, although the world economy depends on the United States, the United States also depends on the rest of the world. It is this interdependence that the United States must fully recognize. U.S. policies and actions in the arena of international finance must always take into consideration their impact on others. Unilateralism, if motivated by shortsighted national interests, will sooner or later invite backlash. The best option for the United States is a positive leadership role based upon the spirit of multilateralism.

14

Turning Its Back to the World?
The United States and
Climate Change Policy

Lucas Assunção

IT IS HARD TO IMAGINE THAT THE UNITED STATES—THE NATION THAT HAS LONG led the world in research, advocacy, and legislative action to protect the natural environment—would suddenly opt out of the challenge of combating global warming. Ever since the protection of the environment and the management of limited natural resources became issues of concern to policymakers, economists, businesses, and the public, the United States has played a leading role in advancing scientific knowledge and setting standards on environmental issues ranging from hazardous waste, air pollution, and acid rain to the disposal of nuclear waste and obsolete spaceship components.

Yet today U.S. policy toward global warming is following a radically different pattern. The United States appears determined to hold itself aloof from the 1997 Kyoto Protocol to the United Nations Framework Convention on Climate Change (UNFCCC), despite global concern about the potentially devastating impacts of human-induced climate change. Is the United States indeed turning its back to the world? Is it consciously choosing a unilateral, inward-looking path? If so, is this position sustainable environmentally or economically at the global level, or even in purely domestic terms? Can the United States afford to step down from the global climate change challenge? Can the Kyoto Protocol survive without the United States?

The unilateral trend in U.S. policy toward climate change has had two high points. The first was U.S. Senate Resolution 105–98 of July 25, 1997, cosponsored by Senators Robert Byrd (D–West Virginia) and Charles Hagel (R–Nebraska).[1] The second was a written response from President George W. Bush, dated March 13, 2001, to a request by Senators Hagel, Jesse Helms, Larry Craig, and Pat Roberts (dated March 6, 2001) requesting clarification of the administration's position regarding the Kyoto Protocol.

In this chapter I argue that the recent trend toward unilateralism in the U.S. position in climate negotiations is nothing new. Since the late 1980s, U.S. policy has oscillated between more progressive (i.e., outward-looking) multilateral periods and more conservative (i.e., inward-looking) unilateral periods. The unilateral tendency can be interpreted as a strategy of self-defense. It reflects a desire to reduce the political responsibility and economic burden that would otherwise fall on the United States, as the world's largest economy and largest emitter of greenhouse gases (GHGs) to take major steps to combat global warming.

Any effective global response to climate change will involve serious economic and energy costs and will carry nontrivial trade implications in the years to come. As scientific uncertainty is reduced to a minimum, policymakers have begun, finally, to understand that climate change represents more than an isolated environmental problem. As scientific knowledge has improved and uncertainty about climate change greatly reduced, the United States has gradually moved toward greater unilateralism in an effort to protect its national economic and trade interests. The question is whether this unilateral trend can be sustained both domestically and internationally.

On the domestic front, the key question is whether any future U.S. administration will commit itself to achieving the bipartisan collaboration with the U.S. Senate required to create international law in this arena while also committing itself to raising domestic public awareness about the causes and potential consequences of climate change (including the costs of U.S. inaction). At the same time, the United States has much to gain from the worldwide adoption of effective climate policies. The private sector in the United States, which enjoys undisputed leadership in technological development and major interests in most developed and developing countries, has a natural interest in exploiting the market opportunities arising from the implementation of the Kyoto Protocol. Private companies are likely to generate significant bottom-up pressure on the United States government as the protocol unfolds and enters into force without U.S. ratification.

At the international level, there is now greater consciousness about the irreversible and unpredictably high costs of inaction on climate change. It is also becoming increasingly clear that the international response will trigger fundamental shifts in energy and transportation policies, with trade impacts across economic borders.

U.S. unilateralism in climate change is most easily explained by three factors: the desire by the United States to protect its trade interests and consumption patterns; the failure of Bill Clinton's administration (1993–2001) to work more cooperatively with Senate Republicans to raise public awareness about climate change; and an apparent neglect on the part of the George W. Bush administration to concerns of global equity and sustainability.

I begin by addressing a few key issues related to the climate change problem, then outline the nature of multilateral efforts that have been undertaken to address it. I then analyze the increasingly isolated and unilateral U.S. position and the international criticism that this generated. Subsequently, I assess the U.S. dilemma and interpret the sudden policy turn at the beginning of the administration of President George W. Bush.

Causes of Climate Change

Scientific uncertainty about anthropogenic climate change has been greatly reduced. Today, there is widespread consensus that human activity across multiple economic sectors has changed—and continues to change—the composition and concentration of gases that form the atmosphere. This is especially true of such key greenhouse gases as carbon dioxide (CO_2), methane (CH_4), and nitrous oxide (N_2O).[2] These naturally occurring gases make up less than one-tenth of 1 percent of the total atmosphere, which consists mostly of oxygen (21 percent) and nitrogen (78 percent). But greenhouse gases are vital because they act like a blanket around the earth. Without this natural blanket, the earth's surface would be some 30°C colder than it is today.[3]

The problem is that human activity is making the blanket thicker, thanks to processes such as the combustion of coal, oil, and natural gas for electricity production, heating, cooling, and transportation; the burning of forests; the disposal of municipal solid waste; and various industrial and agricultural activities.

The United States was an early leader in research into the causes of global warming. Largely at U.S. instigation, the Intergovernmental Panel on Climate Change (IPCC) was created in 1988 to advance scientific knowledge about human-induced climate change and to report its findings regularly through peer-reviewed technical assessment reports. In 1995, the authoritative IPCC estimated that if greenhouse gas emissions continued to grow at current rates atmospheric levels of carbon dioxide would double from preindustrial levels during the twenty-first century. And if no steps were taken to slow down the trend in greenhouse gas emissions, atmospheric levels might triple by the year 2100. The most direct result, according to the developing scientific consensus, was likely to be a global warming of 1.5°–4.5°C over the next century. Such a change would come in addition to an apparent temperature increase of half a degree Celsius since the preindustrial period (before 1850).[4]

In March 2001, the IPCC issued its *Third Assessment Report,* concluding that intensive climate research and monitoring now gave scientists much greater confidence in their understanding of the causes and consequences of global warming. The report, adopted by thousands of scientists from more than 100 countries (including the United States), revised the estimated temperature increase upward to 1.4–5.8°C (2.5–10.4°F). The report presented a compelling and alarming snapshot of what the Earth will probably look like at the end of the twenty-first century. Such a warming would have dramatic impacts on weather patterns, water resources, seasonal cycles, ecosystems, extreme climate events, and much more.

Although developing countries are at greatest risk, climate change will also pose challenges for rich countries such as Japan, the United Kingdom, and the United States. In North America, the IPCC projects an increasing frequency, severity, and duration of weather disasters, including floods, droughts, storms, and landslides. Climate change is likely to stress and potentially overwhelm institutional structures and engineering systems designed for a more stable world, whether they pertain to water, health, food, energy, insurance, governments, or human settlements.

Although the battle to reduce emissions will be costly, some of these costs can be mitigated by technological advances. The crisis thus presents economic opportunities for those actors able to provide and take advantage of new technology. In the words of IPCC Working Group III (which included U.S. government representatives and renowned U.S. economists), "While there will be winners and losers in the marketplace, significant economic and technological benefits can be achieved by reducing emissions."[5] Well-designed market-oriented policies can reduce emissions and the costs of adapting to unavoidable impacts of climate change while simultaneously generating significant economic benefits in the form of more cost-effective energy systems, quicker technological innovation, reduced expenditures on inappropriate subsidies, and more efficient energy markets.

Expected Adverse Climate Impacts

But are costs of inaction sufficiently serious to justify a more constructive U.S. response to climate change? In a word, yes. The economic impact of climate change has been estimated by the IPCC, and by other researchers like William Cline and William Nordhaus at the Massachusetts Institute of Technology, to amount to more than $50–60 billion per year for the United States.[6] This cost is of the same order of magnitude as the bailout costs the U.S. government incurred during financial crises in Mexico and Asia during the 1990s. These estimates, however, do not include costs incurred in other parts of the world, which can be expected to be much higher because they will involve significant sea-level rise, massive flooding, severe droughts, the disappearance of small island states, and losses of valuable natural resources. The IPCC's *Third Assessment Report* has reduced to a minimum any remaining uncertainty about "the discernible evidence of anthropogenic impact on climate." But there is little certainty about how the adverse impacts of global warming will be distributed among different regions and localities around the world or about when and where the resulting random and increasingly severe climate fluctuations will cause the greatest economic losses. In this sense, one can interpret climate change policy as a matter of risk assessment and risk management.

At the same time, the potential destruction that may be brought about by unmitigated climate change calls for a worldwide research and development effort. According to H. E. Ott, this mission would need large financial and human resources.[7] Some of those might be generated through a levy on transactions under the emissions trading system, others through a redirection of the enormous subsidies currently given to fossil fuels. Research and the dissemination of technologies should concentrate on fossil-free technology and an efficiency revolution of at least a factor of four.

Responsibility for Historical GHG Concentrations in the Global Atmosphere

U.S. scientists and academic institutions have played a seminal role in clarifying the causes and estimating the physical and economic impacts of climate change. Similarly, successive U.S. administrations have held an important role in multilateral climate negotiations. Indeed, the United States has been active ever since the climate issue was first addressed seriously by the international community, in early 1990, at a meeting in Chantilly, Virginia, just outside Washington, D.C.

The multilateral effort initiated there led to the adoption and opening for signature, at the 1992 Earth Summit in Rio de Janeiro, Brazil, of the United Nations Framework Convention on Climate Change. This sophisticated piece of international law, the product of multilateral negotiations, established the unifying, mutually agreed framework of institutions and processes needed for global cooperation on climate change. It is also the multilateral environmental agreement that comes closest to universality, as it has been ratified by 187 parties, including the United States.[8] This also means that, whatever disagreements may have arisen over its Kyoto Protocol, the UNFCCC's 187 parties will continue to meet on a regular basis to discuss how to carry out their treaty commitments.

The UNFCCC commits developed as well as developing countries to adopt national programs for mitigating climate change and to develop strategies to adapt to its impacts. They are also to take climate change into account in their relevant social, economic, and environmental policies; to cooperate in scientific, technical, and educational matters; to minimize the effects of response measures on developing countries; and to promote education, public awareness, and the exchange of information related to climate change. Additional commitments, however, apply only to developed countries: They include taking actions aimed at stabilizing GHG emissions at 1990 levels by the year 2000 and at providing financial and technological support to developing countries.

The UNFCCC sets out a number of guiding principles for global cooperation on climate change. The so-called precautionary principle says that the lack of full scientific certainty should not be used as an excuse to postpone action when there is a threat of serious or irreversible damage. The principles of equity and of the common but differentiated responsibilities and respective capabilities of countries imply that developed countries that are party to the UNFCCC should take the lead in combating climate change and its adverse effects. The principle of cost-effectiveness seeks to ensure that the global benefits of minimizing climate change are achieved at the lowest possible cost.

Article 2 of the UNFCCC declares the ultimate objective of the convention to be the "stabilization of greenhouse gas concentrations in the atmosphere at a level that would prevent dangerous anthropogenic interference with the climate system." Significantly, the objective of the treaty pertains to atmospheric concentrations, not emissions. Accordingly, all signatory parties accepted that the developed country parties should take the lead in combating climate change and the adverse effects thereof, given their disproportionate contribution to the current GHG concentrations in the atmosphere. The principle of the common but differentiated responsibilities between Annex I and non–Annex I parties arises from this acknowledgment, as well as from the fact that most developing countries, unlike the United States and other OECD countries, only initiated their industrialization processes (and hence large-scale fuel combustion) in the early 1950s. This historical gap of virtually a century between developing and developed countries' contribution to current GHG concentrations was duly addressed in the Rio Principles[9] and is a cornerstone principle of the UNFCCC.[10] The UNFCCC also acknowledges that the per capita emissions in developing countries remain relatively low and that the share of global emissions originating in developing countries will need to grow to meet their social and development needs.

Table 14.1, prepared by the UNFCCC in April 2001, shows the most recent 1998 data on total CO_2 emissions and per capita emissions of both developed (Annex I parties) and developing countries (non–Annex I parties). The discrepancy in CO_2 emission levels is shockingly clear and unequivocal.

Based on 1996 carbon emissions from fossil fuel burning and cement manufacturing, the Carbon Dioxide Information Analysis Center at Oak Ridge National Laboratory in Tennessee has estimated that global per capita carbon emissions average about 1 ton per year. U.S. per capita emissions exceed 5 tons of carbon per year (tC/year), whereas Western Europe and Japan emit 2–5 tC/year per capita. By contrast, average per capita emissions in the developing world are about 0.6 tC/year, and more than fifty developing countries have emissions below 0.2 tC/year. The Oak Ridge lab report further estimates that "in order to prevent atmospheric GHG concentration levels from exceeding twice pre-industrial levels, average worldwide emissions must be stabilized at levels below 30,000 MtC/year, or 0.3 tC/year per capita for a future world population anticipated to stabilize near 10 billion people."

The issue of relative contributions to global warming is a complicated one, in part because changes in the climate system occur due to increases in atmospheric GHG concentrations, not GHG emissions. To clarify the role of developed country emissions in global climate change, a few scientists have sought to measure the relative contribution to global warming of

Table 14.1 Emissions of CO_2 (in Mt) in 1998 from Fuel Combustion

	Total CO_2 emissions (Mt*)	CO_2 emissions per capita (t/inhabitant)
World**	22,726	3.9
Non–Annex I parties	8,622	1.9
Annex I parties	13,383	11.0
Annex II parties	10,972	12.0
Economies in transition	2,592	8.2

Top Twenty Countries (based on 1998 emissions level) Plus EU

	Total CO_2 emissions (Mt)	CO_2 emissions per capita (t/inhabitant)
United States	5,410	20.1
China (including Hong Kong)	2,893	2.3
Russian Federation	1,416	9.6
Japan	1,128	8.9
India	908	0.9
Germany	857	10.4
United Kingdom	550	9.3
Canada	477	15.8
Italy	426	7.5
France	376	6.4
Republic of Korea	370	8.0
Ukraine	359	7.1
Mexico	356	3.7
South Africa	354	8.5
Poland	320	8.3
Australia	311	16.6
Brazil	296	1.8
Saudi Arabia	271	13.1
Islamic Republic of Iran	260	4.2
Spain	254	6.5
European Union	3171	8.5

Source: IEA CO_2 emissions from fuel combustion, 1971–1998, Paris, 2000.
Notes: *Mt = metric tons
**"World" includes all parties and nonparties to the UNFCCC

Annex I countries and non–Annex I countries as separate groups. According to estimates, whereas annual emissions from non–Annex I countries will "grow to be equal to those of Annex I countries by 2037, the resulting induced change in global temperature from non-Annex I countries are estimated to equal that of Annex I countries only in 2147."[11]

Both the Byrd-Hagel Senate resolution of 1997 and President Bush's letter on Kyoto in March 2001 declared the Kyoto Protocol to be unfair to the United States. Both the U.S. Senate and the Bush administration have made a more positive U.S. approach to the climate issue contingent on the meaningful participation of developing countries in emission reduction targets.

Both fairness and political logic based on significant differences in current and historical emission levels, however, suggest that the United States and other large emitters of GHGs must set a prior example by engaging in an effective and coordinated policy response to climate change before developing countries can conceivably accept commitments to reduce GHG emissions. In all fairness, the multilaterally adopted Kyoto Protocol represents such a step forward.

The Kyoto Protocol and Its Entry into Force

The 1997 Kyoto Protocol builds on the UNFCCC and constitutes a first, pragmatic step in the global multilateral campaign to address climate change. It was negotiated under the UNFCCC's auspices on the basis of the so-called Berlin Mandate agreed by all UNFCCC parties in 1995. The original two years of talks that led to the Kyoto Protocol's adoption in December 1997 in Japan have been followed by several additional years of complex negotiations, because many of the operational details of the protocol's mechanisms still need to be finalized. Under the protocol, Annex I parties agree to reduce their 1990 GHG emission levels by an average of 5.2 percent during the first commitment period (2008–2012). At the eleventh hour in Kyoto, and to a large extent due to the personal initiative of Vice President Albert Gore, the United States agreed to a reduction of 7 percent from its 1990 GHG emission level by 2008–2012.

The protocol sets a double trigger for its entry into force. First, it enters into force ninety days after it has been ratified by at least fifty-five parties to the UNFCCC. Second, these ratifying parties must include industrialized countries representing at least 55 percent of total 1990 carbon dioxide emissions by Annex I countries.

The report of the Kyoto conference sets out baseline percentages of CO_2 emissions: 24.2 percent for the European Union countries (which could be expected to ratify as a group), 7.4 percent for the countries in economic transition, 8.5 percent for Japan, 17.4 percent for the Russian Federation, and 36.1 percent for the United States.[12] Any combination adding up to 55 percent would trigger the treaty's entry into force, whereas any combination adding up to 45 percent would prevent it.

Contrary to the perception in the United States that Kyoto targets can be achieved only with a disproportionate cost borne by the United States, the Kyoto Protocol offers developed nations a lot of flexibility to achieve their targets. The three flexibility mechanisms under the Kyoto Protocol—emissions trading, the clean development mechanism, and joint implementation—have been the subject of intense negotiations among all UNFCCC parties, including the United States, and have attracted a lot of attention from private-sector companies worldwide.[13] It is expected that these market mechanisms could lead to substantial investment opportunities in Eastern

European and developing countries, as well as trigger the birth of a global market of carbon allowances and credits obtained through offshore GHG offset projects. But most important, they allow for sufficient policy flexibility and much lower mitigation costs for developed countries when compared to costs they would have incurred if all GHG emission reductions had to be achieved domestically.

The sixth session of the UNFCCC Conference of the Parties was held at The Hague, Netherlands, in November 2000: The chief U.S. negotiator in Kyoto, Stuart Eizenstat, described the climate negotiations as the most complex negotiations in the world, apart from those on trade and disarmament. Climate negotiations have since been compared with the Uruguay Round trade negotiations, due to their complexity and scope, the myriad of parallel groups that meet almost nonstop in formal and informal settings, and the profound implications they have for economic prosperity and equity within and across national economies.[14] The complexity of recent negotiations has been exacerbated by the introduction of so-called sink activities (carbon absorption in growing trees) into the process. Jan Pronk, president of the Conference of Parties, identified no less than thirty-nine controversial crunch issues in the global warming negotiations at The Hague in November 2000. If one multiplies this number by the number of major players in the negotiations—approximately fifteen—one gets an idea of the potential complexities and the dense web of cross-cutting interests and possible compromises.

In recent years, and especially since the adoption of the Kyoto Protocol in 1997, climate negotiations have attracted the attention of a multitude of stakeholders from a growing number of countries involved in key economic sectors. Many have been attracted by business opportunities that will open up after the Kyoto Protocol enters into force. Others are genuinely concerned about fundamental equity aspects that pervade the climate debate, whereas others have been primarily concerned about their own short-term economic interests, as in world trade negotiations.

Much has been written about the collapse of negotiations at The Hague. The United States was not the only country to blame for this outcome. Generally speaking, the failure of these negotiations were a product of a severe EU-U.S. disagreement on the role of carbon sink management in developed countries, on the role of sinks in the clean development mechanism, and on the operational rules for the three Kyoto mechanisms. According to Michael Grubb and Farhana Yamin, the collapse of The Hague highlighted all the intrinsic weaknesses of the EU as a negotiating entity on such complex issues of mixed competence and demonstrated that many of the lessons that it should have learned from Kyoto have yet to be taken to heart.[15] Still, the United States delegation was once again hesitant, waiting for a real direction from the next administration (still unknown by the end of the Hague talks).

Recent Data and GHG Emission Projections

In preparation for high-level consultations convened by Minister Jan Pronk in New York in April 2001, the UNFCCC secretariat announced the latest data on current emissions of CO_2 from fuel combustion, which is the largest and most easily measurable source of GHGs.[16] The latest projections indicate that for all GHGs covered by the Kyoto Protocol, GHG emissions from Annex I parties in 2010 are now likely to be on average some 5–10 percent above 1990 levels, under a business-as-usual scenario (i.e., without measures to implement the Kyoto Protocol; this is a measure of the collective effort called for by the protocol and is about half the effort estimated at the time the protocol was adopted). In contrast, recent information on U.S. emission levels indicates that the United States might need to reduce GHG emissions 20–25 percent by 2008–2012 to meet its Kyoto target of 7 percent less than 1990 levels. According to scenarios used by the IPCC, GHG emissions from developing countries may catch up with emissions from developed countries around 2015–2020, although emissions per capita will still be much lower in developing countries.

There is also precedent for the principle of equity. Ironically, the nations that have contributed the least to climate change will likely be the least able to adapt to its negative impacts, having the fewest available resources and being generally the most dependent on the land and existing climate patterns for day-to-day subsistence. In the view of some,

> this disparity between the largest emitters and those most vulnerable to the climate change impacts directly contravenes international environmental law. Principle 21 of the Declaration of the 1972 UN Conference on the Human Environment in Stockholm, cited in article 1 of the UNFCCC, states that the exercise of nations' sovereign right to exploit their own resources must not cause environmental damage to other states or to areas beyond that state's national jurisdiction. The U.S. and other industrialized countries accordingly have a legal as well as ethical obligation not to harm more vulnerable nations through their disproportionate use of the atmospheric commons.[17]

From an ethical perspective, it is difficult to sustain the argument that some are entitled to a larger claim or right to the global atmospheric commons than others. The fact that all people have equal rights is a fundamental principle of most modern ethical and legal codes. The idea is enshrined in the U.S. Constitution and in the Universal Declaration of Human Rights, even though the use and distribution of common goods like the atmosphere fall outside the legal control of individuals or nation-states.

Perhaps more important, governments have adopted egalitarian principles in allocating resource rights even in cases where there were large pre-existing claims. For example, "The United States has on several occasions used egalitarian principles to modify entitlements based on historic use.

The Public Trust Doctrine is a powerful part of Anglo-American common law ensuring access to inland water resources on egalitarian principles."[18] Air pollution rights have also been subject to such principles: Under the U.S. Clean Air Act Amendments of 1990, allowances to emit SO_2 were not simply grandfathered but rather granted on a significantly egalitarian basis, with decreasing consideration granted over time to historic emission levels. Conceivably, a long-term per capita allocation of CO_2 emission rights would build on these established egalitarian precedents.

Other important equity considerations would include intergenerational equity, the complexities raised by comparing different GHGs, or the issue of compensation for unequal distribution of damages. These issues still require further consideration among scholars, policymakers, and the public.

Explaining the Wrong Signal Sent by the United States

Thanks to its attitude toward the Kyoto Protocol, the United States now faces a debacle that threatens to undermine its diplomatic relations with a number of countries and regions, most notably Japan, the EU, and island nations from the Pacific to the Caribbean. It also threatens to harm international relations and cooperation in other areas, such as disarmament, the World Trade Organization, and human rights. When the Bush administration announced its intent in March 2001 to pull out of the Kyoto Protocol negotiations, the worldwide response was immediate and deeply negative. At the same time, supporters of more stringent international action on climate change, whether in the public, the private sector, academia, or the NGO community, agreed that President Bush succeeded, albeit unwittingly, in elevating climate discussions higher on global political and economic agendas. Climate change, which has typically been labeled as an environmental and thus secondary issue, suddenly gained international prominence. It is now featured, alongside trade liberalization and regional integration, on the short list of key issues during bilateral discussions between President Bush and heads of state and governments. Perhaps the first political setback of Bush's first 100 days in office,[19] the president's inept handling of climate change as well as other environmental issues caused many commentators to speculate that the environment, so important to suburban swing voters, might prove to be the administration's Achilles' heel.[20]

On the surface, the Bush administration's policy on climate change is partly a response to the president's perception of a U.S. energy crisis. As rolling blackouts plagued California in early 2001, Bush reversed a campaign promise not to seek major reductions in CO_2 emissions from U.S. power plants. The administration also began to push for the development of new sources of petroleum, announcing that existing environmental regulations for the energy sector might be scaled back to generate more electricity.

Perception of U.S. unilateralism became more acute after Bush's letter of March 13, 2001, stating that the Kyoto Protocol was "unfair and harmful to U.S. consumers and that his Administration officially opposes it."[21] Although not totally surprising, this turn in the U.S. position was radical in implying that the United States would for the first time opt out of the multilateral climate change process. At a time of growing international awareness and scientific certainty about climate change, the Bush administration signaled its belief that ongoing multilateral action to curb global warming would be detrimental to U.S. interests.

The administration's reluctance to pursue the Kyoto Protocol may also reflect other internal considerations. Opposition to climate change is not restricted to the oil and coal sectors: Domestic labor interests also oppose it. Many unions perceive the protocol as portending a dampening of economic growth, an increase in production costs in energy-intensive sectors, losses in the trade competitiveness of U.S. goods, and growing unemployment.

Second, the climate debate in the United States has reflected disagreements between the executive and legislative branches of government. Vice President Gore's eleventh-hour push at Kyoto to have the United States adopt a more stringent emissions reduction target left scars in Congress. At the same time, the Clinton administration did not employ enough energy—either before or after Kyoto—to engage Congress in the worldwide effort to combat global climate change. In fact, it laid no groundwork on Capitol Hill for a possible compromise. If the administration had done so, it might have raised awareness in the genuine interests of the United States in participating in the Kyoto Protocol and would have made it more difficult for the Bush administration to bias policy subsequently toward national oil and coal interests.

Finally, U.S. reluctance to adopt the Kyoto Protocol has reflected concerns about burden-sharing, that is, the fairness of the distribution of costs of adjustment between the United States and other countries. The Bush administration insists, arguably with weak justification, that developing countries must participate early on, during the first reporting period of the Kyoto Protocol.

The principle of meaningful participation is another important element. The message coming from the administration is that the Kyoto Protocol is particularly tough on the United States, requiring sharp limitations on the country's GHG emissions. President Bush's letter portrays the Kyoto Protocol as "unfair to the U.S. consumers," indirectly requesting that countries like China, India, Indonesia, and Brazil show meaningful participation in GHG reduction targets.

The administration, however, did not set a good example for other UNFCCC parties by choosing to opt out of the ongoing multilateral process. The administration failed to think strategically on how to involve large developing countries in a truly global effort. Developing countries cannot reasonably be expected to restrict their emissions without being assured of a fair allocation scheme that will not impair their ability to pursue a sustainable development path. This so-called development restriction is particularly relevant at a time that developing countries need, and are actively seeking, real insertion into the world economy through enhanced trade liberalization.

The clean development mechanism (CDM) in the Kyoto Protocol proved to be a clever compromise that responds to some of these concerns. It enables developed countries to meet some portion of their Kyoto targets by offering fresh direct investment in developing countries, specifically targeted to GHG emission mitigation projects, against offset credits and, most important, at a lower cost of abatement. At the same time, developing nations gain access to new sources of funding to upgrade energy efficiency systems and initiate projects in the areas of renewable resources, transportation, waste disposal, biomass, the diversification of energy carriers, and so forth. In effect, CDM promises a meaningful start to developing countries' participation by introducing a trend toward lower reliance on fossil fuels and greater efficiency in the transport sector and in electricity generation.

As a framework convention, the UNFCCC is precisely designed to address the evolution of the climate problem and the policy response to it through the negotiation of individual protocols. The Kyoto Protocol is the first, but not the last, specific binding agreement in the global effort to combat global warming. There has never been any doubt that the largest developing countries will eventually have to face up to their share of responsibility once their emission levels and induced responsibility for temperature increases reach those of developed nations.[22] At the same time, in ratifying the UNFCCC in October 1992, the U.S. Congress committed the United States to the principle that nations with earlier industrialization— and, hence, greater historical use of atmospheric global commons—would need to take the first steps and confront their responsibility for the problem (UNFCCC, article 4.2[a]).

The fact that aggregate CO_2 emissions from developing country parties to the UNFCCC, which accounted in the late 1990s for some 38 percent of global emissions, are estimated to equal those of developed countries in twenty to thirty years is still insufficient to warrant the expectation of early commitments from developing nations. It seems equally unrealistic to request voluntary commitments without any corresponding increase in aid to enable such an early participation in this global effort. Existing official sources of funding, such as the Global Environmental Facility, have been under growing scrutiny to meet developing countries' funding needs.

It is intuitively evident that the recent bias toward U.S. unilateralism aims to protect current consumption patterns among the U.S. domestic public, without giving much consideration to the longer-term and international consequences of this move. From a U.S. perspective, protecting the American way of life is obviously a legitimate objective. However, even if one leaves aside considerations of global equity, it is not entirely clear that an inward-looking policy path will advance the long-term welfare of the U.S. public. For one thing, such disregard of the urgency of formulating an effective domestic and international policy on climate change does not give the people choices to exert their economic and technological leadership or to fulfill their moral obligation to reduce the human-induced impacts on the global climate. Neither are U.S. citizens being offered options to pursue a less fossil fuel–intensive pattern of consumption. Finally, continued U.S. isolationism will prevent U.S. businesses from participating in the emerging carbon market through emissions trading, joint implementation, and the clean development mechanism. By giving in to the lobbying of domestic interests with very specific short-term interests, particularly in the oil and coal sectors, the current administration may in fact overlook the damage of its policies to the medium- and longer-term interests of U.S. citizens, U.S. private-sector companies, and key U.S. allies abroad.

By abandoning the Kyoto Protocol, the United States is unwittingly giving the reluctant sectors in large developing countries a premium for their similar inward-looking attitude. The Bush administration has lost the political credibility required to press major developing nations for early commitments and has signaled to China, India, and other developing countries that they were absolutely right in not engaging earlier in climate policy responses. Had they done so, they would have been fooled and possibly left with embarrassing international commitments and, worse yet, without the new investments expected through CDM.

Climate as an Economic, Energy, and Trade Challenge

Australia, Canada, Japan, and most European nations, much like the United States, are unable to meet their Kyoto targets without introducing domestic mitigation policies and measures and having the option to buy credits and allowances through the Kyoto mechanisms. But unlike the United States, these nations were unwilling to give up on negotiations about how best to meet these targets.

The Kyoto talks never progressed to the point that detailed rules could be adopted governing sectoral mechanisms to meet emissions targets. But negotiators agreed that changes in the transportation sector of most countries would be critical to the protocol's success. More than 27 percent of total carbon dioxide emissions in OECD countries are produced by the transport sector, and there are signs that transportation energy use is still peaking up. This is particularly relevant in the case of the United States, because the country's geography, large population, cheap energy policy, and prevalent individual preferences makes the U.S. transport sector one of the single largest sources of GHGs on the globe.

But the climate change challenge is not only about transportation patterns. GHG emissions arise from a large number of emission sources and sectors of the economy. Although the bulk of the GHG emissions originate from fuel combustion in the energy and transportation sectors, GHGs are also emitted in varying degrees in sectors such as agriculture, forest, cement, chemical, heating, waste disposal, and elsewhere. This is in sharp contrast to other environmental issues, such as the ozone layer problem, which is triggered by emissions of chlorofluorocarbons (CFCs). CFC emissions can ultimately be banned or greatly reduced by technical regulations, whereas GHGs cannot be banned and their emission is a recurring externality in many, if not all, known processes and production methods. Thus, any effective global climate policy will necessarily require technological development (i.e., changes in the way goods and services are produced) and possibly result in significant shifts in production costs, particularly in energy-intensive industries, with expected foreign trade implications.

Yet some bottom-up approaches are emerging. From the very beginning of the climate talks, the U.S. private sector has played a leading role in exploring market-based mechanisms to meet environmental objectives. The United States pioneered the joint implementation initiative back in the early 1990s in the search for business opportunities through credit projects in developing countries. The private sector also steered the U.S. position toward adoption of the three Kyoto flexibility mechanisms.

Given the current level of scientific knowledge on the issue, it is only logical to assume that the climate change problem will not go away. In fact, several large U.S. and international businesses in a growing number of sectors have understood that it makes economic sense to take climate change seriously, for failing to do so now may be more costly in the future. Many large companies such as Shell, BP, Ford, Daimler/Chrysler, General Motors, TransAlta, Dow Chemical, and Texaco have seen tremendous opportunities for market expansion.[23] Several U.S. and international companies have been investigating opportunities to develop technologies that might facilitate a transition to less carbon-intensive modes of production and processing. The United States has historically been at the forefront of technological development, particularly in response to emerging market demand. In spite of the Bush administration's position, a growing number of private U.S. and European groups—and even some companies in middle-income countries—have begun to see advantages in taking the lead now instead of waiting for consensus at the intergovernmental level.

In his March 13, 2001, letter to congressional leaders, President Bush stated his optimism that "we will be able to develop technologies, market incentives and other creative ways to address global climate change . . . in the context of a national energy policy that protects our environment, consumers and economy."[24] It remains to be seen whether the United States will take advantage of its great capacity to find innovative and profitable technological responses to the climate challenge.

Conclusion

I would like to conclude with some final comments and take a look at the steps ahead. The uncooperative U.S. attitude vis-à-vis the Kyoto Protocol has its parallels in other areas of international relations, such as disarmament. It contradicts the liberal ideals so often preached by U.S. representatives in multilateral negotiations, particularly the importance of cooperation—as opposed to blunt confrontation—as a means to achieve a set of international rules and institutions. Instead, it seems to emphasize a realist approach, reflecting the notion that we live in an anarchic world run by states that are in permanent competition for power. By turning away from the global climate problem, the United States is not only rolling the clock backward but also sending a signal to other reluctant countries that they can behave the same way. What signal is the United States sending to China, India, and Brazil? Put simply: that they were right to be skeptical about real U.S. engagement in the world effort to combat global warming—a problem that they have not created.

U.S. unilateralism in climate negotiations is not new and is directly linked to the deep economic and trade implications of the issue. The recent U.S. relapse toward unilateral isolationism is not totally surprising, as the U.S. position has been marked by hesitation since the late 1980s. The question now is whether the current unilateralist, inward-looking position can be sustained indefinitely. In all likelihood, there will be a reaction, either from the domestic front—led by the public opinion and/or progressive U.S. business interests—or from abroad—led by a coalition between other developed country parties and the developing world. The future of the Kyoto Protocol will depend on whether such a reaction can convince the U.S. Senate and the Bush administration (or its successor) that the United States has more to gain than to lose by exerting its technological and economic leadership.

As scientific uncertainty is greatly reduced, policymakers finally understand that climate change represents more than an isolated environmental problem. It can have irreversible and unpredictably high costs if nothing is done, and at the same time, the international response to it will necessarily entail fundamental shifts in energy and transportation policies, with relevant trade impacts. The recent stall in U.S. involvement in climate talks reflects: a U.S. need to assess the potential trade implications of the emerging climate regime; a disguised strategy to gain time to prepare U.S. industry and other sectors for "Kyoto shock"; and an apparent neglect on the part of the United States as to broader concerns of global equity and sustainability.

In an increasingly globalized world, trade liberalization has become a driving force for economic development and for greater insertion in the global economy. To the degree that the climate externality is gradually internalized in economic policies (i.e., GHG emissions are capped by an multilaterally negotiated agreement), climate policy becomes ultimately a matter of assessing risks and opportunities in trade competitiveness. Because the United States will have to assume high initial costs in the global effort to introduce domestic policies and measures to mitigate climate change, U.S. policymakers are conscious of the potentially negative effect on its exports, due to the increase of energy and other production costs, and the likely effects on consumption patterns in the country.

At the domestic level, increasing U.S. unilateralism is likely to prevail until there is greater bipartisan cooperation—essential for enacting international law in the United States—and the U.S. government makes a resolute effort to raise public awareness on both the risks—including the costs of U.S. inaction—and opportunities for a more proactive foreign and domestic U.S. climate policy. President Clinton could conveniently pursue a strategy of participating in but not agreeing to lead in the necessary steps in the global climate change challenge. In contrast, the Bush administration is greatly exposed and compelled to act, even though it fears that domestic climate policies may only result in additional inflationary pressures and possibly affect consumption patterns of average U.S. households. At the moral level, however, the United States has defaulted on its responsibility, as possessor of the world's biggest economy, in doing its share to combat climate change. As this book goes to press, the international community has taken a bold step toward the ratification of the Kyoto Protocol without the United States. In July 2001, at the resumed session of the sixth Conference of the Parties, all the parties to UNFCCC except the United States agreed on a political deal that would enable them to move the Kyoto Protocol forward in their national legislatures. In November 2001 in Marrakesh, the Conference of the Parties at its seventh session made further elaborations to the agreement reached in July and translated them into legal text. The so-called Marrakesh accords effectively pave the way for a sufficient number of countries to ratify the protocol, likely in time for the Rio+10 conference scheduled for Johannesburg, South Africa, in September 2002.

At the international level, President Bush needs a way out of the predicament that he has created. The White House recently said that Bush's cabinet would conclude a thorough internal review by July 2001 and seek an alternative to the Kyoto pact that would include the world in an effort to reduce GHG emissions. But while the administration flounders, angry world leaders have declared their intent to continue with the Kyoto implementation. President Bush succeeded in elevating the climate issue to the highest political and economic agendas. In doing so, it will be difficult to avoid commitments already assumed through UNFCCC ratification, including the historical responsibility and global equity issues. At the same time, Bush has lost the moral authority to request any early action from developing countries, as he seems to be unable to strike a balance between domestic short-term oil and coal interests and U.S. strategic interests in technological development, international emissions trading, joint implementation, and the CDM.

As long as the United States opts out of the Kyoto Protocol, U.S. businesses will be prevented from participating in international emissions trading, joint implementation, and the CDM, each of which offers new opportunities for innovative investments abroad. The lack of a climate policy aborts the possibility of setting in motion market mechanisms that could trigger rapid technological development (and new achievements in energy use) in a series of GHG emission-intensive sectors. It also places U.S. business at a comparative disadvantage in the future, depriving the country of the ability to exploit its undisputable leadership in technology development. To take advantage of such opportunities, U.S. political leaders will need to embrace multilateral coordination and develop the domestic political vision to expand the U.S. role in international affairs and place the country in a position of world leadership. Plausibly, Bush's unilateral policy is intended as a strategy to gain time and prepare the U.S. private sector for the Kyoto shock.

Kyoto Protocol commitments apply to developed nations only, recognizing their disproportionate share of current and past GHG emissions and the greater resources available to them to reduce emissions. This differential treatment embodies the international consensus that industrialized countries should take the lead in mitigating climate change and that participation by developing countries should not impair their ability to develop.

Developing countries recognize that the industrialized nations have based their own development on unrestricted fossil fuel use, so they see restrictions on their own emissions to per capita levels below those of industrialized countries as perpetuating global inequality. A fair long-term agreement involving all countries will require a transition from an allocation method based on grandfathering past emissions to one based on equal per capita emissions limits.[25]

The U.S. Senate's demand for meaningful participation by developing countries denies the historical responsibility of the United States as well as other industrialized countries in creating the problem of climate change. Undoubtedly, the eventual participation of developing countries will be decisive for the long-term success of the climate change regime. Today, the emissions growth trends of several developing countries already look better than those of most developed countries. For any strategy to succeed, developing countries need the assurance that the North is serious about combating the impacts of climate change (adaptation costs) and that countries and companies in the South can also profit from a global market of allowances and credits. But it is essential that developed countries implement the ratified text of UNFCCC by taking the first steps. The Kyoto Protocol represents a first, multilateral step in precisely this direction. Then, mutual confidence must be built so that there is an open and transparent dialogue on the fair and equitable allocation of emission rights, possibly on a per capita basis.

In the end, is the United States gaining or losing by isolating itself? The history of the U.S. climate policy shows that typically, after an extreme act of unilateralism, some attempt is made to bring the country back to the multilateral path. The discussion in this chapter suggests that pressure in this direction is mounting both domestically—from the general public and progressive U.S. business circles—and internationally—with a worldwide reaction against Bush's inward-looking approach and the now imminent ratification of the Kyoto Protocol by mid-2002. Significantly, the Bush administration was the first to break openly with the multilateral climate change negotiations. As in the case of the WTO, the largest GHG emitter can afford to throw its weight around in an attempt to steer the process and adjust it to fit domestic conditions and interests. This strategy, however, cannot be pursued indefinitely. It will require wisdom to know when to go back to the negotiating table. The United States cannot pretend to be a climate free-rider on the commitments taken by other developed countries.

Most likely, the United States will launch domestic initiatives and stay away from the multilateral negotiating process for a while. In the meantime, many businesses perceive value in seizing market and political opportunities early on. Private-sector companies in the United States and elsewhere increasingly see climate change as a cause for risk management and are willing to hedge against greater economic losses in the future—without waiting for governments to act. In the leadership vacuum left by Bush, the EU has launched its own leadership initiative by convincing other major emitters like the Russian Federation and Japan to ratify the protocol, possibly ensuring that Kyoto will soon enter into force. The initiative has counted on strong support from a sufficient number of developing countries. With the ratification of Kyoto, this strong alliance would isolate the United States even more. With Kyoto entering into force without the United States, the unilateralists might be badly burned. It seems that many have raised concern that Bush has lost more than he has gained domestically, as the majority of the U.S. public now sees climate change as a serious threat and might soon call for a more responsible attitude from Bush.[26] Just as reality passed by the domestic opponents of the New Deal, the Republicans might be left behind by a new global deal.

Notes

1. According to Harold K. Jacobson, "The Clinton administration was caught off guard by the Byrd-Hagel resolution. It did not learn of the resolution until shortly before it was to be considered by the Senate, with little time for its lobbyists to act; they could not prevent the resolution's adoption. The situation was complicated by the fact that Byrd is a prominent Democrat and the administration had to rely on Hagel, a moderate Republican, for support on a number of issues. The production of coal is an important component of the economy of Senator Byrd's state, West Virginia. Agriculture is the most important economic activity in Nebraska, Senator Hagel's state. The mechanized agriculture that is practiced in Nebraska is very sensitive to fuel prices." Jacobson, "Climate Change: Unilateralism, Realism, and Two-Level Games."

2. Water vapor is the most important greenhouse gas, but human activities do not affect it directly.

3. UNFCCC *Guide*, see www.unfccc.de.

4. IPCC *Second Assessment Report: Climate Change*, 1995, see www.ipcc.ch.

5. UNEP, Press Release, "Governments Seek Greenhouse Gas Cuts at Kyoto Climate Talks," December 1, 1997, Kyoto, www.unep.ch/convetions/press/climate/pr11-97.htm.

6. See a comparison of their estimates of impact of global warming—CO_2 doubling—on U.S. incomes in "Reflections on the Economics of Climate Change" in *Journal of Economic Perspectives*, 1993.

7. H. E. Ott, "Climate Change."

8. Significantly, the United States was the fourth Party to ratify the UNFCCC in October 1992.

9. UNCED Principle 7: "States shall cooperate in a spirit of global partnership to conserve, protect and restore the health and integrity of the Earth's ecosystem. In view of the different contributions to global environmental degradation, States have common but differentiated responsibilities. The developed countries acknowledge the responsibility that they bear in the international pursuit of sustainable development in view of the pressures their societies place on the global environment and of the technologies and financial resources they command."

10. UNFCCC article 3.1: "The Parties should protect the climate system for the benefit of present and future generations of humankind, on the basis of equity and in accordance with their common but differentiated responsibilities and respective capabilities. Accordingly, the developed country Parties should take the lead in combating climate change and the adverse effects thereof."

11. See Brazilian proposal, FCCC/AGBM/1997/Misc.1/Add.3.

12. See http://www.unfccc.int/resource/docs/cop3/07a01.pdf.

13. *International emissions trading* allows for unlimited trading of allowance units among eligible developed countries toward their Kyoto targets, i.e., one Annex I country that met its target can transfer some of its "surplus" allowable emissions, assigned amount units (AAUs), to another Annex I country. Under *joint implementation,* one Annex I country (through the government or a company) can invest in an emissions reduction or sink enhancement project in another Annex I country to earn emission reduction units (ERUs) that the investor can credit toward its emission targets. Under the *CDM* a project to mitigate climate change in a developing (non–Annex I country) would generate certified emissions reductions (CERs) that can be used by an Annex I country toward its emissions limitation commitment. At present, investors are engaged in pilot CDM projects with a view to obtaining credits once rules are in place. The CDM allows developed countries to receive offsets against their caps by investing in projects that reduce emissions in developing countries. In the absence of developing country emissions caps, the reductions from a project must be calculated against a baseline, which is both difficult to calculate and provides incentives for both the host and investor countries to overstate the baseline and the reductions. This in turn increases the complexity and cost of monitoring and enforcement.

14. The process has the potential to become even more complicated because the climate change problem is not only about emissions and, certainly, not only about today's emissions. Much still remains to be negotiated about the historical responsibility for current GHG concentration levels and the equal human right to atmospheric global commons.

15. Michael Grubb and Farhana Yamin, "Climatic Collapse at The Hague."

16. The Netherlands minister of environment and current president of the Conference of the Parties, in charge of carrying out all climate negotiations and seeing

a way out from the apparent U.S. unilateral and isolated decision to trash the Kyoto Protocol.

17. See Baer et al., "Equity and Greenhouse Gas Responsibility," p. 2287.

18. See Baer et al., "Equal Per Capita Emission Rights: The Key to a Viable Climate Change Policy," Energy and Resources Group, University of California–Berkeley, October 2000.

19. The Bush administration, from all reports, was astonished by the intense reaction around the world to its decision to pull out of the Kyoto Protocol on climate change. "They did not expect this to stay on the front pages and in the news for three weeks, as has been the case," said European Union Environment Commissioner Margot Wallstrom, *Reuters*, April 5, 2001.

20. "Challenges in Bush's first 100 days" *Wall Street Journal*, April 20, 2001.

21. The White House, "Text of a Letter from the President to Senators Hagel, Helms, Craig, and Roberts," www.whitehouse.gov/news/releases/2001/03/20010314.html.

22. See Meira and Goldemberg, "Some Reflections on the Issue of Supplementarity Associated with the Mechanisms of the Kyoto Protocol," photocopy.

23. As an example, in early 2000 a group of companies created the International Emissions Trading Association to carry on activities towards the establishment of an efficient plurilateral international emissions trading system drawing from the experience in a few Annex 1 parties. Several companies have announced internal emissions trading schemes and many have set up offices to explore opportunities for joint implementation and the clean development mechanism, study project profiles, and lobby country positions so that can participate early on in the emerging global carbon market.

24. White House, "Text of a Letter from the President to Senators Hagel, Helms, Craig, and Roberts."

25. See Baer et al., "Equity and Greenhouse Gas Responsibility," p. 2287.

26. Indeed, a new poll from ABC News reveals that 61 percent of Americans believe that the United States should sign the Kyoto treaty, whereas only 26 percent oppose the agreement. The treaty is overwhelmingly favored by Democrats and Independents, but Bush doesn't even have the support of his party on this one—52 percent of Republicans favor the treaty, whereas 37 percent oppose it. ABCNews. com, April 17, 2001.

PART 4

U.S. REGIONAL POLICIES

15

The United States and Latin America: Multilateralism and International Legitimacy

Gelson Fonseca, Jr.

IN A WORLD OF SOVEREIGNS, UNILATERAL ACTIONS ARE PERMANENTLY OPEN TO all states. The realization of this hypothetical has, however, been conditioned by historical situations. In broad terms, it may be said that different patterns in the distribution of power and in the intensity of interaction among states condition the level of adherence to international institutions, creating different incentives or inhibitions to the recourse to unilateral moves.[1] In the current era, the preeminence of the United States in the international system poses often, for the superpower, the temptation of acting alone. For many other states, the natural attitude would then be either to contain these unilateral trends or to attract the United States to multilateral and shared solutions. Of course, it would be simplistic, and even false, to oppose an alleged U.S. unilateralism to a "multilateral" inclination on the part of all other states.[2] Nevertheless, the question of how unilateralist and multilateralist tendencies coexist is central to any understanding of today's world order.

The inter-American system offers a unique setting to analyze the dynamics of unilateralism, precisely because of its long-standing unipolar characteristics and the extensive and deep historical connections linking the United States and its hemispheric neighbors. Indeed, the regional system has combined, since the days of the Monroe Doctrine, a strong normative tradition with the reality of U.S. hegemony—and consequently the unilateral temptation. In this chapter, after briefly discussing the concept of unilateralism, I analyze how Latin American diplomacy has reacted to the trends of U.S. unilateralism in the hemisphere.

The Concept of Unilateralism

To frame the argument on the current meaning of unilateralism and its implications for diplomacy—and especially how to react against its negative consequences—one needs first to consider four broad sets of factors.

First, the *instinctive reaction* of a diplomat from a developing country to unilateralism is to prevent it from taking place in the future. The argument is both simple and obvious. The option of unilateral action depends initially and mainly, albeit not only, on the power of the nation that would choose this path. In a world without any rules, the victor in a clash between strong and weak states would almost inevitably be the former.[3] In such an anarchical, or Hobbesian, situation, power would always tend to triumph over reason.[4] To take an example from trade, the possibility that a developing country would prevail in a commercial dispute with a developed country, in the absence of the WTO regulations, is virtually nonexistent. By contrast, the developing country would enjoy greater odds of success under the WTO regime, even though its rules are far from perfect.[5]

Thus, the question of how to prevent unilateralism is relatively easy to answer in general terms: The antidote to unilateralism is *more multilateralism*—or more rules and more respect for those rules. The problem becomes more difficult, however, when one deals with specific situations and the variety of manifestations of unilateralism as well as the multiple dimensions of multilateralism.[6]

Second, due to the expansion of normative rules and principles in the international system, adherence to multilateral rules tends to offer a high degree of legitimacy.[7] This trend has drastically reduced the possible courses of action available in the classic international system that existed before the creation of the League of Nations, when the "reason of state" was sufficient to justify any government policy, including the breach of contractual obligations. The old idea that the reason of state acquits all crimes must be seen today against a new backdrop: the notion of duties beyond borders. Moreover, the duties that in theory justify certain moral or legal constraints on state behavior are ultimately defined by multilateral mechanisms.[8] In other words, the various multilateral types of decisions— such as charters, treaties, conventions, declarations, and resolutions—are nowadays the least unequivocal body of reference of what is right or wrong in the behavior of a state.[9]

Third, the modes and possibilities of acting unilaterally have varied in time and space. The inter-American system provides a useful framework to examine the evolution and characteristics of unilateralism, because this system developed, to a certain extent, as a barrier to the unilateral tendencies of the United States. This system combines a situation of inequality between a strong state and other, less powerful members, on the one hand, with an intricate and consolidated set of juridical rules that aims to limit their behavior on the other.

For an illustration of how this system has evolved, one can compare the history of U.S. interventions in Central America throughout the twentieth century. Even if we admit that comparisons between different historical moments are somewhat artificial, it is clear that the undisguised U.S.

occupation of Haiti in 1915 answered to a logic of power completely distinct from the multilateral intervention in the same country in the 1990s. At the beginning of the last century, unilateral actions corresponded to a mere projection of internal needs, with minimal (if any) concern to international rules or constraints. The legitimating patterns and their institutional architecture have undergone an enormous change over time, as exemplified by the creation of the Organization of American States in 1948.[10]

Even so, we should recall that until the 1980s the model of intervention approximated the earlier crude one, with slight variations. In the case of Grenada in 1983, for instance, the United States attempted to justify its unilateral decision to intervene a posteriori by the resort to a multilateral organization, even if one with no clear competence in the matter (the Organization of Eastern Caribbean States). The invasion of Panama in 1989 also resembles a more blunt model of intervention. A provisional hypothesis would be that the end of the Cold War led to the obsolescence of the crude model of U.S. unilateralism.

Fourth, unilateralism is, in our days, a primarily U.S. issue, and it would be difficult to imagine any analysis of this concept that did not focus on the United States, even if it takes into account the importance of the so-called great powers in general.[11] In fact, unilateralism in this context goes beyond the classic resort to self-help under conditions of an anarchical international system—something that is (at least in theory) within the reach of any sovereign state due to the nature of sovereignty (and its acceptance by the United Nations Charter).[12]

Unilateralism today is something different. The international system has at its disposal a collection of rules and common attitudes that tend toward universal acceptance. Such norms and attitudes have been adopted through multiple rounds of negotiation; they are comprehensive and cover a wide range of aspects of international relations, from security to the environment, human rights, and trade. They are expanding mainly due to globalization.[13] In such a context, unilateralism can be defined as the decision to act in violation of such rules or as self-exemption from these rules and common attitudes; that is, it is the resort to self-help in areas in which, at least hypothetically, diplomatic solutions would suggest or oblige compliance with the existing rules and agreed attitudes.[14]

The tendency toward unilateralism has, in the U.S. case, been reinforced by a sense that the United States is an "exceptional state" within the international system. As Edward Luck argues, this U.S. sense of exceptionalism involves four components:

> 1) a willingness to go it alone on a variety of issues, along with apparent immunity to the pressures and criticisms of others; 2) an assumption that its national values and practices are universally valid and its policy positions are moral and proper, not just expedient; 3) a strong tendency to look

inward, to domestic political considerations and processes, when determining how to act in international fora, in some cases coupled with a willingness to adopt national legislation that contradicts the rules and responsibilities imposed by international arrangements; and 4) a belief by national policymakers and legislators that they have other options for pursuing their nation's interests and that acting through multilateral institutions is only an option, not an obligation.[15]

An additional and less visible manifestation of unilateralism can emerge during negotiations, when a strong power uses political pressure to constrain multilateral partners to accept specific decisions. This occurs, for instance, in discussions over proposed resolutions in multilateral fora. The powerful—by linking different issues, promising reward, or hinting of harmful consequences if their interests are not met—are able to narrow the margin of maneuver of smaller countries. Formally, this unilateral action results in victory through the vote, but substantially it derives from the imposition of the will of the stronger party. Such "unilateralism" is often hard to discern, partly because it is difficult to determine a state's ideal goals during negotiations, as opposed to attainable goals. In theory, diplomacy is based on the rule of equality among negotiating parties and the prevalence of the "best" argument. But we know that this is only partially true in practice.[16]

Unilateralism is a mode of international behavior, a particular way to use power in the international arena, affecting a country or a group of countries or even bringing about systemic consequences. So if American unilateral actions are carried out, one might conceive of regional responses to this phenomenon. In this paper I examine the Latin American response to U.S. unilateralism to explore how unilateral actions affect developing countries and what means they have to counter unilateralism.[17]

As presented in this chapter, unilateralism and multilateralism should be considered two ideal-types, in the Weberian sense; that is, both terms represent theoretical categories that are used as tools to gauge the empirical realities of international relations. They should not be confounded with reality itself, although both concepts are based on specific characteristics and empirical evidence synthesized in an analytical framework. Depending on the historical circumstances and on a number of intervening variables— among which power and values play an important part—international reality may resemble, more or less, certain characteristics of one or the other ideal-type. Historically, U.S. attitudes toward hemispheric neighbors have varied greatly, from a more unilateralist stand to multilateral-friendly policies and back to unilateral decisions. At times, both unilateral and multilateral attitudes have coexisted.[18] Any analysis of these issues must therefore be grounded in a solid historical account and avoid the hypostatization of theoretical categories.

The Post–Cold War
International System and the United States

An essential characteristic of the modern international system, as it has evolved since the Treaty of Westphalia of 1648, is the unequal distribution of power resources. Of course, the modalities of inequality have changed over time. We know, for instance, that it is no longer possible to reinstate the juridical differences between sovereign states and colonies extant in the 1950s. Under colonial rule, domination had its heyday, and the goal of liberation movements was to rupture the link between the metropole and the colonial territory. Today, the scenario for developing countries is far more complex, and the possibilities of autonomy from the powerful vary in accordance with such factors as economic advantages and technological development. Political independence is a condition for autonomy but no longer its ultimate goal.

In an era of globalization, true rupture—or detachment from the international system—is not a realistic option. In contrast, there is a vast array of ways to pursue autonomy, to decide about one's own future, and to influence the shape of the international system (including its patterns of legitimacy). For a developing country, autonomy no longer means a protective distance from the superpower conflict or radical plans to reorganize the world economy to correct the global inequities. Rather, the challenge for developing countries today is to broaden autonomy through increased participation, both in shaping the solution of security problems and in articulating proposals for viable reforms of the international institutions so that they could better serve the goals of improving national social and economic situations. Better global governance could foster better national governance.

Increasing autonomy—in the sense of opening and guaranteeing opportunities for broad participation in international decisionmaking—is an important strategy for decisively containing unilateralism. But how open are international institutions to this broad participation? How effective could such participation be?[19]

The ongoing heated debate on the power distribution and systemic effects of today's international system is partly a product of the end of the neat bipolar logic of the Cold War, which left the United States as the preeminent world power. On the one hand, it is generally accepted that the United States will play a pivotal role in the definition of the future of the international system. To begin with, it is hard to think of any issue on the international agenda over which the United States has no influence, and this is valid in particular with regard to the adoption and implementation of international regimes. On many occasions, the United States has taken a positive stance toward the establishment of multilateral mechanisms and rules, such as the creation of the United Nations, the negotiation of the

1948 Universal Declaration of Human Rights, and the initial movement to set up the International Criminal Court (ICC).

On the other hand, such positive actions are frequently contradicted by a U.S. reluctance to abide by the standards it helps to shape. Conspicuous recent examples of this tendency have been the U.S. decisions to disregard the Kyoto Protocol on climate change, to withhold UN-assessed contributions, to reject ratification of the Comprehensive Nuclear Test Ban Treaty (CTBT), to refuse to accept some verification clauses in the biological arms convention, and to oppose ratification of the 1998 Rome Statute of the ICC.[20] One might also add the earlier U.S. withdrawal from UNESCO in 1984.[21]

It is clear that the active involvement of the United States is fundamental for the success of multilateral institutions. The unique U.S. position means that a more benign attitude on its part toward multilateralism will favor the consolidation of a more rule-oriented order in which the less powerful will be more likely to achieve significant autonomy. A U.S. attitude contrary to multilateralism is likely to have the opposite effect and to foster, through a sort of mimetic effect, a preference for power solutions. The ICC, for instance, will be stronger or weaker depending on whether the United States chooses to adhere to its rules. This is not to say that the will of the United States is the same as the will of the system. Certainly, for example, the consolidation of human rights on the international agenda has been due to many factors and, to a large extent, has come about despite a lack of U.S. enthusiasm in ratifying several important treaties adopted in this field. But the unavoidable presence of the United States in all areas of international relations allows it to link issues and establish connections among interests in different areas. And though this power can be used in a positive way, there is a risk that such capacity will reinforce a more selective multilateralism shaped by political interests, rather than serving the objective of giving a universal character to multilateral rules.

In short, U.S. behavior has been ambivalent, to say the least. To use professor Luck's apt expression, the United States has offered "mixed messages" to the international community. There has been a general preference for multilateralism, with different degrees of enthusiasm and commitment, depending on specific issues and historical circumstances. But this preference does not rule out unilateral actions (such as the frequent use of sanctions), and when in specific circumstances the United States abandons multilateral institutions, its attitude tends to have systemic consequences. The mere lack of U.S. participation, however, does not necessarily doom multilateral mechanisms to failure. The treaties regarding the Law of the Sea and the Maritime Tribunal, to cite two examples, are in place despite the fact that the United States has never adhered to them. The preliminary conclusion to be drawn is that the U.S. influence is universal but is not always absolute.

If one looks at the international agenda *à vol d'oiseau* (from a bird's-eye view), it is possible to distinguish between two paradigmatic attitudes:

issues in which the United States has high stakes or absolute interest and thus moves unilaterally, such as in matters of security (like Iraq), even if such action is against established UN rules; and issues in which the United States has interests but where the stakes are not too high, allowing U.S. foreign policy makers to advance the agenda from within a multilateral framework. Of course, intermediary situations between these two extremes tend to prevail.[22]

Given the growing strength of multilateral institutions as providers of international legitimacy, one can hypothesize that the U.S. tendency toward unilateralism is increasingly less absolute. The unilateral bombardment of Iraq in 1998, for example, did not prevent the United States from negotiating with its partners in the UN Security Council to pass resolutions on the return of international inspectors to Iraq.[23] Conversely, the active involvement of the United States in adopting Security Council resolutions on African conflicts has not eliminated implicit special rules. These include the requirement of a fifteen-day period to allow the U.S. delegation to the UN to consult with the U.S Senate and the House on cost implications before any resolution concerning the establishment of peacekeeping operations can be adopted and enter into force. In the same vein, the rejection of the Kyoto Protocol on emission of greenhouse gases has been accompanied by hints from U.S. officials that a new and more realistic treaty on climate change is necessary. Unfortunately, the United States has never presented its ideas, and an agreement was reached in November 2001 in Marrakech on the mechanisms of implementation of the Kyoto Protocol. The United States is not a party to the agreement, leading an optimist commentator to say that "the fact that the world could agree despite the absence of the United States may prove promising. No single country, even the largest economy in the world, can stop the cooperation of others. Sometime soon the United States is likely to rejoin these international discussions."[24]

From a political and diplomatic standpoint, the question is how to ensure the prevalence of the paradigm of U.S. multilateralism in its highest degree of purity. And here we touch on the dynamics of unilateralism. The origins of U.S. unilateralism may be traced back to certain historical peculiarities of the U.S. political system and explained with reference to the country's unique power position in the international system. Today, however, these unilateral U.S. tendencies are complicated by the complexity of the contemporary international landscape, characterized, among other things, by the presence of NGOs that advance crosscutting issues, the role of corporations, the importance of worldwide communications, the widespread disparities among countries and regions, and so on. Although the implications of this more complex world on multilateralism are not straightforward, one logical conclusion is that these forces will tend to constrain attempts to make unilateralism politically viable. Political viability, in this context, means the existence of both a space of legitimacy, which allows for a minimal degree of acceptance for unilateral decisions, and a space of power, which ensures that unilateral acts are pursued at a low and affordable cost.

The need for legitimacy constrains U.S. policy. Given its power, the United States can do a lot, but it is not allowed, for instance, to propose torture as a method of police investigation or to advocate the end of the United Nations, because such courses of action would go well beyond the limits of contemporary legitimacy (both domestic and external).[25] In terms of the space of power, the imposition of sanctions against Cuba is a low-risk policy and thus politically viable—although it has been challenged on political and legal grounds—because that country cannot retaliate against the United States. But the legitimacy of the argument that such measures are necessary as a defense against the spread of communism disappeared with the end of the Cold War.[26]

In addition, we should bear in mind that the option of resorting to unilateralism is available to all countries—just in different degrees. Ethiopia and Eritrea, for instance, were able to disregard for a time the appeals from the Security Council for conciliation, for it seemed that they could bear the costs of such a behavior. However, for those two countries—and even for a medium-sized country—the high costs of noncompliance with the outcome of a WTO panel or with the obligations of the nuclear nonproliferation regime would almost certainly induce observance of the established rules.[27] From these observations, we may conclude that there are two kinds of unilateralism: a weak one, practiced, in our example, by Ethiopia and Eritrea, which consists of refraining from complying with multilateral demands; and a strong one, practiced publicly by the United States, which is not limited to merely disobeying multilateral rules but also involves the active bending of rules and other forceful interventions that change power relations and the overall strategic balance in a much more profound way.[28]

U.S. unilateralism thus tends to carry an inherent ambivalence. It has some pure manifestations, but most of the time it seeks the blessing of multilateralism. It is as if there exists a sort of ideal multilateralism from the U.S. perspective, one that accepts the wishes of the United States with no deviation. In effect, this would amount to unilateralism being enshrined as the will of the international community. The U.S. attitude toward the ICC illustrates this kind of perspective. During President Bill Clinton's administration, U.S. negotiators sought a special guarantee to exempt fellow U.S. citizens from the court's jurisdiction. This position went beyond reasonable limits. Its acceptance would have created a privilege for the United States that was unacceptable for the majority of countries and would have denied an essential aspect of the rule of law: its universality. The administration of George W. Bush, in deciding to "unsign" the Rome Statute of the ICC in 2002 and threatening to withhold U.S. approval for peacekeeping missions unless U.S. military personnel were guaranteed immunity from ICC prosecutors, adopted an even more uncompromising stance on this question.

The dilemma is to arrive at a level of accommodation to U.S. concerns acceptable both to other countries and to the United States. The dominant impression today is that there is no universal rule on this matter. During the Uruguay Round of multilateral trade negotiations, the United States accepted commitments on the liberalization of trade in agriculture. By contrast, the United States took many years to adhere to the International Covenant on Civil and Political Rights, and so far it has not become party to the Convention on the Rights of the Child. And as we will see below, some thirty years elapsed before the United States was in a position to accept in explicit terms the rule of nonintervention in the inter-American system.

We may conclude that unilateralism is not an option that always prevails in U.S. policy. One of the most formidable diplomatic problems we face is how to deal with the ambivalence of U.S. foreign policy, with a view to restraining, through diplomatic instruments, the space of legitimacy for unilateralism.

Multilateralism and the Prevention of Unilateralism

It is exactly because unilateralism projects itself on the international order that it is possible to deal diplomatically with its actions, that it is possible, to a certain extent, to use diplomatic instruments to contain it. How is this so?

Legitimacy and Sovereign Equality

First, it is possible to contain unilateralism at the level of patterns of legitimacy. Any act of power, even a unilateral one, depends on a plausible justification as a precondition for legitimacy. Such justification is fully obtained today only at the multilateral level.[29] For this precise reason, one of the first possible steps to contain unilateralism resides in the field of shared values. Therefore, the first step consists of enshrining the fundamental limit to unilateralism: reaffirming the idea that states are equal as a basis for legitimacy. The challenge is to depict unilateralism as an exception in every case, thereby forcing the "unilateralist" into a defensive position.

The issue is not new. It is worth recalling an episode that took place during the International Peace Conference at The Hague in 1907, an event that anticipated discussions on the question of the permanent seats on the Security Council in San Francisco in 1945.[30] During the meeting at The Hague, in which a tribunal of arbitration was under discussion, the main goal for medium-sized countries like Brazil was to prevent great powers from gaining a permanent seat at such a tribunal, in violation of the rule of equality.[31] In reality, the sharpest means to preventively deconstruct unilateralism is to advance the idea of the juridical equality of states and its embodiment in fora in which sovereign states find symbolic expressions of equality, as is the case when their votes in multilateral organizations carry the same weight.[32]

Any unilateral action may be seen as a denial of equality, as it implies that the interests of a particular state are superior to those of its partners. It could be said that unilateralism implicitly carries with it a doctrine of hierarchy of interests, where national objectives are given priority over universally accepted multilateral rules.[33] The doctrine of sovereign equality is an essential precondition to multilateral diplomacy; it is the guarantee that the values and interests to be pursued will be those that enjoy legitimacy, those that the community of nations helps to build collectively.[34]

Nonintervention

The second step toward the preventive deconstruction of unilateralism consists in enshrining the rule of nonintervention. Once more, the pattern is repeated: resorting to multilateralism to create an ideological antidote to unilateralism. We can identify this process in the inter-American system, notably in the conferences held during the 1930s. On the one hand, that era saw the U.S. "good neighbor" policy designed by Franklin D. Roosevelt. On the other hand, it also witnessed a repetition of historic demands from Latin American countries for the consolidation of the rule of nonintervention, which finally occurred at the seventh International Conference of the American States held in Montevideo in 1933. The Convention on Rights and Duties of States, adopted during that conference and ratified by the United States, states the following in article 6: "States are juridically equal, enjoy the same rights, and have equal capacity in their exercise. The rights of each do not depend upon the power it possesses to assure its exercise, but upon the simple fact of its existence as a person under international law." And in article 8, the convention continued: "No state has the right to intervene in the internal or external affairs of another."

It is also interesting to recall what President Roosevelt said on that occasion:

> The definite policy of the United States from now on is one opposed to armed intervention. The maintenance of constitutional government in other nations is, not, after all, a sacred obligation devolving upon the United States alone. The maintenance of law and the orderly process of government in this hemisphere is the concern of each individual nation within its borders first of all. It is only if and when the failure of the orderly process affects the other nations of the continent that it becomes their concern, and the point to stress is that in such an event it becomes the joint concern of the whole continent in which we are all neighbors.[35]

Diplomatic Activism

A third way of dealing with unilateralism is through diplomatic activism, which means using the rule of nonintervention in a consistent, precise, and positive way, proposing courses of actions alternative to the prospective unilateralism of the United States. A good recent example was the articulation of the Contadora Group (later Rio Group) in the 1980s. A group of democracies (some recently democratized) were able to propose means to reach peaceful solutions for the Central American conflicts, in which the United States was a major player. What were the origins of the successful actions of the Rio Group in creating alternatives to U.S. unilateralism? Success reflected a combination of four factors: a sound normative basis; a focused and clear objective; a set of real alternatives for conciliation; and, finally, strong democratic legitimacy.[36]

What is the real effect of these barriers of legitimacy to unilateralism? It is certainly not absolute. Following World War II, the United States carried out a number of different types of unilateral interventions: with different degrees of a posteriori multilateral legitimacy (as in the Dominican Republic in 1965); with precarious resort to legitimacy mechanisms (Grenada in 1983); with no legitimacy whatsoever (Cuba in 1961, Chile in 1973); and even against a decision of the International Court of Justice (as in that court's 1984 decision on the mining of Nicaraguan ports). All these events occurred during the Cold War, which gave greater leeway for interventions.

The Cold War provided, to some degree, grounds for breaking the multilateral rule of legitimacy. The threats that demanded unilateral responses were no longer defined as "internal disorder" but as losses suffered by one side in the bipolar struggle, losses that could mean gains for a competing model of social organization. Any partial gains by the Soviet Union or of the socialist bloc were interpreted as affecting not only U.S. security but also the very idea of Western civilization, especially in the Americas.[37] The preservation of the rule of nonintervention was balanced, and compromised, by the dramatic character of potential strategic losses. This argument was sufficient to rally the Western European allies on the U.S. side (and Eastern European governments to the Soviet Union when socialism was "threatened" in Hungary, Czechoslovakia, or Poland). But, of course, the third world condemned these interventions.

The U.S. invasion of Panama in 1989 offered the first signal that this pattern of unilateralism was becoming exhausted.[38] There were many possible accusations against Panamanian strongman Manuel Noriega, but the allegation that he embodied a communist threat was no longer plausible. The intervention was justified, rather, by Noriega's alleged involvement with drug-trafficking. This explanation or justification marked a turning point. Under the new framework for unilateral actions, strategic and civilizational reasons would give way to reasoning related to respect for values.[39]

This created new dilemmas and additional problems, both for those who wished to intervene and for those who wanted to prevent interventions. During the Cold War, the advantages of legitimacy were clearly on the side of the party that suffered an intervention, as no clearer rule existed in international law than that of nonintervention. Sovereignty was an absolute only to be supplanted by an illegal act. In such situations, there could have been strong political or ideological reasons to justify interventions, but the legitimacy of such actions was very weak. Today, the situation is considerably more complex, and the advantages and disadvantages are distributed in a different fashion.

One consequence of the end of the Cold War has been the fragmentation of the strategic space. For the United States, this has meant a certain indifference to winners in regional confrontations. In contrast to the Cold War, a regional "winner" is not perceived to serve the interests of a global rival, because no global ideological rivalry exists. This has mitigated the perceived U.S. need to intervene for global strategic reasons. Symptomatically, the military strategy of the administration of George W. Bush is based upon defensive notions, as exemplified so clearly in his insistence on establishing nationwide missile defense.[40] Nevertheless, such indifference to intervention is not absolute, and regional strategic interests help explain, for example, the bombing of Iraq. Yet the U.S. attitude toward multilateral interventions in Haiti, Somalia, and East Timor was significantly influenced by a preference for certain values. Was the military action against Afghanistan beginning in October 2001 a different case? The reaction has not been motivated by a regional interest but by a universal concern with terrorism. The U.S. interest in responding to the attacks converges with the attitude of the international community of condemning terrorism (clearly expressed in this case). Military action could be taken within the boundaries of the UN Charter, and the Security Council adopted a new role in organizing the counterterrorism efforts (Security Council Resolution Nos. 1368 and 1373).

Thus, with the dissolution of the Cold War rivalry, two possibilities have arisen: first, the possibility of using—with credibility—a universalist argument for legitimizing interventions; and second, the possibility of resorting to multilateral instruments. At least in theory, multilateral institutions, especially the Security Council, are no longer subject to power politics to the degree that they were during the Cold War. Structural reasons for paralysis no longer prevail.[41] There are no objective reasons to suspect that the Security Council will favor a side that no longer exists. The case of Central America is instructive in this regard. We can compare the unilateral and illegal interventions that the United States led in this region during the 1980s to combat purported communist infiltration with the multilateralization of the international presence in the 1990s. As Susan Burgerman summarizes in discussing El Salvador,

> After 1989, changes in domestic political conditions (the emergence of an elite with the authority to subordinate the military and a concern for El Salvador's international reputation) combined with a permissive international context (the post Cold War withdrawal of U.S. military support) to produce conditions for a UN mediated settlement to the civil war, which resulted in a human rights–based peace keeping operation.[42]

Thus, even if the end of the Cold War did not erase the century-old strategic interests of the United States in Central America, the means of defending these interests have drastically changed.

In order to act unilaterally, one must now make two moves in the process of argumentation: justify the action in the name of inestimable values, as well as argue that resorting to multilateralism (the natural protective home of such values) is impossible due to the paralysis and incapacity of multilateral institutions to act expeditiously in situations of grave emergencies. The NATO decision to bomb the Federal Republic of Yugoslavia during the Kosovo war of 1999 is emblematic of this line of reasoning.

It is also worth noting that there is another unilateralism, a preventive variety that seeks to avoid the adoption of multilateral rules seen as potential constraints on a state's freedom of action. Again, examples are the reluctance of the United States to sign and ratify the ICC, the Ottawa Convention that bans antipersonnel landmines, and the Convention on the Rights of the Child. Multilateralism has to do with common attitudes that tend to crystallize into rules. That is why the above definition equates unilateralism with solitary discrepancy from common attitudes.

What are the new dimensions of the problem of the diplomatic struggle against unilateralism? What has changed since the end of the Cold War, besides the hypothetical strengthening of multilateralism and the parallel weakening of the legitimacy of resorting to unilateralism?

Developing Countries and U.S. Unilateralism

Let us look at the problem from the perspective of developing countries. We have a *negative* and a *positive* challenge. To begin with the negative, are developing countries in a better or worse ideological and juridical position to defend themselves from the unilateralism that manifests itself through intervention and other concrete and specific actions? The positive challenge could be summarized in another question: Are there means to persuade the superpower to adhere to new multilateral rules? Both challenges coexist and must be tackled at the same time, but they lead to two different sorts of policy problems, as described below.

The answer to the first question is a multifaceted one. In a certain way, the premises of the equality of states and of nonintervention remain untouched. But it is undeniable that the perception of this equality has changed alongside the possibilities of intervention. After the Cold War, the ways of defining what a state *is* in the international system have been widened. States are no longer defined solely by their membership in groups or blocs or by their adherence to a certain type of social organization. States now are viewed by world public opinion and by multilateral institutions according to new criteria. They can now be labeled as violators of human rights, as enemies of the environment, as hosts to criminal organizations, as agents in the proliferation of arms of mass destruction, as being incapable of preventing humanitarian tragedies, and so forth.[43] The degree of international legitimacy and the defense of sovereignty now depend on elements other than the stability of national frontiers. This also ushers in a new notion of inequality—at the level of legitimacy—in international relations and raises a greater possibility of corrective interventions against states failing to meet basic standards.

A few qualifications are necessary. First, during the Cold War, interventions were motivated ideologically and, for this reason, were subject to an almost automatic condemnation. The principle of nonintervention had an absolute validity and was always seen as positive. Once the interventions undertaken under the banner of universal principles such as the defense of human rights became a tangible hypothesis, however, the meaning of intervention was altered to encompass the theoretical possibility of being a positive action. The great challenge, for countries possessing scant power resources, does not consist of rejecting the new patterns of international legitimacy. The real challenge is to avert the unilateral use of patterns that clearly bypass the multilateral mechanisms entrusted with the mandate to uphold them.

Second, although the patterns of *substantive* legitimacy are altered, there has been no similar modification in the mechanisms that define the *procedural* legitimacy (i.e., in those institutions that declare what is legitimate in the international system). In contrast with what happened after World War I and World War II, the end of the Cold War has engendered few new political institutions, except in the area of trade with the establishment of the WTO.[44] In most areas, rather, existing multilateral institutions were adapted, basically through the expansion of the competence of their organs. (For example, the work of the Security Council was expanded to cover areas such as the restoration of democracy in Haiti and the solution to internal conflicts in Mozambique.) Today, there is a gap between what is considered to be legitimate—bearing in mind that the limits of legitimacy are subject to controversy—and the mechanisms for bringing about such legitimacy. Moreover, the proliferation of NGOs has contributed to the emergence of new sources of legitimacy. As a matter of fact, the agendas of multilateral organizations are to a certain extent shaped by civil society.

Third, as a direct consequence of the above-mentioned gap and of the consolidation of new criteria of legitimacy for state behavior, it is now more difficult to oppose unilateralism undertaken in the name of universal values. Because the institutions remain the same, the unilateralist argues that their lack of effectiveness justifies unilateral actions in situations apparently requiring an urgent response. The challenge here again is not to reject the values considered to be universal—which, by the way, many developing countries helped to consolidate—but to avoid the emergence of self-proclaimed privileged interpreters. The interpretation of legitimacy is necessarily selective when it hinges on unilateral actions. To put it differently, it is selective when freed from the system of checks and balances of multilateral institutions.[45]

There is, however, a positive aspect for developing countries: the fact that existing multilateral organizations, which are based on the rule of equality, are still the centers of the legitimizing process. Even the alternative sources of legitimacy, such as NGOs, try to influence the outcome of multilateral negotiations and the behavior of multilateral organizations. The fact that states undertaking unilateral actions seek frequently not only the substantive legitimacy of values but also the formal endorsement of multilateral organs (procedural legitimacy) shows that multilateralism remains a necessary reference point in virtually all situations. Unilateral interventions, even in the name of universal values, tend to seek the blessing of the competent multilateral organs, even if such a blessing is only sought a posteriori. Of course, the blessing does not suspend the possible pernicious effects of the intervention itself.

The second challenge in deconstructing unilateralism goes beyond a preventive or defensive attitude. It has to do with the hypothesis of inducing the United States to accept multilateral rules in those areas in which there is a deep and universal consensus, broken only by the exceptionalism of the U.S. attitude. We are talking now of reconstructing multilateralism. Viewed from outside and in broad terms, this would imply no profound contradiction between the U.S. position in the world and the ratification of the Convention on the Rights of the Child, the Ottawa Convention on landmines, the ICC, and so on.

As Ed Luck indicates, "the roots of American ambivalence are many and deep."[46] Moreover, in the current circumstances, the problem is aggravated by two factors: The center of resistance to the adoption of a more multilateralist attitude can be identified in specific conservative sectors of U.S. domestic society that are virtually immune to any kind of appeal from the international community; and the costs of U.S. unilateralism in specific issues are low in diplomatic terms. If we combine these two factors, taking into consideration the strength of unilateralism in the U.S. foreign policy tradition, a plausible conclusion is that the international community will simply have to forsake any expectation of changes in U.S. unilateral trends.

Furthermore, we are dealing with an abstract entity—the international community—that seldom acts in unison, on the one hand, and a very concrete reality—U.S. foreign policy—on the other. The theoretical possibilities that the former may shape the latter are limited, but even so they should not be ignored. The issue of the UN scale of assessed contributions and how U.S. multilateralists forged direct ties between the international community (the UN) and the Senate is a case in point. In the same vein, it is important to reflect on the consequences of September 11 for the general U.S.

attitude regarding multilateralism. In the wake of the 2001 attacks, multilateral support for the United States was prompt and positive, both by the Security Council and by the General Assembly. It remains to be seen whether this strong international support has any deep and lasting effect on the willingness of the United States to adopt a more multilateralist attitude. In addition, we should not forget that U.S. unilateralism is conditioned by the fact that it is a democracy and a historical proponent of multilateral institutions. Democracies, moreover, tend to learn with experience, reflecting changes in the internal and external debate on the virtues and shortcomings of multilateralism. If the benefits of multilateralism become more obvious, certainly the constraints for unilateralism will increase. The complexity of the U.S. political system also leads to the conclusion that it would be easier for the international community to constrain unilateralism by another country, though this would likely require different instruments.

Conclusion

For developing countries, especially in Latin America, it is important to evaluate the paths that may lead to the strengthening of multilateralism. These paths must include the reaffirmation of the equality of all states and the consolidation of universal institutions as legitimate interpreters of the implementation of internationally accepted standards. The antidote to unilateralism and the imposition by force of decisions does not lie in the outright rejection of the values that are used to justify humanitarian interventions but in the renewal of the belief that such values can only be duly realized through multilateral institutions.[47] In other words, it is essential to reconcile the *substantive* legitimacy with the *procedural* legitimacy.

There are at least three evident obstacles in the way of this strategy to combat unilateralism. The first is the force of the argument of the inefficiency and political paralysis of existing multilateral institutions. The example of Kosovo serves as an illustration: In the face of the paralysis of the Security Council, the argument runs, NATO had to act to safeguard the basic rights of the Kosovars who were being targeted by the Serbian security forces in their attempt to carry out ethnic cleansing. The basic values of human rights and the principles of international humanitarian law, following this argument, were in danger, and an immediate intervention was needed by those actors who had the necessary resources to impose a change in the behavior of the perpetrators of these violations.

This argument is frequently combined with an assertion of the alleged inefficiency of multilateral mechanisms. International institutions not only suffer from political paralysis; often they also lack the material and strategic resources to intervene in a situation of high complexity. According to this point of view, only powerful countries could carry out with a real chance of success even those interventions authorized by competent multilateral institutions. Accordingly, so-called coalitions of the willing would have to be considered the natural substitutes for traditional peacekeeping operations, particularly given the lack of human and material resources of the UN Department of Peacekeeping Operations to plan and execute increasingly complex and multidimensional missions.

These arguments—political paralysis and inefficiency—offer powerful obstacles to multilateralism because they can constitute a sort of self-fulfilling prophecy. If one begins with the assumption that the Security Council has grave limits, it becomes easy to set aside the path of diplomacy and negotiation, thereby increasing the chances that political paralysis will continue to exist. Similarly, the argument of inefficiency can be used as an excuse for unilateral actions—rather than as grounds for reforming multilateral institutions by providing them with the tools required for the implementation of their mandates. The Brahimi Report on reforming multilateral peace operations is, in this sense, an auspicious development that can help overcome the obstacle of inefficiency.

A third obstacle to multilateralism is a tendency to endorse a version of the maxim that the ends justify the means. Unilateral actions, after all, may lead to positive outcomes. One can think of examples where unilateral action united the national interest of specific countries with the objective of halting massacres, such as the Vietnamese intervention against the Pol Pot regime in Cambodia and the Tanzanian role in overthrowing Idi Amin in Uganda. It is difficult, though, to ensure such a virtuous and harmonious coincidence between interests and values when the arbiter is the intervener. Moreover, the means—unilateral actions, usually undertaken from a power position—can too easily contaminate the virtuous goals they are alleged to serve. Such goals may be distorted in practice to favor less noble objectives.

A great effort has been made in the United Nations over the last fifty years to create, to the extent possible, a legal basis to ensure an acceptable degree of predictability, stability, and rationality in international relations. The assumption behind this exercise is the understanding that the unilateral action usually generates instability. It is so precisely because of its unpredictable character and its subjection both to the domestic political game and to considerations of national interests that may or may not coincide with universal values. The rules adopted under the aegis of the UN and other multilateral organizations are intended to express the interest of the international community, whose only authorized interpreter is the international community itself through the multilateral institutions.

How can the Latin American countries help reconcile substantive legitimacy with procedural legitimacy? First, it is essential to stress that today most Latin American countries cherish the values and objectives of democracy, human rights, disarmament, respect for the environment, pursuit of peaceful settlement of disputes, and the acceptance of international law as regulator of interstate relations. To put it differently, Latin American countries are not passive targets of values that emanate from multilateral institutions. On the contrary, they are largely coparticipants in the adoption and definition of values that are the core of legitimacy patterns nowadays—values, by the way, that are Western and close to U.S. ones. A good example of this convergence was the initiative to approve a resolution, based upon the Rio Treaty, to consider the September 11 attacks against the United States "as attacks against all American States" (RC.24/Res.1/01, September 21, 2001). This is not to say that such countries are immune to the unilateral manipulation of universal values, but their domestic systems, combined with the fact that they are a sort of Westernized middle class in the international system, predisposes them to strengthen multilateral institutions.

This active, supportive stance meets the initial requirement of legitimacy and bestows authority on the discourse of these Latin American countries, which become in turn valid interlocutors at the international level. Consequently, Latin Americans are in a position to demonstrate—partly due to their history as targets of many kinds of interventions—the concrete benefits of multilateral institutions. They can make the argument that the lack of procedural legitimacy will ultimately lead to the loss of substantive legitimacy, as universal values turn out to be seen as mere tools to dissimulate the private interests of the powerful. The a posteriori legitimacy of benign unilateralism constitutes an exception, and given its inherent unpredictability, it is very unlikely that this form of unilateralism can become the rule.

For all these reasons, it is in the interest of Latin American countries to ensure the efficacy of the multilateral institutions (by reforming them if necessary), to renew their willingness to engage in dialogue and to negotiate, and to persuade the strong that unilateral action, even in the name of universal values, tends in the long run to discredit such values. This position stems not only from the relative lack of power resources at the disposal of Latin America, although this is obviously an important reason, but also mainly from the social and political systems of these countries.

As democratic societies, Latin American countries naturally want to project onto the international scene a legitimate conception of power as being formed from the bottom up and as one that can constitute itself as the concerted action of the international community.[48] To make a comparison with political theory, it is not enough to say that power is wielded on behalf of the collectivity; it is necessary to ensure that the mechanisms for the participation of all in the affairs of the community are in place. The source of legitimacy for decisions taken by multilateral mechanisms resides not only in the content of the decision but also in the observance of procedural rules previously accepted by those who are supposed to abide by the decision.

The outstanding problem continues to be how to induce the United States to take up a more proactive role in strengthening multilateral institutions. Is it possible to create conditions that would lead the United States to choose multilateral rules and regulations instead of succumbing to the temptation of unilateral actions? How can Latin America contribute to a new attitude on the part of the United States, in particular in those areas where the United States is going it alone in refusing to adhere to multilateral institutions? The obstacles, as we have seen above, are huge and cannot be underestimated, but this does not mean that a change is not possible.

The conservative sectors of U.S. society that deny the advantages of multilateral rules are not the only ones that have a say in U.S. foreign policy. Other worldviews can affect the domestic balance of power to favor a more multilateralist approach to international relations. In this regard, public opinion plays a pivotal role in our era of real-time, global communications. If a majority of the public is eventually convinced that unilateral actions undermine the long-run stability of the international order and consequently the vital interests of the United States itself, there may be a chance to change course. In this sense, domestic public opinion could be the most important barrier to U.S. unilateralism.

Latin American countries could contribute to this change of attitude, first and foremost, by making their views on this issue better and more widely known. Force is not a sufficient factor to keep the international order free from instability. Real leadership exists when it is accepted as legitimate and is largely based on positive incentives. In other words, leadership depends upon the leader being able to remain as a role model. The refusal to adhere fully to many multilateral rules and institutions could undermine the U.S. ability to be such a model.

From the first meeting of the Pan American Union in 1889 until the Inter-American Conferences of the 1930s, it took more than fifty years for the United States to accept the rules of equality and nonintervention, both of which were enshrined in the charters of the UN and of the OAS. These are overarching rules or principles that in theory should not leave room for ambivalence. But reality is much more complex than that, and the problem is how to interpret, in specific situations, the limitations imposed by these principles in a way that preserves the pattern of legitimacy.

Despite the conflicting interpretations that may arise, there is always the possibility of negotiating a common perspective in some politically delicate issues. The acceptance of the democratic clause by the OAS, for instance, created the framework for restraining U.S. interpretations as to when and how to intervene in cases of institutional breakdown. In the area of trade, there is a similar tendency to set up rules that are powerful incentives not to resort to unilateral actions, such as the multilateralization of the antidumping legislation that is part of the discussions on the Free Trade Area of the Americas.

It is important to adopt a case-by-case approach for dealing with unilateralism. There are some forms of unilateralism that can be influenced by diplomatic pressure, whereas others cannot. Following this argument, perhaps it will be easier to change the U.S. attitude regarding the Kyoto Protocol than its position on the CTBT. One must also consider, as an additional variable in this analysis, the possibility that the international community will in some cases adopt a virtually unanimous view against the United States. There is an extremely complex interaction between international public opinion and U.S. domestic politics, one that in theory could lead to a positive outcome, if the conservative segments of the U.S. society were persuaded that they had nothing to fear from active engagement in multilateral institutions.

The strengthening of multilateral institutions is essential for developing countries. Procedural legitimacy is in a certain way even more important than substantive legitimacy, as the latter is more easily subject to controversy. The existence of predictable mechanisms to settle disputes and solve conflicts of interest is so important precisely because a certain dose of controversy is always inevitable. Legitimate procedures offer the only way to ward off the crystallization of the principle of might makes right and to start building a solid basis for international relations in the twenty-first century. In this context, Latin American countries are committed to pursuing autonomy through participation, which means that they will continue to seek the consolidation of multilateralism and international law as the keystones of cooperation among states.

Are there lessons to be drawn from the inter-American experience in dealing with unilateral actions?

The nature of the problem and of its possible solution has changed over time. In the 1930s, it was necessary to struggle to reach some basic legal understandings with the United States. Today, the legal foundation is in place, and the question is how to improve and use it. The essential factor permitting solid conditions for diplomatic dialogue with the superpower was the democratization of Latin American societies in the 1980s. This created a common space of legitimacy throughout the hemisphere, with important consequences. It helped renew regional institutions devoted to democracy and human rights. Once a common view of the international system was obtained and a common perception of fundamental values established, the reasons for unilateral behavior were curtailed, at least in principle. The transposition of such a model to the international order, or even to the relations of the superpower with developing countries in other regions, is limited because of the unique hemispheric combination of shared values, institutional traditions, and, today, lack of conflicts that could invite intervention in the inter-American context. The set of common goals and values binding the United States and Latin America represent the outcome of a long process of mutual learning.

But the convergence and the pedagogy of understanding are still incomplete. The democratization of Latin America has made those countries closer to the United States by shaping the democratic institutions of the former along the lines of the institutions of the latter. The liberal democracies of Latin America were inspired by the vitality of the democratic principles in the United States. The completion of the process of mutual learning and the deepening of the convergence now could depend on a similar move— but in a different direction. The United States would come to adopt an attitude toward multilateral institutions along the lines of the commitment that Latin American countries show toward those institutions. U.S. democracy has inspired Latin American constitutionalism; convergence would be complete if the United States became inspired by Latin America's endorsement of multilateralism. The logical outcome would be not the weakening of U.S. leverage in world affairs but rather the strengthening of U.S. leadership by increasing the cohesion of the hemisphere and the removal of the distrust generated by prior unilateral attitudes. Looking at the tremendous progress achieved since the Monroe Doctrine, the possibility of such an outcome in the future is not farfetched.

Notes

This chapter was written with the collaboration of Benoni Belli and Leonardo Fernandes. I would like to thank Alexandra Barahona de Brito, David Malone, Shepard Forman, Yuen Foong Khong, Stewart Patrick, and Danilo Turk for their comments and suggestions, which have always improved the quality of the argument. Professor Ed Luck was a rigorous and careful reader, and I tried to incorporate many of his suggestions, always pertinent, in my final version. This chapter expresses the personal views of the author.

1. In his classical article, "Variants on Six Models of the International System," Morton Kaplan makes some useful remarks about the relations of power distribution and compliance with the nonintervention rule.

2. For an analysis of the complexities of the U.S. attitude toward multilateralism, see Luck, "American Exceptionalism and International Organization: Lessons from the 1990s."

3. It is evident that calculation of power available, especially prior to the engagement in conflicts, is an exercise full of uncertainties. The paradigmatic example was the resistance of North Vietnam to the U.S. armed intervention.

4. The possibilities of an international society that supplants the Hobbesian are studied in Bull, *The Anarchical Society*. A pure Hobbesian world is a Weberian ideal-type that would exist only in situations of war, in which the rules limiting warfare are easily broken.

5. See the example of the panel on gasoline. This was one of the first WTO cases, brought by Venezuela and later Brazil against the United States. The central question was about discrimination—specifically, whether U.S. environmental measures discriminated against imported gasoline and in favor of domestic refineries. Although the panel's ruling in 1996 was favorable to Venezuela and Brazil, the United States managed to minimize its defeat at the level of the appellate body. It is clear that the existence of norms, such as those of the WTO, that induce the transformation of conflict in judicial disputes does not rule out the advantages of power, which now can be shifted to other arenas, such as access to information, resources to hire

the best international attorneys, and so forth. United States—Standards for refor-mulated and conventional gasoline—Panel established at the request of Brazil-WTO-WT/DS4/95-1820—04/07/1995.

6. Multilateralism has multiple institutional expressions, each one with a dif-ferent capacity to enforce decisions. Rather than discussing multilateralism in all its forms and manifestations, this chapter will focus mainly on multilateralism within the United Nations.

7. See Held et al., *Global Transformations*, pp. 62–63.

8. On the original meaning and reach of the *reason of state* see Etienne Thuau, *Raison d'Etat et pensée politique à l'epoque de Richelieu* [Reason of state and political thought in the age of Richelieu].

9. Multilateral decisions are certainly not the only source of legitimacy. Social movements and civil society at large can also play this role but with weaker sanc-tioning mechanisms. Another qualification should be pointed out: the fact that we can conceive the possibility of unfair or unjust decisions by multilateral institutions. Nevertheless, because they are necessarily the result of debating processes, such de-cisions tend to incorporate at least a minimal democratic ingredient that is the most accurate, albeit imperfect, mechanism to unveil the will of the international com-munity. Still, we have to accept, in certain very rare circumstances, that unilateral acts taken in contradiction to international norms possess some legitimacy. One ex-ample might be the interventions of Tanzania in 1979 to correct massive violations of human rights in Uganda.

10. The OAS has often been accused of being an "instrument of American im-perialism," in a curious symmetry with the "tyranny of the majority" at the UN. Of course, both phenomena could distort the aims of multilateral institutions.

11. It is not my intention here to offer a sociology of the exceptionalism that many argue lies at the heart of U.S. unilateralism. Other countries, of course, have invoked the peculiarities of their particular civilization as a justification of the de-cision not to adhere to certain ideas that have won near-universal legitimacy.

12. Article 2.1 of the UN Charter establishes the principle of sovereign equal-ity of all UN member states, whereas article 51 recognizes "the inherent right of in-dividual or collective self-defense if an armed attack occurs against a Member of the United Nations." This could be interpreted as opening a window for legal uni-lateralism.

13. "The development of international agencies and organizations has led to significant changes in the decision-making structure of world politics. In 1909 there were 37 IGOs and 176 INGOs, while in 1996 there were nearly 260 IGOs and 5,472 INGOs. In addition, it is interesting to note that during the period 1946–1975 the number of international treaties in force between governments more than doubled form 6,351 to 14,601, while the number of such treaties embracing intergovern-mental organizations expanded from 623 to 2,303." These figures are presented by Held et al., *Global Transformations,* p. 53.

14. I will not enter here into the debate over the weight of the rules, which en-tail different levels of obligations, and of their legitimacy. Similarly, it is not my in-tention here to discuss in detail the issue of the fora in which the rules are negoti-ated and imposed.

15. Luck, "American Exceptionalism and International Organization."

16. In some situations, it is clear that are *no options.* That was the case of Latin America in 1965, when the countries of the hemisphere voted in the OAS to give le-gitimacy to the U.S. invasion of the Dominican Republic. At that time, many argued that it would be better to join the intervention despite its illegality because the mul-tilateralization of the process was considered to be the best way to somehow limit the U.S. will.

17. The analysis is focused on symbolic and diplomatic means to constrain unilateralism; it does not take into consideration the instruments of power traditionally employed to oppose manifestations of power, which are not normally available to developing countries.

18. One of the best analyses of the history of the U.S. attitude regarding multilateralism is found in Luck, *Mixed Messages.*

19. The answer to these questions would require a broad analysis of all the characteristics of the current international system. That is not the purpose of this chapter, which is only focused on the consequences of the U.S. presence in the multilateral system—a decisive but far from exclusive theme to understand the pillars of globalization.

20. The origins of the attitude were sometimes in the executive branch but most often in the Congress during the Clinton presidency. The trend may be reversed with President George W. Bush.

21. The House International Relations Committee opened the door for reversing such a decision by adopting in May 2001 two amendments to the State Department budget authorization bill directing President George W. Bush to rejoin the organization.

22. For a more elaborate view on this categorization, see Patrick, "America's Retreat from Multilateral Engagement."

23. This was a case of so-called shared unilateralism due to the participation of the United Kingdom in the intervention. Besides, the multilateral discussions were never abandoned and the *unilateral spasm* (the bombardment) was justified on the basis of multilateral rules (the argument of a *material breach* of Security Council resolutions by Iraq).

24. *Yomiuri Shimbun* (The Daily Yomiuri) (Tokyo), November 29, 2001, "Globalization and the United Nations."

25. The domestic legitimacy derives from the internal social and political system of the United States. It would be unlikely, to say the least, that torture could be adopted by the United States as a method of investigation without being challenged and overturned through domestic political institutions and civil society. The external legitimacy stems from the country's general observance of universally accepted standards having to do with the content of specific policies and the rules for the decisionmaking process. There is always the possibility, especially in the case of the United States, that internal processes will wind up trumping external standards of legitimacy. The U.S. opposition to the Kyoto Protocol is widely seen, for instance, as a consequence of the powerful influence of sectors of U.S. domestic industry on the Bush administration.

26. We must remember that a sequence of resolutions in the General Assembly over eight consecutive years was condemned by a large majority the U.S. embargo against Cuba.

27. The reasons why states abide by certain rules is a subject of significant debate. Let us admit, for the sake of the argument, that the most visible motive is the cost of a different behavior.

28. Alexandra Barahona de Brito proposed this distinction between weak and strong multilateralism. Another example of strong unilateralism, but coming from a developing country, is the resistance of India and Pakistan to adhere to the NPT. This attitude is juridically acceptable, as any country has the sovereign right not to adhere to a treaty or a convention. Nevertheless, we may admit that legitimacy goes beyond the realm of law, and there are also identifiable legitimate grounds for decisions of eliminating nuclear weapons that should include all the nuclear powers.

29. It is true that it has not always been like that. In pre-Westphalian Europe, the legitimacy of an action could derive from dynastic titles.

30. It is not my intention to provide a detailed historic account on the ideal of equality of states. The reference to the Hague is arbitrarily illustrative, simply demonstrating a recurrent pattern.

31. See the Preface by Hildebrando Accioly to volume 34, *Obras completas de Ruy Barbosa* (Complete works of Ruy Barbosa) (Rio de Janeiro: Ministério da Educação e Cultura, 1966).

32. This is especially true regarding the UN General Assembly, which has a broad mandate to discuss any matter pertaining to the overall configuration of the international order.

33. The justification of unilateralism was originally based on the notion of *difference*. The qualitative change represented by the transformation of difference into superiority is a natural risk of this kind of attitude.

34. The breach of the rule of inequality, as we have in the Bretton Woods institutions or in the Security Council, was accepted by assemblies of equals, and that is the foundation of their legitimacy.

35. Mechan, *The United States and the Inter-American System,* p. 116.

36. We must remember that under Noriega Panama was not invited to a meeting of the Group of Eight (later the Rio Group) in June 1988.

37. It is clear that there were differences in the legitimating process and even in the way that the blocs confronted or conciliated each other, as one could see during the Nixon détente. I would like simply to highlight the possibility of a legitimating resource that is abandoned after the end of the Cold War.

38. The case of Panama is curious because the fact that the Noriega administration was seen as illegitimate, the condemnation by the OAS notwithstanding, decreased the political costs of the invasion.

39. During the Cold War, "values" were a sort of by-product of the bipolar conflict. The novelty of the post–Cold War world consists in the new "autonomy" of the field of values, which cannot be equated simply with ideological weapons at the hands of the superpowers but rather gain a stature of their own. This is not to say that there is unanimity on the practical implication of adopting the values of democracy and human rights but to assert that the claim of the universality of such values is not inextricably linked to strategic considerations (although they can still be used to advance strategic interests).

40. For a discussion of several factors that changed the nature of U.S. intervention in the third world, see Schraeder, *Intervention into the 1990s.* This book emphasizes the costs of intervention in a world of strong nationalisms.

41. Paralysis is now confined to areas of high interest of the permanent members, which can veto any proposed action that concerns themselves and their allies, and to problematic situations that would involve unpredictable difficulties for peace operations.

42. See Burgermam, *Moral Victories.* A similar pattern of solution through multilateral means of regional problems occurred, for instance, in Namibia, Angola, and Mozambique.

43. See Barahona de Brito, "New Sovereignties and Old Territorialities: Regional Integration and Expanding Universal Jurisdiction," 2001, photocopy.

44. It is interesting to note that one of the main innovations for the Uruguay Round was to introduce a dispute settlement mechanism that would be much more intrusive than the previous GATT mechanism.

45. Sometimes, international institutions can also "selective." African countries, for instance, accused the Security Council of being selective in approving stronger means for the peacekeeping operation in Kosovo than those adopted to deal with regional conflicts in Africa. In the 1970s, Americans blamed the tyranny of

majority for U.S. defeats in the General Assembly. Of course, selectivity is quite different, conceptually and politically, from a unilateral course of action. In the latter, there is an original sin, and by definition a unilateral action will always be selective. Selection within multilateralism is, in most cases, a political choice, inherent in all sorts of public policies. For example, a mayor with a limited budget who uses his resources to build a school in zone A is making a selection that certainly would be criticized by the dwellers of zone B who also need a school. But the selection will be legitimate if the authority of the mayor is legitimate and if he has good *public* reasons to postpone the building of the second school.

46. See Luck, *Mixed Messages,* p. 280.

47. There may be interventions carried out in the name of values that are not universal. Due to the new configuration of the international relations, however, such a hypothesis is becoming increasingly unlikely.

48. An interesting development is the launching of the idea of a strategic partnership between MERCOSUR and the European Union, guided by the idea of struggling for a more democratic international society.

16

The United States and Africa: Malign Neglect

Christopher Landsberg

AFRICA REMAINS AT THE BOTTOM OF U.S. FOREIGN POLICY PRIORITIES—A FACT that has major implications for U.S. engagement with the continent. In this chapter I explore African perceptions of the mixture of unilateralism, bilateralism, and multilateralism in U.S. Africa policy. I examine the internationalist and isolationist impulses in U.S. policy toward the region and analyzes how U.S. political, economic, and security interests interact with African actors. Beginning with an investigation of the broad pattern of U.S. engagement in and disengagement from Africa, I also explore the extent to which the United States undertakes prior consultations before articulating foreign policy initiatives affecting the interests of other regions and states. In addition, I highlight the possible negative consequences of U.S. unilateralism on the country's friends, allies, and partners.

I then turn to specific themes and case studies, examining the balance between unilateralism and multilateralism in U.S. policy toward Africa in three spheres: economics and trade, regional security, and the management of the global commons. I look closely at U.S. policy toward the Africa Growth and Opportunity Act (AGOA), the African Crisis Response Initiative (ACRI), and the challenge of the AIDS pandemic.

I conclude that U.S.-African relations are characterized by considerable ambivalence on both sides. I document a pattern of benign neglect by the United States, whereby the latter often embarks on unilateral action, only to disengage subsequently from continental affairs. For their own part, African states invariably seek U.S. multilateral engagement to meet the challenges of development, peace, and security. At the same time, there is significant suspicion in many African quarters that the United States is pursuing an imperialist grand strategy toward the continent. This presumed strategy may conflict with Africans' perceptions of their own collective and diverse national interests.

U.S. Foreign Relations: Perceptions and Misperceptions

Writing in the journal *Survival,* French foreign policy expert Francois Heisbourg contends that global "[p]erceptions of the U.S. are contrasted and indeed contradictory."[1]

> Foreign perceptions of the U.S. . . . are not only divergent; they are to a large extent incompatible in logical terms. They include a U.S. intent on minding what it sees as its own business; the dark, satanic U.S. of Islamic conspiracy theorists who see deliberate purpose and focused aim in every aspect of what America does (or indeed, does not do); a unilateralist U.S. which has made military power its tool of choice; and an America with a network of allies around the world, ensuring strategic stability in the key areas of Asia, Europe and the Middle East.[2]

It is not surprising that a view from Africa does not even feature on Heisbourg's list of foreign images of the United States, a hint at just what a low priority Africa is on the U.S. foreign policy radar screen.

Determining the rhythm of overall U.S. foreign policy can be a complex undertaking, especially following a change in presidential administrations, because U.S. hegemony does not always translate into a discernible grand strategy. It is a more straightforward exercise in the African context, however, because U.S. policy takes a predictable pattern. The United States alternatively embarks on unilateral action, disengages on U.S. terms, fails to consult properly with its partners, and rarely opts for genuine multilateralism.

For more than ten years, African countries have had to deal with the reality of the unrivalled hegemony of the United States in the post–Cold War world. Because the international system revolves around the proclivities of the U.S. hyperpower, African leaders must factor into their foreign policies the inclinations of whatever administration holds office in Washington.[3] Jendayi Frazer, National Security Council director for African affairs, has warned foreign observers of the perils of interpreting U.S. Africa policy from the outside:

> Regional critics approach the U.S. government as a unitary actor whose every action reflects an intended purpose rather than acknowledging that like all governments, U.S. policy is the (often incoherent) product of multiple competing interests and its actions sometimes reflect the failed or partial execution of policy directives.[4]

From an African perspective, however, U.S. policy has been less mysterious and can be easily deciphered. Prior to September 11, 2001, Americans should not be surprised to learn that widespread suspicion existed in Africa of an alleged grand strategy behind U.S. dominance.

Today, there is great concern in Africa that the United States will take unilateralist actions that will complicate its relations with friend and foe alike. Many Africans perceive U.S. conduct toward the continent as an obstacle to, rather than promoter of, international cooperation. It is possible that such unilateralism will become less pronounced now that the United States has discovered that it is vulnerable to global threats like terrorist attacks and understands that it can fight them only in collaboration with others.

Regardless of which party occupies the White House, African observers remain preoccupied with perceived unilateralist tendencies in U.S. foreign policy. U.S. unilateralism in Africa, and selective disengagement from Africa, is a function of both the rise of the so-called imperial presidency—in which the president and his administration's foreign and national security policy formulation and execution have become increasingly concentrated in the White House—and the inclinations toward disengagement ascendant in the Department of State and the Pentagon. In addition, unilateralism and disengagement are also functions of parochial impulses at work in the U.S. Congress, where members of the House and Senate can exert a negative drag on U.S. intentions at the executive level.

Thus, there are mixes of unilateral and disengaging tendencies at both the executive and legislative levels. After the passage of the Clark Amendment preventing U.S. support to the Union for the Total Independence of Angola (UNITA), no administration, whether Democratic or Republican, was able to take unilateral initiatives in this regard. This, in turn, has made for multilateral compatibility in terms of dealings with most African states. But as soon as the Clark Amendment was repealed, Ronald Reagan's administration, just defeated on the issue of South African sanctions, had a green light to revert to old-style unilateralism and implement the Reagan Doctrine of support for anticommunist guerrillas in Angola. Moreover, the repeal of Clark happened in spite of Democratic control of Congress, reflecting the conservative-liberal tensions within the party, which often played to conservative Republican benefit, especially among southern Democrats. With the Cold War over, such partisan divisions have largely disappeared, and with the United States vulnerable to terrorist attacks, such divisions may disappear, at least in the short term.

But apart from Congress, and regardless of the political tendencies of the party occupying the White House, there remained a propensity, before September 2001, for the United States to go it alone in Africa. This was driven both by calculated design and the political-cultural impulse of the U.S. hegemon to act on its own terms and interests, irrespective of the interests of others. It was reinforced by the mistaken notion that Africa was of no strategic significance to the United States. The U.S. conception of hegemony did not—and still does not—appreciate the importance of multilateral cooperation and burden-sharing; it supports burden-shifting, the passing on of responsibility for peacekeeping, peacemaking, and stabilizing Africa to "pivots" or "anchors" like South Africa and Nigeria, and disengagement. So again, the rhythm of U.S. policy toward Africa is easy to decode.

Setting the African Scene

Historically, multilateralism has not been a strong component of U.S. foreign policy toward the African continent. But if U.S. policymakers are really serious about engaging Africa constructively in the aftermath of September 11, multilateralism must become a more important tenet of U.S. Africa policy. The United States should come to appreciate multilateralism as an important means of building and constructing coalitions and alliances in which others will feel they have a stake, are taken seriously, and are respected as partners. This could represent a historical paradigm shift for African international relations. Since World War II, African countries have been preoccupied with the successive challenges of winning independence from European colonialism, building stable domestic regimes, and developing their national economies.[5] During the Cold War, U.S. involvement with Africa was dominated by the recognition that Africa contained a critical supply of raw materials for military and industrial purposes, and Washington started playing a strategic role in Africa to advance its own interests.

The objectives pursued by the United States involved preserving its access to strategic resources and containing the Soviet Union in Africa as the continent became a theater for balance-of-power games between the superpowers.[6] For example, the basis for U.S. involvement in the Congo crisis of 1960–1964 was the dependence of the United States on strategic minerals (e.g., cobalt and uranium) for use in its growing nuclear weapons program. In stark contrast to the professed U.S. commitment to liberty and human rights, the legacy of this early involvement in the Congo (Zaire) was a sustained period of U.S. support for the dictatorial regime of President Mobutu Sese Seko, who reciprocated by acting as an agent for U.S. interests in southern Africa.[7] U.S. relations in West Africa were focused on Nigeria, which became the second leading exporter of oil to the United States in the early 1970s. The U.S. stance began to turn briefly during the presidency of Jimmy Carter in the late 1970s as concern for human rights became an important dimension of U.S. foreign policy.[8]

In southern Africa, U.S. policy had a number of foci. Washington sought to protect U.S. business investments, maintain access to a superior supply of strategic minerals (especially diamonds, manganese, chromium, and platinum-group metals), protect oil routes around the Cape of Good Hope and along the eastern and western shores of the region, and of course check Soviet influence and perceived expansionism in the subcontinent.[9] Particularly when Republicans occupied the White House, Washington's strongly anticommunist posture led the United States to support rebel movements like UNITA, South African–sponsored guerrillas, and military incursions by South Africa itself (as part of the latter's destabilization policies).[10]

These historical developments laid the foundation for the U.S. pursuit during the 1980s of what the Reagan administration called constructive engagement. This policy aimed, ostensibly, at brokering peace deals and ending regional conflicts without cutting U.S. ties to regimes like South Africa. Engaging Pretoria was the centerpiece of this policy. The doctrine set out to "maintain public opposition to racial repression but relax political isolation and economic restrictions" on Pretoria.[11] It further sought to challenge Soviet influence by bringing poorer African nations closer to the mainstream of the free-market economy that Washington regarded as the surest way to growth. Reagan's policy emphasized private investment, bilateral aid as opposed to multilateral assistance, a preoccupation with security, and special attention to a selected grouping of states such as Egypt, Sudan, Somalia, Kenya, Senegal, Botswana, Gabon, and Rwanda.[12] But critics saw the policy as little more than "piecemeal, quiet, carrot-but-no-stick diplomacy" that gave succor to Pretoria in its fight against the "total Marxist onslaught."[13]

With the dramatic end of the Cold War in the late 1980s, Africa essentially slipped off the U.S. foreign policy radar screen; Africa fell to the bottom of the U.S. foreign policy agenda, where it remains today. It is undoubtedly true that at various times certain non-African countries and regions have despaired of persuading the United States to engage their agendas to a satisfactory degree. But the task for African states was even more daunting: to impress upon the United States the importance of taking the continent seriously as a regional entity in world affairs.

There is a clear disjunction between how the United States engages Africa versus how it engages the rest of the world. Contemporary U.S. liberal internationalism expresses itself in varying degrees of commitment to international cooperation through multilateral institutions that are global, regional, or subregional in scope. To the extent that the United States possesses a strategy for engaging Africa, it is founded on selective disengagement, energetic unilateralism, or active engagement in bilateral relationships and commitments. This pattern has raised two sets of suspicions among Africans.

First, there is a view that the U.S. is primarily interested in engaging those pivotal states, or, as Colin Powell, U.S. secretary of state under George W. Bush, called them, "anchor" or "key" states like South Africa and Nigeria that are capable of advancing U.S. foreign policy goals in Africa.[14] As Henry Kissinger, one of the foremost exponents of the school of power politics, recently wrote:

> No state except Nigeria or South Africa is in a position to play a major role outside its immediate region. . . . . African security issues—largely civil wars and ethnic conflicts—should be left largely to African nations, with South Africa and Nigeria playing the principal roles.[15]

Similarly, John Stremlau has written that "only with lasting democracies—especially in South Africa and Nigeria, sub-Saharan Africa's major powers—will Africa have a realistic chance at conflict prevention." Because South Africa "is the continent's most advanced democracy by far, with an economy that that accounts for 40 percent of sub-Saharan Africa's total GDP," Stremlau argues, it "is of singular strategic significance to U.S. Africa policy."[16] Likewise, U.S. Ambassador Howard Jeter has declared that the United States considers Nigeria "the essential nation in Africa." In the hopes that the country would become an "anchor of stability," the United States had decided "to increase its bilateral assistance to Nigeria in the last two years from an almost non-existent level to $190 million."[17] Such a pattern suggests a third orientation in U.S. policy toward Africa: bilateralism.

In addition, the U.S. approach toward South Africa and Nigeria during the latter years Bill Clinton's administration and the first years of George W. Bush's administration suggests yet another dimension to U.S. policy: a "trilateral" approach whereby the United States might engage the two African great powers in concert.

A second, related perception has grown out of the first. It is that U.S. interests in Africa are largely economic and that Washington, in collaboration with such pivotal states, desires to play an imperialist game in Africa. To take this idea one step farther, international cooperation with Africa, from the vantage point of the sole superpower, is not the same thing as multilateralism, whereby national interests would be subordinated to a multilateral power or authority. Rather, U.S. foreign and national security policy toward Africa, whether under liberal or conservative administrations, deliberately resists subordinating U.S. interests and authority to multilateral political burden-sharing or military command. Foreign policy toward Africa in essence becomes a matter of how the United States cooperates—or fails to cooperate—with friend and foe alike, even within given multilateral organizations like the United Nations.

Africa and U.S. National Interests

What stood out in the U.S.-Africa relationship before September 11, 2001, was the glaring gap between rhetoric and reality, promise and delivery, thinly disguised as commitment to Africa. Although the relationship was characterized by heavy doses of symbolism and public relations, in Africa the United States was rarely viewed as playing fair. Instead, it was the pursuit of poorly defined U.S. national interests that typically led the United States either to disengage from the continent or to cooperate with its carefully selected partners. This view was based on the belief that in a world without the Cold War's balance-of-terror considerations, Africa possessed little strategic significance. For example, the U.S. National Security Strategy of 1998 listed Africa as last among the world's regions in degrees of strategic importance.[18]

This tendency to marginalize Africa ignored the fact that it is clearly in the interests of the United States (as well as of other industrialized powers) to help stabilize the continent, end its deadly conflicts, and secure an environment in which economic growth, trading opportunities, and global burden-sharing can flourish.[19] Thus, it is disturbing that when it comes to Africa the United States has a propensity not only to engage in unilateral action (and in the process disregard its partners) but also to disengage from African commitments altogether.

The United States has also followed a strategy of dividing Africa into good guys versus bad guys. As the Ugandan scholar Paul Omach argues, "In the United States policy perspective, African states are classified as 'failed,' 'rogue,' and 'focus' states or 'anchors of stability.'"[20] Washington singles out what it sees as pivotal states—notably South Africa and Nigeria—and tries to build lasting partnerships with them. The rationale behind engaging such states is one of burden-shifting, not burden-sharing. As argued above, burden-shifting is a strategy in which the U.S. singles out African powers like South Africa and Nigeria to assume the responsibility for burdens such as peacekeeping, peacemaking, and promoting peace and security while the U.S. and other European powers would focus primarily on advancing their economic and other interests. The burden-shift approach is captured, for example, in the statement made by Colin Powell during his Senate confirmation hearing when he said: "We know also that Africans must do more for themselves."[21] Another problem with the anchor or key states approach, as Jeffrey Herbst has argued, is that it presupposes collusion in U.S. interests by such carefully chosen partner states.[22] The results of such an approach are mixed, as reflected in U.S. policy in East Africa, particularly with countries like Uganda, Rwanda, Ethiopia, and Eritrea.

Given the absence of Cold War competition, and the fact that the continent contains no potential challengers to U.S. hegemony, U.S. Africa policy under George W. Bush was shaping up, before September 11, to be quite similar to that pursued by the Clinton administration. This continuity included a prominent reliance on key countries headed by new-generation leaders. The two most important countries in this regard were South Africa and Nigeria. Nigerian President Olesegun Obasanjo's state visit to the United States in March 2001, and Colin Powell's visit in May of that year to South Africa, where the secretary of state gave an important speech, suggested that the administration would continue to give these two countries priority. Powell's visit to Mali, by contrast, underlined that country's key role in the Sahel, where the United States remains concerned about Libya's aspirations along the Sudan-Sahelian border areas and in West Africa. Otherwise, a continuity of interest in expanding trade with Africa, coupled with fashioning an as yet unclear security relationship extending to postconflict peacebuilding and combating the HIV/AIDS pandemic, appears to define what will be forthcoming from the Bush administration. It is within this context that Africa policy will be assessed from the perspective of the United States as a benign hegemon or one whose policy will reflect benign neglect.

How should this be turned around? Jendayi Frazer has argued that advancing a U.S.-Africa relationship beyond "symbolic dialogue" requires "articulation of an explicit strategic rationale for partnership, commitment to organizational change, and provision of adequate resources from all sides to establish strong institutional linkages."[23] Frazer went farther to suggest that U.S.-Africa relations should be framed in terms of the need for both parties to define basic assumptions and interests and, as far as African partners are concerned, to gain a realistic understanding of the U.S. policy process.[24] Although the relationship needs fleshing out, the United States needs to recognize that continued African suspicions about the motives of U.S. policy render cooperation difficult. Cooperation between the United States and Africa is further complicated by a deterioration in the political and security environment in much of the continent since the end of the Cold War, which has strengthened negative perceptions of Africa in Washington and the United States more broadly. Some U.S. constituencies and policymakers see little value in investing resources in Africa when such sharp divisions and armed conflicts exist within the region.

As stated above, there are perceptions within some African countries that Washington harbors imperialist designs on the continent, even though the resources that the United States commits to Africa are negligible.[25] This perception is mainly fueled by the style and conduct of U.S. diplomacy. On the one hand, the United States has disengaged from peacekeeping and peace-enforcement commitments, and on the other hand it seeks to pursue aggressively its economic interests through instruments like a free trade agreement with South Africa and the latter's Southern African Customs Union partners—Botswana, Lesotho, Namibia, and Swaziland—while at the same time putting in place antidumping measures to curtail imports of South African steel into the U.S. market. Despite Frazer's argument that there is no U.S. grand strategy regarding Africa generally, many African observers believe that one exists. One way of dispelling such African suspicions would be for the United States to commit itself to burden-sharing and to engaging African partners on a concerted multilateral basis. Although Frazer is right to argue that U.S. post–Cold War policy initiatives in Africa have been both ad hoc and reactive, the overriding rhythm before September 11 was for the United States to do as it pleased, without due regard to the views, perceptions, and interests of its African partners.[26] That is certainly not the way to dispel widespread African views of selfish U.S. conduct.

Yet Frazer usefully points out that U.S. national security strategy needs to be understood as operating at three levels of analysis.[27] First, homeland defense (especially after September 11) and NATO; second, economic and commercial interests, which prioritize Europe, Asia, and Latin America;

and, only in the third instance, humanitarian interests, which focus mainly on Africa. In other words, Africa ranks at the bottom of the U.S. foreign policy radar screen: low priority, low objectives. Although African governments and observers often complain about the continent's marginalization in U.S. foreign policy, they are not necessarily aware of how low the continent actually ranks in U.S. thinking.

Broadly speaking, U.S. interests in Africa include the advancement of prosperity, in terms of promoting and encouraging trade, economic integration, and foreign investment; democratization, in the sense of promoting democratic stability and the rule of law; and, especially of late, security, in terms of addressing the challenge of transnational threats (terrorism, crime, and arms proliferation).[28] In the realm of security, Frazer argues, the United States and Africa need to arrive at certain trade-offs if they are to advance an agenda that will satisfy Africa's security interests within the context of overall U.S. priorities.[29] But it is important to note that U.S. security strategy is based first and foremost on the premise that Africa itself must bear the burden of sorting out its security problems. Specifically, the United States will not engage in any troop deployments in Africa, either for peacekeeping or peace enforcement, and it will consider direct military engagement only against terrorism. Under the rubric of training, the United States and other industrialized democracies will increasingly shift the peacekeeping burden to, not share it with, Africa. The United States would not deploy troops in Africa anymore, but it would share part of the financial and material burden for peace operations. African observers, however, often argue that the United States should be more forthcoming in terms of the size and levels of its contributions. There are therefore limits to the trade-offs that Frazer is calling for. It is the United States, not Africans, who are largely reluctant to identify common interests. Indeed, we are likely to witness a review of the antimilitary engagement posture, but only to the extent that the military option would become a tool in the post–September 11 war against terrorism.

Benign Hegemony or Benign Neglect?

The fact that the political classes in most African countries were ambivalent about U.S. power did not change the generally favorable view that Americans themselves held about their country's hegemony before September 11, 2001. Whether it was former Secretary of State Madeleine Albright, who touted the United States as the indispensable nation, or neoconservatives, who advocated a benign hegemon role for the country, there was a general feeling in the United States that the world was indeed fortunate to be dominated by a democratic superpower that U.S. power was a force for good in the world and that U.S. allies could not do without U.S. involvement in the affairs of their regions. Although the liberal internationalist Clinton administration made a rhetorical commitment to multilateralism in general and greater cooperation with Africa in particular, even it fell back on unilateralism when events in the world did not go Washington's way. It was only when that image of the United States as an indispensable and arrogant superpower came under attack—as on September 11—that the United States was likely to appreciate its friends in Africa as well as the benefits of multilateralism more generally.

One might contrast U.S. hubris about its global hegemony with South Africa's more reluctant regional hegemony. Whereas the status of the United States as the world's preeminent superpower status has fueled unilateralist tendencies, South Africa has adopted a more modest approach in its region, seeking to compensate for the predatory unilateralism it often exhibited during its troubling past. Despite its overwhelming dominance in the Southern African Development Community (SADC) and its primacy in Africa as a whole, postapartheid South Africa has been very sensitive not to be seen as a big brother or giant in the region. In a similar fashion, Nigeria's president Obasanjo feels the need to understate his country's hegemonic status in order to solicit the cooperation of other West African states on matters of peace and security.[30]

Prior to September 11, a unilateralist impulse in U.S. African policy complicated U.S. relations with South Africa. The United States often failed to appreciate Pretoria's wariness of being seen in Africa (and especially southern Africa) as Washington's surrogate. Following the attacks on the United States, South Africa, under the leadership of Thabo Mbeki, is likely to show even greater independence from the United States, and this relationship could become even more complicated. Given South Africa's apartheid-era history of regional destabilization, the democratic government in Pretoria has developed an antihegemonic posture, not unlike that of post-Nazi Germany and postimperial Japan in the wake of their World War II depredations. Yet the new governing elites in South Africa, unlike the elites in Germany and Japan, were the victims of the same regime that destabilized neighboring states. They and the black majority do not bear the burden of guilt in relating to their fellow members of SADC.

The government of the African National Congress (ANC) is anxious to be seen as a good regional citizen and, mindful of the sacrifices that Africans in neighboring countries had to endure on their behalf, feels duty-bound to downplay South Africa's power. Under the leadership of Thabo Mbeki, the ANC government has an ingrained impulse toward multilateralism and, indeed, plays the role of antihegemon to the perceived hegemony of the United States. For Pretoria, being a good hegemon means carrying the rest of Africa's baggage while pursuing its own national interest in its dealings with the United States and the broader international community. Multilateralism also serves Pretoria's fundamental strategic interest of integrating South Africa, long isolated from the continent by apartheid, into the rest of Africa via SADC. South Africa is also keen to integrate the rest of Africa (or at least the SADC) into its foreign policy under a multilateral cover. For example, with respect to the African Crisis Response Force (ACRF), Pretoria made its involvement conditional on a formal SADC position and endorsement on the ACRF.

Security in Africa:
The African Crisis Response Initiative

The saga of the African Crisis Response Initiative is a good example of how, in the security field, U.S. efforts at international cooperation can feed perceptions of superpower unilateralism and going it alone.[31] It is important here to distinguish between a propensity toward burden-shifting and a true commitment to multilateralism, which appears to have much less support among U.S. liberals and conservatives alike. The underlying U.S. motivation for ACRI was essentially corrective: It was an effort to improve responses to African conflicts in reaction to policy disasters in Somalia (1990–1993) and Rwanda (1994). As a policy initiative, ACRI's genesis was entirely unilateral: It was proposed by the United States, which sought to opt out of security commitments in Africa. The initiative quickly landed into trouble, where it remained until the United States adopted a more cooperative approach to retrieve it from utter failure.

One also has to distinguish here between approach and substance. Washington's frantic consultations with the UN, the Organization of African Unity (OAU), and various African subregional organizations, as well as with France and Britain, which occurred only after the United States had already decided on the mechanics of such a scheme, were motivated more by the desire to secure as wide as possible support for this U.S. initiative than with transforming it into a genuinely multilateral initiative. Although Washington devised a corrective strategy of broad consultation and coordination (especially with Britain and France), the ACRI took the form of bilateral agreements between the United States and individual African governments that chose to buy in to it. The ACRI saga helped feed into the perception in Africa that the United States embarks on African initiatives only in ad hoc fashion.

The South African case shows that the unilateral propensity in U.S. security policy can complicate U.S. relations with African partners. After the fallout from the Somalia experience in 1993, the United States started to disengage from involvement in peace efforts in Africa. Washington's proposal for the ACRF emerged as a thinly disguised initiative to shift the burden of peacekeeping to African players while the United States opted out. What drove policy were domestic political pressures impinging on U.S.

policymakers as much as any considerations they had for the interests of various African actors.

What is particularly telling here is that the Democratic Clinton administration was widely perceived in Africa, as well as in the United States, as being the most sympathetic to Africa in memory. Yet because of the unilateralism attached to the ACRF proposal (later changed to the ACRI for "Initiative" instead of the provocative-sounding "Force"), the Clinton administration experienced a singular policy defeat from which it did not recover. South Africa, in particular, would remain deeply cynical about U.S. intentions behind ACRI.

The Somalia-ACRF experience revealed certain tensions within U.S. foreign policy and in U.S. relations with other countries. Initially, Clinton's policy toward Africa held out the hopeful prospect that U.S.-Africa relations would benefit from greater U.S. activism in UN-led humanitarian intervention and peacekeeping initiatives. The initial phase of U.S.-UN involvement in the humanitarian operation in Somalia was widely judged successful.[32] But the operation's transformation into a mission of peace enforcement and peacebuilding, coupled with resistance from Somali warlords, revealed the limits of applying U.S. liberal internationalism to UN operations in Africa. The rapid U.S. withdrawal following the deaths of eighteen members of the U.S. intervention task force in a Mogadishu firefight also highlighted the extent to which U.S. policy could be subject to wild swings under the pressure of crosscurrents in Washington.

Fearful of a domestic backlash, spearheaded by a highly skeptical U.S. Congress, against U.S. involvement in UN operations, the Clinton administration quickly became a major inhibiting force in future UN interventions in Africa. The United States determined not only that U.S. troops must be spared a repeat of the humiliation suffered in Mogadishu but also that African troops too should be spared such risks. In the aftermath of the Somali fiasco, the Clinton administration invoked Presidential Decision Directive 25 (PDD-25), the new guide to U.S. peacekeeping policy.[33] In its attempts to cope with a string of failed peacekeeping missions, the United States chose to shift the burden to African countries. The goal of PDD-25 was to define the terms under which Washington would approve participating in peacekeeping missions on the continent.[34] According to PDD-25, "If U.S. participation in a peace operation were to interfere with our basic military strategy . . . we would place our basic military strategy uppermost."[35]

Rwanda became the first casualty of the post-Somalia backlash. The horrendous magnitude of the Rwandan genocide of 1994 generated yet another reaction in the Clinton administration's Africa policy. The United States not only decided not to intervene in Rwanda but also persuaded the UN Security Council to pull out of Rwanda altogether. The resulting Rwandan genocide and the horror that this provoked led to Washington's hasty launch of the ACRF as an instrument for humanitarian intervention and security in Africa.

Although ACRI was a well-meaning initiative, intended to help build African capacities for peacekeeping, it came up short in its presentation to some African states, largely because the United States failed to engage its prospective African partners in a process of prior consultations. Had the United States done so, the initiative might have taken on a multilateral character, and its chances of success would have been far greater. The problem, however, is that Washington tends to insist on its freedom of maneuverability and to shun having its options subordinated to multilateral dictates.

The initiative suffered from another shortcoming. According to Omach, it failed to anticipate that states that perceived the primary threats to their national security "as emanating from external sources [would be] generally reluctant to participate in ACRI."[36] Omach said, "The practical feasibility of establishing an African Crisis Response Initiative was received with skepticism."[37] (Chances are, just like some regimes viewed ACRI as a means to be exploited for short-term gain, so the war against terrorism is likely to be exploited by autocratic regimes in Africa, who have military scores to settle with foes in their countries.)

In the end, ACRI came across as a take-it-or-leave-it fait accompli; as such, it was bound to be rejected by a South Africa that was, and remains, sensitive to being perceived by other African states as doing Washington's bidding on the continent. Some Washington observers described ACRI as a panicky U.S. response to an anticipated emergency in Burundi that might follow the genocide in Rwanda. The initial ACRF proposal had not involved consultations with likely European or African partners in what was aimed at being a program of humanitarian intervention.[38]

Furthermore, the timing was unfortunate, for it surfaced on the eve of the 1996 presidential election and was conveyed by a secretary of state making his swan-song voyage to Africa. Another factor undermining the ACRF message was the heavy-handed U.S. campaign to deny UN Secretary-General Boutros Boutros-Ghali a second term in office, an effort abrasively spearheaded by Clinton's envoy to the UN, Madeleine Albright. Hence, the ACRF almost immediately came under French as well as South African criticism, at a time when the European Union was emphasizing its relations not only with Pretoria but also with SADC.

The SADC multilateral dimension was crucial in the South African response to the ACRF. As noted, Pretoria has embraced multilateralism to counter any impression that it is imposing its will on weaker neighbors and the rest of Africa. To be successful in South African eyes, ACRF would need to have the support of SADC and the OAU, a factor that the Clinton administration did not fully appreciate. In Africa it is politically more prudent for regional and subregional actors to buy in to a multilateral initiative than one that would require endorsing the approach of a single power. The Clinton administration never recovered from its bad start. The administration's course-correction, accompanied by after-the-fact consultations in Europe and Africa, was intended to downplay the notion of a U.S.-backed, all-African standing army by shifting the focus to capacity-building, but it failed to impress Pretoria.

Washington seemed unable to appreciate the fear that some African countries have of being seen as a proxy for the United States. If Washington and pro-African constituencies in the United States were to develop a common vision of the U.S. interest in Africa, as well as a strategic plan for engaging Africa on a bipartisan basis, African suspicions about a selfish U.S. grand strategy might dissipate, and South Africa and other African actors might be less reluctant to engage Washington on sensitive initiatives like ACRI.

As it turned out, for many African states, such as Uganda, Ethiopia, and Senegal, whose leaderships were not burdened by Pretoria's special circumstances and could afford to take a pragmatic approach, buying in to ACRI was not a problem. But what emerged from such buy-ins was not a multilateral program or structure as much as a U.S.-African regional initiative geared to a series of bilateral arrangements. Prospects of ACRI evolving into a U.S.-African Crisis Response Forum are slim; ACRI remains essentially a regional program of U.S. international security cooperation.

From Pretoria's vantage point, the goodwill that Clinton had built up early with the new South Africa through the U.S.–South Africa Bi-National Commission (BNC) was not transferable to the ACRF. The contrasting U.S. and South African approaches to their unique hegemonies are instructive. Whereas South Africa's rulers are increasingly viewed as sensitive to African concerns, the United States continues to be viewed with suspicion and as acting in unilateral fashion.

Washington adopted a somewhat different approach in establishing the Pentagon's African Center for Strategic Studies (ACSS). Like the ACRI, ACSS is a capacity-building program, though it focuses on conducting seminars and workshops traversing a range of themes in civil-military relations. Unlike the creation of ACRI, in which Africans were consulted after the fact, ACSS was established after a thorough consultation process—although the extent to which this consultation influenced the design of the program is unclear.

The Economic Dimension: Trade Versus Aid

Unlike in the security field, where the United States has a clear interest in a multilateral approach (albeit underappreciated until the attacks on U.S. soil), a more ambivalent mix of motives drives policy in U.S. foreign economic relations. There can be no doubt that Africa's stabilization requires burden-sharing, which involves African players and external partners. On the one hand, supporting Africa's recovery from its many economic woes should be a multilateral project. African leaders spearheading the Millennium Africa

Recovery Plan (MAP) and the New African Initiative (NAI)—now the New Partnership for Africa's Development (NEPAD)—are hoping for a multilateral commitment to this "mini–Marshall Plan" blueprint for African renewal.[39] These initiatives are based on the principle that in exchange for an agreement by African governments to hold one another accountable and promote democratization and good governance measures, the United States and other industrialized powers should promote foreign direct investment, debt-relief and debt-forgiveness measures, and market access to the industrialized North.

Different Western powers, however, have specific economic interests, and these will determine how they pursue economic engagement with the continent. Western economic relations with Africa are essentially competitive, especially when it comes to trade and investment, and these interests could clash with initiatives like MAP, NAI, and NEPAD.

Furthermore, the United States perceives agreements like the EU–South Africa Trade and Development Pact as competing with U.S. interests. The United States fears that the EU will gain a head start by concluding free trade agreements with African states. Instead of being concerned about such competition, the United States should promote the role of African countries in designing their own initiatives. An approach based on African ownership and critical external support serves to legitimize initiatives; it also ensures that Africans take responsibility—and therefore assume accountability—for projects. The call is for genuine partnerships between the United States (plus other industrialized powers) and their African counterparts.

As for the Africa Growth and Opportunity Act, one can interpret this initiative in one of two ways: as opportunity, or as opportunism. The lack of priority given to Africa in U.S. policy calculations facilitates a benign unilateralism, whereby Washington designs initiatives for Africa rather than consulting Africans early on to produce initiatives that reflect joint ownership. The recent history of the AGOA and its attendant trade-versus-aid message is a case in point. As an independent task force sponsored by the Council on Foreign Relations in New York remarked, "Unfortunately, the convergence of these developments (declining aid levels and increased interest in trade) has led to an often simplistic 'trade versus aid' debate over which is the more constructive approach for changing U.S. economic policies toward Africa."[40]

This false debate revealed that South Africa and other African states adopted opposing stances toward the United States, just like with ACRI. The AGOA initiative similarly emerged without prior consultation with African partners. Also known as Lugar-Crane, the proposed legislation called for a trade and investment approach to African development that would serve the interests of African countries as well as those of the United States.[41] As Clinton acknowledged during his 1998 visit to Africa, U.S. involvement in the continent was not about charity but enlightened self-interest.

AGOA sought to give the United States the opportunity to broaden trade in Africa and create domestic jobs by improving on a status quo in which the United States enjoys less than 8 percent of the African market compared to the EU's 41 percent.[42] It was also an effort to challenge a potential EU monopoly in Africa that could result from a renegotiation of the Lomé Convention with Africa, a process subtly dominated by France.[43] Put bluntly, AGOA had a lot to do with the ostensible antagonisms between the United States and France and their respective spheres of influence.

Moreover, AGOA contained conditionalities that were attractive to the United States. It promised debt relief to African countries that pursued free-market liberalization and democratic reforms.[44] It also directed the Overseas Private Investment Corporation to create a $150 million equity fund and a $500 million infrastructure fund for Africa, as well as to establish a U.S.-Africa forum for economic cooperation.[45]

Section 4 of AGOA contained political and democratization conditions that would disqualify many African countries from participation in the opportunities created by AGOA.[46] The South African government did not hide its reservations about these requirements, which became an act of Congress without any African input. Pretoria wanted African states to play a role in devising aid conditionalities and programs.

Moreover, all of the provisions of the AGOA bill could have been implemented by the administration without legislation, thereby providing opportunities to build credible partnerships.[47] For example, one of the bill's provisions called for the establishment of the cabinet-level U.S.-Africa Economic Cooperation Forum. This did not have to be legislated, and it would have provided an ideal vehicle for consultations between the administration and its African counterparts in establishing the parameters of AGOA. Such a lack of consultation on Washington's part fed African perceptions of U.S. unilateralism, irrespective of the actual content of the U.S. initiative.

At the same time, there is a major difference between AGOA and ACRI. Unlike ACRI, AGOA emerged out of a legislative initiative in which the Clinton administration jumped on the bandwagon. In a sense, there was a measure of consultation, in the form of House and Senate hearings, that was not the case with ACRI, where such transparency was lacking. Yet such consultation remained largely between two branches of the U.S. government and was not extended to the broader African constituency. The United States cultivates close ties with the five countries that make up 80 percent of all U.S. trade with Africa: Nigeria, Gabon, Angola, Guinea Bissau, and South Africa.[48]

The United States ultimately has a number of economic instruments and forums at its disposal for direct trade and investment relations with the continent. The Export-Import Bank, the Overseas Private Investment Corporation, and the Trade and Development Agency—along with the U.S.

Agency for International Development—can better coordinate economic interaction with Africa.[49] The United States should not underestimate the potential for economic intercourse with Africa, and these agencies should seize the opportunity to promote mutually beneficial trade. In 1996, for example, U.S. trade with twelve southern African countries totaled more than $9 billion (dominated by South Africa, of course). This was trade at a level comparable to trade with the fifteen republics of the former Soviet Union combined.[50] According to Steven Metz, "While U.S. exports to Sub-Saharan Africa account for less than 1% of U.S. exports, they do exceed those of the former Soviet Union and currently account for 100,000 jobs."[51] Between 1994 and 1995, U.S. exports to Africa have grown more than 20 percent. In 1995, U.S. businesses increased their exports to sub-Saharan Africa by 23 percent to total $5.4 billion, and in 1996 that figure rose to $6.1 billion.[52] The International Monetary Fund reported that African economies grew at an average of more than 5 percent in 1996 and continued that pace in 1997.[53]

The United States is in a position to utilize the above-mentioned agencies and economic instruments to accomplish a number of critical economic aims: to increase two-way trade between the United States and African countries and U.S. direct investment in Africa; to increase and strengthen U.S. development assistance to create conditions for greater investment and enhanced trade; to improve debt reduction as an important tool for restoring the creditworthiness of African countries; and to strengthen international cooperation in support of development in Africa.[54]

The New Regionalism and the "New" Africans

Perhaps more fundamental to the problem of the perceived unilateralist hegemony of the United States in Africa may be just how little Africa's interests figure in U.S. global policy. Policies that may not be Africa-specific typically influence developments on the ground in Africa. The issue of terrorism is a case in point, amplified by the September 11, 2001, attacks in New York and Washington, which highlighted the terrorist Osama bin Laden and his Al-Qaida network as the chief U.S. nemesis. By way of background, Washington's bombing of the Islamist regime in Sudan in 1998, in retaliation for their hosting of bin Laden, who was allegedly responsible for the bombings of the U.S. embassies in Kenya and Tanzania in 1997, exacerbated instabilities in East Africa by reinforcing the region's militarized politics. This development was underwritten by U.S. assistance to Ethiopia, Eritrea, and Uganda, as part of U.S. support for the new Africans who also formed an anti-Khartoum coalition. However, the brittleness of this alliance of the new generation of African leaders exacerbated interconnected problems in the Great Lakes region once Ethiopia and Eritrea engaged in their own hostilities. The anti-Khartoum coalition shattered, along with U.S. policy in the Great Lakes.

In hindsight, it would appear that U.S. strategy in this part of Africa was influenced more by the dictates of U.S. antiterrorism policy, linked in opposition to Islamic fundamentalism, than by the requirements of stabilizing northeastern Africa—and notably the urgent problem of resolving the civil war in the Sudan. Rather, the U.S. emphasis was on destabilizing or, more ambitiously, toppling the Khartoum regime. This will require a more concerted U.S. diplomatic strategy of multilateral engagement with all of the major actors involved in the Sudan conflict.

The events that develop in the aftermath of September 11 will complicate maneuvering in this region. As Washington's overriding foreign policy and national security preoccupation became one of building a global antiterrorist coalition, this opened up a new vista for the Islamist regime in Khartoum to advance its diplomatic offensive by rallying behind the U.S. campaign. The leaders of the Khartoum regime believed that the pressures that were building up on it to pursue a political settlement of its civil war may have been greatly alleviated by the aggressive U.S. antiterrorism stance.

A resolution of Sudan's civil war, which is of paramount interest among Khartoum's neighbors, could at the same time end Sudan's status in Washington as a terrorist state. In the wake of Secretary of State Powell's first visit to Africa in May 2001, the State Department's influence in structuring a considered diplomatic approach involving a UN special envoy appeared to be in ascendancy. This would favor the least controversial path, given the volatility of some of the domestic U.S. constituencies that have taken an interest in Sudan. But the September 11 events may have substantially eclipsed these calculations.

My Friend's Enemy Is My Friend

Washington's unilateralist impulses may, now and then, provide opportunities for others to step into seemingly intractable and highly visible disputes in the international arena. Such actors could play what might be termed a "counterunilateralist" role on issues of major importance to the United States. South Africa has been uniquely placed to fill such a niche. The international popularity of its celebrated transition from apartheid to democracy, under the heroic leadership of Nelson Mandela, provided Pretoria with a unique moral high ground in international affairs, one that enabled it to punch above its weight on global issues ranging well outside the universe of African international relations. In fact, the Mandela factor, during the first five years after the electoral transition in 1994, was characterized by personal leadership initiatives by Mandela himself that ventured very close to a brand of South African unilateralism; it backfired in some instances, especially in Africa.

In 1995, President Mandela's anger at the Sani Abacha regime's execution of Ongoni activist Ken Saro Wiwa led him—and South Africa—to spearhead Nigeria's suspension from the Commonwealth. This episode exposed South Africa to a backlash from other African states; the United States remained ambivalent in view of its dependence on Nigerian oil. Mandela's campaign broke the mold of behind-the-scenes consensus politics and diplomacy in addressing problems on the continent. The fallout from this episode, in fact, wound up reinforcing the new government's dominant multilateralist tendencies, especially in inter-African politics. For as long as Nigeria and South Africa remained at loggerheads, there would be no progress in reordering Africa's affairs. Mandela's actions over Abacha threatened a renewed isolation of Pretoria within the continent.

Later in Mandela's presidential tenure, his singular leadership in breaking the Lockerbie deadlock, which resulted in the lifting of sanctions against Libya and the return of Muammar Qaddafi's regime from isolation, balanced the slate. Unlike in the Nigerian case, Mandela's role in Lockerbie combined an element of counterunilateralism, as South Africa opposed the United States and Britain's position on how the issue should be handled. Mandela mediated between these two countries, and Libya and acted in concert with other actors, to bring the issue to a conclusion that extricated Tripoli from sanctions and isolation.

Such counterunilateralism was grounded in African multilateralism, as the Mandela initiative grew out of the OAU's opposition to sanctions. The Mandela initiative was coordinated with the OAU, and this gave Mandela important multilateral backing in Africa, which was united in resisting what was considered U.S. and British bullying on an issue that affected one of its own member states. The Lockerbie issue provided Pretoria with an opportunity to display leadership in solidarity with the rest of Africa against Anglo-U.S. hegemony. It also helped pay Libya back for support during South Africa's liberation struggle.

Another instance of South African counterunilateralism has arisen in the Middle East. In this regard, U.S. hegemony has taken the form of a mediation monopoly in refereeing the Arab-Israeli stalemate, despite the obvious role that the United States plays as Israel's protector. All other actors have been shunted to the sideline in the wake of the Cold War's end; no longer is there a Soviet Union to provide balance on the Arab side of the equation. The failure of the Oslo peace process to resolve the Israeli-Palestinian conflict and the outbreak of a renewed Palestinian intifada has raised anew the question of whether Washington can truly serve as an honest broker in the Middle East. President Thabo Mbeki and former President Mandela have led South Africa in openly declaring the need for a wider, more multilateral intervention in the Middle East peace process to offset the U.S. tilt toward Israel.

As in the case of Libya, Pretoria is influenced by the history of solidarity between the South African and Palestinian struggles. Nevertheless, in spite of the alliance that existed between the apartheid regime and Israel, South Africa has steered away from a hard-line anti-Zionist posture, a reflection of both Jewish as well as Muslim constituencies within the ruling ANC and in the wider South African society. By the same token, this aspect of South Africa's plural makeup gives Pretoria as much a stake as Washington in the Middle East conflict. South Africa's vocal support for the multilateralization of the Middle East peace process, including a more visible role for the UN, parallels the posture of the EU, especially of France, which sees itself as having a special relationship with the Arab world.

A Power Struggle Between Major Powers?

France requires special mention, as its history and role in Africa presents another dimension to the issue of U.S. hegemony and unilateralism. Paris typically tends to offer itself as an alternative model of influence and leadership on the international stage and, in particular, to regard itself as an African power. France has sought to parlay its African connection into a special relationship with both South Africa and Nigeria. Thus far, Pretoria has avoided gravitating toward French realpolitik as an alternative to its engagement with the United States.

France clearly has an obsession with U.S. hegemony, one that has taken on added force during the current period of cohabitation between Gaullist President Jacque Chirac and Socialist Prime Minister Lionel Jospin—and in the statements of Jospin's highly expressive foreign minister, Hubert Vedrine. In the pecking order of world politics, Vedrine regards the United States as a "hyperpower" with "worldwide influence."[55]

Perhaps Pretoria suspects that an alliance between itself, as a "mere state," and France as a power with "worldwide influence" is little different from, and maybe less in its interest than, forging a partnership with the United States during the age of globalization. As it is, Vedrine's articulation of the defects of globalization is also instructive. According to Tony Judt, they include: "ultraliberal market economy, rejection of the state, nonrepublican individualism, unthinking strengthening of the universal and 'indispensable' role of the USA, common law, *anglophonie,* Protestant rather than Catholic concepts."[56]

This is all suggestive of globalization as America's imperium, which Vedrine sees "most assuredly as a 'project.'"[57] Whereas the United States has global power, Washington "lacks a conception of what such power means, and what to do with it," something that French public figures like Vedrine find hard to believe.[58] But France's political and economic strategy in Africa has not retarded the momentum of U.S. influence. Yet Vedrine's anti-Americanism strikes a chord with African thinking and converges with the sensitivities of South African leaders, who do not want their country to be seen as the gateway to U.S. penetration of the continent.

On the African front, however, there has been a display of pragmatism in engaging the United States. Such pragmatism may benefit the nurturing of a more multilateralist U.S. approach to Africa. Washington should support the proactive initiatives displayed by Presidents Thabo Mbeki of South Africa, Olusegun Obasanjo of Nigeria, Abdoulaziz Bouteflika of Algeria, Benjamin Mkapa of Tanzania, Abdoulaye Wade of Senegal, Festus Mogae of Botswana, and Joachim Chissano of Mozambique. These leaders have all joined to spearhead a campaign aimed at ensuring that Africans assume more responsibility and mutual accountability for the continent's future. This is already forming the basis for engaging the United States and other powers of what Vedrine considers worldwide influence, like France.

The AIDS Pandemic and Prospects for Multilateralism

Based on Secretary of State Powell's remarks at the University of the Witwatersrand in May 2001, prospects for a U.S.-Africa partnership on the global issue of HIV/AIDS are promising, provided that the United States is more forthcoming in meeting the challenge laid down by UN Secretary-General Kofi Annan. Annan is on record as saying that to seriously combat the AIDS pandemic the UN will need $10 billion for a global trust fund. Although Powell touted his country as being the largest bilateral donor in combating AIDS, malaria, and tuberculosis, he was quick to add that the United States will contribute only an additional $200 million to the AIDS global trust fund. This is a paltry sum that goes against the grain of the designation, by the Clinton administration, of HIV/AIDS in Africa as a U.S. national security threat.

One factor that might produce an enhanced U.S. commitment is the activist constituency in the United States and South Africa (as well as farther a field) generated by the HIV/AIDS threat, one that transcends partisan political lines. This constituency has been mobilized by sobering statistics, including some 13.2 million AIDS orphans worldwide, 95 percent of whom live in Africa.[59] Within southern Africa, the AIDS crisis is acute: Nigeria, Uganda, Malawi, the Democratic Republic of Congo (DRC), Botswana, Zimbabwe, and South Africa are particularly hard-hit. In 1990, hospital bed occupancy for AIDS patients in Zimbabwe alone was roughly 7 percent; by 2000, this figure had ballooned to roughly 68 percent.[60] In Botswana, where 33 percent of the adult population is estimated to have HIV/AIDS, the president recently said his country faces "mass extinction—a blank slate, unless drastic steps are taken now to combat HIV/AIDS."[61] In South Africa, too, the rate of HIV/AIDS infections is said to hover around 25 percent. According to Metz, "Some 1,500 more South Africans are infected with AIDS every day."[62] He also stated that "the Health Minister of Nigeria estimated that 5.8 million Nigerians were HIV positive or had AIDS."[63] Ugandan President Yoweri Museveni admitted frustration with his hard-pressed efforts to spend money to train military officers only to see them die of AIDS in the short to medium term. Estimates of HIV infection among regional armies include 50 percent in the DRC and Angola, 66 percent in Uganda, 75 percent in Malawi, and a staggering 80 percent in Zimbabwe.[64]

It is clearly on the HIV/AIDS front—a global commons issue—that bipartisan cooperation in the U.S. Congress, a prospect enhanced by the Democrats controlling the Senate, may make a difference. As some argue, "Less immediately threatening to the United States, but even more important for African nations, the cross-border spread of infectious diseases, such as AIDS, also requires a cooperative approach."[65] An enhanced U.S. commitment to match that made by African leaders, who pledged to give the fight against AIDS the highest priority in their national development plans, would provide a solid basis for a U.S.-Africa partnership in combating the pandemic.

To place this challenge in perspective, however, it is important to note that the United States has barely ever been able to fund its entire assistance program for Africa at a level approaching $700 million—compared to the $3 billion and $2 billion, respectively, in U.S. aid to Israel and Egypt. One serious policy dilemma is whether any developed country's Africa policy should essentially boil down to AIDS policy or whether—given the magnitude of funding involved on the AIDS pandemic combined with other challenges facing Africa—bilateral assistance to Africa should not be largely multilateralized. For example, the United States and other G8 countries could channel aid through regional and subregional organizations.

Conclusion

In this chapter, I have attempted to provide an African perspective of United States unilateral and multilateral engagement of Africa. There are a number of vehicles at the disposal of U.S. decisionmakers and policymakers, which they can use to pursue multilateral engagement with Africa. These include global institutions like the UN Security Council and the Bretton Woods institutions, which Africans perceive to be instruments of U.S. power, as well as important African multilateral institutions like the African Development Bank and Fund, the Organization of African Unity, the African Union, and above all Africa's subregional organizations. However, such a change in U.S. strategy may not materialize because it runs counter to Washington's tendency toward bilateral engagement with carefully chosen allies, so-called anchor states, and above all a penchant for unilateral conduct and even disengaging from Africa's affairs.

U.S. engagement has presupposed the presence of willing and credible African partners, particularly leaders deemed to have special qualities. In practice, such partners have often proven elusive. Such was the case with the purported new generation of East African leaders, the former president of the DRC, Laurent Kabila, Rwandan President Paul Kagame, Ugandan President Yoweri Museveni, Ethiopian President Meles Zenawi, and Eritrean President Azaias Efewerki. The idea of these leaders constituting a so-called new generation of African leaders ultimately turned out to be a mirage. Accordingly, the United States has come to depend on relations with new democracies in Africa, what some have called African pivots, or key states, especially after the democratic transition in South Africa in 1994. South Africa emerged as a special case, as Washington sought to court the new Mandela government in navigating U.S. relations on the continent and in the developing world generally. As soon as the civilian regime of Olusegun Obasanjo emerged in Nigeria after democratic elections in 1999, Washington quickly moved to adopt the same strategy toward the West African state.

Washington's bilateral strategy in relation to Africa is problematic. At the same time, there were some stumbling blocks for U.S. tactics. Some of the longtime foes of the United States, such as Cuba's Fidel Castro and Libya's Muammar Qaddafi, were longtime friends of the ANC, and this influenced South Africa to display its independence from Washington. To some extent, this independent posture by South Africa and others became caught up in a perceived competitive relationship between France and the United States on the continent. This, in turn, affects relations of major African powers like Nigeria and South Africa with France as well as with the United States. The French dimension is, therefore, an important consideration from an African standpoint of navigating relations with the United States. Apart from this, can the United States move beyond a perceived unilateralism toward a multilateral approach to its relations with Africa?

Turning now to future challenges, the point of departure for relations between the United States and Africa in the coming years should be based on reinforcing initiatives that Africa's leadership is undertaking to bolster the continent's future, as embodied in the New Partnership for African Development, spearheaded by African powers like South Africa, Nigeria, Algeria, and Senegal and backed by African states like Tanzania, Botswana, Mozambique, Mali, Egypt, Mauritius, Ethiopia, among others.[66] The hope is that the United States and other industrialized powers will play a role in the areas of debt relief, overseas development assistance reforms, private capital flows, and market access for agriculture, mining, tourism, and services. In exchange, African states commit to holding one another accountable for political and economic good governance and to help create an enabling environment for socioeconomic development and economic growth.

There exists a window of opportunity for the United States to respond positively to the NEPAD and the AIDS challenge; it could find its credibility as a full-fledged partner in the African renaissance, an ambitious bid for continental renewal, eroding. Importantly, the continent's regional and sub-regional organizations—especially the African Union (the successor to the

OAU), SADC, the Inter-Governmental Authority on Development, and the Economic Community of West African States (ECOWAS)—must have important roles to play.[67]

To the extent that George W. Bush's administration buys into NEPAD, Africans will be able to influence U.S. policy and choices of action on Africa. To South Africa's benefit, the mutual downgrading of the BNC to (in effect) a bilateral joint commission may make its relationship with Washington more manageable by lowering the profile of the bilateral relationship from one where South Africa comes across as having been anointed by the United States as its chief ally in Africa.

However, as a complement to this adjustment in the BNC relationship, Washington and Pretoria should show a greater commitment to multilateralism by investing more time and energy in the U.S.-SADC forum. That forum, in turn, could serve as a model for structuring subregional multilateral relationships between the United States and other parts of the continent—in East and West Africa, for example. This could, among other things, make for more effective implementation of that part of the AGOA that calls for period meetings of the U.S.-Africa subregional groupings. This forum could be subregionalized.

Similar subregional economic cooperation forums could be incorporated into U.S. forums with ECOWAS and the East African Community (EAC). Subregional multilateralism between the United States and Africa could also benefit programs like ACRI and AGOA. In southern Africa, for example, now that a consensus within SADC has been reached on the SADC organ and the Protocol on Politics, Defence, and Cooperation has been adopted, the U.S.-SADC forum might be able to revisit ACRI in a less sensitive context, one that is informed by the Brahimi Report on UN peace operations in areas of conflict prevention, peacekeeping, and peacebuilding. In fact, because of a lower-key style on Africa, the Bush administration may be able to more systematically multilateralize U.S.-Africa policy while building on the initiatives of the Clinton administration. In the case of the Sudan, which is shaping up as a high-profile Bush initiative, a subregional multilateral relationship between the United States and the EAC and/or the Inter-Governmental Authority for Development might advance Washington's diplomatic strategy in pursuing a political settlement to the Sudan civil war.

It is ultimately in the U.S. national interest to place a greater priority on getting Africa policy right. As it embarks on organizing itself into the African Union, Africa seems to be heading into a natural alignment of the South with Asian powers like India and China; Latin American powers like Brazil; and possibly Russia as well. So far, this tendency is motivated more by a commonality of economic interests in transforming the international trading system than by a clearly articulated political agenda. However, the possibility that this could become a polarizing alignment cannot be ruled out entirely.

At the same time, these prospects have been muted recently as a result of the new multilateralism emerging out of Washington's frenetic antiterrorist coalition-building. In fact, September 11, tragic as it was, may have been the historical watershed that, for all practical purposes, ended U.S. unilateralism, or at least ended the illusion that the United States could cut itself off from the rest of the world and adopt a take-it-or-leave-it approach to friend and foe alike. To what extent this will benefit Africa is unclear.

Certainly, G8 powers like Canada and the EU appear to be holding fast, assuring Africans that antiterrorism priorities will not marginalize the NEPAD agenda. Otherwise, somewhere down the line, if the U.S. antiterrorism campaign and coalition falter amid the marginalizing of the NEPAD agenda, renewed polarizing tendencies cannot be ruled out. This might especially occur if Washington allows for the low priority it affords Africa to continue. Such a continued posture could influence major African actors like Nigeria and South Africa to solidify a natural alignment of the developing world into an actual alliance. This does not necessarily mean that there is an automatic unity of the developing world or even that major Southern powers will bend over backward to placate Africa's agenda in the name of Southern solidarity.

Many African and other developing countries have their own overriding agendas and are indeed making their own accommodations with Washington, especially in the wake of September 11. This was especially evident in the case of key powers like India, though Washington's renewed reliance on Pakistan is a complicating factor here, as well as an indicator of what fluid global alignments have actually become. Otherwise, the South is obviously not monolithic. However, to the extent that African powers are successful in reorganizing the inter-African terrain into a more disciplined bloc, Africa's voice projected through major powers such as South Africa and Nigeria will become a factor not to be ignored in the international balance of forces affecting Western, including U.S., interests. The Canadians and Europeans appear committed to seeing that this does not happen, and there are indications that Washington is not losing sight of these concerns either given the major AGOA forum hosted by President Bush in October. Therefore, partnership building between the United States, its allies, and Africa may not be sidelined. But nothing is guaranteed.

There is no guarantee that multilateralism may now be gaining ascendancy in Washington. Even if it did, there are already three areas of U.S. policy engagement that may raise a red alert in creating a genuine partnership between, say, the United States and South Africa. As South Africa prepares to host the Earth Summit in 2002, the Bush administration has already polarized the global commons surrounding the issue of global warming in its rejection of the Kyoto Protocol. The Kyoto rejection was a particularly defining episode in an emerging perception of the United States as embarking on a unilateralist course under the Bush administration. This, in turn, was reinforced by U.S. ambivalent disengagement from the World Conference on Racism based on objections to African demands for reparations for slavery and colonialism and on the contentious Israeli-Palestinian conflict that resurfaced attempts to equate Zionism with racism. Indeed, it appeared that the historical pendulum of U.S. foreign policy had swung toward a definitive unilateralist cycle before September 11.

The other issue is all the talk and growing speculation that the United States is planning an attack on fragile Somalia, a move that would surely hurt the relations between Washington and most of NEPAD countries.

To conclude, the jury is still out on whether or not the United States will come to learn that one way of coping with tragic events like the terrorist attacks of September 11, 2001, is to appreciate multilateralism and engagement more than it has done thus far.

Notes

The author thanks Francis Kornegay and David Monyae for their inputs and assistance on this chapter.

1. Heisbourg, "American Hegemony? Perceptions of the US Abroad," p. 5.
2. Ibid., p. 6.
3. The term "hyperpower" has been popularized during the past five years by French Foreign Minister Hubert Vedrine.
4. Frazer, "The United States and Southern African Development Community," p. 3.
5. See Bender, Coleman, and Sklar, *African Crisis Areas and U.S. Foreign Policy*, p. 10.
6. Ibid., p. 18.
7. Walters, "U.S.-Africa Relations," p. 945.
8. Ibid.
9. Ibid.
10. For analyses of South Africa's destabilization policies, see Turok, *Witness from the Frontline*; also see Hanlon, *SADCC in the 1990s*.
11. Crocker, *High Noon in Southern Africa*, p. 21.
12. Philips, *The African Political Dictionary*, p. 189.
13. Ibid., p. 79.
14. Author's discussion with Jendayi Frazer, May 25, 2001, Pretoria, South Africa; also see Colin Powell, Opening Statement at the Confirmation Hearing Before the Senate Foreign Relations Committee, Washington, D.C., January 17, 2001.
15. Kissinger, *Does America Need a Foreign Policy?* pp. 207, 209.
16. Stremlau, "Ending Africa's Wars," p. 126.
17. Public Affairs Section, U.S. Consulate, Lagos, Nigeria, *Crossroads* 7, no. 4 (April 2001).
18. The White House, *A National Security Strategy for a New Century*, pp. 54–57.
19. For an assessment of the role the United States can play in ending Africa's deadly conflicts, see Stremlau, "Ending Africa's Wars."
20. Omach, "The African Crisis Response Initiative," p. 83.
21. Colin Powell, Opening Statement.

22. Discussed in Mills, "Pillars, Keys, Anchors, and Legs," pp. 198–199.

23. Frazer, "The United States and Southern African Development Community," p. 3.

24. Ibid.

25. Kornegay and Chesterman, *Southern Africa's Evolving Security Architecture*, p. 26.

26. Ibid.

27. Frazer, "The United States and Southern African Development Community," p. 5.

28. Ibid.

29. Kornegay and Chesterman, *Southern Africa's Evolving Security Architecture*, p. 26.

30. For an analysis of South Africa and Nigeria's hegemonic ambitions, see Adebajo and Landsberg, "Prophets of Africa's Renaissance: South Africa and Nigeria as Regional Hegemons."

31. For two good analytical accounts on ACRI, see Frazer, "The African Crisis Response Initiative," and Campbell, *The U.S. Security Doctrine and the Africa Crisis Response Initiative.*

32. For an assessment of lessons learned from the Somalia debacle from one U.S. perspective, see Crocker, "The Lessons of Somalia," pp. 2–8.

33. See Wurst, "Global Peacekeeping Hits a Blockade"; also see *Diplomatic World Bulletin* 5, no. 7 (July 25–31, 1994).

34. Landsberg and de Coning, *From "Tar Baby" to Transition*, p. 22.

35. *Diplomatic World Bulletin* 5, no. 7 (July 25–31, 1994).

36. Omach, "The African Crisis Response Initiative," p. 73.

37. Ibid.

38. Kornegay, "The African Crisis Response Initiative," p. 23.

39. As stated, NEPAD is a merger of the Millennium Partnership for Africa's Recovery Program (MAO) and the Omega Plan. This merger came about on July 3, 2001. Out this merger was born the New Africa Plan (NAI). NAI was then approved at the OAU Summit of Heads of State and Government on July 11, 2001. The NAI framework was finalized and formed and adopted as the NEPAD. The goals of NEPAD are to accelerate growth and development; eradicate widespread and severe poverty; and halt the exclusion of Africa from global economic integration.

40. Dulany, Savage, and Booker, *Promoting U.S. Economic Relations with Africa*, p. 9.

41. Kabemba and Landsberg, *Opportunity or Opportunism*, p. 1.

42. Ibid.

43. Ibid.

44. Ibid., p. 2.

45. Ibid.

46. Ibid.

47. Unpublished paper, "Partnership for Economic Growth and Opportunity in Africa: The Evolution of US-Africa Policy" (n.d.), p. 3.

48. See Stremlau, "Forward," p. x.

49. Dulany et al., "Promoting U.S. Economic Relations with Africa," p. 11.

50. Ibid., p. 7.

51. Metz, *Refining American Strategy in Africa*, p. 3.

52. Ibid.

53. See Gordon, Miller, and Wolpe, *The United States and Africa*, p. 18.

54. Ibid., p. 5.

55. Judt, "The French Difference," p. 18.

56. Ibid., p. 19.
57. Ibid.
58. Ibid.
59. Public Affairs Section, U.S. Consulate in Nigeria, *Crossroads* 7, no. 4 (April 2001).
60. Ibid.
61. Ibid.
62. Metz, *Refining American Strategy in Africa*, p. 21.
63. Ibid.
64. Bisseker, "Africa's Military Time Bomb," *Financial Mail* (Johannesburg), December 11, 1998.
65. Gordon, Miller, and Wolpe, *The United States and Africa*, p. 92.
66. Judt, "The French Difference," p. 106.
67. Kornegay, Landsberg, and McDonald, "Participate in the African Renaissance," p. 105.

17

The United States and the Asia-Pacific: Bilateralism Plus "Multilateralism à la Carte"

Andrew Mack

THE U.S. SECURITY ENGAGEMENT WITH THE ASIA-PACIFIC IS BOTH LONG-standing and deeply rooted. From the aftermath of World War II until the end of the Cold War, this commitment was driven primarily by the perceived imperative of containing Soviet communism. In the very different circumstances of the twenty-first century, the U.S. commitment to the region appears, to the surprise of some, to be as robust as it was during the Cold War. Its putative benefits are, however, treated as givens and are rarely subjected to any deep reflection.

It is true that U.S. force levels have been reduced in East Asia, but these reductions have been less than in Europe—an indication both of the importance that the United States attaches to the region and of the greater potential for violent conflict in Asia. Although bilateral relationships between the United States and regional states are subject to frequent minor—and sometimes major—strains, the U.S. presence has been generally welcomed as a force for stability in the region. This is not least because of deeply felt regional concerns about the instability that could be generated by a U.S. withdrawal.

Michael Ignatieff recently observed of contemporary U.S. foreign policy that "it is unilateral when it wants to be, multilateral when it must be."[1] This is not the case in the Asia-Pacific, however. Here, it is truer to say that U.S. policy is multilateral when it wants to be and unilateral only when it cannot operate in its preferred bilateral mode, which most of the time it can and does.

The pattern of bilateral engagement reflects U.S. preferences as well as the skepticism of key East Asian states toward far-reaching, institutionalized multilateralism. In the 1990s, the deep antipathy that the United States had shown to multilateral security arrangements during the Cold War diminished dramatically, and U.S. officials began participating in the newly created Association of Southeast Asian Nations (ASEAN) Regional Forum (ARF), the only official-level multilateral security mechanism in the region.

Today, the U.S. presence in this and other multilateral regional forums is taken for granted. But presence should not be confused with enthusiasm, and the United States remains skeptical about the value of these forums, for reasons that are explained later in this chapter.

The profound differences between the East Asian and European alliance systems, with the former characterized by bilateralism and the latter by multilateralism, arose because tensions between U.S. allies—in particular between Japan and Korea—and opposition from Britain, Australia, and New Zealand precluded the creation of a NATO-style multilateral alliance in East Asia in the years following World War II. In addition, there remains an underlying uneasiness among friends and allies of the United States about the depth of U.S. commitment to the region. This is due in large part to the U.S. abandonment of its ally in South Vietnam in 1975. No comparable event undermined the confidence of U.S. allies in Europe.

The unilateral impulses of the United States are partly, but by no means completely, constrained by the web of close bilateral relationships the country maintains in the region. In 1994, these impulses estranged Washington from its longtime South Korean ally and embroiled the United States in a crisis over an intransigent North Korea's nuclear weapons program. That crisis could well have led to a violent confrontation that would have almost certainly engulfed the whole Korean Peninsula. Fortunately, an intervention by former President Jimmy Carter with the North Korean leadership, plus pressure on Washington from Seoul, helped to defuse the crisis and to set in motion a diplomatic process that culminated in the negotiation of an Agreed Framework between the United States and North Korea and the creation of the Korean Economic Development Organization (KEDO). Today, KEDO is the most important multilateral security agreement in the Asia-Pacific region. At the time of this writing, it appeared that U.S. unilateral impulses and North Korean intransigence were again putting Washington on a possible collision course with Pyongyang and deeply alienating Seoul.

Despite such tensions and occasional crises, most regional analysts would agree that U.S. security engagement in East Asia has served U.S. interests well—even if U.S. isolationists (and some realists) would certainly demur.

The most likely scenario for the near and medium terms is that the future of security multilateralism in the region will resemble its recent past. U.S. engagement will continue to receive broad regional support despite constant irritations and occasional crises. But a major rupture is not impossible, including one possible scenario discussed later in this chapter.

The Impact of September 11

Many analysts have commented on a newfound U.S. enthusiasm for multilateral engagement in the aftermath of September 11, 2001, as George W.

Bush's administration scrambled to piece together a global alliance against terrorism. But the impact of the terror attacks on U.S. policy in East Asia has been rather different. There has been little U.S. effort in the region to foster multilateral collaboration against terrorism, although relations between the United States and key Northeast Asian states improved noticeably in the weeks following the attacks.

China and Russia, as well as Japan, had their own domestic reasons for supporting the U.S.-led war on terrorism. Washington's tough response to September 11 made it difficult for it to oppose Chinese and Russian campaigns against domestic Islamic militants while also facilitating the push by the government of Junichiro Koziumi for greater Japanese involvement in regional and global security. In the wake of the terrorist attacks, Tokyo's unprecedented decision to send Maritime Self-Defense Force ships to the Indian Ocean to aid the United States was relatively uncontroversial, both at home and in the Asia-Pacific region. Significantly, neither Beijing nor Seoul complained about the deployment. North Korea, predictably enough, was not supportive of the U.S. campaign against terrorism.

In Southeast Asia, ASEAN issued a declaration in November 2001 offering rhetorical support for the U.S. position. The statement was short on substance, however, in part because of differing views among ASEAN members. The Philippines has been the most vocal supporter of the U.S. antiterrorism campaign in Southeast Asia, in large part because the government of President Gloria Macapagal-Arroyo confronts its own violent Islamic opposition, the 800-strong Abu Sayyaf group based on Basilan Island. Although the group has had links with Al-Qaida in the past, most observers believe that it is motivated more by the prospect of criminal gain than by religious zeal or political ideology.

The United States responded positively to President Macapagal-Arroyo's professions of support for the antiterrorism campaign and is now providing some $100 million of military assistance to the Philippine government. This is by far the largest amount of assistance Manila has received since 1991, when the Philippine Senate voted to close down the two huge U.S. bases at Clark Field and Subic Bay in response to nationalist pressures. Radical nationalists remain opposed to U.S. armed forces operating on Philippine soil.

Singapore has been quietly supportive of the U.S. antiterrorism campaign, but the official Indonesian and Malaysian response has been tempered by concerns among the majority Muslim populations in both countries that Islam itself should not be targeted, as well as by deep antipathy to U.S. policies in support of Israel. Both Indonesia and Malaysia are moderate Islamic states, but each contains a hard core of deeply anti-U.S. militants. In Indonesia, President Megawati Sukarnoputri condemned the September 11 terror attacks, but she also warned against the risks of "open war" against Afghanistan. Both Megawati and Malaysian Prime Minister

Mahathir Mohamed were worried that the U.S. war in Afghanistan could increase support for the Islamic radicals, who are among their bitterest domestic opponents.

Thailand's support for the U.S. campaign has also been lukewarm and for essentially the same reason: governmental concern to avoid inflaming Islamic sentiments. Thousands of Muslims in the south of the country demonstrated against the U.S. war in Afghanistan.

The most gung-ho regional response has come from the conservative Australian government, whose prime minister in 1999 likened Australia's role in the region to that of deputy sheriff to the United States. Australia sent special forces to Afghanistan to assist U.S. troops in the military campaign against the Taliban government and Al-Qaida.

New Zealand offered to send special forces, and some media reports indicate that they have been deployed, although the government has not confirmed this. Wellington also made a contribution of twenty-five armed personnel to the International Security Assistance Force (ISAF), the UN-authorized and British-led force created to keep the peace in post-Taliban Afghanistan. The ISAF is quite separate from the U.S.-led military campaign, in which Australia has been participating. At the time of this writing, New Zealand was the only Asia-Pacific nation to be participating in the ISAF.

Notwithstanding NATO's support for the U.S. antiterrorism campaign, the United States has chosen to enlist European countries to its cause on a case-by-case basis rather than via the often unwieldy institutional mechanisms of the transatlantic alliance. The same is true in the Asia-Pacific, where neither the United States nor regional states have sought to use the only official regionwide multilateral regional security organization, the ARF, as a tool to coordinate antiterrorism operations.

Perhaps the most unexpected consequence of September 11 has been the creation of a U.S. military presence in, and engagement with, several countries in Central Asia—long a region that both China and Russia have considered part of their spheres of influence. At the time of this writing there are thought to be at least 1,500 U.S. armed forces personnel in Uzbekistan, a smaller number in Tajikistan, and others due to be sent to Kyrgyzstan. Apparently, the Bush administration does not regard this deployment as a temporary move. In congressional testimony in December 2001, Assistant Secretary of State for European and Eurasian Affairs Elizabeth Jones said that the administration hoped to create a permanent U.S. presence in Central Asia in order to boost regional economic development and sustain democratic reforms in the region.[2]

There is an obvious potential for this unprecedented U.S. presence in Central Asia to increase tensions with Russia and China. Tajikistan, Kyrgyzstan, and Kazakhstan, along with Armenia and Belarus, are members of the Russian-led Collective Security Treaty of the Commonwealth of Independent States. Kazakhstan, Kyrgyzstan, Tajikistan, and Uzbekistan are also members of the Shanghai Cooperation Organization, an economic and security forum that also includes Russia and China.

Post–Cold War U.S. Engagement in Northeast Asia: A Puzzle for Realists

Washington perceives Northeast East Asia as the most important security region in the Asia-Pacific. This is not surprising. The subregion contains:

- The most dangerous military confrontations in all of East Asia—those between the two Koreas and across the Taiwan Strait. If either confrontation crossed the threshold into armed conflict, the United States would almost certainly be drawn into the fight.
- Unresolved territorial conflicts—most obviously between the two Koreas and China and Taiwan but also between China and Japan as well as China and various Southeast Asian states, Russian and Japan, and Korea and Japan over disputed islands.
- China, the only country in the region that the United States sees as a strategic rival.
- Two states (South Korea and Taiwan) that have sought to acquire nuclear weapons and may well seek to do so again; two (China and North Korea) that already have them; and one (Japan) that could acquire them very quickly should it chose to do so.
- And two states (China and North Korea) that have been actively involved in exporting missile technology, and one (Japan) that could build nuclear-capable medium-range missiles very quickly if it so wished.

Despite these potential flashpoints, many realist students of international relations consider continued U.S. security engagement in Northeast Asia to be paradoxical. After all, the Soviet Union—the enemy that provided the traditional rationale for U.S. forward presence in the Pacific—no longer exists, and U.S. allies in the region have more than enough resources to provide for their own defense.[3]

What puzzles realists is not the attachment of Korea and Japan to their alliance relationships with Washington; for those two countries, the U.S. military presence provides them with defense on the cheap. The real puzzle is why the United States should continue to take the risks and pay the costs of protecting allies in an alliance that has lost much of its original rationale.

Some realists—and most isolationists—argue that U.S. security relationships in the region are "entangling alliances" that risk embroiling the United States in conflicts not of its own making and wars it does not have to fight.[4] Thus, even though North Korea can pose no military threat to the

United States, the U.S. military presence in South Korea and the security agreements between Washington and Seoul ensure that U.S. forces would be involved in any armed conflict between North and South, regardless of how it started.

A similar logic leads critics to argue that U.S. security relationships also increase the likelihood of an armed clash between the United States and China. The least improbable scenario for such an armed confrontation would be one in which the United States intervened on behalf of Taipei in an armed confrontation across the Taiwan Strait. Such a confrontation could easily by triggered by miscalculation. In the absence of security ties between Washington and Taipei, critics note, there would be little risk of armed conflict with China.

Absent the Soviet threat, the U.S. commitment to Japan is particularly difficult for realists to explain. Under the current arrangement, the United States is committed to defend Japan, yet the Japanese are under no reciprocal obligation to aid the U.S. militarily if the latter is attacked. Indeed, Japan is constitutionally prohibited from so doing outside its own borders.

Realist-versus-isolationist arguments notwithstanding, the continued U.S. commitment to the region is both deep and likely to continue for the foreseeable future. Kenneth Waltz and other neorealists who predicted that the demise of the Soviet Union would lead to the dissolution of U.S. anti-Soviet alliances relied too much on what their theories predicted *should* be the case and paid insufficient attention to what actually *was* the case.

The reality is that more than a decade since the Cold War ended there is no sign of any diminution of support for existing alliances within the foreign policy communities in Japan, Korea, and the United States and few signs of declining support among the citizenries of those countries for such alliances.

There is no simple explanation of why support for the Pacific alliance system should have outlasted the traditional rationale for its existence. Rather, there is a complex of reasons that receive differing degrees of support from different elements within United States—and regional—policy-making circles.

For the Pentagon, the containment of rising military Chinese power is the critical issue, followed closely by the necessity to defend South Korea in the event of an armed conflict with the North. In neither case is the U.S. commitment the product of deep reflection: It is simply taken as a given. Asia-Pacific security planners simply do not address isolationist arguments about entangling alliances no matter how logical these may be. Such arguments have no impact whatsoever on the official U.S. discourse on regional security.

The Pentagon's 2001 *Defense Guidance* makes it very clear that U.S. security policy is oriented toward countering emerging capabilities rather than intentions.[5] In sum, the U.S. strategic posture focuses on countering the developing military forces of potential adversaries rather than on estimates of their current intentions. After all, intentions can change quickly, especially in so-called one-bullet regimes. Thus, even if China or North Korea harbor no aggressive intentions toward either their neighbors or the United States today, no one can be sure that this will still be the case in five years. This means that the U.S. military posture vis-à-vis China will be determined by emerging Chinese military capabilities, regardless of the current status of the politico-diplomatic relationship between Beijing and Washington or relations with regional allies.

Within the State Department there is a strong predisposition toward seeking engagement with China and North Korea rather than pursuing the military containment policy that underpins the *Defense Guidance*. But the State Department's natural affinity for options that stress diplomacy is always held hostage to the ideological and strategic preferences of different administrations—and sometimes the Pentagon. This was strikingly evident in President George W. Bush's State of the Union address in January 2002. The message of that speech, which included a hard-line depiction of North Korea as part of an "axis of evil," was radically at odds with the strategy of multilateral diplomatic engagement with Pyongyang preferred by the State Department's regional specialists as well as the South Korean government.

Whether U.S. policies in Northeast Asia stress deterrence and coercion or engagement, and whether they are unilateral, bilateral, or multilateral, it is highly likely that the United States will continue to stay fully engaged in the region for the foreseeable future. But it is not certain.

Even though Washington's friends and allies are all strongly committed to a continued U.S. presence in the region, there are persistent underlying worries about how sustainable the U.S. commitment would be if the United States were drawn into a major regional conflict. Critics note that Washington abandoned its allies in the Vietnam War, although more than 50,000 U.S. personnel were killed before withdrawal took place. Over time, U.S. willingness to sustain casualties appears to have diminished. In Lebanon in 1983, a terrorist attack that killed 241 Marines precipitated a U.S. withdrawal shortly afterward. In Somalia in 1994, the United States withdrew not long after eighteen U.S. Rangers had been killed. If push comes to shove, pessimists argue, the casualty-averse United States cannot—and should not—be relied on to stay to course.

In fact, the cases of Lebanon and Somalia are misleading. In neither country did the United States possess either alliance commitments or any vital interests. But regional worries persist, and the alliance system confronts other significant risks.

Consider the scenario noted briefly above, in which the United States finds itself drawn into an armed confrontation with China during a new crisis in the Taiwan Strait. Consider further what would happen in such a crisis if the United States called on Japan to provide some of the relatively far-reaching assistance measures spelled out in the revised 1997 "Guidelines for U.S.-Japan Defense Cooperation."[6] Past precedent suggests that the Japanese government might take so long to make up its collective mind that the fighting would have ceased before Tokyo reached a decision.

If U.S. blood was spilled in a regional conflict while Japan sat on its hands, the consequences for the alliance could be very serious. As Hisahiko Okazaki warned in 1996, "If American boys are dying for Taiwan and we don't help, we destroy the alliance."[7]

The Sources of Support for U.S. Engagement

The arguments for continued U.S. commitment to East Asia appear compelling to all but U.S. isolationists, a few realists, and a numerically small number of radicals within the region itself. The reasons are not difficult to determine.

U.S. regional allies provide the United States with forward-basing options, various forms of military and political support, and access to intelligence on adversaries and potential adversaries in the region. This serves U.S. interests at what Washington perceives to be an affordable cost. But the cement that binds regional alliance relationships together also contains a considerable element of bureaucratic interest—on all sides. The Pacific Command, the Japan-based U.S. Seventh Fleet, and the U.S. forces based in South Korea would all lose much of their rationale in the absence of alliance commitments. Similarly, allied armed forces would lose partners for military exercises and access to U.S. intelligence and advanced military hardware and software that would not otherwise be available.

China is the only power in East Asia capable of threatening the continental United States directly, but it lacks any long-range conventional power-projection capability and can strike at the United States only with some twenty nuclear-armed intercontinental ballistic missiles (ICBMs). U.S. armed forces in the Pacific cannot defend the United States against an ICBM threat; they can only defend U.S. allies and interests in the region itself. This gives all the armed services, but particularly the U.S. Navy, a vested bureaucratic interest in the continuation of alliance relationships. The interests of the U.S. armed services and the regional security policies of successive administrations have been complementary, not least because the services have been highly successful in selling their vision of what regional security policy ought to include.

Alliance relationships are also sustained by a considerable element of inertia. On both sides of the Pacific, networks of influential military officers, bureaucrats, and politicians have formed close and comfortable relationships over several decades that have helped sustain the alliance in the aftermath of the Cold War. Moreover, bringing the military personnel and their equipment back home would save little money unless these forces were also demobilized, as Japan pays a major share of U.S. basing costs.

Some alliance boosters—and left-wing critics—argue that U.S. economic interests dictate the need for continued U.S. military engagement in the region. But although this argument is frequently reiterated, it remains unpersuasive. No other government in the world believes that it is necessary to station military forces around the globe simply to protect economic interests, no matter how vital. The United States also has extensive economic interests in Latin America and elsewhere, without perceiving any need to station armed forces in these regions to protect these interests.

Support for regional engagement in political Washington, the Pentagon, and the Beltway think tanks is nurtured not only by its perceived benefits but also by the anticipated costs of the possible dissolution of alliance relationships. To begin with, the United States has an image of itself as a world power, indeed, as *the* world power. Maintaining this self-image requires Washington to sustain its key global commitments even when their original rationale may have disappeared. To abandon its allies would be to diminish the standing of the United States in its own eyes, to say nothing of the huge reputational costs that it would incur.

But this is not all. Many in Washington and in East Asia itself are also concerned about the potentially disastrous consequences of a U.S. military withdrawal from the region. The most prevalent regional concern is the possible reemergence of aggressive nationalism in a Japan that is no longer constrained by a U.S. embrace. (The fact that no serious arguments have been put forward to show how it could possibly be in Japan's interest to embrace militarism once again does not seem to reduce this concern.)

A comparison between Japan and Germany and the nature of the alliance structures in Europe and East Asia is instructive. At the end of World War II, a major concern of the victorious Allies was to prevent Japan and Germany from ever posing another threat to regional and global security. As often observed, the purpose of NATO was multifaceted: to keep the Americans in, the Russians out, and the Germans down. But Germany was not only enmeshed and constrained by NATO's *multilateral* alliance system; increasingly, it was also embedded in and constrained by a web of economic interdependencies and other multilateral institutions, from the European Union to the Conference for Security and Cooperation in Europe (CSCE; later the Organization for Security and Cooperation in Europe [OSCE]).

Even if the United States were to pull out of Europe, Germany would remain enmeshed in and constrained by economic interdependence as well as the dense network of multilateral institutions that has become one of the hallmarks of postwar Europe. In addition, successive German governments have gone to great lengths to reassure their neighbors and address concerns about Germany's past. For these and other reasons, European worries about German revanchism have been largely assuaged.

The contrast with Japan is marked. First, Japan's continued failure to address its aggressive past in a manner that assuages the fears of its neighbors remains a source of deep regional concern and resentment. Second, there is no network of European-style multilateral relationships—military, political, or economic—that would enmesh Japan were the United States to withdraw. Some East Asians worry that a Japan that is no longer held in the restraining embrace of the U.S. alliance could again embark on a militarist path. Even if the inevitable changes in Japan's force posture resulting from a U.S withdrawal were not determined by any aggressive intent, they could nevertheless be highly destabilizing.

One reason that the U.S.-Japan relationship helps allay regional concerns about Japanese revanchism is that the alliance is based on a military division of labor that gives the United States sole responsibility for all the major offensive capabilities. Japan's force structure is essentially defensive, lacking any long-range power-projection capabilities. Were the alliance relationship to be severed, Japan would be on its own, facing even stronger domestic pressures from right-wing nationalists to become a "normal" country. In military terms, this would imply that the Japanese Defense Forces should acquire the long-range power-projection capabilities currently provided by the United States.

Such a step would be seen as deeply alarming by most states in the region, and it could well lead to a destabilizing regional arms race and a series of "security dilemmas."[8] More important, the removal of the U.S. nuclear umbrella would create intense domestic pressures to build a Japanese nuclear deterrent to counter China's nuclear arsenal.

U.S. withdrawal from the region and the removal of the nuclear umbrella over Taiwan and South Korea would almost certainly lead both of those countries to acquire nuclear deterrents of their own. Both Taiwan and South Korea have pursued nuclear weapons programs in the past. They were prevented from carrying through by U.S. pressure, not by any lack of technical capability.

It is widely acknowledged that Japan has the capability to go nuclear relatively quickly should it so wish. The Japanese already have enough weapons-grade plutonium for a dozen or so nuclear weapons, and Japan's space-launch vehicles could be converted relatively easily into a medium-range missile capability.[9]

For all of these reasons, and barring the sort of violent crisis over Taiwan outlined above, the U.S. commitment to the region seems assured for at least for the medium term.

U.S. Engagement in Southeast Asia, Australasia, and South Asia

The United States still has formal treaty relationships with Thailand and the Philippines, but these are of relatively little consequence today compared with the core U.S. relationships in Northeast Asia. It is true that U.S. assistance is now flowing to the Philippines as part of the U.S. antiterrorism campaign, but this has little to do with the alliance relationship. Similarly, Washington has made it clear to Manila that Philippine forces cannot count on U.S. support, notwithstanding the bilateral alliance, should they use force to support territorial claims to the Spratly Islands in the South China Sea.

Southeast Asia

There are several reasons for Washington's now modest level of strategic engagement in Southeast Asia. First, U.S. interests in the subregion declined with China's withdrawal of support for regional insurgencies and with the winding down of the Cold War. The latter reduced the perceived need for U.S. basing facilities in Southeast Asia. Second, U.S. forces had been withdrawn from both Thailand and the Philippines at the request of those countries.[10] Third, unlike Northeast Asia, there is little risk of interstate conflict that could embroil U.S. forces.

Militarily, the United States remains modestly engaged in the subregion, but this is not a function of alliance relationships. Regular meetings of senior officers and officials, ship visits, and military exercises take place with most Southeast Asian states, regardless of whether or not they are formal allies (the Singapore-Washington relationship is particularly warm). Here, as elsewhere in the region, the U.S. preference at the political level is for bilateral relationships. Neither is multilateralism strongly opposed; indeed at the workaday military level it has quietly flourished. Under the leadership of Admiral Dennis Blair, commander in chief of the Hawaii-based Pacific Command, what were bilateral military exercises have become multilateral and now involve not only more subregional participants and Australia but also observers from as far afield as Mongolia and South Korea. This low-key military-to-military multilateral cooperation has little or nothing to do with what goes on in the ARF.

Australasia

The current state of the fifty-year-old Australia–New Zealand–United States (ANZUS) Treaty alliance provides an interesting example of how ruthless the United States can be toward small allies that challenge it. Since the early 1990s, Australia and the United States have rarely disagreed on security matters. The security relationship between the George W. Bush administration and the John Howard government is particularly close, but with New Zealand, the other ANZUS alliance partner, it is virtually nonexistent. Ever since New Zealand refused to admit U.S. nuclear-armed ships in the mid-1980s, the United States has treated New Zealand as a security pariah. Although the alliance still exists on paper, it has ceased to exist in fact since 1986.

The fact that New Zealand had been an model alliance partner in every other respect and that the United States had no need to visit it with nuclear-armed ships in the 1980s made no difference to Washington. Today the only U.S. vessels carrying nuclear weapons are missile-firing submarines, which never patrol south of the equator, rendering New Zealand's nuclear ban wholly irrelevant. But this has not made any difference, either.

Australia sided strongly with the United States in the row over nuclear ships, and the security relationship with New Zealand has been further soured by Canberra's claims that Wellington is not pulling its weight in the common defense relationship. Australia spends nearly 2 percent of its gross domestic product on defense compared to New Zealand's 1 percent. In March 2000, the new Labour government in New Zealand added insult to injury by canceling its lease-purchase of twenty-eight F-16 fighters from the United States. It is now restructuring its forces so that they will be more suitable for what is without doubt going to be their most important future mission, namely, peacekeeping. Even though this makes perfect strategic sense for a country that confronts no military threats, and even though the performance of New Zealand's forces in Timor and elsewhere has been widely praised, neither Canberra nor Washington has been mollified.

Telling evidence of just how bad the security relationship between New Zealand and the United States had become was provided at the conference on the fiftieth anniversary of ANZUS in May 2001. Speakers referred only to the "U.S.-Australia alliance," and, not withstanding the tripartite nature of the alliance, New Zealand was not mentioned once by senior U.S. officials, whose speeches ranged over the fifty-year history of ANZUS. The third party to the ANZUS Treaty might just as well have not existed. Washington's attitude was as petty as it was spiteful.

It is difficult to avoid the conclusion that New Zealand has been punished, not because its policies compromised U.S. security—they did not—but because the United States wanted to demonstrate that any challenge to its strategic hegemony would come at a high cost. Small, weak, and strategically inessential New Zealand was the perfect target.

South Asia

Although South and Central Asian security issues are normally considered separately from those of East Asia, there are a number of important linkages. India, though not Pakistan, is a member of the ASEAN Regional Forum, as is Mongolia. India has fought a border war with China and developed nuclear weapons primarily to deter perceived Chinese threats. Pakistan's nuclear program, which has received support from China, was a response to the Indian bomb. The United States has been, and continues to be, deeply concerned about nuclear and missile technology transfer from China and North Korean to Pakistan.

The Bush administration has accepted the reality that there is no way that India and Pakistan are going to give up their nuclear weapons programs. A major U.S. concern is now to increase the security of both countries' nuclear programs and arsenals. The sanctions imposed by Bill Clinton's administration on both countries in 1998 have since been waived, and defense cooperation has been increased. The events of September 11, 2001, of course, transformed the U.S. relationship with Pakistan almost overnight, but they also strengthened the relationship with India. Recent U.S. efforts to mediate the bitter dispute over Kashmir have been no more successful than previously, however. India resists internationalizing the conflict, which it regards as a purely domestic matter, and it deeply resents the long-standing U.S. refusal to declare Pakistan a state sponsor of international terrorism.

The issue of multilateral security cooperation in South Asia does not really arise, for the major regional institution, the relatively weak South Asian Association for Regional Cooperation (SAARC), has no mandate to deal with security issues, which are much too sensitive. In terms of security multilateralism, SAARC has been described as being "at the point where ASEAN was thirty years ago."[11] The fact that Pakistan is not a member of the ARF means that India-Pakistan security issues are not discussed in the ARF. Even if Pakistan were to join the ARF, India would certainly veto any discussion of the Kashmir issue.

The United States, the Asia-Pacific, and Security Multilateralism

In the early 1990s, the United States strongly opposed initiatives by Australia and Canada to create multilateral security institutions in the Asia-Pacific region. Washington subsequently tempered its opposition, given the changed strategic realities of the end of the Cold War and the growing regional acceptance of the idea of what might be called "soft multilateralism"—namely, the ASEAN preference for relatively informal dialogue mechanisms rather than institutionalized multilateral organizations.

Today, U.S. participation in the ARF—the only official-level multilateral security mechanism in the region—is taken for granted. (Notwithstanding its name, the ARF includes all the states of Northeast Asia, with North Korea having been recently admitted. India and Mongolia are also members.)

The long-standing U.S. preference for bilateralism in the region is not difficult to explain. In Washington's hub-and-spokes relationship, the United States constituted the hub, its allies, the spokes. This suited the United States, for it was unambiguously the dominant partner in each bilateral relationship. Absent a multilateral security organization, there was no way that the country's Pacific allies could combine to resist U.S. policies, as the European allies could—and sometimes did—in NATO.

The deep U.S. opposition to the initial Australian and Canadian proposals for cooperative approaches to regional security in the late 1980s and
early 1990s did not simply reflect an antipathy to multilateralism. In Europe, after all, the United States had embraced a multilateral security
agenda, using the CSCE and the Conventional Forces in Europe Treaty
talks to engage the countries of the Warsaw Pact. But in East Asia, the Pentagon was totally opposed to the same policies that it supported in Europe.

Again, it is important to draw attention to differences in strategic geography and force postures between Europe and East Asia. In Europe, the
Soviets had a clear numerical advantage in offensive conventional land
forces along the Central Front. The United States favored conventional
arms control as a means of shifting the balance in Washington's favor. In
East Asia, U.S. maritime forces were vastly superior to those of the Soviet
Union, and so the United States was wholly uninterested in arms control—
or any other form of restraint on U.S. naval operations.

By the mid-1980s, the Soviets were trying with increasing persistence
to export the CSCE model to the Asia-Pacific. In Vladivostok in 1986, Soviet premier Mikhail Gorbachev advocated regional confidence-building
measures (CBMs), including a "Pacific conference along the lines of the
Helsinki conference"; the ostensible rationale was to reduce the risks inherent in a possible military confrontation between the superpowers in
Northeast Asia.[12]

The U.S. bitterly opposed this proposal, for the Soviets wanted—perfectly reasonably from their point of view—CBMs to include restraints on
the sort of provocative military exercises that were a regular element in the
U.S. Navy's forward-offensive Maritime Strategy. The U.S. Navy's standard response to any calls for naval arms control was, "Just say no!" Navy
spokesmen argued that any restriction of their naval exercise program,
which included mock attacks against the Soviet homeland, would diminish
the navy's operating efficiency. The Soviets would see this as a sign of
weakness, deterrence would be undermined, and the risks of war would
thus increase. From this perspective, CBMs, far from enhancing security,
actually undermined it. The U.S. Navy, which appeared oblivious to the obvious risks of its provocative posture, also argued against any other CBMs
on the grounds that they would lead to a slippery slope, culminating in that
worst of all possible worlds, namely, naval arms control.

Given the Pentagon's hard-line stance on constraining CBMs and on any
importation of CSCE-type multilateralism, it is not difficult to see why Washington was less than amused when Australian Foreign Minister Bill Hayden
warned in 1987 of the risks inherent in the provocative strategies of the superpowers in the North Pacific[13] and went on to argue for a variety of CBMs
similar to those that had emerged in the CSCE negotiations in Europe.[14]

The end of the Cold War created a certain amount of space for new
ideas, however, and in 1990 a new Australian foreign minister, Gareth

Evans, put forward a proposal for a new regionwide multilateral security institution inspired by the CSCE. Evans even used the phrase "Conference on Security and Cooperation in Asia." The Canadian external affairs minister, Joe Clark, also made the case for a new multilateral security dialogue, but only for the subregion of Northeast Asia. Clark also invoked the CSCE model.

Washington rejected both proposals out of hand, with U.S. officials arguing that all such CBM proposals were solutions in search of a problem and that change should be resisted on the grounds that if it isn't broke, don't fix it. Canberra and Ottawa were reminded sharply that U.S. policy in the region was based on forward-deployed forces, overseas bases, and bilateral security arrangements.

Initially, regional states echoed U.S. reservations, if less vehemently. Japanese Prime Minister Toshiki Kaifu, for example, described CSCE-type proposals as "premature."[15] Regional critics of the Australian and Canadian proposals pointed out that territorial disputes in Europe had been resolved, whereas those in Asia had not, and that the nature of alliance relationships was quite different in the two regions. Contributing to Asian irritation was the fact that a Western-inspired institution was being promoted by Western states as a solution to Asian security problems.

Ironically, no sooner had Australia and Canada retreated from their original bold proposals than the ASEAN states themselves began to embrace the idea of multilateral security dialogues. In July 1991, the ASEAN Post-Ministerial Conference (PMC) stated that the PMC was an "appropriate base" for discussion of regional security issues.[16] In 1994, ASEAN established the ARF, which meets each year at the ministerial level just before the PMC. The ARF is the only official-level multilateral security forum in the region.

Although the region has now embraced soft multilateralism, Asian wariness about more institutionalized forms of multilateralism remains. This is most obvious in the reluctance of key member states in the region to give the two key multilateral institutions in the region strong secretariats. The Singapore-based Asia-Pacific Cooperation (APEC) Secretariat, whose mandate is to promote trade and investment and economic and technical cooperation, has a mere twenty people working for it and a tiny budget. The contrast with the Organization for Economic Cooperation and Development, which has a not dissimilar, albeit broader, mandate could not be more striking. The ARF has no permanent secretariat at all.

The Limits of Soft Multilateralism

Many critics believe that neither ARF nor APEC has lived up to its much-heralded beginning. According to Richard Haass, director of policy planning at the U.S. State Department, the ARF "is a frequently frustrating exercise in 'convoy diplomacy'—always moving at the speed of the slowest member"; APEC, by contrast, seems "to have lost its way and is in danger of descending into formalism."[17]

The admitted limitations of these institutions comes at some real cost. APEC was irrelevant in the Asian financial crisis of 1997–1998, as was the ARF in the crisis over East Timor in 1999. In the former, the U.S.-dominated International Monetary Fund (IMF) and World Bank were the key multilateral players. In the latter, Indonesia's eventual, reluctant agreement to allow the Australian-led multilateral force into East Timor was achieved by what has been aptly described as "coerced consent." It resulted from intense U.S. pressure on Jakarta, which involved threats that World Bank–IMF support for Indonesia would be withdrawn if the Indonesians persisted in their recalcitrance. Regional states sat on the sidelines and did little to try and avert or manage the crisis. It would have been inconceivable for the ARF to have attempted to play a crisis-prevention or -management role. Doing so would have been seen as an unwarranted intrusion into the domestic affairs of ASEAN's most powerful state, something diametrically opposed to the cherished ARF principle of nonintervention.

Supporters of both APEC and the ARF argue that neither institution should be criticized for failing to act where it had no mandate for action. APEC was not designed to deal with regional financial stability, and the ARF is predicated on the sanctity of sovereignty and the norm of nonintervention. But this defense serves only to underscore the weakness and very limited utility of both multilateral instruments.

The ARF's self-imposed proscription from dealing with intrastate conflicts means that it can play no role in preventing, stopping, or managing the conflicts within the region that kill most people, namely, those that take place within, not between, states. In addition, China will not countenance any multilateral discussion of the China-Taiwan conflict or any formal moves to resolve the territorial disputes over islands in the South China Sea. The recent admission of North Korea will not lead the ARF to start dealing with the Korean conflict either: This remains the domain of the two Koreas and the United States.

It is interesting in this context to contrast East Asia with West Africa, where states with just as much reason to oppose intervention in their internal affairs, but with much lower levels of state capacity, have nevertheless managed to set up and run regional peacekeeping and peace-enforcement operations. Any such initiatives would be unthinkable in East Asia.

In these circumstances it is not surprising that since coming to office Bush administration officials, who had never been enthusiastic multilateralists, should profess skepticism about APEC and the ARF, seeing both as little more than ineffectual "talking shops."[18] If the hostility with which the United States greeted the emergence of multilateral security dialogues in the early 1990s has long since disappeared, Washington still declines to accord the ARF any great importance.

However, the inability of APEC, or the ARF to have a substantive impact on critical economic and security crises in the region does not mean that they have no utility. They can be—and indeed are—used by the United States and other governments for a range of purposes other than those for which they were ostensibly created. Thus, although APEC is ostensibly an institution committed to enhancing trade openness and economic cooperation, its annual leaders' summits also serve as important informal forums for discussing political issues. In October 2001, for example, the United States used the Shanghai summit very effectively to rally support for its global campaign against terrorism. Moreover, high-level multilateral meetings also provide political leaders and senior officials with opportunities for bilateral side meetings that can be held with minimum publicity.

Southeast Asian analysts sometimes argue that Western participants in regional dialogues often miss the true import of the ASEAN way of consensus-based multilateralism. Forums for multilateral dialogue, they argue, are intended not so much to negotiate verifiable and enforceable agreements, formal institutions, and rule-based procedures—as the lawyer culture of the West prefers—but to build better relationships. When relationships are good, legal agreements are not necessary; when relationships are bad, such agreements are often unworkable.

The consensus approach has two consequences that are worrying, however, and not only to the United States. First, the stress on consensus means that great effort is put into creating language that obfuscates disagreement. This often creates the impression of progress when it fact there is none. Second, progress is made hostage to the wishes of those who seek minimal change. As a recent Brookings Institution study noted, "The ARF's inability to significantly affect the sovereign decisions of its members means it will remain a forum which plays to the lowest common denominator."[19]

The ARF's mandate is to focus successively on CBMs, preventive diplomacy, and finally conflict resolution. The first goal has been relatively easy to achieve. In practice it has involved large numbers of meetings, which are seen as CBMs in themselves, and a commitment to greater transparency in security affairs, not least via an increase in the number of states publishing defense white papers. But years after its formation, the ARF has still not agreed on what should be pursued under the rubric of preventive diplomacy. This is partly because some ARF members worry that pressures on states to accept preventive diplomacy missions could threaten the sacred principle of noninterference in the internal affairs of member states. Ironically, despite the ARF's hesitancy to engage decisively with this issue, there have been a number of successful initiatives at preventive diplomacy in the region. These include: the negotiation of various border agreements between Russia, China, India, and their neighbors; the negotiation of the 1995

Southeast Asian Nuclear-Weapon-Free Zone; and ASEAN's intervention in the dispute between Malaysia and the Philippines over Sabbah in 1968.[20]

Finally, interest in multilateral institutions and processes in East Asia has grown, at least in part because some problems can be effectively addressed only via cooperative solutions. APEC, for example, has been modestly successful in pursuing win-win technical solutions to what are essentially technical economic and trade problems. Somewhat ironically in view of past U.S. Navy attitudes, the most articulate official U.S. proponent of security multilateralism in recent times has been Admiral Dennis Blair, the commander in chief of Pacific Command. Blair has argued against balance-of-power mind-sets and in favor of the promotion of pluralistic security communities—a situation that exists when states share dependable expectations that conflicts will be managed peacefully. These arguments are very similar to those made by the Australians and Canadians at the beginning of the 1990s.[21] Blair's views are certainly not shared by the hard-liners in the Bush administration, and it would be remarkable if his successor at Pacific Command were to espouse similar policies. The civilian side of the Pentagon is certainly far more hostile to security multilateralism than is Pacific Command, but multilateral military-to-military relationships—exercises, dialogues, and multinational conferences—will likely continue.

The fact that the sort of cooperative multilateral approaches that Admiral Blair advocates may be cost-effective in some contexts does not guarantee that they will succeed in all. Power imbalances, historical antagonisms, and sometimes radically different approaches to security, trade, and regulatory policies make attaining multilateral agreement in East Asia far more difficult than is the case within NATO or the European Union, where shared values, the resolution of ancient interstate rivalries, and similar levels of political and economic development have facilitated the achievement of consensus.

Where vital interests are perceived to be at stake in regional conflicts and where there is a real asymmetry of power between the players, as is the case with the territorial disputes between China and its ASEAN neighbors over the Spratly Islands, the prospects for multilateral solutions diminish rapidly.

Soft multilateralism in the security realm is now well established in the region, with the United States now actively engaged in various regional dialogue processes—but rarely leading or demonstrating much commitment to them. But whereas past U.S. hostility and current ambivalence are part of the reason that more far-reaching multilateral security cooperation has not been achieved, in Northeast Asia the creation of any form of official-level subregional security cooperation has been precluded primarily by the attitudes of Northeast Asian states themselves.

Enduring and deep-seated Chinese suspicions of Japan (and vice versa) continue to preclude security cooperation across the East China Sea. And although South Korea and Japan are each close U.S. allies, it remains inconceivable that they will agree to turn their long-standing bilateral alliance relationships into a formal trilateral alliance. This has as much, or more, to do with domestic politics in both countries than it does with the views of their respective foreign policy communities. There is in fact a good deal of quiet trilateral security cooperation already going on, the U.S.–South Korea–Japan Trilateral Coordination and Oversight Group that focuses on North Korea being an important example. This three-way relationship is sometimes described as a "virtual alliance," although Ambassador Stephen Bosworth's term "enriched bilateralism" is probably more accurate.

The Four Party Talks involving China, North Korea, South Korea, and the United States focus on security on the Korean Peninsula are interesting precisely because they include China and North Korea. Thus far they are notable not so much for their achievements, which have been very modest, but for the fact that they have been held at all.

There have been a series of proposals, mostly from scholars and retired officials, for the creation of more institutionalized, official-level, multilateral economic and security regimes for Northeast Asia. These include proposals for the Association of Northeast Asian Nations, a nuclear-weapons-free zone, and a regional development bank. None of these have gone anywhere. The Tumen River Development Program, which brings together North and South Korea, China, Russia, and Mongolia, provides a one very rare example of institutionalized official-level economic and environmental cooperation in Northeast Asia. But progress has been both modest and painfully slow.

There are also a number of so-called Track II mechanisms for multilateral dialogue in Northeast Asia, forums in which government officials may take part in their private capacity (as the polite fiction has it). These include the Northeast Asia Economic Forum, the Northeast Asia Cooperation Dialogue, and the Working Group of the Council for Security and Cooperation in the Asia-Pacific. The latter two institutions have focused on security issues.

These Track II initiatives, which proliferated in the 1990s, are now generally welcomed and can occasionally be used by governments that want to float particular trial balloons. But their ability to effect change is obviously constrained by their nonofficial nature. South Korea has made a number of proposals for official-level dialogue mechanisms to embrace Northeast Asia, but none have come to fruition.

As for the United States, the Bush administration's admonition that "the mission should define the coalition, not the coalition the mission" reflects what has long been U.S. practice in East Asia. Although the United States has never shown any of the enthusiasm for multilateralism tout court that Canada, Australia, and many European governments profess, this has not prevented Washington from opportunistically creating ad hoc multilateral mechanisms when they suit U.S. purposes.

The Most Important
Multilateral Security Agreement in East Asia

The 1994 Agreed Framework between Pyongyang and Washington defused a crisis over the North's nuclear facilities at Yongbyon and led to the creation of what is without doubt the most important multilateral security (though not military) institution in the subregion: the relatively unknown Korean Energy Development Organization. KEDO, a classic example of issue-specific, ad hoc multilateralism à la carte, was created by the United States, Japan, and South Korea in 1995.

KEDO is, in effect, the implementing mechanism for the 1994 Agreed Framework. Under its terms, Pyongyang agreed first to freeze and then to dismantle its nuclear program at Yongbyon in exchange for the provision of 500,000 tons of heavy fuel oil per year and the building of two proliferation-resistant light-water reactors in North Korea. Since 1995, KEDO's membership has grown from three to thirteen, with sixteen nations providing financial support.

The KEDO agreement is not perfect, and the North Koreans have long been difficult to deal with, but without the agreement the North would likely have an arsenal of some two dozen or more nuclear weapons by now. KEDO has been a stunningly successful multilateral exercise in nuclear nonproliferation.

Now that success may be put at risk by the Bush administration's inclusion of North Korea as one of three poles of the "axis of evil." The connecting link between Iraq, Iran, and North Korea for the administration is not so much their support for international terrorism (Lebanon and Syria would be far better candidates than North Korea in this case) as their pursuit of nuclear weapons programs.

On terrorism, the evidence suggests that North Korea, after perpetrating terrorist acts against South Korea in the 1970s and 1980s, had abandoned this sort of violence by the early 1990s. The change in policy did not arise out of any sudden moral squeamishness but because terror had proven to be manifestly counterproductive from a political standpoint.

No evidence has been produced to demonstrate that North Korea has exported any WMD materiel or expertise. Pyongyang has kept its promise to freeze its nuclear facilities at Yongbyon and, since 1998, has also maintained a self-imposed moratorium on flight tests of its missiles. Partly for these reasons, just prior to leaving office the Clinton administration was contemplating removing North Korea from its list of states that sponsor terrorism.

Creating the 1994 Agreed Framework was not easy. Prior to 1994, a number of hawkish retired officials and commentators in the United States were arguing for a unilateralist hard-line policy against the North that would include surgical strikes against the Yongbyon nuclear facilities. This policy option reportedly had enjoyed support, though not uniform, within the Pentagon.

It is conceivable that Washington could have embraced a more reckless and dangerous policy, but it is not clear how. Such a U.S. attack would have been a gross violation of international law and would almost certainly have plunged the peninsula into a war in which tens or even hundreds of thousands of people would have been killed. Because Seoul is within artillery range of the border, civilian casualties in the South would have been particularly high. Moreover, bombing the reactor and spent fuel stores at Yongbyon would have risked generating deadly fallout. Finally, while the North had almost certainly produced enough weapons-grade plutonium to build at least one nuclear weapon at this stage, this material could—and surely would—have been removed from Yongbyon in anticipation of the strikes. This, of course, would have negated the point of military action.

Most commentators have concluded that Bush's axis-of-evil speech signaled a new unilateralist hard-line U.S. approach to North Korea and its axis counterparts. It certainly caused great concern in Seoul. But the conditions that made military strikes against the North dangerously counterproductive in 1994 have not changed. United Nations sanctions against North Korea are not an option, because China would veto any sanctions resolution. The United States could certainly try to use its economic leverage to break the terms of its agreements with Pyongyang and cut the supply of fuel oil to the North. But this would almost certainly lead North Korea to restart its weapons program and resume its missile testing program, which analysts believe could eventually produce a missile capable of striking the United States. This, in turn, could re-create the situation that led to the crisis of 1994. Illegal unilateral military strikes against the North are every bit as foolhardy now as they would have been in 1994.

Fortunately, at the time of this writing, wiser heads in the administration appear to have prevailed. In his visit to South Korea in February 2002, President Bush went to some lengths to reassure both Koreas that the United States was not planning military assaults against the North and that it was committed to supporting Seoul's policy of engagement.

The point here is not that unilateralism should always be opposed, or that multilateralist options should always supported, but that in this instance there is no coherent alternative to multilateral engagement that would not risk a disastrous war. KEDO and the Agreed Framework face challenging problems, but KEDO remains the sole example of successful U.S.-led multilateral security engagement in a subregion where any form of effective security multilateralism is extraordinarily rare.

Conclusion

The U.S. commitment to and engagement in East Asia are unlikely to diminish for the foreseeable future for the reasons outlined in this chapter. Washington will continue to prefer dealing with its allies, friends, and adversaries bilaterally, partly because that is an established and comfortable way of doing business, partly because that is what U.S. allies want, but not least because in all bilateral relationships it is the United States that is unambiguously the dominant power. Washington likes it that way.

The United States is unlikely to demonstrate any greater commitment to soft multilateralism in the future than it has in the past, in part because the ARF's emphasis on consensus gives other countries veto power (albeit nonbinding) over U.S. policy preferences, and in part because Washington is skeptical about the ARF's utility. Multilateral meetings will, however, continue to provide opportunities for sensitive, high-level, bilateral side meetings.

We may also expect the U.S. preference for ad hoc, issue-specific multilateralism to be sustained. The antiterrorism coalition that the United States assembled after September 11, 2001, as well as U.S. support for the coalition of the willing that Australia organized to intervene in East Timor prior to UN authorization, provide obvious recent examples.

Washington, not surprisingly, finds the current security arrangements in the Asia-Pacific highly convenient, but privately U.S. friends and allies voice many of the same concerns about U.S. policies that are heard in other parts of the world. The United States is accused of insensitivity, inconsistency, ignorance, and arrogance. On occasion, all of these accusations have been true. Yet perceiving that they need the United States more than it needs them, and with no other alliance options being feasible, U.S. allies in the region rarely raise their objections publicly. Meanwhile, the exclusion of New Zealand from the ANZUS alliance serves as a cautionary tale for any other country that might be tempted to challenge the hegemony of the United States over regional strategy.

Notes

1. Ignatieff, "Barbarians at the Gate."
2. See Radio Free Europe, http://www.rferl.org/nca/features/2002/01/11012002091651.asp.
3. For a classic statement of this position, see Waltz, "The Emerging Structure of International Politics."
4. See Johnson, *Blowback*; Carpenter, "Smoke and Mirrors"; Johnson and Keene, "The Pentagon's Ossified Strategy"; Doug Bandow, "Japan Plays America for a Sucker," *Los Angeles Times*, December 31, 1995.
5. In fact, the *Defense Guidance* notwithstanding, the United States does *not* base its force planning purely on capabilities. If it did so it would be arming against Japan and Western Europe as well as China and North Korea.
6. These measures included minesweeping and helping monitor sanctions embargoes.
7. Cited in Carpenter, "Smoke and Mirrors," p. 2.
8. A security dilemma arises when the defensive preparations of one state are perceived by other states as potentially threatening, leading them to increase their

military outlays that are seen by the first state as threatening, causing it to further increase its military outlays. The result may be an arms race—a spiral of self-fulfilling increases in apprehension and hostility and considerable risks of crisis instability. For example, in the event of a U.S. withdrawal, Japan might feel it necessary to increase its military capability as a counter to a Chinese military buildup. Such a move could, however, be seen as highly threatening by the South Koreans, leading them to build up their military forces.

9. For a detailed description of nuclear proliferation risks in Northeast Asia, see Mack, *Proliferation in Northeast Asia.*

10. The military rift between the United States and the Philippines that followed the closure of the U.S. bases at Subic Bay and Clark Field has been lessened by the Philippine senate's ratification of the Visiting Forces Agreement in 1999.

11. Blair and Hanley, "From Wheels to Webs," p. 12.

12. See text of speech by Mikhail Gorbachev in Vladivostok, July 28, 1986, reprinted in Thakur and Thayer, *The Soviet Union as an Asian Pacific Power,* p. 223.

13. Hayden, "Security and Arms Control in the North Pacific," p. 4.

14. The first CSCE was held in Helsinki in 1975.

15. *Toronto Star,* July 25, 1990. Japanese Foreign Minister Nakayama had a slightly different response, saying that Tokyo was interested in new security frameworks and envisaged a larger grouping of states than that in the Canadian proposal. See Edith Terry, "Canadian Proposal Pacific Security Rejected by Tokyo," *Globe and Mail,* July 24, 1990; Edith Terry, "Japan Cuts Loose from Old Isolation," *Globe and Mail,* July 25, 1990.

16. Joint Communiqué of the Twenty-fourth ASEAN Post-Ministerial Meeting, Kuala Lumpur, July 19–20, 1991, p. 5.

17. Remarks by Richard N. Haass, director of policy planning, U.S. State Department, at conference entitled "The U.S.-Australian Alliance in an East-Asian Context," University of Sydney, June 29, 2001.

18. Barry Desker, "The Future of the ASEAN Regional Forum," Institute of Defence and Strategic Studies, Singapore, September 7, 2001, http://www.ntu.edu.sg/idss/research_05e.htm.

19. Dalpino and Gill, "Introduction," http://www.brookings.edu/fp/cnaps/papers/survey01.htm.

20. For a comprehensive analysis of this issue, see Ball and Acharya, *The Next Stage.*

21. Blair and Hanley, "From Wheels to Webs."

18

The United States and NATO:
A Selective Approach to Multilateralism

Sophia Clément

SINCE THE END OF THE COLD WAR, U.S. POLICY WITHIN THE NORTH ATLANTIC Treaty Organization (NATO) alliance has reflected a complex and shifting mixture of unilateral and multilateral tendencies.[1] Until 1995 and the signing of the Dayton accords ending the Yugoslav wars, the United States favored a policy of unilateralism by default. Such an approach stemmed from a variety of domestic constraints in the United States, from the prioritization of U.S. interests, and from the fact that NATO had not yet adapted to low-intensity conflicts such as those in the Balkans. After 1995, U.S. unilateralism tended to be subordinated to multilateralism within the Western alliance. Power projection by the United States tended to strengthen NATO, which was adapted and transformed to the benefit of allies. NATO was at the center of U.S. policy.

Following the terrorist attacks on the United States of September 11, 2001, the United States embraced unilateral military action. This new unilateralism reflected the perceived nature of the terrorist threat and the growing evidence of U.S. technological superiority. The United States had been the target of the attacks and was now engaged in a global campaign against terrorism, and its military supremacy allowed it to respond alone, at least at the outset. Yet it continued to rely on a variety of multilateral frameworks, including standing alliances like NATO, which embodied a permanent framework of shared interests, as well as an extensive web of flexible, adaptable, ad hoc coalitions tailored to particular missions.

Within this framework, the institutionalized multilateralism of NATO provided the United States with political and logistical support for U.S. military action and, over the longer term, a privileged forum in which to develop principles and mechanisms for cooperation among the allies. The U.S. commitment to multilateralism in NATO continues to be driven by one major reality: U.S. technological superiority, which ensures the supremacy of the United States in the alliance and permits it to pursue nationally defined objectives within a multilateral framework. However, in this chapter

I point to the inherent limits of an exclusively unilateral response to terrorism thanks to a combination of external factors—most notably the transnational and fluid nature of the terrorist threat, which requires a multidimensional and multilateral response—and of internal constraints—including budgetary requirements, public opinion, and potential long-term military overstretch.

Finally, U.S. thinking on the appropriate balance between unilateral and multilateral responses to national security threats is not monolithic. Rather, U.S. policy emerges as the product of complex internal debate and institutional balances. Even within the George W. Bush administration, a major debate was under way in early 2002 between unilateralists, led by Donald Rumsfeld's Defense Department, and multilateralists, led by Colin Powell's State Department.

Between Unilateralism and Multilateralism in the 1990s: Lessons from the Balkans

During the first phase of the 1990s, during the Bosnian conflict, the U.S. choice of unilateralism by default was driven by strong external and internal constraints. NATO was not adapted to the post–Cold War setting, to address low-intensity conflicts and out-of-area missions, or otherwise redefine its raison d'être. Domestic constraints included a new prioritization of national interests, budgetary constraints, and fear of casualties and opposition to military involvement abroad in both Congress and the wider public. Given such pressures, Europeans faced the real possibility that they would be asked to manage crises on the European continent alone without NATO involvement.

Viewed from Europe, the Bosnian crisis was the first case in which the United States unilaterally chose not to become involved, despite repeated requests from its European allies. Domestic constraints on the United States, including an aversion to casualties and a reorientation of U.S. interests outside of Europe, discouraged Bill Clinton's administration from adapting NATO's Article 5 provisions to low-intensity conflict in the Balkans. This U.S. unilateralism by default in post–Cold War European crises created a quandary for Europeans, who had not yet set up any of the decisionmaking tools and operational defense capabilities inherent in the vision of an independent European foreign and security identity. As a consequence of this experience, Europeans drew two major lessons. First, they came to perceive NATO as intrinsically linked to U.S. willingness to act; accordingly, multilateral action was subordinated to unilateral U.S. decisions. Second, although NATO was not employed as a tool for military action, the United States used the alliance to exercise political and strategic control over European collective action. In parallel with this political control over NATO, the United States pursued its own unilateral policies toward Bosnia-Herzegovina, policies that reflected strategic priorities different from those of the Europeans. These policies included the Train and Equip program for the Bosnians and the decision to launch air strikes in 1994—a step that led the Serbs to take hostage European soldiers serving in the UNPROFOR mission.

From this frustrating experience, Europeans drew some lessons about burden-sharing and the division of labor between the European Union (EU), on one side, and the United States and NATO on the other. First, for real multilateralism there had to be greater coherence between political control, strategic objectives, and military guidance, and these all had to be decided and pursued collectively. At the level of principles, the allies had to determine at an earlier stage whether stability would be better achieved through the partition and rearming of the sides in the Balkan conflict or through their integration and a commitment to multiethnicity. At the operational level, it was essential to ensure a unified command in NATO, to eliminate dual-key arrangements, to provide a clear mandate and common rules of engagement, and to define the end stage of any military involvement.

Second, burden-sharing implied accepting a share of risk and responsibility. There should be no functional or geographic division of labor, with peacekeeping reserved for Europeans deployed on the ground and warmaking reserved for U.S. personnel over the horizon. Coercive diplomacy remained important, but it also had its limits. It must be part of a broader incremental strategy, and it must be used only as a last resort. In addition, there had to be greater coherence in the use of diplomacy, coercive diplomacy, and force, which had to be regarded as complements rather than as substitutes. When armed force was used or threatened, it had to be credible, based on political will, military capability, actual deployments, and an equitable sharing of risks. Finally, the crises underlined the need for NATO to develop new functional and geographic mechanisms to better manage out-of-area operations and non–Article 5 missions. NATO thus had a new raison d'être, and its fate would depend on its ability both to deal with challenges in the Balkans and to embody so-called real multilateralism. The Bosnian crisis transformed NATO from a collective defense grouping to something more akin to a collective security organization.

For Europeans, a strong NATO was a way to cement U.S. engagement in the Balkans and Europe and to temper Washington's unilateral inclinations. NATO adapted by establishing a European dimension within the alliance, the European Security and Defense Identity (ESDI) and by creating new tools for common action. At the same time, the Bosnian experience generated greater momentum, led by Great Britain and France, toward creating a defense dimension within the EU, through the European Security and Defense Policy (ESDP). Perceptions of these initiatives were different on opposite sides of the Atlantic, however. The United States understood all

European efforts as remaining within a NATO framework and ESDI, whereas most EU partners viewed ESDP as separate from, although complementary with (and reinforcing) NATO. The ESDP would allow the EU to undertake action either with NATO, by borrowing the alliance's capabilities, or independently, through autonomous action, if so decided by Washington and European capitals and between the two organizations.

The Kosovo operation of 1999 embodied a complex mixture of unilateralism and multilateralism, and its lessons were perceived differently from the vantage points of the United States and the European Union. EU partners regarded this opportunity to act under NATO's chain of command as proof of their credibility and efficiency as allies and as a way to ensure U.S. participation in collective responses to high-intensity contingencies. For the U.S. public, the experience increased fears that the alliance might place constraints on the conduct of military operations, including in intelligence and targeting. For Washington, one of the major lessons of Kosovo was the need to avoid too much political involvement in the conduct of military operations.

For Europeans, Kosovo reconfirmed the lesson of Bosnia that the United States must be tied in to European security, both geographically and functionally. At the operational level, NATO's value as a military alliance was confirmed through an enhanced military role and the success of its first major engagement. It was the sole organization able to undertake a military operation in a difficult security environment and to play a key role in high-intensity contingencies. Above all, it was able to combine multilateralism with power projection and to ensure that diplomacy was backed by a credible military capability. At the political level, unity of action was ensured through consensus and rapprochement of most EU allies with NATO. Kosovo bridged the twin concepts of a European Europe and a NATO-Atlantic security community. It confirmed that the evolution of ESDP would neither cripple NATO nor result in U.S. disengagement. At a military level, Europeans were determined to act together, as the main U.S. allies.[2] France, often sensitive to U.S. unilateralism, recognized the importance of a continuing strategic relationship between Europe and the United States, acting as a full partner in the first major operation under NATO's chain of command. A true sense of coresponsibility emerged at a Euro-Atlantic level. Rambouillet—a European diplomatic initiative supported by a NATO threat of military action—symbolized this partnership.[3] Rather than take an exclusive military approach to the crisis, Western strategy had an important politico-diplomatic dimension.

Yet U.S. technological superiority—so obvious in Kosovo—seemed to allow the United States some unilateralist action within NATO's collective framework in shaping planning, the chain of command, a low tolerance for casualties, policy toward collateral damage, and the selection of targets. The result was to strain relations among allies on strategic objectives and military guidance.[4] In addition, Europeans believed that only a UN mandate could provide the necessary legal basis and international legitimacy for military action. In the European view, NATO had no automatic right of intervention, and the United States should not regard Kosovo as a precedent for future alliance interventions in the service of nationally defined (i.e., U.S.-defined) policies. On the contrary, European consensus for collective action in NATO was based on the belief that the U.S. presence in Europe should give way to a more permanent multilateral framework for negotiation and transparent consultation within NATO, in which Euro-Atlantic relations would be mutually reinforcing. NATO should not be understood simply as a facilitator for managing the Western alliance but as a forum where a common policy was formulated through negotiated compromise.

U.S. Foreign Policy in the Twenty-First Century: A Selective Commitment to Multilateralism

The events of September 11, 2001, have changed the premises of U.S. policy toward multilateral security cooperation. To begin with, as the target of an attack on its homeland, the United States has the right to act in self-defense. For the purposes of conducting the war on terrorism, moreover, Washington believes that multilateral institutions and alliances cannot be permitted to constrain U.S. action. It is sufficient, for U.S. purposes, to assemble a flexible coalition with variable membership, small or large, loose or tight, depending on the particular mission. In Afghanistan, the United States tried to limit the engagement of partners—whether bilateral or multilateral—in order to avoid any political constraints in the conduct of its operations. The United States, which occupies a dominant position in the current international system thanks to its technological superiority, prefers unilateral action and ad hoc coalitions to the detriment of multilateral security organizations such as the United Nations and even NATO.

Unilateralism as an Ideal Approach to Military Action: The Lessons of Afghanistan

In Afghanistan, the United States has shown a clear preference for unilateral military action without the support of allies. Although the NATO allies invoked Article 5 of the NATO Treaty after the attacks on the United States—the first time in history that article had been activated—Washington chose to opt out of NATO for the purposes of military action rather than acting collectively. This choice corresponded to U.S. strategic doctrine. It was already integrated in the 2001 *Quadrennial Defense Review*, which anticipated a military answer to an asymmetrical threat. The U.S. unilateral response was shaped not only by prior historical lessons—from the attack on Pearl Harbor to the war in Kosovo—but also by the unprecedented nature of the terrorist attack, by far the most damaging on U.S. soil. Finally, the United States had little practical need for allied military assistance in the first phase of its response.

U.S. strategic doctrine calls for heavy reliance on military power. Although any military response will reflect the nature of the threat, it is also encouraged by the overwhelming technological and military dominance of the United States in the contemporary world. The armed forces of the United States have an unmatched capacity to exercise strategic control thanks to unquestioned superiority in intelligence, precision-guided munitions, and armed forces. Given this superiority, which outstrips even that of its closest allies, Washington is reluctant to share views on how to conduct warfare, fearing that collective action will lead to a dilution of its political objectives and constraints on its extensive military options. The military preponderance of the United States is reinforced by the country's economic power, which allows an enormous share of the budget to be devoted to defense purposes and underpins rapid technological developments. In the case of Afghanistan, the priority of the United States has been to retain the ability to conduct operations independently in support of the objectives President Bush defined on September 20, 2001: tracking down Osama bin Laden, destroying the Al-Qaida terrorist network, and punishing countries that harbor terrorists.

Domestically, the unilateral use of force has enjoyed strong support in the administration, in Congress, and among members of the public. As the target of the terrorist attacks, the United States decided—as was its recognized right—to respond in self-defense, not only against the terrorists but also against the states that harbored them, and to adopt a position of leadership in this struggle, defining the objectives as well as the means to accomplish them. The international community recognized this as a situation of self-defense in UN Security Council Resolution 1373, taken under chapter VII auspices, and (more narrowly) in NATO's invocation of Article 5 of the NATO Treaty.[5]

Among the lessons that Washington had taken from the Kosovo experience were that multilateral control of the use of force could introduce political constraints and complicate decisionmaking and that the EU's military capacities remained marginal, given Europe's modest defense budget, lack of strategic capabilities, and uncertain political will. Accordingly, after the September 11 attacks, the United States made no effort to secure allied military support and even proved reluctant to accept offers of allied troops and military assets, whether through the auspices of NATO or an ad hoc form, during the early days of the campaign in Afghanistan. By responding unilaterally, the United States obviated political constraints in the conduct of military operations and avoided inevitable delays in forging consensus with allies on appropriate objectives and strategies.

Afghanistan itself would provide additional lessons for the United States regarding the wisdom of unilateral action and the potential value of coalitions and alliances. The outcome of the campaign reinforced the central position of the United States within the international system—and particularly in Central Asia, which had suddenly become a vital area of U.S. interest—even as it increased Europe's marginalization.

First, the unilateral U.S. approach to military action worked. The United States succeeded in achieving ambitious military and political goals: ending the Taliban regime, dismantling local Al-Qaida networks, and installing a new government. The United States demonstrated its clear technological supremacy by deploying a combination of extremely sophisticated means—such as precision-guided munitions and advanced communications—with traditional material—such as B-52 heavy bombers and conventional arms. The war also reinforced U.S. strategic doctrine, including the projection of military forces over long distances; the use of precision-guided air strikes with minimal risks of casualties and collateral damage; and the enlistment of local forces.

Second, the Afghan experience suggested that unilateral military action had few significant political consequences. Muslim solidarity was revealed to be a myth, with little reaction coming from the much-feared Arab street, and U.S. action garnered support from several countries in the region. Moreover, international reactions against U.S. unilateral withdrawal from the Anti-Ballistic Missile (ABM) Treaty, including from Russia and China, were far more muted than many had anticipated.

Although the Europeans sympathized with the unilateralist U.S. approach to the military campaign, their support was qualified by a broader worry that the United States was seeking to redefine the global legal rules that structure international relations, for instance, by unilaterally rejecting multilateral frameworks like the Kyoto Protocol on global warming or the ABM Treaty, without prior consultations with concerned parties. With respect to terrorism itself, most European governments were uncomfortable with the axis-of-evil formulation in President Bush's January 2002 State of the Union address and with perceived U.S. plans to extend the war against terrorism unilaterally to Saddam Hussein's Iraq. They worried that the United States might seek to shape the emerging international order permanently in ways that were not necessarily in European interests. They feared that the legitimate right of the United States to defend itself from terrorism, which they had endorsed, might be confused with a broader right, which the United States arrogated for itself, to define international order unilaterally entirely outside existing collective frameworks.

New Regulatory Principles of U.S. Foreign Policy:
Specific and Selective Multilateralism

Despite its unilateralist preference, the United States has continued to rely on multilateral cooperation on a selective basis. It has done so out of necessity in response to: the slowdown of the military campaign in Afghanistan; the need for international cooperation in rebuilding Afghanistan; opposition from Western allies and regional countries to unilateral U.S. strikes on Iraq; the fluid and multidimensional nature of the terrorist threat, which requires significant collective action; and the insistent requests of allies to have a say in the antiterrorism campaign. To respond effectively to the terrorist challenge, Washington has been obliged to define a coherent international strategy that combines a wide range of diplomatic, economic, and legal tools and in which allies are essential partners. Allies were needed to provide help in addition to political legitimacy for U.S. action locally or within international organizations, to provide military support for U.S. operations in Afghanistan and the Arabian Sea, and, as part of a new division of labor, for instance, to contribute to reconstruction and peacekeeping in Afghanistan. Second, despite its military redeployment to Afghanistan, Washington maintains a general geopolitical interest in preserving the vigor of the NATO alliance as the key forum for Euro-Atlantic dialogue, as the main vehicle for U.S. interests in Europe, and, above all, as a reservoir of interoperable forces for future coalitions.

Bilateral Multilateralism:
Coalitions of Coalitions in the War Against Terrorism

As noted, the U.S. mode in Afghanistan is based primarily on unilateral action. When the United States has sought collective action, it has shown a clear preference for flexible coalitions outside existing alliances and other institution structures that might constrain decisions and actions. It embraces multilateral cooperation on a selective and functional basis, creating coalitions on an ad hoc basis around particular activities, tailoring these groupings to the nature of the mission, and allowing them to evolve in membership and level of commitment. The result has been an extensive web of flexible and adaptable coalitions of coalitions. According to Secretary of Defense Donald Rumsfeld, the Bush administration is committed to the principle that the mission determines the coalition rather than the reverse. At any one time, the coalition may include nations prepared to join for certain purposes (but not for others) and at particular levels of commitment. Some countries will bring extensive assets to the table, others only limited ones.

Integration into the overall terrorist coalition has been based on a fundamental division of the world into states that are either with us or against us, a dichotomy determined in Washington and one that leaves little room for divergent attitudes or nonalignment. Finally, coalitions are treated as temporary expedients created for specific missions. In this sense, U.S. multilateralism is more tactical than strategic. This modular approach allows the United States to maintain a quasipermanent antiterrorism coalition that provides essential political and practical support for U.S. action and a lever to legitimize U.S. policies. It remains to be seen whether this coalition approach will continue to define the strategic posture of the United States over the long term.

Concretely, the U.S. approach has resulted in a web of bilateral coalitions with the United States at its core in a dominant position. The broad antiterrorism coalition can be subdivided into smaller groupings, forming multilayered concentric circles containing different categories of allies. In the case of Afghanistan, the first circle was composed of countries from the region, reflecting a U.S. desire to ensure political and military support around the immediate theater of operations. These countries offered the United States diplomatic support, logistical and staging areas, and military bases. The continued support of Central Asian states will be necessary to secure the economic and political stability of Afghanistan and of its immediate surroundings, to track down Al-Qaida networks and constrain regimes in the region, and to permit a longer-term U.S. military presence on the ground, including access to bases, in Uzbekistan and Afghanistan.

Arab-Muslim countries constitute a second circle that the United States seeks to manage, both to consolidate the overall antiterrorism coalition and to minimize the capacity of these countries to block U.S. action. Were the United States to enlarge the scope of the current campaign, some of these countries could become members of the first circle.

The third circle is composed of NATO allies, countries that Washington believes possess the political will, shared values, and military strength to cooperate in military operations if required. For the United States, NATO has long been the most important multilateral collective defense arrangement, and NATO activated Article 5 obligations following the attack on the United States. Nevertheless, wishing to avoid the political constraints that the multilateral alliance might place on its actions, the United States requested only limited logistical support from allies within the Article 5 framework. For instance, it made use of NATO AWACS planes to secure U.S. airspace, but it did not request direct allied involvement—and indeed rebuffed early offers of assistance—in the military operation in Afghanistan. Washington requested only strategic resources from the alliance as a complement to the massive national means at U.S. disposal. The United States made no formal requests for NATO support for the operation itself beyond certain specific bilateral requests.

For political and tactical reasons, Washington has used a range of direct and indirect strategies to co-opt local governments, offering financial aid, advice, intelligence, training, and equipment to secure bilateral cooperation in the antiterrorism campaign. The specific strategies pursued have been differentiated, adapted to the particular target state. The United States has offered aid and technical assistance to secure cooperation from weaker countries like Yemen and Georgia and has in some cases—such as the Philippines—sent U.S. military advisers to assist forces combating local terrorist elements with possible links to Al-Qaida. Overall, the United

States has modified its military deployments and bilateral security arrangements to exert greater control over volatile regions, to increase the support of local governments, and to ensure base rights and prepositioning of materiel for possible military contingencies.

Within the United States itself, domestic support for the Bush administration's war on terrorism has been overwhelming. Internal issues of domestic policy, such as the health of the U.S. economy, have not been subject to major divergences despite some opposition in Congress. Seven months after September 11, 2001, domestic disagreements remained subordinated to the imperatives of homeland security and the war against terrorism.

The ongoing debate in Washington over what to do about Iraq, a major focus of U.S. attention during 2002, perfectly illustrated the new blend of unilateralism and multilateralism in U.S. foreign policy. Although the decision about when and how to act against Iraq has not yet been taken, there was a natural, instinctive predisposition in the United States that any such decision—even though it carried great implications for U.S. partners and allies—should be taken unilaterally by Washington before being raised at a multilateral level either within NATO or with other major allies. Over time, as domestic and international criticism grew, U.S. officials began to consider military options and to explore the degree of regional and international support for regime change in Iraq. Washington discovered that many of its allies were reluctant to expand the antiterrorist campaign to Iraq. In addition, the dramatic escalation of Israeli-Palestinian violence in 2002 made it unlikely that any Iraq operation could be insulated from the Middle East peace process. Still, the decisionmaking process regarding Iraq remained fundamentally unilateral: Washington insisted on maintaining complete margin of maneuver, so as to define for itself the ends of any military operation there and the means of executing it.

NATO: U.S. Unilateralism Within a Multilateral Framework

Washington's attitude toward the NATO alliance provides a case study of the U.S. vision of multilateralism. The United States is strongly committed to NATO's collective defense framework, regarding the alliance as an embodiment of shared transatlantic interests, one that provides security guarantees in times of peace and ensures the continued political cohesion of its members. It helps to sustain, reinforce, and legitimize U.S. foreign policy. The NATO alliance can also be adapted as necessary. The United States has strongly backed the reform efforts of NATO Secretary-General Lord Robertson, and it has sought to improve the alliance's capacity to coordinate the response to terrorism. Above all else, Washington views NATO as an indispensable framework within which the United States and its allies can meet to elaborate common standards and strategic doctrine, improve the interoperability of their forces, undertake joint training and exercises, and reinforce transatlantic solidarity through routine daily interaction. At a regional level, the alliance has had an invaluable stabilizing role in keeping the peace in the Balkans. In sum, the alliance remains the most important framework for common action. It is the reservoir for future coalitions, a forum from which partners can be chosen for future operations, whether they occur through the NATO structure itself or through ad hoc arrangements.

Although NATO did not participate in military operations in Afghanistan, it retained its importance to the United States as an alliance. For the first time in its history, the alliance activated Article 5 of the NATO Treaty. In addition, several allies participated in the operations in Afghanistan on a bilateral basis. From Washington's perspective, the alliance provided an important expression of moral and political solidarity in the struggle against terrorism, as well as certain practical assets, such as infrastructure, logistical support, and overflight rights. Washington took advantage of the alliance as a credible political framework in which to explain its purposes, convince allies of the worthiness of its goals, and legitimize its actions. Article 5 is critical in this regard, as the permanent collective commitment it symbolizes provides, along with UN Security Council Resolution 1368, a foundation for continuing the war on terrorism beyond Afghanistan.

One of Washington's primary goals regarding NATO is to transform the alliance so that it can better respond to the new challenges of the twenty-first century, particularly transnational terrorism and weapons of mass destruction. Article 5 remains at the core of the alliance's functions in this view, but the alliance must adapt its mandate to the new conditions, broadening its agenda to include nontraditional threats and adapting its structures to respond more flexibly to them.[6] Washington considers the alliance an ideal forum to discuss and promote principles for action against terrorism, as well as a promising instrument to arrive at a better division of labor among the Western allies. Washington seeks European allies that are more credible and efficient, better prepared to deal with the terrorist crisis, and more politically ready to undertake responsibilities in neighboring regions, most notably the Balkan theater. To achieve these broad goals, Washington must take steps to restore the confidence of its allies in the U.S. commitment to NATO, particularly with respect to Germany and the newer incoming allies. Finally, NATO provides an ideal framework in which the United States and its allies can approach external partners like Russia, Ukraine, and the other members of the Partnership for Peace, as well as a framework of stability for the countries of Southeast Europe.

Prospects for a smooth evolution of the NATO alliance have been complicated by Washington's unilateral tendencies within the alliance. Although the United States has continued to engage NATO in the aftermath of September 11, 2001, it has shown a determination to constrain the evolution of the alliance in several ways. The Prague summit scheduled for autumn

2002 should provide an opportunity for the United States to reaffirm U.S. commitments to the alliance as one of the pillars of U.S. foreign policy.

Limitations on NATO's geographic and functional missions. The United States contributed to NATO's military marginalization in Afghanistan. Although the nineteen NATO allies agreed unanimously to Lord Robertson's proposal to activate Article 5, Washington surprised the allies by insulating the alliance from the effective conduct of operations. Contrary to its long-standing advocacy for an expanded NATO mandate, Washington rebuffed any suggestion that NATO's functional and geographic missions should be extended to intervention in Afghanistan on the grounds that NATO was unlikely to do better what the United States was doing alone. Washington similarly rejected any role for the alliance in supporting the subsequent peace operation there—fearing that the consensus-based decisionmaking would interfere with U.S. operational control.

Externalization of national issues within a multilateral reform process. The overwhelming power of the United States, which stems in large part from the country's technological superiority, leads Washington to regard itself as the primus inter pares within NATO and to adopt behavior that can limit, in practice, the range and the scope of multilateralism within the alliance. The overall U.S. approach to NATO suggests an attempt to subordinate the alliance's new agenda to policies defined by the United States itself. A prime example of this pattern included Washington's reform proposals for NATO. Aimed at redistributing burden-sharing tasks with the alliance, they appear to be closely linked to reforms within the U.S. defense establishment itself. Although introduced in NATO, U.S. proposals regarding matters such as force structure, the internal adaptation of the alliance, and the respective roles of the U.S. and European forces in the Balkans are driven by U.S. national preoccupations. These include Washington's capability-defined approach to threat assessment, its need to ensure homeland security, and the ongoing reform of U.S. defense structures.

Strategic Concept. The implementation (rather than reform) of NATO's strategic concept is necessary in order to respond to the new threats. Additional missions for the alliance were proposed at the Washington summit in 1999, and a prolonged debate among nineteen members (with more joining soon) would be counterproductive given the lack of consensus between allies and the risk of weakening the cohesion of the alliance. It is likely that NATO action to respond to unconventional and out-of-area threats will be considered only on a case-by-case basis, so as to reduce systematic interference with U.S. operations around the world.

Defense Capabilities Initiative. The stagnation of the Defense Capabilities Initiative (DCI) and the lack of political will among European countries to increase defense budgets have hampered efforts to develop European strategic capabilities that might allow the allies to act in concert to address new threats. From the viewpoint of Washington, a rationalization process within the alliance would bolster and coordinate efforts, ensuring concrete results as well as interoperability with the United States in future contingencies. To address these concerns, the alliance must establish a smaller version of the DCI that focuses on a few key fields, such as communications, transport, biological issues, and theater missile defense. This process must be harmonized with developments in EU capabilities and accommodate the expansion of NATO.

A new command structure. From Washington's perspective, the NATO command structure should be made more flexible and reorganized along new lines to respond functionally and geographically to new threats. To these ends, Washington has proposed eliminating one of the two NATO strategic commands, the Supreme Allied Command Atlantic (SACLANT). This would correspond to the planned creation next autumn, in the U.S. defense establishment, of a single integrated Northern Command responsible for North American homeland defense (covering the United States, Canada, and Mexico). Washington proposes to dissociate this new Northern Command from the U.S. Joint Forces Command, which will then focus exclusively on force transformation and joint training. The Northern Command would be dissociated from SACLANT, effectively separating the defense of U.S. national territory from NATO's integrated military structure.[7] This would allow SACLANT's mandate and operations to be subsumed within SACEUR, which would centralize all the functions of NATO's strategic command. In addition, Russia should be integrated into the European Command, and not addressed by the Joint Forces Command (as it was during the Cold War).

For most of Washington's NATO allies, and especially Germany, this apparent willingness on the part of the United States to protect itself alone is a worrisome trend. The allies fear that this step will weaken NATO's collective structure by decoupling European security from the protection of U.S. territory. From a U.S. perspective, SACEUR is perfectly capable of serving as Washington's sole military interlocutor on NATO issues, assuring the linkage between European and U.S. headquarters and guaranteeing the transatlantic link. A movement in this direction would reinforce a new geographic distribution of responsibilities, decided by the United States alone, and remain consistent with the development of coherent NATO-Russia relations.

A new force structure. Washington is also promoting the creation of a special pool of forces, contributed by particular alliance members, that might address new missions. Beyond its Article 5 commitments, Washington believes NATO members must be capable of assembling forces for coalitions of the willing, whether organized under NATO, on an ad hoc basis, or under the leadership of the EU.

NATO and Russia. The United States has proposed intensified relations between NATO and Russia, according to a new strategic concept. In the short term, Washington believes, Russia must be rewarded for its participation in the coalition against terrorism, that is, for its political and operational support for the war. Over the longer term, Washington seeks to alter Russian perceptions of the alliance and to create institutional ties that embody the concept of permanent shared interests between Russia and NATO. The United States envisions close cooperation on a number of substantive issues, such as weapons of mass destruction, joint military exercises, and regular discussions on security issues. At the same time, Washington insists that the evolving U.S.-Russia relationship not weaken NATO's internal cohesion or dilute decisionmaking among the current allies.

One of the implications of the U.S. reform agenda will be to diminish allied maneuvering room. In the long run, the NATO reform process should not end up being tailored simply to U.S. domestic conditions; neither should it merely legitimate internationally the national objectives of the United States. Rather, it must also embody and reflect the preoccupations and priorities of other NATO allies.

A New Euro-Atlantic Division of Labor in the Balkans

Washington's strong support for a EU-led operation in the Balkans, especially in the Republic of Macedonia, is motivated by a series of broader considerations. One of Washington's concerns is to ensure the implementation of an operational capability on the part of the EU. From Washington's perspective, concrete steps toward the development of ESDP can help Europe assume some of the burden for providing collective defense in a post–September 11 world. An improved European capability could also permit the United States to reduce its Balkan presence significantly in order to facilitate a global redeployment of U.S. troops to other theaters. In sum, the development of European capabilities in the Balkans would advance a functional and geographic division of labor at a Euro-Atlantic level. The EU would deal with peace implementation, peacekeeping, and postconflict reconstruction (i.e., so-called soft security) in Europe and the Balkans, whereas the United States would address military operations (hard security) in the rest of the world. When necessary, Europeans would enter coalitions of the willing with the United States to address out-of-area military challenges.

Under such a formula, any EU-led operation would remain within NATO's chain of command and under the strategic control of SACEUR, rather than taking an autonomous form. Such a framework would allow the United States to preserve a minimal military presence on the ground while maintaining (as was the case in Bosnia in the past) a considerable level of control through its domination of allied decisionmaking structures and its military capacity to respond to terrorist networks.[8]

Consequently, Washington has supported the EU's takeover of Operation Amber Fox within NATO's chain of command. For Washington, a strong NATO presence in carrying out this mission is necessary for several reasons. First, it is skeptical that Europeans have either the political will or the military capacity to carry out their responsibilities in the Balkans outside of the NATO framework. In addition, Washington maintains control over such an operation through the commander in chief, Allied Forces Southern Europe, in case of a deterioration of the situation, and is reluctant to engage national forces outside a NATO framework, to avoid problems of inefficiency and dual chains of command. Operationally, NATO provides an effective centralized mechanism to manage information and threats. Politically, it allows the United States to maintain control over the alliance's integrated military structure while responding to allied requests for a strong U.S. presence. Finally, the permanence of the NATO framework would allow the United States to slowly promote the reforms in favor of a regionalization of the Balkan theater, which reinforce Allied Forces Southern Europe.

Conclusion

This analysis permits us to draw some conclusions about U.S. foreign policy. First, unilateralism represents an ideal mode of action from Washington's perspective. The United States generally has the technological and material capacity to act alone, and unilateralism is its preferred orientation. Second, the United States tends to adopt multilateralism only when necessary or when its preferred unilateral option collides with certain constraints. These constraints are sometimes political, as in practice the United States may need outside political support to legitimize its action, especially in certain parts of the world like the Middle East, where its motives are suspect. More generally, the United States often finds it politically desirable to include the participation of allies and partners who are willing and able to contribute in a common endeavor. Their integration within the antiterrorism coalition has resulted from political necessity rather than from military needs and imperatives.

Third, U.S. multilateralism tends to take two forms. One is the coalition of coalitions approach, a selective and sequenced type of multilateralism whereby the United States unilaterally tailors and builds, on an ad hoc and flexible basis, an extensive web of bilateral relationships to carry out particular missions. The result is a hub-and-spokes arrangement with the United States at its core. Individual coalitions are temporary, coalescing, evolving, and disintegrating with the life of the particular mission—as

defined by Washington. This form of multilateral cooperation is more tactical than strategic. It looks more like disguised unilateralism, as it places
few constraints on U.S. action: The decision to act remains unilateral, and
coalitions are conjectural, as they are delimited in time as well as in scope.

The NATO alliance, by contrast, is a permanent multilateral framework. It is the premier venue for Euro-Atlantic political and military dialogue, and it groups credible, reliable, and loyal allies. Contrary to coalitions, which can appear and disintegrate quickly, investment is long-term.
It is, however, limited by certain political constraints, such as the rule of
consensus, and may not be as flexible as a coalition in responding to military contingencies. Accordingly, U.S. policy aims to shape the alliance to
meet U.S. expectations while maintaining some pressure on Europeans to
improve their capabilities for burden-sharing.

The analysis I present in this chapter has several implications. To begin
with, acting unilaterally within a multilateral framework—that is, using the
NATO alliance to pursue national priorities or objectives—can have positive results for the United States. It can also serve the purposes of the
NATO allies, for whom strong U.S. engagement is necessary for the credibility and efficiency of the alliance, especially after September 11. By taking the initiative in the NATO reform process, the United States can help
strengthen the alliance to improve collective action, helping NATO adapt to
new realities and better address global challenges. The overwhelming technological superiority of the United States encourages unilateral U.S. attitudes and underlines the limits of a permanent alliance. Although other
members maintain equal rights in a formal sense ("one-country, one-vote"),
they cannot hope to exercise the same influence over the NATO agenda or
to have their proposals treated with equal consideration.

However, the U.S. preference for unilateral action within NATO could
raise the issue of the sustainability of the alliance over the long term. The
balance between egalitarian principles and hierarchical privileges in NATO,
and the balance between commitments and obligations, is a delicate and
controversial one. Too much unilateralism could lead to a decoupling of
European allies. Relegated to a subordinated role, they might be increasingly forced to act outside NATO's framework (e.g., through ESDP) and
duplicate its missions. This would weaken the collective consultative
process, diminish solidarity within the alliance, and create dividing lines at
the expense of efficiency. More broadly, U.S. unilateralism can undermine
multilateralism as a framework for legitimate action if the allies perceive
U.S. policy to be insufficiently sensitive to European national interests and
values. Such a situation could end up having negative consequences on collective action, for instance, in arriving at a common policy with regard to
the Middle East.

Similarly, the United States should be careful about taking too much
unilateral action outside the framework of NATO. Further marginalization

of the alliance as well as allies could diminish U.S. leadership in NATO as well as NATO's credibility and efficiency. First, it could increase the technological gap between the United States and its allies, reducing the allies' willingness to develop European capabilities within NATO. Second, the lack of institutional and operational interaction would greatly diminish the level of interoperability that has been until now developed on the basis on joint operations. Third, if Article 5 continues to be activated but not implemented, NATO might wind up becoming an essentially political organization to the detriment of its military dimension.

U.S. unilateralism might also have negative consequences for allied perceptions and attitudes. Although the Europeans have accepted a functional and geographic division of labor over the short term, on a case-by-case basis, and reflecting the necessity for burden-sharing after September 11, such a division is unlikely to be sustainable in the long run. A division of labor in which the Europeans manage European soft security issues while the United States addresses global hard security challenges would limit considerably the future international role of the EU. In addition, it would relegate the EU to the status of a mere banker and reconstructor that moves in to deal with the aftermath of global policies determined elsewhere that do not necessarily match Europe's own specific interests. Europeans are likely to resist such an arrangement. At the same time, one must acknowledge the ambivalence of European attitudes toward U.S. technological capabilities, which the allies find at once reassuring and worrisome. A more determined European approach to improving Europe's collective capabilities might be a first, valuable step toward correcting this imbalance. If the allies wish to convince Washington that NATO multilateralism enhances rather than hampers U.S. policy potential and options, they must refine their own positions and articulate clear and coordinated ideas about the future of the alliance.

An effective response to the terrorist threat requires close multilateral cooperation among the Western allies. The multidimensional, fluid nature of the threat requires a variety of financial, legal, diplomatic, and military responses that can be undertaken only collectively—for instance, in the tracking of terrorist financial flows, or the definition of legally binding frameworks for nonproliferation.

The strength of coalitions is based upon a jointly identified goal, a convergence of interests at a given time, and an initial consensus around a specific objective. Coalitions are flexible and can be established rapidly to meet given situations. However, their weakness lies in the absence of constraints they involve and the fact that they are essentially based on the goodwill or interest of their members to commit to the common undertaking. Their long-term sustainability can be uncertain, as initial agreed premises and objectives evolve or change without collective consultation.

In the short term, U.S. unilateralism has proven positive for U.S. goals in the war against terrorism. It allowed for immediate action, the control of strategic objectives, the use of preferred military means, and flexibility of action with few constraints.

In the long term, however, it is unclear whether unilateral U.S. action in the war against terrorism will be sustainable or whether there are internal and external limits to its effectiveness. During the first phase of the antiterrorism campaign, there was significant support for Washington's leadership. As the campaign moves to other fields, however, it may be harder to ensure consensus within the NATO alliance and the broader coalition. More generally, there is a discrepancy between the U.S. tendency toward a unilateral response and the widespread sentiment that terrorism, as a transnational challenge, requires a more collective approach. Unilateral approaches are unlikely to succeed and may lead to overextension. Unilateralism is not a politically viable or realistic solution for the United States over the long term. Obviously, the United States will maintain its potential to use force unilaterally, as it retains technological readiness and the willingness to do so. But the legitimacy of U.S. actions is likely to clash with the notion of shared allied values or the fundamental strategic premises of NATO if U.S. policy appears to reflect an imposition of U.S. interests.[9] This is especially true because the implicit bargain that has long governed transatlantic relations—European subordination in return for U.S. protection—appears to be increasingly outdated and inconsistent with united Europe's economic and political developments.[10] Perceived U.S. unilateralism may progressively undermine the legitimacy of U.S. global action and claims for Western leadership. This will be especially likely if U.S. actions have consequences for European interests, especially on Europe's immediate periphery. Finally, a variety of U.S. domestic factors, including budgetary considerations, uncertain economic conditions, and volatile public opinion, may place limits on significant unilateralism in U.S. foreign policy. If there are significant failures or setbacks in the U.S.-led war on terrorism, one might expect these domestic constraints to grow.

Consequently, the United States will need to solve two major dilemmas. First, Washington will need to evaluate whether a more consistent policy of multilateral action might not better serve, complement, and support U.S. national goals. A more thoroughgoing commitment to multilateralism might enhance the war against terrorism by increasing prospects for burden-sharing with allies, by developing allied capabilities, and by ensuring interoperability and enhancing political consensus within NATO.

Second, Washington will need to consider the optimal form of multilateralism (in this chapter I argue that multilateralism is essential and inevitable for the United States, for a combination of internal and external reasons). The short-term benefits include greater cohesion of the NATO alliance, more effective implementation of U.S. policy, and greater international support. The long-term benefits include improved prospects for sustainable and successful policies. The NATO action in Kosovo and the

Coalition assembled prior to the 1991 Gulf War point to the value of multi-lateral approaches to common security challenges.

Notes

The author writes in a strictly personal capacity, and the views expressed in this chapter represent her own only.

1. Patrick, "Multilateralism and Its Discontents."
2. France was the first European contributor to Operation Allied Force in Kosovo. It was joined by the United Kingdom, Germany, Italy, and the Netherlands, among others. There was also a firm commitment of countries close to the theater, including Greece, Hungary, and Turkey.
3. Gnesotto, "L'OTAN et l'Europe à la Lumière du Kosovo" (NATO and Europe in the light of Kosovo).
4. Ministère de la Défense, *Enseignements du Kosovo* (Lessons of Kosovo), pp. 10–12.
5. According to the White House website, some 136 countries had announced their intention to contribute militarily to the antiterrorism coalition by April 2002.
6. Comments of Nicolas Burns, U.S. ambassador to NATO, NATO Defense College, Rome, February 8, 2002.
7. SACLANT, the NATO strategic command currently responsible for the defense of Canada and U.S. territory, as well as the Atlantic zone and Portugal, is linked to the Joint forces Command within NATO's military structure.
8. Clément, ed., *Lessons of Bosnia and the Transatlantic Debate.*
9. Patrick, "Multilateralism and Its Discontents."
10. Wallace, "American Unilateralism: A European Perspective."

PART 5

CONCLUSION

19

Resisting the Unilateral Impulse: Multilateral Engagement and the Future of U.S. Leadership

David M. Malone and Yuen Foong Khong

ALMOST HALF A CENTURY AGO, PRESIDENT DWIGHT EISENHOWER WAS CON-fronted with one of the Cold War's momentous decisions: whether to inter-vene militarily in Vietnam to stave off a French defeat in Dien Bien Phu at the hands of the Vietminh. Virtually all his advisers, from Vice President Richard Nixon to Chairman of the Joint Chiefs Admiral Arthur Radford, urged him to use military force. A French defeat would mean the collapse of North Vietnam and a defeat for the free world. In the end, Eisenhower rejected the arguments of his advisers and decided against military inter-vention, thus sealing the fate of the French garrison at Dien Bien Phu and countenancing the fall of North Vietnam to Ho Chi Minh's forces. A major reason why Eisenhower refrained from using military force was Britain's refusal to join the U.S. fight in Vietnam. Despite Eisenhower's emphasis on the importance of "acting in concert with some other nations," his advisers continued to press the point about the vital stakes in Vietnam. At a decisive stage in the debate, Eisenhower cut off his advisers' importunities by lec-turing them on his notion of leadership. For Eisenhower, "The concept of leadership implies associates. Without allies and associates the leader is just an adventurer like Genghis Khan."[1]

Although Eisenhower's analogy to Genghis Khan may be overwrought, the thrust of his remarks remains pertinent today. In this concluding chap-ter, we seek to address two issues: the implications of our findings for United States leadership; and the implications of the terrorist attacks of September 11, 2001, for our findings.

A Lonely Hyperpower?

Most of the contributors to this book implicitly or explicitly accept, and welcome, U.S. leadership in international affairs. Yet a central finding of this book is that in exercising that leadership the United States seems increasingly disinclined to act in concert with its allies. Our main thesis is that there has been a discernible trend in United States foreign policy in the last decade: The United States has been increasingly prone to adopting unilateral strategies across a wide variety of issues, with potentially negative consequences for itself. Our findings do not constitute a linear trend sloping unambiguously in the direction of unilateralism, since there is much U.S. action to and fro between multilateral and unilateral approaches to the same issue over time. But a trend it is, and the George W. Bush administration's prosecution of the war on terrorism since September 11, 2001, has underscored it. Our identification of this trend in post–Cold War U.S. diplomacy may be at odds with, and indeed offensive to, the self-perception of some Americans, but it is advanced by the majority of our authors.[2] What is most striking is the wide range of issues on which the United States is seen to be moving in a unilateral direction.

The issue areas in which our authors detect strong U.S. predilections for unilateral behavior include international law (U.S. refusal to sign or ratify treaties and opting out of others), the United Nations (where a case-by-case commitment to multilateralism is increasingly evident, e.g., in the use of force in Kosovo), nuclear policy (the abandonment of the ABM Treaty and the pursuit of nationwide missile defense), nonproliferation (nonratification of the CTBT), international monetary coordination, and the environment. In the areas of human rights and peacekeeping, however, it is possible to detect a greater willingness on the part of the United States to pursue multilateral approaches. In the late 1980s and early 1990s, the United States signed onto several multilateral human rights regimes, although the U.S. Senate qualified U.S. commitments by attaching reservations. Moreover, the United States remains outside several important human rights regimes.

On the issue of peacekeeping, the United States vacillates between multilateral and unilateral strategies, although on balance it took multilateralism very seriously in the 1990s. U.S. approaches to peace enforcement in Kosovo were more controversial, with one of our authors (Ramesh Thakur) focusing on the imperative of rapid action (and thereby bypassing multilateral consensus beyond NATO), and the other (Ekaterina Stepanova) emphasizing the importance of always obtaining approval of the UN Security Council before using force. U.S. policies toward the various regions of the world also exhibit a mix of unilateral and multilateral measures. The U.S. policy toward Africa in the 1990s was perceived by regional actors as evincing a unilateral streak in lacking commitment to consultation, as confirmed by the way in which the U.S. promoted several well-intentioned initiatives in the fields of peacekeeping and commerce. In Latin America, the United States seems more open to multilateral options (notably on trade and democratization), especially in contrast to the 1980s, when it undertook two unilateral and highly contested military interventions. Democratization has altered the political landscape of Latin America, and the conditions for unilateral U.S. military intervention mostly no longer exist. As such, the U.S. move toward multilateralism is as much a product of changed circumstances as it is a change of heart. Furthermore, U.S. policies toward Colombia inspire considerable regional foreboding.

In the Asia-Pacific region, the United States continues to rely on a mix of bilateral and multilateral alliances and arrangements to keep the peace. In the early 1990s, the United States pursued a unilateral drawdown of its military presence. Between 1990 and 1994, the United States withdrew 35,000 troops from the region, and U.S allies fully expected this withdrawal to continue. However, the Nye Report of 1995 put a stop to it and foreshadowed the maintaining of a regionwide troop level of 100,000. Whether events in the region (such as North Korea's attempt to go nuclear), unilateral U.S. calculations, or remonstrations by U.S. allies caused this reversal is beyond the scope of this book, but the most plausible answer is that the switch in U.S. strategy reflected a mix of these factors.

Since the end of the Cold War, the United States has adopted a varying mixture of multilateral and unilateral approaches in its relationship toward NATO. On the one hand, it continues to value the alliance as a critical foundation for U.S. national security. NATO provides an institutional expression of Western solidarity and a means to seek consensus on legitimate U.S. foreign policy purposes. On the other hand, there have always been tensions between the egalitarian principles upon which the alliance is based and the hierarchical reality of U.S. domination in determining strategy, force structure, and military operations. As Sophia Clément argues in Chapter 18, the United States faces the challenge of forging consensus with its allies on the evolution of the alliance to confront new security challenges, including the threat of terrorism and missions outside NATO's historical geographic area of concern. The largely unilateral U.S. response to the terrorist attacks of September 11, 2001, which saw the alliance largely on the sidelines, and Washington's apparent determination to control the nature of NATO's adaptation to this new environment, have raised concerns in Europe about prospects for a smooth evolution to a more equitable transatlantic relationship.

It should be clear that the United States has not rejected multilateralism. However, the United States exhibits increasingly strong unilateralist tendencies. In March 2002, for example, after receiving considerable European support for the war on terrorism, the United States unilaterally imposed tariffs of up to 30 percent on imported steel from the EU. Thus, the Bush administration seemed to have yielded to domestic political pressures in an area—trade—where it had committed itself to demonstrating multilateral leadership (as it did at the Doha conference launching a new round of multilateral trade negotiations in late 2001). U.S. trading partners were outraged, and some retaliated; others (e.g., China) sought compensation through the World Trade Organization.

As of early 2002, the Bush administration seemed increasingly committed to the use of military force—over objections from its allies in Europe and the Middle East—to remove Iraqi strongman Saddam Hussein from power. Perhaps in part due to the fallout of the attacks of September 11, our findings go beyond those of the earlier companion volume (*Multilateralism and U.S. Foreign Policy* by Stewart Patrick and Shepard Forman) that characterized the United States as being ambivalent about multilateralism in the past decade. Indeed, these events seem to have accelerated the U.S. movement toward unilateral policies, especially in areas relevant to homeland security.

What explains this U.S. preference for unilateralism? Although factors specific to each of the issue areas are important in understanding U.S. policies, our authors identified three crosscutting factors as especially pertinent. They are the power position of the United States; the domestic political processes and institutions of the United States; and U.S. exceptionalism.

The United States is preeminent on virtually all the most important indicators of power: economic wealth, military prowess, technology, and so-called soft power. The natural tendency of a mighty state is to see its views, wishes, and interests prevail, and this goes some way in explaining U.S. approaches to the International Criminal Court (ICC), the Kyoto Protocol, drug certification, missile defense, and the role of the United Nations. Domestic political structures and processes—the roles of Congress and the frequency of congressional elections in particular—also contribute to U.S. unilateralism. The Senate's refusal to ratify treaties that the executive has signed, such as the CTBT, and its attempt to attach reservations to human rights conventions signed by the executive, instill fear among negotiating partners of a United States that may opt out at the last minute or seek to dilute its treaty commitments. U.S. explanations about the constraints imposed by its executive-legislative interaction or competition often get a sympathetic hearing but when deployed too often invite cynicism and doubt about the reliability of the U.S. executive branch in delivering on its promises. Finally, U.S. exceptionalism sometimes justifies, in Washington's eyes, the decision to go it alone while greatly irritating partners and allies. Such exceptionalism appears to foreigners to conform to a "city on the hill" mind-set and also suggests U.S. attitudes of overall superiority.

What of the consequences of U.S. unilateralism? On rare occasions, it can improve prospects for international cooperation. Ramesh Thakur, for example, argues that U.S. unilateralist tendencies helped bring about a quicker solution in Kosovo, saving countless lives. Yet even there the support of eighteen NATO partners provided the United States with good company and hence a large degree of legitimacy, if not international legality, to the operation.[3] The instances where unilateralism is beneficial would appear to be exceptions. By and large, our authors argue that U.S. unilateralism has led to suboptimal solutions to common problems and hurt the institutions the United States has chosen to neglect or bypass but that matter to other countries. Washington's reluctance to sign onto regimes that the United States has had a role in negotiating, such as the ICC and the Kyoto Protocol, have had the effect of weakening these institutions. To the extent that these regimes contribute to international peace, security, and prosperity, foreign friends of the United States perceive U.S. behavior as shortsighted. The tendency of the United States to opt out has also damaged its reputation with key partners. (This may explain Vladimir Putin's apparent lack of confidence in the U.S. policy directions enunciated by George W. Bush during their summit of November 2001: It is now Moscow, not Washington, that seeks to trust but verify.) Reputation is an intangible but valuable asset. The Soviet Union, for example, was hated and feared by its satellite states. The architects of U.S. foreign policy need to think long and hard about allowing the country's own international reputation to decline. This was one of several lessons that the tragic events of September 11, 2001, brought home. Double standards will always exist in international relations, but they should be addressed and reduced to the extent possible. In the human rights field, the United States has done a poor job of projecting its own values internationally. As Rosemary Foot put it, when U.S. diplomats lecture others on their poor human rights record, a common and powerful rejoinder has been "If you attach so much importance to human rights, why have you not even ratified the United Nations' conventions and covenants on this subject?"

The United States that has been willing to go it alone on a wide range of issues—for a variety of power political, domestic, and ideological reasons—may have garnered some short-term gains for itself, but only at the price of immediate and long-term costs for many of its partners and the regimes (such as the ICC, CTBT, etc.) that they thought they were building together with the United States. Of the two models of leadership outlined by Dwight Eisenhower, international partners continue to hope that the United States will choose the one that "implies associates" over the temptation of solo adventures.

The Impact of September 11

How have the terrorist attacks on the U.S. homeland in September 2001 changed, if at all, the U.S. foreign policy outlook documented in this volume? The attacks foisted a new mission on the United States: to counter and defeat international terrorism. Before these events, U.S. officials, strategists, and thinkers were engaged in animated debates about the nature of the country's post–Cold War challenges. Was the new fault line to be found where civilizations met and clashed? Or did China, the rising power, pose a serious strategic challenge for the United States? After September

11, these debates have a theoretical ring to them. The country's mission in the first decade of the twenty-first century will be to take on international terrorism and related concerns.

In a stark way, September 11 confirmed the argument of the earlier volume that "the U.S. foreign policy agenda is being transformed by transnational challenges that no single country, even one possessing the unchallenged power of the United States, can resolve on its own." The nature of the terrorist threat is such that the United States will need the cooperation of many state and nonstate actors, some of whom will need to absorb substantial political, financial, and human costs, over a sustained period of time, in order to win. This requires the United States to embark on a multilateral venture of unprecedented complexity. It calls for a strategy of eliciting the cooperation and sacrifices of numerous states of different political and cultural complexions, as well as those of international institutions and nongovernmental organizations. The spiral of violence that gripped Israelis and Palestinians during 2002 served as a reminder that actors elsewhere do not conceive of their own policies principally for the convenience of Washington and that small-scale regional conflicts dismissed by the Bush administration early on as not meriting high-level involvement in Washington can urgently require firefighting of the most demanding sort. Indeed, this particular conflict, featuring highly lethal suicide bombings, posed conceptual, as well as diplomatic, challenges for Washington, for the terrorism involved was, even by President Bush's own admission, of a very different sort than that of Al-Qaida and one that called for very different policies.

In building the coalition against terror, the United States embarked on possibly the largest and most demanding multilateral diplomatic exercise in recent memory (Operations Desert Shield and Desert Storm in 1990–1991 were huge undertakings of a different sort). The closest U.S. allies, the members of NATO, have invoked Article 5 of the NATO Treaty, thereby construing the attack on the World Trade Center and the Pentagon as an attack against all members of the alliance. Yet the military operation of the international coalition assembled with great skill by the administration after September 11 to combat terrorism, to defeat the Taliban, and to eliminate the Al-Qaida network is revealing. The partners in the coalition had never met as such. Washington had created a hub-and-spoke operation, over which it retained complete military control and political domination (with strong support from British Prime Minister Tony Blair). Indeed, the fight against terrorism evoked a Wild West scenario in which the United States, as sheriff, deputized posses of allies to achieve certain tasks while remaining at the center of decisionmaking. Elite British units joined U.S. Army Rangers in the ground attacks against Taliban assets in Afghanistan; in an initial phase, Canada, Australia, and France also offered reinforcements. Some weeks later, Germany and Italy offered to provide military support. Depending on future targets (e.g., Iraq), NATO solidarity could come under stress. Much of the Islamic world has remained ambivalent, sympathizing with the United States over the September 11 attacks and providing diplomatic support at the UN but criticizing the air attacks against Afghanistan and their impact on Afghan civilians. Overall, the military strategy in Afghanistan proved highly effective, but strains among the allies were rapidly in evidence over peacebuilding efforts there aimed at inducing a revival of economic activity and consolidation of the government of Hamid Karzai.

The essentially (and perhaps necessarily) unilateral nature of Operation Enduring Freedom was underscored within the UN Security Council. The United States repeatedly resisted attempts to define what, specifically, the Security Council was authorizing Washington and its allies to do in Afghanistan and elsewhere. The sheriff-and-posse approach was accepted at the UN as a reasonable method of exercising self-defense in extreme circumstances and elicited little protest, but over time a more genuinely multilateral strategy may be required in order to sustain international support.

Meanwhile, the U.S. position on climate change (as expressed during negotiations among parties to the Kyoto Protocol in October and November 2001 in Morocco) and on a treaty-based approach to nuclear testing (as advanced during discussions in New York in November 2001) remained unchanged. Washington's position against the ICC hardened, and it even introduced a negative policy line on the international criminal tribunals for the former Yugoslavia and Rwanda (which the United States had been instrumental in creating within the Security Council).

Hence, it is hard to argue that Washington's international response to the attacks swung the United States away from the unilateral tendencies documented by many of the contributors. Even though the United States foreign policy agenda is being transformed by transnational challenges, official Washington has not yet accepted the policy and diplomatic implications of issues requiring multilateral strategies at least in part.

The United States has demonstrated that it is prepared to make tactical concessions to the requirements of the moment. It quickly paid the bulk of its financial arrears to the UN in the aftermath of September 11. It also responded to criticism of its plans for prosecution of suspected terrorists by building in a number of legal safeguards. However, to win the war against terrorism it will need more systematically to induce the cooperation of non-U.S. intelligence agencies, coordination among security officials of the coalition, and support of as many Muslim leaders as it can marshal. Such active (as opposed to reluctant, sullen, and limited) support cannot be compelled.

As this book goes to press, the war in Afghanistan appears to be winding down, though air strikes and casualties continued to occur. With the Taliban regime gone and a new Afghan government installed under Hamid Karzai, and with Al-Qaida most definitely on the run, the U.S.-led coalition against terror has gained the upper hand militarily. The United States is already moving into the second phase of the war on terrorism, which appears to involve efforts to achieve regime change in Iraq. This also will require active support of some allies and at least the tacit concurrence of several Arab governments. The problem with this next stage is not only that a U.S. attack is likely to be in contravention of international law but also that the United States is unlikely to command easily the support of its allies, as much as many of them would be pleased to see power in Baghdad change hands.

Writing about the nuclear strategy of the Bush administration in May 2001, conservative U.S. columnist Charles Krauthammer characterized it as a "soft unilateralism": it was "not in your face" and "not defiant" but rather "deliberate and determined."[4] In the initial months after September 11, the U.S. paid tactical heed to multilateral diplomacy as it sought to fashion a response. Several months on, it is clear that a wounded United States has reverted back to its original disposition: From tariffs on steel to war plans against Saddam Hussein, it is certainly proceeding in a deliberate and determined way. But the administration's rhetoric on terrorism, which declares "Either you are with us or with the terrorists" and makes allusions to an "axis of evil," grates on U.S. allies and other partners. It seems to reflect a sense of impatience and self-righteousness that is incompatible with the "humility" in foreign policy of which President Bush spoke during the 2000 elections campaign.

Josef Joffe, editor of *Die Zeil* and a European opinionmaker friendly to the United States, recently penned an open memo to President Bush in which he remonstrated with him about the importance of allies. Joffe argued: "Even the one and only superpower needs allies. . . . But corralling them requires the old techniques: listening, bargaining, give-and-take." He then went on to argue: "Of course, No. 1 can always ignore the yapping of the lesser nations and go it alone. But History offers a nasty warning. Throw your weight around, and the others will coalesce into a counterweight. That is what they used to call balance-of-power politics."[5] Joffe's admonition may sound overly dramatic and premature, but the thrust of his thinking is also shared by leading U.S. foreign policy figures. In a recent essay, a former assistant secretary of defense, Joseph Nye, Jr., acknowledges that concerts against the United States are not impossible to envision. In a cautionary note, Nye pointed out that "while potential coalitions to check American power could be created, it is unlikely that they would become firm alliances unless the United States handles its hard coercive power in an overbearing unilateral manner."[6]

The United States is the preeminent power of our age, and its defense spending will continue to be greater than that of its major allies combined if the Bush administration secures congressional support for its current plans. The United States is the preponderant power not only globally but also in each of the regions it sees fit to position its military assets. In many regions of the world, U.S. power continues to be viewed as benign. Historically, other countries have tended to balance not against power but against threat. What Joffe and Nye suggest is that the United States already possesses the power to frighten others into coalescing against it; yet U.S. allies remain steadfast, and the United States should work hard to keep it that way. However, most of the chapters in this book see a gradual U.S. retreat from taking the needs and worries of its friends seriously. These perceptions and the realities underlying them are ones the United States needs to counter effectively.

A less ambivalent posture toward multilateralism and a more cautious attitude toward unilateralism will go a long way in answering charges of overbearing behavior. The first step in effective multilateralism must consist of appreciating the concerns of one's interlocutors. Although U.S. partners acknowledge U.S. power, they desire to be treated as members of the club. (Whereas nobody much takes the sovereign equality of UN member states seriously, except at a symbolic level, the United States would be wise to mitigate perceptions of this inequality when dealing with weaker partners.) An acknowledgment by the United States that they too are sovereign and have interests is often at the heart of the matter. Leonid Brezhnev's Soviet Union believed it could attain sovereign equality with the United States only by achieving strategic nuclear parity. We would be loath to see today's emerging world powers believe they can relate respectably to the United States in the future only by competing with it. Indeed, foreign governments are extremely sensitive to how the United States conducts itself diplomatically; friends and allies wish to be engaged and to be brought along as associates in the search for security and prosperity in our complicated world. Dwight Eisenhower would view the genuine engagement of these associates as the very essence of wise leadership.

Notes

1. U.S. Department of State, *Foreign Relations of the United States, 1952–1954*, vol. 13 (Indochina), p. 1440.

2. Compare the essays on the same issue areas in Patrick and Forman, eds., *Multilateralism and U.S. Foreign Policy.*

3. The agreement among G8 countries to seek Security Council legitimization of the NATO-led KFOR presence on the ground in Kosovo, enshrined in Security Council Resolution 1244 of June 10, 1999, once Belgrade had yielded militarily, put an end to the awkward legal status of NATO's activity on Kosovo.

4. *Washington Post,* May 4, 2001, p. A25.

5. Josef Joffe, "Viewpoint: Don't You Forget About Us," www.time.com/europe/eu/printout/0_98699713100 html.

6. *The Economist,* March 23, 2002, pp. 24–25.

Acronyms and Abbreviations

AAUs	assigned amount units
ABA	American Bar Association
ABM	Anti-Ballistic Missile (treaty)
ACRF	African Crisis Response Force
ACRI	African Crisis Response Initiative
ACSS	African Center for Strategic Studies
AGOA	African Growth and Opportunity Act
AIDS	Acquired Immune Deficiency Syndrome
ANC	African National Congress
ANEAN	Association of Northeast Asian States
ANZUS	Australia–New Zealand–United States (treaty)
APEC	Asia-Pacific Economic Cooperation (forum)
ARF	ASEAN Regional Forum
ASEAN	Association of Southeast Asian Nations
BITs	Bilateral Investment Treaties
BMD	Ballistic Missile Defense
BNC	Bi-National Commission
BWC	Biological and Toxin Weapons Convention
CAT	Convention Against Torture
CBD	Convention on Biological Diversity
CBMs	confidence-building measures
CD	Conference on Disarmament (Geneva)
CDM	clean development mechanism
CEDAW	Convention on the Elimination of All Forms of Discrimination Against Women
CENTCOM	Central Command (U.S.)
CERD	Convention on the Elimination of All Forms of Racial Discrimination
CERs	certified emissions reductions
CFCs	Chlorofluorocarbons

CFE	Conventional Forces in Europe (treaty)
CH_4	methane
CICAD	Inter-American Drug Abuse Control Commission
CO_2	carbon dioxide
CRC	Convention on the Rights of the Child
CSCE	Conference on Security and Cooperation in Europe
CTBT	Comprehensive Nuclear Test Ban Treaty
CTBTO	Comprehensive Nuclear Test Ban Treaty Organization
CWC	Chemical Weapons Convention
DCI	Defense Capabilities Initiative
DEA	U.S. Drug Enforcement Administration
DPKO	Department of Peacekeeping Operations (UN)
DRC	Democratic Republic of Congo
DRL	Democracy, Human Rights, and Labor (Bureau, U.S. State Dept.)
DSB	Drug Supervisory Body
DSU	Dispute Settlement Understanding (WTO)
EAC	East-African Community
ECOWAS	Economic Community of West African States
EFTA	European Free Trade Area
ERUs	emission reduction units
ESDI	European Security and Defense Identity
ESDP	European Security and Defense Policy
EU	European Union
EXIM	Export-Import (Bank)
FBN	Federal Bureau of Narcotics
FCCC	Framework Convention on Climate Change
FMCT	Fissile Material Cut-Off Treaty
FTA	free trade agreement
FTAA	Free Trade Area for the Americas
G-7	Group of Seven
G-8	Group of Eight
GATS	General Agreement on Trade in Services
GATT	General Agreement on Tariffs and Trade
GHG	greenhouse gas
HIV/AIDS	Human Immunodeficiency Virus
IAEA	International Atomic Energy Agency
ICBM	intercontinental ballistic missile
ICC	International Criminal Court
ICCPR	International Covenant on Civil and Political Rights
ICESCR	International Covenant on Economic, Social and Cultural Rights
ICJ	International Court of Justice
ICTR	International Criminal Tribunal for Rwanda

ICTY	International Criminal Tribunal for the Former Yugoslavia
IFOR	Intervention Force (Bosnia)
ILO	International Labor Organization
IMF	International Monetary Fund
INF	Intermediate-Range Nuclear Forces (treaty)
IPCC	Intergovernmental Panel on Climate Change
ISAF	International Security Assistance Force (Afghanistan)
ITC	International Trade Commission (previously International Tariff Commission)
ITO	International Trade Organization
KEDO	Korean Peninsula Energy Development Organization
KFOR	Kosovo Force
MAP	Millennium Africa Recovery Plan
MEM	Multilateral Evaluation Mechanism
MTCR	Missile Technology Control Regime
N$_2$O	nitrous oxide
NAC	New Agenda Coalition
NAFTA	North American Free Trade Agreement
NAI	New African Initiative
NAM	Non-Aligned Movement
NATO	North Atlantic Treaty Organization
NEPAD	New Partnership for Africa's Development
NGO	nongovernmental organization
NIEO	New International Economic Order
NIIO	New International Information Order
NPT	Nuclear Non-Proliferation Treaty
NSG	Nuclear Suppliers' Group
OAS	Organization of American States
OAU	Organization of African Unity
ODA	Official Development Assistance
OECD	Organization for Economic Cooperation and Development
OPEC	Organization of Petroleum Exporting Countries
OSCE	Organization for Security and Cooperation in Europe
P-5	permanent five (members of UN Security Council)
PCOB	Permanent Central Opium Board
PDD	Presidential Decision Directive
PKO	Peacekeeping Operation
PKOs	peacekeeping operations
PMC	Post-Ministerial Conference
PNA	Palestinian National Authority
PRD	Policy Review Directive
RTAA	Reciprocal Trade Agreements Act
RUDs	reservations, understandings, and declarations
SAARC	South Asian Association for Regional Cooperation

SACLANT	Supreme Allied Command Atlantic
SADC	Southern African Development Community
SFOR	Stabilization Force
START	Strategic Arms Reduction Treaty
TAA	Trade Adjustment Act
TMD	Theater Missile Defense
TPA	Trade Promotion Authority
TRIPs	Trade-Related Intellectual Property agreement
UDHR	Universal Declaration of Human Rights
UN	United Nations
UNCED	United Nations Conference on Environment and Development
UNCHR	United Nations Commission on Human Rights
UNDHR	Universal Declaration of Human Rights
UNDP	United Nations Development Program
UNEF	UN Emergency Force
UNESCO	United Nations Educational, Scientific, and Cultural Organization
UNFCCC	United Nations Framework Convention on Climate Change
UNHCR	United Nations High Commission for Refugees
UNICEF	United Nations Children's Fund
UNITA	Union for the Total Independence of Angola
UNITAF	Unified Task Force
UNOSOM	United Nations Operation in Somalia
UNPROFOR	United Nations Protection Force (Bosnia-Herzegovina)
UNSC	United Nations Security Council
UNSCOM	United Nations Special Commission on Iraq
USAID	United States Agency for International Development
USTR	United States Trade Representative
WHO	World Health Organization
WMD	weapons of mass destruction
WTO	World Trade Organization

Bibliography

Abbott, K. W., and D. Snidal. "Hard and Soft Law in International Governance," *International Organization* 54 (2000): 421–456.

Abott, F. M. "NAFTA and the Legalization of World Politics: a Case Study," *International Organization* 54 (2000): 519–547.

Accioly, Hildebrando. "Preface," *Obras completas de Ruy Barbosa* (Complete works of Ruy Barbosa), vol. 34 (Rio de Janeiro: Ministério da Educação e Cultura, 1966).

Ackerman, B., and D. Golove. "Is NAFTA Constitutional?" *Harvard Law Review* 108 (1995): 799–929.

Addo, M. K. "Vienna Convention on Consular Relations (*Paraguay v. United States of America*) ('Breard') and LaGrand (*Germany v. United States of America*), Applications for Provisional Measures," *International and Comparative Law Quarterly* 48 (1999): 673–681.

Adebajo, Adekeye, and Chris Landsberg. "Prophets of Africa's Renaissance: South Africa and Nigeria Regional," in Mwesiga Baregu and Chris Landsberg, eds., *From the Cape to Congo: Southern Africa's Evolving Security Architecture*, a project of the International Peace Academy (Boulder: Lynne Rienner Publishers, forthcoming).

Agarwal, A., and S. Narain. *Global Warming in an Unequal World: A Case of Environmental Colonialism* (New Delhi: Center for Science and Environment, 1991).

Albright, Madeleine. "Use of Force in Post–Cold War World," *U.S. Department of State Dispatch* 4, 39 (September 27, 1993).

Alston, Philip, ed. *The EU and Human Rights* (Oxford, UK: Oxford University Press, 1999).

Alvarez, J. E. "Do Liberal States Behave Better? A Critique of Slaughter's Liberal Theory," *European Journal of International Law* 12 (2001): 183–246.

Andreas, Peter. "Free Market Reform and Drug Market Prohibition: U.S. Policies at Cross Purposes in Latin America," *Third World Quarterly* 16, 1 (1995): 75–87.

Arend, A. C. "Do Legal Rules Matter? International Law and International Politics," *Virginia Journal of International Law* 38 (1998): 107–153.

Arsanjani, Mahnoush H. "The Rome Statute of the I.C.C.," *American Journal of International Law* 93, 1 (1999): 22–42.

"Asia-Pacific Security Relationships," *Washington Quarterly,* Winter 2001.

"Aspin's Formula for U.S. Defense," *Congressional Quarterly Weekly Report* 51, 2 (January 9, 1993).

Aspin, Les. "The Use and Usefulness of Military Forces in the Post–Cold War, Post-Soviet World," September 21, 1992, in Richard N. Haass, *Intervention: The Use of American Military Force in the Post–Cold War World* (Washington, DC: Carnegie Endowment, 1994), pp. 183–190.

Assunção, Lucas. "The Buenos Aires Tango: What Trade-Related Consequences?" in *Bridges Between Trade and Sustainable Development* 2, 8 (Geneva: International Centre for Trade and Sustainable Development, December 1998).

———. "The Climate Change Externality and Competitiveness: Implementing the FCCC Kyoto Protocol at the Firm Level," Harvard Institute for International Development (EEPA Workshop, 1998).

———. "Presentations on Issues related to Climate Change and Trade," seminars at the Royal Institute of International Affairs, London, 1998 and 1999.

———. "Trade Rules and Climate Change Policy: Some Issues of Synergy and Conflict," in *Trade, Environment and Sustainable Development* (New York: United Nations University Institute of Advanced Studies, 2000).

Austin, J. *The Province of Jurisprudence Determined* (Indianapolis, IN: Hackett, 1998).

Baer, P., et al. "Equal Per Capita Emission Rights: The Key to a Viable Climate Change Policy," Energy and Resources Group (University of California–Berkeley, October 2000).

———. "Equity and Greenhouse Gas Responsibility," *Science,* 289 (2000): 2287.

Baldwin, Robert E. "U.S. Trade Policy since World War II," in Robert E. Baldwin and Anne O. Krueger, eds., *The Structure and Evolution of Recent U.S. Trade Policy* (Chicago and London: University of Chicago Press, 1984).

Baletsa, S. J. "The Cost of Closure: a Reexamination of the Theory and Practice of the 1996 Amendments to the Foreign Sovereign Immunities Act," *University of Pennsylvania Law Review* 148 (2000): 1247–1301.

Ball, Desmond, and Amitav Acharya. *The Next Stage: Preventive Diplomacy and Security Cooperation in the Asia-Pacific,* Canberra Papers on Strategy and Defence, no. 131 (Canberra: Strategic and Defence Studies Centre, Australian National University, 1999).

Barnes, Ambassador Harry G., Jr. "Preface," in David P. Forsythe, ed., *The United States and Human Rights: Looking Inward and Outward* (Lincoln: University of Nebraska Press, 2000).

Barrett, Matthew A. "Ratify or Reject: Examining the U.S.' Opposition to the I.C.C.," *Georgia Journal of International and Comparative Law* 28, 1 (1999): 83–110.

BASIC Papers. *US Policy Leading Into the NPT Conference,* Occasional Papers on International Security Issues, no. 10, March 24, 1995.

BASIC Publications. *NPT Plenary in Review: Campaign for the Non-Proliferation Treaty,* April 26, 1995.

Bassiouni, M. Cherif. "From Versailles to Rwanda in Seventy-Five Years: The Need to Establish a Permanent International Criminal Court," *Harvard Human Rights Journal* 10 (1997): 11–62.

———. *The Statute of the I.C.C.: A Documentary History* (New York: Transnational Publishers, 1998).

———. "Negotiating the Treaty of Rome on the Establishment of an I.C.C.," *Cornell International Law Journal* 32, 3 (1999): 443–470.

BBC. *Summary of World Broadcasts.* Asia-Pacific, FE/3166/S1/5, March 4, 1998, FE/3481 G/4, March 12, 1999, FE/3526 G/1 May 5, 1999, FE/3535 G/7, May 15, 1999, FE/4084, and March 2, 2001.

Beijing Review. March 13–19, 1995, October 21–27, 1996, and March 22–28, 1999.

Bemis, S. F. *A Diplomatic History of the United States*, 5th ed. (New York: Holt, Rinehart, and Winston, 1965).

Bender, Gerald J., James S. Coleman, and Richard S. Sklar, eds. *African Crisis Areas and U.S. Foreign Policy* (Berkeley: University of California Press, 1985).

Betsill, M. M. "The United States and the Evolution of International Climate Change Norms," in P. G. Harris, ed., *Climate Change and American Foreign Policy* (New York: St. Martin's Press, 2000), pp. 205–224.

Bhagwati, Jagdish. "After Seattle: Free Trade and the WTO," *International Affairs* 77, 1 (January 2001).

———. *The World Trading System at Risk* (London: Harvester Wheatsheaf, 1991).

Bianchi, A. "Immunity Versus Human Rights: The Pinochet Case," *European Journal of International Law* 10 (1999): 237–277.

Blacker, Coit D., and Gloria Duffy, eds. *International Arms Control: Issues and Agreements*, 2d ed. (Stanford: Stanford University Press, 1984).

Blair, Admiral Dennis C., and John T. Hanley, Jr. "From Wheels to Webs: Reconstructing Asia-Pacific Security Arrangements," *Washington Quarterly* 24, 1 (Winter 2001).

Blechman, Barry M. "Emerging from the Intervention Dilemma," in Chester A. Crocker and Fen Osler Hampson with Pamela Aall, eds., *Managing Global Chaos: Sources and Responses to International Conflict* (Washington, DC: United States Institute of Peace, 1996), pp. 287–295.

Blum, John Morton. *Woodrow Wilson and the Politics of Morality* (Boston: Little, Brown, 1956).

Bodansky, D., "What's so Bad about Unilateral Action to Protect the Environment?" *European Journal of International Law* 11 (2000): 339–347.

Boensitan, Lichade, and Luosi Mangluo (Richard Bernstein and Ross Munro. *Jijiang daolai de meizhong chongtu* (The coming conflict with China) (Beijing: Xinhua Publishing House, 1997).

Bolton, John R. "The Risks and Weaknesses of the International Criminal Court from America's Perspective," *Law and Contemporary Problems* 64, 1 (2001): 167–180.

———. "Wrong Turn in Somalia," *Foreign Affairs* 73, 1 (January/February 1994): 56–66.

Boutros-Ghali, Boutros. *An Agenda for Peace: Preventive Diplomacy, Peacemaking, and Peace-keeping* (New York: United Nations, 1992).

———. *Unvanquished* (New York: Random House, 1999).

Bowring, Philip. "Bush's America Is Developing an Image Problem," *International Herald Tribune*, May 31, 2001.

"Brazilian Proposal," in *Implementation of the Berlin Mandate: Additional Proposals from Parties, Addendum, Note by the secretariat*, FCCC/AGBM/1997/MISC.1/Add.3, May 30, 1997: 1–45.

Brierly, J. L. *The Law of Nations*, 6th ed. Ed. H. Waldock. (New York: Oxford University Press, 1963).

Brownlie, Ian. *Basic Documents on Human Rights*, 3d ed. (Oxford, UK: Oxford University Press, 1992).

Bull, Hedley. *The Anarchical Society: A Study of Order in World Politics* (London: Macmillan, 1977).

Bunn, George, and John B. Rhinelander. "Extending the NPT: What are the Options," *Arms Control Today* 25, 2, March 1999.

Burgermam, Susan. *Moral Victories: How Activists Provoke Multilateral Action* (Ithaca, NY: Cornell University Press, 2001).

Bush, George. *Address to the United Nations General Assembly*, September 21, 1992.

Bush, President George W. Letter from U.S. President of 13 March 2001 in Response to the Letter from U.S. Senators Hagel, Helms, Craig, and Roberts of 6 March 2001.

Busse, N. "Und wieder sind die Amerikaner die bösen Buben: Streit über das Verbot biologischer Waffen," *Frankfurter Allgemeine Zeitung*, July 23, 2001.

Byers, M. *Custom, Power, and the Power of Rules* (Cambridge, UK, and New York: Cambridge University Press, 1999).

———. "International Law and the American National Interest," *Chicago Journal of International Law* 1 (2000): 257–261.

Cambone, Stephen A., and Patrick J. Garrity. "The Future of US Nuclear Policy," *Survival* 36, 4 (Winter 1994–1995).

Campbell, Horace G. *The U.S. Security Doctrine and the Africa Crisis Response Initiative*, Africa Institute of South Africa, Occasional Paper 62 (Pretoria, South Africa, December 2000).

Canner, S. J. "The Multilateral Agreement on Investment," *Cornell International Law Journal* 31 (1998): 657–681.

Caplan, L. M. "The Constitution and Jurisdiction over Foreign States: The 1996 Amendment to the Foreign Sovereign Immunities Act in Perspective," *Virginia Journal of International Law* 41 (2001): 369–426.

Carpenter, Ted Galen. "Smoke and Mirrors: The Clinton-Hashimoto Summit," Cato Foreign Policy Briefing No. 41, May 16, 1996.

Carter, Ashton, and William Perry. *Ashdun kate he weilianmu peili, Yufangxing fangyu: yixiang meiguo xin anquan zhanlue* (Preventive defense: a new security strategy for America), translated by Hu Liping and Yang Yunqin (Shanghai: Shanghai Renmin Publishing House), p. 11.

Cerna, C. "The United States and the American Convention on Human Rights: Prospects and Problems of Ratification," in D. P. Forsythe, ed., *The United States and Human Rights: Looking Inward and Outward* (Lincoln: University of Nebraska Press, 2000), pp. 94–109.

Chayes, Abram, and Antonia Handler Chayes. *The New Sovereignty: Compliance with International Regulatory Agreements* (Cambridge: Harvard University Press, 1995).

Chellaney, Brahma. "Nuclear Deterrent Posture," in Brahma Chellaney, ed., *Securing India's Future in the 21st Century* (New Delhi: Orient Longman, 1999).

Chinen, M. A. "Presidential Certifications in U.S. Foreign Policy Legislation," *New York University Journal of International Law and Politics* 31 (1999): 217–306.

Claussen, Eileen, and Lisa McNeilly. "Equity and Global Climate Change: The Complex Elements of Global Fairness," Pew Center on Global Climate Change, 1998; available online at www.pewclimate.org/projects/pol_equity.cfm.

Clément, Sophia, ed. *Lessons of Bosnia and the Transatlantic Debate.* Chaillot Paper, EU (WEU) Institute for Security Studies, 1998.

Cleveland, S. H. "Norm Internalization and U.S. Economic Sanctions," *Yale Journal of International Law* 26 (2001): 1–102.

Climate Equity Observer, "Europe at the Crossroads," April 2001.

Clinton, William J. *A National Security Strategy for a New Century,* The White House (December 1999).

Clutterbuck, Richard. *Terrorism, Drugs, and Crime in Europe After 1992* (New York: Routledge, 1990).

Coate, Roger A. *Unilateralism, Ideology, and U.S. Foreign Policy: The United States in and out of UNESCO* (Boulder: Lynne Rienner, 1988).

Cortright, David, and George Lopez. *The Sanctions Decade: Assessing UN Strategies in the 1990s* (Boulder: Lynne Rienner Publishers, 2000).

Cousens, Elizabeth M., and Charles K. Cater. *Toward Peace in Bosnia: Implementing the Dayton Accords* (Boulder and London: Lynne Rienner Publishers, 2001).

Crocker, Chester A. *High Noon in Southern Africa: Making Peace in a Rough Neighborhood* (Johannesburg: Jonathan Ball, 1992).

———. "The Lessons of Somalia," *Foreign Affairs* (May/June 1995).

Crocker, Chester A., and Fen Osler Hampson with Pamela Aall, eds. *Managing Global Chaos: Sources and Responses to International Conflict* (Washington, DC: United States Institute of Peace, 1996).

Crossette, B. "Effort by U.N. to Cut Traffic in Arms Meets a U.S. Rebuff," *New York Times,* July 10, 2001.

Daalder, Ivo. "Knowing When to Say No: The Development of U.S. Policy for Peacekeeping," in William J. Durch, ed., *UN Peacekeeping, American Policy, and the Uncivil Wars of the 1990s* (New York: St. Martin's Press for the Henry L. Stimson Center, 1996), pp. 35–67.

Dalpino, Catharine, and Bates Gill. "Introduction," *Northeast Asia Survey,* Brookings Institution, March 2001.

Das, Dilip K. "Debacle at Seattle: The Way the Cookie Crumbled," *Journal of World Trade* 34, 5 (October 2000).

Davey, William J. "The WTO Dispute Settlement System," *Journal of International Economic Law* 4, 1 (March 2001).

David, Marcella. "Grotius Repudiated: The American Objections to the I.C.C. and the Commitment to International Law," *Michigan Journal of International Law* 20, 2 (1999): 337–412.

Davis, Zachary S. "The End of the Beginning or the Beginning of the End?" *Arms Control Today* 25, 2 (March 1995).

Department of Defense (U.S.). *Quadrennial Defense Review Report,* September 30, 2001.

Desker, Barry. "The Future of the ASEAN Regional Forum," Institute of Defence and Strategic Studies, Singapore, September 7, 2001, http://www.ntu.edu.sg/idss/research_05e.htm.

DeSombre, E. R. "Environmental Sanctions in U.S. Foreign Policy," in P. G. Harris, ed., *The Environment, International Relations, and U.S. Foreign Policy* (Washington, DC: Georgetown University Press, 2001), pp. 197–216.

Destler, I. M. *Making Foreign Economic Policy* (Washington, DC: Brookings Institution, 1980).

Dicker, Richard. "Issues Facing the International Criminal Court's Preparatory Commission," *Cornell International Law Journal* 32, 3 (1999): 471–476.

Dodds, Shona E.H. "The Role of Multilateralism and the UN in Post–Cold War U.S. Foreign Policy: The Persian Gulf, Somalia, and Bosnia-Herzegovina," Ph.D. thesis, Australian National University, 2001.

Domínguez, Jorge. "US–Latin American Relations During the Cold War and Its Aftermath," in Victor Bulmer-Thomas and James Dunkerley, eds., *The United States and Latin America: The New Agenda* (London: Institute of Latin American Studies in association with the David Rockefeller Center for Latin American Studies, 1999).

Donnelly, Jack. *Universal Human Rights in Theory and Practice* (Ithaca, NY: Cornell University Press, 1989).

Dorsey, Ellen. "U.S. Foreign Policy and the Human Rights Movement: New Strategies for a Global Era," in David P. Forsythe, ed., *The United States and Human Rights: Looking Inward and Outward* (Lincoln: University of Nebraska Press, 2000), pp. 175–198.

Doyle, Kate. "The Militarisation of the Drug War in Mexico," *Current History* 92 (1993).

Drezner, Daniel W. *The Sanctions Paradox: Economic Statecraft and International Relations* (Cambridge, UK: Cambridge University Press, 1999).

Dulany, Peggy, Frank Savage, and Salih Booker. *Promoting U.S. Economic Relations with Africa*. Report of an Independent Task Force, sponsored by the Council on Foreign Relations (New York: Council on Foreign Relations, 1998).

Durch, William J. "Introduction to Anarchy: Humanitarian Intervention and 'State Building' in Somalia," in William J. Durch, ed., *UN Peacekeeping, American Policy, and the Uncivil Wars of the 1990s* (New York: St. Martin's Press for the Henry L. Stimson Center, 1996), pp. 311–365.

———. "Keeping the Peace: Politics and Lessons of the 1990s," in William J. Durch, ed., *UN Peacekeeping, American Policy, and the Uncivil Wars of the 1990s* (New York: St. Martin's Press for the Henry L. Stimson Center, 1996), pp. 1–34.

Durch, William J., ed. *UN Peacekeeping, American Policy, and the Uncivil Wars of the 1990s* (New York: St. Martin's Press for the Henry L. Stimson Center, 1996).

Eban, Abba. "The UN Idea Revisited," *Foreign Affairs* 74, 5 (September/October 1995).

Elliott, Kimberly Ann, and Gary Clyde Hufbauer. "Ambivalent Multilateralism and the Emerging Backlash: The IMF and the WTO," in S. Patrick and S. Forman, eds., *Multilateralism and U.S. Foreign Policy: Ambivalent Engagement* (Boulder: Lynne Rienner Publishers, 2002).

Evans, Tony. *US Hegemony and the Project of Universal Human Rights* (Basingstoke, UK: Macmillan, 1996).

Falkner, R. "Regulating Biotech Trade: The Cartagena Protocol on Biosafety," *International Affairs* 76 (2000): 299–313.

Finger, Michael, ed. *Antidumping: How It Works and Who Gets Hurt* (Ann Arbor: University of Michigan Press, 1993).

Feng, Zhu. "Meiguo dandao daodan fangyu jihua yu emei guanxi" (U.S. BMD program and Russo-American relations), paper delivered at the conference on the BMD in Fudan University, Shanghai, December 20–21, 2000, pp. 1–5.

Flood, Patrick. "Human Rights, UN Institutions, and the United States," in David P. Forsythe, ed., *The United States and Human Rights: Looking Inward and Outward* (Lincoln: University of Nebraska Press, 2000), pp. 348–376.

———. "U.S. Human Rights Initiatives Concerning Argentina," in David Newsom, ed., *The Diplomacy of Human Rights* (Lanham, MD: Institute for the Study of Diplomacy/UPA, 1986): 129–139.

Foot, Rosemary. *Rights Beyond Borders: The Global Community and the Struggle Over Human Rights in China* (Oxford, UK: Oxford University Press, 2000).

Foreign Broadcast Information Service (FBIS). Daily Report, China, 94–110, June 8, 1994.

Forsythe, D. P. *The Politics of International Law: U.S. Foreign Policy Reconsidered* (Boulder and London: Lynne Rienner Publishers, 1990).

———. "Human Rights and US Foreign Policy: Two Levels, Two Worlds," *Political Studies* 48 (1995): 111–130.

———. "U.S. Foreign Policy and Human Rights: The Price of Principles after the Cold War," in Forsythe, ed., *Human Rights and Comparative Foreign Policy* (Tokyo: United Nations University Press, 2000), pp. 21–48.

Franck, T. M. *The Power of Legitimacy Among Nations* (New York: Oxford University Press, 1990).

Franck, T. M., and M. J. Glennon. *Foreign Relations and National Security Law,* 2d ed. (St. Paul, MN: West, 1993).

Frazer, Jendayi. "The African Crisis Response Initiative: Self-Interested Humanitarianism," *World Affairs* 4, 2 (Summer/Fall 1997).

————. "The United States and Southern African Development Community," paper presented at the conference entitled "Enhancing Southern Africa's Regional Security Architecture: Problems and Prospects," Gabarone, Botswana, December 11–13, 2000.

Frowein, J. A., and N. Krisch. "Introduction to Chapter VII," in B. Simma et al., eds., *The Charter of the United Nations: A Commentary*, 2d ed. (Oxford and New York: Oxford University Press, forthcoming).

Funabashi, Yoshi. *Alliance Adrift* (New York: Council on Foreign Relations, 1999).

Gamarra, A. Eduardo. "Transnational Criminal Organizations in Bolivia," in T. Farer, ed., *Transnational Crime in the Americas* (London and New York: Routledge, 1999).

————. "The United States and Bolivia: Fighting the Drug War," in Victor Bulmer-Thomas and James Dunkerley, eds., *The United States and Latin America: The New Agenda* (London: Institute of Latin American Studies in association with the David Rockefeller Center for Latin American Studies, 1999).

Glennon, Michael J. "Accountability in the Use of Force: The United States," in Charlotte Ku and Harold Jacobsen, eds., *Accountability and Use of Military Forces Under International Law* (Cambridge, UK: Cambridge University Press, forthcoming).

Gnesotto, Nicole. "L'OTAN et l'Europe à la Lumière du Kosovo, Politique Etrangère" (NATO and Europe in the light of Kosovo), September 1999.

Goldemberg, J., and L. Gylvan Meira Filho. "Some Reflections on the Issue of Supplementarity Associated with the Mechanisms of the Kyoto Protocol," photocopy (n.d.).

Gordon, David F., David C. Miller, Jr., and Howard Wolpe. *The United States and Africa: A Post–Cold War Perspective.* The American Assembly (New York: Columbia University and W. W. Norton, 1998).

Gordon, M. R. "Bush's Missile Plan: Military Analysis—Grand Plan, Few Details," *New York Times*, May 2, 2001.

————. "Germ Warfare Talks Open in London; U.S. Is the Pariah," *New York Times*, July 24, 2001.

Gowlland-Debbas, V. "The Functions of the United Nations Security Council in the International Legal System," in M. Byers, ed., *The Role of Law in International Politics* (Oxford and New York: Oxford University Press, 2000), pp. 277–313.

Graham, Thomas, Jr., and Damien J. LaVera. "Nuclear Weapons: The Comprehensive Test Ban Treaty and National Missile Defense," in Stewart Patrick and Shepard Forman, eds., *Multilateralism and US Foreign Policy: Ambivalent Engagement* (Boulder: Lynne Rienner Publishers, 2002).

Grewe, W. G. *Epochen der Völkerrechtsgeschichte,* 2d ed. (Baden-Baden: Nomos, 1988).

Groombridge, Mark A. "America's Bittersweet Sugar Policy," *Trade Policy Brief No. 13* (Washington, DC: Cato Institute, December 2001).

Grubb, Michael, and Farhana Yamin. "Climatic Collapse at The Hague: What Happened, Why, and Where We Go from Here," *International Affairs* 77, 2 (2001): 261–276.

Grubb, M., C. Vrolijk, and D. Brack. *The Kyoto Protocol* (London: Royal Institute for International Affairs and Earthscan, 1999).

Gu Guoliang. "Kelindun zhengfu duichao zhengce: he yu daodan wenti" (Clinton administration's Korea policy: nuclear and missile questions), *Meiguo Yanjiu* (American Studies Quarterly) 1 (2001).

Guymon, C. D. "International Legal Mechanisms for Combating Transnational Organized Crime: The Need for a Multilateral Convention," *Berkeley Journal of International Law* 18 (2000): 53–101.

Guzman, A. T. "Why LDCs Sign Treaties That Hurt Them: Explaining the Popularity of Bilateral Investment Treaties," *Virginia Journal of International Law* 38 (1998): 639–688.

Haass, Richard. *The Reluctant Sheriff: The United States After the Cold War* (New York: Council on Foreign Relations, 1997).

Hafner, Gerhard, Kristen Boon, Anne Rübesame, and Jonathan Huston. "A Response to the American View as Presented by Ruth Wedgwood," *European Journal of International Law* 10, 1 (1999): 108–123.

Halperin, Morton H. "Guaranteeing Democracy," *Foreign Policy* 91 (Summer 1993).

———. "Dodging Security," *The American Prospect* 12, 18 (September 22, 2001).

Hanlon, Joseph. *SADCC in the 1990s: Development on the Frontline* (London: Penguin, 1989).

Harris, P. G.. "International Environmental Affairs and U.S. Foreign Policy," in Harris, ed., *The Environment, International Relations, and U.S. Foreign Policy* (Washington, DC: Georgetown University Press, 2001): 3–42.

Hart, H. L. A. *The Concept of Law,* 2d ed. (Oxford, UK: Oxford University Press/ Clarendon Press, 1994).

Hayden, Bill. "Security and Arms Control in the North Pacific," in *Security and Arms Control in the North Pacific,* in Andrew Mack and Paul Keal, eds. (Sydney: Allen and Unwin, 1988).

Heisbourg, Francois. "American Hegemony? Perceptions of the US Abroad," *Survival* (Winter 1999–2000): 5–19.

Held, David, et al. *Global Transformations* (Stanford: Stanford University Press, 1999). Kaplan, Morton. "Variants on Six Models of the International System," in James Rosenau, ed., *International Politics and Foreign Policy* (New York: The Free Press, 1969): 291–303.

Hellman, Christopher. "Congressional Leaders Looking to Increase Pentagon Budget," *Weekly Defense Monitor* 4, no. 9 (March 3, 2000), http://www.cdi.org/ weekly/2000/issue09.html#2.

———. "Pressure Growing to Boost Pentagon Spending," *Weekly Defense Monitor* 2, no. 37 (September 17, 1998), http://www.cdi.org/weekly/1998/Issue37/#3.

Helms, Senator Jesse, Chairman, U.S. Senate Committee on Foreign Relations, Address Before the United Nations Security Council, January 20, 2000, available at www.usinfo.state.gov/regional/af/unmonth/t0012005.htm.

Helms, Jesse. "American Sovereignty and the UN" (excerpts), *National Interest* 62 (Winter 2000/2001).

Henkin, L. *How Nations Behave: Law and Foreign Policy,* 2d ed. (New York: Columbia University Press, 1979).

———. "U.S. Ratification of Human Rights Conventions: The Ghost of Senator Bricker," *American Journal of International Law* 89, 2 (April 1995): 314–350.

———. *Foreign Affairs and the United States Constitution,* 2d ed., (Oxford, UK: Clarendon Press; and New York: Oxford University Press, 1996).

Herkin, Greg. *The Winning Weapon: The Atomic Bomb in the Cold War, 1945–1950* (Princeton, NJ: Princeton University Press, 1988).

Hirsch, John, and Robert Oakley. *Somalia and Operation Restore Hope: Reflections on Peacemaking and Peacekeeping* (Washington, DC: United States Institute of Peace, 1995).

Hudec, Robert. "Section 301: Beyond Good and Evil," in Jagdish Bhagwati and Hugh Patrick, eds., *Aggressive Unilateralism: America's 301 Trade Policy and the World Trading System* (Ann Arbor: University of Michigan Press; and London: Harvester Wheatsheaf, 1990).

———. *Enforcing International Trade Law: The Evolution of the Modern GATT Legal System* (Salem, MA: Butterworth, 1993).

Hufbauer, Gary Clyde, and Ben Goodrich. "Steel: Big Problems, Better Solutions," *International Economics Policy Briefs No. 01-9* (Washington, DC: Institute for International Economics, July 2001).

———. "Time for a Grand Bargain in Steel?" *International Economics Policy Briefs No. 02-2* (Washington, DC: Institute for International Economics, January 2002).

Hull, Cordell. *Memoirs* (New York: Macmillan, 1948).

Human Rights Watch World Report 1998 (New York: December 1997).

Human Rights Watch World Report 1999 (New York: December 1998).

Human Rights Watch World Report 2001 (New York: December 2000).

Huntington, Samuel P. "American Ideals Versus American Institutions," in G. John Ikenberry, ed., *American Foreign Policy: Theoretical Essays,* 3d ed. (New York: Longman, 1999), pp. 221–253.

Ignatieff, Michael. "Barbarians at the Gate," *New York Review of Books,* February 28, 2000.

Ikenberry, G. John. *After Victory: Institutions, Strategic Restraint, and the Building of Order after Major Wars* (Princeton, NJ: Princeton University Press, 2001).

———. "Multilateralism and U.S. Grand Strategy," in Stewart Patrick and Shepard Forman, eds., *Multilateralism and U.S. Foreign Policy: Ambivalent Engagement* (Boulder: Lynne Rienner Publishers, 2002).

Intergovernmental Panel on Climate Change (IPCC). Summary for Policy-makers, Third Assessment Report, Working Group III, February–March 2001.

———. Climate Change 1995: Economic and Social Dimensions of Climate Change. Contribution of Working Group III to the Second Assessment Report of the Intergovernmental Panel on Climate Change. Ed. J. P. Bruce, H. Lee, and E. F. Haites (Cambridge, UK: Cambridge University Press, 1996).

International Herald Tribune, March 29, 1999.

International Institute for Strategic Studies. *The Military Balance, 1999–2000* (London: Oxford University Press, 1999).

Jacobson, Harold K. "Climate Change: Unilateralism, Realism, and Two-Level Games," in Stewart Patrick and Shepard Forman, eds., *Multilateralism and U.S. Foreign Policy: Ambivalent Engagement* (Boulder: Lynne Rienner Publishers, 2002).

Jensen, L. Eric, and Jurge Gerber. "The Social Construction of Drug Problems: An Historical Overview," in Jensen L. Eric and Jurge Gerber, eds., *The New War on Drugs: Symbolic Politics and Criminal Justice Policy* (Cincinnati: Anderson Publishing, 1998).

Jensen, L. Eric, and Jurge Gerber, eds. *The New War on Drugs: Symbolic Politics and Criminal Justice Policy* (Cincinnati: Anderson Publishing, 1998).

Johnson, Chalmers. *Blowback: The Costs and Consequences of American Empire* (New York: Henry Holt, 2000).

Johnson, Chalmers, and E. B. Keene. "The Pentagon's Ossified Strategy," *Foreign Affairs* 74, 4 (July–August 1995).

Johnson, Rebecca. "The 2000 NPT Review Conference: A Delicate, Hard-Won Compromise," *Disarmament Diplomacy,* no. 46 (May 2000).

———. "Nuclear Disarmament Priorities," *Sixth NPT Review Conference,* Briefing No. 9, May 9, 2000.

————. "Midnight Oil on Troubled Waters," *Sixth NPT Review Conference*, Briefing No. 14, May 16, 2000.

————. "The NPT Review: Disaster Averted," *Bulletin of the Atomic Scientist* 56, 4 (July/August 2000).

Joyce, Elizabeth. "Conclusion," in Elizabeth Joyce and Carlos Malamud, eds., *Latin America and the Multinational Drug Trade* (London: Macmillan, 1998).

————. "Packaging Drugs: Certification and the Acquisition of Leverage," in Victor Bulmer-Thomas and James Dunkerley, eds., *The United States and Latin America: The New Agenda* (London: Institute of Latin American Studies in association with the David Rockefeller Center for Latin American Studies, 1999).

Joyce, Elizabeth, and Carlos Malamud, eds. *Latin America and the Multinational Drug Trade* (London: Macmillan, 1998).

Judt, Tony. "The French Difference," *New York Review of Books,* April 12, 2001.

Kabemba, Claude, and Chris Landsberg. *Opportunity or Opportunism: Behind the Africa Growth and Opportunity Act* (Johannesburg: Centre for Policy Studies, Policy Brief 6, September 1998).

Kahler, Miles. "Conclusion: The Causes and Consequences of Legalization," *International Organization* 54 (2000): 661–683.

Kahn, P. W. "Speaking Law to Power: Popular Sovereignty, Human Rights, and the New International Order," *Chicago Journal of International Law* 1 (2000): 1–18.

Kaufman, Natalie Hevener. *Human Rights Treaties and the Senate: A History of Opposition* (Chapel Hill: University of North Carolina Press, 1990).

Kaul, Hans-Peter. "Towards a Permanent I.C.C.: Some Observations of a Negotiator," *Human Rights Law Journal* 18, 5–8 (1997): 169–173.

————. "The Continuing Struggle on the Jurisdiction of the International Criminal Court," in H. Fischer, C. Kress, and S. R. Lüder, eds., *International and National Prosecution of Crimes under International Law* (Berlin: Berlin-Verlag, 2001), pp. 21–46.

Keeny, Spurgeon M. Jr. "The NPT: A Global Success Story," *Arms Control Today* 25, 2 (March 1995).

Kent, Ann. "China and the International Human Rights Regime: A Case Study of Multilateral Monitoring, 1989–1994," *Human Rights Quarterly* 17, 1 (1995): 1–47.

Keohane, Robert. "Reciprocity in International Relations," *International Organization* 40, 1 (Winter 1986): 1–27.

Kerrey, Robert, and William D. Hartung. "Towards a New Nuclear Posture: Challenges for the Bush Administration," *Arms Control Today* 31, 3 (April 2001).

Kimball, Darryl. "Holding the CTBT Hostage in the Senate: The 'Stealth' Strategy of Helms and Lott," *Arms Control Today* (June/July 1998).

————. "What Went Wrong: Repairing the Damage to the CTBT," *Arms Control Today* 29, 8 (December 1999).

Kinder Clark Douglas. "Nativism, Cultural Conflict, Drug Control: United States and Latin America Antinarcotics Diplomacy through 1965," in Donald J. Mabry, ed., *The Latin American Narcotics Trade and US National Security* (New York: Greenwood, 1989).

King, Henry T., and Theodore C. Theofrastous. "From Nuremberg to Rome: A Step Backward for U.S. Foreign Policy," *Case Western Reserve Journal of International Law* 31, 1 (1999): 47–106.

Kingsbury, B. "The Concept of Compliance as a Function of Competing Conceptions of International Law," *Michigan Journal of International Law* 19 (1998): 345–372.

Kirkpatrick, Jeanne. "Where Is Our Foreign Policy?" *Washington Post*, August 30, 1993.

Kirsch, Philippe. "Keynote Address," *Cornell International Law Journal* 32, 3 (1999): 437–442.

Kirsch, Philippe, and John T. Holmes. "The Birth of the I.C.C.: The 1998 Rome Conference," *Canadian Yearbook of International Law* 36 (1998): 3–39.

———. "The Rome Conference on an I.C.C.," *American Journal of International Law* 93, 1 (1999): 2–11.

Kissinger, Henry. *Does America Need a Foreign Policy? Toward a Diplomacy for the 21st Century* (New York: Simon and Schuster, 2001).

Klare, Michael. *Rogue States and Nuclear Outlaws: America's Search for a New Foreign Policy* (Delhi: Universal Book Traders, 1997).

Koh, H. H. "Review Essay: Why Do Nations Obey International Law?" *Yale Law Journal* 106 (1997): 2599–2659.

———. "On-the-Record Briefing on U.S.-China Human Rights Dialogue," released by U.S. Department of State, Washington, DC, January 13, 1999, available at www.mtholyoke.edu/acad/intrel/koh.htm.

———. "Promoting Human Rights in the Pursuit of Peace: Assessing 20 Years of U.S. Human Rights Policy," remarks before the United States Institute of Peace, March 17, 1999.

———. "America Gets a Wake-Up Call on Human Rights," *International Herald Tribune*, May 9, 2001.

Kornegay, Francis. "The African Crisis Response Initiative," unpublished paper, National Policy Institute of South Africa, Johannesburg, 1999.

Kornegay, Francis, and Simon Chesterman. "Southern Africa's Evolving Security Architecture: Problems and Prospects" (New York: International Peace Academy Report, December 2000).

Kornegay, Francis, Chris Landsberg, and Steve McDonald. "Participate in the African Renaissance," *Washington Quarterly*, 24, 3 (Summer 2001).

Krisch, N. "The Unilateral Enforcement of the Collective Will: Kosovo, Iraq, and the Security Council," *Max Planck Yearbook of United Nations Law* 3 (1999): 59–103.

Lamb, Susan R. "The UN Protection Force in Former Yugoslavia," in Ramesh Thakur and Carlyle A. Thayer, eds., *A Crisis of Expectations: UN Peacekeeping in the 1990s* (Boulder: Westview, 1995), pp. 65–84.

Landsberg, Chris, and Cedric de Coning. *From "Tar Baby" to Transition: Four Decades of U.S. Foreign Policy Towards South Africa*, Center for Policy Studies, *Policy: Issues and Actors*, 8, 6 (March 1995).

Latin American Program. "Drug Certification and US policy in Latin America" (Washington, DC: Woodrow Wilson Center for Scholars, April 1998).

Lavergne, Philipe. "The Political Economy of U.S. Tariffs," Ph.D. thesis, University of Toronto (1981).

Lawrence, Robert Z. "Emerging Regional Arrangements: Building Blocks or Stumbling Blocks?" in *International Political Economy: Perspectives on Global Power and Wealth* (New York: St. Martin's Press, 1995).

Lawson, R. J., et al. "The Ottawa Process and the International Movement to Ban Anti-Personnel Mines," in M. A. Cameron, R. J. Lawson, and B. W. Tomlin, eds., *To Walk Without Fear: The Global Movement to Ban Landmines* (Toronto, Oxford, and New York: Oxford University Press, 1998): 160–184.

Lee, Roy S., ed. *The International Criminal Court, The Making of the Rome Statute: Issues, Negotiations, Results* (The Hague: Kluwer Law International, 1999).

Leibowitz, Lewis E. "Safety Valve or Flash Point? The Worsening Conflict between U.S. Trade Laws and WTO Rules," *Cato Institute Trade Policy Brief No. 17* (Washington, DC: Cato Institute, November 2001).

Leigh, Monroe. "The United States and the Statute of Rome," *American Journal of International Law* 95, 1 (2001): 124–131.

Lepgold, Joseph. "Hypotheses on Vulnerability: Are Terrorists and Drug-Traffickers coerceable?" in Lawrence Freedman, ed., *Strategic Coercion: Concepts and Cases* (Oxford, UK: Oxford University Press, 1998).

Levi, Michael, and Tom Naylor. "Organized Crime, the Organization of Crime, and the Organization of Business." Office of Science and Technology Foresight Directorate Crime Prevention Panel DTI, 2000.

Levitin, Oleg. "Inside Moscow's Kosovo Muddle," *Survival* 42, 1 (Spring 2000).

Lindau, Juan D. "El narcotráfico y las relaciones México-Estados Unidos," in Bernardo Mabire, ed., *México Estados Unidos Canadá* (México, D.F.: El Colegio de México, 2000).

Luck, Edward C. *Mixed Messages: American Politics and International Organization, 1919–1999* (Washington, DC: Brookings Institution, 1999).

———. "American Exceptionalism and International Organization: Lessons from the 1990s," in Rosemary Foot, Neil McFarlane, and Michael Mastanduno, eds., *The United States and Multilateral Organizations* (Oxford, UK: Oxford University Press, 2002).

Lupsha, A. Peter. "Drug Lords and Narco Corruption: The Players Change but the Game Continues," in A. W. McCoy and A. A. Block, eds., *War on Drugs: Studies in the Failure of US Narcotics Policy* (Boulder: Westview, 1992).

———. "Transnational Narco-Corruption and Narco Investment: A Focus on Mexico," *Transnational Organized Crime* 1, 1 (1995): 84–101.

———. "Transnational Organised Crime Versus the Nation-State," *Transnational Organised Crime* 2, 1 (1996): 21–24.

Lyons, Gene M. "The UN and American Politics," *Global Governance* 5 (1999).

M'Gonigle, R. M., and M. W. Zacher. *Pollution, Politics, and International Law* (Berkeley: University of California Press, 1981).

MacCoun, Robert, and Peter Reuter. "Drug Control." (Santa Monica, CA: Rand/RP 731, 1998).

Mack, Andrew. *Proliferation in Northeast Asia* (Washington, DC: Henry L. Stimson Center, 1996).

MacKinnon, Michael G. *The Evolution of US Peacekeeping Policy Under Clinton: A Fairweather Friend?* (London: Frank Cass, 2000).

Madison, J., A. Hamilton, and J. Jay. *The Federalist Papers*. Ed. I. Kramnick (London: Penguin Books, 1987).

Mahbubani, Kishore. "UN: Sunrise or Sunset Organization in the 21st Century?" in Kamelesh Sharma, ed., *Imagining Tomorrow: Rethinking the Global Challenge* (compiled for the United Nations Millenium Assembly, New York, August 15, 2000).

Makinda, Samuel M. *Seeking Peace from Chaos: Humanitarian Intervention in Somalia* (Boulder: Lynne Rienner Publishers for the International Peace Academy, 1993).

Malanczuk, P. "The International Criminal Court and Landmines: What are the Consequences of Leaving the US Behind?" *European Journal of International Law* 11, 1 (2000): 77–90.

Mallaby, Sebastian. "The Bullied Pulpit," *Foreign Affairs* 79, 1 (January/February 2000).

Malone, David. *Decision-Making in the UN Security Council: The Case of Haiti, 1990–1997* (Oxford, UK: Clarendon, 1998).

———. "Goodbye UNSCOM: A Sorry Tale in US-UN Relations," *Security Dialogue* 30, 4 (December 1999): 393–411.

———. "Iraq: No Easy Response to 'The Greatest Threat,'" *American Journal of International Law* 95 (2001): 236–245.

Manish. "Negotiating the Comprehensive Test Ban Treaty, 1994–1996," Ph.D. thesis, CIPOD, School of International Studies, Jawaharlal Nehru University, New Delhi.

Marland, G., et al. "Global, Regional, and National Fossil Fuel CO_2 Emissions," in *Trends: A Compendium of Data on Global Change*. Carbon Dioxide Information Analysis Center, Oak Ridge National Laboratory, U.S. Department of Energy, Oak Ridge, TN (1999).

Martin, Larry, Vincent Amanor-Boadu, and Fiona Sterling. "Countervailing and Antidumping Actions: An Evaluation of Canada's Experience with the United States," *American Review of Canadian Studies* (Autumn 1988).

Mastandano, Michael. "Extraterritorial Sanctions: Managing 'Hyper-Unilateralism' in U.S. Foreign Policy," in Stewart Patrick and Forman Shepard, eds., *Multilateralism and U.S. Foreign Policy: Ambivalent Engagement* (Boulder and London: Lynne Rienner Publishers, 2002).

Maynes, Charles William, and Richard S. Williamson, eds. *U.S. Foreign Policy and the United Nations System* (New York: W. W. Norton, 1996).

McAllister, William. *Drug Diplomacy in the Twentieth Century* (London: Routledge, 2000).

McCormack, Timothy L. H., and Gerry J. Simpson, eds. *The Law of War Crimes: National and International Approaches* (The Hague: Kluwer Law International, 1997).

McDonald, F. William. "The Globalisation of Criminology: The New Frontier is the Frontier," *Transnational Organised Crime* 1, 1 (1995).

McLean, Denis. "Peace Operations and Common Sense," in Chester A. Crocker and Fen Osler Hampson with Pamela Aall, eds., *Managing Global Chaos: Sources and Responses to International Conflict* (Washington DC: United States Institute of Peace, 1996): 321–332.

McNerny, Patricia. "The International Criminal Court: Issues for Consideration by the United States Senate," *Law and Contemporary Problems* 64, 1 (2001), 181–192.

Mechan, Apud J. Lloyd. *The United States and the Inter-American System* (Austin: University of Texas Press, 1961).

Meiguo guofang daxue guojia zhanlue yanjiusuo (Institute of National Strategic Studies of the U.S. National Defense University), *Qingli fenluan de shijia: meiguo kuashiji quanqiu zhanlue pinggu* (Priorities for a turbulent world: strategic assessment), translated by Lin Dong et al. (Beijing: National Defense University Press, 2000), p. 167.

Metz, Steven. *Refining American Strategy in Africa* (Carlisle, PA: Strategic Studies Institute, U.S. Army War College, February 2000).

Mills, Greg. "Pillars, Keys, Anchors, and Legs: Emerging U.S. Africa Policy under Bush," in *South African Yearbook of International Affairs, 2001/2002* (Braamfontein: South African Institute of International Affairs, 2002).

Ministère de la Défense. *Enseignements du Kosovo—Analyses et Références* (Lessons of Kosovo: Analyses and References) (Paris: November 1999), pp. 10–12.

Mirchandani, G. G. *India's Nuclear Dilemma* (New Delhi: Popular Book Services, 1968).

Missbach, A. "Regulation Theory and Climate Change Policy," in P. G. Harris, ed., *Climate Change and American Foreign Policy* (New York: St. Martin's Press, 2000), pp. 131–149.

Moravcsik, A. "Conservative Idealism and International Institutions," *Chicago Journal of International Law* 1 (2000): 291–314.

————. "The Origins of Human Rights Regimes: Democratic Delegation in Postwar Europe," *International Organization* 54, 2 (Spring 2000): 217–252.

————. "Why Is U.S. Human Rights Policy so Unilateralist?" in Stewart Patrick and Shepard Forman, eds., *Multilateralism and U.S. Foreign Policy: Ambivalent Engagement* (Boulder: Lynne Rienner Publishers, 2001).

Morris, Madeline. "High Crimes and Misconceptions: The ICC and Non-Party States," *Law and Contemporary Problems* 64, 1 (2001): 13–66.

Mower, A. Glenn, Jr. *Human Rights and American Foreign Policy* (Westport, CT: Greenwood, 1987).

Murphy, S. D. "United States Practice in International Law," *American Journal of International Law* 93 (1999): 470–501.

Nadelmann, Ethan A. "The Case for Legalisation." *The Public Interest* 92 (1988).

————. "Global Prohibition Regimes: The Evolution of Norms in International Society." *International Organisation* 44, 4 (1990): 470–526.

————. *Cops Across Borders: The Internationalisation of U.S. Criminal Law Enforcement* (University Park: Pennsylvania State University Press, 1993).

————. "Commonsense Drug Policy," *Foreign Affairs* 77, 1 (1998): 111–127.

Naylor, R. Tom. "From Cold War to Crime War: The Search for a New 'National Security' Threat," *Transnational Organised Crime* 1, 4 (1995): 37–56.

de Neufville, Judith Innes. "Human Rights Reporting as a Policy Tool: An Examination of the State Department Country Reports," *Human Rights Quarterly* 8, 4 (1986).

Neville-Jones, Pauline. "Dayton, IFOR, and Alliance Relations in Bosnia," *Survival* 38, 4 (Winter 1996–1997): 45–65.

Noland, Marcus. "Learning to Love the WTO," *Foreign Affairs* 78, 5 (September/October 1999).

Nolte, Georg. "The Limits of the Security Council's Powers and its Functions in the International Legal System: Some Reflections," in M. Byers, ed., *The Role of Law in International Politics* (Oxford, UK: Oxford University Press, 2000), pp. 315–326.

Nolte, Georg, and Stefan Oeter. "European Commission and Court of Human Rights: Inter-State Applications," in R. Bernhardt, ed., *Encyclopedia of Public International Law*, vol 2. (Amsterdam: Elsevier, 1995), pp. 144–159.

Nordhaus, William D. "Reflections on the Economics of Climate Change" in *Journal of Economic Perspectives* 7, 4 (1993).

————. *Managing the Global Commons: The Economics of Climate Change* (Cambridge: MIT Press, 1994).

O'Neill, Paul H. U.S. Secretary of the Treasury's Memorandum for the U.S. President on Global Climate Change of 27 February 2001.

Odell, John, and Barry Eichengreen. "The United States, the ITO, the WTO: Exit Options, Agent Slack, and Presidential Leadership," in Anne O. Krueger, ed., *The WTO as an Organization* (Chicago: University of Chicago Press, 1998), pp. 181–209.

Oellers-Frahm, K. "Pacta sunt servanda—Gilt das auch fuer die USA? Ueberlegungen anlaesslich der Missachtung der einstweiligen Anordnungen des IGH im Breard- und im LaGrand-Fall durch die Vereinigten Staaten," *Europaeische Grundrechte-Zeitschrift* 26 (1999): 437–449.

Oliver, Kendrick. *Kennedy, Macmillan, and the Nuclear Test Ban Debate, 1961–1963* (New York: St. Martin's Press, 1998).

Olson, E. "U.S. Rejects New Accord Covering Germ Warfare," *New York Times*, July 26, 2001.

————. "U.S. Calls for Global Action to Counter Germ Weapons," *New York Times*, November 20, 2001.

Omach, Paul. "The African Crisis Response Initiative: Domestics Politics and Convergence of National Interests," *African Affairs* 99, 394 (January 2000).

Oppenheim, L. *International Law, Volume 1: Peace* (London: Longmans, Green, 1905).

Osgood, Robert E. *Ideals and Self Interest in American Foreign Policy* (Chicago: University of Chicago Press, 1965).

Ott, H. E. "Climate Change: An Important Foreign Policy Issue" in *International Affairs* 77 (2001).

Patman, Robert G. "The UN Operation in Somalia," in Ramesh Thakur and Carlyle A. Thayer, eds., *A Crisis of Expectations: UN Peacekeeping in the 1990s* (Boulder: Westview, 1995), pp. 85–104.

Patrick, Stewart. "America's Retreat from Multilateral Engagement," *Current History* (December 2000): 430–439.

———. "Multilateralism and Its Discontents: The Causes and Consequences of U.S. Ambivalence," in Stewart Patrick and Shepard Forman, eds., *Multilateralism and U.S. Foreign Policy: Ambivalent Engagement* (Boulder: Lynne Rienner Publishers, 2002).

Perkovich, George. *India's Nuclear Bomb: The Impact on Global Proliferation* (New Delhi: Oxford University Press, 2000).

Pfaff, William. "Europe Is Unqualified for the World Role It Seeks," *International Herald Tribune*, May 26–27, 2001.

Philips, Claude S. *The African Political Dictionary* (Oxford, UK: ABC-CLIO, 1984).

Popovski, Vesselin. "International Criminal Court," *Survival* 31, 4 (December 2000).

Pronk, Jan (President of the UNFCCC Conference of the Parties). Briefing at the High Level Consultations, New York, April 20–21, 2001.

Puckett, A. L., and W. L. Reynolds. "Rules, Sanctions, and Enforcement Under Section 301: At Odds with the WTO?" *American Journal of International Law* 90 (1996): 675–689.

Rabkin, J. A. *Why Sovereignty Matters* (Washington: AEI Press, 1998).

Reisman, W. Michael. "The United States and International Institutions," *Survival* 41, 4 (1999): 62–79.

Report of the Panel on United Nations Peace Operations. UN doc., A/55/305-S/2000/809, August 21, 2000.

Report of the Secretary-General Pursuant to General Assembly Resolution 53/35 (1998). New York: UN Secretariat, November 1999, www.un.org/News/ossg/srebrenica.html.

Reuter, Peter. "The Decline of the American Mafia," *The Public Interest* 120 (1995): 89–99.

Reuter, Peter, and David Ronfeldt. "Quest for Integrity: The Mexican-US Drug Issue in the 1980s," *Journal of Inter-American Studies and World Affairs* 34, 3 (1992): 89–153.

Rice, Condoleezza. "Promoting the National Interest," *Foreign Affairs* 79, 1 (January/February 2000).

Roberts, Adam. "NATO's 'Humanitarian War' over Kosovo," *Survival* 41, 3 (Autumn 1999).

Rose, Michael. "The Bosnia Experience," in Ramesh Thakur, ed., *Past Imperfect, Future UNcertain* (Basingstoke, UK: Macmillan, 1998), pp. 135–146.

Rosen, M. "The Alien Tort Claims Act and the Foreign Sovereign Immunities Act," *Cardozo Journal of International and Comparative Law* 6 (1998): 461–517.

Roshandel, Jalil. "Iran's Foreign and Security Policies," *Security Dialogue* 31, 1 (March 2000): 110–113.

Rubin, Alfred P. "Challenging the Conventional Wisdom: Another View of the International Criminal Court," *Journal of International Affairs* 52, 2 (1999): 783–794.

———. "The International Criminal Court: Possibilities for Prosecutorial Abuse," *Law and Contemporary Problems* 64, 1 (2001): 153–165.

Rubio, Mauricio. *Crimen e Impunidad: Presiciones sobre la Violencia* (Bogotá, Colombia: Tercer Mundo Editores in association with CEDE, 1999).

Ruggie, John Gerard. "Multilateralism: The Anatomy of an Institution," in Ruggie, ed., *Multilateralism Matters: The Theory and Praxis of an Institutional Form* (New York: Columbia University Press, 1993).

Sanger, D. E. "Bush Links Trade with Democracy at Quebec Talks," *New York Times*, April 22, 2001.

Schabas, William A. "Invalid Reservations to the International Covenant on Civil and Political Rights: Is the United States Still a Party?" *Brooklyn Journal of International Law*, no. 277 (1995).

———. "Spare the RUD or Spoil the Treaty: The United States Challenges the Human Rights Committee on Reservations," in David P. Forsythe, ed., *The United States and Human Rights: Looking Inward and Outward* (Lincoln: University of Nebraska Press, 2000), pp. 110–125.

Schachter, O. "Self-Defense and the Rule of Law," *American Journal of International Law* 83 (1989): 259–277.

Scharf, Michael P. "The ICC's Jurisdiction over the Nationals of Non-Party States: A Critique of the U.S. Position," *Law and Contemporary Problems* 64, 1 (2001): 67–117.

Scheffer, David J. "The U.S. and the International Criminal Court," *American Journal of International Law* 93, 1 (1999): 12–21.

———. "U.S. Policy and the I.C.C.," *Cornell International Law Journal* 32 (1999), pp. 532 ff.

Schnabel, Albrecht, and Ramesh Thakur, eds. *Kosovo and the Challenge of Humanitarian Intervention: Selective Indignation, Collective Action, and International Citizenship* (Tokyo: United Nations University Press, 2000).

Schott, Jeffrey J., and Jayashree Watal. "Decision-making in the WTO," *International Economics Policy Briefs No. 00-2* (Washington, DC: Institute for International Economics, March 2000).

Schraeder, Peter J., ed. *Intervention into the 1990s* (Boulder: Lynne Rienner Publishers, 1992).

Serrano, Mónica. "Transnational Crime in the Western Hemisphere" in Jorge I. Domínguez, ed., *The Future of Inter-American Relations* (London: Routledge, 2000).

Serrano, Mónica, and María Celia Toro. "From Drug-Trafficking to Transnational Organized Crime in Latin America," in Mats Berdal and M. Serrano, eds., *Transnational Organized Crime and International Security: Business as Usual?* (Boulder: Lynne Rienner Publishers,).

Sewell, Sarah B. "Multilateral Peace Operations," in Stewart Patrick and Shepard Forman, eds., *Multilateralism and U.S. Foreign Policy: Ambivalent Engagement* (Boulder: Lynne Rienner Publishers, 2002).

Shalikashvili, John M. "Report on the Findings and Recommendations Concerning the Comprehensive Test Ban Treaty," *Arms Control Today* 31, 1 (January/February 2001): 18–28.

Shanker, Thom. "Bush's Way: 'A la Carte' Approach to Treaties," *International Herald Tribune*, August 1, 2001.

Sharpe, E. Kenneth. "The Military, the Drug-War, and Democracy in Latin America," in Gabriel Marcella, ed., *Warriors in Peacetime. The Military and Democracy in Latin America* (Ilford, UK: Frank Cass, 1994).

Sherwin, Martin. *A World Destroyed: The Atomic Bomb and the Grand Alliance* (New York: Vintage Books, 1977).

Sikkink, Kathryn. "The Power of Principled Ideas: Human Rights Policies in the United States and Western Europe," in Judith Goldstein and Robert O. Keohane, eds., *Ideas and Foreign Policy* (Ithaca, NY: Cornell University Press, 1993): 139–170.

Simmons, B. "International Efforts against Money Laundering," in D. Shelton, ed., *Commitment and Compliance: The Role of Non-binding Norms in the International Legal System* (New York: Oxford University Press, 2000), pp. 244–263.

Simon, Herbert A. "The Architecture of Complexity," in Simon, *The Sciences of the Artificial* (Cambridge: MIT Press, 1969), pp. 84–118.

Sitaraman, S. "Evolution of the Ozone Regime: Local, National, and International Influences," in P. G. Harris, ed., *The Environment, International Relations, and U.S. Foreign Policy* (Washington, DC: Georgetown University Press, 2001), pp. 111–133.

Smithson, A. E. "The Chemical Weapons Convention," in Stewart Patrick and Shepard Forman, eds., *Multilateralism and U.S. Foreign Policy: Ambivalent Engagement* (Boulder: Lynne Rienner Publishers, 2002).

Spiermann, O. "Lotus and the Double Structure of International Legal Argument," in L. Boisson de Chazournes and P. Sands, eds., *International Law, the International Court of Justice, and Nuclear Weapons* (New York: Cambridge University Press, 1999), pp. 131–152.

Spiro, Peter J. "The New Sovereigntists: American Exceptionalism and Its False Prophets," *Foreign Affairs* 79 (November/December 2000): 9–15.

———. "Treaties, Executive Agreements, and Constitutional Method," *Texas Law Review* 79 (2001): 961–1035.

Steiner, Henry J., and Philip Alston. *International Human Rights in Context* (Oxford, UK: Oxford University Press, 1996).

Steiner, Roberto. "Hooked on Drugs: Colombian-US Relations," in Victor Bulmer-Thomas and James Dunkerley, eds., *The United States and Latin America: The New Agenda* (London: Institute of Latin American Studies in association with the David Rockefeller Center for Latin American Studies, 1999).

Stephens, B., and M. Ratner. *International Human Rights Litigation in U.S. Courts* (Irvington-on-Hudson, UK: Transnational Publishers, 1996).

Stern, B. "Vers la mondialisation juridique? Les lois Helms-Burton et D'Amato-Kennedy," *Revue Générale de Droit International Public* 100 (1996): 979–1003.

Stremlau, John. "Ending Africa's Wars," *Foreign Affairs* 79, 4 (July/August 2000).

———. "Forward: Putting Principles into Practice in the SA-U.S. Relationship," in Greg Mills and John Stremlau, eds., *The Reality Behind the Rhetoric: The United States, South Africa and Africa* (Johannesburg: South African Institute of International Affairs and The Center for International and Strategic Studies, 2000).

Subrahmanyam, K. "Nuclear India in Global Politics," *World Affairs* (New Delhi) 2, 3 (July–September 1998).

Tessitore, John, and Susan Woolfson, eds. *A Global Agenda: Issues before the 52nd General Assembly of the United Nations,* 1997–1998 ed. (Lanham, MD: Rowman and Littlefield, 1997).

―――. *A Global Agenda: Issues Before the 53rd General Assembly to the United Nations*, 1998–1999 ed. (Lanham, MD: Rowman and Littlefield, 1998).

Thakur, Ramesh. *Peacekeeping in Vietnam: Canada, India, Poland, and the International Commission* (Edmonton: University of Alberta Press, 1984).

―――. *International Peacekeeping in Lebanon: United Nations Authority and Multinational Force* (Boulder: Westview, 1987).

―――. "From Peacekeeping to Peace Enforcement: The UN Operation in Somalia," *Journal of Modern African Studies* 32, 3 (September 1994): 387–410.

―――. "A Future Role for the U.N.," *Japan Times*, September 29, 1999.

Thakur, Ramesh, ed. *Past Imperfect, Future UNcertain* (Basingstoke, UK: Macmillan, 1998).

Thakur, Ramesh, and David Malone. "Rich and Afraid of Peacekeeping," *International Herald Tribune*, October 25, 2000.

Thakur, Ramesh, and Albrecht Schnabel. "Cascading Generations of Peacekeeping: Across the Mogadishu Line to Kosovo and Timor," in Ramesh Thakur and Albrecht Schnabel, eds., *United Nations Peacekeeping Operations: Ad Hoc Missions, Permanent Engagement* (Tokyo: United Nations University Press, 2001), pp. 3–25.

Thakur, Ramesh, and Carlyle Thayer, eds. *The Soviet Union as an Asian Pacific Power* (Boulder: Westview, 1987).

―――. *A Crisis of Expectations: UN Peacekeeping in the 1990s* (Boulder: Westview, 1995).

Thakur, Ramesh, and Hans van Ginkel. "An International Perspective on Global Terrorism," *United Nations Chronicle* 38, 3 (September–November 2001): 71–73.

Thompson, Robert. *Defeating Communist Emergency: Experiences from Malaya and Vietnam* (London: Chatto and Windus, 1966).

Thuau, Etienne. *Raison d'Etat et Pensée Politique à l'Epoque de Richelieu* (Reason of state and political thought in the age of Richelieu) (Paris: Albin Michel, 2000 [1966]).

Toro, Maria Celia. *Mexico's "War" on Drugs: Causes and Consequences* (Boulder: Lynne Rienner Publishers, 1995).

Treaties and Other International Agreements: The Role of the United States Senate—A Study Prepared for the Committee on Foreign Relations, United States Senate (Washington, DC: Congressional Research Service, Library of Congress, 2001).

Trebilcock, M. J., R. and Howse. *The Regulation of International Trade*, 2d ed. (New York: Routledge, 1999).

Tribe, Laurence H. *American Constitutional Law*, 3d ed., vol. 1 (New York: Foundation Press, 2000), pp. 643–646.

Tschäni, Hanspeter, and Ossi Tuusvuori. *Principles and Elements of Free Trade Relations: 40 Years of EFTA Experience* (Zürich: Verlag Rüger, 2000).

Turok, Ben, ed. *Witness from the Frontline: Aggression and Resistance in Southern Africa* (Bloomington: Indiana University Press, 1993).

Tyler, P. E. "Russia and China Sign 'Friendship' Pact," *New York Times*, July 17, 2001.

United Nations Commission on Human Rights (UNCHR). Summary record of the 13th meeting, 48th session, 5 Feb. 1992, E/CN.4/1992/SR.13.

United Nations Development Program. *Climate Change and Development*. Ed. L. Gomez-Echeverri. New Haven, CT: Yale School of Forestry and Environmental Studies, 2000

United Nations Framework Convention on Climate Change. *In-Depth Reviews of Annex I Parties First National Communications (of several Annex I Parties),*

FCCC, the Kyoto Protocol and other documents. Available online at www.un-fccc.de.

U.S. Department of State. *Foreign Relations of the United States, 1952–1954, Volume 13: Indochina* (Washington, DC: U.S. Government Printing Office, 1982).

Vagts, D. F. "Taking Treaties Less Seriously," *American Journal of International Law* 92 (1998): 458–462.

————. "The United States and its Treaties: Observance and Breach," *American Journal of International Law* 95 (2001): 313–334.

Vlassis, Dimitri. "The United Nations Convention Against Transnational Organised Crime: Origins and Content," in Mats Berdal and M. Serrano, eds., *Transnational Organized Crime and International Security: Business as Usual?* (Boulder: Lynne Rienner Publishers, in press).

von Hebel, Herman, and Darryl Robinson. "Crimes Within the Jurisdiction of the Court," in Roy S. Lee, ed., *The International Criminal Court* (The Hague: Kluwer Law International, 1999), pp. 79–126.

von Weizsäcker, E. U., A. Lovins, and L. Hunter Lovins. *Factor Four: Doubling Wealth—Halving Resource Use* (London: Earthscan, 1997).

Wallace, William. "American Unilateralism: A European Perspective," in Stewart Patrick and Shepard Forman, eds., *Multilateralism and U.S. Foreign Policy: Ambivalent Engagement* (Boulder: Lynne Rienner Publishers, 2002).

Walters, Ronald. "U.S.-Africa Relations," in Joel Krieger, ed., *The Oxford Companion to Politics of the World* (Oxford, UK: Oxford University Press, 1993).

Waltz, Kenneth. "The Emerging Structure of International Politics," *International Security* (Fall 1993).

Wang Zhongchun and Wen Zhonghua. *Busan de he yinyun: hezuqi yu hezhanlue cong zuotian dao mingtian* (Undispelled cloud of nuclear weapons: nuclear weapons and strategies from yesterday to tomorrow) (Beijing: National Defense University Press, 2001).

Washburn, John. "The Negotiation of Rome Statute for the I.C.C. and International Lawmaking in the 21st Century," *Pace International Law Review* 11 1 (1999): 361–377.

Wedgwood, Ruth. "Fiddling in Rome," *Foreign Affairs* 77, 6 (1998): 20–25.

————. "The International Criminal Court: An American View," *European Journal of International Law* 10, 1 (1999): 93–107.

————. "The U.S. and the I.C.C.: Achieving a Wider Consensus Through the 'Ithaca Package,'" *Cornell International Law Journal* 32, 3 (1999).

White, G. E. "The Marshall Court and International Law: The Piracy Cases," *American Journal of International Law* 83 (1989): 727–735.

The White House. *A National Security Strategy for a New Century* (Washington, DC: The White House, October 1998).

Wijkman, Per Magnus. "Managing the Global Commons," *International Organization* 36, 3 (Summer 1982).

————. "Informal Systemic Change in the GATT," *The World Economy* (March 1986).

Wilkie, Wendell L. *One World* (New York: Simon and Schuster, 1943).

Wilmshurst, Elizabeth. "Jurisdiction of the Court," in Roy Lee, ed., *The International Criminal Court* (The Hague: Kluwer Law International, 1999), pp. 127–141.

Wines, M. "NATO Plan Offers Russia Equal Voice on Some Policies," *New York Times,* November 23, 2001.

World Trade Organization. *Trading into the Future* (Geneva: WTO, April 1999).

Wurst, Jim. "Global Peacekeeping Hits a Blockade," *Toward Freedom* 43, 4 (June/July 1994).

Zammit Cutajar, M. "The Climate Protectors Need U.S. Leadership and Ingenuity," *International Herald Tribune,* 20 March 2001.

Zoellick, Robert B. "A Republican Foreign Policy," *Foreign Affairs* 79, 1 (January/February 2000): 63–78.

———. Statement Before the Committee on Finance of the U.S. Senate, January 20, 2001.

———. "Free Trade and the Hemispheric Hope," remarks to the Council of the Americas, Washington, DC, May 7, 2001.

———. "A Time to Choose: Trade and the American Nation," June 29, 2001.

———. "Five U.S. Reasons for Liberalizing Trade," *International Herald Tribune,* November 8, 2001.

Zwanenburg, Marten. "The Statute for an International Criminal Court and the United States: Peacekeepers Under Fire?" *European Journal of International Law* 10, 1 (1999): 124–143.

———. "The Statute for an International Criminal Court and the United States: Peace Without Justice?" *Leiden Journal of International Law* 12, 1 (1999): 1–8.

The Contributors

Lucas Assunção is coordinator of climate change and biotrade programs at the United Nations Conference on Trade and Development in Geneva. He was previously research director at the International Center for Trade and Sustainable Development and staff member of the 1992 Earth Summit and Climate Convention Secretariats. He is the author of numerous papers on trade and climate change issues.

Kanti Bajpai is professor of international politics at the School of International Studies, Jawaharlal Nehru University, New Delhi. He is coauthor of *Brasstacks and Beyond: Perception and Management of Crisis in South Asia* and of *Jammu and Kashmir: An Agenda for the Future.* He recently coedited the book *Kargil and Beyond: Challenges for Indian Policy.* He is finishing a book on Indian grand strategic thought.

Sophia Clément is head of the U.S. and Transatlantic desk at the Delegation of Strategic Affairs of the French Ministry of Defense. She teaches international relations at the Institut d'Etudes Politiques in Paris and is associate research fellow at the Centre d'Etudes de Géostratégie of the Ecole Normale Supérieure. Previously, Clément was a senior fellow at the Institute for Security Studies of the (Western) European Union and affiliated to the Centre d'Etudes et de Recherches Internationales. She has published extensively on crisis management and transatlantic security issues.

Gelson Fonseca, Jr., is the permanent representative of Brazil to the United Nations. A career diplomat, he taught international relations at the Instituto Rio Branco (Brazilian Diplomatic Academy) from 1979 to 1993. His most recent publication is "Legitimacy and Other International Problems: Power and Ethics Among Nations."

Rosemary Foot is professor of international relations and the John Swire Senior Research Fellow on the international relations of East Asia, St.

Antony's College, University of Oxford. In 1996, she was elected a fellow of the British Academy. She is the author of four books, including *Rights Beyond Borders: The Global Community and the Struggle over Human Rights in China* and *The Practice of Power: U.S. Relations with China Since 1949*. She is also coeditor (with Andrew Hurrell and John Lewis Gaddis) of the forthcoming volume *Order and Justice in International Relations.*

Toyoo Gyohten is president of the Institute for International Monetary Affairs and concurrently senior adviser of the Bank of Tokyo–Mitsubishi, Ltd. Formerly, he was chairman of the Bank of Tokyo and, before that, vice minister of finance for international affairs in the Japanese Finance Ministry. Gyohten has been a visiting professor at Harvard and Princeton universities and is coauthor, with Paul Volcker, of the book *Changing Fortunes.*

Qingguo Jia is professor and associate dean of the School of International Studies of Peking University. He received his Ph.D. from Cornell University in 1988 and has taught at the University of Vermont, Cornell University, the University of California–San Diego, and the University of Sydney. He is the author of *Wei shixian de hejie: lengzhan chuqi de zhongmei guanxi* (Unmaterialized rapprochement: Sino-American relations during the early phase of the Cold War) and numerous articles on U.S.-China relations, relations between the Chinese mainland and Taiwan, Chinese foreign policy, and Chinese politics.

Yuen Foong Khong is the John G. Winant university lecturer in American foreign policy and a fellow of Nuffield College, Oxford University. He taught U.S. foreign policy at Harvard University (1987–1994) and has also served as professor and director of the Institute of Defense and Strategic Studies in Singapore. His publications include *Analogies at War: Korea, Munich, Dien Bien Phu, and the Vietnam Decisions of 1965* and a jointly authored volume entitled *Power in Transition: The Peaceful Change of International Order.*

Nico Krisch is visiting senior fellow at the Center for International Studies at the New York University School of Law and postdoctoral fellow of the Max Planck Society for the Advancement of Science. He is the author of *Selbstverteidigung und kollektive Sicherheit* and of several articles on international law, in particular on the law of the United Nations and the use of force in international affairs.

Christopher Landsberg is codirector of the Center for Africa's International Relations at the University of the Witwatersrand in Johannesburg, where he is also senior lecturer in international relations. During 1999–2000, he was Hamburg Fellow at Stanford University's Center for International

Security and Cooperation. He holds M. Phil. and D. Phil. degrees from Oxford, where he was a Rhodes Scholar. Between 1997 and 1999, he was deputy director of the Center for Policy Studies in Johannesburg.

Andrew Mack is director of the Human Security Center at the University of British Columbia. Previously, he was visiting scholar at the Program on Humanitarian Policy and Conflict Research at Harvard University and, before that, director of Strategic Planning in the Executive Office of the Secretary-General of the United Nations. The author or editor of eleven monographs and books and more than fifty scholarly articles, he is working on a major project to create an annual *Human Security Report* and chairing the multiyear International Peace Academy project Economic Agendas in Civil Wars.

Kishore Mahbubani, diplomat and author, is currently serving as Singapore's ambassador to the United Nations and is the author of *Can Asians Think?* Mahbubani majored in philosophy at universities in Singapore and Canada, served as a fellow at Harvard, and has had diplomatic postings in Phnom Penh, Kuala Lumpur, Washington, D.C., and New York. He was permanent secretary in the Foreign Ministry and dean of the Civil Service College before coming to New York.

David M. Malone is president of the International Peace Academy, an independent research and policy development institution in New York. Currently on leave from the Canadian Foreign Service, he served as director general of the Policy, International Organizations, and Global Issues Bureaus in the Canadian Department of Foreign Affairs and International Trade (1994–1998). He holds a D. Phil. from Oxford University and teaches at the New York University School of Law.

Georg Nolte is professor of law and director of the Institute of International Law at the University of Goettingen. He is a member of the European Commission for Democracy Through Law (the Venice Commission) of the Council of Europe. He has written on *Intervention upon Invitation: Use of Force by Foreign Troops in Internal Conflicts at the Invitation of a Government Under International Law* and on the law of the United Nations, human rights, and comparative constitutional law.

Mónica Serrano is a research professor at the Colegio de México and MacArthur research fellow at the Center for International Studies at Oxford University. Serrano has published extensively on Mexican politics and the international relations of Latin America, with particular reference to security. Her current research focuses on the privatization of violence in Latin America, and her recent publications include "Latin America: The Dilemmas of Intervention" and *Transnational Crime and International Security: Business as Usual* (coauthored with Mats Berdal).

Ekaterina Stepanova is a senior researcher at the Center for International Security, Institute of World Economy and International Relations (Moscow), where she heads a research group on Non-Traditional Security Threats. During 1994–2000, she worked as a researcher on foreign policy and security issues at the Moscow Center of the Carnegie Endowment for International Peace. She is the author of *Civil-Military Relations in Operations Other Than War* and coeditor and coauthor of *Kosovo: International Aspects of the Crisis*.

Ramesh Thakur is vice rector of the United Nations University. A member of the International Commission on Intervention and State Sovereignty, he also serves on the advisory boards of the UN Intellectual History Project, the Bonn International Center for Conversion, and the Harvard Program on Humanitarian Policy and Conflict Analysis. He is the author or editor of several books on peacekeeping, the most recent being *United Nations Peacekeeping Operations: Ad Hoc Missions, Permanent Engagement*.

Per Magnus Wijkman is adjunct professor of international economic policy at the School of Economics and Commercial Law at the University of Göteborg, Gothenburg, Sweden. He was previously chief economist at the Federation of Swedish Industries, Stockholm, and at the European Free Trade Association Secretariat, Geneva. He is currently a member of the board of the Centre for Economic Analysis. He is coeditor of *Principles and Elements of Free Trade Relations*.

Index

About the Book

From the war on terrorism to global warming, from national missile defense to unilateral sanctions, the United States has been taken to task for coming on too strong—or for doing too little. This important new book explores international reactions to U.S. conduct in world affairs.

Authors from around the world address the tensions between unilateralism and multilateralism in U.S. foreign policy. Their careful analysis suggests that the U.S. inclination to go it alone may undermine not only long-term international support for U.S. leadership but also the sustainability of valuable international institutions.

David M. Malone is president of the International Peace Academy. Currently on leave from the Canadian Foreign Service, he has served as director general of the Policy, International Organizations, and Global Issues bureaus in the Canadian Department of Foreign Affairs and International Trade. Among his recent publications are *From Reaction to Conflict Prevention: Opportunities for the UN System* (coedited with Fen Osler Hampson) and *Decision-making in the UN Security Council: The Case of Haiti.* **Yuen Foong Khong** is John G. Winant University Lecturer in U.S. Foreign Policy and a fellow of Nuffield College, Oxford University. His publications include *Analogies at War: Korea, Munich, Dien Bien Phu and the Vietnam Decisions of 1965* and a coauthored volume, *Power in Transition: The Peaceful Change of International Order.*